Leadership in Leisure Services: Making a Difference

Third Edition

by Debra J. Jordan

Leadership in Leisure Services:
Making a Difference

Third Edition

by Debra J. Jordan

Venture Publishing, Inc.
State College, Pennsylvania

Production Manager: Richard Yocum
Manuscript Editing: Michele L. Barbin, Christina Manbeck

Library of Congress Catalogue Card Number 2007928237
ISBN-10:   1-892132-69-9
ISBN-13:   978-1-892132-69-7

Table of Contents

Section I
The Foundation:
Developing the Underlying Construct

Chapter One
Understanding Leadership

Chapter Two
Leadership Theories and Styles

Chapter Three
Leadership and Human Development

Section II
Working with People:
Essential Skills of Leadership

Chapter Four
Group Dynamics:
The Essence of Leadership

Chapter Five
Communication Skills for Leaders

Chapter Six
Nonverbal Communication

Section III
Synergy in Leadership:
Pulling It All Together

List of Figures

List of Tables

Preface

Leadership is a process and an experience that impacts all of us in our roles as leaders and as followers. Generally, leadership is a positive opportunity that enables us to learn about ourselves and others. Most of us look up to leaders, honor leaders, and strive to become more like them. There is something about a leader that draws our attention and influences our intentions. We know leaders are good people who make a difference in the lives of others. What we often don't fully understand is how leaders make that positive impact—That is part of the allure of leadership.

Throughout this text you will read about leadership as a personal journey that requires conscious effort to undertake. Each one of us, if we wish to be like those who make a positive difference in others' lives, will need to step forward and claim our own leadership journey. To do so, we will increase our self-awareness and become more alert and receptive to new knowledge and understanding.

This text begins by addressing the intentionality of leadership. Each one of us can decide today, tomorrow, or the next day to take a step toward increasing our personal leadership skills. We alone decide the seriousness of our intentions, the intensity behind those intentions, and the true goal of those intentions. If we truly desire to become more effective leaders, we must begin with ourselves.

Leadership is one of the keystones of successful parks, recreation, and leisure services agencies, organizations, and programs. How we deal with people, and how we interact with fellow staff, supervisors, participants and the general public all make an incredible statement about who we are and what our profession is about. Those interactions are very much like the ripple created in a pond by a thrown stone. They reach far and wide.

Thus, if we are serious about making a positive difference in the lives of others, we must begin with study and personal reflection. This text is designed to help students of leadership to begin (or renew) their personal journey toward leadership. The text is divided into three major sections. *Section I, The Foundation: Developing the Underlying Construct* provides information to serve as a framework around which the other two sections are built. This section offers background material such as definitions, theories, and material about human development. These are essentially the bedrock upon which the other elements of leadership are built. The information found in this section will serve as the foundation for all the material that follows.

Section II, Working with People: The Essential Skills of Leadership provides the developing leader with information about the interpersonal side of leadership. Many argue that leadership is all about interpersonal components; after all, a leader interacts with others through everything she or he does. Here you will begin to consider issues surrounding communication, motivation, behavior management, and group dynamics. All of these areas are heavily interrelated and have a large impact on successful leadership.

The goal of *Section III, Synergy: Pulling it All Together* is to bring together the foundational material from Section I, blend it with the information in Section II, and challenge yourself to think about the application and practice of leadership. Thus, diversity, leader values and ethics, risk management, and professional and social issues are topics of discovery in this section.

Leadership is best developed and refined through experience. Therefore, during the studying process associated with this text, you are encouraged to seek out as many opportunities for leadership practice as possible. Practice your public communication skills, your conflict resolution skills, and your motivation skills. Expose yourself to issues and experiences outside of your comfort zone to stretch yourself and increase your self-awareness. As much as possible, practice, reflect on your experiences, seek out feedback, and practice some more.

Leadership is a never-ending journey.

—DJJ, 2007

Acknowledgments

Leadership is not something any one of us can develop in a vacuum, and I owe a debt of gratitude to the many teachers in my life for what they have shared intentionally and through living their lives. I recognize that my views and thoughts about leadership have evolved over the course of my life in ways of which I am not yet aware. Thus, while I would like to be able to do so, I am unable to name each individual who has helped to develop the concept of leadership I have come to understand. Hopefully, those people know who they are and accept my appreciation for touching my life.

To compensate for some of this, in this edition of the text I have included profiles of leaders—peers and colleagues who each demonstrate excellence in leadership—who represent the many influences in my life. I also wish to specifically acknowledge several individuals who have contributed to this process in various ways: Michele L. Barbin, Christina Manbeck, Richard Yocum, Kay Whiteside, and Geof Godbey at Venture Publishing continue to be wonderful professionals with whom to work. Margie Arnold, Lowell Caneday, Don DeGraaf, Linda Kotowski, Michal Anne Lord, Phil Rea, and Beth Wilson are some of the finest examples of colleagues engaged in leadership—and to them I owe a good deal of appreciation. I would like to thank Paul Jordan, Steven Nanton, Gywnn Powell, Vicki Proctor, and Nina Roberts for their contributions to this edition of the text. Tyler Tapps undertook a big task with very short notice and has done an outstanding job with the instructors' CD. My students and the groups with which I work are also wonderful teachers about leadership and followership—theirs and mine. In addition, I am indebted to my nieces and nephews for all that they teach in the playfulness and honesty of childhood. Thank you Chris, Nicole, Holley, Matthew, Sarah, and Carter.

—DJJ, 2007

Section I
The Foundation:
Developing the Underlying Construct

Leadership is a complex process which is culturally based and not fully understood. Yet through study and practice, information can be learned to aid in the understanding of what leadership is and how to use it effectively. To help in the study of the various elements of leadership this text is divided into three sections, all of which are inextricably intertwined. Successful leadership requires more than technical skills; it also requires an understanding of why and how the practice of leadership influences the people with whom we work. In addition, it requires a conscious understanding of the culture through which one expresses leadership.

In this section, the foundation is laid to help place later materials into perspective and to provide a context for learning more specific skills. Basic definitions, values, theories and models of leadership, and material about human development form the frame around which other leadership skills are built.

By examining and understanding the evolution of how leadership has been defined and illustrated, one can more easily view leadership as a process. Without this understanding it can be difficult to understand the *why* of leadership. Therefore, in order to provide the necessary foundation upon which to build, the early section of this book will deal with definitions used throughout the book; leader competencies, traits, and qualities; as well as how leaders are identified.

In addition, as a basis for developing one's own leadership style preferences, one should have a sense of what leadership appears to be. Several alternative ways of viewing leadership are presented in this section as theories and models of leadership. It often is easier to integrate practical knowledge into one's own experience base if a model or representation of a phenomenon feels like it fits one's experiences.

Once exposed to background information about leadership, it is just as important to have a solid knowledge base about people—people, after all, define a leader. The people whom we call clients, guests, customers, participants, users, players, and others make leisure services exciting, challenging, and highly rewarding. Thus, the text examines physical, socioemotional, intellectual, and moral development across the life span and how cultural differences affect that development.

This first section provides a basis for understanding leadership. It may be read and discussed early in one's leadership education, and returned to after learning and practicing specific leadership skills. In this manner, a model (or philosophy) of leadership can be further developed to provide guidance in a wide variety of leadership opportunities. Recreation and leisure services is an exciting field!

Leader Profile

Nina S. Roberts, Ph.D.
Assistant Professor, Department of Recreation and Leisure Studies • San Francisco State University

Nina has three years in higher education, and 24 years in the parks, recreation, and leisure services profession,

Volunteer leadership positions she has held include:

- Cultural Diversity Transition Planning Team—U.S. Forest Service
- Advisory Council Member—GirlVentures, Inc., San Francisco, CA
- Advisory Committee, Subcommittee for Environmental Justice—George Wright Society
- Associate Editor—Leisure Sciences
- Association Liaison—Society for Park & Recreation Educators and the Association for Experiential Education (AEE)
- Board of Directors, Member—Girls Outdoors, Inc. (Fort Collins, CO)
- Women's Professional Group Representative—AEE Board of Directors
- Vice President, Recreation Division—Massachusetts Association for Health, Physical Education, Recreation, and Dance

What is the meaning of leadership?

For me, leadership is the key dynamic force that encourages, gives confidence to, and coordinates individuals, groups or organizations in achieving goals and objectives. Leadership involves inspiring, motivating, and influencing others, and spearheading useful changes or some desired course of action.

What are the most important leader qualities?

A leader comprehends different types of leadership styles, sets realistic and attainable goals, has solid communication skills, the ability to resolve conflicts and solve problems, engages in active listening, is safety conscious, gives and solicits feedback, inspires trust and confidence, has proficiency in helping others think more creatively (and in some instances, more critically), builds teamwork, learns how to be a "courageous follower," and knows how to give constructive advice and emotional support.

What advice do you have for students who aspire to leadership in parks, recreation and leisure services?

Understand who you are as an individual and be clear about your personal as well as professional aspirations and desires. One of the best ways to build leadership skills is to seek new ways to be a leader; this should occur through volunteerism, community involvement, professional associations and committees, and taking initiative towards some defined action or by creating change, to name a few…. Become a master at communication by developing an ongoing desire to always keep fresh regarding how language impacts others, the benefits of analogies and metaphors, and why nonverbal communication is crucial to being an effective leader. Furthermore, become adept at crosscultural communication and embrace multiculturalism—It is absolutely essential.

Favorite book(s): The Power of Now by Eckhart Tolle and All I Need to Know I Learned in Kindergarten by Robert Fulghum

Favorite activities: Biking, hiking, backpacking, camping, photography, walking on the beach/ kite-flying, basketball, racquetball, and strength training.

Chapter One
Understanding Leadership

Learning Opportunities

Through studying this chapter readers will have the opportunity to

- Mull over the various definitions of leadership and followership.
- Explore common leadership skills and competencies.
- Identify qualities and traits of successful leaders.
- Examine three layers of leadership.
- Explain how leaders are identified from within groups.
- Describe the various forms of power and how they can be used.

Photo courtesy of Gwynn Powell

Practitioners work with all types of people in a variety of settings. Leisure services professionals help women and men, the elderly and children, those with disabilities and those without, people with low incomes and people with very high incomes, and people representing diverse ethnic backgrounds to achieve a higher quality of life. We do this through recreation and leisure activities in the out-of-doors, hospitals, resorts, recreation centers, eldercare facilities, at tourist destinations, after-school programs, military bases, and other settings. As you might imagine, being a leader of recreation and leisure services can be a demanding, yet highly enjoyable task.

The field of recreation and leisure services directly impacts the health and well-being of all individuals in various ways. We often talk about the positive impacts of leisure on quality of life for both individuals and communities—they are many! People engage in recreation activities for many reasons, including to learn new skills, to refresh themselves, and to share in fellowship with friends and family. For most people, recreation and leisure services are important elements of their lives. They engage in self-initiated activities as well as those provided by leisure service practitioners.

In the delivery of leisure services, recreation and leisure service practitioners interact with participants in ways that may enhance or detract from the leisure experience. A quality recreation experience results in positive feelings and mental well-being, as well as a wide variety of physical, social, and spiritual benefits. On the other hand, a poor recreation experience may leave a participant with negative feelings and a desire to avoid other similar leisure opportunities.

Quite often the difference between quality and poor leisure experiences can be traced back to the people involved. In particular, the leadership provided at an event has a tremendous influence on its success or failure. Because leadership is an inherent factor in structured recreation experiences, all leisure services professionals need this skill. Examples of leadership in recreation and leisure services surround us: a Certified Therapeutic Recreation

Specialist (CTRS) facilitates a leisure education session; a lifeguard provides informal feedback about a swimmer's stroke; an executive director makes a presentation to the board; and an event coordinator gives out assignments to volunteers. In each of these instances, someone engages in certain behaviors and exudes certain qualities that result in others identifying her or him as a leader.

This chapter will explore many of the basic concepts related to leadership. As you will quickly learn, leadership comprises many concepts, theories, and practical skills. Initial discussions will revolve around defining terms. Next, leadership qualities and competencies will be addressed. Finally, classifications of leadership and how leaders are identified will be presented.

Definitions

Leisure and Recreation

There are many varied definitions of *leisure* and *recreation* used in the field today. To laypeople (i.e., non-leisure services professionals), the terms recreation and leisure generally mean the same thing. Frequently, these terms are used interchangeably to refer to nonwork activities engaged in during one's free time. Sometimes, recreation has a more active connotation to it than leisure, but for the most part, they share similar meanings for the general public.

For ease of use, this text takes a layperson approach to defining leisure and recreation. Therefore, throughout this text *leisure* and *recreation* are used interchangeably and refer to those socially acceptable non-work activities in which people voluntarily engage during their unobligated time. This might include such things as arts and crafts, small and large group games, patient-chosen activities undertaken during physical rehabilitation, reading, exercise routines, sports, music, table games, camping, high-risk activities, special events, and others.

Defining Leadership

On the surface, *leadership* may seem to be an easy term to define. After all, most everyone reading this text has been in some type of leadership position at some time in her or his life, and it is a safe bet that everyone reading this text has been a follower to someone else's leadership. If each person in a leisure services leadership class was asked to define leadership, however, the answers would certainly be varied and most likely ambiguous and difficult to "get a handle on." Because individual experiences and culture influence one's view of concepts, defining leadership is not as easy as it might first seem.

A well-phrased definition helps in coming to a basic understanding of a term, in this case, leadership. Prior to defining leadership, one must appreciate the difficulty people have had over the years in agreeing on a single definition of leadership. While not covered in depth here, those studying leadership should know that over the years leadership has been defined as

- a group process
- the personality of the leader
- the inducement of compliance in followers
- the exercise of influence by one person (designated as the leader)
- the behaviors one exhibits (e.g., planning, organizing, directing)
- a power relationship between one individual and others
- an effect of interaction (e.g., when certain people come together, one emerges as the leader)
- a differentiated role (e.g., leader, follower)
- the initiation of structure (e.g., taking initiative, getting a task started)
- an exchange or transaction between two people
- charisma
- both art and skill
- a combination of two or more of the above definitions. (Bass, 1990)

These definitions evolved from interpretations of observations and studies of various groups and leaders. The definitions are fluid; that is, based on one person's

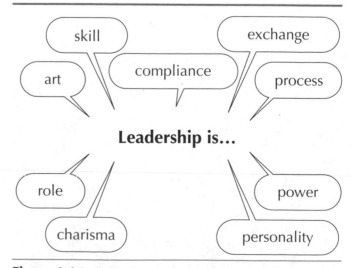

Figure 1.1 Individual experiences and culture influence one's views of leadership.

perceptions, leadership is one thing and in another person's eyes leadership is something slightly different. In the following chapter, which deals with leadership theories, you will see these definitions based on the models and theories that people developed in an attempt to better understand leadership.

It is critical to gain an appreciation for how the term *leadership* is used throughout this text so that everyone operates from a common basis of understanding. Remember, defining leadership is no easy task, and definitions have changed and evolved over many years of study. It makes sense to define leadership as a combination of many elements. Throughout this book, leadership is viewed as

> a dynamic process of influence which occurs in the interactions between two or more members of a group and involves recognition and acceptance of leader-follower roles by group members within a certain situation. Leadership includes activities by the leader and followers that facilitate meeting group goals.

In the next chapter you will be exposed to various theories of leadership which will help to further explain this definition. In the meantime, examining each component of the definition will be helpful.

Leadership is a dynamic process...

Dynamic process refers to the fact that leadership changes constantly; it is never stagnant. In any group, leadership fluctuates based on internal and external factors affecting the group. It is heavily influenced by one's cultural perspectives. In addition, as a process, leadership consists of a series of actions which evolve over time. In other words,

a single act or behavior that might relate to leadership does not necessarily define a leader.

...of influence which occurs in the interactions between two or more members of a group...

Influence may be thought of as the power that one person exerts over others that affects a course of action, thought process or attitude. The term *interaction* refers to reciprocal actions which occur between people. For instance, a reciprocal action occurs when one person says hello and another person nods her or his head in response. It is an action-response process. Typically, leadership interactions include verbal and nonverbal communication, a sharing of tasks, and the establishment of relationships. The term *group* refers to two or more people who together form a complete unit and share common goals.

...and involves recognition and acceptance of leader-follower roles by group members...

To be a leader, one must first be recognized as a leader. If others do not see and accept that person as the leader, leadership does not exist (Hare & O'Neill, 2000; Shipper & White, 1999). Leader-follower roles are differentiated from one another by intent (i.e., what one has her or his mind set to do), interpersonal skills (i.e., commonly called *people skills*), task orientation (i.e., the ability to motivate involvement by others in a task or job), and an understanding of how to work toward goal achievement (i.e., leaders take an active initiating approach; followers work cooperatively with the leader to make things happen). In the definition of leadership used for this text, leaders and followers fulfill different roles within a group, all necessary for effective group functioning.

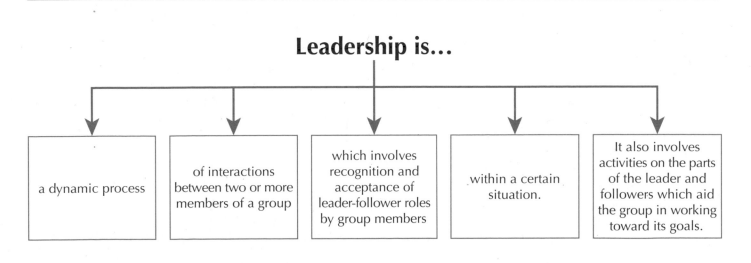

Leadership is...

| a dynamic process | of interactions between two or more members of a group | which involves recognition and acceptance of leader-follower roles by group members | within a certain situation. | It also involves activities on the parts of the leader and followers which aid the group in working toward its goals. |

Figure 1.2 Elements of leadership

...within a certain situation.

This will be discussed in later chapters, but be aware that while there is "carry-over," leadership tends to be situational. That is to say that in one situation one person may be a leader, yet in another situation she or he may not be the leader. Some of this is based on the skills and experience of the leader; some is based on the skills and experience of group members. Yet other influences include elements such as formal position titles, safety issues, and environmental forces such as time and weather. Whatever the reason, leadership roles often change with the situation.

Leadership includes actions by one or more leaders, which facilitate meeting group goals.

Leadership is goal directed. Typically, an effectively functioning group will exhibit compatible and shared goals among the leader(s) and the followers. The leader facilitates the group in moving toward those goals. The followers apply their skills and talents toward achieving those same goals. For the leader(s), this often involves working closely with and managing the people in the group, the tasks to be accomplished, and the outside forces that may enhance or interrupt a group's progress. Leaders fill a role to support, encourage, and assist group members in such ways as to advance the group agenda in a positive fashion.

Followership

"The crux of leadership is concern for the needs and goals of followers" (Krishnan, 2003, p. 345). Thus, it seems that to discuss leadership without discussing followership would be missing half of the leadership equation. Without followers there would be no leaders—Followers act as active partners in pursuit of the group goals. Our staff, participants, fellow employees, and even the leader may all serve in followership roles at one time or another. In effective groups, followers recognize, acknowledge, and accept one (or more) person(s) as the leader. They impact the leader and her or his effectiveness through the synergy that emerges from their interactions with the leader (Bratton, Grint & Nelson, 2005). Without followers agreeing that an individual is the leader, little leadership will be accomplished.

Despite the importance of followers, the concept of followership has been receiving study and attention only recently. It is commonly believed that to be an effective leader one must first be a good follower. Therefore, a good follower shares many traits with effective leaders (Banutu-Gomez, 2004; Lu, 2004).

Followership and leadership are interrelated and neither makes sense without the other. While many perceive followers as being passive receptacles, leadership and followership are mutual acts of influence and counter-influence (Bratton, Grint & Nelson, 2005). The reinforcement of behaviors, attitudes, and values goes both ways. In addition, followers are motivated by many of the same things that motivate leaders: personal goals, relationships, a desire to express themselves, and the use of followership opportunities as a means to transform themselves (Miller, Butler & Cosentino, 2004). Followers' expectations affect the performance of leaders (i.e., what followers expect leaders to do affects the way leaders behave) and the leader's expectations affect the way members of a group behave. Furthermore, followers' perceptions of the leader's motives and actions constrain or facilitate what the leader can accomplish. For example, if followers perceive a leader to be self-serving, they may block that individual's efforts at leadership. On the other hand, if followers perceive that a leader acts for the good of the group, they often will work harder to help the leader accomplish those common goals. Leaders exert the same types of influence on followers.

Good followers are as important, if not more important, than good leaders. Capable followers use their skills to help "get the job done" and work cooperatively, putting pieces of a task together to achieve a shared goal. Self-led followers are self-motivated, take initiative, and take on even undesirable tasks to further the goals of the group (Nelson & Quick, 2005). They collaborate with the leader and make effective use of one another's skills in the group effort. Followers work within groups in several ways. Examples in the leisure services profession include: to help a sports team to win, to successfully prepare for a special event, or to prepare a budget. Within the group the leader serves in the role of group guide, director, counselor, resource, authority, and others as needs dictate. Followers serve in supportive roles that enhance the total group effort.

The research about followership indicates that effective and desirable followers share similar characteristics (Bratton, Grint & Nelson, 2005; Kellerman, 2005). First, they are independent, think for themselves, and manage themselves well. They commit to the leader, organization, and purpose. Furthermore, effective followers know and build upon their own competence and apply these talents

Capable followers use their skills to help "get the job done" and work cooperatively, putting pieces of a task together to achieve a shared goal.

for the good of the group or organization. In addition, desirable followers control their own egos to work cooperatively with the leader and other followers. They play key roles in planning and implementing courses of action. Effective followers make very conscious contributions to the central purpose and good of the organization. The leader takes an active role in assisting followers to be as effective as possible.

In addition to relating to leaders, followers also relate to other followers. Exemplary followers do this by:

- being alert to the needs of others;
- appreciating follower differences, and recognizing the power of those differences;
- respecting each other's (followers) boundaries;
- building strong lateral communication and coordination efforts;
- participating in creative thinking;
- remembering who is being served—this helps followers maintain common ground; and
- being willing to both lead and follow peers toward the common good. (Chaleff, 1995; Kellerman, 2005)

Because the role of follower is so important, a wise leader practices good followership when appropriate. Jax (2000) suggests times when a leader should follow: (1) if another individual has more/better judgment, experience, or skills than the leader; (2) if an individual's growth requires that the leader facilitate their leadership development over her or his own; (3) if the work of the team requires that the leader "get in there" and do the work

with the group; and (4) if the organization's purpose and goals warrant it. In follower roles, leaders might ask questions instead of giving answers, provide opportunities for others to lead, serve as a resource to the group, do the task with the group, and facilitate the group's work.

Chaleff (1995) has characterized the most capable follower as a *courageous follower.* This type of follower has the courage to do several things:

1. *Assume responsibility* for themselves and the organization. They discover and create opportunities to fulfill their personal potential; they initiate values-based action.

2. *Serve*—They are not afraid of hard work and they often assume new duties to free up the leader. They stand up for their leader, and they pursue the common purpose.

3. *Challenge*—They speak up when something goes against what they believe. They are willing to stand up, stand out, risk rejection, and initiate conflict when appropriate. They value organizational harmony, but not at the expense of the common purpose and integrity.

4. *Participate in transformation*—Courageous followers recognize the need for transformation. They champion the need for change, and they become full participants in the change as appropriate.

5. *Leave*—Followers know when it is time to separate from a leader and group. When leaders are ineffective or actions are detrimental to the common purpose, courageous followers are prepared to withdraw their support and disavow the leader despite high personal risk.

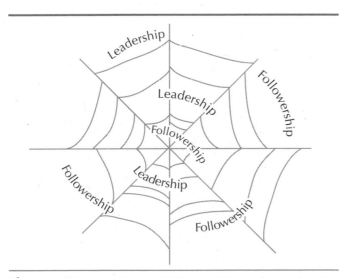

Figure 1.3 Leadership and followership are interrelated and interdependent.

The Follower Creed

"I will follow you, if you—
    Treat me with respect,
    Inspire me with your vision,
    Teach me,
    Are tolerant of my mistakes,
    Are visible and available,
    Talk with (and listen to) me,
    Allow me to grow,
    Don't give up or change course arbitrarily,
    Have the courage of your convictions,
    Tell me the truth, and
    Practice what you preach."

Figure 1.4 The Follower Creed (O'Toole, 1999, p. 111)

Capable leaders and followers share many traits, skills, and competencies. Leaders typically possess stronger conceptual, relationship-building, and initiative skills than followers because these are the ingredients that help groups to function well. In this next section, the various types of skills associated with effective leadership—and followership—are discussed.

Leader Skills

Successful leaders exhibit skills in many areas, which distinguish them from followers. Skills consist of the knowledge and abilities we gain throughout life. Effective leaders continually work on their skills to become better at what they do. In fact, innumerable authors discuss the need for and importance of lifelong learning in an effective leader (Clark, 2006b; Ruderman & Ernst, 2004). It might be helpful to view leadership development as a personal journey—a path that each one of us is on every day of our lives. Everything we do, everything we say, and every decision we make all constitute part of our own leadership development. Thus, it is wise to be very aware of the decisions we make, as well as the things we do and say. We should ask ourselves, "Is *doing this* going to help make me the type of leader I want to be?" Three skill areas have been identified by numerous authors which combine to make a highly skilled leader: *conceptual skills, interpersonal skills,* and *technical skills.*

Conceptual Skills

Conceptual skills include the ability to analyze, anticipate, see the big picture, and use sound judgment. A leader scans, makes note of subtleties observed in a situation, and uses her or his judgment to decide about a course of action. Leaders have long-range vision and continually look for what is best for the future. Critical thinking, problem solving, creativity, and being able to handle ambiguity are commonly considered conceptual skills. Being able to articulate a philosophy of recreation and how it guides one's use of leadership styles, contributing to the agency, and striving to better society are other competencies that fit within this skill group (Russell, 2005). In addition, conceptual skills comprise following the organizational mission through one's actions and decisions, adhering to internal values, and understanding one's role in promoting the leisure services profession. Without conceptual skills it would be difficult to integrate interpersonal and technical skills into leadership situations.

Interpersonal Skills

Interpersonal skills are those skills and leadership techniques that involve relationships with people. Understanding group dynamics, facilitating cooperation and trust building among participants, and being a good communicator all fit within the interpersonal skills of leadership. Understanding and being able to resolve conflicts, and making people feel welcomed, valued, and respected also fit within the interpersonal component. Success in leisure services requires strong interpersonal skills. Leisure services professionals work with people as participants in the community, as peer professionals in the community, and as peers, subordinates and superiors in the workplace. Thus, these skills must become well-honed for successful recreation leaders. In addition to conceptual and interpersonal competencies, being able to do the work is another important skill for successful leadership.

Photo courtesy of Deb Jordan

Leadership as a personal journey involves self-awareness and reflection.

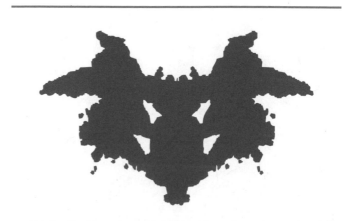

Figure 1.5 Creativity requires leaders to see many different things in one situation.

Technical Skills

Technical skills relate specifically to accomplishing tasks. These are the skills needed for professional competence. They enable a person to do a particular job or task. As we think about those skills necessary for jobs in parks, recreation, and leisure, among other things, leaders plan, implement, and evaluate programs and services (Hersey, Blanchard & Johnson, 2001). Leaders also deal with logistics, safety and legal issues, and office tasks. Other technical skills used by leisure practitioners in direct leadership positions include leading songs, games, and activities in a variety of settings. Technical skills are readily taught to most leaders-to-be. It should be noted that a person who is successful at technical tasks may be an excellent technician, yet a poor leader. An effective leader also needs strong interpersonal and conceptual skills.

❖   ❖   ❖

All three domains of leadership skills are critical to success in parks, recreation, and leisure services. Much study, practice, and real-world experience are necessary to become proficient in these three areas. As with all elements of success, to be truly good at what we do we need ongoing study, learning, and refinement of the skill domains that characterize leadership. Becoming a leader is a lifelong journey; it should also be a conscious one.

Impact of Gender, Ethnicity, and Age

Because early research about leadership primarily utilized white males as subjects, the influences of gender, ethnicity, or age on the effective use of the three skill domains were not examined. As these influences became more prominent

in terms of the study of leadership, researchers began to investigate their impact on the delivery of leisure services.

Stereotypes, which are fixed ideas (often unfavorable) about members of a particular group, are related to demographic variables such as ethnicity, age and gender, and they often influence the acceptance of leadership by followers (Bratton, Grint & Nelson, 2005); Dubrin, 2004). They are ways that we categorize others, causing us to assume and expect what people of a certain group will be like and how they will act. When individuals identify and acknowledge a leader, they mix expectations (i.e., stereotypes) of leadership with expectations about the group that person appears to represent (e.g., elderly, Hispanic, disabled). If the expectations and stereotypes do not appear to be in sync, group members may not follow that person, or will do so with some hesitation.

For instance, teenagers are often perceived (and therefore, expected) to be irresponsible, immature, impatient, and unable to make sound decisions. Leaders are expected to be very responsible, mature, patient, and able to make good decisions. These two short lists are stereotypes—negative expectations for teens and positive expectations for leaders. Someone who believes these stereotypes will automatically assume that every teenager has the negative traits and that every leader has the positive traits. Therefore, the expectations or stereotypes about teens and leaders are perceived as incompatible. While the stereotype is not accurately applied to all teens, a person who believed the stereotypes would not view teenagers as leaders. Obviously, this would eliminate leadership opportunities for many talented teens before giving them a chance to demonstrate their skills. Similar scenarios could be devised relating the influences of gender, ethnicity, and physical impairment on perceived leadership ability.

Generally, U.S. society prescribes roles for women and men, old and young, for those who have disabilities and those who do not, and for people of color and those who are white. On the surface, some of these roles would seem incompatible with the competencies identified as necessary for leadership. For instance, it has long been noted that in U.S. culture, women are expected and perceived to be better at interpersonal skills (i.e., better with relationships) than men, and men are presumably better than women with technical and conceptual skills (i.e., better with doing and thinking; Groves, 2005). Hogue, Yoder & Ludwig (2002) and Sczesny, Boask, Neff & Schyns (2004) report that in many instances women are less likely to be seen as leaders than are men. Others have found that women in leadership roles tend to use an empowering type of leadership rather than a "command-and-control" type of leadership (Groves, 2005; Northouse, 2001).

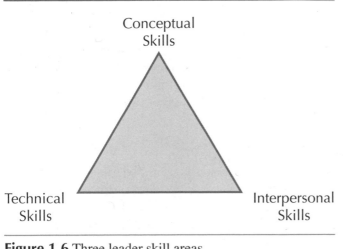

Figure 1.6 Three leader skill areas

An effective leader, therefore, might be anyone: a 10-year-old, a person of Hispanic heritage, an individual who is blind, a woman, or anyone else with the skills and initiative to fill a leadership role.

Eagly and colleagues (1995) found that, in general, men have had more opportunities for formal leadership than have women; at the same time women have gained much experience in informal settings and in followership roles. This difference in access to leadership roles is thought to be one of the reasons that people view women and men differently in terms of competence and experience in leadership positions.

Some researchers have found that perceptions of differences in leadership abilities based on gender and ethnicity are really due to perceived differences in status and power. Women and people of color tend to have a lower social status and less access to resources (i.e., power) in U.S. society than white males (Bartol, Martin & Kromkowski, 2003). Leadership is perceived as being a high status/high power position. Thus, those with high social status and perceived power are more likely be accepted as leaders than those with less recognized status and power. We should be alert to this "gendering" or "ethnicizing" of leadership as each of us moves into various leadership roles. Group expectations must be managed to facilitate effective leadership for a woman, an elderly person, someone with a disability, or a person of color.

To make a generalization that one gender, age, or ethnic group excels at leadership is inaccurate and not particularly constructive. To be an effective leader—rather than a woman leader, elderly leader, or Native American leader—one must be skilled in the three primary leadership competencies and have the ability to use those skills appropriately. An effective leader, therefore, might be anyone: a ten year old, a person of Hispanic heritage, an individual who is blind, a woman, or anyone else with the skills and initiative to fill a leadership role.

Leader Traits and Qualities

In addition to the types of skills necessary for successful leadership, many qualities or traits have been identified as being important to leadership. Traits are qualities or characteristics of an individual. Generally, people believe that leaders possess many positive qualities. If you were asked to make a list of leadership qualities, you would very likely identify a list similar to that reported in the research literature about leadership. The challenge lies in determining which traits and qualities are of most importance to a leader. While researchers still struggle with this, there is some level of concurrence; agreed upon traits are discussed below.

Self-Awareness and Identity

An effective leader is one who is self-aware (Brocato, 2003; Tubbs, 2006). Effective leaders understand the notion of leadership development as a journey. They practice self-reflection to learn more about themselves. Effective leaders develop awareness of their attitudes, talents, weaknesses, biases, strengths, and predispositions. They willingly work on developing their talents and learning how to apply them in the best light. They have inwardly decided to grow more conscious, developed, and skilled in the ways of leadership.

Because of this inward examination, an effective leader has a sense of identity—an understanding of who she or he is and is not. A strong sense of self allows a leader to be in many different situations and remain true. Identity is based on a set of core values, the guiding beliefs in one's life, and is related to integrity. It is what allows a person to feel a sense of wholeness and integration. A leader with a strong sense of self exudes self-confidence and a sense of who she or he is no matter the situation. These leaders tend to be easy to follow because they are consistent in their leadership efforts.

Courage

An effective leader has courage to do what she or he believes is right, to stand up for her or his convictions, and to go against the grain when needed; she or he has the courage to take risks (Dixon & Westbrook, 2003; Stone, Russell & Patterson, 2004). Courage involves the willingness to make difficult decisions, to try new things, and to make and admit mistakes so that as much as possible can be learned from every situation. Being willing to take risks and accepting responsibility for one's own actions are elements of courage. Some believe that courage is a

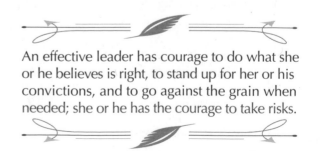

An effective leader has courage to do what she or he believes is right, to stand up for her or his convictions, and to go against the grain when needed; she or he has the courage to take risks.

force within a person. In an effective leader, courage must be accompanied by consideration. Being considerate of others in the face of courage is necessary to achieve a balance in leadership.

Creativity

According to several authors, leaders are creative (Banutu-Gomez, 2004; Clark, 2006a; Tubbs, 2006). Creativity involves thinking broadly, a willingness to try new ideas, and not being afraid to look silly. Creative people can usually think in abstract terms and see one thing from many different perspectives. Creative people color outside of the lines (and are proud of it), challenge others to think in a fluid fashion, and have a good sense of humor. They use their imagination to create meaningful and new ideas and interpretations as they go beyond traditional ideas, rules, relationships, and patterns. Being creative is necessary whether one is leading an activity, solving a facility-related problem, or planning a program.

Drive and Determination

A successful leader has drive and determination to see tasks through to completion (Clark, 2006c; Tubbs, 2006). This resolve helps a leader to focus and meet her or his commitment to the group as well as the group goals. Leaders with drive seem compelled to continue their quest and to help the group move forward. In the face of difficulties or challenges, leaders with drive and determination persevere—they move through the challenge, learn from the struggle, and continue to work toward the desired end.

Focus and Commitment

Two other key characteristics of leaders mentioned throughout the leadership literature are focus and commitment (Banutu-Gomez, 2004; Dixon & Westbrook, 2003; Lu, 2004). Effective leaders have a focus; they know what they are aiming for and they can articulate that focus to others. In fact, effective leaders are often individuals who clarify that focus for followers. Commitment refers to being committed to the ideal (which is often the ultimate focus), as well as to one's group or organization. It is so important to leadership development that one author suggests that leaders need to "show *uncommon* commitment" (Cohen, 1998, p. 32, emphasis added). This commitment, in conjunction with focus, helps to drive leaders and move groups forward.

High Expectations

Effective and respected leaders have high expectations of themselves as well as others (Leavy, 2003; Schruijer, 2002). They expect quality, work for quality, and thereby achieve quality. High expectations carry over into all aspects of leadership—conceptual skills (e.g., expecting to be able to find solutions to dilemmas), interpersonal skills (e.g., expecting positive and upbeat things from people), and technical skills (e.g., striving for a perfect safety record). The self-fulfilling prophecy suggests that what people expect, they receive. This means that a leader who expects a great deal and who has high standards commonly finds that followers meet those high expectations. At the same time, a leader with low standards and expectations of others may find that followers rise only as high as those expectations. High expectations give followers a target for which they can aim.

Honesty

Dixon and Westbrook (2003) and Lu (2004) report the most important trait or quality of a leader is honesty. Being upfront and telling the truth in a kind and compassionate manner is an important aspect of developing trust between leaders and followers. If a group feels as though the leader is not being completely honest, is holding back information that affects them, or is purposefully deceiving

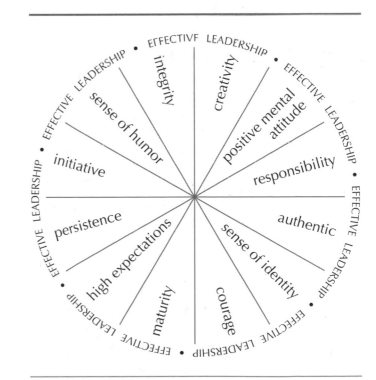

Figure 1.7 Many qualities are associated with effective leadership.

them, she or he will not be accepted as the leader for long. A leader who is viewed as honest will also be viewed as being trustworthy, and the group will be likely to accept her or his skills and talents as the leader.

Integrity

Every day people face ethical choices and decisions that impact others. Integrity means doing what is right rather than what is the easiest. In addition to honesty, integrity is another building block that forms the basis for trust between people. Respected and effective leaders have the integrity and courage to be honest with themselves and others. If a group does not trust a leader, the leader will be ineffective in working with the group. Like a person with a strong sense of self, a leader with integrity has a solid core of values and ethical principles upon which she or he bases decisions, actions, and thoughts. These values are apparent to others and remain consistent across situations (Stone, Russell & Patterson, 2004; Storr, 2004).

> Like a person with a strong sense of self, a leader with integrity has a solid core of values and ethical principles upon which she or he bases decisions, actions, and thoughts.

Positive Mental Attitude

Highly sought-after leaders maintain a positive attitude in the midst of not-so-positive situations. A positive mental attitude (PMA) allows a leader to always see the bright side of situations. They have high energy and know how to use it (Dupuis, Bloom & Loughead, 2006; Krishnan, 2004). These leaders celebrate both success and failure because those experiences help them to learn (McDermott, 2004). People with PMAs are fascinating people. They always seem upbeat and look for the good in others and in situations. They tend to be good listeners and want to help others. People desire to be around those who have a positive attitude; leaders who can maintain this tend to be well-respected and successful. Leaders with PMA typically have confidence in themselves and in others.

Other Leader Qualities

Other research has reported desirable leader qualities to include competence, vision, inspiration, intelligence, fairness, tolerance, straightforwardness, imagination, and

professionalism (Brocato, 2003; Lu, 2004). Nelson and Quick (2005) identified additional items for the list of leader qualities: a sense of friendliness, self-motivation, supportive of group tasks, control over one's own emotions, dominance, great physical energy, a willingness to take risks, strong values, and maturity. According to numerous other authors, desired leader qualities also include the following:

- adaptability
- can be a follower
- communication skills
- compassionate
- cooperativeness
- curiosity
- empathy
- emotional intelligence
- emotional maturity
- enabling personality
- sense of fairness
- flexibility

- good health
- high energy
- strives for justice
- initiative
- insightfulness
- persistence
- persuasive
- pleasing appearance
- sense of humor
- stamina
- tact
- warm personality

(Groves, 2005; Hultman, 2006; Kanter, 2005; Tubbs, 2006)

❖ ❖ ❖

Many people have given a good deal of thought to leader traits and qualities (and many people like to make lists!). While particular qualities are important, one must have a solid knowledge base to be a truly effective and respected leader. Continuous self-development and self-improvement are the hallmarks of an exemplary leader. In and of themselves, leadership qualities will not result in effective leadership.

Values

Values have been described as the attitudes about the worth of people, concepts, and things (Clark, 2006c; Krishnan, 2004). They are central to effective leadership, and leaders need to be conscious of their personal, organizational, and cultural values. Discussions about values often arouse controversy—some believe it is not right for any one person or agency to assert her or his values on another; others believe this to be absolutely necessary. One belief position asserts that all values are equally good; another belief paradigm judges values by religious or philosophical tenets. People commonly question where (and by whom) values should be taught—the home, church, school, playground, or other social institutions.

Values are everywhere; none of us operates in a values vacuum. Everything we say and do reflects our values and the larger values of our culture. The way we wear our hair, our choice of clothing, even the language we use reflects our personal and cultural values. Leaders in leisure services must know and understand the values they promote covertly (i.e., subtly) as well as overtly (i.e., purposefully) through their work and chosen leadership styles. We should also remember that it is important for leaders to acknowledge, understand, and be considerate of others' cultural values in order to be a compassionate leader. Many of these values serve as the foundation for various leadership theories presented in the next chapter.

In addition to values related to right and wrong, there are other values that effective and well-respected leaders exhibit in their work. Krishnan (2004) offers ten value types that indicate a commitment to positive leadership opportunities. Because there is no stated order of importance, they are presented here in alphabetical order.

An Achievement Orientation

Achievement orientation is a value that indicates a sense of initiative or taking action and follow-through. It includes values related to personal success, ambition, and intelligence. A leader who exhibits an achievement orientation and focuses on successfully achieving goals (i.e., societal, organizational, or personal) tends to be well-respected. An achievement orientation can help a leader see a task through from beginning to end (including cleanup and evaluation). It involves staying focused on the task and working with people to ensure each individual's strengths are being utilized to achieve group goals throughout the entire process.

Benevolence

Leaders who value benevolence tend to be helpful, honest, forgiving, loyal, and responsible individuals. A person who values benevolence often engenders a similar sense of helpfulness and "other" orientation in group members. Successful and effective leaders know their group members' needs and focus on the group's needs, rather than their own. This means that the needs of others are put ahead of the needs of the leader. The leader's primary responsibility is to help others do their jobs well and successfully. For instance, as a leader moves about and observes others at work, she or he constantly wonders, "What can I do to make that person's job easier? What does that person need right now to make things move smoothly? How can I make that happen for them?" In this way, the leader manifests an *enabling personality* (Ross & Offerman, 1997).

Conformity

In some respects leaders are a paradox—they are conformists and revolutionaries at the same time. Leadership requires innovation, imagination, creativity, and a willingness to take risks. At the same time, it requires an understanding and agreement with what is socially acceptable. As a value category, conformity includes being polite, obedient, self-disciplined, and honoring one's elders. Clearly, respect for self, others, and institutions is embedded in this value type.

Hedonism

Many are surprised to see hedonism included in a list of values related to leadership. Hedonism has a connotation of being nothing but self-indulgent and self-satisfying. With a broader look, however, hedonism refers to enjoying life and experiencing pleasure. There is no doubt that leaders who exude a love of life and pleasure in what they do attract followers who want to share a similar outlook on life. When taken out of the selfish context, this value is important for leaders to demonstrate.

Power

Elements of power include authority, wealth (broadly conceived), and social recognition or status. By the position they fill, leaders are viewed as having power. As with hedonism, however, leadership is not about the selfish accumulation or use of power. Rather, it is about using power in appropriate ways to facilitate group development and task accomplishment. It also is about using one's position as leader to *empower* others—to help others

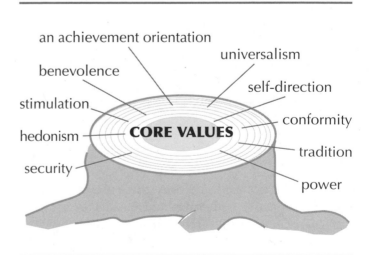

Figure 1.8 Effective leadership requires a leader to have a solid core of values.

discover and make use of their own strengths and gifts in the group's work.

Security

One of the responsibilities of a leader is to make others feel safe—physically, psychologically, and emotionally. This value type includes safety, social order, health, and cleanliness. Leaders who value these aspects of this value demonstrate it personally through actions as well as their sense of being. Maintaining personal health and cleanliness (e.g., physical, mental, emotional, spiritual) serves as a foundation for group members to feel secure. Ensuring group safety through relationship building and maintenance are other elements of this value.

Self-Direction

The fact that leaders lead by example and model behaviors is important to remember. Self-direction includes displaying independent thought, freedom, self-discipline, and a sense of personal identity—all traits members of effective groups exhibit. Effective leaders know who they are and where they want to go. They also usually have good ideas about how to reach their goals. The contradiction of self-discipline and freedom, for instance, gives us an idea about the need for balance in being self-directed.

Stimulation

Previously it was mentioned that effective leaders are innovative, creative, and have positive mental attitudes. Leaders engage in stimulating activities to enhance these traits. The activities might be intellectual (e.g., generating new ideas) or physical (e.g., hang gliding) or a combination of both. Included within this type of value is a desire or need for challenge, daring exploits, novelty, excitement, and variety. Through seeking stimulation leaders not only keep themselves invigorated and rejuvenated, they also energize group members. Lively groups tend to be actively involved in the task at hand and work together in ways that develop synergy.

Tradition

Because sudden change can cause anxiety among group members, effective leaders remain grounded. In this instance, being grounded refers to understanding and respecting the customs, conventions, and mores of a group or agency. When people feel as though their traditions are understood and valued, they are more open to taking risks and trying something new. Thus, while it is necessary to

Effective leadership requires a solid core of values.

be creative and "think outside of the box," it is also necessary to acknowledge and honor "the way things have been" to effect change and move a group forward.

Universalism

The last type of value presented by Krishnan includes important, yet often neglected factors. Universalism includes being broad-minded, expressing a commitment to social justice and equality, and protecting the environment. Being open to new ideas, new ways of doing things, new types of thinking, and new people are hallmarks of an effective leader. Working for social justice and equality for all helps a leader to appreciate and respect group members from all "walks of life" and to address each person with dignity. Being aware of one's own impact on the environment as well as the group impact on the environment acknowledges the role of steward that we all play with regard to limited resources.

❖ ❖ ❖

Leaders fill a variety of complex roles. They have all of the qualifications and limitations of followers. They have good days and bad days. Some have a lot of leadership experience and some do not. Those who strive to be the most effective in leadership work to develop the skills, qualities, and values of leaders deemed by researchers as necessary for effective leadership. As leaders, we evolve over time and continually improve our skills—leadership is a lifelong journey. Those who strive to be the strongest leader possible practice self-reflection, stay focused, and engage in ongoing personal development.

Levels of Leadership

So far, we have examined definitions of leadership, explained the types of skills needed for successful leadership, and identified leader qualities and values, which are important to followers and group members. These traits and values are important whether leading a recreational activity or developing a budget because they permeate everything leaders do. Leading an activity and developing a budget are very different tasks and typically are the responsibility of individuals at different levels of leadership. The following will discuss three levels of leadership that exist within an organization: administrative, supervisory, and direct.

Administrative Leadership

The administrative level of leadership also is referred to as the *managerial* or *executive level*. Administration typically includes the agency director and assistant directors or president and vice presidents. In a hierarchical organization this would be the top level; in a web or spoke-shaped organizational structure the administration may be either at the center or the outer edge. This level of leadership primarily concerns itself with what would be considered administrative matters such as the budget, organizational structure, establishment of a vision and agency philosophy, raising funds, and writing grants.

Typically administrative leaders have responsibility for the entire organization or a large department. Thus, a solid knowledge of all aspects of an organization, including supervisory and direct leadership, is required for an administrative leader to be most effective. People at this level of leadership need strong conceptual skills, good technical skills, excellent interpersonal skills, and the ability to make sound decisions in the midst of much activity.

Supervisory Leadership

Supervisory leadership is commonly thought of as the middle level of leadership within an agency or organization. Supervisory leaders report to administrators and supervise or help guide those in direct leadership positions as well as other staff members. Common titles for this level of leadership include division head, program director, unit leader, district manager, and director of contract services.

Supervisory leaders typically have responsibility for staff members in a particular department, program area, or unit within an agency. Individuals in this type of leadership position make some decisions directly related to their particular unit and must be able to work with people and be strong problem solvers. When needed, supervisory leaders will step into the role of direct leader. Therefore, a good foundation of direct leadership is necessary to be successful at the supervisory level.

Direct Leadership

In leisure service agencies and organizations, the individuals in direct leadership roles provide service directly to participants. If an agency conducts recreation programs, the direct leader plans, prepares for, implements, and evaluates the specific program. Common titles for people in direct leadership positions include recreation aide,

naturalist, recreation technician, activity leader, recreation therapist, camp counselor, and instructor (e.g., martial arts, aerobics, canoe).

Direct leaders also are called *face-to-face leaders* because they interact on a one-on-one basis with participants. To be successful, direct leaders must have a solid knowledge of the activities appropriate to the position (e.g., swim instructors must know stroke techniques), understand safety hazards and how to manage them, and practice excellent people skills. Direct leaders are considered front-line staff and, because they interact closely with participants, are vital to quality offerings. This text focuses on information and skills primarily needed by those involved in direct leadership.

❖   ❖   ❖

Although the three basic levels of leadership are distinct, similar skills, traits, and values are desirable for leaders at all levels. The skills will be utilized differently as required by the particular groups of followers for each level of leadership. While it is not a hard-and-fast rule, generally administrative leaders work directly with supervisors; supervisors work with direct leaders; and direct leaders work with participants. Within each of these levels, groups recognize different people as leaders through different mechanisms. There are situations where the same person fulfills all three leadership roles for one leisure services agency.

Figure 1.9 Organizations have three levels of leadership.

How Are Leaders Identified?

A person may have the title of leader and still not be accepted as such by the group she or he is to be leading. For instance, in a school classroom a substitute teacher may be the leader—in title. However, if the students do not accept and reinforce that role, the substitute teacher might not be perceived as the actual leader. In fact, when a substitute teacher is in the classroom it is not uncommon for a student in the class to be the true leader of her or his classmates. To be a leader, one must be recognized and accepted as such by the group. Individuals become recognized and reinforced as leaders by the group in several ways. A leader might be appointed, the leader may be elected, she or he might emerge from the group, the person's charisma might cause others to follow, or leadership might be attributed to the "halo effect."

Appointment

A leader may be appointed to a titled position that identifies her or him as the leader. This may occur from the administrative level within an agency or from within a group. The agency director, for instance, may hire (i.e., appoint) a person to be a leader in a position of lifeguard. In another case the group might appoint a leader (e.g., chairperson) to facilitate completion of a task. Once appointed, that person must fulfill the roles and responsibilities of a leader and utilize leadership skills and techniques to the best of her or his ability. Appointed leaders often earn respect as a leader through their actions and attitudes related to the group goals. Appointed leaders, however, are not always automatically accepted as such by followers.

Election

Many groups elect leaders to leadership positions. In many sporting events, for instance, individuals may be elected leaders and given the title of "team captain." Team captains are expected to guide team members, set the tone for the team, and serve as a motivating force. Respect and admiration may be given at first, but it must continue to be earned through leadership actions. It should be remembered that some people elected to leadership positions are chosen for their popularity, financial status, or intimidation tactics. Therefore, an elected leader is not necessarily the best person for the leadership role.

Emergence

In the early stages of group development, there are times when a group has no clearly identifiable leader. No one

To be a leader, one must be recognized and accepted as such by the group.

has been appointed or elected, and initially, the group is somewhat adrift. Then, from within the group, one person emerges as the leader. As the task or group continues to exist, it becomes apparent that one person "rises to the top" in terms of leadership. That individual may be recognized as the leader by group members for her or his knowledge of an activity, her or his skills at mediating conflict, or her or his understanding of what the group needs to accomplish. A leader who emerges from a group often has the respect of the group members because she or he is first a group member who became the leader.

Charisma

Charisma is defined as personal magnetism or charm. A leader with charisma induces group members to follow with ease, and greatly influences them. A charismatic leader arouses a great deal of enthusiasm and loyalty from within the group. In informal leisure settings, charismatic leaders seem to draw group members to them. Followers often work hard to be noticed by a charismatic leader, and

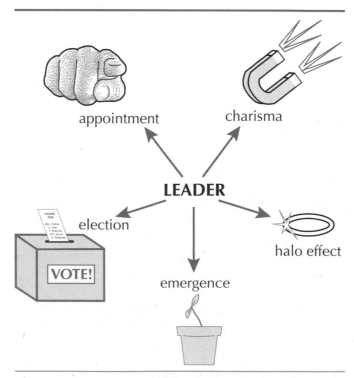

Figure 1.10 Leaders are identified in five different ways.

tend to respect such a person out of a sense of loyalty. As with elected leaders, people with charisma may be very positive role models and leaders (e.g., Jane Addams), or they may be individuals who use their personal charm to the detriment of others (e.g., Adolf Hitler). Care must be taken in the accolades given a leader selected based solely on personal charisma.

The Halo Effect

The halo effect refers to how certain attributes or thoughts about a person carry over into other situations. For instance, the class clown in one classroom is often perceived to be the class clown in other classes—even if she or he does not engage in clowning behaviors. The same effect occurs in leadership situations. The halo effect describes a scenario where a person is a leader in one group and others look to her or him to be the leader in other groups in which she or he is involved. As with other ways that leaders are recognized, this may or may not be the best situation for the group.

❖　❖　❖

There are several avenues through which individuals may be identified as leaders. No matter how a person gained the position or title of leader, however, she or he may not be the best suited for the needs of the group and situation. A skilled leader will constantly adapt and develop as situations warrant. In recreation and leisure settings, being aware of how one is perceived as a leader may help in guiding the use of leadership skills and techniques to move the group forward. Once a person becomes a group leader, she or he needs to understand how her or his (and their group members') power is perceived and utilized.

Power

Power is a phenomenon related to leadership; in fact, many people confuse leadership with power. Some think that the one with the most power automatically becomes the leader; however, this is not always the case. Power can be defined as the influence an individual (or group) wields over another, and as the ability to overcome resistance and get things done (Krishnan, 2003; Ward, 2001). Power is the capacity to influence others, and it is inherent in all relationships. A common notion is that powerful people are strong, aggressive, knowledgeable, intelligent, empathetic, and somewhat ruthless (Preston, 2005). However, power exists in all relationships and is more often than not exercised in a subtle and constructive fashion.

Power is commonly perceived to be a finite construct where in order for one person to have power, another has less or none. Typically, a leader has more power than group members; it is the group members who confer power on the leader. This means that if a group does not want to defer to a leader (i.e., bestow power on her or him), the leader will experience difficulty in influencing group members.

With this viewpoint in mind, one of the dilemmas associated with the use of power is that a power relationship is often an unbalanced relationship—one person has more power than another; this creates a "one-up, one-down" relationship. Johnson and Johnson (2003) note that inappropriate use of power in these cases can result in resistance from group members. Further, they note that the effectiveness of a group is improved when power is relatively balanced among group members and that power is based on competence, expertise and information. Balanced power leads to a sense of commitment and cooperation by all members of the group.

This balanced view of power typically arises when power is viewed as infinite—it is shared among all group members (including the leader). In this way leaders are challenged to *empower* group members to meet their individual potentials. This involves providing the social support, resources, time, and opportunities to exercise one's personal power; it often manifests in the leader serving as a facilitator.

To understand the various manifestations of power, a taxonomy of social power was suggested by French and Raven in 1959 (as cited in Koslowsky & Stashevsky, 2005; Politis, 2005). It is commonly used throughout leadership literature and has been expanded upon since it was first introduced. Individuals, groups, and leaders all use one or more of these types of power in different situations.

Coercive

Followers of people who use coercive power believe a coercive leader has the capability to punish them and withhold resources. Also included in this type of power is an individual's fear that someone will disapprove or dislike her or him (as social beings, we have a strong desire to be liked). A coercive leader, for example, could be one who has the ability to suspend participants from a sports league, to withhold a paycheck, or to make an individual sit in time-out. This tends to be the least effective form of power over time.

Connections/Networking

In this day and age when networking is considered vital to one's professional development, an individual who has varied and strong connections with others in the field is often perceived as having this type of power. Networking is characterized by the adage, "It's not what you know, but who you know." Certainly, connections and networking can increase an individual's information base and ability to influence. People who "name drop" at gatherings are often trying to assert this type of power.

Empowerment

Empowerment is power to do—power that is shared with others. In this view power is not seen as finite, but rather as expansive. Giving power to followers enables them (and the leader) to accomplish more and experience a sense of self-esteem. Leaders empower people when they teach them the skills, provide them the social support, and give them the resources to meet group goals. Empowerment involves people having the authority to make appropriate decisions for the situation at hand without having to get permission every step of the way. As an example, a front desk staff member might be empowered to handle customer complaints by listening and giving free pool passes to allay irate patrons.

Expert Power

Some people attribute a person with power because they believe this individual has special knowledge or expertise about the best way to do something. This type of power is usually attributed to an individual in a specific situation.

Figure 1.11 Leaders use eleven different types of power in various situations.

For example, an individual who has the knowledge to understand the meaning of gang symbols will likely be granted power when in gang-tagged (with graffiti and symbols) territory. If a leader creates the perception that she or he has expertise in a particular area and then fails to demonstrate the expected knowledge, she or he would lose power very quickly.

Helplessness

Helplessness power is used by all of us at one time or another. People claim to be infirm or helpless to induce others to do something for them. This is a form of indirect power and can be quite successful in terms of influencing others to action. Examples of this include seeking help with a crafts project by claiming a lack of skill to complete it, and requesting help with heavy equipment by acting helpless when trying to move it. It is not uncommon for group members or participants to demonstrate helplessness power, but it is not a form of power recommended for leaders.

Indirect Power

In groups where power may be relatively balanced, there may be times when a faction of group members will use indirect power to influence another member of the group who is perceived to be an outlier. In this case, the subgroup would subtly use group norms to convince the other member to join with them on a particular endeavor. For instance, a group member may say to another, "You know, around here, we follow this process…" This is a subtle way of telling a group member to stop doing something in one manner and follow previously established group customs.

Informational

A person with informational power has access to information that can impact another individual. For example, a secretary or administrative assistant takes phone messages (and can "lose" them), files paperwork (which can be "misplaced"), and knows when meetings are being held (but can "forget" to tell you). This is often an unrecognized form or source of power, yet is crucial to organizational success.

Legitimate

In this situation the one with legitimate power is seen as having the right and/or authority to do something (usually by way of position), and others are obliged to follow. For instance, students generally confer legitimate power on teachers, and participants generally attribute this type of power to leisure services leaders. It is important to note that just because an individual holds a position with a title and authority does not necessarily mean that the leader will have influence over the group.

Referent (Charisma)

People admire, respect, and look up to a person with referent power; she or he may have warmth, personal charisma, and charm that draws others to her or him. Followers typically want to be associated with a leader who has this type of power. Examples of referent power have been attributed to people such as John F. Kennedy, Mahatma Gandhi, and Eleanor Roosevelt.

Reward

Reward power is often viewed as the converse of coercive power. Followers believe this individual has the capability to reward them; the powerful person has control of resources that are perceived as rewards or as being useful to the group. For instance, if a recreation leader has the ability to give free spa passes to well-behaved participants, she or he would be perceived as having reward power.

Social Status

Often those with higher levels of social status, as indicated by their position in the community, their occupation, or their history of altruism, are perceived to have more power than those with low social status. Social status and the power that goes with it may be attributed to people who are team captains, gang leaders, and the president of an organization (e.g., class president, president of the state recreation association).

❖ ❖ ❖

Understanding power as well as one's personal style of influence is an important tool for leisure services leaders. Braynion (2004) has found that those leaders who understand and know how to use power are more effective than those who do not. In support of that idea, Preston (2005) offers several strategies for exercising one's power in positive ways. Among those strategies are words of advice to remain calm in the face of negativity—be unflappable. Powerful people, while they show human vulnerability, do not react emotionally when things are not going the way they would like. Sharing information with others and being deliberate in decision-making are other power strategies. Giving careful thought to a situation, making a decision, and sticking to it are further signs of power. At the same time, people with power do not make commitments they

will be unable to keep. Preston notes that powerful people have large networks; thus, building one's professional network is important to being viewed as powerful by others. Finally, engaging in ongoing learning opportunities to expand one's understanding and use of power are significant strategies to conveying and sharing power wisely.

Power can be used in both positive and negative ways. Power often implies an imbalance in perceptions of capabilities and as such can leave those who are perceived to lack power feeling less than adequate. Leaders, however, can use power positively to enable others and help them reach their full potential. Wisely used, power is a valid aspect of leadership and group dynamics. An effective leader will use power appropriately (to the group and the situation) and consistently consider the impacts of various types of power on group members.

Summary

Leisure services practitioners interact with participants in many ways. These interactions may enhance or detract from the leisure experience. Because leadership is an inherent factor in structured recreation experiences, all leisure services professionals need leadership skills. Leadership can be defined as a dynamic process of interactions between two or more members of a group which involves recognition and acceptance of leader-follower roles by group members within a certain situation. It also involves activities on the part of the leader and followers that aid the group in moving toward its goals.

After establishing a definition of leadership for use in this text, this chapter presented information about necessary competencies and skills of leaders. Leadership skills fall into three categories: conceptual, interpersonal, and technical skills. Leader traits and qualities were reviewed, as were the values of effective and successful leaders. Because it is not possible to live in a "values vacuum," it is important for leaders to understand and appreciate the values they promote through action, attire, and attitude.

After examining traits and characteristics of successful leaders, three levels of leadership were presented: administrative, leaders who interact directly with supervisors; supervisory leaders, who report to administrators and interact directly with face-to-face leaders; and direct leaders, who also are considered face-to-face leaders because they interact directly with participants. Leaders at all levels of leadership may have a tremendous impact on a successful leisure experience; therefore, learning about leadership is vital for all who intend to work in the leisure services profession.

Lastly, leaders may be identified through a variety of mechanisms, each of which has its advantages and disadvantages. Some leaders are recognized by title, while others are conferred by the group. No matter how one is identified as a leader, she or he must continue to act like and be a leader to maintain group respect and followership. Furthermore, understanding power and how it can be used contributes to continued, successful leadership. Power may be viewed as finite or infinite and is shared with group members to the extent a leader is comfortable.

Beginning the Journey

As mentioned in the introductory materials of this text, leadership is a personal journey. For each one of us, this personal journey consists of lifelong learning about ourselves as well as our understanding of leadership as a construct. To assist you in understanding the material in this chapter and how it relates to you as a leader, these end-of-chapter critical thinking questions are provided for your consideration. You are encouraged to use these questions as part of your own journey to leadership.

1. Choose five of the ways leadership has been defined over the years and discuss them with others. With which do you agree or disagree most strongly? Back up your thoughts. Give examples of how leadership is defined this way.

2. Leadership is defined in one specific way for this text. Do you agree with the entire definition? Are there other elements you think should be added? If so, what? Should any of the elements be omitted? Which ones, and why?

3. Why is it so important that leadership be goal directed? What does it mean that leadership is goal directed? Draw a diagram of what this concept looks like.

4. What or who are followers? How do they differ from leaders? What do effective followers do? How can you become a more effective follower? What lessons can leaders learn from being followers?

5. When should leaders become followers? How do they make this switch? Why is this (or is it not) important?

6. Explain and give examples of when you have engaged in leader competencies and skills. In which are you most skilled? least skilled? Give examples from your leadership experiences. What can you do to continue improving in each area? Name specific strategies.

7. How do stereotypes impact leadership and followership? What specific examples of this have you seen in leadership? Which stereotypes do you inadvertently perpetuate? How can you overcome the stereotypes you hold?

8. Why is self-awareness so important for effective leadership? What sorts of attitudes, thoughts, and behaviors does a leader exhibit if she or he is self-aware? How do you demonstrate your self-awareness?

9. What are the primary qualities of effective leaders? Which ones are your strong qualities? Which do you need to work on most? How can you go about doing this? Have a close friend or family member respond to these questions for you; compare your responses.

10. Values are an integral part of leadership. Where have you learned your most important values? What are those most important values? How do these make you a more effective leader? How do they interfere with your leadership? How do you manifest or model these values for others?

11. Select a local recreation agency or organization and give examples (by position title) of the three different levels of leadership. At what level do you envision working initially? In five years? Ultimately? What do you need to do to become prepared for that level of leadership?

12. Of the five different ways leaders are identified, which do you think would make a leader the most effective? Explain. Think of the times when you were identified as a leader in a group—how did that happen? Did that help or hinder your leadership effectiveness?

13. How and when have you used the various types of power? Which was most successful for you? Can you describe types of power that are less effective for a leader than others? How would you, as a leader, empower others?

References

Banutu-Gomez, M. (2004). Great leaders teach exemplary followership and serve as servant leaders. *Journal of American Academy of Business, 4*(1/2), 143–151.

Bartol, K., Martin, D., and Kromkowski, J. (2003). Leadership and the glass ceiling: Gender and ethnic group influences in leader behaviors at middle and executive managerial levels. *Journal of Leadership & Organizational Studies, 9*(3), 8–19.

Bass, B. (1990). *Bass and Stogdill's handbook of leadership* (3rd ed.). New York, NY: The Free Press.

Bratton, J., Grint, K., and Nelson, D. (2005). *Organizational leadership*. Mason, OH: South-Western.

Braynion, P. (2004). Power and leadership. *Journal of Health Organization and Management, 18*(6), 447–463.

Brocato, R. (2003). Coaching for improvement: An essential role for team leaders and managers. *The Journal for Quality and Participation, 26*(1), 17–23.

Chaleff, I. (1995). *The courageous follower.* San Francisco, CA: Berrett-Koehler.

Clark, D. (2006a). *Core or essential competencies*. Retrieved March 18, 2006, from http://www.nwlink.com/~donclark/hrd/case/chart1.html

Clark, D. (2006b). *Introduction to competencies*. Retrieved March 18, 2006, from http://www.nwlink.com/~donclark/hrd/case/compet1.html

Clark, D. (2006c). *Leadership—Character and traits.* Retrieved March 18, 2006, from http://www.nwlink.com~donclark/leader/leaderchr.html

Cohen, W. (1998). *The stuff of heroes: The eight universal laws of leadership*. Marietta, GA: Longstreet.

Dubrin, A. (2004). *Leadership: Research findings, practice, and skills* (4th ed.). New York, NY: Houghton Mifflin.

Dupuis, M., Bloom, G., and Loughead, T. (2006). Team captains' perceptions of athlete leadership. *Journal of Sport Behavior, 29*(1), 60–78.

Eagly, A., Karau, S., and Makhijani, M. (1995). Gender and the effectiveness of leaders: A meta-analysis. *Psychological Bulletin, 117*(1), 125–145.

Groves, K. (2005). Gender differences in social and emotional skills and charismatic leadership. *Leadership & Organization Development Journal, 11*(3), 30–46.

Hare, L. and O'Neill, K. (2000). Effectiveness and efficiency in small academic peer groups: A case study. *Small Group Research, 31*(1), 24–53.

Hersey, P., Blanchard, K., and Johnson, D. (2001). *Management of organizational behavior* (8th ed.). Upper Saddle River, NJ: Prentice-Hall.

Hogue, M., Yoder, J., and Ludwig, J. (2002). Increasing initial leadership effectiveness: Assisting both women and men. *Sex Roles, 46*(11/12), 377–384.

Hultman, K. (2006). Leadership as genuine giving. *Organization Development Journal, 24*(1), 41–56.

Jax, J. (2000). A critical interpretation of leadership for the new millennium. *Journal of Family and Consumer Sciences, 91*(1), 85–88.

Johnson, D. and Johnson, F. (2003). *Joining together: Group theory and group skills* (8th ed.). Boston, MA: Allyn & Bacon.

Kanter, R. (2005). How leaders gain (and lose) confidence. *Leader to Leader, Winter*(35), 21–27.

Kellerman, B. (2005). How bad leadership happens. *Leader to Leader, Winter*(35), 41–46.

Koslowsky, M. and Stashevsky, S. (2005). Organizational values and power. *International Journal of Manpower, 26*(1), 23–34.

Krishnan, V. (2003). Power and moral leadership: Role of self-other agreement. *Leadership & Organization Development Journal, 24*(5/6), 345–351.

Krishnan, V. (2004). Impact of transformational leadership on followers' influence strategies. *Leadership & Organization Development Journal, 25*(1/2), 58–72.

Leavy, B. (2003). Understanding the triad of great leadership—Context, conviction, and credibility. *Strategy & Leadership, 31*(1), 56–61.

Lu, X. (2004). Surveying the topic of "effective leadership." *Journal of American Academy of Business, 5*(1/2), 125–129.

McDermott, L. (2004). Exploring intersections of physicality and female-only canoeing experiences. *Leisure Studies, 23*(3), 283–301.

Miller, R., Butler, J., and Cosentino, C. O. T. (2004). Followership effectiveness: An extension of Fiedler's contingency model. *Leadership & Organization Development, 25*(4), 362–368.

Nelson, D. and Quick, J. (2005). *Understanding organizational behavior* (2nd ed.). Mason, OH: South-Western.

Northouse, P. (2001). *Leadership: Theory and practice* (2nd ed.). Thousand Oaks, CA: Sage.

O'Toole, J. (1999). *Leadership A to Z: A guide for the appropriately ambitious*. San Francisco, CA: Jossey-Bass.

Politis, J. (2005). The influence of managerial power and credibility on knowledge acquisition attributes. *Leadership & Organization Development Journal, 26*(3/4), 197–214.

Preston, P. (2005). The power image: Strategies for acting and being powerful. *Journal of Healthcare Management, 50*(4), 222–225.

Ruderman, M. and Ernst, C. (2004). Finding yourself: How social identity affects leadership. *Leadership in Action, 24*(3), 3–7.

Russell, R. (2005). *Leadership in recreation* (3rd ed.). New York, NY: McGraw Hill.

Schruijer, S. (2002). Leader, leadership, and leading: From individual characteristics to relating in context. *Journal of Organizational Behavior, 23*(7), 869–872.

Sczesny, S., Boask, J., Neff, D., and Schyns, B. (2004). Gender stereotypes and the attribution of leadership traits: A cross-cultural comparison. *Sex Roles, 51*(11/12), 631–645.

Stone, G., Russell, R., and Patterson, K. (2004). Transformational versus servant leadership: A difference in leader focus. *Leadership & Organization Development Journal, 25*(3/4), 349–361.

Storr, L. (2004). Leading with integrity: A qualitative research study. *Journal of Health Organization and Management, 18*(6), 415–434.

Tubbs, S. (2006). Exploring a taxonomy of global leadership competencies and meta-competencies. *Journal of American Academy of Business, 8*(2), 29–34.

Ward, E. (2001). Social power bases of managers: Emergence of a new factor. *The Journal of Social Psychology, 141*(1), 144–147.

Leader Profile

Christopher K. Jarvi
Associate Director; Partnerships, Interpretation/Education, Volunteers and Outdoor Recreation • National Park Service

Chris has four years in this position, and 35 years in the parks, recreation, and leisure services profession.

On providing leadership to the profession: I have always believed in giving back to both the profession and the community in which I live through service. We cannot ask others to be involved with our organizations if we don't provide the model and experience what they will experience as volunteers.

Leadership positions he has held include:
- Director for Anaheim Community Services Department
- Head Park Planner, Los Angeles County Parks and Recreation
- President of California Parks and Recreation Society
- President of the National Recreation and Parks Association

What is the meaning of leadership?
You are a leader at the point where you firmly decide who you are and what you stand for in the world. I really like that concept and find that it most aligns with what I believe. You cannot be a leader until you are firmly grounded in your own beliefs and philosophy. Most of my career, I have been in search of my own personal philosophy rather than that provided by others. Leadership does not confine itself to a profession. It can be part of everything we do. That is why our beliefs are so important to the appropriate exercise of leadership.

What are the most important leader qualities?
I am firmly in agreement with the philosophy of Robert Greenleaf who first described *servant leadership*. Servant leadership is a practical philosophy which supports people who choose to serve first and then lead as a way of expanding service to individuals and institutions. Servant leaders may or may not hold formal leadership positions. Servant leaders encourage collaboration, trust, foresight, listening and the ethical use of power and empowerment. The servant leader uses his or her influence to make sure that other people's highest priority needs are being serviced first.

What advice do you have for students who aspire to leadership in parks, recreation, and leisure services?
Education doesn't end with school. It begins there. My personal and professional life has been enriched by continual reading, continuing education and a constant questioning of the status quo. Further, the key skills to leadership include personal skills such as flexibility, integrity, self esteem, decisiveness, creativity and resiliency…. One needs good interpersonal, reading and comprehension, and oral and written communication skills…. One needs facilitation, conflict management, negotiations and team-building skills…. Collaboration, leveraging, cultural awareness, community collaboration and customer-orientation skills. Finally, a leader needs a good sense of belief in one's self, systems thinking, strategic planning, financial management, program evaluation, entrepreneurship, and performance measurement skills.

Favorite book: Last Child in the Woods: Saving Our Children from Nature Deficit Disorder by Richard Louv

Chapter Two
Leadership Theories and Styles

Learning Opportunities

Through studying this chapter readers will have the opportunity to:

- Better understand how leadership has been viewed.
- Examine several theories of leadership.
- Understand the progression of thoughts related to leadership theory.
- Relate leadership theory to their own life experiences.
- Begin to explore the impact of culture on leadership.

True comprehension of any new concept or idea only comes when a person knows and understands how and why something is the way it is. Knowing and understanding why something is the way it is begins with examining underlying thoughts, ideas, and theories about what makes it work. This applies to understanding how a car works, how birds fly, and the construct of leadership. In Chapter 1 we explored definitions, traits, and skills of leadership; we will now examine leadership models and theories in an attempt to gain a solid foundation of the leadership concept.

Since the beginning of humankind, in all cultures in all parts of the world, some people have led while others have followed. Some of those efforts were successful; others were not. Some efforts moved society forward, yet others interfered with social evolution. As people began to realize that this phenomenon of leading and following occurred in every group of people, the study of leadership began.

This chapter will examine various perspectives of leadership, the construct of leadership, and why leadership occurs. In addition, changes in thinking about leadership will be examined as theories and people's understanding of leadership have grown more sophisticated over the years. Understanding leadership theories and models will enhance the usefulness of direct leadership techniques to be discussed in later chapters. Furthermore, making sense of theories helps individuals to make conscious and sound decisions related to leader-follower interactions.

Photo courtesy of Vicki Proctor

True comprehension of any new concept or idea only comes when a person knows and understands how and why something is the way it is. This begins with examining underlying thoughts, ideas, and theories about what makes it work.

A variety of theories are presented here in anticipation that one or more of them will help you (as a future leisure services leader) make sense of what you will do. Very often, individuals select various pieces of several theories or models to help in understanding this very complex phenomenon. No one theory or model perfectly represents leadership, and individuals should choose a model that makes the most sense based on their experiences and view of the world.

Early Theories

Early theories of leadership developed from observations of early leaders and their accomplishments, such as Julius Caesar, Peter the Great, and Joan of Arc. As social movements emerged and researchers became increasingly sophisticated, the complexities and understandings of leadership deepened. Early leisure services theories include trait theories, attribution theories, and behavioral theories.

Trait Theories

Trait theories define leadership as a function of an individual's characteristics or traits (Dubrin, 2004; Gillespie & Mann, 2004). Those characteristics might consist of superior physical, intellectual, or personality traits that differentiate an individual from other group members. For instance, in the United States recognized leaders have greater cognitive ability, physical fitness, prior influence experiences, and self-esteem than do followers (Bartol, Martin & Kromkowski, 2003; Van Wart, 2004).

One of the most common examples of trait theory is the Great Man theory of leadership. This theory explained leadership by focusing on the greatness of the leader. Greatness was socially defined and used to describe a renowned individual: a male, perceived as virtuous, magnanimous, industrious, and famous. Researchers theorized that leaders (i.e., great men) were born with specific characteristics that would result in their later emergence as highly effective leaders (Chemers, 1997; House & Aditya, 1997).

According to the great man theory, factors such as birthing order, family background (e.g., royalty, wealth), level and type of education, and overall upbringing could predestine a leader. In this model of leadership, if one were born into a good and virtuous family, received the best education, and was raised well (usually on the military model), one would become a great leader (Nelson & Quick, 2005).

In some cultures, valued traits of a leader might include creativity, superior intellect, and a petite physical stature. In yet another culture, highly valued traits might include a large physical stature, brute strength and the ability to be physically aggressive. According to the trait theory, in some cultures only men would be accepted as leaders, in others only women would be accepted as leaders, and in other cultures individuals of either sex might be perceived as having leadership traits. Due to strict role expectations and a European influence, in the early United States it was highly unlikely that a woman would be considered a leader. Some cultures, however, such as the Native-American tradition, socially defined and accepted women as tribal leaders. In fitting with the great man

Margaret Thatcher

Mohandas Karamchand "Mahatma" Gandhi

Joan of Arc

Great "Man" Theory

Queen Elizabeth II

Martin Luther King, Jr.

John F. Kennedy

Figure 2.1 According to the great man theory of leadership, successful leaders are born with innate leader qualities.

theory, others recognized their talents, skills, and deep understanding of the culture. It was also related to personality characteristics they exhibited, their family lineage, and training (Napier, 1999).

The scientific evidence to support trait theories of leadership has been contradictory. That is, some research supports the model, while other research refutes it (Appelbaum, Audet & Miller, 2003; Van Wart, 2004). Van Wart found that a person's height (e.g., relatively tall), gender (e.g., male), and attractiveness (e.g., slightly above average) had an impact on whether or not an individual was perceived as a leader. In fact, if one were to line up and observe the leaders of most technological nations, one could develop a trait profile of a leader. The leaders of Canada, the United States, Japan, Great Britain, China, Russia, Germany, and most other European nations are (or have been) male, tall (relative to their respective constituents), between 40 and 60 years old, light-skinned, and somewhat fit looking. It might be said that people from those respective countries see those traits as being indicative of successful leadership and thus, elect these people into office.

While recognizing that many accept this theory of leadership on some level, this model of leadership has limited scientific support in terms of what makes an effective leader. Many nations are led by excellent leaders who are people of color, women, short, introverted, and lacking in charisma. Leadership is much more than the physical or personality traits one exhibits.

Attribution Theory

Similar to the trait theory, attribution theory explains leadership through the belief that leadership is attributed to

Leadership is often attributed to a person who looks like a leader.

one who looks and acts like a leader. Van Wart (2004) talks about an individual having a "leadership presence" that instills confidence in others. Attribution theory also refers to how people tend to attribute "good" leadership to a leader of a group that has done something well regardless of the leader's actual impact. Observers assume that if the group did well, then it must have had a good leader. Conversely, if things do not go well in a group, observers attribute the leader with poor leadership abilities regardless of her or his actual skill level (Bratton, Grint & Nelson, 2005; Nelson & Quick, 2005).

It is important to understand attribution theory because these types of beliefs can impact the acceptance and success of a leader. Attributions are judgments or evaluations of another person. All people make judgments; for instance, we attribute kindness to some and stinginess to others. In group settings participants make judgments of the leader and the leader makes judgments of the participants. The judgments or attributions may be based on fact, perceptions, feelings, and stereotypes. Attribution theory can be utilized to help explain why people attribute leadership to certain individuals based on overall perceptions, regardless of whether or not that person is actually the designated leader. Usually leadership is attributed to those with good interpersonal skills (Dubrin, 2004; Moorhead & Griffin, 2004).

Behavioral Theories

Behavioral theories encompass those ideas that explain leadership on the basis of behaviors exhibited by the leader. This belief about leadership suggests that an effective leader will manifest certain leadership behaviors at a particular time (Burke & Collins, 2001; Hersey, Blanchard & Johnson, 2001). Recreation leader behaviors might include actions such as problem solving, teaching a song, or managing participant behaviors. If one believed in this explanation of leadership, one would simply have to act like a leader to be perceived as one.

Many broad-based leadership theories include behavioral elements. As an example, in their leadership theory House and Aditya (1997) identified the following tasks as leadership behaviors: planning, organizing, directing, and evaluating; as well as communicating vision, serving as a role model, resolving conflicts, and maintaining cohesion. These behaviors and functions of leadership are certainly integral to successful leadership, yet leadership goes beyond the "doing" of these functions (see Figure 2.2, p. 28).

Yukl's (1989) theory of leadership also included behavioral elements. He developed a model of leadership typology that explained leadership through four primary leader tasks: making decisions, influencing people, building relationships, and giving-seeking information (see Figure 2.3). Within each of these four behavior categories specific behaviors were identified which essentially encompass task and human relations skills. This model may be suitable for use in our field, because in recreation settings, leaders engage in all of these behaviors at one time or another with both colleagues and participants. Generally, researchers have found no difference between the leader behaviors of women and men (Appelbaum, Audet & Miller, 2003; Hogue, Yoder & Ludwig, 2002).

The Influence of Stereotypes

While short-sighted in explaining leadership from a scientific perspective, the trait and behavioral theories carry some weight with laypeople, particularly in the early stages of developing leader-follower relationships. Because stereotypes often cloud the way people perceive others, both the trait and behavioral theories of leadership have implications for a variety of people in leadership roles. Ruderman and Ernst (2004) have found that a person's social identity (i.e., how we see ourselves in terms of the groups to which we belong) not only impacts the way an individual looks at others, but also at how others view that individual. People interpret emotions, words, and behaviors differently depending upon the perceived background of the individual.

In most cultures in the United States, people attribute leadership traits to men more often than women, and commonly view leadership as a masculine endeavor (Hogue, Yoder & Ludwig, 2002; Sczesny, Boask, Neff & Schyns, 2004). For instance, women who exhibit the desirable leadership traits of assertiveness, being analytical, and being task-focused are often perceived as cold, aloof, and aggressive. Furthermore, women in direct leadership positions in recreation and leisure services find that they may not be as readily accepted as "voices of authority" because of their higher pitched voices. In the predominant U.S. culture, authoritative voices are perceived as being low-pitched, deep, and male. One only has to listen to the voice-overs on television commercials to recognize that male voices are perceived as having more authority than female voices.

The research shows some interesting findings about the realities of female and male leaders. Appelbaum, Audet, and Miller (2003) and Stelter (2002) reported that female and male leaders are more alike than different, and both can be extremely effective or ineffective. They agree with Eagly and colleagues (1995) on a couple of basic points. When females and males are engaged in leadership tasks that are congruent with their gender roles (i.e., females leading tasks that are typical for females and males leading tasks typical for males), both women and men are perceived as effective with a wide range of acceptable leadership behaviors. In addition, women are perceived as effective leaders at the mid-management level, while men are perceived as more effective at the direct and administrative levels of leadership (Bass, 1998; Carless, 1998).

Others have found that sometimes women who are leaders find themselves in a "double-bind." In much of North America leaders are expected to be assertive, competent, bold, and confident—stereotypical masculine traits.

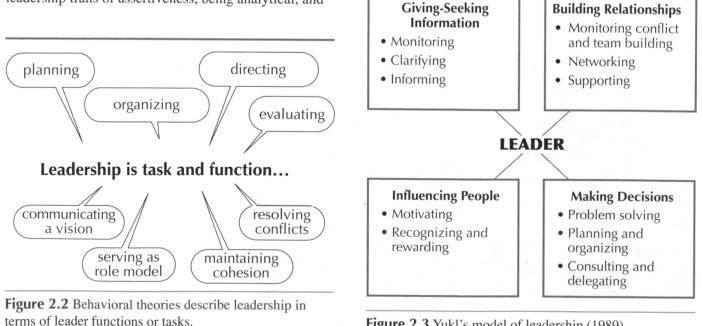

Figure 2.2 Behavioral theories describe leadership in terms of leader functions or tasks.

Figure 2.3 Yukl's model of leadership (1989)

On the other hand, women are expected to be nurturing, relationship-oriented and deferential—stereotypical feminine traits. Thus, if a female acting like a leader is expected to act masculine, she may be evaluated negatively because she is not acting in a feminine manner. Further, people of color and others who use styles of communication other than the socially prescribed Eurocentric style (e.g., street talk, jargon, heavy accents) may not be perceived or accepted as leaders even if they hold legitimate leadership positions. As can be seen, leadership is very much culturally defined.

Leadership Styles

Early on as people looked for ways to understand the leadership phenomenon, at least three primary types of leadership were observed: autocratic, democratic, and laissez-faire. In 1939 Lewin, Lippitt, and White (as cited in Bass, 1990) studied the impacts of those primary styles of leadership on group productivity and perceptions of group members.

Autocratic

Autocratic or authoritarian leadership is unidirectional. An autocratic leader directs, or orders, participants to do various tasks and does not accept input from group members. In this style, the leader does not reveal reasons behind her or his decision making or actions and believes that participants should do as they are told because she or he is the leader. The leader directs, and followers are expected to follow those directions.

An autocratic leader takes on a role of determining all decisions, policies, and directions for the group. She or he usually has very little trust or faith in group members and expects them to react to directions as given. The leader promotes herself or himself as the authority figure, and as the only one with answers. In autocratic relationships group responsibility tends to be low, and people merely do what they are told. Often, when the leader is gone, participants "cut loose" and act out. When a leader uses this style of leadership, group members' feelings of anger, hostility, and aggression may increase (Chemers, 1997).

Humphreys and Einstein (2003) suggest that people will accept an order from a leader if the following conditions exist:

- The communication is understood.
- The communication is in harmony with the purpose of the activity.
- The communication is consistent with the individual's (or group's) personal interest.
- The respondent(s) has the physical and cognitive ability to comply.

Thus, being aware of the conditions surrounding the need to use this style would assist the leader in its effective use.

While many perceive the autocratic style to be a negative style of influence and ineffective in the long run, there are times when an autocratic style of leadership or autocratic behaviors are appropriate. For example, when the group requires a quick, sharp, immediate response to protect someone or something from harm, an autocratic style works well. In this type of setting, the group generally accepts the leader as having the necessary expertise and acts willingly on the directive.

After the safety issues have been resolved and things have calmed down, a leader concerned with group affect and learning would share with the group information regarding the use of leadership styles, decision-making behaviors, and any other issues of concern related to the situation. Generally, participants of all ages appreciate being informed and treated with respect. By sharing the reasoning behind decisions and the use of autocratic techniques, participants learn about leadership, safety issues, judgment, and responsibility.

Photo courtesy of Deb Jordan

Autocratic leadership involves a command style of leadership.

Democratic

In a democratic style of leadership, the leader and the group share in decision making. The leader shares the reasoning behind decisions and asks for and receives group input. Group members make decisions based on information supplied by the leader; together they decide both the process and content of decisions. This is often accomplished by voting and accepting the majority opinion. In a democratic group, criticism and praise are given objectively and group members generally feel a sense of responsibility within the group. A trust relationship between the leader and group members, as well as mutual respect, develops.

Although a democratic society perceives democratic leadership style as best, at times such a style is inappropriate. If a group is underskilled, immature or has little knowledge about a situation, using a leadership style that places decision making in the group's hands is not appropriate. In addition, if a democratic style of leadership were used and a "majority rules" attitude were followed to make decisions, some people (i.e., the minority) would always be left out and their input would be nullified. Furthermore, because of the group input, a democratic style often takes more time than other approaches.

Laissez-faire

In French, laissez-faire means to "let it be," to leave it alone. In this style of leadership the leader tends to shy away from the group and decision-making responsibilities. In fact, many describe this style of leadership as "an absence of leadership" or non-leadership (Bass, 1998). Laissez-faire leaders seem to avoid the leadership role and associated tasks. Complete freedom is given to group members without any participation from the leader. The

---

Autocratic Leader:

"Do it this way, please. We'll have no discussion on the matter."

Democratic Leader:

"I'd like your opinions about how we should do this. Group input is important to me."

Laissez-faire Leader:

"It doesn't matter to me how you do it, just leave me out of it."

Figure 2.4 Leadership styles might be characterized by these leaders' words.

leader provides information or materials when asked, but otherwise stays out of the group process.

These behaviors may indicate a lack of confidence in oneself, and may leave a group feeling as though it has little or no direction. Because of this, following a laissez-faire style of leadership may result in low group morale. In addition, the "true" leader of the group becomes whomever makes decisions and does the work. Bass (1990) reported that

> more activity by leaders, regardless of style, is usually associated with the greater satisfaction and effectiveness of their followers. (p. 551)

As might be imagined, laissez-faire leadership may be viewed as a weak form of leadership because of the low level of involvement by the leader. However, when used with a purpose (e.g., to enhance group development), this style can be highly effective in helping a group to mature and grow in its decision-making abilities. In a positive approach to a laissez-faire style the leader is available to the group and shows interest in the group's needs. While she or he allows the group to struggle through decision-making and task accomplishments, the leader provides guidance and assistance when needed. Group members are empowered and group dynamics can be extremely strong when facilitated with a laissez-faire approach to leadership.

Tannenbaum and Schmidt Continuum of Leader Behaviors

Rather than taking an either/or approach, Tannenbaum and Schmidt placed leadership styles on a continuum from democratic to autocratic (Hersey, Blanchard & Johnson, 2001). On this continuum leader behaviors range from being very group-oriented (similar to a positive laissez-faire style) to very leader-oriented (with the leader being very directive and authoritarian). Four elements influence the use of a particular style over others: leader values, leader confidence in the group, leader preferences, and the group's feelings of security about getting the job done. (See Figure 2.5)

Later Theories

Later theories include those that were developed in the twentieth century. Primarily based on business management and military leadership frameworks, these models of leadership have aided our understanding of how leaders work with groups. They offer a view of leadership that may fit our needs in recreation and leisure services.

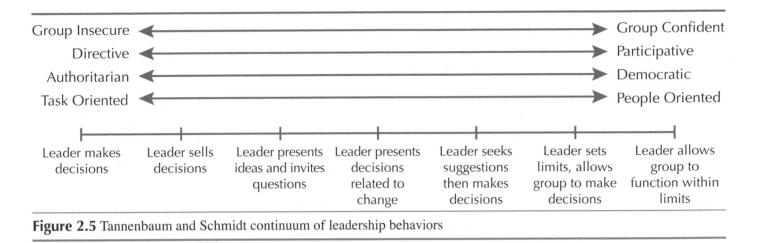

Group Insecure ⟵————————————————⟶ Group Confident
Directive ⟵————————————————⟶ Participative
Authoritarian ⟵————————————————⟶ Democratic
Task Oriented ⟵————————————————⟶ People Oriented

| Leader makes decisions | Leader sells decisions | Leader presents ideas and invites questions | Leader presents decisions related to change | Leader seeks suggestions then makes decisions | Leader sets limits, allows group to make decisions | Leader allows group to function within limits |

Figure 2.5 Tannenbaum and Schmidt continuum of leadership behaviors

Situational Theories

Situational theories take into account the leader, the followers, and the situation and explain leadership as emerging based on the situation. If the skills of an individual match the group task and fit within the structure of the group, she or he will emerge as the leader. Simply put, a person emerges as the leader when a certain situation arises that draws her or him out. For example, if an Emergency Medical Technician (EMT) were taking an aerobics class, she or he would follow the lead of the aerobics instructor because the instructor has more knowledge, expertise and skills than the EMT in this situation. The EMT would follow directions and suggestions based on these factors. During class, however, if one of the participants experienced severe breathing or heart problems, the EMT would likely emerge as the leader of that situation. Others would defer to the EMT's directions and commands because, at that time, she or he would be the most appropriate leader.

Hersey and colleagues (2001) present a model of leadership that aligns task behaviors and follower maturity resulting in particular leadership behaviors (See Figure 2.6). If the task requires a great deal of focused activity and the group maturity is low, a telling or directing leadership style is required. On the other hand, if task needs are low and individual/group maturity is high, a participative leadership style is most appropriate. A leader would select a leadership style based on her or his own preferences, group maturity, and the demands of the task. While

a number of people like this conceptualization of leadership, research since 1982 has shown very little support for this model (Bratton, Grint & Nelson, 2005; Chen & Siverthorn, 2005).

Contingency Theory

Fiedler (1967) developed a contingency theory that explained leadership in terms of an individual's style of leadership and the response of the group she or he was leading. The style of leadership used by a leader interfaces with the situation in which the group (leader and followers) finds itself. This style is contingent upon the situation and the relationship between the leader and the group.

Fiedler (1967) suggested that a leader is motivated from either a task or interpersonal perspective. That is,

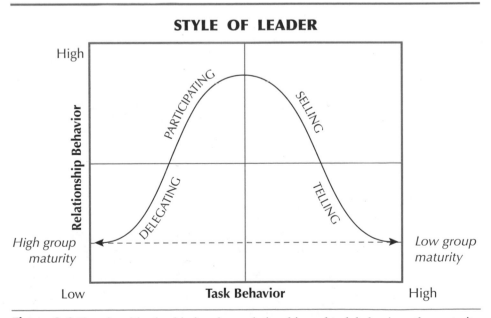

Figure 2.6 Situational leadership involves relationship and task behaviors, the maturity of the group, and leadership style.

different leaders prefer and focus on either the job to be done or the people in the group. Three other elements help explain this theory:

- *the relationship between the leader and the group,* where the more liked a leader is by group members, the easier it is for her or him to exert influence;

- *the task structure*, where the more clear goals and tasks are, the easier it is for the leader to exert influence; and

- *the power of the leader*, whereby the more powerful (e.g., having access to resources) the leader is, the easier it is for the leader to exert influence over the group.

According to this theory, leadership effectiveness is contingent upon the appropriateness of the leader's style to the task. A well-liked leader who has clear goals for the task at hand, and who has power by virtue of her or his position, would be highly effective using most any style of leadership with the group. As is the case with other models and theories, research on this view of leadership has resulted in contradictory findings (Bass, 1997).

Leadership Factors

Two early theories about leadership have had a great deal of impact on the study of modern leadership. They are mentioned here because the findings lay the groundwork for later and contemporary views of leadership. The two groundbreaking models were developed out of experiential research: the leadership styles research conducted by Lewin et al. in 1939, and the leadership factor studies performed at Ohio State University in the mid 1940s. The leadership factor studies found (using an instrument called the Leadership Behavior Development Questionnaire) two leadership factors that define leadership. These two factors are called *consideration* and *initiation of structure* (Northouse, 2001).

Consideration refers to interpersonal skills such as communication, trust, and respect between leaders and followers; follower participation in decision making; and other behaviors that enhance and maintain interpersonal relations within a group. We sometimes label these as people skills or interpersonal skills, and a leader who has strengths in this area is considered to be people-oriented. *Initiation of structure* refers to leader behaviors focused on tasks. These behaviors might include setting rules, assigning tasks or jobs, giving directions, defining roles, and goal setting. A leader who is strong in these skills is often considered to be task-oriented.

Managerial Grid

Blake and Mouton's managerial grid is one of the leadership models built on the two leadership factors found in the Ohio State studies. Blake and Mouton (1964, as cited in Clark, 2006) see leadership as consisting of two elements: a concern for task, and a concern for people (the group). See Figure 2.9. The horizontal axis of the grid represents a concern for task, and the vertical axis represents a concern for people. The concern for task relates to getting a job done and producing outcomes and products. The concern for people relates to developing trusting relationships, establishing a friendly atmosphere, and being concerned for the well-being of others.

Using this grid, a person could be rated as to her or his degree of concern for people and concern for task.

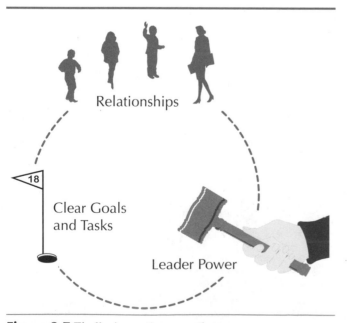

Relationships

Clear Goals
and Tasks

18

Leader Power

Figure 2.7 Fiedler's contingency theory

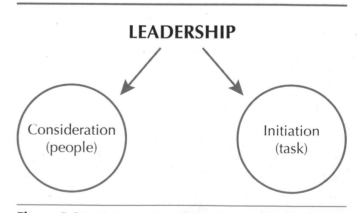

LEADERSHIP

Consideration
(people)

Initiation
(task)

Figure 2.8 Initiation and consideration are two dimensions of leadership.

Through this process leadership strengths and weaknesses may be identified. A leader overly concerned with people might never complete a task because she or he is focusing so much on the relationships, yet a leader overly concerned with task might act like an authoritarian and alienate participants. Most people strive for a balance of the two concerns (5, 5); the "ultimate leader" strives for a 9, 9 orientation—she or he would strive for task excellence along with a well-satisfied team.

Likert System of Management

The Likert System of Management (Moorhead & Griffin, 2004; see Figure 2.10, page 34), model allows for the view that leaders behave in different ways, with different motivations, for a variety of reasons at different times.

Exploitive Autocratic

On one extreme is a leadership style labeled *exploitive autocratic* where the message from the leader is, "You will do it." The motivation for leadership comes from the leader's need for security and status and the results show the leader in the best possible light, even at the expense of others. The leader does not trust the group, communicates little, and makes all the decisions.

An example of this approach may be seen in the following (slightly exaggerated) scenario. A young, relatively inexperienced lifeguard sits on his stand, whistle at the ready. He is very proud of being a lifeguard and has heard all the myths about how girls respond to male lifeguards. He believes some of those myths and feels rather narcissistic. The young lifeguard decides to impress the teenaged girls nearby. He sees two youngsters playing (within the rules) in the water and blows his whistle at them, shouting through the bullhorn to stop the horseplay. He then sits back feeling all eyes on him, and imagines that the teenaged girls are impressed by his show of authority and power.

There was no real need for the whistle and horn, but the acts of using those tools and fulfilling his leadership role helped make the young lifeguard look larger than life. In exploiting his position of leadership and authority to get attention, he was exhibiting an exploitive autocratic leadership style.

Benevolent Autocratic

Moving to the right on the Likert continuum, a leader moves into a benevolent autocratic mode, where a parental-like attitude is evidenced through leadership acts. Here, the message from the leader to participants might be, "Do it, please." Some follower variance is allowed from the leader's directions, but participants know when the leader means business. Often, this style is used when a leader believes people should do something for their own good. The style is still directive, but the leader will often add commentary. The leader does not trust group members, and her or his motivation is in the best interest of others, rather than self.

If, in the previous scenario, the young lifeguard simply asked the youngsters to ease up on the horseplay because someone might get hurt, he would have exhibited a benevolent autocratic style of leadership. He would have been directive, but with the well-being of the young people foremost in his mind.

Consultive

At the consultive point along the continuum, the leader might ask for input: "How would you like to do it?" Yet at this stage the leader's decision is still final. Here, leaders allow group input and show some interest in group members, but still retain the decision-making power. A consultive style of leadership implies some level of trust between leader and group members. Leaders consider participant knowledge and feelings and sincerely try to make people feel included.

If the young lifeguard were to exhibit a consultive style of leadership with the playful youngsters, he might have asked them to get out of the water and talked with them about their perceptions of the danger of their play. In a consultive style the lifeguard would listen to the youth,

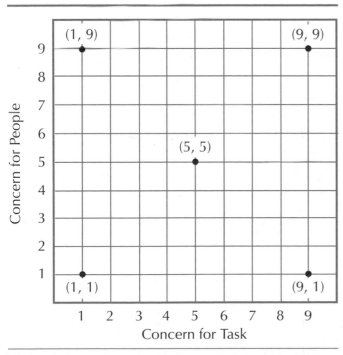

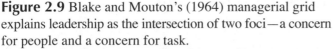

Figure 2.9 Blake and Mouton's (1964) managerial grid explains leadership as the intersection of two foci—a concern for people and a concern for task.

Exploitive autocratic	Benevolent autocratic	Consultive	Participative
"You will do it."	*"Do it, please."*	*"How would you like to do it?"*	*"What do you think we should do?"*

Figure 2.10 The Likert system of management illustrates leadership as a continuum.

then make a decision to either ask them to stop or let them return to their water play.

Participative

At the right extreme on the continuum, the leader has a lot of trust in the group members and includes group members in the decision-making process. The message from leader to participants is, "What do you think we should do?" This style allows for full group involvement throughout the leadership and decision-making processes. Leadership is truly a group effort.

A participative style of leadership is somewhat similar to a democratic style, yet the focus of decision making in Likert's system of management is consensus-oriented rather than by vote. All group members come to a decision that everyone can accept—quite time-consuming, but excellent for group development.

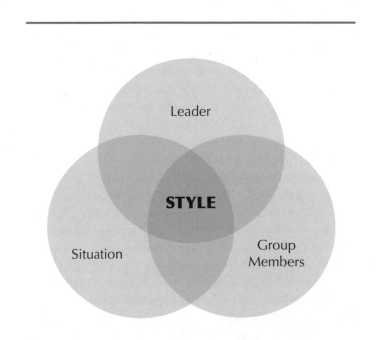

Figure 2.11 The comprehensive view of leadership suggests leadership is a combination of leaders, followers, and the special circumstances of the situation.

Comprehensive View of Leadership

The comprehensive view of leadership is somewhat similar to situational leadership in that it identifies the interactions of the leader, followers, and the situation (Jordan, 1989; Napier, 1999). The intersection of these three elements results in the identification of an appropriate leadership style. In this model, one must bear in mind that the *leader* is a composite of her or his knowledge, values, skills and abilities, cultural beliefs, need disposition, experiences, motivation, sense of spirituality, personal style, history, personal "baggage," and sources of power.

Similarly, the *group* includes characteristics of each individual as well as the group as a distinct entity. These traits include knowledge, skills and abilities, cultural beliefs, experience, maturity, group goals, group methods and processes, and group norms. The *situation* encompasses all the external factors that influence a group: environment, time, temperature, external stresses, cultural attitudes, and the physical setting. As the elements of these three components interact, an appropriate leadership style is identified (e.g., autocratic, democratic, laissez-faire, participative, consultive).

Contemporary Views of Leadership

Research and study have evolved a great deal over the years and led to three contemporary views of leadership. These all take into account leadership as a personal journey of growth and development. Khatri, Ng, and Lee (2001) believe that these newer theories of leadership emphasize emotions and values. They also report that these theories envision leadership as "encouraging the heart" or spirit of followers. The three contemporary theories are transactional leadership, transformational leadership, and servant leadership.

Transactional Leadership

As the most commonly used type of leadership today, transactional leadership is viewed as an exchange between a leader and followers (Humphreys & Einstein, 2003). Within a given situation a leader uses particular leadership techniques while engaged in some type of interaction with followers. This exchange is based on a subtle agreement between leaders and followers: if followers will acknowledge and validate the leader (usually by performing well), the leader will give the followers recognition and status for their efforts (e.g., reward them with money, public accolades, increased responsibilities). In this way, both leaders and followers influence one another and both benefit from the transaction (Smith, Montagno & Kuzmenko, 2004; Stone, Russell & Patterson, 2004).

Three basic components of transactional leadership have been well-documented in the literature: contingent reward, management by exception (active), and management by exception (passive) (Bratton, Grint & Nelson, 2005; Moorhead & Griffin, 2004). The *contingent reward* element refers to the leader's ability and power to give rewards (or punishments) for the efforts and effectiveness of followers. In effect, participants work hard and the leader rewards their accomplishments. The *management by exception (active)* component describes the leader as she or he actively watches and searches for deviations from rules and standards; she or he tries to catch people doing something wrong and then takes corrective action. This has been found to be relatively effective in many instances. In the *management by exception (passive)* approach, the leader only steps in if standards are not being met and then takes corrective action. Research has found that in groups where leaders primarily use this type of transaction, followers are dissatisfied (Humphreys & Einstein, 2003).

A transactional leader focuses on rules, policies, and procedures and typically relies on power, position, and formal authority to enhance effectiveness (Vinnicombe & Singh, 2002). It would come as no surprise then, to learn that in the United States men are more likely than women to use transactional leadership behaviors. Fertman and van Linden (1999) and Walumbwa, Wu, and Ojode, (2004) view transactional leaders as people who focus on goals and objectives, problem identification and solving, making decisions, using standards and principles as guides for behaviors, getting things done, and taking charge (with personal power).

Transformational Leadership

Another contemporary view of leadership, *transformational leadership,* has also received a lot of attention in the last ten to fifteen years. To transform means to change the nature, function, or condition of something. In terms of transformational leadership, the term describes a model of leadership that changes the nature or function of others in such a way that they become more concerned with collective (i.e., group) rather than personal (i.e., individual) interests.

Transformational leadership is based on the personal values of the leader, inspires followers to commit to a common purpose, empowers group members to reach their potential, and promotes nontraditional thinking (Gillespie & Mann, 2004; Krishnan, 2004). Where leaders strive to elevate followers to a higher good and to act in the best interest of the group's goals, followers are being transformed into moral agents. That is, followers become messengers for the leader, helping to spread the leader's ideals, values, and convictions. Transformational leadership has four components: *leader charisma, inspirational motivation, individualized consideration,* and *intellectual stimulation* (Bass, 1998).

Leader Charisma

Charisma is defined in the dictionary as a "rare personal quality attributed to leaders who arouse fervent popular devotion and enthusiasm," and as "personal magnetism or charm." As an element of transformational leadership, leader charisma serves as an outlet for visionary and inspirational abilities of the leader. A leader who is considered a visionary sees the big picture; takes risks; generates a great deal of enthusiasm, emotion, and confidence in her or his followers; and is considered a transformational leader. These leaders are sensitive to the needs of the group, are masters of social skills, and develop emotional bonds with

Contingent reward:
Leader gives rewards based on follower efforts.

> **Management by exception—Active:**
> Leader tries to catch followers doing something wrong and gives feedback.

>> **Management by exception—Passive:**
>> Leader waits and if standards are not being met, gives feedback.

Figure 2.12 Transactional leadership has three components.

Transformational leaders are excellent communicators and instill high ethical standards in group members.

followers (Khatri, Ng & Lee, 2001). It is common for followers to want to be just like the leader. Sometimes participants even start dressing, acting, and talking like the leader. In recreation settings leaders with charisma seem to electrify the room. Everyone is well-behaved, participant enthusiasm is high, and followers seem to gravitate toward the leader.

Inspirational Motivation

Leaders act in ways to motivate and inspire others by providing both meaning and challenge in their work. Transformational leaders are excellent communicators and instill high ethical standards in group members (Stone, Russell & Patterson, 2004). Team spirit, enthusiasm, and optimism run high in groups that are led by a transformational leader. These leaders help others to envision the future, clearly communicate their expectations to followers,

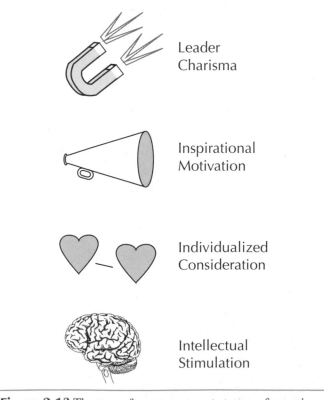

Leader Charisma

Inspirational Motivation

Individualized Consideration

Intellectual Stimulation

Figure 2.13 There are four components to transformational leadership.

and demonstrate commitment to goals and the shared vision. Vision and the ability to get others "fired up" are hallmarks of a transformational leader. You might think of Pat Summitt, coach of the Tennessee Lady Vols basketball team, as a good example of a person engaged in inspirational motivation. Her team commitment is incredibly high, the players know they are going for a national championship each year, and they believe that they can win it (and often, they do!).

Individualized Consideration

In a global sense, transformational leaders appeal to ideological values of followers. This means that they can connect with followers at a "heart" level. While appealing to these common values and ideals, transformational leadership allows for followers to be treated as individuals, generating a great deal of follower confidence. Leaders empower followers to engage in a variety of tasks, and they celebrate individual accomplishments and growth (Smith, Montagno & Kuzmenko, 2004; Tucker & Russell, 2004). Transformational leaders believe in and work toward the personal and professional development of their followers—they help others to grow and develop their potential as individuals. Recreation leaders who allow for individual consideration make each person genuinely feel special. Furthermore, leaders hold each person to high expectations and let her or him know that they have great confidence in her or his ability to meet those challenges.

Intellectual Stimulation

A visionary and transforming leader challenges existing thinking about the way things have been done. She or he encourages new ways of looking at things, generates innovative ideas, asks a lot of questions, and gives followers the opportunities to participate in discoveries. Intellectual stimulation tends to make transforming leaders people who are exciting to be around; they are not afraid to take risks. A transforming leader challenges people to think differently than they are used to thinking. Elements ranging from activity rules to social policy are challenged and the intellectual excitement is high among group members.

Research has shown that leaders who engage in transformational behaviors are viewed as effective leaders, and have satisfied and highly motivated followers (Groves, 2005; Hayashi & Ewert, 2006). These researchers have also shown that women are high in transformational leadership.

It certainly would be easy to see how someone with charisma, who treats people as though they are each special and unique and who challenges people to think, would be well-liked and well-respected. Transformational leaders use many leadership styles and exhibit a transformational philosophy that influences both leadership tasks and people. Humphreys and Einstein (2003) and Tucker and Russell (2004) talk about a transformational leader as one who is involved in several tasks: visioning, valuing, coaching, motivating, team building, and promoting quality. In addition, they report that transformational leaders are more compassionate, flexible, insightful, pragmatic, and less forceful and tough than nontransformational leaders.

Transformational Leadership and Emotional Intelligence

Transformational leadership has been found to correlate highly with emotional intelligence (EQ; Schruijer, 2002; Zohar, 2005). In fact, one aspect of emotional intelligence, self-awareness, is integral to transformational leadership effectiveness. Being self-aware and being willing to look inside oneself is a critical skill for highly effective leaders. According to Groves (2005) and Kunnanatt (2004) the key aspects of emotional intelligence include: self-awareness, emotional management, self-motivation, empathy, and relationship management.

Self-awareness. Being self-aware means being attentive to inner thoughts and feelings, having a sense of purpose in life, and having a public self-consciousness (i.e., being generally aware that you are a social object—that other people notice and respond to you). Self-awareness enables individuals to develop resilience, adaptability, and self-confidence. This sense of self-awareness enables a leader to develop and grow throughout the course of her or his leadership life.

Emotional Management. This aspect of emotional intelligence involves self-monitoring. It includes regulating personal moods, emotions, and other expressions of behavior and being sure that we express ourselves in socially appropriate ways. Emotionally intelligent leaders know when it is appropriate to joke around, be serious, address others' emotional needs, and so on.

Self-motivation. Being self-motivated arises from an optimism and belief that one has the ability to influence events and consequences in her or his life. This is often referred to as having an internal locus of control—we accept responsibility for the consequences of our actions. Self-motivated leaders are also self-starters and they persevere. They get involved, do what needs to be done without being asked, and see projects through to the end.

Empathy. The capacity to be empathetic includes the ability to recognize and respond to changes in the emotional states of others by being sensitive, having social self-confidence, and being even-tempered. People who have empathy understand the emotional state of others and can articulate that to the individuals involved. Those high in EQ are well attuned to others' moods, emotions,

Being self-aware and being willing to look inside oneself is a critical skill for highly effective leaders. The key aspects of emotional intelligence include: self-awareness, emotional management, self-motivation, empathy, and relationship management.

and readiness levels. These leaders make good use of group member strengths and talents.

Relationship Management. Being able to effectively manage relationships is an important element of emotional intelligence. This includes understanding the differences between formal (e.g., business) and social (e.g., family, friends) relationships and how to interact with each. Leaders who are skilled in relationship management move consciously and freely between several types of groups. Related to empathy, relationship management involves perceiving others accurately and being able to respond within group norms.

Individuals high in EQ and high in transformational leadership know that one often needs to give up short-term benefits on the way to more beneficial, but longer-term goals. They also have strong positive affect, positive relationships with people, and they treat individuals with dignity and respect. Leaders who possess EQ exhibit transformational leadership when they demonstrate determination, farsightedness, a willingness to put the needs of others before their own, and strength in their convictions. Self-awareness, self-sacrifice, and self-control are required for both transformational leadership and EQ. By providing followers with purpose and meaning, a leader high in

Transformational Leadership	Emotional Intelligence
Self-awareness	Self-awareness
Inspirational motivation	Emotional management
Visionary, excited	Self-motivation
Connects with followers, sees them as individuals	Empathy
Long-term goals	Long-term goals
Positive affect	Upbeat, positive affect

Figure 2.14 Transformational leadership has much in common with emotional intelligence.

emotional intelligence exhibits inspirational motivation to move others to perform beyond their expectations.

Transformational leadership is a well-respected view of leadership, and many consultants and popular press books seek to train corporate leaders along these lines. Those authors cited in this chapter suggest, however, that combining transformational and transactional leadership proves most effective over the long term.

Servant Leadership

Another theory of leadership that has been seen frequently in the literature over the past several years is that of *servant leadership*; some view it as a philosophy or a way of living. Servant leadership was something first conceptualized in the early 1970s and is now making a resurgence in business, education, and other institutions of our society.

Robert Greenleaf first conceived of the idea of servant leadership after he read a story by Herman Hesse (Greenleaf, 1977). The central figure of the story was a character named Leo, who accompanied a traveling party on a journey as a servant to do menial chores. In addition to his tasks, Leo also sustained the group with his spirit and song—he was a person of extraordinary presence. Everything went well until Leo disappeared, then the group fell into disarray and the journey was abandoned. The group could not make it without Leo.

After many years of wandering a group member found Leo, and they travelled to the home of the Order that first sponsored the journey. There he discovered that Leo, whom he first had known as a servant, was in fact the head of the Order—its guiding spirit, a great and noble leader. By serving others in meeting their needs as they moved toward their goals, Leo exhibited leadership. Rather than lead from an "out front" position, he helped the group move to meet their goals from the "back" or "inside." Greenleaf (1991) captured the essence of servant leadership when he stated

> The servant leader is servant first. It begins with the natural feeling that one wants to serve, to serve first. Then conscious choice brings one to aspire to lead. The best test is: Do those served grow as persons; do they, while being served, become healthier, wiser, freer, more autonomous, more likely themselves to become servants? And, what is the effect on the least privileged in society; will they benefit or, at least, not be further deprived? (p. 7)

The most distinctive element of servant leadership is that the leader's priority and motivation is to serve others (Russell, 2002; Sendjaya & Sarros, 2002). This one focus drives the leader's thoughts, words, and deeds. Follower needs are placed ahead of the leader's needs and the leader is dedicated to serving others. A servant leader views her or his role as a trustee or steward—she or he has been entrusted to elevate the lives and potentials of others (Sendjaya & Sarros, 2002; Smith, Montagno & Kuzmenko, 2004). Eicher-Catt (2005) talks about servant leadership as encompassing the "head, heart, and hands" of those who follow. It is a leadership philosophy that is grounded in morality and ethical behaviors.

Servant leaders inspire hope and encourage the best in others. They are excellent communicators and deeply believe in the value of active listening. Servant leadership has a lot in common with transformational leadership. Like transformational leaders, servant leaders make followers feel significant and celebrate what each person brings to the group (Russell, 2002). Servant leaders have charisma, challenge old ways of doing things, and have a great deal of influence over followers. Stone, Russell, and Patterson (2004) report that the primary difference between transformational and servant leadership is the focus of the leader. The overriding focus or drive of a servant leader is on service to followers. Transformational leaders have a greater focus on helping followers to achieve group goals. A servant leader focuses on the followers; transformational leaders focus on the group goals.

Spears (1998) characterized ten traits of a servant leader, building on the foundation that Greenleaf had established twenty years earlier:

1. *Listening.* Leaders need a deep commitment to listening intently to others; this requires receptive listening—both to what is said and not said. Receptive listening involves getting in touch with one's own inner voice and seeking to understand with one's body, spirit, and mind. This type of listening should be coupled with reflection about all aspects of what was heard.

2. *Empathy.* Servant leaders strive to understand and empathize with others. This includes accepting people for their own "wonderful and unique spirits;" a servant leader assumes good in other people and operates from that perspective.

3. *Healing.* Servant leadership has a potential for healing self and others. A servant leader and those led search together for wholeness.

4. *Awareness.* Both general awareness and self-awareness strengthen a servant leader. This aids in understanding one's ethics and values. It helps servant leaders to be alert to their surroundings; that way a servant leader can act out of understanding the whole.

5. *Persuasion.* Servant leaders rely on persuasion rather than positional authority to make decisions. They convince people rather than coerce them. Servant leaders effectively build consensus in groups and prefer to work toward group understanding and acceptance of decisions.

6. *Conceptualization.* Servant leaders seek to nurture their abilities to "dream great dreams." They strive to see the big picture, have a long-range view, and utilize conceptual thinking in their leadership process.

7. *Foresight.* The ability to foresee is important in servant leadership. A servant leader understands past lessons, the realities of the present, and the likely consequences of future decisions. This judgment is deeply rooted in the intuitive mind and related to conceptual thinking.

8. *Stewardship.* The notion of stewardship is one of holding something in trust for present and future generations of people (and the planet). Servant leaders have this attitude toward their group, organization, constituents, and the environment.

9. *Commitment to the growth of people.* A servant leader believes that all people have intrinsic value beyond their contributions as group members. Servant leaders do everything they can to nurture the personal, professional, and spiritual growth of group members. One's spiritual nature is defined as everything not physical, their inner being, or the essence of who they are; it is not meant to be equated with religion.

10. *Building community.* A servant leader builds community—both within the group as well as in the larger community.

Fairholm (1998) characterized servant leadership as the "soul of leadership." This soul of leadership encompasses a spiritual wholeness that includes a leader's heart, mind, and body. It creates a mindset, defines the leader's values, determines her or his actions, and predicts future behaviors. Fairholm says

> We engage our spirit in all we do. Spirit lies at the heart of all life. Our spirit defines meaning for self and motivates our actions individually, and in the groups we join. It expresses itself in beauty, aesthetics, and in our relationships with others (Jacobson, 1995). In aggregate, spirit is what makes up our idea of who we are. In truth, it determines who we are. Spirit, along with mind and body, compose the soul—the whole person. (1997, p. 5)

As he reflects on the writings about the soul of leadership, spiritual leadership, and servant leadership, Kouzes (1999) suggests that these are all elements of exemplary leadership. Exemplary leaders challenge the process, inspire a shared vision, and enable others to act. These leaders model the way and "encourage the heart." Encouraging others includes setting clear standards, expecting the best, paying attention, giving personal recognition, telling the story, celebrating together, and setting an example.

Batten (1998, p. 44) summarized the concept of servant leadership saying that servant leaders should make a promise to

- Exemplify a passion for excellence.
- Ask, listen, and hear—to determine the wants, needs, and possibilities of my customers and my team.

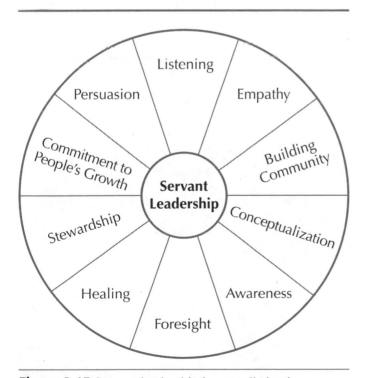

Figure 2.15 Servant leadership has ten distinctive characteristics.

Exemplary leaders challenge the process, inspire a shared vision, and enable others to act. These leaders model the way and "encourage the heart."

- Provide an example of accountability, commitment, and integrity.
- Follow a path of continual empowerment for myself and others.
- Consistently look for a [*sic*] focus on the strengths rather than the weaknesses of all with whom I come in contact.
- Cultivate optimum physical, mental, and spiritual fitness.
- Lead as I would like to be led.
- Savor the flavor of each passing moment.
- Infuse every thought and relationship with faith, hope, love, and gratitude.
- Dare to be all I can be.

Relating servant leadership to the field of recreation and leisure leadership, DeGraaf, Tilley, and Neal (2000) discussed the importance of leisure services practitioners being able to serve and lead in the new millennium. This becomes especially important as the field of leisure services moves away from simply providing services to community development and empowerment. People who have been taught leadership skills or who have been placed in positions of leadership need to be willing servants to those around them. DeGraaf, Tilley, and Neal (2000) and Jordan, DeGraaf and DeGraaf (2005) say that leadership should call us to be something beyond ourselves—to the higher purpose of improving the quality of life of those we serve.

Leadership and Culture

It was mentioned earlier that leadership is a process of being perceived by others as a leader; thus, it is culturally defined. Culture both inspires and constrains the understanding, enactment, and acceptance of leadership (Ruderman & Ernst, 2004). Within each culture leadership means different things. For example, leadership perceived by a traditional aboriginal tribe differs from leadership perceived by a highly technological society. The group roles are different, how a person becomes the leader is different, and how a leader acts (and is expected to act) is different.

Within one country there are many cultures; therefore, within each country there are several definitions and ways of looking at leadership. In addition, culture is viewed as a multidimensional and complex construct. One way to explore the impact of culture on leadership is to consider the dimensions of culture. Cultures have been found to differ on four primary facets: collectivism/individualism, power distance, masculinity/femininity, and

Culture both inspires and constrains understanding, enactment, and acceptance of leadership.

uncertainty avoidance (Hofstede, 2001). While all four of these factors differentiate cultures from one another, perceptions of leadership are clearly influenced by whether a group has a collectivist or individualist foundation.

Collectivist Cultural Perspective

Collectivists tend to look for similarities in people and consider the group to be more important than the individual. This view emphasizes a "we" perspective and interdependent values and mores are the norm (Fujimoto & Hartel, 2004). Cooperation, self-control, social order, loyalty, and group cohesion determine how groups and leaders function. A leader who puts the group before herself or himself, who works within a consensus model, and who helps the group achieve its collective goals would fit well within this philosophy. The group is the primary focus, and the leader's role is to help the group reach its potential. When the group is successful, the accomplishments are attributed to the group, rather than the leader.

Two examples of collectivist cultures in U.S. society include Native-American and African-American cultures. Bryant (1998) examined several people from six different Native-American tribes and Napier (1999) investigated several groups of indigenous people from the United States, New Zealand, Australia, and Central America. They

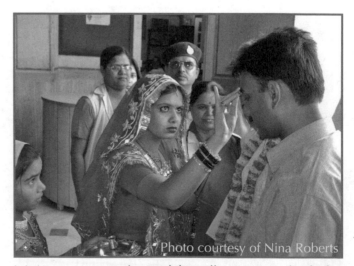

It is important to understand the collectivist or individualist nature of various cultures.

found decentralized and fluid leadership in both cultures—different people move into and out of leadership roles as needed. Everyone leads through the work that they do—no one person is more important than another. A person is first recognized by the larger community for her or his wisdom, concern for other members of the community and their personal strengths, and then they are recognized and accepted into leadership positions. A leader of these groups is not "the star;" rather they are quite humble, self-deprecating, and modest. Leadership is viewed as a way of living demonstrated in the process of acknowledging and developing relationships with the community, the environment, the past, present, and future.

Individualist Cultural Perspective

Differing from collectivists in many respects, individualists emphasize an "I" perspective; individual rights are valued above duty and the primary concern is for self (Fujimoto & Hartel, 2004). Individualists tend to look for differences in people and promote and value individual achievement over group accomplishments. The role of leader is viewed as very important and leadership is seen as vital to group success (Ndubisi, 2004; Yan & Hunt, 2005). Competition, personal exhibition, individual style differences, and achievement of personal goals form the foundation of this leader-group philosophy. Euro-Americans tend to favor this approach to working within a group. An individualist leader would promote competition within a group, encourage individuation, and look to put forth a group member as "the best." Group members are encouraged to do their individual best—regardless of the impact on the overall group performance. Leaders are concerned with people as well as task, and look for individual initiative. Leaders have a goal, a focus, a vision, and objectives, and they guide others toward this end. When group success occurs, it is commonly attributed to the skills of the leader.

Choosing the Appropriate Leadership Style

People view and understand leadership in many different ways, and use many styles and models of leadership in their roles as leaders. Most people feel more comfortable with one or two approaches to leadership than others. For instance, one person may feel very comfortable using a participative style where group decisions are made through consensus. Another person may not feel comfortable with that much group involvement and prefer to exert a bit more leader control. How can a person determine the best leadership style?

Most people who study leadership believe that choosing a particular leadership style depends upon several factors including the leader, the group, the situation, and the task. Leader experience, maturity, knowledge, and skills will have a strong impact on which styles of leadership are within her or his repertoire, as will one's cultural perspective. The maturity of the group, as well as group size, experience level, and other factors influence which styles of leadership will be most effective in what situations. The situation includes the task to be done (i.e., activity), time constraints, the environment, equipment, temperature, and other external forces that influence a group.

With experience, a leader can tell which styles of leadership have potential to be effective and which styles do not. Take a close look at Figure 2.17 (p. 42) for ideas on how to determine appropriate leadership styles to be most effective. Not all leadership styles are listed.

Summary

Understanding leadership requires a thorough examination of how others have viewed it in the past, envision it in the present, and how it functions in a given situation. As may be seen from this chapter, leadership theories are models of the leadership construct that enable an understanding of the many aspects of human interactions. Leadership theories range from quite simplistic to very facilitative. They address a leader's physical traits (e.g., great "man" theory and trait theories), behaviors and actions (e.g., behavioral theories), and situations in which leaders find

Individualism emphasizes the individual over the group.

Collectivism centers around a group; everyone is equally important.

Figure 2.16 Collectivism and individualism

themselves (e.g., situational and contingency theories). Leadership also has been viewed from transactional, transformational, and servant leadership perspectives.

Each model of leadership explains a variety of leadership styles. These styles help explain how leaders and followers interact and develop personal judgment related to use of leadership styles. Contemporary views of leadership generally support a transformational model where the leader uses her or his charisma to share ideologies, treats individuals as unique and important, and stimulates others to think and challenge the status quo. Research indicates that individuals who exhibit characteristics of both transformational and transactional leadership are perceived as effective and competent.

Choosing an appropriate leadership style is an ongoing effort for leisure services leaders. Each group, each situation, and each day require unique responses by the leader. In choosing a style, leaders strive to match their own needs with those of the followers, the situation, and the environment. When safety or time is a concern, or when participants are extremely young, an autocratic style of leadership may be appropriate. In another setting where the group is mature, committed to the task, and knowledgeable, a consultive leadership style may be most appropriate. Time, experience, and practice will help leaders to determine which leadership style to utilize in what circumstances.

Choosing an Appropriate Leadership Style

One of the biggest challenges leaders face is to select an appropriate leadership style or technique based on the situation at hand. It may help if leaders become familiar with the various dimensions along which leadership situations vary and consider the choices among them.

First, it may be helpful to draw a continuum of leader styles or behaviors such as below:

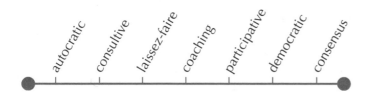

Next, **consider the leader and participant dimensions**; the appropriate style would move along the continuum from left to right based on the level of leader and participant:

- maturity (from immature to mature)
- skill level—in both content and process (from unskilled to highly skilled)
- judgment (poor judgment to excellent judgment)
- experience level—in both content and process (no experience to a great deal of experience)
- knowledge base—in both content and process (no knowledge to expert knowledge)
- emotional stability (has good control to no control of emotions)

The next step is to **consider the environment** in which the leadership situation takes place. Again, leader style or approach would move along the continuum based on:

- environmental complexity (complex to simple)
- structure and control of the environment (uncontrolled to highly controlled)
- concern over hazards (many potential hazards to few or no potential hazards)
- time constraints (from tight constraints to no time limits)
- familiarity with the environment (totally unfamiliar environs to very familiar environs)

Finally, a leader would want to **consider the activity dimension**. Leader style or approach moves along the continuum from left to right based on how the activity varied in:

- rule or strategy complexity (highly complex to very simple)
- level of importance (activity is critical to group success to very low importance)
- level of structure to activity (no structure to activity to much structure)
- degree of familiarity (totally new activity to a longtime favorite)

By **considering one's own comfort level** with various leadership styles and by attending to this checklist, leisure services leaders may decide upon the most appropriate level of leader involvement in the leadership situation. Practice and exposure to a variety of situations will also be extremely helpful.

Figure 2.17 Choosing an appropriate leadership style

Beginning the Journey

The journey to developing one's leadership potential is lifelong. You began the personal reflection process when you considered the questions asked of you at the end of Chapter 1. To assist you in understanding the underlying foundations of leadership and what they have to do with you and your leadership development, you are encouraged to reflect thoughtfully on the reflective questions in this chapter.

1. How would you characterize the early theories of leadership? Can you identify contemporary leaders who may be thought of as viewing leadership this way? How does culture interact with these early views of leadership? How do stereotypes impact people's attribution of leadership?

2. What are the similarities between the Leadership Styles, and Tannenbaum and Schmidt's Continuum of Leadership Behaviors? Give examples of when different leadership styles are best used. What is your preferred or most commonly used leadership style? How do you exhibit this?

3. Which of the Later Theories makes the most sense to you? Why do you think the Lewin et al. and Ohio State Studies were thought to be so important and groundbreaking in their times? How does the Likert System of Management relate to the Leadership Styles?

4. What makes Contemporary Views of Leadership so different from earlier views? Talk about how these three theories relate to one another. Do any of these leadership views "speak to you?" In what way and why? What is it that draws you to one (or more) of these views? What can you do to become an exemplary leader following one of these theories?

5. What are collectivism and individualism, and how do they relate to leadership? Which is your primary world-view? Explain why you believe this to be so. How do you manifest this in your thoughts, actions, values, attitudes, and relationships? How does your primary world-view influence you as a leader? What, if any, adjustments do you need to make if your participants hold a different world-view than you? How could you do this?

6. Develop a chart of all the leadership styles discussed throughout this chapter and describe the situations when it would be best to use each of the styles. Also give a recreation and leisure leadership-related example for each situation.

References

Appelbaum, S., Audet, L., and Miller, J. (2003). Gender and leadership? Leadership and gender? A journey through the landscape of theories. *Leadership & Organization Development Journal, 24*(1/2), 43–51.

Bartol, K., Martin, D., and Kromkowski, J. (2003). Leadership and the glass ceiling: Gender and ethnic group influences in leader behaviors at middle and executive managerial levels. *Journal of Leadership & Organizational Studies, 9*(3), 8–19.

Bass, B. (1990). *Bass & Stogdill's handbook of leadership* (3rd ed.). New York, NY: The Free Press.

Bass, B. (1997). Does the transactional-transformational leadership paradigm transcend organizational and national boundaries? *The American Psychologist, 52*(2), 130–139.

Bass, B. (1998). *Transformational leadership: Industry, military, and educational impact.* Mahwah, NJ: Lawrence Erlbaum Associates.

Batten, J. (1998). Servant-leadership: A passion to serve. In L. Spears (Ed.), *Insights on leadership* (pp. 38–53). New York, NY: John Wiley & Sons.

Bratton, J., Grint, K., and Nelson, D. (2005). *Organizational leadership.* Mason, OH: South-Western.

Burke, S. and Collins, K. (2001). Gender differences in leadership styles and management styles. *Women in Management Review, 16*(5/6), 244–256.

Chemers, M. (1997). *An integrative theory of leadership.* Mahwah, NJ: Lawrence Erlbaum Associates.

Chen, J. and Silverthorn, C. (2005). Leadership effectiveness, leadership style, and employee readiness. *Leadership & Organization Development, 26*(3/4), 280–288.

Clark, D. (2006). *Concepts of leadership.* Retrieved March 18, 2006, from http://www.nwlink.com/donclark/leader/leadcon.html

DeGraaf, D., Tilley, C., and Neal, L. (2000). Servant-leadership. *Leisure Management, 20*(1), 60–61.

Dubrin, A. (2004). *Leadership: Research findings, practice, and skills* (4th ed.). New York, NY: Houghton Mifflin.

Eagly, A., Karau, S., and Makhijani, M. (1995). Gender and the effectiveness of leaders: A meta-analysis. *Psychological Bulletin, 117*(1), 125–145.

Eicher-Catt, D. (2005). The myth of servant-leadership: A feminist perspective. *Women and Language, 28*(1), 17–25.

Fairholm, G. (1997). *Capturing the heart of leadership: Spirituality and community in the new American workplace.* Westport, CT: Praeger.

Fairholm, G. (1998). *Perspectives on leadership: From the science of management to its spiritual heart*. Westport, CT: Quorum.

Fiedler, F. (1967). *A theory of leadership effectiveness*. New York, NY: McGraw-Hill.

Fujimoto, Y. and Hartel, C. (2004). Culturally specific prejudices: Interpersonal prejudices of individualists and intergroup prejudices of collectivists. *Cross Cultural Management, 11*(3), 54–69.

Gillespie, N. and Mann, L. (2004). Transformational leadership and shared values: The building blocks of trust. *Journal of Managerial Psychology, 19*(6), 588–607.

Greenleaf, R. (1977). *Servant leadership*. New York, NY: The Paulist Press.

Greenleaf, R. (1991). *The servant as leader*. Indianapolis, IN: The Robert K. Greenleaf Center.

Groves, K. (2005). Gender differences in social and emotional skills and charismatic leadership. *Leadership & Organization Development Journal, 11*(3), 30–46.

Hayashi, A. and Ewert, A. (2006). Outdoor leaders' emotional intelligence and transformational leadership. *Journal of Experiential Education, 28*(3), 222–242.

Hersey, P., Blanchard, K., and Johnson, D. (2001). *Management of organizational behavior* (8th ed.). Upper Saddle River, NJ: Prentice-Hall.

Hofstede, G. (2001). *Culture's consequences: Comparing values, behaviors, institutions, and organizations across nations*. Thousand Oaks, CA: Sage Publishing.

Hogue, M., Yoder, J., and Ludwig, J. (2002). Increasing initial leadership effectiveness: Assisting both women and men. *Sex Roles, 46*(11/12), 377–384.

House, R. and Aditya, R. (1997). The social scientific study of leadership: Quo vadis? *Journal of Management, 23*(3), 409–473.

Humphreys, J. and Einstein, W. (2003). Nothing new under the sun: Transformational leadership from a historical perspective. *Management Decision, 41*(1/2), 85–95.

Jordan, D. (1989). A new vision for outdoor leadership theory. *Leisure Studies, 8*, 35–47.

Jordan, D., DeGraaf, D., and DeGraaf, K. (2005) *Programming for parks, recreation, and leisure services: A servant leadership approach* (2nd ed.). State College, PA: Venture Publishing, Inc.

Khatri, N., Ng, H. A., and Lee, T. (2001). The distinction between charisma and vision: An empirical study. *Asia Pacific Journal of Management, 18*(3), 373–384.

Krishnan, V. (2004). Impact of transformational leadership on followers' influence strategies. *Leadership & Organization Development Journal, 25*(1/2), 58–72.

Kunnanatt, J. (2004). Emotional intelligence: The new science of interpersonal effectiveness. *Human Resource Development, 15*(4), 489–495.

Moorhead, G. and Griffin, R. (2004). *Organizational behavior: Managing people and organizations* (7th ed.). Boston, MA: Houghton Mifflin.

Ndubisi, N. (2004). Understanding the salience of cultural dimensions on relationships and aftermaths. *Cross Cultural Management 11*(3), 70–89.

Napier, L. A. (1999). *An alternative model on the practice of leadership: An indigenous people's perspective*. Paper presented at the American Educational Research Association meeting. April 22, 2000. Montreal, Quebec.

Nelson, D. and Quick, J. (2005). *Understanding organizational behavior* (2nd ed.). Mason, OH: South-Western.

Northouse, P. (2001). *Leadership: Theory and practice* (3rd ed.). Thousand Oaks, CA: Sage.

Ruderman, M. and Ernst, C. (2004). Finding yourself: How social identity affects leadership. *Leadership in Action, 24*(3), 3–7.

Russell, R. (2002). A review of servant leadership attributes: Developing a practical model. *Leadership & Organization Development Journal, 23*(3/4), 145–157.

Schruijer, S. (2002). Leader, leadership, and leading: From individual characteristics to relating in context. *Journal of Organizational Behavior, 23*(7), 869–872.

Sczesny, S., Boask, J., Neff, D., and Schyns, B. (2004). Gender stereotypes and the attribution of leadership traits: A cross-cultural comparison. *Sex Roles, 51*(11/12), 631–645.

Sendjaya, S. and Sarros, J. (2002). Servant leadership: Its origin, development, and application in organizations. *Journal of Leadership & Organizational Studies, 9*(2), 57–64.

Sivanathan, N. and Fekken, G. C. (2002). Emotional intelligence, moral reasoning and transformational leadership. *Leadership & Organization Development Journal, 23*(3/4), 198–204.

Smith, B., Montagno, R., and Kuzmenko, T. (2004). Transformational and servant leadership: Content and contextual comparisons. *Journal of Leadership & Organizational Studies, 10*(4), 80–91.

Spears, L. (Ed.). (1998). *Insights on leadership: Service, stewardship, spirit, and servant-leadership*. New York, NY: John Wiley & Sons.

Stelter, N. (2002). Gender differences in leadership: Current social issues and future organizational implications. *Journal of Leadership & Organizational Studies, 8*(4), 88–99.

Stone, G., Russell, R., and Patterson, K. (2004). Transformational versus servant leadership: A difference in leader focus. *Leadership & Organization Development Journal, 25*(3/4), 349–361.

Tucker, B. and Russell, R. (2004). The influence of the trans-formational leader. *Journal of Leadership & Organizational Studies, 10*(4), 103–111.

Van Wart, M. (2004). A comprehensive model of organizational leadership: The leadership action cycle. *International Journal of Organizational Theory and Behavior, 7*(2), 173–208.

Vinnicombe, S. and Singh, V. (2002). Sex role stereotyping and requisites of successful top managers. *Women in Management Review, 17*(3/4), 120–129.

Walumbwa, F., Wu, C., and Ojode, L. (2004). Gender and in-structional outcomes: The mediating role of leadership style. *The Journal of Management Development, 23*(2), 124–140.

Yan, J. and Hunt, J. (2005). A cross-cultural perspective on perceived leadership effectiveness. *International Journal of Cross Cultural Management 5*(1), 49–66.

Yukl, G. (1989). *Leadership in organizations*. Englewood Cliffs, NJ: Prentice Hall.

Zohar, D. (2005). Spiritually intelligent leadership. *Leader to Leader, 38*, 1–4.

Leader Profile

Bob Roadarmel
**All Army Sports Specialist, Department of Morale, Welfare, and Recreation
Department of Defense**

Bob has five years in this position, and 35 years in the parks, recreation, and leisure services profession.

Some leadership positions he has held include:

- Family and Youth Sports Specialist, Department of the Army, Nuremburg, Germany
- Sports official for most sports
- Community Intramural Director
- Youth Sports Director
- Fitness Specialist

What is the meaning of leadership?
Know when to lead and when to follow; be strong enough to do both well. If you are in charge, take charge.

What are the most important leader qualities?
Integrity, honesty, discipline—Only expect it of others if you can live it yourself. Adhere to the idea of "tough talk for tough times;" call it like it is and be honest about it, but you can do this gently as well. Praise sincerely and publicly, and do your best to discipline one-on-one. Notice what people do well and let them, and others, know about it. Set a positive tone; this can be matter of fact; you can't *always* be jumping around and going crazy with energy (Energy is good though!). I've always believed if you're not moving forward, you're sliding back. Grow leaders; always give people the chance to excel, but learn from failure.

What advice do you have for students who aspire to leadership in parks, recreation, and leisure services?
Be willing to do any task at any time, no matter what. Always be willing to get your hands, and the rest of you, dirty—and do it with a bright attitude and a smile. Jump in, the mud is warm! You are never too good or too high on the food chain to be past doing anything that needs doing. Acknowledge people in a sincere way—Folks are important and you can't do anything without them. Do nice things for people; it doesn't have to be big. It makes for a better workplace and a better world in general. Fight for your people; stand up for them. Get certified as an official in multiple sports; it helps with every aspect of your job. At your job site, introduce yourself around *before* you need anything from anybody. That way you'll have some solid footing to work from when you do need to interact with others.

Favorite book: Raptor by Gary Jennings

Favorite activities: Playing soccer, swimming, mountain biking or hiking with Gussie, my chocolate lab. Also downhill skiing, SCUBA diving, snorkeling, baseball, softball, squash, reading, going to plays, canoeing, whitewater rafting, coaching, and learning to kayak.

Chapter Three
Leadership and Human Development

Learning Opportunities

Through studying this chapter readers will have the opportunity to

- Be exposed to major theories of human development.
- Examine the role of environment in influencing human development.
- Discover underlying reasons for cognition, actions, and affective behaviors.
- Integrate knowledge of ages and stages of life into leadership concepts.
- Consider the implications of human development on leadership.

Photo courtesy of Paul Jordan/WEBSPORTSPHOTO

Leaders who truly understand human development are more successful than those who do not. Learning about how people grow, mature, and develop across the life span helps leaders understand the thoughts, behaviors, and preferences of participants. For instance, a young child who refuses to share equipment does not necessarily do so out of selfishness. Rather, it is not until a certain stage of development that a child learns to share and cooperate with others. The social, psychological, emotional, and physical evolution of individuals influences development. Growth, a term often used in conjunction with development, results in new potential in specific time periods of an individual's life. Many external factors influence human development including cultural mores, generational events, family experiences, socioeconomic status, health, and personal talents and liabilities.

While human development is a complex and extensive field, leaders who understand the basics have a foundation from which to draw when applying various leadership skills. Knowledge and understanding of general principles of human development are necessary to lead in a developmentally appropriate fashion. This is needed because at different stages of development, different techniques are more effective than others. For instance, when dealing with a child who has not yet fully reached Piaget's concrete operations stage, an effective leader must use concrete rather than abstract directions and instructions. Once a person develops the capability to understand literal language a leader may be a little more creative with her or his use of terms and phrases. It should be noted that everyone does not move through developmental stages at the same time in life, and some people have arrested development in certain stages. Those people who are well above the chronological age most typical of a particular development stage (e.g., have slowed or stopped in development) are usually considered to have a developmental disability.

The behaviors, skills, and abilities described within each developmental stage are simply more typical of one age group than another—they are not hard and fast rules of when every person should go through each stage or developmental phase. Therefore, while information about human development can be extremely helpful in understanding people in general, it cannot be used to predict individual behaviors or reasons behind individual behaviors. It can be useful in matching leader expectations with participant capabilities. This is developmentally appropriate leadership.

This chapter summarizes research about human development, providing a basis for understanding people and making leadership decisions when working with people across the life span. This chapter sets the stage for understanding by first presenting an overview of popular development theories. The theories discussed here include Piaget's model of development, which focuses on various cognitive abilities; Kohlberg's theory of moral development over the life span; and Gilligan's position on moral development. The remainder of the chapter is designed to provide information and material related to physical and social development across age groups and life stages. Implications for leadership are presented to help leaders make the best use of this information.

Theories of Human Development

Development According to Piaget

Although they sometimes seem to be miniature grownups, children have unique ways of learning and understanding. These differences are based on developmental stages and involve cognitive abilities and limitations. Levels of understanding and cognitive abilities evolve over time and impact the way an individual deals with others, approaches tasks, and makes decisions. According to Piaget, knowledge is constructed gradually through interactions with the environment. Responses to the environment depend upon how the individual understands the situation in which she or he finds herself or himself. Piaget theorized that four general stages of development exist: sensorimotor intelligence stage, preoperational stage, concrete operations stage, and formal operations stage (Beilin, 1992; Howe, 1993).

Sensorimotor Intelligence Stage (0–24 Months)

The sensorimotor stage occurs within the first two years of life. What occurs at this stage of development may not impact recreation leadership directly, but knowledge of this stage provides an important foundation for understanding people. The sensorimotor stage includes human learning through reflexes and exploration of the world (e.g., infants explore things through the five senses—taste,

Knowledge of human development is useful to match leader expectations with participant capabilities, and leader actions with various groups. This is **developmentally appropriate leadership.**

smell, touch, sight, and sound). Through this type of exploration, babies recognize their own position in the world. As one might imagine, at this stage repetition is the primary method of learning. Through multiple exposures children learn object permanence (i.e., the knowledge that things do not cease to exist simply because they are hidden from view), physical causality (i.e., the knowledge that things do not happen at random), and that intentional acts are required to achieve a desired goal.

Preoperational Stage (2–6 Years)

Children enter the preoperational stage between ages two and six. At this stage children learn how to use language, but are limited in understanding various constructs. For instance, a child in this stage believes that water poured from a short wide glass becomes more (in volume) when poured into a tall thin glass. Further, the child becomes egocentric—believing that everyone sees things the same way she or he does. Knowledge of this egocentricity helps in modifying leader expectations about social capabilities of young children (i.e., sharing). As part of this stage children think they cause events of nature. For example, if in anger, a child were to wish ill of someone and something bad were to happen, youngsters at this stage would believe that their wish caused the negative action to occur.

Friendships are important to a child's sense of belonging.

Leaders who recognize this can be sensitive to a child's potential feelings of self-doubt. Further, at this stage children believe in animism, the belief that inanimate objects (e.g., stuffed animals) have feelings.

Concrete Operations Stage (7–11 Years)

In middle childhood youngsters learn to classify and group objects, and begin to understand abstract notions and logical reasoning. At this stage, children can focus on more than one thing at a time and can handle multiple directions. In middle childhood, young people learn that general principles apply across a variety of situations, and that basic principles apply to everyone. They also learn how to retrace their thought processes and keep track of their thoughts. They begin to understand that merely changing the form of an object does not change the nature of it. Understanding what occurs developmentally during this stage helps leaders to communicate, assign tasks, and use increasingly sophisticated behavior management techniques. For instance, at this age children understand what it means to play within activity rules. Prior to this stage children commonly feel free to make up rules as they go along (usually to avoid failing or losing).

Formal Operations Stage (11+ Years)

The development and acquisition of formal operations is gradual. While it generally begins around age 11, the skills acquired in this stage do not become consistently learned and applied until approximately age 16. The formal operations stage includes the development of problem-solving

abilities and hypothesis testing. People have the ability to wonder, "What would happen if…?" and then test that notion. When moving through this stage, young people learn best when confronted with novelty and a desire to understand. For example, as children develop the ability to solve problems, leaders might engage them in leadership decisions, conflict management, and the development of new games and activities.

❖   ❖   ❖

In cultivating his four-stage theory of development, Piaget studied boys as they moved from infancy into adolescence and noted that enough similarities existed to define the four stages of human development as described above. Piaget's model focuses on how people learn, what they learn, and the beliefs they hold about their place in the world ("Stages of socioemotional development in children and teenagers," 2006). Piaget provided a framework for understanding how and why people develop, think, and behave the way they do. It is generally accepted that all people follow similar patterns of development across the life span, although the actual age at which one reaches a particular stage varies.

Kohlberg's Theory of Moral Development

While many have attempted to understand how a sense of morality (learning about right and wrong) develops over the life span, the model proposed by Kohlberg is the most commonly discussed today. According to Barger (2000), Kohlberg believes people of all cultures experience moral

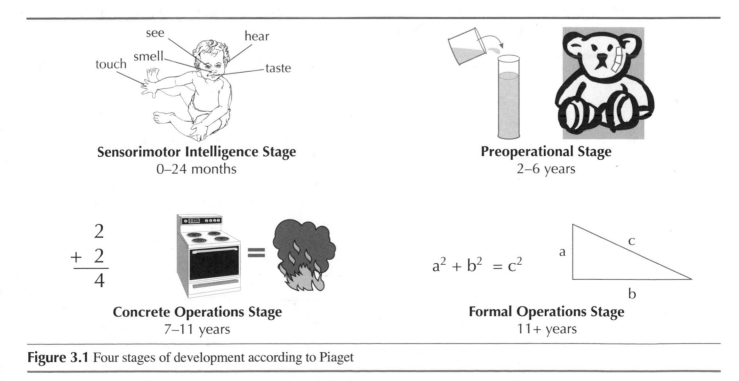

Figure 3.1 Four stages of development according to Piaget

development through the same stages, although perhaps at different rates. Further, we learn about morality through thinking about moral problems and through interaction with others. As people grow through the various moral stages, they integrate what they learned at earlier stages into more global frameworks.

Leaders understanding moral development will better understand the thinking behind participant actions and be in a position to intervene, if desired. It is generally thought that as people grow and mature, they move through various stages of moral development, from an egotistical position ("me" orientation) to a more objective position ("other" orientation). It should be noted that all people do not move through all stages of moral development, but individuals do evolve progressively over the life span (Barger, 2000; Hardy & Carlo, 2005).

Stage 1: Early Childhood

In Stage 1 moral decisions are based on a desire to avoid punishment. People in this stage of moral development decide not to violate social norms because they fear or want to avoid the consequences. Authority figures rule and obedience is a result of fear of punishment from the authority figures. For example, a child at this stage would behave as asked by a leader because she or he fears disapproval or punishment. Children begin to understand delayed gratification and to exercise self-control in Stage 1 (Hardy & Carlo, 2005; Murray, n.d.).

Stage 2: Early/Middle Childhood

In Stage 2 people make decisions about how to behave based on a desire to obtain rewards; they want to know *What is in it for me?* Morality is viewed somewhat as an exchange or a transaction—youngsters believe that if they do something for someone else, the moral thing to do would be for that individual to reciprocate in some fashion. A person in this stage might resolve a dilemma by determining what rewards would be gained by following instructions (and vice versa). Individuals in this stage of moral devel-

opment might behave as expected if they believed they would be rewarded for doing so (e.g., with extra attention or a prize).

Stage 3: Adolescence

As people move through the stages of moral development, they move from being self-centered (i.e., holding an ego-centric view) to becoming aware of society and their place in it. In Stage 3 people make decisions based on a desire to gain social approval—They strive for good interpersonal relationships (Barger, 2000; Crain, 1985). At this stage, people value trust, loyalty, and respect. The effects of peer pressure provide an example of individuals making decisions to gain social approval. Youth want to live up to others' expectations. They also begin to take into consideration good intentions and motivations when judging others' actions. For many, this is the highest moral development stage attained; across the life span people look to others to serve as their "moral barometers" (Jaffe, 1998). This means that when an individual is about to make an ethically difficult decision, she or he first looks around, seeks counsel from peers, and tries to think about how others would handle the situation before making a decision.

Stage 4: Adolescence/Young Adulthood

At this phase of development, individuals consider the importance of morality in maintaining social order; thus, what society says is right, is so (Hardy & Carlo, 2005). The thought is that those in legitimate authority positions determine morality and do so out of a desire to manage social existence. What is legal is moral; what is illegal is immoral. A person at this stage would follow rules (because the leader said so) and act in legally appropriate ways (because the law so dictated). It can be seen as a very either/or, and rigid moral stance.

Stage 5: Young/Middle Adulthood

In Stage 5, individuals broaden their view of the role of society in determining morality and look to think and act

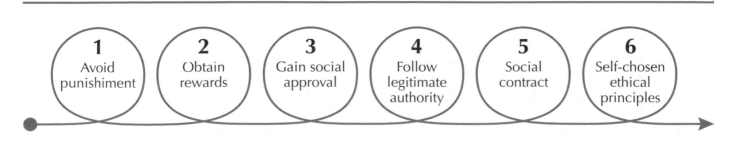

Figure 3.2 Kohlberg postulated about moral development across the life span and viewed this development as progressive and integrative.

in ways that result in the greatest good for the greatest number. Morality is based on an assumption that an unwritten contract exists among members of society whereby people agree to behave in an acceptable and appropriate manner. The concern is not for the consequences of one's actions, but for the welfare of society. At this stage a person would make decisions and engage in behaviors that are in the best interest of others. For instance, an angry individual at this stage would prefer to talk out the issues rather than engage in a fistfight. Someone in this stage might repeatedly ask if her or his beliefs contributed to the common good.

Stage 6: Adulthood

When Kohlberg first developed his theory of moral development, he envisioned six stages. In the sixth and final stage of moral development he believed that individuals based decisions on self-chosen ethical principles directed toward the good of humanity. A person at this stage would operate within a consistent system of values and principles and with integrity. She or he would utilize abstract thinking and carefully consider the greater good prior to acting. According to Barger (2000), however, because research support for this stage of moral development is lacking, Kohlberg now views this stage only as a theory.

❖   ❖   ❖

Kohlberg envisioned moral development as maturing over six stages across the life span. He viewed Stage 6 as the highest moral order and observed that many people never reach this stage of morality. Life stages do not necessarily correlate to a particular moral development stage. It may be viewed however, that as one matures, one moves away from a fear-based morality to a moral viewpoint that focuses on the good of humanity.

Morality Based on an Ethic of Care

It was common practice in early years of science to conduct research with only males as subjects; thus, it is not surprising that Kohlberg worked only with boys in the initial development of his theory. As might be imagined, this raises questions related to the viability of moral development theories for girls and women. Concerned about the exclusion of females in studies related to moral development, Gilligan (1982) engaged in research to examine the moral development of girls.

Gilligan found that girls and women are taught to value relationships and remain connected to others while boys and men are taught to value independence and autonomy from others. Another way to characterize this is to note that the female approach to morality is that people have responsibilities toward others; thus, the moral imper-

ative is to care for others. This may require self-sacrifice as the focus is on others' needs, rather than one's own. On the other hand, the male approach to morality is that all people have certain (and the same) rights. The moral imperative is to respect those rights; thus, rules are necessary to maintain fairness for all (Cypher, n.d.).

Gilligan termed the female approach to morality as an "ethic of care." In contrast, the moral development process presented by Kohlberg has been characterized as an "ethic of rights and justice." For example, an individual in an adult sports league adhering to an ethic of rights and justice might avoid an argument or fight with others because it is against the rules. On the other hand, an individual who subscribes to the ethic of care would avoid an altercation out of a concern for hurting the individual emotionally and/or physically. We might notice that when boys argue during play, they actively resolve the problem. Girls who get into an argument during play often stop playing in order to protect the relationship. This difference highlights one of the distinctions between the two views of ethical positions.

Research findings related to the differences found between the models presented by Kohlberg and Gilligan have been contradictory. Initially some thought that females and males learned about and achieved moral development differently. Research based on Gilligan's work has continued, however, and now it appears that rather than developing differently, males and females perceive dilemmas differently. Females perceive moral dilemmas as more important to their lives than do males. In addition, females and males tend to focus on different

Figure 3.3 Ethic of rights and justice, and the ethic of care.

issues within the same moral dilemma. Furthermore, rather than finding that women and men have different internal predispositions to morality, the dilemma itself is what leads one to view it from a viewpoint of caring or of justice (Wark & Krebs, 2000).

Gender and Development

Genetics, as well as one's environment, influence cognitive, social, physical, and moral development. One of the elements is gender, or the notion of what is feminine and masculine. Children are taught what is feminine and what is masculine by the media, peers, parents, church, and through play. They come to understand their own gender by age three or four (Eagly, Karau & Makhijani, 1995). By this age, children know the difference between girls and boys and can identify "girls' games/toys" and "boys' games/ toys." Gender is one characteristic that is evidenced in all aspects of human development; girls and boys face different biological, psychological, and socioemotional changes across the life span.

Society has determined acceptable behaviors for girls and boys, and these sex-based stereotypes lead to differences in expectations based on sex. For example, boys are expected to show more aggression, dominance, and competitiveness than girls. In addition, boys are expected to show more risk-taking behaviors (willingness to try more on their own) than girls. On the other hand, girls face expectations to be more dependent on others than are boys. Furthermore, girls are expected to be more nurturing, helping, and generous than boys (Eagly, Karau & Makhijani, 1995). Leaders should be careful, however, to avoid the traps of stereotyping, as labeling people tends to limit their potentials. In leisure services settings females and males are often victims of stereotypes and face social

and structural constraints to full engagement in a variety of recreation and leisure services.

Life Stages and Age Groups

Life stages describe general classifications of people based on physical, mental, social, and emotional levels of maturity. While there are exceptions, in general people in similar age groups fall into similar stages of development. With their knowledge of human development, leaders can make well-informed choices about grouping people by age for activity participation. At times it may be wise to mix ages in a group, while at other times it may best to separate by age.

With a foundation in the basics of human development, this text next considers age groupings based on similar categories found in the education and human development literature. Much of the information related to age groups is based on extensive research, including interviews with school teachers, parents, and youth, and observations of youth over extended periods of time (*Growth 4–5 year olds*, 2005; *Growth 6–12 year olds*, 2005; *Growth 13–18 year olds*, 2005; *Normal adolescent development*, 2005; *Stages of socioemotional development in children and teenagers*, 2006; *Understanding the teen years*, 2004; Yan & Fischer, 2002). Each section describes information related to physical, mental or cognitive, socioemotional, and moral development

Behavior results from a combination of physical, mental, socioemotional, and moral aspects of a person— It is both a process and a product. Generally speaking, *physical* development includes energy and growth, the acquisition of fine and gross motor skills, activity preferences, and physical coordination. *Cognitive* development includes the ability to think in the abstract, academic

Young Childhood (< 5 years)

Middle Childhood (5–7 years)

Older Childhood (8–11 years)

Early Adolescence (12–14 years)

Adolescence (15–17 years)

Young Adulthood (18–25 years)

| | | | | | | Middle Adulthood (26–40 years) | Older Adulthood (41–60 years) | Seniors (61–74 years) | Elderly > 75 years |

Figure 3.4 Timeline with developmental stages identified

People who are close in age tend to have similar mental, physical, social, and emotional capabilities.

achievement, reasoning and logic, and mental abilities. *Socioemotional* development consists of relationships with others (peers and adults), fears, worries, and moods. The other element of development discussed in this chapter is *moral* development. This involves the thought process behind decision-making, and how individuals define what is good and right and what is bad and wrong.

Childhood

The idea of *childhood* (as well as the other life stages) is a social construct which varies by culture, ethnicity, gender, and class (Gurstein, Lovato & Ross, 2003). Generally speaking, in the United States childhood spans toddlerhood to adolescence. It captures the period of time when youngsters begin to have an understanding of the world, enter the public school system, and develop a social self. A great deal of unstructured time, large developmental changes, and a strong dependence on adults for subsistence, safety, and security characterize childhood. It has three stages: young, middle, and older childhood. Young childhood usually encompasses preschool children, and since parks and recreation practitioners rarely service that age group as individual constituents, this stage is not addressed here.

Middle Childhood (5–7 years)

Physical Development. In terms of physical development, children ages five to seven years grow about two inches per year. They have a lot of energy that comes in spurts and can be difficult to keep under control. As they continue to practice large motor skills, children at this age enjoy a great deal of running, hopping, skipping, climbing, and catching. In addition, chasing and being chased are favorite activities. Because children at this age struggle with fine-motor control, there may be frustration surrounding these efforts (such as tying shoes); yet they need to practice these skills. The high level of physical activity complements a similar need for rest as youngsters in this age group tend to tire easily.

Cognitive Development. This period of life characterizes the fastest cognitive growth of any age group. Five to seven-year-olds tend to be concrete thinkers and very literal in interpreting meanings. At this age, children operate from perception and intuition rather than logic. Young children have difficulty focusing on more than one thing at a time, and they see things primarily from their own perspective. They believe everyone sees things as they do, as well. Young children can accept and work with basic rules, but they will change rules when needed to avoid failure or losing a game. Due to the heavy reliance on concrete thinking, movement is often necessary for learning and understanding directions. At this age children have wonderful capabilities for fantasy and active imaginations.

Socioemotional Development. Young children do not have strong social skills (e.g., communication, conflict resolution, other orientation, empathy) and tend to be egoistic. In this age group, children begin to demonstrate the ability to share and to engage in interactive play; they are learning to take turns. In addition, there tends to be a

Young children engage in dress up and make-believe as part of the developmental process.

Children of all ages need to be physically engaged to maintain healthy living.

separation of the sexes with boys and girls playing apart from one another. Children at this age generally are very honest, due in part to a lack of mastery over the nuances of lying. These young children lack strong organizational skills, often losing or leaving items behind.

Youngsters at this stage of development (preoperational, according to Piaget) can be overly sensitive to comments and actions of others. For example, they may be very hurt if a child sticks out her or his tongue at them. Youngsters of this age can be easily frustrated by difficulty in understanding directions. They need a good deal of encouragement and support from adults and seem to crave adult affection. Children of this age are very impulsive and unable to control their emotions. They tend to use physical aggression to resolve problems, and start and stop crying quickly.

Moral Development. Generally, children between five and seven years of age are at the first and second stages of moral development as described by Kohlberg. They base decisions to do or not do as the leader asks on a fear of punishment and a desire for rewards. They come from a self-centered perspective yet believe that authority figures set the tone for morality.

Implications for Leaders. Successful leaders understand that knowledge of human development will provide a basis for understanding why people act the way they do. This is not meant to serve as an excuse for behaviors, however. One of the most fascinating things about humans

---

Table 3A Middle Childhood (ages 5–7 years)

Piaget's Theory of Cognitive Development: Preoperational Stage
Kohlberg's Moral Development Theory: Stage 1 and Stage 2

Characteristics	Description	Leadership Implications
Physical	• Lots of energy balanced with need for rest. • Struggle with fine motor skills; developing gross motor skills. • Enjoy running, hopping, chasing, catching, and climbing.	• Teach through physical demonstration; allow for practice of large motor skills; give opportunities for practicing fine-motor skills; build in rest opportunities. • Provide opportunities for success in social skills; give children a good deal of attention; lead simple activities with minimal and unsophisticated rules; be flexible.
Cognitive	• Concrete, literal thinkers. • Operate from perception and intuition; logic and reasoning abilities are limited. • Tend to see things only from their own perspective. • Can only focus on one or two things at a time. • May change rules to avoid failure or losing; movement is necessary for learning. • Creativity and imagination are active.	• Take care to treat all youngsters with love and attention; be sensitive to their fragile emotional nature. • Remember the power of words; behavior management can be relatively basic as youngsters generally respond quickly to adults. • Make sure there is enough appropriate equipment to keep children occupied; minimize wait time when leading; get the youngsters moving and keep them active and involved.
Socioemotional	• Poor social skills; impulsive in emotional reactions. • Tend to be egotistical; do not share well. • Very honest; do not tell lies well. • Sensitive to comments of others; can be easily frustrated. • Poor organizational skills; high need for adult love and affection. • Emotions can swing quickly and widely.	
Moral	• Decisions based on desire to avoid punishment or on hopes for rewards. • Authority figures set the tone for morality.	

is that we can learn. Thus, in addition to providing leaders a basis for understanding, this knowledge allows leaders to establish environments in which people can be challenged to grow and develop.

For instance, when working with a young child who becomes frustrated and hits another child, a leader first will be able to understand that this is not necessarily a purposeful act of aggression. Hitting among young children is often due to poor impulse control and the inability to reason through a conflict. Once the leader addresses the inappropriate behavior (in a developmentally appropriate way), she or he can then begin to help the youngster develop control over her or his emotions through examples and repetitive practice.

Due to their physical nature, young children learn best by doing. Leaders would be wise then to present activity instructions in such a way as to incorporate physical engagement of the children. Bear in mind that activities need to be balanced with rest; youngsters tire easily. Both fatigue and a need to move may be underlying reasons for inappropriate behaviors; the leader will need to make a judgment based on her or his understanding of the entire situation. Logic and reasoning capabilities of young children are limited; therefore, extended lessons in reasoning will not be very effective when addressing various difficulties. In addition, youth at this stage are very literal thinkers and will follow directions literally rather than figuratively; therefore, explicit leader instructions are necessary.

Preventative behavior management with this age group may be accomplished by thorough preparation of the physical and social environments. At this age children have difficulty sharing, so being fully prepared with enough equipment to go around is important. Flexibility in adjusting activities based on physical capabilities (e.g., establishing environments for success), mental capabilities (e.g., providing opportunities for youth to show mastery in creative areas), socioemotional skills (e.g., structuring social interactions to address low level of maturity), and moral development (e.g., establishing just a few easy-to-follow rules) will help set a tone for leader and participant success.

Relationships with adults are important to children in the five- to seven-year-old age range. Often youngsters become very dependent on leaders and compete for leader attention. Leisure services leaders will need to be sensitive to this and aware of how they treat the attention-seeking youngsters.

Older Childhood (8–11 years)

Physical Development. As children move into older childhood they continue to grow about 2.5 inches per year. Physical coordination improves as do abilities in gross-motor and fine-motor skills. High energy levels are still apparent, although children at this stage do not tire as easily as young children. While children at this age can be still for longer periods of time, active participation is still needed for optimum learning to occur. It is not uncommon for signs of puberty to occur in girls between eight and thirteen years of age (e.g., onset of menstruation, change in body shape). For boys, first signs of puberty tend to occur later.

Cognitive Development. As youth move into the concrete operations stage (Piaget), logic and reasoning abilities begin to appear. In addition, the ability to effectively deal with abstractions develops. One of the characteristics of eight-year-olds to eleven-year-olds is that they ask a lot of "why" questions as they begin to sort out and understand issues of cause and effect. During this stage the development of self-concept begins. Youngsters in this age group tend to be easily motivated and able to work within activity rules.

Older children can consider more than one aspect of a situation, and they understand general concepts better than when younger. Problem-solving skills improve and youngsters can work independently for short periods of time. When five to seven years of age, children often would give up if faced with frustration; at eight to eleven years of age, children tend to persevere longer—they begin to believe that they can make something happen if they try hard and long enough.

Socioemotional Development. As children move out of the egoistic phase, they gain impulse control and begin to understand social mores. Because children are beginning to form attachments to groups, they become very concerned about fairness and equality. They share better, yet the sexes (for the most part) remain separate (e.g., girls/boys have "cooties"). Those children in this age group who are maturing more quickly than others may describe girlfriend/boyfriend relationships. As groups develop, so too do relationship skills; youngsters at this age develop some tact, but are not always sensitive to others' needs. Adults remain important figures in the lives of these youth, although older children begin to test adults in their desire for independence.

Children between the ages of eight and eleven do not take criticism from peers or adults very well (i.e., they tend to be sensitive and defensive), and are easily embarrassed. An increased awareness of peers' and others' expectations impacts the development of self-esteem. This may be seen in an increase of girls "primping" and boys striving to look "cool."

Moral Development. Youth in this stage of development begin to form and articulate personal values. They recognize that there is more than one viewpoint, and often, more than one "right" way to do things. While still acting out of their own interests, older youngsters in this age group begin to consider the consequences of their actions before acting. At the same time, youth are striving to gain social approval and often base decisions of morality on peer or social approval. Most youngsters at this age are in Kohlberg's Stage 2, and some are beginning to exhibit characteristics of Stage 3.

Implications for Leaders. Leaders working with eight-year-olds to eleven-year-olds face young people at a time of many changes, particularly in social development. Physical coordination is improving, and children are beginning to understand reasoning and logic; therefore, leaders might experience increased success in using logic and reasoning when explaining activity directions or rules. These youngsters are not quite so literal as when younger, and can better understand nuances in communication.

Table 3B Older Childhood (ages 8–11 years)

Piaget's Theory of Cognitive Development: Concrete Operations Stage
Kohlberg's Moral Development Theory: Stage 2 and Stage 3

Characteristics	Description	Leadership Implications
Physical	• Lots of energy balanced with reduced need for rest. • Improved coordination skills. • Active participation needed for learning. • Can sit still for a variety of engaging activities. • Early signs of puberty in girls.	• Provide opportunities to practice and achieve success with both gross- and fine-motor skills, as well as interpersonal skills. • Explain the reason behind leader decisions; help youth to understand the processes that leaders go through in decision making. • Talk to youth like people—They need the adult attention and they need to continue to practice their communication skills. • Be aware of frustration and impulsive acting out (i.e., emotional regression) if things are not going well. • Provide lots of opportunities for exploration and learning new things. • Provide structured choices; engage youth in conflict resolution situations. • Encourage all youth to try new things and work toward their potential; be aware of and ready to act on self-esteem challenges (particularly in girls).
Cognitive	• Logic and reasoning abilities are being developed and practiced. • Curiosity abounds; children ask a lot of "why" questions and are easily motivated. • Youth learn to deal with abstractions and general concepts. • Youth can consider situations from more than one view; problem-solving skills are improving. • Children begin to work independently and exhibit persistence.	
Socioemotional	• Social skills are improving; peer groups begin to become important; girls and boys tend to be in separate groups although they begin to talk about girl- and boyfriends. • Concern with fairness and equity. • Friendships develop and change quickly; the focus on peer group results in easy embarrassment. • Adults remain important figures. • Self-esteem development becomes apparent; self-concept is forming and observable; youth become concerned with how others (especially peers) see them.	
Moral	• Values development is initiated; children begin to think of consequences prior to acting. • Decisions are based on a desire for tangible rewards and social acceptance/approval.	

Thus, communication with adults becomes easier as these abilities develop. The ability to work independently away from adult supervision often frees leaders to take care of other issues and allows youngsters to grow and develop.

In this age group, best friends come and go, and children may be sensitive to these changing relationships. Leaders who are aware of social development can help youth through the difficult times and help them practice new social skills. This may be accomplished by manipulating group membership and structuring activities to facilitate the practice and development of interpersonal skills.

Knowing that at this age youngsters begin to test adult limits enables the leader to understand that various behaviors are not personal or motivated out of malice, but out of learning to gain a sense of self and independence. Therefore, when it appears that preadolescents are acting to disrupt a leader's efforts, the leader should remember that many possible reasons exist for the behaviors. When working with all people we must be aware of the impact of leadership on the self-esteem of participants; this is particularly true at this age. Specifically, self-esteem issues for preadolescent girls are fragile; many begin to lose self-esteem during this period. The values that leaders model in behaviors, words, and style of presentation have a big impact on the development and esteem of young people.

Adolescence

The period of adolescence can be explained in several ways. Some define it from a biological perspective, as that which occurs between puberty and physical maturation. Others suggest that adolescence is the age range of eleven to eighteen years. Still others take a more sociological approach and define adolescence as the transition from dependence on adults to autonomy (e.g., working on one's own, taking care of oneself). It may not be critically important to come to a particular agreement on the exact period of adolescence as long as leaders have a general understanding of the changes that occur during this developmental period.

Early Adolescence (12–14 years)

Physical Development. In the early teen years youth experience a balance in their energy output; the impulsivity of the previous years has lessened. At twelve to fourteen years of age most girls have experienced the onset of puberty and the development of secondary sex characteristics. There is great variation with boys; some boys have reached puberty, others are just beginning the sexual maturation process. For many young people in this age group, abilities related to coordination and fine-motor and gross-motor skills are well-developed.

Cognitive Development. Most teenage youth gain experience in the formal operational stage as described by Piaget. Logic, reasoning, and problem-solving skills develop, and organizational skills and rules management improve. Twelve-year-old to fourteen-year-old youth have the capabilities to understand multiple perspectives (i.e., they can see and begin to appreciate others' viewpoints) and to deal with abstractions. Teens begin to develop the ability to formulate and test hypotheses (i.e., "What if?" situations). In this period of early adolescence many youth find themselves facing an early identity crisis; they begin to develop a sense of self-identity separate from family and friends. Individual attention is focused on the present, rather than the future; thus, these are years of exploration (i.e., drugs, sexuality, risk-taking behaviors) as the search for self continues.

Socioemotional Development. Peers are a very important source of support for young teens as they strive to make the transition from family dependence to independence. The peer group strongly influences this age group, and the need for belonging seems all important. At this stage, adolescents turn to their friends more than their parents for recreation, companionship, and understanding. Sociosexual relationships (attractions to others based on sexuality) begin to develop, as does sexual exploration.

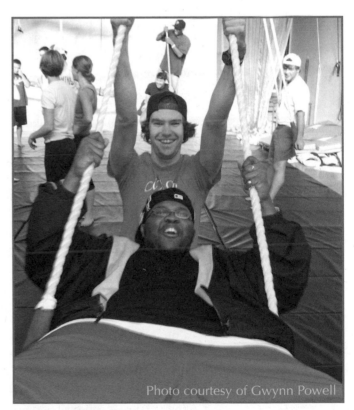

Photo courtesy of Gwynn Powell

People of all ages seek fun and enjoyment through recreation and leisure services.

Adolescents are learning about their identity and self-concept and deciding who they want to be—it can be a confusing time.

Emotions and moods can range widely as changes in hormones interfere with cognitive, social, and physical changes. Self-esteem, particularly for girls, fluctuates tre-

---

Table 3C Early Adolescence (ages 12–14 years)

Piaget's Theory of Cognitive Development: Beginning of Formal Operations
Kohlberg's Moral Development Theory: Stage 3 and Stage 4

Characteristics	Description	Leadership Implications
Physical	• A balance of energy output occurs. • Abilities related to coordination and fine motor skills are well-developed. • Most girls have reached puberty and experience the development of secondary sexual characteristics. • Most boys are just beginning to experience sexual maturation. • Focus on body image for both girls and boys.	• Provide opportunities for individual and peer group leadership development. • Try purposeful laissez-faire, democratic, or consultive leadership styles. • Model positive social relationships and human relations skills. • Lead and facilitate a variety of sophisticated activities; lead for success. • Allow for and accept mood swings; understand lashing out at the leader is not personal.
Cognitive	• Logic and reasoning abilities are developed and continue to be practiced. • Organizational skills and rules management skills are honed. • Can understand abstractions and various viewpoints. • Begin to learn how to test hypotheses. • Early identity crisis may occur—search for self as separate from parents; risk-taking behaviors are common.	• Encourage nonstereotypical leisure pursuits; act as a guide, mentor, counselor. • When leading activities that involve physical contact or exposure (e.g., swimming), be aware of and plan for self-consciousness by both girls and boys. • Involve youth in decision-making and behavior management processes. • Communicate with these young people; talk to them, listen to them, treat them with respect.
Socioemotional	• Peers are a very important source of support. • Teens are seeking independence from adults and family; are developing a sense of self. • Sociosexual relationships develop; self- and other-acceptance is often related to body image. • Moodiness may be apparent; self-esteem for many girls begins to plummet. • Boys strive to be "cool;" girls often follow media stereotypes for body image/success. • Exploration in many areas is common. • Issues are compounded by ethnicity, sex, disability, and sexual orientation.	
Moral	• Values clarification continues; teens are able to understand actions and consequences. • Decisions are based on rewards and social acceptance/approval. • Approval, loyalty, respect and trust are important aspects of self.	

mendously in this age group. Concerns with body image (as body shape changes with physical maturity) and embarrassment are important issues to this age group. Privacy issues are also apparent. Boys often work through determining a sense of self through being "cool" and engaging in between-boy competitions. Teenage boys often engage in showing off behaviors and spontaneous public competitions (e.g., basketball "jam" contests at the neighborhood court). Teen girls often subscribe to social images of beauty and may experience negative effects on their own psyche (e.g., anorexia, bulimia). The types of issues and concerns that impact youth at this life stage are compounded by ethnic, sex, disability, and sexual orientation issues.

Moral Development. At this age, teens understand intention and consequences; they have the ability to accept responsibility and blame for their own misbehaviors. As young people further develop their values and belief systems they often project a sense of absoluteness (either/or) in moral judgments. They believe that people should act in ways that are deemed to be "good." Social approval, loyalty, trust, and respect remain important in decision-making processes. Most youth at this age may be found in Stage 3 of Kohlberg's moral development theory.

Implications for Leaders. Leaders should be aware of issues surrounding body image for both girls and boys. Participant embarrassment and acceptance of these changes can be difficult to acknowledge and address. It is during these years that teasing from peers based on differences occurs; teens can be very sensitive to this. As they work through breaking away from parents, young teens often project this wrestling with independence onto other adults. Therefore, all adults may experience teens talking back and testing limits as the young people strive to identify how they define themselves as independent beings.

Social and group opportunities are important to teens; therefore, leaders who address these issues will be more successful than those who do not. Teens recognize and are concerned with unfairness, inconsistency, jumping to conclusions, not being liked, and being criticized in front of others. Thus, leaders will want to establish policies and develop leadership techniques to proactively address these concerns.

To be most effective in working with young teens, leaders should be cognizant of their own influences (both purposeful and unintentional) on the lives of these adolescents. Opportunities for success, and protection and security from negative social influences are strongly desired. Helping teens to explore many facets of their skills, abilities, and personality in a safe environment can make a tremendous difference in young teens' development.

Adolescence (15–17 years)

Physical Development. Well into being teenagers, fifteen-year-olds to seventeen-year-olds tend to be very concerned about their physical development and body image. Most girls and boys have reached their adult height. Body shape will continue to change for girls; boys will continue to develop muscle. Most males reach puberty during this period; most girls already have reached puberty. As physical growth outpaces their ability to adapt, boys' coordination takes a dip. They may appear gangly—all arms and legs. By this age most girls have accepted their postpubescent bodies. Skills acquisition becomes important and is made possible by physical capabilities—this is the age at which many physical skills are refined.

Cognitive Development. Many teens hold an idealistic view of the world and believe that situations can change if people just try hard enough. At this age the ability to handle abstractions, test hypotheses, and engage in problem solving come together. Cognitive abilities have reached a point of development where further growth results in increasing sophistication rather than the development of new skills. Teens have a wide variety of interests and a strong need to experiment and stretch themselves. They ask a lot of questions and engage in observation and experimentation as they continue to learn.

Socioemotional Development. Moving toward young adulthood, older teens strive to achieve self-identity, freedom from adults, and responsibility for themselves. Group affiliation remains important and mixed-sex activities are sought. This stage of development can be difficult for teens as the pull for independence and desire for familial security coexist. Moodiness might reflect the struggle in maintaining changing relationships. Many teens in this age group often seem like two different people—one mature young adult, and one immature youngster. In addition, a stronger sense of self begins to emerge at this stage of development. In particular, one's sexual identity is being formed. Adolescents begin to self-identify as heterosexual, homosexual, or bisexual; they experience intense love feelings at this life stage (Ryan & Futterman, 2001). This is the period of time when most youth begin to think of the future—their goals and ambitions beyond their teen years.

Moral Development. While many teens remain in the belief that morality is based on peer approval (Stage 3), a large number of teens are moving into the stage of moral reasoning where the desire to maintain social order is the driving force. Morality is defined by legitimate authority as a way to ensure the greatest good for the greatest number (Stage 4). Rules, laws, and leader guidelines become the source of right and wrong. A sense of responsibility develops as many youth at this age begin working and thinking about higher education or self-sufficiency away from the security of family.

Implications for Leaders. Working with teens can be a challenge for recreation and leisure services leaders. The fragility and strength paradox often manifested by teens can be just as confusing for adult leaders as for the teens themselves. Certainly, leaders have much more freedom to communicate using reason and logic when working with teens, as their abilities in those areas are fairly well-developed. Leaders who understand the struggle between needing the social approval of one's peer group and the desire to be one's own self will be more effective than those who do not understand these inherent difficulties.

The compounding factors of ethnicity, disability, and sexual orientation continue to impact this age group; some

Table 3D Adolescence (ages 15–17 years)

Piaget's Theory of Cognitive Development: Formal Operations Stage
Kohlberg's Moral Development Theory: Stage 3 and Stage 4

Characteristics	Description	Leadership Implications
Physical	• Almost all girls and boys have reached puberty; a focus on body image prevails. • Boys' coordination may dip (e.g., they may be gangly). • Skills are well-developed and specific skill (e.g., music, athletics) acquisition is important.	• Practice empathy, maintain high expectations; leaders will want to "choose their battles." • Use open communication patterns; work on developing trust with this age group; teach the reasons and thought processes behind leader recommendations or rules.
Cognitive	• Most teens hold an idealistic view of the world. • Logic and reasoning abilities are developed. • Teens understand abstractions, problem solving, and hypothesis testing. • Sophistication in cognitive abilities increases. • Teens have a wide variety of interests and look for ways to challenge themselves.	• Allow space and time for youth to practice their own leadership skills. • Model positive values and social skills; offer structured opportunities for positive sociosexual relationship development. • Provide skill instruction and activity strategies for honing of skills and cognitive development.
Socioemotional	• Peers remain an important source of support and identity; peer groups are very important to the socioemotional health of teens. • Mixed-sex activities are desired and sociosexual relationships can become serious. • Moodiness is not uncommon; self-esteem for girls may drop. • The struggle for own identity, away from family, continues. • Sexuality becomes established and teens become cognizant of it. • Adolescents begin to think of their future after high school; most have optimistic views.	• Continue to offer a variety of leisure and leadership opportunities; provide opportunities for success and allow for failure.
Moral	• Values clarification continues; decisions are based on social acceptance/approval. • Beginning to believe that morality is based on legitimate authority so as to maintain social order. • Rules, laws and leader guidelines serve as the basis for right and wrong.	

youth may experience isolation and insecurities. The struggle with body image is evident for both girls and boys. Boys often become increasingly physical as they use their bodies in sports, athletics, and demonstrations of physical prowess. Many girls discover that their bodies are capable of being strong and fluent as well, and are active in sports and outdoor activities. As this is a time of varied interests and strong skills, leaders who provide opportunities for trying new things will likely be effective. In addition, this age group must be allowed the freedom to experiment and practice making decisions for themselves by resolving conflicts and working through relationships with minimum leader involvement. At the same time, genuine leader concern and respect for these young people are important.

Adulthood

Once an individual has grown past adolescence they enter the world of adulthood and development continues. As long as physical aging continues and we move through various social and psychological changes, we all continue to grow and change. Adulthood is often marked with additional responsibilities and an orientation away from oneself and toward family, friends, vocation, and society. Adulthood is divided into several subheadings in this text: young adulthood, middle adulthood, older adulthood, seniors, and the elderly.

Young Adulthood (18–25 years)

Physical Development. Young adults are at their physical peak; most physical abilities are well-developed, and increased physical prowess is unlikely. The activity level of young adults is relatively high, but it can be slowed somewhat by life changes (e.g., beginning a career, relocation, establishing a family). Most people in this age group desire structured competition and recreational play. Often a concern for fitness drives physical activity, and activity is typically secondary to college or career. Interests in physical activity often include both individual and group or team activities.

Cognitive Development. Building on the cognitive skills of the late teen years, young adults express creativity and handle abstractions quite well. Cognitive skills are sharp and often considered peak during these years. Problem solving and hypothesis testing are further refined as young adults build on previous knowledge and experience. Intellectual development tends to increase in sophistication. General knowledge, educational knowledge, and workforce knowledge begin to come together.

Socioemotional Development. During the young adult years most people in our culture search for a life partner and a sense of stability. Young adults often experience enjoyment in mixed-sex activities, and one's circle of friends expands through work contacts and neighborhood connections. This stage of socioemotional development is often characterized as a "settling in" as one becomes more secure in her or his sense of personal identity. People take risks at this life stage to develop intimate and social connections with others. Those who are "different" from the group (based on ethnicity, sexual orientation, disability, or some other aspect of identity) may continue to experience isolation in this life stage. As part of an effort to fit in, these individuals will often seek others who are like them.

Moral Development. In young adulthood people gain a perspective on life that, while it certainly addresses personal needs, also shows an awareness of the influences of society. According to Kohlberg, some young adults are in Stage 4, which addresses the acknowledgment of the rights of the legal system in efforts to maintain social order. Other young adults are in Stage 5, which is indicative of an assumption of a social contract where people strive to do the greatest good for the greatest number. A sense of social consciousness develops for many. Stages of moral development are very heterogeneous (mixed) in this life stage.

Implications for Leaders. Leaders who work with young adults can expect a great deal of sensibility and stability in participant choices and actions. In the predominant individualist culture a sense of competition may drive some behaviors, and a knowledge of rules combined with life experiences can make it relatively easy for a leader to present activity instructions and directions.

Photo courtesy of Deb Jordan

Young adults enjoy being challenged, and working and playing in mixed-sex groups.

Participants often follow stereotypical activity patterns, although individuals may step outside of these expectations. This age group, particularly males, tends to engage in the highest frequency of risk-related recreation and leisure opportunities of any age group. An attitude of life and vibrancy is expressed. Leader-participant communication is easier than at previous stages of development, due in part to the developmental stage and in part to the fact that many leisure leaders and participants in this age group are peers. A wide variety of activities and

social groupings would help to meet the leisure needs of this age group. Treating individuals with dignity and respect and allowing them to be involved in leadership and decision-making processes tend to be effective leadership techniques.

Middle Adulthood (26–40 years)

Physical Development. At middle adulthood, many people are still at their physical peak. Some slowing down becomes evident as family and career take priority, and

---

Table 3E Young Adulthood (ages 18–25 years)

Piaget's Theory of Cognitive Development: Formal Operations Stage
Kohlberg's Moral Development Theory: Stage 4 and Stage 5

Characteristics	Description	Leadership Implications
Physical	• Physical peak; most physical abilities are well-developed. • High activity level; structured activities and competitive recreation experiences are desired. • Concern for fitness can influence activity choices and intensity of play.	• Provide opportunities for physical and cognitive prowess to be expressed; provide a variety of structured and unstructured activities. • Creative outlets are desirable; allow flexibility in choices of self-directed activities. • Appeal to social contract in explaining rules and moral issues related to behaviors. • Allow group development to occur naturally; monitor and mediate as necessary. • Bear in mind the competitive nature of many in this age group, and the need for structured, social, competitive situations. • Provide opportunities for risk-taking behaviors and for ready-made groups to engage in recreation activities as an entity.
Cognitive	• Cognitive abilities developed as teens continue to be honed; creativity is thought to be at a peak. • Abstractions and complex thought are easily handled for most. • Tend to have a concern for community and world as much as self.	
Socioemotional	• The search for a life partner and a sense of familial stability occurs. • People enjoy mixed-sex activities; circle of friends expands through work and neighborhood relationships. • Personal identity is firmed up; most in this age group are happy with who they are. • Both group and individual activities are sought and enjoyed. • Risks are taken to enhance life enjoyment as well as intimacy and connections with others.	
Moral	• An awareness of concerns for the greater society is seen; people think in terms of consequences outside of themselves. • Some believe morality is based on legitimate authority while others perceive the notion of an assumed social contract (greatest good for greatest number). • A social consciousness develops.	

finesse generally becomes more important than strength. Physical activities often take on a family orientation. Individual involvement in recreational activities tends to be focused on a few activities in which an individual works to hone her or his skills or to improve fitness. Toward the end of this stage, there is a physical slowing. Some people recommit to being physically engaged, while others allow themselves to slow down and become increasingly sedentary.

Cognitive Development. Cognitive skills and abilities of human beings peak in middle adulthood. One's creativity, use of logic and reasoning, and understanding abstractions reach a high point, and many people enjoy stretching their cognitive skills through mental challenges. An awareness of the influences of greater society and global issues on self and family also occurs.

Socioemotional Development. Persons in middle adulthood generally are settled in their decisions relative

---

Table 3F Middle Adulthood (ages 26–40 years)

Piaget's Theory of Cognitive Development: Formal Operations Stage
Kohlberg's Moral Development Theory: Stage 4, Stage 5, and Stage 6

Characteristics	Description	Leadership Implications
Physical	• Some adults are still at their physical peak; some slowing is evidenced as family and work interfere with activity level. • Finesse becomes more important than strength. • People work to further refine a few physical skills; often they are related to fitness and weight management activities. • Some people have allowed themselves to become increasingly sedentary.	• Recognize the pull of family and work obligations on personal leisure efforts; be flexible with activity prerequisites, scheduling, and leadership techniques. • Be prepared for great diversity in desire for structured and self-directed recreational and competitive activities. • Laissez-faire, participative, and coaching styles are effective leadership approaches for this age group. • Open communication with participants is important to effective leadership.
Cognitive	• Cognitive abilities including creativity, logic, reasoning, problem solving, and hypothesis testing are well-developed. • Mental and cognitive challenges are important and fun for this age group. • Very aware of self in terms of the larger society; often a global perspective is held.	
Socioemotional	• Settled with decisions relative to family structure; often a "couple" orientation. • A concern for both one's children as well as aging parents may be evident. • A focus on social position and status become important as people begin to define themselves in terms of their work and family. • Work stresses may interfere with personal and leisure life.	
Moral	• Some believe morality is based on legitimate authority. • Some perceive the notion of an assumed social contract (i.e., greatest good for the greatest number). • Others wrestle with defining their own sense of principles.	

to children and family. Often, the family orientation goes in two directions—concern for one's children as well as aging parents. For those without children, in the early years of middle adulthood there is often a "couple" orientation, where partners are focused on one another, and an emphasis toward developing one's work and career. Work-related stresses may begin to interfere with one's personal and leisure life.

Moral Development. Generally, by middle adulthood people have realized that for individuals in society to coexist, moral and ethical decisions must be based on an unspoken social contract (Stage 5). People must "buy into" certain social norms for society to flow smoothly. A simplified example of this is the convention of walking on the right side of the road or sidewalk. If the unwritten rule of staying to the right did not exist, navigating a busy sidewalk would be very challenging. At this stage some people wrestle with developing and refining their own sense of ethics and principles (Stage 6). Personal integrity becomes an important factor in the establishment and maintenance of one's values and morals.

Implications for Leaders. Leaders who work with both young and middle adults can expect a good deal of sensibility and stability in participant choices and actions. People strive to do what is best and look to leaders to facilitate a leisure experience free from constraints typical of the workplace. Logic, reasoning, and sound explanations help adults to make behavior choices appropriate to the situation.

With their physical, social, and cognitive capabilities, adults are often able to lead themselves. Leadership then becomes a matter of providing resources and space for adults to determine and engage in their own leisure experiences. It is common when leading adults for the direct leader to become more of an experience facilitator or program supervisor. As the supervisor, the leader might help resolve rule issues, respond to maintenance concerns, and generally oversee the area in which people are engaged in leisure.

Older Adulthood (41–60 years)

Physical Development. As individuals pass middle adulthood, changes in physical abilities become evident. For most people, there is a general slowing down with some changes in eyesight, strength and musculature, and flexibility. Metabolism begins to slow and weight gain is common; for women, menopause occurs. Physical activity tends to decline as personal, work, and family situations change.

Cognitive Development. As with middle adulthood, people in this age group experience strong cognitive skills and abilities. Much of one's focus is on career; creativity and the use of mental capabilities are focused in that direction. An understanding of global and social issues is increasingly important to individuals and families. During these years people begin to experience a sense of their own mortality.

Socioemotional Development. Social position and security in retirement become issues for people in this age

Adults are quite capable of working together to accomplish tasks.

Adults often enjoy individual activities that require concentration.

group. Family, grandchildren, aging parents and extended family also become increasingly important. Social relationships tend to be stable and long-lasting. Concern about the future and work-related stresses may influence one's emotional and mental stability. During this life stage it is common for adults to experience midlife crises—often a radical change in behaviors and attitudes occurs. Both women and men and people from all walks of life experience midlife crises.

Moral Development. Similar to those in middle adulthood, people in older adulthood operate on the assumption that a social contract (Stage 5) is necessary for society to function efficiently. It is thought that some individuals at this stage of life strive to meet their own sense of principles and high ethical standards (Stage 6). Generally, personal integrity is an important personal quality for individuals in this life stage.

Implications for Leaders. Sensibility and stability in participant choices and actions are still primary themes in adult life. Life experiences may take on increased importance as people learn from past events and integrate that knowledge into their lives. Understanding that some physical changes occur as people age is helpful for leisure services leaders. There may be a slowing down in activity level, and physical skills may not be as sharp as they once were.

Adults expect to be able to make their own choices surrounding their leisure experiences and are skilled at doing so. Many adults will balk at rules that seem to have no real purpose. Leader-participant communication and issues related to problem solving tend to be resolved through logic, reasoning, and consideration of each situation. Participative and facilitative styles of leadership tend to be very effective with adults of all ages.

Table 3G Older Adulthood (ages 41–60 years)

Piaget's Theory of Cognitive Development: Formal Operations Stage
Kohlberg's Moral Development Theory: Stage 5 and Stage 6

Characteristics	Description	Leadership Implications
Physical	• Changes in physical abilities occur; eyesight changes, strength and flexibility lessen. • Metabolism slows, muscle mass is lost, and weight gain is common. • Fitness and social contacts are typical motivations for activity; overall physical activity declines.	• Be aware of the tremendous variety in skills, desires, and interests in leisure. • Nuances of strategy and sophistication in activities is appropriate. • Leisure may be viewed as a step to social status and position; be aware of participant motivations and desired outcomes of leisure experiences.
Cognitive	• Abilities including creativity, logic, reasoning, problem solving, and hypothesis testing are well-developed. • Focus is on one's career; an understanding of global and social issues is apparent.	• Leader role moves from active and directive to facilitative and participative; older adults are clearly in charge of who they are and how they want to be—particularly in leisure.
Socioemotional	• Family is often a center of activity although much of the activity is based on children's interests. • Work-related stresses are evident. • A focus on social position and security in old age becomes important. • A sense of one's own mortality is experienced; this may be seen when an individual questions their place in the world and their contribution to it. • Stable, long-lasting social contacts exist.	• Conflict often decreases as people begin to understand perspective and the importance of situations "in the scheme of things."
Moral	• Most agree that an unwritten social contract exists and determines one's sense of morality. • Some are refining their own ethical principles and standards for decision-making.	

Seniors (61–74 years)

Physical Development. As medical and lifestyle changes are introduced and accepted, people live longer, healthier lives. Thus, tremendous variation exists in physical abilities and limitations of adults aged 61 and older. While everyone experiences changes in balance, eyesight, hearing, strength, and flexibility, how each person is affected by and deals with these changes is based on one's own physical makeup, mental attitude, environment, and opportunities. Some people seem as young and vibrant as those many years their junior, while others appear quite frail.

According to the Census Bureau (2002), approximately 52% of seniors 65 years and older have some type of disability. Thirty-seven percent of those are considered to have severe disabilities and just over 16% have disabilities for which they require assistance. Sleep difficulties and weight gain are common physical ailments among seniors. In addition, high blood pressure and hearing impairments affect many in this age range.

Women tend to outlive men in all racial and ethnic groups by about eight years; therefore, in this age group there are higher numbers of female participants than male. The great disparities between well, active seniors and frail seniors require that recreation and leisure services leaders be careful to avoid categorizing all older adults as having limited physical or cognitive abilities.

Cognitive Development. As with the changes and differences in physical condition, similar variation exists in cognitive and mental processes. Eventually mental processes slow, but as a whole, older adults remain sharp and in control of their mental capacities until well into old age. Some seniors are impacted by diseases such as senility and Alzheimer's disease which affect their mental capabilities, but these people are exceptions, and not the norm. Work-related stresses decrease although stresses related to a change in lifestyle (from worker to retiree) can occur.

Socioemotional Development. It has been reported that seniors are the happiest of any age group in the United States (Yntema, 1999). Seniors do not feel rushed, and they experience what they want when they want. In fact, people ages 55 to 64 years of age are more likely than those in any other age group to say that life is exciting—filling their time with hobbies, social activities, and travel. They often enjoy the energy and vitality of grandchildren and the company of their adult children.

As people age social connections become increasingly important. Ironically, this occurs at the same time that people begin to deal with social isolation and death. Conflict in response to the desire for and lessening of social contacts may occur. Much reflection over one's life is common as people recognize their own mortality. Because of this, a renewed interest in religion may occur.

Furthermore, retirement may result in great joy and an apparent rejuvenation, or it may cause new stresses as financial stability and quality of life may become important issues.

For those who are healthy and can afford it, retirement will stretch for two to three decades. Nelson (2000) divides retirement into three phases: (1) the go-go stage, similar to a second childhood without parental supervision; (2) the slow-go phase when people become more introspective and get their affairs in order; and (3) the no-go phase when health and/or dwindling financial resources prohibit active recreation and leisure activities. A survey in 2005 reported that 66% of older Americans currently work or plan to work for pay after retirement (*Retirement anxiety on the rise,* 2005). Some indicated they would continue working to pursue leisure interests in retirement, while others were concerned about personal finances. We face a very active group of seniors in the upcoming years.

Moral Development. By this stage in life, as one's own mortality becomes evident, many people live their lives with a focus on the greater society. After wrestling for many years with their own understanding of morality, many individuals by now have developed and live by a set of ethical principles and standards that follow a consistent system of values (Stage 5) and reflect a concern for the global community.

Implications for Leaders. As with all age groups, leaders are cautioned to not put all older people in one category. The impacts of ethnicity, sex, socioeconomic status, and other elements of diversity are quite evident in older adulthood. Further, the variation in physical abilities, cognitive capacity, and socioemotional states is tremendous across people. The accumulation of life experiences to share and integrate into one's leisure life is vast. Leaders can learn much from those years of experience. In leading,

Photo courtesy of Deb Jordan

Many seniors are active well into their older years.

remain aware of pacing and other physical issues; provide real choices. Opportunities for social interaction and inter-generational activities often work well with seniors.

Facilitation and participative leadership tend to be effective methods of leadership with seniors; these individuals tend to be very self-directed in their leisure choices. A leader might want to take "inventory" of the capabilities of the seniors with whom she or he works. Leading for capabilities and desires rather than leading in a way to fit the leader's expectations of "what seniors want" is important.

Elderly (75+ years)

Physical Development. While physical development continues to decline from one's earlier years, there is still great disparity in physical well-being among the elderly. In this age group hearing and vision impairments are common, as are some other physical ailments (e.g., high blood

---

Table 3H Seniors (ages 61–74 years)

Piaget's Theory of Cognitive Development: Formal Operations Stage
Kohlberg's Moral Development Theory: Stage 5 and Stage 6

Characteristics	Description	Leadership Implications
Physical	• There is tremendous variation in physical capabilities; some seniors are in excellent health while others experience debilitating health problems. • Most people experience some lessening in eyesight, hearing, balance, strength, and flexibility. • Arthritis is a common physical ailment in this age group; sleep patterns and weight gain are other physical concerns.	• Recognize a wide range in physical and mental health, and well-being in people in this age range. • Focus on social interactions; treat all participants with the utmost respect and dignity. • Accept the knowledge, judgment, and experience gained over a lifetime— Utilize those strengths in participants. • Introduce new activities; encourage personal leadership and choice in leisure. • Facilitate or engage in purposeful laissez-faire leadership, rather than more active forms of leadership.
Cognitive	• Some slowing and lessening of cognitive abilities occurs. • Stresses related to retirement and life changes may occur. • Cognitive and mental abilities may be refocused either on work, volunteerism, leisure pursuits or on one's family (e.g., grandchildren).	
Socioemotional	• Social connections and relationships with family and friends become increasingly important. • Happiness is a common emotion experienced by most seniors; they choose to make their lives exciting. • At the same time, disease and death are faced often as friends and cohort groupmates pass on. • Social isolation can occur and many seniors engage in life reflection. • Financial stability and quality of life become prominent issues for seniors. • The effects of ethnicity, sex, disability, socioeconomic, and other status factors are evident.	
Moral	• One's own sense of integrity and ethical principles are usually well-established by this point. • The focus is on the needs of others in society and the role one plays in those efforts.	

pressure, cardiovascular problems, a slowing down in mobility), but not everyone faces these health concerns to the same degree. Issues with balance arise and falls resulting in fractured hips are not uncommon; recovery can be difficult for individuals in this life stage. Poor elderly—24% of Blacks, 23% of Hispanics, and 9% of Whites—face physical and mental dilemmas not faced by those who have a stable income (Yntema, 1999). Recreation leaders must understand the group and individuals they serve to be most effective.

Cognitive Development. As with the changes and differences in physical condition, there is a similar variation in mental processes. Certainly, more elderly than those in other life stages experience a slowing down of mental

Table 31 Elderly (ages 75+ years)

Piaget's Theory of Cognitive Development: Formal Operations Stage
Kohlberg's Moral Development Theory: Stage 5 and Stage 6

Characteristics	Description	Leadership Implications
Physical	• Physical development continues to decline, yet there is tremendous variation in physical capabilities; some elderly are in excellent health, others experience major health problems. • Hearing and visual impairments are common, as are decreases in mobility, increases in brittleness of bones, and circulatory problems. • Balance becomes an issue, and recovery from serious injury or illness can be difficult. • Arthritis is a common physical ailment of people in this age group, and sleep patterns and weight gain are other physical concerns of elderly. • More women than men are alive, as females have longer lifespans than males.	• Recognize a wide variety in physical and mental health, and well-being in people in this age range—focus on individual needs and capabilities. • Focus on social interactions; offer inter-generational programs. • Provide opportunities for independence, and be prepared to assist where needed. • Introduce new activities; encourage personal leadership and choice in leisure. • Facilitate or engage in purposeful laissez-faire leadership, rather than more active forms of leadership.
Cognitive	• Continued slowing and lessening of cognitive abilities occurs. • Increased incidences of mental illnesses occur, such as Parkinson's disease, Alzheimer's disease, and senility. • Many elderly are as cognitively sharp as people many years their junior.	
Socioemotional	• Social isolation affects people in this age group more than any other. • Disease and death are common in the lives of elderly as friends and life partners are affected. • Most elderly women live alone, and over two thirds of men live with their life partner; many are living in care centers. • Financial stability and quality of life are prominent issues for the elderly; almost one quarter live poverty.	
Moral	• One's own sense of integrity and ethical principles are usually well-established by this point. • The focus is on the needs of others in society.	

capabilities. In addition, illnesses such as Parkinson's disease, Alzheimer's disease, and senility increase (but remember, not everyone is afflicted by these illnesses).

Socioemotional Development. Facing the loss of friends and family, the elderly are the most isolated of any age group. Because of the extended lifespan of women, over two-thirds of them will be living alone at this stage of their life—most in their own home. On the other hand, over two-thirds of men in this age group are living with a spouse. A strong need for social interaction and remaining connected to others is of primary importance. Intergenerational interaction is often a vibrant option for the elderly in parks and recreation settings.

Moral Development. Like seniors, as one's own mortality is evident, many people live their lives with a focus on the greater society. After wrestling for many years with their own understanding of morality, many individuals by now have developed and live by a set of ethical principles and standards which follow a consistent system of values (Stage 5).

Implications for Leaders. The elderly are a heterogeneous group in terms of their physical, mental, and socioemotional abilities. Leaders need to pay attention to the individual needs and abilities of their constituents in this age group to serve them well. This can be a very independent group or it can be a group in great need of guidance and support. Certified therapeutic recreation specialists (CTRSs) often work with the elderly in rehabilitation and other care facilities. Effective leaders get in the habit of talking to their participants to learn about their needs, wants, desires, and abilities, and then leading within those parameters.

Leading a mixed generation group is common for recreation and leisure program providers.

Summary

This chapter has provided a basis for understanding people—the one common element in all leisure services settings. Being exposed to different theories or models of human development allows leaders to make effective decisions in their interactions with people of all ages. Being familiar with and understanding well-known models of development such as those presented by Piaget, Kohlberg, and Gilligan provide a firm rooting in learning about human behaviors.

Piaget suggested that individuals move through four stages of development—sensorimotor intelligence, preoperational, concrete operations, and formal operations—whereby one's ability to process information cognitively becomes increasingly sophisticated. In investigating moral development, Kohlberg reported that people make moral decisions differently based on cognitive and emotional maturation. Gilligan examined gender differences in moral development by presenting us with the concept of an ethic of care.

Table 3J Applying human development information

Knowing and applying information about human development when leading leisure services activities can make a big difference in perceived competence and effectiveness of the leader. To this end leaders would be wise to

- Remember that knowledge about human development should be applied to communication with participants, behavior management situations, choice of leadership style, risk management situations, and all other aspects of leadership in leisure services.

- Remember that very young children do not understand figurative language.

- Avoid treating young children as miniature adults.

- Recognize that much "sassing back" from teenage youth is normal and, generally, not personally directed.

- Realize that to learn and improve their own leadership skills, youth need opportunities to practice various forms of leadership.

- Avoid referring to older adults as "cute" (and other paternalistic adjectives).

- Avoid discounting the life experiences of older adults.

- Be careful not to assume that all adults are skilled in communication or conflict resolution.

- Bear in mind that all persons, no matter their age, have potential to develop leadership skills.

While all people pass through the various life stages and develop (cognitively, physically, emotionally, socially, and psychologically), not everyone does so at the same chronological age. In their development people are affected by social mores and stereotypes, genetic disposition, opportunities, their own abilities and limitations, and leader expectations. By understanding the basic elements of human development—physical, cognitive, socioemotional, and moral—leaders can make appropriate choices in communication, activity leadership, conflict resolution, behavior management, and other aspects of direct leadership. Leaders are encouraged to continue to study issues of human development and to apply that knowledge to leadership situations.

Beginning the Journey

Understanding people is a critical element to understanding leadership. The critical thinking questions posed to you below are designed to aid you in better understanding your own knowledge and comprehension of people. This is a repeating theme in any journey to personal leadership.

1. What factors affect human development? With a partner, discuss how these factors have affected and continue to affect your life. Give examples from your life history.

2. Interview two people from generations other than yours (e.g., your children, parents, grandparents). Compare their life histories to yours—what was different? What was the same?

3. Imagine that you are in front of a board of directors—justify why you need to learn and utilize developmentally appropriate leadership.

4. Draw a picture to explain Piaget's view of human development. Make a direct and concrete link to how one should lead.

5. Describe Kohlberg's model of moral development. Can you think of examples from your own life that match these stages? What stage of moral development are you in right now? Is this where you want to be? What can you do to further develop your sense of morality according to Kohlberg's stages?

6. Do you support the notion of an ethic of care? How do you manifest this in your life? Do you believe that females and males see things differently when it comes to moral issues? Give some examples from your own experience. Do you find the understanding of an ethic of care and an ethic of rights and justice to be a useful way to understand people? Why or why not?

7. Over the past century our society has come a long way in terms of equalizing opportunities for females and males. Do you believe there are differences in opportunities and treatment that leisure services leaders should be aware of? Explain your position and what it means in terms of your own leadership development. Do you believe that women and men make better leaders at different things? Explain.

8. Why is it important for leaders to understand life stages? Choose one activity and make modifications in how you would lead it (try to avoid programming tips; think leadership) for each of the different age groups identified in this chapter. Be sure to address the physical, cognitive, socioemotional, and moral aspects of development as you do this.

9. From what you have read in this chapter related to life stages, identify three passive, semi-active, and active recreation activities appropriate for each age group. Make notes about the differences in leadership style you might use for each age group or life stage.

10. Take a personal inventory and examine your own attitudes and skills. With which age groups do you most enjoy working? Why those ages and not the others? What can you do to improve your leadership skills for each age group?

References

Barger, R. (2000). *A summary of Lawrence Kohlberg's stages of moral development.* Retrieved June 22, 2006, from http://www.nd.edu/~rbarger/kohlberg.html

Beilin, H. (1992). Piagetian theory. In R. Vasta (Ed.), *Six theories of child development: Revised formulations and current issues* (pp. 85-132). London, UK: Jessica Kingsley.

Crain, W. C. (1985). *Chapter seven: Kohlberg's stages of moral development.* Retrieved June 22, 2006, from http://faculty.plts.edu/gpence/html/kohlberg.htm

Cypher, A. *Notes on* In a different voice *by Carol Gilligan.* Retrieved June 22, 2006, from http://www.acypher.com/BookNotes/Gilligan.html

Eagly, A., Karau, S., and Makhijani, M. (1995). Gender and the effectiveness of leaders: A meta-analysis. *Psychological Bulletin, 117*(1), 125–145.

Gilligan, C. (1982). *In a different voice*. Cambridge, MA: Harvard University Press.

Growth 4–5 year olds. (2005). Retrieved June 19, 2006, from http://kidshealth.org/parent/growth/growth/growth_4_to_5.html

Growth 6–12 year olds. (2005). Retrieved June 19, 2006, from http://kidshealth.org/parent/growth/growth/growth_6_to_12.html

Growth 13–18 year olds. (2005). Retrieved June 19, 2006, from http://kidshealth.org/parent/growth/growth/growth_13_to_18.html

Gurstein, P., Lovato, C., and Ross, S. (2003). Youth participation in planning: Strategies for social action. *Canadian Journal of Urban Research, 12*(2), 249–274.

Hardy, S. and Carlo, G. (2005). Identity as a source of moral motivation. *Human Development, 48*, 232–256.

Jaffe, M. (1998). *Adolescence*. New York, NY: John Wiley & Sons.

Murray, M. (n.d.) *Moral development and moral education: An overview*. Retrieved June 22, 2006, from http://tigger.uic.edu/~lnucci/MoralEd/overviewtext.html

Nelson, P. (2000). An aging population: The challenges and the opportunities. *Journal of Family and Consumer Sciences, 92*(2), 10–11.

Normal adolescent development. (2005). Retrieved June 19, 2006, from http://www.aacap.org/publications/factsfam/develop.htm

Ryan, C. and Futterman, D. (2001). Social and developmental challenges for lesbian, gay, and bisexual youth. *SEICUS Report, 29*(4), 5–18.

Stages of socioemotional development in children and teenagers. (2006). Retrieved June 19, 2006, from http://www.cdipage.com

Understanding the teen years. (2004). Retrieved June 19, 2006, from http://kidshealth.org/parent/growth/growing/adolescence.html

U.S. Census Bureau (2002). *Americans with disabilities: 2002—Table 1*. Retrieved July 4, 2006, from http://www.census.gov/hhes/www/disability/sipp/disab02/ds02t1.html

Wark, G. and Krebs, D. (2000). The construction of moral dilemmas in everyday life. *Journal of Moral Education, 29*(1), 5–10.

Yan, Z. and Fischer, K. (2002). Always under construction: Dynamic variations in adult cognitive microdevelopment. *Human Development, 45*(3), 141–160.

Yntema, S. (Ed.). (1999). *Americans 55 & older: A changing market* (2nd ed.). Ithaca, NY: New Strategist Publications.

Section II
Working with People: Essential Skills of Leadership

Having recently begun your personal leadership journey and completed the foundational material presented in the first section, you will find this section of the text, *Working with People: Essential Skills of Leadership*, to be more specific. Background information, reasoning, and specific techniques are offered to aid in the usefulness of the material. To be both an effective follower and an effective leader requires skills in working with others. This section includes information and knowledge about people skills necessary for leaders and followers.

This material provides information that can be used in the actual practice of leisure services leadership. Without actual practice and experience with groups, a leader's judgment may be lacking, and she or he may be unsure which direction to turn. Therefore, upon studying the material in this section, you are strongly encouraged to "try out" and practice these essential leadership skills with a variety of groups. This real-life practice is essential in furthering one's journey as a leader.

Leadership is about relationships, and relationships are formed in groups; thus, this section examines group dynamics, communication, managing difficulties, and motivating participant behaviors. Building on the material in Section I, definitional information as well as guiding principles and specific techniques for working with diverse groups of people are presented.

Throughout each chapter an attempt has been made to discuss the influences of demographics—such as gender, age, and ethnicity—on the various interpersonal skills and in the use of specific techniques. In this way, leaders are reminded that to work with participants effectively requires an understanding of all people, especially those who are different from themselves.

Research has shown that individuals who are perceived as effective in human relations are often also perceived as effective leaders. Therefore, an individual committed to learning and improving personal leadership skills will wish to focus in on these areas. This section of the text provides a starting point for learning these types of skills. Combining this knowledge with observations and personal experience enhances effective leadership.

Leader Profile

David Rogers
Graduate Assistant, Outdoor Adventure • Oklahoma State University

David had two years in this position, and four years in the parks, recreation, and leisure services profession. He has since graduated with his master's degree and is working in outdoor recreation in Raleigh, North Carolina.

Some of the leadership positions he has held include:

- Student representative to the Board of Directors of the Oklahoma Recreation and Parks Society (ORPS)
- Vice President of the Student Branch of ORPS
- Presented at the National Recreation and Park Association Congress

What is the meaning of leadership?
Leadership is one of the truest dynamic roles and concepts. It is the ability to accept and/or delegate constantly varying degrees of responsibility, accountability and recognition for successes as well as failures. I believe leadership is a measure of influence among (not over) people. The best leaders know how to follow where someone else knows the path.

What are the most important leader qualities?
An effective leader demonstrates honesty, accountability, confidence, patience, perseverance, openness to new ideas, attention to detail, and effective listening.

What advice do you have for students who aspire to leadership in parks, recreation, and leisure services?
First and foremost, get involved! The best way to learn this field is to dive in. Don't wait until you're getting ready to graduate to start building experience. What you learn in class is readily applicable to the field of recreation right now! Second, take advantage of the knowledge and professional connections of your professors and others in the field. Go to every professional conference you can and introduce yourself to people. And finally, take yourself and your future in this field seriously. If you don't believe in yourself, and in what you are doing, why should anyone else?

Favorite book(s): I can't choose only one favorite.

Favorite activities: Hang gliding and board-related sports like surfing, wakeboarding and snowboarding.

Chapter Four
Group Dynamics: The Essence of Leadership

Learning Opportunities

Through studying this chapter readers will have the opportunity to

- Define group dynamics.
- Understand the components that comprise groups.
- Explore group development across and within stages.
- Evaluate effective and ineffective groups.
- Better understand what constitutes a team.

Photo courtesy of Gwynn Powell

Leaders do not exist in a vacuum—they lead people, usually in a group. It makes sense then, that group dynamics is critical to leadership; without a group of followers, there would be no leader. As noted in earlier chapters, leadership entails interpersonal influences in relation to group tasks and socioemotional concerns. These influences, plus the social, intellectual, and moral forces that produce activity and change in a group, constitute group dynamics. Having a clear understanding of how groups work will greatly enhance a leader's ability to be effective.

Group dynamics is characterized as the scientific study of behaviors in groups, group development, and interrelationships between groups and others (Johnson & Johnson, 2003). Experts in group dynamics study human interactions in specific group settings and describe what is happening in groups to explain why [people in] groups behave the way they do. As one might imagine, this type of study is very helpful to all types of leaders.

Since we work with groups in almost all aspects of our work (e.g., with colleagues, clients, participants, the community), leisure services leaders must be well-aware of group dynamics and what it means in terms of their own leadership, and the growth and development of the group within which they work. If a leader does not understand a group's behaviors, she or he may respond inappropriately to that group and interfere with its effectiveness and satisfaction.

Definitions

As with all phenomena one is trying to understand, it is important to have agreement about meanings of terms; thus, in this section a review of definitions is presented. Several definitions exist for *group*:

- a number of individuals who interact with one another
- a social unit consisting of two or more people who see themselves as members of a group

- a collection of individuals who are interdependent
- a number of people who are trying to satisfy personal needs through joint association
- a number of people who are joined together to achieve a common goal
- a collection of people whose interactions are structured by a set of roles and norms
- a collection of people who influence one another
- a combination of the above-mentioned definitions. (Johnson & Johnson, 2003)

Most agree that for a group to be so identified, the members and outsiders must define themselves as such. A group is more than the sum of its parts—it is a social system with its own structure and culture. Members may come or go and the group will evolve over time, but the base culture generally remains the same.

Another group phenomenon to bear in mind is that social identity is bound up in group memberships; people define themselves and others by the groups to which they belong. In those groups they may take on certain roles such as sibling, teammate, teacher, garden club member, or supervisor. In fact, research shows that when people join and become committed to a group, they show an in-group bias (Sheard, 2004). This means that when people join groups they begin to think and act in ways to reinforce the "my group is better than your group" philosophy. We all seek positive identities, and for most of us, we partially accomplish this through the groups we join. To be successful, leaders need a variety of skills to work with groups; some group skills are fundamental—decision making, trust building, communication, and conflict management—to working with all groups.

Most scholars view a group as a system organized as a set of interrelated and interacting parts that attempt to maintain a balance (Karriker, 2005; Smith, 2001). In other words, external and internal forces act on groups continually, and group members have to balance these forces. *Internal forces* include such things as individual group members and all their baggage (e.g., personalities, motives, emotions, self-esteem), levels and types of participation, overt and covert agendas, group norms, and perceived group status. *External forces* include time, spatial arrangements, lighting, acoustics, external stimuli, and the physical environment. As each of these forces change, so too do the dynamics within a group.

Within all groups, individuals develop and express expectations; in turn group members respond to these expectations. These help to establish the group's internal and external structures—underlying assumptions about how the group operates. There are two general group structures in society which we have already explored—*collectivist* and *individualist*. Collectivist cultures (and groups) work toward complete sharing of group norms and goals while individualistic cultures (and groups) have as a primary focus the goals of individuals (even within the group). No group exudes pure collectivism or individualism, yet groups do seem to be predominantly one or the other.

In collectivist groups the views, needs, and goals of the group are much more important than personal or individual needs, views, and goals. Behavior responds to the needs of the group, and elements such as loyalty, trust, and cooperation within and among group members are considered paramount. Members perceive achievement in a group framework rather than individual accomplishment.

A group is a collection of people who influence one another and interact together.

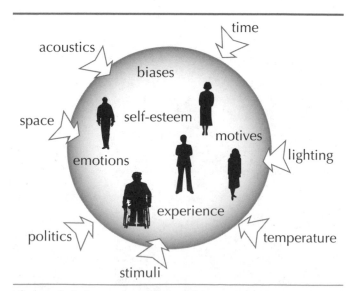

Figure 4.1 Groups are impacted by both internal and external forces.

This may be characterized by the statement, "It's amazing how much gets done when no one cares about who gets the credit." Group members are perceived as homogenous, and the underlying assumption is that all group members have similar needs. Collectivist groups strive for harmony, affiliation, and nurturance. In groups that follow this philosophy a leader would be wise to remember to celebrate and salute the *group* efforts rather than single out individuals for special attention.

Individualistic cultures, on the other hand, emphasize the *individual* within the group over the group effort. Personal rights, the pursuit of pleasure, and achievement are perceived in personal terms—individual achievements are more important than group achievements. Attachment to other group members is minimal because of the emphasis on freedom and equality for individuals. These groups tend to be heterogeneous. Leaders who work with this type of group may need to spend time helping individuals learn how to work within a group, and should remember that participants will likely value individual mastery and achievement.

Groups: The Good and the Bad

Research has been contradictory about whether or not groups are a good thing—some research indicates that groups are extremely beneficial while others report the opposite. Many researchers agree that groups are good because under most conditions the productivity of groups is higher than the productivity of individuals alone (Miles & Mangold, 2002; Sheard, 2004). This phenomenon of the sum being greater than its parts is known as *synergy*. Synergy allows groups to make more effective decisions and solve problems more effectively than individuals acting alone. In addition, research reports that group membership promotes the values of altruism, kindness, consideration for others, and responsibility in people. It would be difficult to argue against these traits!

Group membership enhances a person's quality of life through the emotional bonds of friendship, camaraderie, love, excitement, and joy. In addition, achievement and task accomplishment are greater for group members than for individuals acting on their own. Furthermore, research has shown group membership shapes a person's identity, self-esteem, and social competencies. Humans are social by nature, and without cooperation, social organization, and groups of all kinds, this would be compromised. Belonging to groups then, is a good thing. Groups benefit both individuals and society as a whole.

On the other hand, some research indicates groups are not all good. Many researchers have reported people

Synergy allows groups to make more effective decisions and solve problems more effectively than individuals acting alone.

in groups tend to take greater risks than when alone, and groups tend to take more extreme positions than individuals do alone (Johnson & Johnson, 2003; Sheard, 2004). This can be both positive and negative. Also in groups, members sometimes diffuse responsibility, taking less responsibility for attending to group tasks and the needs of group members. The perception exists that "someone else will do it." This is known as *social loafing* and can have a strong negative effect on the group (Markulis, Jassawalla & Sashittal, 2006; Nelson & Quick, 2005).

Research also shows that when in large groups people have a tendency to feel anonymous; therefore, they may engage in extreme or socially unacceptable behaviors which they would not do when alone. This acting out within a feeling of anonymity is known as *mob mentality*. Another drawback to groups is that perceiving outsiders as members of an out-group makes it easier to depersonalize

---

Table 4A Group qualities: The good and the bad

The Good

- Productivity is high.
- Effective decision-making occurs.
- Effective problem solving supports group efforts.
- Altruism, kindness, consideration for others and responsibility become socialized in group members.
- Emotional bonds enhance quality of life.
- Synergy is a powerful, positive force influencing change.

The Bad

- Group members take greater risks—often without forethought.
- Groups tend to take extreme positions on issues.
- Individuals do not accept responsibility for their actions—social loafing occurs.
- Anonymity can lead to antisocial behaviors.
- Group members depersonalize outsiders and treat them badly.
- Group-think serves as a barrier to creativity and growth.

them and treat them poorly (e.g., stereotyping, discrimination, prejudice). Furthermore, groups often demand conformity, and not always in a positive fashion. This can result in *group think*, where group members fall into the trap of thinking alike, even against evidence to the contrary (Bratton, Grint & Nelson, 2005; Johnson & Johnson, 2003; Moorhead & Griffin, 2004). Examples of this would be hazing and gang initiation activities. People engage in those types of behaviors, even though they know the activities are hurtful or detrimental.

While there are both positive and negative aspects to groups and their existence, groups nonetheless exist and will continue to do so—as social animals, humans need groups. In recreation and leisure services settings, leaders have the opportunity to help form and develop groups that exhibit positive values and benefit the group as well as individual group members. To be most effective in these efforts leaders need to understand why people join groups, what elements constitute a group, and what differentiates effective from ineffective groups.

Why Do People Join Groups?

People join groups for many different reasons. To best understand how groups function and why they act the way they do, leaders would be wise to find out from group members why they joined. Generally, people join groups to form relationships and to meet needs for affiliation; it feels good to belong to something identifiable and to be able to say, "I am a member." An affinity for a particular group may be based on an attraction to other members (e.g., young people may join a group because group members are perceived as "cool;" adults may join because members are interesting and stimulating). Others may be attracted to a particular group because of the nature of the group goals or tasks (e.g., individuals want to help meet the group's goals), perceptions of prestige associated with the group (e.g., members may be perceived as having higher status than nonmembers), and physical proximity to members and facilities (e.g., the closer one lives to a group, the more apt she or he is to join; Johnson & Johnson, 2003).

Generally, people join groups to form relationships and to meet needs of affiliation; it feels good to belong to something identifiable and to be able to say, "I am a member."

In addition to these, there are many other reasons why people join groups, including:

- social reasons (e.g., to meet new people)
- to learn a new skill (e.g., increase personal knowledge)
- self-enhancement or advancement (e.g., résumé builder)
- to share a common activity with a significant other (e.g., achieve intimacy)
- coercion (e.g., parents "force" children to join after-school groups)
- to make a statement (e.g., rebel against the "establishment")
- for self-identity

Elements of Groups

Groups have certain characteristics that define the community of people. All groups share basic components, although the quality of these components differs across groups. As mentioned earlier, a group is a social system consisting of several elements or components which exist to provide structure and form to the group. Group elements typically include common goals (e.g., shared vision), agreed upon rules (i.e., norms), cohesion, various tasks and functions, and differing roles of group members.

Shared Goals

Almost everyone who works with groups indicates that the most important component of a successful group (e.g., the group is fun, effective, efficient) is goals which

Photo courtesy of Steven Nanton

Some people join groups to experience a sense of belonging.

are known and shared by all group members. Common goals serve as the directional beacon toward which groups work. Goals also help groups by providing a standard of excellence, serving as a source of stimulation for involvement, acting as a guide for member actions, serving as criteria for justifying group actions, and clarifying relations with outside groups (LaFasto & Larson, 2001). To reach group goals efficiently, all members must be committed to achieving them.

One reason groups form is to help people achieve goals they would otherwise be unable to achieve by themselves. Goals represent an ideal—a state of affairs that people value and wish to achieve. They give a group focus and direction; goals help to shape and motivate member behaviors. Member commitment to group goals depends upon several factors:

- how desirable the goals seem to individual group members
- how likely it is the group can achieve the goals
- how challenging the goals are (moderate levels of challenge are desirable)
- expected satisfaction when goals are achieved
- extent to which members participated in setting the goals (e.g., the higher the member participation, the higher the commitment)
- level of group cohesiveness. (Hartenian, 2003)

It is important to remember that while groups have goals, so too do individual group members. Thus, it is critical that individuals have enough goals in common with other group members to be effective and successful as a group. Group members should feel comfortable that the group goals are in concert with personal goals and that working toward one goal will support achievement of the other. The relationship between group goals and individual goals is known as *goal interdependence*. There are three basic goal relationships between member and group goals: cooperative, competitive, and independent (Jordan & Mertesdorf, 1994; Tjosvold, Andrews & Struthers, 1992).

Goals may be *cooperative* in nature and positively aligned when reaching one goal supports reaching the other goal. For example, consider an individual who joins a softball team to learn to play softball at a high-skill level (i.e., personal goal). This goal would be positively related to the softball team goal to win games (i.e., group goal). These goals are said to be cooperatively related. This is the ideal goal relationship for effective and well-functioning groups.

The second type of goal relationship is *competitive*. Inversely related goals exist when achieving one goal is done at the expense of achieving the other goal. For instance, if an individual joins a group to increase her or his own status in the community, yet the goal of the larger group is to share all credit for group tasks, then the actions of the individual will be in conflict with the group (and vice versa). In this case, the individual might act in such a way as to take the spotlight and claim credit for achievements which rightly belonged to the group. This would be in direct contradiction to the group's desires. On the other hand, every time the one individual did achieve something

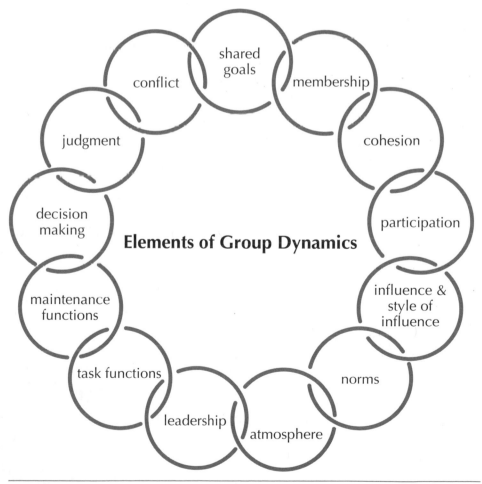

Figure 4.2 All groups consist of similar elements, and all elements impact group success.

for the group and the group claimed credit, this might irritate the individual. A competitive goal relationship is the most damaging and contributes negatively to group success.

The third possible goal configuration is *independent*. This occurs when the goals of the individual have no relationship to the goals of the group. When one acts to achieve one's own goals, the group is not impacted (and vice versa). One might think of an individual who has joined a walking group for the social interaction, yet the group's primary goal is weight reduction for members. In this case the two differing goals do not interfere with one another, nor do they necessarily support one another. An independent goal relationship then, has little impact on group or individual success.

Membership

Individuals who are members of a group define the attributes that make each group unique. As each person is added to a group, the nature of the group flexes to accommodate the change. Leaders should remember that while a group has its own personality, each individual within the group remains unique. Every time the group changes, so too, do the interactions among members. Each member brings to the group her or his own history which includes personal "baggage," expertise, knowledge, biases, attitudes, feelings, and ways of interacting with others.

Cohesion—Social and Task

Social cohesion is viewed as the interpersonal glue that holds a group together. *Task cohesion* is what keeps the group focused in a common direction. In physics, cohesion is characterized as an intermolecular attraction by which the elements of a body are held together; this is similarly true in group dynamics. Without an attraction of some sort to hold individuals in a group, there is no cohesion. Generally, this attraction occurs due to socioemotional aspects (i.e., people in the group like one another), shared interests, common goals, and the meeting of individual needs. The more cohesive a group, the more the group acts with its own distinct identity.

Participation

Observable participation—verbal, physical, and emotional—indicates involvement in and commitment to a group. Every group differs in levels of participation among members. Group members individually and collectively influence who participates, how much, and when. Individuals make decisions based on dedication to the group, perceived ability to accomplish the task, and feelings of belonging. Leaders may wish to monitor levels of participation within a group to ensure inclusion of all members in activities and tasks of the group. Collectivist groups will tend to have greater participation than individualist groups due to the difference in focus (i.e., the group rather than the individual).

Influence

Influence exists and fluctuates within groups, and both leaders and followers influence one another. Different people have differing levels and styles of influence over others in the group. Groups simultaneously influence outsiders

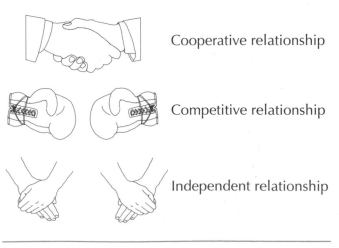

Cooperative relationship

Competitive relationship

Independent relationship

Figure 4.3 There are three primary goal relationship possibilities between leaders and followers.

Social Cohesion

Task Cohesion

Figure 4.4 Social and task cohesion

and are influenced by outsiders. Influence may be positive or negative. Some people try to influence by bullying others into agreement, others use subtle manipulation, while still others use logical arguments and positive motivation.

Norms

Norms are the unwritten rules that guide and control member behavior. They are standards that group members tacitly agree to support. Norms express the beliefs and values of the majority of group members as to what behaviors should and should not take place within the group. Norms may be explicit or implicit; some help a group function, whereas others hinder group functioning. *Explicit norms* are openly expressed by a group. For example, a new group member might be told she or he needs a haircut because group members want to project a particular image. *Implicit norms* are unspoken, but well-understood. For instance, when the recreational therapist enters a group therapy session, clients know they should take their seats.

Atmosphere

Atmosphere describes the climate or general impression of being in a group. All groups have climates—some are quite positive while others are negative; some seem to constantly fluctuate. For instance, one may instantly sense a high level of enthusiasm, excitement, and a positive can-do attitude in one long-term care facility while another has an atmosphere of despair, sadness, and underlying anger and resentment. A leader has tremendous influence and impact on the atmosphere of a group; her or his values, levels of acceptance, and own moods will "rub off" on the group.

Photo courtesy of Vicki Proctor

To be most effective it is important for group members to be heading in the same direction.

Norms express the beliefs and values of the majority of group members as to what behaviors should and should not take place within the group.

Leadership

Styles of leadership and leadership as it emerges from within a group are fundamental elements of a group. Leadership is an integral part of a group and meets one of the role requirements needed to accomplish tasks and meet group and individual needs. As mentioned in previous chapters, leadership styles vary as do the ways individuals within a group become recognized and accepted as leaders. Many approaches to leadership were explained in detail in Chapter 2.

Task Functions

Task functions directly relate to accomplishing the tasks of the group. Task functions tend to be outcome-oriented and include such things as taking initiative, staying on task, and working with resources. An individual who reminds others to stay on track and follow the agenda is engaging in a task function. In parks, recreation, and leisure settings task functions are evident among staff groups as well as participant groups.

Maintenance Functions

In conjunction with task functions, maintenance functions are necessary for effective group functioning. Maintenance functions are those tasks associated with caring for individual group members and concern for the morale of the group. These functions help maintain harmonious working relationships among group members and enable group members to contribute maximally to the effective functioning of the group. For instance, the group member who checks in with others when they arrive and asks about their week is engaging in a maintenance function.

Decision Making

All groups are involved in decision making to some degree. How decision making occurs, who facilitates it, and what type of approach is used are critical to group processes. Johnson and Johnson (2003) indicate that an effective decision is one where:

- The resources of the group are fully utilized.
- Time is well-used.
- The decision is of high quality.
- The decision is implemented in full by all group members.
- The problem-solving ability of the group is enhanced.

Group decision making can be enhanced by:

- positive interdependence (i.e., everyone is needed for success)
- individual accountability
- members encouraging and supporting each others' efforts
- socially skilled members
- debriefing and processing to address group issues
- accepting controversy
- the motivation to make high-quality decisions

On the other hand, effective decision making can be hindered by:

- poor group skills
- a lack of group maturity (e.g., the group is young, or has not been together very long)
- making quick decisions based on the dominant and quickest response of the group
- social loafing
- conflicting individual goals
- a failure to communicate and use information
- egocentrism of members
- lack of heterogeneity
- inappropriate group size
- power differences and distrust
- a lack of time to thoroughly engage in the decision-making process

Several decision-making methods have advantages and disadvantages depending upon the situation. Table 4B presents several methods of decision making and the advantages and disadvantages of each.

Judgment

Judgment is "knowing what you know and knowing what you don't know" (Petzoldt, 1984). Leadership requires skilled judgment. When a group understands and utilizes good judgment, group decisions, actions, norms, and gen-

eral functioning reach a highly effective level. Judgment involves:

- knowledge (i.e., of oneself, others, the environment, similar situations from past experiences)
- skills and abilities needed in the particular situation
- self-confidence (i.e., one believes that whatever decision is made is based on sound reasoning and knowledge)
- selflessness (i.e., the decision made is made with the group needs and welfare foremost in one's mind)
- commitment (i.e., one is committed to the role of leader and is willing to face the consequences for one's decisions)
- expediency (i.e., decisions are made quickly, but without waste)
- experience (e.g., past experiences assist in the use of judgment). (Cockrell, 1991)

Judgment is "knowing what you know and knowing what you don't know."

Conflict

A fully functioning group must experience conflict. Groups primarily experience two types of conflict: task conflict and emotional conflict (Miller, 2003). *Task conflict* focuses on the work of the group. People might disagree over goals, how to accomplish something, when to do it, and so on. This type of conflict, when handled appropriately, is a very healthy component of all groups. A group without task conflict becomes stagnant, where few or no new ideas are formed and forward movement is absent. Disagreements and disharmony help people to think in new directions and consider situations from various viewpoints.

Emotional conflict is personal, and often perceived as a personal attack. In this type of conflict people might experience frustration, dislike, personality clashes, and other negative interpersonal interactions. A leader will want to manage this type of conflict to maintain safety and trust within the group so that the work can be accomplished. Leaders should be aware that task conflict can lead to emotional conflict, and vice versa. Thus, while conflict is necessary, most groups will need a leader (formal or informal) to aid in resolving it in a positive manner.

❖ ❖ ❖

As can be seen, groups consist of many components that define and determine group success. Groups find their identity by emphasizing some aspects and not others, and by uniquely defining each component. Leaders may have a great impact on the effectiveness of groups by being attentive to these components and by helping to define them positively. Successful and effective groups are those in which these elements are acknowledged and consciously developed. While every group has these same elements, each group is comprised of individuals. As such, it can be beneficial to understand individual behavior-style preferences to begin to comprehend why people behave the way they do.

Behavior Styles

Successful groups require diversity. If everyone in a group is similar in style, ideas and energy, accomplishing group tasks would be extremely difficult and accompanied by much conflict. Leaders should look for diversity in backgrounds, individual preferences, ideas, and ways of approaching problems. Examining personal behavior style preferences is one way to look at group diversity. Everyone has a preference for work and behavior styles. Some people approach problems and work very quickly, while others are more successful with a slower approach. Some individuals prefer to focus on the job at hand, while others are

Table 4B Advantages and disadvantages of decision-making styles

Decision-Making Style	Advantages	Disadvantages
Authority without Discussion Leader makes decision with no input from the group.	• useful for simple, routine decisions • good when short on time or immature group • good in emergency or short time frame	• may cause resentment among group members • no commitment to implementing decision • group members not used as resources
Expert Member Group member with expertise makes decision for group.	• good if one member is by far an expert • can begin trust building based on experience levels	• may cause resentment among group members • no commitment to implementing decision • group members not used as resources
Average of Members' Opinions Add opinions and divide by group members.	• good when time is short, but want some member input • good for simple routine decisions	• not enough sharing among members to get needed commitment • conflict and controversy may hinder future decisions
Authority with Discussion Leader asks for input then makes decision on own.	• uses some group resources • group members feel included • uses expertise of leader	• no group commitment to decision • members may feel put aside or discounted • does not resolve group conflicts
Majority Vote The largest number of group members' opinions counts as the entire group's decision.	• good when time is short and desire group input • some commitment by the group is evident • quick and straightforward	• usually leaves disgruntled minority which may impact future decisions • full commitment is absent • full participation is absent
Minority Control A subcommittee or small executive group makes the decision.	• can be used when everyone is not available • delegates responsibilities to a committee • good when only a few members have necessary knowledge	• does not utilize all group members • no commitment by group • decision may alienate some or hinder future decisions
Consensus Entire group talks through the process until a decision is made that all members can accept.	• often creative and innovative • elicits commitment from all • uses resources of all members • useful when entire group involvement is desired	• takes a great deal of time and energy • requires skilled leader to facilitate • not good if short on time or in emergency

Leaders should look for diversity in backgrounds, individual preferences, ideas, and ways of approaching problems.

more concerned with the happiness and satisfaction of the people in the group.

Several models explain personal behavior style differences by examining four dimensions: fast pace, slow pace, task orientation, and people orientation. Utilizing a model popular in business and educational settings, leaders can see that based on these dimensions people may be characterized by four basic styles: director, socializer, relater, and thinker (Alessandra & O'Connor, 1996). In group dynamics people exhibit their personal styles through interactions with other group members, interactions with group leaders, and in how they approach the group tasks. All four styles need to be represented in groups, as their strengths and weaknesses complement one another.

Director

Individuals who favor the director style have a fast-paced, task-oriented approach to life. They prefer to focus on the task to be accomplished rather than the people in the group. People who favor this behavior style:

- work quickly
- think logically
- want facts and highlights
- like personal choices
- enjoy risks
- accept challenges
- prefer control and leadership roles
- enjoy competition
- enjoy conflict and confrontation
- are change-oriented
- are results-oriented
- are independent
- are decisive
- prefer to make a bad decision rather than no decision at all

As a group member, a director prefers fast-paced and independent work. This individual prefers options and alternatives in group activities and the freedom to choose

from among them. Directors tend to be impatient with groupmates, particularly if they make mistakes. In group meetings people who score high on the director scale tend to be intolerant of wasted time and lack of structure. Due to their need for control and independence, directors might emerge as group leaders or participate frequently in group discussions and tasks.

Socializer

Like a director, an individual who favors socializer characteristics operates at a fast pace. With an orientation that emphasizes relationships, however, socializers prefer to be with people rather than accomplish tasks. They enjoy variety and stimulation, tend to think (and react) emotionally, and enjoy having others notice them. In addition, socializers:

- tend to be persuasive with others
- seek recognition
- prefer opportunities to express their creativity
- may not follow through with tasks
- can be impulsive
- are inattentive to detail
- are irritated by routine
- like innovation and change
- are enthusiastic
- may become irritated by a lot of rules and procedures which can be seen as interfering with creativity and expression

Individuals who are primarily socializers like to be in groups; they need people. They enjoy being the center of attention and showing off to others. Because of their fast pace and orientation to others, socializers might need help with getting organized relative to group tasks. People who exhibit socializer traits often enjoy socializing during meetings more than getting a particular task done. Socializers might be late to meetings because they got caught up with people elsewhere. Socializers generally feel comfortable being the spokesperson as they love the spotlight.

Relater

Relater participants prefer a much slower pace than directors or socializers. Like socializers, individuals characterized as relaters are relationship-oriented, although their goal is group harmony and cohesion, not self-recognition. Relaters tend to think logically in a step-by-step progression, care about stability, and dislike conflict. Relaters also:

- enjoy routines and avoid risks
- need a lot of rules and procedures
- prefer the status quo and security
- need reassurance in facing challenges
- enjoy being a member of a group
- want documentation and facts
- strive to maintain peace in groups
- seek consensus from others
- are concerned with inclusion of all
- want to be appreciated by others

As group members, relaters tend to be easy-going, low-key, and strive to please everyone. They are very

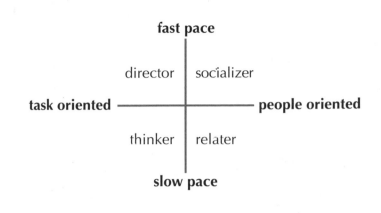

Figure 4.5 Four primary behavior styles fit along two axes.

Table 4C Leaders should consider the needs of the four behavioral styles when deciding on appropriate leadership approaches

Behavior Style	Director	Socializer	Relater	Thinker
Followers need:	Options or alternatives for task completion and freedom	Exciting premiums or incentives	Assurances they will not be left alone to complete tasks	Reasons why they should participate
Followers want freedom to:	*Win* Let them choose the most successful path.	*Gain* Give endorsement and encouragement.	*Relax* Avoid additional relationship tension.	*Breathe* Give time to think and react.
Followers ask:	*What is it?*	*Who else is involved?*	*Why should I do that?*	*How does it work?*
Followers are motivated to save:	*Time* Time is money, and structure saves time.	*Effort* Give shorter and more direct systems for saving effort.	*Relationships* They complete tasks usually as a result of preserving relationships.	*Face* They feel awkward handling relationships and problems.
Followers irritate others by:	Displaying impatience and sarcasm	Not following through	Not being able to make decisions	Expressing negativism and criticism
Followers are irritated by:	Being asked to perform illogical, unreasonable tasks	Rules and procedures	Pressure of any kind	Those who fail to follow regulations and keep deadlines
Followers need to learn:	To listen	To check	To reach	To decide
Followers need leaders who:	Allow freedom	Provide inspiration	Provide direction	Give suggestions
Followers measure progress by:	*Results* They need to reach goals and accomplish tasks.	*Applause* They need to feel love and know their contributions are appreciated.	*Attention* They need to know they are noticed and their work appreciated.	*Activity* They need to be involved in lots of facts, details, and projects.
Followers want appreciation for their:	Capabilities	Cleverness	Contributions	Carefulness

Adapted from Phillips, B. (1989). *The delicate art of dancing with porcupines: Learning to appreciate the finer points of others* (pp. 150–154). Ventura, CA: Regal Books.

people-oriented and friendship-oriented, as well as loyal to the group. Relaters often make excellent managers because they focus on group members and morale. During meetings, relaters feel most comfortable with routine and structure. If there is going to be a change, relaters need to know why and how it affects them—preferably in advance.

Thinker

Individuals characterized as thinkers prefer a slow pace (similar to relaters). Like directors, thinkers prefer tasks over people. They tend to think logically and methodically and seek data to back up group processes and approaches. Because they prefer to have the information at hand before making decisions, thinkers tend to be cautious in their approach to group work. Furthermore, thinkers:

* are low risk-takers
* are perfectionists
* are cautious
* are task-oriented
* are detail-oriented
* need order and organization
* are slow and very deliberate
* need a lot of rules and procedures
* avoid conflict
* need to be right
* believe that no decision is better than a wrong decision

Thinkers prefer to have order and organization in group meetings and prefer to work carefully and alone. As members of a group, thinkers would keep close track of group tasks such as minutes, following an agenda, and obeying the meeting rules. Quality of group work is a prominent concern of thinkers.

Labeling Without Labels

The purpose of identifying these four behavioral styles is not so we can label individuals and place them into "boxes." Administrators, programmers, and leaders must be careful to avoid "writing off" individuals by thinking or saying:

He's always late; what else would you expect from a socializer?

Don't make her the group leader, she's a thinker and will never make up her mind about a strategy.

Give him that job, he's a relater and won't fuss about it.

She's so pushy, she must be a director.

Use and abuse of labels may influence leader and group member expectations of individuals which can constrain individual potential as members of a group. Identifying the four predominant behavioral styles can help leaders to better understand the observable differences in people's behavior so that they can be more tolerant and effective in dealing with others. By understanding the choices of others and self, leaders can avoid making hasty judgments about behaviors and control their own responses to participants based on observable behaviors.

Understanding people is the heart of recreation and leisure services. With increased knowledge of human behavior, recreation and leisure services professionals can provide guidance and leadership direction which meet the needs of a variety of people. Gaining insight into participant needs, desires, and style preferences provides leisure services leaders with information to mold programs and leadership techniques to meet the diverse needs of program constituents. Through sharing information about the dimensions of behavior with participants and recognizing those differences, leisure services professionals can enhance between-participant interactions of group members as well as leader-participant relations. Enhancing group member interactions can have a very positive impact on group development.

Group Development

Groups are like living things—they form and evolve over time. They go through life stages, mature, make mistakes, and learn continuously. Groups continually fluctuate, gaining and losing ground on various occasions. A group is more than a number of people simply sharing time and space; members interact and move through several stages together as they grow and mature into a distinct entity.

Leaders need to go beyond knowing about group development to understanding it. Without truly understanding how groups develop and function, a leader cannot act as effectively as possible. Deciding on the level of leader involvement, the amount of structure to provide, and the appropriate leadership styles all depend upon where a group is in its development.

Group development has commonly been viewed as a linear and sequential process. Researchers now, however, view group development as nonlinear and cyclical. Experience indicates that while groups might move through several stages on their way to high performance, much cycling exists along the way. It certainly is not a neat, easily identifiable process. During each stage of development, internal and external forces impact progress. A group may move "forward" in its development to the next stage and while in that stage group members may experience growing pains similar to earlier stages. They may temporarily regress to an earlier stage. Thus, as effective groups develop, the movement may appear to be unidirectional, but the process is convoluted and intertwined with many subprocesses occurring at each stage.

The labels used to identify the stages a group moves through differ, but the process and group experiences described are very similar. These approaches delineate what typically occurs as groups move through various stages. Models of group development help explain group affect as well as leader roles.

A commonly used model for explaining group development is described by Tuckman and Jensen (1977): forming, norming, storming, and performing; adjourning was added later by other researchers. While this conceptualization has merit in helping people to understand what happens to groups, research has indicated additional stages are necessary. The acronym GROUPD is a mnemonic that explains the various stages through which a group moves: Getting to know one another; Relationship building; Opposition and conflict; Unity; Productivity; and Dissolution.

Getting to Know One Another

During this orientation phase of group development members seek clarification and direction from the leader(s). Individual roles within the group and member status are typically assigned based on the perceived roles one fulfills outside of the group. Issues within the group tend to be discussed on a surface level and often remain quite ambiguous. Mutual respect (on a surface level) is typically evident. This is a time of identity formation—determining who members are, and what is unique about this group.

This stage is similar to the forming stage presented by Tuckman and Jensen (1977).

As they feel their way into a new group, members may experience feelings of concern over their acceptance and sense of belonging in the group. They tend to be tentative in their interactions with others in the group. Dependency on the leader and dependency on an established structure, as well as anxiety, exist in this stage. Group members are often concerned about the leader's competence, as well as their relationship to the leader. At the same time, members depend upon the leader(s) for guidance and direction.

Leaders also experience identifiable feelings and situations when a group is in this phase. At this stage of group development the leader is called upon to provide structure to the group and task clarification to members. The group expects the leader to be dependable, prepared, and somewhat directive in style. In an effort to aid in the transition for each individual group member, leaders may wish to focus on the involvement and participation levels of each individual. The leader and group members share information to facilitate a comfortable environment and form a solid understanding of the direction and goals of the group. At this stage, many leaders serve as facilitators to ensure that the group gets off to a successful start. Establishing the tone—acceptance, tolerance, safety—are primary considerations of a leader in this stage.

Relationship Building

Moving out of the orientation stage, group members now begin to form relationships with one another as well as in relation to one another (i.e., perceived status and within-group rankings commonly known as a "pecking order"). During this phase there is quick agreement on the group norms and atmosphere of the group. This period relates to Tuckman and Jensen's (1977) norming stage. People search for an understanding of how they fit into the group,

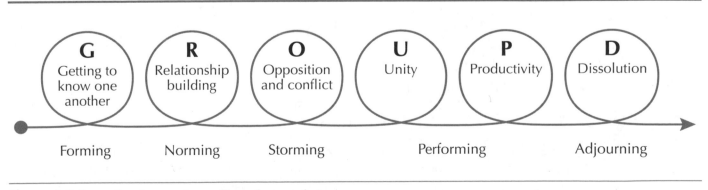

Figure 4.6 Group development goes through several stages.

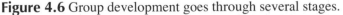

which niches they fill. Some give-and-take is evident among group members as the niche-finding occurs. Individual members make judgments of others relative to personalities, behavior styles, work ethics, and other group concerns.

Group members and leaders build and define relationships between themselves, as well. At this stage leaders and participants have defined their relationships with one another. Some leaders have very close relationships with individual participants and the group, while other leaders feel more comfortable with a sense of formal distance between themselves and the group members. Leader respect and credibility are usually fairly well-established at this stage, although leaders are continually tested.

Opposition and Conflict

Every group (if it is together long enough) goes through an opposition and conflict stage, correlated to Tuckman and Jensen's (1977) storming phase. A normal phase of group development, it may be likened to a teenager in the process of breaking away from parents. Individuals within the group attempt to gain control of the group (i.e., take control away from the leader) and assert themselves as independent and viable in their own right. Leaders are tested and challenged either overtly or covertly. For example, a group in this stage might have strong disagreements and experience anger, frustration, and irritation with other group members (including the leader). These feelings should be addressed with the group at this point with an aim toward working through the issues. If a leader recognizes this as a normal phase of group development, she or he is much more likely to accept the situation as growing pains rather than as a personal affront.

Relationships and a sense of accomplishment are important for all who participate in leisure.

Because various intergroup power issues are the primary focus during this stage, task avoidance often results. Members work to determine their level of autonomy and the level of influence over themselves and others in the group. Individuals try to ascertain the "pecking order" of the group, and as a result not much work toward goal achievement or task accomplishment is undertaken.

For leaders, particularly those who are caught unaware, this stage of group development can be one of the most difficult. Establishing a tone accepting of divergent viewpoints will ensure that all group members feel equally a part of the group activities. Due to the struggles experienced during this phase, the leader must also encourage members to engage in frequent and open communication about their feelings. This assumes, of course, that the leader has already established the group as a safe place to express and accept feelings as valid. In addition, knowing that this is a healthy phase of group development may make it easier for the leader to become less directive and more participatory in her or his chosen leadership style.

Unity

This is a period of reconciliation, integration and cohesion. Group members have experienced and survived feelings of discord, and can now clearly focus on the tasks at hand. Goals have recently been restated and clarified. Often informal leaders reemerge, more widely accepted than in earlier stages. Having been through difficult times, intimate discussions are likely to occur as the cohesion process begins. Risk taking and trust building are evident within the group.

In this phase of development, the desire to be a group member is noticeable—if things are going well people are proud of their group affiliation. Group members exhibit a positive bias toward their own group and other group members (Reynolds, Turner & Haslam, 2000). Members learn to disagree without being disagreeable, and laugh and enjoy one another's company while working toward group tasks. Group loyalty and an implicit agreement to abide by group norms is evident; a real sense of "we-ness" develops. Norms are solidified, roles are accepted, and a unique group culture is recognizable to outsiders. Group members also accept roles and present a recognizable culture to outsiders.

At this stage leaders might wish to disengage themselves from the internal workings of the group and allow the group to achieve its potential. One leader role is to solicit and respond to positive and negative feedback from group members. Group members take on additional tasks and delegation becomes an important leader skill. In this stage, the leader's primary function is to be supportive and provide needed resources as the group is relatively self-sufficuent.

Productivity

In the productivity phase, the group works toward shared goals with enthusiasm and a solid understanding of one another's strengths and limitations. The group functions effectively and efficiently, and accepts and utilizes the different strengths of group members. Members take initiative toward accomplishing the goal. The group is performing (Tuckman & Jensen, 1977).

Similar to the opposition and conflict stages, member challenges often recur during this phase of group development. Unlike the earlier stages, however, at this stage of development groups use the challenges to increase creativity and effective problem solving. Functional and personal relationships are strong, and the group accomplishes what needs to be done. As group members seek feedback from the leader and other members, the group becomes self-regulating and self-determining.

The leader may wish to assist (as needed) with restating or restructuring goals to aid the group in meeting its needs. With a fully functioning group, the leader might play the role of the devil's advocate and question traditional or habitual ways of doing things. The leader also facilitates the development of ongoing assessment methods for the group in this stage of development. The leader's role has evolved from one of setting the tone and providing direction to one of helping members develop their fullest potential through monitoring and evaluation of task and maintenance functions.

Dissolution

All groups cease to exist at some time. Some groups reframe and reinvent themselves, while others simply dissolve. This may occur gradually or abruptly. In this stage some groups experience an overoptimism about the power of the group (We can do anything!) followed by denial of the impending dissolution. Authors have referred to this stage as adjourning (Bratton, Grint & Nelson, 2005; Miller, 2003).

Group leaders need to understand what occurs at this stage because it is not uncommon for a well-functioning group to seem to fall apart—members fight, withdraw, or appear to self-destruct. These behaviors are normal and not necessarily the fault of poor leadership or selfish group members. The pool of emotions is often difficult for members to address, and they may react by withdrawing or striking out.

❖ ❖ ❖

All groups grow, develop, and mature through several intertwined phases and are subject to internal and external forces. The intensity and impact of the growth process experienced by group members influences leader preparation, group tasks, group skills, and the effect of internal and external forces. A basic knowledge and understanding of groups and how they develop can be beneficial to leaders as they attempt to positively influence the group growth. Solid leadership skills and a willingness to help individuals in groups work through the various stages can increase the effectiveness of the group in both task and maintenance functions.

Group members often express their unity through logos on clothing.

All groups grow, develop, and mature through several intertwined phases and are subject to internal and external forces.

Strong and Effective Groups

Leaders desire strong and effective groups (so do group members!). Strong groups have more stability, have greater control over member behaviors, do a better job of servicing member needs, and generate high-levels of participation and loyalty than do weak groups (Hartenian, 2003; LaFasto & Larson, 2001). To be successful, groups must have:

- shared goals that every group member knows
- the "right sort" of leadership (it should fluctuate)
- complementary roles and skills among group members
- open and candid communication
- member commitment to the group and its goals
- concern and caring for all group members
- appropriate challenges and opportunities to meaningfully contribute
- social and task cohesion
- conceptual, interpersonal, and technical skills
- celebrations of team success.

In addition to understanding and being cognizant of these many elements of effective groups, in such groups members also interact freely, depend upon one another, want to remain as members, and as a group have social power (Karriker, 2005). Personal need satisfaction of members determines the strength and solidarity of a group. If a group meets the personal needs of its members, satisfaction is high and the group is strong. It has been found that the size of a group impacts its strength and effectiveness; five to thirteen people are considered to be more cohesive and effective than larger or smaller groups. A participative leadership style, such as transformational or servant leadership, increases satisfaction, as do common goals and things that make people feel special (Markulis, Jassawalla & Sashittal, 2006). Other characteristics of effective and ineffective groups are found in Table 4D.

Effective group efforts require work; groups do not develop without some struggle with tasks and socioemotional factors. The group skills and characteristics listed in Table 4D do not necessarily come naturally to people. Group members must learn the necessary skills, attitudes, and belief structures to work through the rough spots and persevere. Individual group members must be convinced that this group is for them, will meet their needs, and that cohesion will occur with the efforts of all. Effective groups are those in which members have a commitment to growth, and experiencing and utilizing the effects of synergy.

Effective groups are those in which members have a commitment to growth, and experiencing and utilizing the effects of synergy.

Barriers to Effective Groups

As mentioned previously, effective groups do not just happen—the group leader and group members must have some level of commitment to making things work to achieve group goals. As one might imagine, many barriers to developing effective groups exist. Some of these barriers exist without conscious effort on the part of the individuals engaging in the behaviors. Nonetheless, the barriers affect not only individuals but also the functioning of the group.

Petzoldt (1984) believed that an ineffective group results from a breakdown in human relations caused by selfishness. In this sense, selfishness is characterized as being overly focused on oneself so that what is best for the group is set aside in efforts to do what is best for the self. Unfortunately, individualist cultures, like the predominant culture of the United States, tend to perpetuate this mindset. Good leadership requires letting go of this type of self-absorption and focusing on the group and its needs. A leader who is not involved with and cognizant of the group will be ineffective in helping group members achieve their goals. As can be seen in Table 4D, other reasons for group ineffectiveness exist. Poor group skills, a lack of commitment to group efforts, and the lack of a common goal all negatively impact group functioning.

One of the strong points of group dynamics, which when overused becomes a weakness, is peer (or group) pressure and the influence to conform. Used in a positive sense, group pressure assures that group members adhere to norms, agree to group goals, and share a common focus. When overused or overemphasized, however, group pressure can squelch individual ideas and creativity, force individuals to comply with situations with which they do not agree, and subsume individual identity within the group (Moorhead & Griffin, 2004; Sheard, 2004). This "group think" mentality can be a real detriment to positive group functioning.

Groups that have obvious status differences between group members may experience difficulties in becoming fully functioning. As an example, Knouse and Dansby (1999) found an optimal level of minority status in a group before it becomes detrimental to the group's effectiveness. They found that group membership that has 11% to 30%

minority representation allows for the minority group to experience a sense of inclusion (i.e., there are enough other people "like me" for me to feel comfortable), while at the same time enabling the larger group to utilize the strengths of that diversity.

As with having too much diversity, having too much sameness can cause problems as well. Pelled and colleagues (1999) investigated very similar and very dissimilar groups. They found a great deal of in-group comparison, which often resulted in jealousy and emotional conflict, in highly similar groups. Similar people often fought over resources, promotion tracks (in a workplace setting), and the attention of the group leaders.

Furthermore, an unacceptable physical environment (e.g., too hot, too cold, too stark, too dilapidated) will likely have a negative effect on group functioning. If people are uncomfortable in their physical surroundings they are unlikely to be concentrating on the task or fellow group members. As one might imagine, poor leadership also presents problems for effective group functioning. Being overly dictatorial with a mature, highly experienced group

may result in a stifling of group abilities, boredom, or irritation. On the other hand, being too removed from the group when it is in need of guidance can also result in a group not functioning up to its potential.

Group Roles

In addition to the many factors identified earlier, group roles may serve as a barrier to a group's effectiveness. Group roles are fluid; people change the role they fulfill from time to time. One day someone may be clowning around and entertaining the group and on another day that same individual may be seeking information and opinions from group members. While it might be true that one group member might be more apt to fill a certain role than another, on any given day each group member has the capability of filling one or more positive or negative roles. The behaviors, attitudes, thoughts, and moods of each group member influence the position one will play within the group at a given time. If negative group roles are

---

Table 4D Characteristics of effective and ineffective groups

Effective Groups	Ineffective Groups
• Are between five and thirteen people in size.	• Form cliques (i.e., subgroups)
• Share common goals which are clarified and change as the need arises.	• Have no focus or goals; goals may be imposed on group members.
• Meet the needs of group members (e.g., inclusion, control, affection).	• Ignore the contributions of select individuals.
• Communicate openly and in all directions.	• Communication is one-way (or nonexistent).
• Feelings and affect are accepted and addressed as needed.	• The affective component is downplayed, suppressed, or ignored.
• Decision making is mutual; group memebers are involved as much as the situation will allow.	• Decision making is by authority with little or no discussion.
• Controversy and conflict are viewed as signs of a healthy group and are dealt with from a positive learning approach.	• Controversy and conflict are viewed as negative and are ignored, suppressed, or denied.
• Cohesion is a primary focus, and a real "we" approach to group tasks is taken.	• Cohesion is ignored; group members are controlled by authority; a "me" stance is adopted.
• Feedback and evaluation are ongoing and viewed as exciting learning opportunities.	• Feedback and evaluation are done sporadically, if at all; group members fear evaluation and feedback.
• Alternative ways of looking at things are encouraged and nurtured.	• Creative thoughts and approaches are squelched; the leader has rigid control.
• Leadership rotates based on the situation and group need.	• Leadership is hoarded and used as power and self-enhancement or aggrandizment.
• Participation is shared across all members of the group; involvement is high.	• Participation is by a select few; some monopolize, others withdraw.

allowed to dominate the group process, the group will be ineffective in its efforts.

Positive Group Roles

Positive roles help a group achieve its goals while at the same time maintaining high group morale. By fulfilling these roles individuals contribute to the effective functioning of the group. Positive group roles include:

Clarifier: Seeks clarification and assists others in seeing things more clearly; simplifies complex issues; strives to reduce confusion.

Compromiser: Seeks the middle road; helps members see ways of agreeing through disagreements; ensures that everyone understands the issues as well as individual group member needs.

Consensus seeker: Assures that all members are equally involved in the group and decision-making processes.

Encourager: Supports and encourages group members to do their best.

Gatekeeper: Checks in with group members as tasks move ahead to be sure that tasks are being completed and that everyone is being included.

Harmonizer: Helps people smooth over conflicts and helps the group recognize similarities among members.

Initiator: Initiates task and people functions; gets the action started.

Opinion/information giver: Shares her or his own opinions and knowledge in group sessions when appropriate.

Opinion/information seeker: Strives to include group members through asking them to express their thoughts and opinions.

Problem solver: Identifies and addresses problems and issues as they arise and helps group members to solve problems.

Summarizer: Provides a summary of what has occurred and helps to keep things in perspective.

Timekeeper: Keeps tasks on time and the group moving toward group goals in a timely fashion.

Negative Group Roles

Because groups consist of many members, all of whom are unique and experience a variety of influences, some members fill negative roles. Negative roles impede or hinder group functioning; these roles may interfere with group tasks and/or group morale. Any positive role taken to the extreme could have a negative impact on the effectiveness of a group. Negative roles also include the following:

Blocker: Stops forward movement by arguing, resisting, and disagreeing beyond reason with comments such as "Yeah, but…" and "We've always done it this way."

Clown/Entertainer: Interrupts group functioning with inappropriately placed humor and antics, which serve as a disruption and move the group off task.

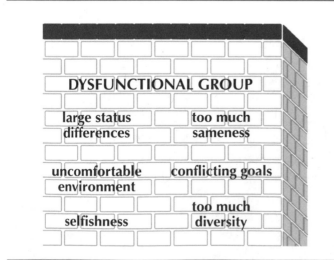

Figure 4.7 A leader must be aware of and try to minimize the many barriers to effectively functioning groups.

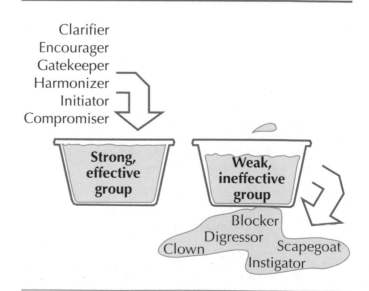

Figure 4.8 Positive and negative group roles enhance and detract from a group.

Digressor: Takes group members off-task and into un-related tangents. The behaviors may be friendly and open, but disturb group goal achievement.

Disassociator: Disengages from working toward group goals; tends to daydream, talk to others, or leave the room for no apparent reason.

Instigator: Initiates irritations in others and gets them excited or upset about topics irrelevant to the tasks at hand; enjoys (and sometimes thrives on) conflict.

Scapegoat: Gets blamed for everything that does not go well within the group; accepts responsibility; acts helpless.

❖ ❖ ❖

Leaders who understand group roles and what constitutes an effective group will likely be successful in their leadership efforts. This takes time, skills, and conscious effort. Many groups desire to further develop their effectiveness and efficiency and move from being a group to becoming a team. Teams are highly effective and successful groups, and experience a unique brand of cohesion; thus, it is beneficial to examine the unique elements of team building.

Team Building

In conjunction with knowledge of group elements, group development, group roles, and leadership, leaders need to understand the concept of team building. People often use the word team when describing a group, yet differences exist between what constitutes a group and what makes a team. A group is a number of people sharing space (and, perhaps, resources), often engaged in an activity, but having no sense of "belonging to one another," and not necessarily sharing a common goal. A team is a group of people who are interdependent—they need each other to be successful—and they know it. A team has visible cohesion, a team identity beyond the individuals on the team, a common goal, and similar ideas about how to achieve that goal. In addition, a team has team leadership, team motivation, and team competencies (LaFasto & Larson, 2001).

When working with teams, team leaders are typically involved in assisting the team in developing its goals, even if formal goals are already identified. This usually leads to increased team performance, because team members take ownership of what they create. Leaders of teams participate by establishing challenges, facilitating improvement of team member skills, aiding in the development of cohesion, and actively celebrating team successes. Participants of high-performance teams feel involved, committed, and valued by the leader and other team members.

A team is a group of people who are interdependent—they need each other to be successful—and they know it. A team has visible cohesion, a team identity beyond the individuals on the team, a common goal, and similar ideas about how to achieve that goal.

Good team members are just as important as a good team leader. Good team members have been characterized as people who: (a) participate fully in team discussions; (b) motivate themselves; (c) are open and willing to try new things; (d) are sensitive to others' points of view; (e) cooperate and collaborate with teammates; (f) know their own as well as teammates' strengths and limitations; (g) are committed to resolving team conflicts; and (h) celebrate team successes (Druskat & Wheeler, 2004).

To develop an effectively functioning team, group leaders and group members must be committed to the process and willing to accept responsibility to make things happen. It must be understood that team building is a process, not a one-shot approach to group development. In many instances the leader takes on the role of a coach—encouraging, teaching, modeling, and helping individual members to understand how to best use their talents to help the team achieve its goal. In developing a team, group members strive to meet the following team essentials.

Take Care of One's Self

In the event of an emergency, airline flight attendants direct capable individuals to put on their own oxygen masks before attempting to assist others so that the helpers do not lose consciousness before helping either the individual needing assistance or themselves. This self-help concept is needed for team members, as well. If individual team members do not first take care of themselves, they will be unable to adequately tend to teammates.

Take Care of Each Other

If everyone takes care of everyone else, each person will receive the benefit of the others' concern. This is the positive aspect of the norm of reciprocity, or "what goes around comes around." This approach to life tends to enhance and encourage cohesion and team building. In addition, this is an important element in developing social capital—rich resources of people in our lives who care for us and support us.

Take Care of Facilities, Equipment, and Supplies

A team without the tools and resources necessary to accomplish its tasks will be ineffective. Teams know what resources and equipment are necessary and they take care of them. Often, team members take great pride in having excellent facilities, equipment, and supplies (e.g., uniforms). These items facilitate the development of a distinct identity. Team members understand that these types of tools are important for long-term success.

Have Balance in One's Life

Another component of taking care of oneself is balance; it enhances individual well-being. Healthy people are balanced and tend to be happy, physically well, and capable of taking on a variety of tasks. People with balanced lives make positive contributions to teams. Balance involves health in all aspects of one's life—physical, emotional, mental, spiritual, and social.

Give the Other Person the Benefit of the Doubt

Effective and supportive team members avoid harsh or quick judgments of others and situations; they are open and accepting of the uniqueness of each team member. Being too quick to judge is one of the most insidious barriers to effective teams. Remember to allow people to be human, including yourself. Everyone makes mistakes, and we often learn much from our failures.

Photo courtesy of Gwynn Powell

Team members share a common goal and work as one unit to achieve it.

Bring Your Best to Each Situation

If each person on the team consistently presents herself or himself to do the best possible in every situation, the synergy and energy will expand and great things will happen. This involves using all of one's talents and energies to achieve the group goals—it requires ongoing self-monitoring. This is positive social involvement, rather than social loafing.

Put the Other Person First

By putting the other person first, no one will be left out and everyone will be on equal footing. This "other-esteem" will enhance self-esteem for all. It might be wise to follow the Platinum Rule: "Do unto others as they would want to be done unto." (Note how this differs from the Golden Rule: "Do unto others as you would have them do unto you"). Be supportive of individual team members and their efforts; generally speaking, we all try to do our best.

Think "We" and Support Other Team Members

If people support others (even in their disagreements), trust will build and people will be willing to take risks. Open communication will occur and individual team members will feel valued for what they bring to the team. Trust and risk-taking behaviors are two components necessary for team building. These both take time to develop, yet are easily damaged. Being alert to this will aid positive team growth.

Meld Personal Goals with the Team Goals

With shared goals, each team member has a better opportunity to know the reasoning behind, and to understand the consequences of her or his actions. If one member's individual goals are distinctly incompatible with team goals, perhaps it is time for that person to find a more compatible team. Interdependent and cooperative goals can lead to synergy and a sense of belonging.

Appreciate the Strengths, Diversity, and Limitations Each Person Brings to the Team

Without the ability to take advantage of and integrate the differences, limitations, and strengths brought by each team member, conflicts are likely. While some conflict is a positive aspect of team development, too much conflict can derail a team from its goals. Diversity enriches groups, and teams are enriched by diversity. Leaders who are

Developing and maintaining a strong team requires mutual understanding, goal agreement, trust, risk-taking, safety within the group, an understanding of diversity, and effective decision-making processes.

skilled and knowledgeable about issues of diversity are likely to be highly successful in facilitating team growth.

❖ ❖ ❖

Effective teams do not simply "happen." They take attention, nurturing, and ongoing evaluation throughout the life of the team. Team building is a continuous process—it takes time and commitment by all those involved. Developing and maintaining a strong team requires mutual understanding, goal agreement, trust, risk-taking, safety within the group, an understanding of diversity, and effective decision-making processes. By taking care of self, others, and equipment, and by addressing all team essentials, a leader can help develop an exciting and effective team.

Summary

Leisure services leaders work with groups in a variety of settings and in a variety of situations. Therefore, understanding group dynamics becomes a critical skill for leisure services leaders. Groups consist of many elements and have internal and external forces acting on them. Task and social cohesion are both important to group development and group success. Collectivist groups focus on the collective self; individualist groups perceive individual freedoms as more important than the collective group.

People join groups for a variety of reasons. By understanding the reasons people have for joining, leisure services leaders can be well-prepared for group and individual behaviors. People join others to engage in social behaviors, to learn new skills, for self-enhancement, to achieve intimacy, because they were coerced into doing so, for self-identity, and to make a statement. Leaders can utilize this knowledge to increase comprehension about group structure. Group structure consists of membership, cohesion, participation, influence, norms, atmosphere, leadership, task and maintenance functions, decision making, judgment, conflict, and goals.

Individuals within groups have preferred behavioral styles. Some tend to be fast-paced while others are slow-paced; some people are task-oriented, yet others are more people-oriented. All groups pass through many stages of

When working with groups, leaders will often be in positions to help group members learn about the process of being a group and developing into a team. By asking group members a variety of questions about the dynamics observed within the group, leaders can facilitate learning so that group members experientially discover what is needed for effective functioning. Leaders might consider asking the following types of questions:

Participation: Did all group members participate equally? Who participated the most? the least? How were silent group members treated? How was participation defined? Who contributed the most to the task? to the affect of the group?

Influence: Who were the most influential members of the group? What made them influential? Who had more influence—the talkers or the nontalkers? What outsiders influenced the group? How could you tell? Did any one group member seem to manipulate others? How?

Norms: What were the group norms? How were norms defined by the group? Who seemed to define the norms? Did everyone adhere to the norms? What happened when individuals did not follow the norms? Which norms were implicit? Explicit?

Atmosphere: How would you describe the atmosphere of the group? What makes you define it that way? Who influenced the climate of the group? How did they do that?

Leadership: Who was the leader of the group? What made her or him the leader? What leadership style was primarily used? Did anyone not follow this leader? What impact did that have on the group? Did leadership fluctuate?

Task Functions: What were the tasks of the group? Who served to develop group goals and objectives? Who kept the group on task and on time? Who initiated the group work? How did others react to these individuals?

Maintenance Functions: Who appeared to take care of the group members? Was there one person who ensured member involvement? Did the leader exhibit more task or maintenance functions? Who was concerned for the well-being of the group members?

Decision Making: What style of decision making was used most often? Were all group members included in all decisions? Were all ideas heard and acknowledged? How did those who were excluded react? Was the decision-making process effective? How could you tell? What impeded effective decision making?

Communication: Describe the communication process. Was it effective or ineffective? Why? What hindered/helped effective communication? What would you suggest as guidelines to enhance communication?

Figure 4.9 Leaders can facilitate team development through considering many factors.

development, which intertwine throughout the development process. Group members first get to know one another, then build relationships. Next opposition and conflict occur, after which unity is restored. Once re-formed, group productivity tends to be high, and then the group dissolves or recommits. Understanding how groups develop helps a leader to more effectively lead, facilitate, and encourage group growth.

Identifiable differences between effective and ineffective groups exist. Group members play distinct roles which change regularly. Team development focuses on establishing a successful group of people who are interdependent, share goals, are committed, care for one another, and celebrate team successes. If leaders want to work with teams, they will need to work on facilitating team skills.

Beginning the Journey

Learning about human development in Chapter 3 provided a foundation for understanding people as individuals. Interestingly, however, parks and recreation leaders generally interact with people in groups. Thus, this chapter provided basic knowledge about groups and how to work with them. As you continue your personal journey to leadership, reflect on your understanding of and abilities in working with groups through the following questions.

1. Explain the notions of task and social cohesion—give examples of each of these from a group of which you are a current member. Which do you think is more important in a group—social or task cohesion? Why do you believe that?

2. How is a group different from a nongroup? Explain how you can tell the difference. Which do you see in parks, recreation, and leisure services leadership (groups, teams, neither, both)? Give examples.

3. Explain what is meant by collectivist and individualist cultures or groups. Which one do you favor the most? How is this manifested? Develop a bumper sticker slogan for each type of culture. How would your leadership be different if you were leading a primarily collectivist group versus a primarily individualist group?

4. Develop an easy-to-read chart of the good and the bad of groups. Compare synergy, group think, and social loafing. Which do you want to encourage/discourage? Why? How would you go about doing this?

5. Visit a local parks, recreation, and leisure services agency and determine which programs have groups. Informally ask group members why they joined that group. Are those reasons compatible? Are some of them in conflict? Are any independent? Explain how you, as a leader, would address these individual reasons within the group.

6. Why are group goals important? Look at the list of factors that impact group commitment to goals found on page 79, and discuss each one in terms of how you, as the leader, can impact those factors. What can you do to enhance group commitment to goals?

7. Give examples of the three different goal orientations. Indicate what your role as a leader would be in each of these situations.

8. Draw a conceptual map of the various elements of a group. Next to each element, identify leadership skills that are necessary for successful leadership of this group element.

9. What are behavior styles and why is it helpful for leaders to have some understanding of them? As you read through these styles, try to identify the one that best seems to represent you, and the one that supports that style (your second strongest style). What does this mean in terms of your strengths and limitations as a leader? What type of assistance do you need from others to be your best?

10. Draw up your own chart describing the changes that groups go through as they develop into fully functioning units. Identify specific leadership strategies that you can use with a group in each stage of development to help them be fully functional. Which areas do you need to work on most?

11. Compare and contrast an effective group with an ineffective group. What can you do to ensure that all the groups you work with are effective? From your experience, what size group do you prefer to work with and why? What size group is "too big" to be effective? Why?

12. Make a chart with a list of the barriers to effective groups down one side. In the column to the right, identify what leadership style or strategies you can use to break down that barrier and help a group be more effective.

13. Have a look at the group roles identified in this text (both positive and negative, pp. 91–93). Which role(s) do you most often fill? Why is that? Are there times when you think you should consciously change roles? As the leader, do any of those group roles concern you? If so, which ones

and why? How can you encourage people to take on positive roles?

14. How does team building fit with group development? Explain. How are teams and groups different? Which would you rather lead and why? How does a leader help a group become a team? Have a look at the characteristics of a good team member (pp. 93–94). How often do you practice good team membership? As a leader how can you facilitate this?

References

Alessandra, T. and O'Connor, M. (1996). *The platinum rule: Discover the four basic business personalities.* New York, NY: Time Warner.

Bratton, J., Grint, K., and Nelson, D. (2005). *Organizational leadership.* Mason, OH: South-Western.

Druskat, V. and Wheeler, J. (2004). How to lead a self-managing team. *MIT Sloan Management Review, Summer,* 65–71.

Hartenian, L. (2003). Team member acquisition of team knowledge, skills, and abilities. *Team Performance Management, 9*(1/2), 23–30.

Johnson, D. and Johnson, F. (2003). *Joining together: Group theory and group skills* (8th ed.). Boston, MA: Allyn & Bacon.

Jordan, D. and Mertesdorf, J. (1994). The effects of goal interdependence between leisure service supervisors and employees. *Journal of Applied Recreation Research, 19*(2), 101–116.

Karriker, J. (2005). Cyclical group development and interaction-based leadership emergence in autonomous teams: An integrated model. *Journal of Leadership & Organizational Studies, 11*(4), 54–64.

Knouse, S. and Dansby, M. (1999). Percentage of work-group diversity and work-group effectiveness. *Journal of Psychology, 133*(5), 486–494.

LaFasto, F. and Larson, C. (2001). *When teams work best.* Thousand Oaks, CA: Sage Publications.

Markulis, P., Jassawalla, A., and Sashittal, H. (2006). The impact of leadership modes on team dynamics and performance in undergraduate management classes. *Journal of Education for Business, 81*(3), 145–150.

Miles, S. and Mangold, G. (2002). The impact of team leader performance on team member satisfaction: The subordinate's perspective. *Team Performance Management, 8*(5/6), 113–121.

Miller, D. (2003). The stages of group development: A retrospective study of dynamic team processes. *Canadian Journal of Administrative Sciences, 20*(2), 121–130.

Moorhead, G. and Griffin, R. (2004). *Organizational behavior: Managing people and organizations* (7th ed.). Boston, MA: Houghton Mifflin.

Nelson, D. and Quick, J. (2005). *Understanding organizational behavior* (2nd ed.). Mason, OH: South-Western.

Pelled, L., Eisenhardt, K., and Xin, K. (1999). Exploring the black box: An analysis of work group diversity, conflict, and performance. *Administrative Science Quarterly, 44*(1), 1–28.

Petzoldt, P. (1984). *The new wilderness handbook.* New York, NY: W.W. Norton & Co.

Phillips, B. (1989). *The delicate art of dancing with porcupines: Learning to appreciate the finer points of others.* Ventura, CA: Regal Books.

Reynolds, K., Turner, H., and Haslam, S. (2000). When are we better than them and they worse than us? A closer look at social discrimination in positive and negative domains. *Journal of Personality and Social Psychology, 78*(1), 64–80.

Sheard, A. (2004). A process perspective on leadership and team development. *The Journal of Management Development, 23*(1), 7–56.

Smith, G. (2001). Group development: A review of the literature and a commentary on future research directions. *Group Facilitation, Spring*(3), 14–45.

Tjosvold, D., Andrews, I., and Struthers, J. (1992). Leadership influence: Goal interdependence and power. *Journal of Social Psychology, 132*(1), 39–50.

Tuckman, B. (2001). Developmental sequence in small groups. *Group Facilitation, Spring*(3), 66–81.

Tuckman, B. and Jensen, M. (1977). Stages of small group development revisited. *Group & Organization Studies, 2*(4), 419–427.

Leader Profile

M. Kathleen (Kathy) Perales, CPRP
Research Biologist • U.S. Army Corps of Engineers

Kathy has 25 years with this agency in the parks, recreation, and leisure services profession.

Some of the many leadership positions she has held include:

- Board of Trustees, National Recreation and Park Association
- President of the Armed Forces Recreation Society (AFRS), NRPA
- Board member, National Society for Park Resources (NSPR)
- Liaison between AFRS and NSPR boards of directors

What is the meaning of leadership?
To me, leadership is a combination of vision, skill, communication, and service. To use a musical analogy, a business plan could be compared to a melody that is already in place. As a leader, your role is to add the harmony or the descant. Other times you realize there is not enough melody to stand out, so you switch from harmony to melody. Harmony may be nice, but it is not a substitute for the melody. You have to be able to hear the melody line. Think of the vision (or action) as thinking of the song; you should be able to hear it in your head (or see it in your mind's eye) before you start singing. You know the melody and the rhythm before you start. Getting others to sing along means you have to teach them the melody (direction of the action), and this can be a communication challenge. The leader needs to ensure that everyone has a copy of the score and knows which part is theirs. Although a certain level of skill is required, those with talent can be trained. The higher your role in the organization (leadership role), the more people you have to serve to ensure they understand and support the effort. Leadership is not telling people what to do; it is communicating the vision of the outcome and mobilizing the masses to join in and sing along. If you do it right, it becomes their song as well.

What are the most important leader qualities?
People skills. A leader needs to be able to read, understand, respect, and work with people. A leader must understand what drives other people to see how they can best participate.

What advice do you have for students who aspire to leadership in parks, recreation, and leisure services?
Get involved, listen, learn, and volunteer. Get involved in your professional organizations or on campus. Pay attention to "how" an office operates. Teach yourself people skills and volunteer to help on things that help you learn. See volunteering as a development of a skill set you don't have, and use it as a training ground for others to depend on you. Then work on that job or skill set until you have it down. As you move up the service line, get a feel for each job and its challenges. Don't be afraid to start with little things. Others will recognize talent.

Favorite book(s): Right now I'm reading books that can teach me and help me finish my dissertation. I buy business books and books that tell a story. I buy everything from knowledge management to business books, things I did not learn in school. I have a couple of autographed Maya Angelou books and a couple of books autographed by instructors that have taught me in the past. Reading for the soul is good. For fun, I read mysteries – crime-solving types, Greg Iles or Nevada Barr.

Favorite activities: SCUBA diving; BJ (my miniature schnauzer) has me share in the beauty and wonder of pre-dawn and starlight walks. BJ has also given me the gift of friends; friends that like walking and friends that like dogs. Every day is a new walking adventure. Walks help me think, rest, socialize and be on the watch for wildlife (It's a terrier thing).

Chapter Five
Communication Skills for Leaders

Learning Opportunities

Through studying this chapter readers will have the opportunity to:

- Examine the communication process.
- Evaluate effective and ineffective communication.
- Identify requisite skills of active listening.
- Understand how elements of culture interact with the communication process.
- Explain how one can improve communication effectiveness.
- Explore facilitation and processing as special communication techniques.

In anger a small child may stomp her or his foot and exclaim, "I'm not talking to you!" This sends a powerful message. In fact, we send messages—communicate—through everything we do. We can never not communicate. We communicate through the way we walk, the clothing we wear, the tone of our voice, the use of silence, and the words we use. People constantly read, decipher, and listen to what we have to say. A leader would be wise to pay attention to what she or he is saying—through words, body movements, silences, and external coding (e.g., the way one dresses). Learning about and practicing various communication skills can help us develop communication competence—skills in effective communication.

Payne (2005) reported that communication competence is directly related to job mobility, upward mobility, job level, and salary. The more competent in communication skills one is, the more apt she or he is to be successful in the workplace. She cited seven important skills to becoming competent in communication:

- empathy (i.e., the ability to demonstrate understanding of others' feelings)
- attentiveness (i.e., paying attention, being present in the moment)
- listening (i.e., demonstrating both behavioral as well as cognitive components)
- articulation (i.e., use of appropriate grammar and the ability to clearly express one's ideas)
- other-orientation (i.e., being cued into others, rather than focused on oneself)
- interaction management (i.e., fluency, verbal ability)
- adaptability (i.e., being flexible in communication style, approach)

Leisure services leaders communicate with supervisors, peers, participants, and the general public throughout their careers. To maximize communication effectiveness, leaders need to be articulate and accurate. Effective

Photo courtesy of Gwynn Powell

communication consists of much more than simply talking. It also involves listening, speaking, delivering, selling, giving, and receiving information. Communication is used to manage conflict, create and maintain relationships, persuade others, understand group dynamics, and transmit cultural norms. It is both an art and a science—a critical skill for leaders.

Shared meanings are the very crux of effective communication. When I say, "It's raining cats and dogs," we must have a shared agreement that this means it is raining quite heavily or some people will be looking for animals to drop from the sky. Without shared meanings based on shared experiences, communication is full of confusion and misinterpretations. Shared meanings develop over time when people learn to agree on the meaning of certain sounds. By changing one's voice tone, volume, or pitch, these meanings can change. For instance, a change in voice tone can change a simple statement from a request to a command. We key in on power differences and the nuances of verbal language.

Effective leadership requires knowledge of basic communication skills and practice with communication in a variety of settings. It occurs when the message is received the way it was intended. This chapter presents information related to the communication process focusing on verbal communication. Chapter 6 will address paraverbal and nonverbal forms of communication—vocalizations, body language, writing skills, and symbolic language.

Defining the Communication Process

Communication is a process of exchange and interaction directed at conveying meaning and achieving understanding. It occurs within, between, and outside of groups and is an essential component of human relationships. Ideas, opinions, facts, and feelings are shared in this process. Communication is multichanneled. It may be verbal, nonverbal, written, sensory, demonstrative, or two or more of these at once. Many believe that communication is a core competency of leadership (Joseph & Winston, 2005; Kratzer, Leenders & van Engelen, 2005). Because it is so important to individual and group success, leisure services leaders are encouraged to develop strong communication skills.

Neuliep (2006) suggests that communication has eight properties. First, it is a process rather than a product. Thus, it is a series of actions that are directed toward an aim (to be understood). Second, communication is dynamic— alive, active, and involved. Third, it is interactive; it requires more than one individual to be considered com-

Communication is used to manage conflict, create and maintain relationships, persuade others, understand group dynamics, and transmit cultural norms. It is both an art and a science—a critical skill for leaders.

munication. The fourth and fifth properties are that communication is symbolic, and it is intentional. Sixth, it is contextual—it is related to the environment as well as those involved in the process. Next, communication is everywhere, done by everyone, all the time. Lastly, communication is culture; through it we define culture. The inverse is also true—culture defines communication.

Communication has a visible structure to it and a model of the communication process is presented in Figure 5.1. Most models include similar elements: (1) a sender of the message; (2) a message or intended communication; (3) a channel through which the message is sent; (4) noise which interferes with the process; (5) a receiver of the message; and (6) feedback from the receiver to the sender. Each of these components has a function directly related to making the intended message understood as sent. Whether a person is a sender or a receiver primarily depends on time and circumstance rather than any firmly defined role. In the same interaction the same person is both the sender and receiver depending upon the flow of the communication.

Sender

The sender initiates an interaction and has a message she or he wishes to send to a receiver. Before the message can be sent the sender must first have an intention to communicate. Next, the sender goes through various cognitive processes to encode, or put into words, what she or he wants to say. Both the intended message and the motivation for sending the message are important in the encoding process. Sender intentions and motivations can influence the tone and manner in which a message is sent (and subsequently received).

Message

Many feel that the message is the most important element of communication; it is after all, the object of the interaction between people engaged in the process. Messages may take many forms: verbal and overt (e.g., person says exactly what is on her or his mind), verbal and hidden (e.g., double entendres), nonverbal (e.g., through body language), written (e.g., memoranda, text messages), and symbolic (e.g., hair style and clothing choices). To ensure effective communication, the various forms should complement, rather than contradict, each other. Problems arise when there is confusion about the message as it gets sent to the receiver. Confusion and misinterpretations are quite common because communication and language are culturally based; common meanings are generally a result of shared culture.

Channel

The channel is the medium through which a message is sent. The channel might be a written memo, person, video recording, audiotape, telephone, or computer network. Each type of channel has advantages and drawbacks to effective communication, and there are informal "rules" about the appropriateness of the use of certain channels. For instance, it would be inappropriate to fire someone through text messaging. Some of the channels intend to be primarily one way, while others encourage two-way communication. Some, such as the use of written memos, are two-way channels, but have periods of delay where the receiver must first have the memo in hand before the communication cycle may be completed.

Receiver

To continue the process, once a sender crafts a message and selects a channel, a recipient of the message must exist. This receiver perceives the incoming message and then must attend to the message and decode or interpret what is being communicated. For the receiver to interpret the message as intended, the sender and receiver must understand the context as well as the actual message.

Feedback

Feedback rounds out the communication process. Feedback is the reaction given by the receiver which tells the sender that the message was either understood or further clarification was needed. As with all methods of communication, feedback may be verbal, nonverbal, written, symbolic, or a combination. To be effective

To be effective feedback should be given freely, expeditiously, and succinctly.

feedback should be given freely, expeditiously, and succinctly.

People often consciously give feedback when observing or monitoring behaviors or actions of another (e.g., behavior management). To be most effective feedback should be very specific and focused on the particular behavior or words in question. For example, consider the following exchange:

Sender: "It's time to go; I'd like everyone to help pick up."

Receiver provides feedback seeking clarification: "What would you like us to pick up, and what should we do with it after picking it up?"

In many ways feedback provides clues about the accuracy of the sent message, motivation of the receiver, clarification of the message, and interest level of the receiver. If culturally understood, nonverbal cues such as a hand to the back of the ear (i.e., "I can't hear you") are often effective means of providing feedback to speakers. An effective communicator constantly scans the audience and looks for cues from listeners. Picking up on and

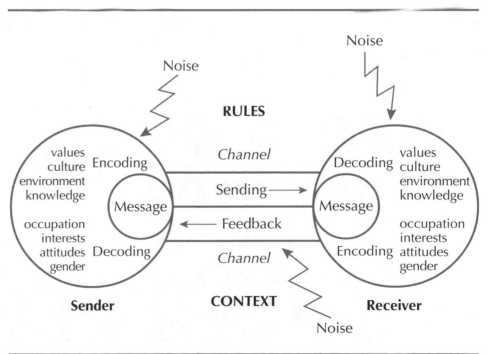

Figure 5.1 A basic communication model (York, Jordan & Safford, 1995)

responding to feedback helps the effectiveness of the communication process.

Noise

Anything that is not directly a part of the communication cycle and interferes with the successful sending and receiving of a message is called *noise*. Noise may be internal to the communicating parties (e.g., personal biases, practicing one's response, thinking about something else), or external to the communicators (e.g., sounds from passing vehicles, bright lights, other people fidgeting). If not addressed, noise can render communication efforts ineffective.

❖ ❖ ❖

To be complete, communication should cycle through all elements of the process. If any one element is lacking, incomplete or misinterpreted, communication efforts will be negatively impacted. In striving for effective communication, leaders will want to seek to enhance their skills in all aspects of the communication process. In addition to this, it may be helpful to understand the various functions of communication.

Functions of Communication

Like group dynamics, communication is a dynamic process—always changing and involving different people. It consists of both a task (i.e., content) and an affective component (i.e., feelings related to group processes; Gudykunst, 2004; Neuliep, 2006). Within the task and process components, communication has several different functions. An effective leader understands which function of communication is being utilized at any given time.

While all communication has multiple levels of meanings and serves several purposes simultaneously, function provides some cues as to the intent of the sender and ongoing motivations of those involved in the communication process. It helps focus and clarify the intent of the message. Communication may be used as persuasion, to share information, to express oneself, to command others, and to resolve conflicts.

Persuasion/Influence

Communication may be used to persuade or influence others in their thoughts or actions. Persuasion is communication designed to cause an individual (or a group) to adopt an idea as their own, which they would not otherwise support (Preston, 2005a). For example, a recreation aide might wish to persuade or influence elderly residents in a care facility to participate in recreational activities, a youth services director might wish to persuade parents to enroll their child in upcoming special events, or a park ranger might wish to persuade canoeists to pack out all their trash. Since ethical issues can arise when persuading others to certain courses of action, leisure services leaders would be well-served to adhere to strong ethical principles when engaging in this type of communication.

Information Sharing

Recreation and leisure services leaders do a lot of information sharing with people—exchanging facts and information with colleagues, supervisors, treatment team members, town council members, participants, and non-participating constituents. Often this communication is one-way, whereby a leisure services leader simply informs others about schedules, policies, upcoming events, or how

Communication involves verbal and nonverbal language.

We send messages through how we dress and what we say.

to play a particular game. Other times, information sharing is two-way, as in activity instruction or town hall meetings about sensitive issues.

Social/Expressive

Social/expressive communication is at the heart of interpersonal communication. People communicate with others to engage in social interaction and to express themselves creatively and emotionally. Social/expressive communication efforts comprise a large part of human communication patterns, yet many have limited skills in this area. This may be due in part to the predominant U.S. culture commonly suppressing and ignoring feelings, and operating on a cognitive (rather than an emotional) plane. Nonetheless, expressing oneself socially and creatively is important and a legitimate function of communication. Some people pride themselves on their ability to express themselves creatively and to make connections with others.

Command/Instruct

Another common purpose of communication is to command, direct, or instruct others. Most often utilizing a one-way approach, leaders engage in this function when they dictate or instruct participants or subordinates to do something—stop an activity, pick up equipment, attend a meeting, or follow rules. Often this type of communication is used when safety is an issue or time is short.

Conflict Resolution

Resolving problems positively and creatively is critical to task accomplishment, effective group growth, and personal

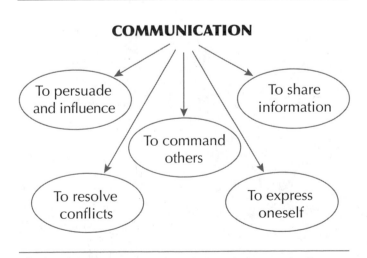

Figure 5.2 There are five functions of communication.

development. To be effective, conflict resolution must be desired by those involved and be a conscious goal of communication. Effective leadership requires conflict management skills; this is addressed in detail in Chapter 7.

Communication effectiveness varies in each interaction. As people, messages, channels, and noise change, the effectiveness of communication may be affected. The next section addresses identifiable factors that influence the communication process.

Effective Communication

Many factors influence the communication process; they may be elements internal to those communicating or external to the communication process. *Internal factors* that influence the communication process include the need for shared meanings between the sender and receiver, sender and receiver biases and prejudices which might impact the communication process, individual readiness, and the individual communication skills of those involved. *External factors* that might influence the effectiveness of communication include the physical environment, timing issues, and noise. The physical environment (e.g., room temperature, arrangement of furniture) can also have an impact on participant readiness to receive communication messages.

Other factors that influence communication effectiveness are the varying emphases placed on either task accomplishment or morale within a group. If a group is very focused on task completion, for instance, communication related to emotions, affect, and group feelings would not only be unwelcome, but perhaps, distracting. In addition to group focus, personal factors such as credibility and trustworthiness, impact the communication process.

Both senders and receivers must be credible and trustworthy for effective communication to occur (Joseph & Winston, 2005; Limon & La France, 2005). Credibility is addressed through issues such as task competence, communication, character, composure under stress, sociability, likableness, and extroversion (Brocato, 2003). Using appropriate grammar, considering the emotional impact of what is said, being aware of possible ambiguity, and understanding the needs of the sender and receiver contribute to one's perceived competence (Nelson & Quick, 2005).

Both senders and receivers must be credible and trustworthy for effective communication to occur.

Using appropriate grammar, considering the emotional impact of what is said, being aware of possible ambiguity, and understanding the needs of the sender and receiver contribute to one's perceived competence.

Effective communication requires an understanding of professionalism and a sound knowledge of written, oral, and nonverbal skills. A sense of professionalism is communicated in the way one dresses, wears one's hair, and carries oneself. For example, participant confidence in leaders tends to be greater when leaders are dressed in uniforms (sometimes as simple as a polo shirt and matching shorts), or neatly pressed clothes (e.g., a nice shirt, tucked into neat slacks) than in a leader who wears cutoff jeans and a T-shirt that reads, "Who me?"

In addition to exuding professionalism, leisure services leaders convey messages through basic communication skills, which must be developed and continually improved upon throughout one's lifetime. Leisure services professionals tend to stress oral presentation skills (e.g., leading songs or games, giving instructions, speaking on the telephone) and place less emphasis on other forms of communication. In addition to being accomplished speakers and presenters, however, leisure services leaders must also be skilled in listening skills and in written communication. Reports, inventories, memos, promotional materials, policy manuals, websites, and schedule books are just a few of the areas in which a solid command of the written language is necessary.

Increasing Communication Effectiveness

Effective communication occurs when the message is received as intended and the exchange is accomplished efficiently. As can be seen from the model of communication presented earlier, there are many places where effectiveness might be strengthened or compromised. To increase the quality of the communication process, leaders will want to subscribe to the following principles.

Speak and Write at the Audience Level

Children require different communication patterns than do adults, and teens require an approach different from

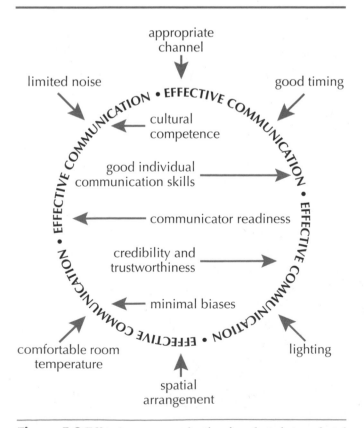

Figure 5.3 Effective communication involves internal and external influences.

Participant confidence increases when a leader communicates professionalism.

children. Leaders should be well aware of cultural differences, and attempts should be made to reach the audience at its level of readiness, not where the leader thinks the group should be. For example, when communicating with adults for whom English is a second language, the choice of words and word arrangements should be carefully considered to maximaize understanding.

Communicate to Share Ideas

Many young leaders get caught up in communicating to "puff" themselves up and to make an impression on those around them. This type of impression management can interfere with effective communication because it is egocentric rather than being other-oriented. The message is not content-focused, but rather self-focused. Being conscious of the function, reason for communication, and the intended audience will aid in maintaining clarity of purpose.

Consider Both Fact and Feeling Aspects of Communication

Too often people choose words or deliver information in a way that offends, shocks, or hurts the receiver. All communication has an emotional component to it, and matching one's words and message to the audience lends itself to effective communication. Leaders should also bear in mind that potential audiences often extend beyond those who are immediately present. What is communicated in one situation "gets around" in short order.

Consider Intent vs. Interpretation

There can be a big difference between intent and interpretation of what is being communicated. Simply because a sender meant to send a particular message does not mean that was the message received. What becomes important, then, is the message as interpreted and perceived by the receiver. This is particularly true when working with young children who are still in the stage of literal understanding. Using a figure of speech would be ineffective in communicating an intended message because youngsters interpret messages literally.

Good communicators choose what to say from a variety of options. They understand the other person's point of view, monitor their own behaviors to better understand how others perceive them, and choose the most appropriate way to converse. Furthermore, leaders understand the cultural context in which communication occurs (Gudykunst, 2004; Neuliep, 2006). In addition to these traits of good communicators, Johnson and Johnson (1991)

Good communicators choose what to say from a variety of options. They understand the other person's point of view, monitor their own behaviors to better understand how others perceive them, and choose the most appropriate way to converse.

presented the six Cs of effective communication. Leaders should note that as with all communication efforts, these style issues are culturally based:

- *Clear:* Language and messages should be unambiguous.
- *Concise:* Being succinct and concise minimizes misinterpretation.
- *Correct:* Effective communication is accurate communication.
- *Complete:* The communication cycle should be complete for a message to be fully understood.
- *Courteous:* Being courteous and considerate of receivers and their needs enhances communication.
- *Convincing:* To be effective, communication should be convincing in its logic and reasoning.

In any culture, effective communicators are very aware that words have tremendous power. People take to heart very much the words and tone that leaders use. The use of "I," for instance, sets the stage to share personal opinions and feelings; "you" can project blame or pride; "we" sets the stage for inclusion. "But" is a negating word that sinks the heart of listeners as in, "You did well, but…" (but negates everything that came before it); while "and" often serves the same purpose yet is not judgmental. "Yes," is a very positive can-do word; "no," a word that should

Figure 5.4 The Six Cs of Communication

be used sparingly; "should" and "ought" are two words that infer a heavy responsibility (What happens if one does not do…?) Leaders have tremendous power and influence over their constituents through various ways of communicating.

No matter how much one knows about and practices effective communication, misinterpretations and miscommunications are bound to occur, because so much of the communication cycle is out of the control of any one person. Knowledge of miscommunication can aid in avoiding common pitfalls. Preparing for miscommunication can minimize its negative effects.

Miscommunication

To minimize miscommunication people must first come to understand five basic principles of communication relationships: (a) we can never know the state of mind of others, (b) we depend on ambiguous symbols to explain others' attitudes, (c) we use our own (often defective) coding system to decipher signals, (d) we may be biased in interpreting others' behaviors, and (e) we are not as accurate as we think in interpreting others' messages (Gudykunst, 2004). Keeping in mind these principles, it is easy to see how miscommunication might occur. In fact, we might wonder how we ever manage to communicate well!

A breakdown in the communication process can occur in several ways:

- The sender may improperly encode the message.
- The message may be ambiguous or culturally erroneous.
- The channel may not be the best choice for the message.
- The noise may be too intrusive.
- The receiver may misinterpret the message.
- The feedback may be inadequate.

The result of miscommunication, of course, is that the intended message is not the message received. This results in actions on the part of the receiver that do not coincide with the intent of the sender. Frustration, anger, inefficiency, and lack of task completion result from such communication miscues.

To improve communication one must practice. This is true for oral, written, and nonverbal language. In addition, being open to learning and feedback is critical for improvement to occur. Along with repeating an important message three times (Research shows that people remember something after hearing or seeing it three times — That's right, memory is increased if a person is exposed to a concept three times), using demonstration and practice

To improve communication one must practice. This is true for oral, written, and nonverbal language.

by receivers are desirable to overcome potential barriers to communication.

Barriers to Communication

Communication is incredibly complex and while we engage in it constantly, most people do not communicate well (Beavin & Chovil, 2000). The good news is that communication skills are learned—poor communication habits can be minimized and good communication skills can be enhanced. In spite of this, barriers to communication exist in many places. In fact, people often interject barriers into the communication process without realizing it.

Whether one is a sender or receiver, "people issues" may arise which act as barriers to communication. The sender might put up barriers through engaging in one or more of the following behaviors:

Photo courtesy of Paula Dohoney

One barrier to communication is shutting down before receiving all the feedback.

- having a lack of credibility
- prejudging the receiver
- avoiding the real and immediate concerns of the receiver
- experiencing disorganized thoughts
- experiencing strong emotions
- trying to share too much information at one time
- using inappropriate language or nonverbal signs
- mismatching communication style with receiver

Receivers also put up barriers to effective communication. Receiver barriers include:

- a lack of trust in the sender
- prejudgment of the sender
- poor listening skills
- defensiveness
- strong emotions
- incorrect assumptions
- different connotations and intonations
- mismatched communication styles with sender

Group problems also contribute to communication problems:

- lack of cohesiveness
- lack of openness to different and opposing views
- lack of willingness to talk
- unacknowledged cultural differences
- biases inherent within the group
- ineffective leadership

Verbal Language

Communication occurs through verbal, nonverbal and paraverbal language. In fact, while we tend to examine these elements separately, they really cannot be studied in isolation from one another. People form opinions of us based on our verbal skills—our use of the language, our ability to articulate, and the clarity of our message. This is true whether engaging in one-on-one communication, giving a presentation, or being overheard in a casual conversation by passersby. Limon and La France (2005) found that leadership was attributed to the more verbal (to a point) individuals in a group. Further, we know that frequent (at least one to three times per week) communication is necessary for effective team functioning (Kratzer, Leenders & van Engelen, 2005). Therefore, leaders will

People form opinions of us based on our verbal skills—our use of the language, our ability to articulate, and the clarity of our message.

want to learn and practice good verbal communication skills as much as possible.

Language is imprecise. Words have both a denotation (i.e., dictionary definition), and a connotation (i.e., personal or cultural meaning). To improve the use of language, communicators should strive to expand their vocabulary, use straightforward language, choose action words, illustrate abstract ideas, and use compare and contrast techniques to aid in comprehension (Pell, 1999; Ting-Toomey, 1999).

Verbal communication involves many specific skills. Internalizing these skills into one's communication patterns and seeking feedback about use of these skills will improve one's ability to communicate with a variety of people. Effective communicators:

- Know how to say the right thing at the right time.
- Know the necessity of sometimes remaining silent.
- Work on improving verbal skills (e.g., increase vocabulary, reading, exposure to other cultures).
- Know how to protect information when necessary.

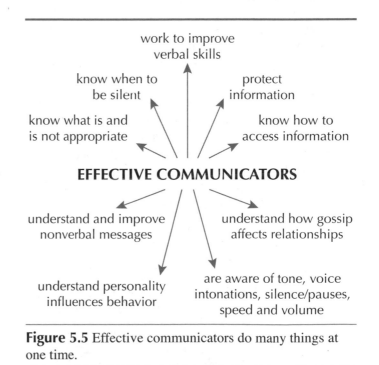

Figure 5.5 Effective communicators do many things at one time.

- Know what information is and is not appropriate for each unique situation.
- Understand that personality influences behaviors.
- Understand gossip and how it affects relationships.
- Know how to access information.
- Know the importance of nonverbal messages and how to improve them.

In addition to these skills effective communicators are aware of how tone of voice, intonations, use of silence/pauses, speed, and volume affect verbal communication. For instance, lowering the pitch of one's voice and "clipping" one's words may convey an attitude of authority; asking a question such as, "Would you please help get set up?" conveys a different message than a flat command, "Please help with the setup."

Effective communicators are very cognizant of the impact of their language on others. Leaders must always bear in mind that using sexist, racist or other demeaning language will affect how and what is being conveyed. Noninclusive language will send messages about the sender, the agency she or he represents, and how receivers are perceived. Care should be taken to respect all individuals in communication efforts.

Listening

In order for verbal language to have any influence, someone must be listening. As most people have learned over time, to truly listen requires work—it does not simply happen. Listening takes up more waking hours than any other activity, yet 75% of oral communication is not listened to (Worchel & Simpson, 1993). This is an amazing statistic! Listening does take effort, and it is a reciprocal and active process. This means that someone has to be listening in order for communication to have an effect. Everyone can learn to be a good listener. To be most effective, leisure services leaders should work to develop their listening skills. To fully utilize the communication process no aspect of it can be passive—every step requires active, conscious effort on the part of those involved. Nelson and Quick (2005) summarize several types of active listening:

Everyone can learn to be a good listener. To be most effective, leisure services leaders should work to develop their listening skills.

Empathic listening: This form of active listening involves relationships and sharing feelings. Empathic listening is an intimate process and involves understanding and reflecting feelings, needs, and intentions of others. It requires that we understand others' points of view, and their feelings. For instance, when listening to an irate customer an empathic listener might say (in a calm, well-modulated voice), "I see you feel strongly about this."

Comprehensive listening: Listening to understand the material presented—listening for facts, ideas and themes the speaker is trying to share—is the goal of comprehensive listening. Students commonly use this form of listening when learning in classes. It involves a "holistic" style of listening where the message and its context are considered.

Critical listening: This involves listening to evaluate ideas as they are expressed. Generally, it is used when trying to make judgments about the persuasive messages of others. For example, when engaged in the fact-finding period in the problem-solving process, leaders will use critical listening skills to ascertain pieces of truth from those involved in the conflict.

Appreciative listening: Appreciative listeners engage in listening for pleasure. Appreciative listening stimulates the mind and senses through listening to others. Leaders often use this when listening to elderly participants reflecting on their lives, and participants use it as they listen to music or the sounds of nature.

❖ ❖ ❖

To understand intended messages of any kind, one needs to *want* to listen. This desire and commitment to listen

Photo courtesy of Vicki Proctor

There are several types of active listening. These women are engaged in comprehensive listening.

enables the receiver to pay attention to the context as well as identify and interpret the feelings of the speaker. Receivers can improve listening skills by practicing the three primary skill clusters of listening: attending, following, and reflecting.

Attending Skills

Attending is the process of deciding which sounds one should focus on and try to discern. It describes how listeners pay attention to what is being said and how the message is being conveyed. To best attend to a speaker, listeners often model an attending posture. In an attending position, the listener faces the speaker **S**quarely, has an **O**pen posture (no arms and legs crossed), **L**eans toward the speaker, maintains **E**ye contact, and appears **R**elaxed. Many professionals in the therapeutic recreation field refer to this as the SOLER technique. At times, the listener's body may mirror the posture of the speaker. When listening to children, the leader may wish to "hunker down" to get on their level; with teens, the leader may do the "teen lean" (i.e., leaning back on a piece of furniture or tree to indicate nonverbally that one intends to stick around; Brandwein, 1999) to show their interest and commitment to listening. Attending nonverbally indicates that a listener is staying put, paying attention, and focused on the speaker.

Following Skills

Once a listener indicates attentiveness toward the speaker, following skills become important. Exhibiting nonverbal door-openers (e.g., eyebrows raised, an inviting look on face), making interpretive statements for clarification and acknowledgment (e.g., "I see" and "You mean…?"), using verbal prompts to continue talking (e.g., "tell me more," "describe that for me"), and attentive silences are all examples of these skills. Being attentive and following what is being said indicate active listening.

Reflecting Skills

The third cluster of active listening skills consists of reflecting skills. Used to ensure understanding, reflecting skills include paraphrasing, reflecting meanings and feelings back to the speaker, and summarizing what has been said. Reflecting skills provide an opportunity for the speaker to restate issues if needed, and to ensure that the listener truly comprehends the message. When restating, listeners should be careful to avoid inappropriate responses. Inappropriate responses include those that are irrelevant (i.e., ignores the speaker and message), tangential (i.e.,

some acknowledgment of the speaker, then the subject is changed), incongruent (i.e., the response is in opposition to the statement), and interruptive (i.e., breaking in before another finishes; Verderber & Verderber, 1992).

As with verbal language, effective listening requires much practice. It can be difficult to learn at first because many of us have picked up poor listening habits. Problems with listening may originate with the receiver, the sender, or any part of the communication cycle.

Factors Influencing the Ability to Listen Effectively

Listener problems include not listening (or poor listening skills), a lack of motivation to listen, and an inability to make sense of the message. Speaker difficulties include speaking too quickly or too slowly, being unclear, and choosing an inappropriate time or place for communication. In addition, the message may be poorly structured, have too much or too little detail, or be based on incorrect assumptions (especially if there are cultural differences). Furthermore, a noisy or uncomfortable environment negatively affects listening.

Listening, speaking, and sending messages occur among and between all types of people. Due to the diverse nature of society, effective leaders understand that communicating with others may not be as simple as we would like. We have a tendency to assume others are like ourselves in values, thoughts, and attitudes. These assumptions are not always accurate, however, and can lead to ineffective communication. Effective communicators strive to identify their own assumptions about others and

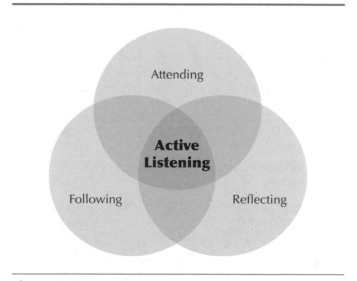

Figure 5.6 Attending, following, and reflecting skills are all components of active listening.

to learn more about the values, beliefs, and attitudes of those different from themselves.

Intercultural Communication

Culture affects communication and communication affects culture. Intercultural communication occurs any time the communication process is initiated by an individual who holds one set of cultural beliefs and is received by an individual who holds a different set of cultural beliefs. For purposes of this text *culture* is defined as an identifiable group of people who share customs, language, patterns of speech, norms, meanings, religion, relationships, or values. Intercultural communication occurs between

Intercultural communication occurs any time the communication process is initiated by an individual who holds one set of cultural beliefs and is received by an individual who holds a different set of cultural beliefs.

teenagers and older adults, women and men, and people of various racial and ethnic backgrounds.

Language can be used to impress, influence, and exert power over people. Power in speaking comes from the receiver's perceptions and stereotypes about the status, prestige and competence of the person communicating. Listeners perceive speaker status based on factors such as speed, intonations, word choices, or accent. For instance, low-power speakers tend to use tag questions, qualifiers, and a questioning tone of voice when speaking. Tag questions such as "...don't you think?" or "...if you agree?" are tacked on the end of a sentence. Rate of speech is related to perceived speaker competence; those who speak quickly are perceived as more competent than slow talkers. In addition to speech rate, voice intonations and intensity also relate to speaker power; those in high power are perceived as being intense communicators—they make assertions, are firm, and have a conviction to their communication (Preston, 2005b).

Generalizations can be very helpful in that they help us order and make sense of the world; however, inappropriate use of generalizations can result in unfair and inaccurate stereotypes. Thus, all of us should be concerned with making generalizations about people because these global statements often become accepted as truth. To be the best communicators possible, leisure services leaders should understand how various groups tend to communicate while avoiding the trap of believing that *all* members of a group communicate

Table 5A Effective and ineffective feedback behaviors

Effective Feedback	Ineffective Feedback
• Describes the behavior which led to the feedback	• Uses evaluative, judgmental, or generalized statements
• Comes as soon after the behavior as is appropriate	• Is delayed, saved up, and "dumped" in a destructive way
• Goes directly from sender to receiver	• Passes indirectly through a middle person or group
• Is "owned" by the sender (i.e., "I" statements are used.)	• Is not "owned" by the sender (e.g., "You are..."; "We think ...")
• Includes sender's feelings, when relevant, about the behavior (e.g., "I feel... when....")	• Conceals, denies, and/or distorts personal reactions and feelings
• Is checked for clarity to ensure that the receiver understands what is being conveyed	• Is not checked out with the receiver to ensure the receiver understands
• Asks questions of the receiver when more information is needed to provide constructive, realistic feedback	• Asks questions which are rhetorical or confrontive in nature (e.g., "Do you really think I'm going to let you get away with that?")
• Specifies consequences of the behavior (both present and future)	• Does not provide specific examples of present and future consequences
• Is solicited or to some extent desired by the receiver	• Is imposed on the receiver or at the least, not well-timed
• Refers to behaviors about which the receiver can do something	• Refers to behaviors over which the receiver has little or no control
• Reflects a sensitivity for the impact feedback can have on the receiver	• Does not reflect a sensitivity for how difficult feedback can sometimes be for the receiver to hear

Adapted from Project Adventure, Inc. (1994). *Executive Reach Train the Trainer Workshop materials*. Covington, GA: Author.

that way. Our perceptions about language and communication differ from others' because learning contexts differ; the cultures in which people are raised vary tremendously (Gudykunst, 2004).

As we examine intercultural communication, it becomes evident that the greater the cultural and linguistic knowledge, and the more one's beliefs overlap with others (i.e., the more we have in common), the more effective the communication will be.

Ethnic Variations in Verbal Communication

Ethnocentrism is the belief that one's own culture is correct and proper while other cultures are incorrect and improper. Unfortunately, many people adhere to this position, oftentimes unconsciously. Ethnocentrism results in stereotypes, overgeneralizations, and inaccurate judgments about various groups. It also can interfere with effective communication.

Cross-cultural confusion in communication goals or in interpreting the main point of a conversation may occur. This is because cultures differ in how precise and candid they are in verbal communication (Neuliep, 2006). For instance, people who live in collectivist cultures commonly use an indirect style of communication, while individualists tend to be explicit and straightforward in their communication. As an example, in Asian cultures one typically begins a conversation with background material and then moves on to the main point. The main point is often subtle and somewhat hidden in the discourse.

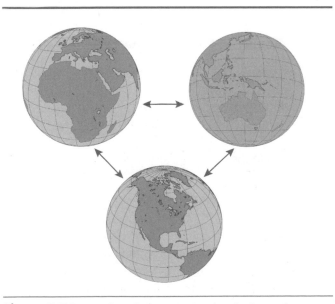

Figure 5.7 Intercultural communication is dependent upon our cultural worldviews.

Language is ambiguous by nature, and people draw inferences about meaning based on their worldview.

This helps to maintain harmony in the relationship. In the dominant U.S. culture, the point is made first and the explanation follows; the discourse is straightforward. Depending upon one's cultural background, expectations and perceptions might lead one to believe that Westerners are frank and rude and that Asians are difficult to understand (Gudykunst, 2004; Neuliep, 2006).

Language is ambiguous by nature, and people draw inferences about meaning based on their worldview. They draw inferences from the language, tone, nonverbal language, and other communication cues used. Therefore, depending upon the culture in which one was raised, one might arrive at the conclusion that a speaker is highly intelligent, manipulative, confident, or concerned only about the task at hand.

Neuliep (2006) indicates that three styles or approaches to communication exist: (a) an elaborate style that emphasizes flashy and embellished language; (b) an exacting style where the speaker uses only the words needed to get the message across; and (c) a succinct style where silence or very short verbalizations are commonly used. Many Arab, Middle Eastern, and African-American cultures use the elaborate style of communication. Most Euro Americans prefer the exacting style of communication, and many Asian and American Indian cultures use a succinct style of communication.

Furthermore, how one uses language expresses degrees of familiarity (e.g., "Yo!"), politeness (e.g., "Yes, ma'am"), and shared knowledge/worldview (e.g., "My bad"—a term meaning "sorry, that was my fault"). Intonation changes the meanings associated with those words, as does timing. For example, the way one asks the question, "Did you do that?" changes based on whether or not the one asking is pleased, angry, perturbed, or mildly amused that you "did that." Thus, different interpretations arise out of not knowing or understanding other's communication styles—meanings of words, intonation, nonverbal language, and so on.

Other ways that language across ethnic groups affects communication is in the use of family or street language. In the study of African-American dialects (termed *African American vernacular English [AAVE], ebonics,* or *Black English*), for instance, it has been learned that certain aspects of the language differ from standard English. Consider the following examples of Black English:

- The word "be" is used in place of am, is, or are.
- The "sk" sound is often reversed as in "I aksed you a question."
- The use of double negatives is common; "Nobody knows nothing."
- The "l" sound is dropped in words like "help," and the "r" sound is dropped in words like "door."
- The last consonant cluster is often dropped. (Neuliep, 2006)

These differences become understandable when one knows that African-American vernacular English has its roots in the days of enslavement when Africans were forcibly taken from their tribes and prohibited from speaking any language. Some standard English sounds (e.g., "th") were not a part of the tribal languages, and as those who were enslaved began to communicate, they had to develop their own usable language. Sounds and intonations became distinct from the now "standard" (i.e., white, middle class) English. For recreation and leisure services leaders, understanding Black English (and other ethnic forms of standard English) is important to more effectively communicate with staff, participants, and the general public.

It is important for leaders to note that not all styles and forms of communication are perceived equally. For instance, Gudykunst (2004) reports that those who speak with a standard dialect (e.g., national television newscasters) are more likely to receive help on the phone than those who speak with an ethnic dialect. People who speak with this standard dialect are perceived as more competent, intelligent, industrious, and confident than those who speak in an alternative dialect.

Racism in Verbal Communication

Language perceived as racist, sexist, or exclusive in some other fashion may alienate or irritate listeners so that they are no longer able to discern the intended content of the message. We should be aware that covert and subtle racism can exist in all forms of communication. An underlying message being sent by a speaker using racist language is one of exclusion and disregard for listeners. Therefore, leaders will want to be cognizant of such exclusionary language. While racism can be observed throughout the communication process it is most obvious in one's choice of words. Being aware of the meanings of words across cultures is necessary to eliminate this problem. For example, identifying all people of Hispanic heritage as Mexican does not

Language perceived as racist, sexist, or exclusive in some other fashion may alienate or irritate listeners so that they are no longer able to discern the intended content of the message.

acknowledge that some have origins in Latin countries, others in the South Atlantic, and still others in Spain. This misidentification negates distinct cultural groups.

In other racist communication one might hear blatantly racist words in arguments or fights (e.g., calling each other names based on ethnic group affiliation). In addition, it is important to recognize and put a stop to more subtle uses of racist language as in the phrases, "yellow coward," "Indian-giver," or to "Jew someone down." These phrases all have historically racist roots and continue to be a negative use of language. Not knowing what a phrase means or where it came from does not absolve one of the hurt listeners might feel with its use.

Other subtle forms of racism in communication occur when a person is defined by her or his ethnic heritage when it has no relevance. This is common in news reports where individuals are identified as Black or Asian in crime stories, but White perpetrators are not identified as being Caucasian. In leisure leadership this could be a issue when describing individual behaviors to others: "The Black boy shoved Tommy." "Wow! Look at the fine crafts project that Kim did! She's Hmong, you know." Leisure services

---

Examples of Racist and Biased Language

- The presentation of reconstructed history where Whites "discovered" America.
- The omission of any mention of people of color and their impact on the parks and recreation profession (and other contributions to society).
- Referencing the skin color or ethnicity of only those who are not White in stories or articles.

Derogatory connotations in common words or phrases:

Blacklist	Black market
White lie	Blackmail
White knight	Indian giver
To Jew down	Yellow bellied
Sitting Indian style	Yellow coward

Figure 5.8 Racism and bias in language comes in many forms.

leaders would be wise to examine their own cultural biases and prejudices, and to listen to themselves and others when speaking to avoid "innocent" (but hurtful) remarks.

Gender Variations in Verbal Communication

In examining communication between women and men, many believe that the differences result from varying socialization patterns and/or power imbalances between the sexes. Others view the differences as due to socialization. Researchers have reported that women tend to use more empathic styles of communication than men (Appelbaum, Audet & Miller, 2003; Groves, 2005; Koch, 2004).

Extensive studies of female and male communication patterns reported that females tend to use language to build and maintain relationships while males tend to use language to establish and maintain personal power (Appelbaum, Audet & Miller, 2003; Vinnicombe & Singh, 2002). Women use language to focus on the connections between people. They tend to smooth hurt feelings, be concerned about group morale, and address issues of people liking one another. Men, on the other hand, use language to establish positions of power, status, and prestige among others involved in the communication process. Tannen (1990) identified nine dimensions of communication on which women and men differ:

Intimacy-Independence: Women desire intimacy in communication while men strive for independence.

Connection-Status: Women are involved in connecting with others while men are engaged in communication to enhance their status.

Inclusion-Exclusion: Women have a tendency to be inclusive and men exclusive in group-task accomplishment.

Relationship-Information: Women are relationship-oriented while men are information-oriented.

Rapport-Report: Women are concerned with developing rapport with others while men have a tendency to focus on outcomes.

Community-Contest: Women's communication conveys sense of community and cooperation while competition and contest are more evident in men's language.

Problems-Solutions: Women often present situations as problems to be worked through together while men are drawn toward devising quick solutions to those problems.

Novice-Expert: Women often perceive and present themselves as novices while men perceive and present themselves as experts.

Listening-Lecturing: When communicating, women are more apt to listen and men are more apt to lecture.

Some would argue that these distinctions also exist in relationships between low-power and high-power people (e.g., worker-supervisor relationship; child-parent relationship). Speech patterns of people in low-power situations (e.g., women, children) include a greater use of the following types of statements than for high-power individuals (e.g., men, supervisors):

- use of word qualifiers such as "kind of," "I guess," and "maybe"
- tag questions placed at the end of assertions as in, "… don't you agree?"
- compound requests such as adding "… if you would like" to one's thought

Women tend to	Men tend to
• Build/maintain relationships	• Establish/maintain personal power
• Be more empathetic	• Be less empathetic
• Establish connections between people	• Establish positions of power
• Desire intimacy	• Strive for independence
• Connect with others	• Enhance their status
• Be inclusive	• Be exclusive
• Be relationship-oriented	• Be information-oriented
• Establish rapport	• Develop reports
• Convey a sense of community/cooperation	• Convey an attitude of contest/competition
• Work through problems together	• Devise quick solutions independently
• Present themselves as novices	• Present themselves as experts
• Listen	• Lecture

Figure 5.9 Women and men have different cultural filters through which they communicate.

- polite forms of language such as saying, "thank you for your time"
- disclaimers, usually stated at the beginning of a statement such as, "This might not be right, but…"
- intensifiers such as "very," "really," and "surely"
- verbal fillers which are often linked to a tentative speech pattern: "well," "okay," and "um"
- requests that might serve to discount one's ideas as in, "I'd like to hear from others on this." (Gudykunst, 2004; Tannen, 1990)

Sexism in Communication

Sexist language is used by females and males alike, often without an understanding of the impact of such language. Generally there are three types of sexism in language:

1. ignoring one gender (e.g., using a supposedly generic "he")
2. defining a gender in relation to something else (e.g., using the phrase "women and children" puts women in the same light as children; i.e., weak and in need of protection)
3. deprecating a gender (e.g., "women's work" is not desirable work).

Research has shown that using the male pronoun "he" when addressing mixed groups sets a tone of exclusivity (DeVito, 1999; Pearson, West & Turner, 1995). This is also true if leaders consistently use male-based examples as in, "the Director, he …" and, "the Firefighter and his dog…" This technique of ignoring females is a sexist use of language.

The other two ways in which sexism is identified in language are by defining a gender in relation to something else, and in deprecation of a gender (when adjectives discredit one gender as in "That's a girl's toy!" or "You throw like a girl!"). The most common way women are defined in relation to something else is seen in the phrase "women and children." This grouping subtly places women on the same level as children—vulnerable, without power, with few skills, and little to contribute. To avoid the first pitfall

leaders should be careful to use parallel terms. Examples of paralllel terms include women and men (not girls and men), girls and boys, and ladies and gentlemen (not ladies and men). Generally, in the predominant U.S. culture females and males are labeled as girls and boys as children; as they mature they are identified as either young women and young men or women and men in their mid-teen years. Just as identifying adult males as boys is inaccurate (and often a put-down), so too is referring to a woman as a girl; this is considered a sexist use of language.

Communication serves a variety of functions, one of which is to wield power over others. Language in the form of sexist or racist remarks, no matter how "innocent," denigrates members of the targeted group. Leaders can combat racism and sexism in language by doing the following:

- Examine personal verbal, written, and symbolic language for inclusiveness (e.g., both sexes, people with disabilities, people of color, and people of various ages).
- Be aware of works, images, and situations that suggest that everyone of one race, sex, or ethnic group is the same. Leaders will want to pay particular attention to promotional materials.
- Avoid qualifiers that reinforce stereotypes (e.g., "She's smart—for a woman.").
- Identify by sex, race, or ethnicity only when relevant.
- Be aware of language that has sexist, racial or ethnic overtones or connotations to some people.
- Avoid patronizing others (e.g., "cute" elderly).
- Substitute substantive information for sexist or racist clichés.
- Review all media, office, and promotional materials to be sure representation of people is broad.

Facilitation and Processing

Facilitation and processing are special communication skills used by leaders who work with groups in therapeutic settings, adventure settings, corporate settings, and a wide variety of other areas of our field. Typically, these skills are used with small groups of six to twenty people and focus on helping others to learn from their experiences, to build a sense of team, and to aid in the therapeutic process. Facilitators often work in teams of two, although many work with smaller groups individually.

The primary work of facilitation is that of helping a group of people to work together to achieve a common

Research has shown that using the male pronoun "he" when addressing mixed groups sets a tone of exclusivity.

goal. That goal might be individually based, where group members decide what they each wish to get out of the experience; group-based, where the group as a whole decides what its goals and objectives will be; or externally imposed, where a leader (e.g., manager, employer, therapist) decides upon the primary learning objectives for the experience.

Furthermore, the goals might be: conceptually focused, where the aim is to help the group gain a better understanding of the whole; interpersonal, where the group might be working on improving interpersonal skills such as conflict resolution, communication or behavior management issues; or task-focused, where the group works on task skills such as problem solving, improving productivity, or learning how to better serve customers.

Essential skills for facilitators include thorough preparation; fostering a caring attitude among group members; personal communication skills such as questioning, providing feedback, and general communication strategies; and solid conceptual, interpersonal, and task skills (Luckner & Nadler, 1997; Martin, Cashel, Wagstaff & Breunig, 2006). In addition, remaining objective and minimizing one's own biases are also highly important skills. Leaders who facilitate and process groups must only do so with activities they know are within their skill level.

Gass (1995), and Priest and Gass (1997) presented six generations of facilitation techniques; the five most commonly used by recreation leaders are addressed below. The first three techniques commonly occur after (and sometimes during) an experience or activity. The latter two techniques are used before and during an activity to aid in bringing about change.

Let the Experience Speak for Itself

In this fashion, the facilitator sets up and programs activities assuming that participant learning will take place by the mere fact that they have gone through the experience.

Essential skills for facilitators include thorough preparation; fostering a caring attitude among group members; personal communication skills such as questioning, providing feedback, and general communication strategies; and solid conceptual, interpersonal, and task skills.

After the event, a facilitator using this technique might say something like, "Nice job! That was quite the experience, wasn't it?"

Speak for the Experience

Also done after an activity has been completed, with this technique the facilitator interprets the experience for the participants. She or he might tell the participants what they've learned and how they might apply that new knowledge in their lives, or in upcoming activities. For instance, the facilitator might say, "Well done! You learned how to listen to one another during that activity; listening can help people to better understand in all sorts of situations."

Debrief the Experience

Debriefing is a very common technique and can be done during and after an experience. Here, the facilitator engages in processing—helping the group to learn through reflection. The facilitators ask questions to guide the group to an

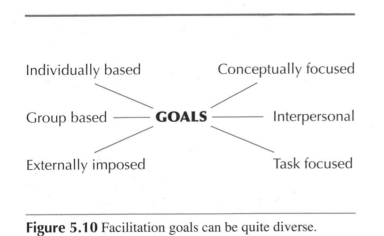

Figure 5.10 Facilitation goals can be quite diverse.

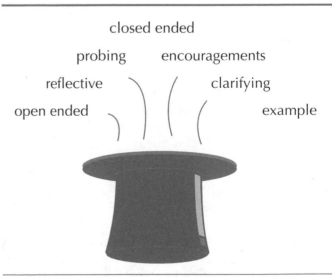

Figure 5.11 Types of questions asked during debriefings.

understanding of their experiences. Sometimes a facilitator will stop a group in the middle of an activity to debrief an important occurrence. Thus, questioning skills become very important. Facilitators can ask seven different types of questions to elicit various responses:

- *closed-ended questions* (e.g., yes/no answers)
- *open-ended questions* (i.e., require more than yes/no to be answered)
- *clarifying questions* (i.e., seek additional information to help something make sense)
- *probing questions* (i.e., dig deep to discern underlying issues)
- *encouragements* (i.e., short questions that encourage group members to add more)
- *reflective questions* (i.e., encourage group members to think back and reflect on their involvement in the experience)
- *example questions* (i.e., ask for a particular instance or example of something that occurred; Cameron, 1998)

Directly Frontload the Experience

This is essentially *prebriefing* (as opposed to debriefing) an experience. The facilitator talks to the group prior to beginning an activity and sets the stage by doing several things. The facilitator can highlight what the group "should" learn from the upcoming experience—this helps to focus the group. She or he can revisit a previous activity and help the group determine how that knowledge and

experience can be used to make the upcoming activity more successful. Restating the goals and objectives of the experience might be useful, as might focusing on the group's motivations for the activity. Lastly, a facilitator can help the group to focus on what has aided the group's success and/or what has interfered with their success and strategies that the group might use to capitalize on this information.

Frame the Experience

Framing helps a group make sense of what they are learning in terms of "real world" experiences. Prior to the beginning of an activity, the facilitator might use metaphors and analogies to help a group understand how the upcoming activity can be similar to their lives outside of this experience. For instance, the facilitator might ask the group how the upcoming activity is like their family or work life. After participants have identified similarities (e.g., processes, relationships) the activity is undertaken. Debriefing follows, with the facilitator guiding the group through their earlier comments and the discoveries of the activity.

❖ ❖ ❖

In addition to these techniques it is helpful to understand that processing and learning occurs on several different levels (Luckner & Nadler, 1997). First, the facilitator can help raise individual and group *awareness* about certain issues. Next, the facilitator can help the group to accept *responsibility* for understanding and taking action based on that awareness. Third, group members can *experiment* with this new knowledge. Finally, facilitating the *transfer* of this new information into one's life occurs.

Facilitating and processing can be helpful communication tools when used appropriately by individuals who have learned and practiced the skills in a variety of settings. Be aware, however, that leaders can easily get in over their heads by asking questions and raising issues for which a group is ill-prepared. A strong understanding of group dynamics, interpersonal and questioning skills, and strong self-awareness are necessary for effective facilitation.

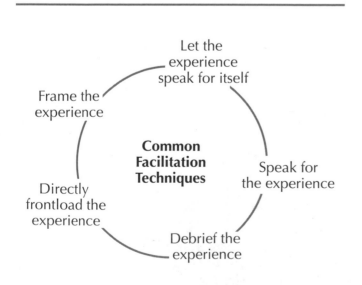

Figure 5.12 The five most common types of facilitation techniques.

Facilitating and processing can be helpful communication tools when used appropriately by individuals who have learned and practiced the skills in a variety of settings.

Summary

Communication skills are fundamental to effective leadership. The communication process includes a sender, message, channel, receiver, feedback, and noise. For effective communication to occur, there must be agreement between the sender and receiver in terms of the underlying meanings of the message. Sender and receiver roles change as positions in the communication process change.

Leaders utilize five basic functions of communication: persuasion, information sharing, social/expressive, command, and conflict resolution. Effective communication must be developed and continually practiced to improve one's skills. It entails understanding the receiver, communicating to share ideas, attending to the message one sends, and actively listening.

Miscommunication may occur at any stage of the communication process due to barriers put up by the sender, receiver, or the environment. Barriers to communication may arise due to many factors: a breakdown in the communication process, poor listening skills, lack of motivation, and inept skills. To be an effective communicator one must overcome these issues. One of the most important aspects of effective communication is listening. There are several types of listening; empathic listening, comprehensive listening, critical listening, and appreciative listening. Each requires the listener to attend to the sender, use following skills, and reflect the communication back to the sender.

In addition to these elements, effective communicators understand issues related to intercultural communication, which occurs any time the process begins in one set of cultural expectations and must be interpreted in another. Ethnicity and gender (as well as other elements of diversity) influence the communication process. Word usage, voice quality, and other variations in language may exist between individuals of different cultures. Effective leaders take into consideration their own skills, levels of awareness, and the audience when engaging in the communication process.

As a special form of communication, facilitation and processing can be highly effective in helping individuals and groups to learn from a wide variety of experiences. There are five commonly used facilitation techniques and four general levels of processing in which a good facilitator engages. An effective facilitator knows herself or himself, understands group dynamics, and possesses strong interpersonal skills.

Beginning the Journey

While the journey to leadership development is indeed a personal one, it occurs in the context of others. As such, communication and facilitation skills become very important tools for successful leaders. Use the questions below to help you reflect on your communication skills and consider how they influence the journey on which you are traveling.

1. Explain what is meant by the concept that "we can never not communicate" in the simplest terms possible. How do we communicate? Take an inventory of yourself right now—what are you (and your body) communicating? What messages are you sending to someone who might see or hear you?

2. What is communication? What is meant when it is said that communication is "multi-channeled?" Give an example of what this means. Look around the room you are currently in and choose several props (e.g., a book, pencil, piece of string). Now take those props and use them to make a three-dimensional model of the communication process. Explain it out loud (either to yourself or another).

3. Identify the five general functions of communication. Practice these by choosing one topic of conversation and altering the function of your message. For example, you might decide to talk about the impacts of television on American youth. First, try to persuade another that it is positive (or negative); next alter your message so you simply share information with your audience about television and American youth; now try to alter your communication to express yourself and tell a classmate something about who you are (while talking about television and American youth); next, change your communication to instruct or command another about the topic; finally, engage in a conflict with another about the impacts of television on American youth and work to resolve that conflict.

4. Revisit the material about factors that influence communication. First, imagine that you have the resources and authority to do what is needed. Next, be very specific and tell a classmate what you would do in terms of making your communication the most effective it can be (limit negative factors and enhance positive factors). How can you exude professionalism through your communication? Be very specific in your response.

5. Take a personal inventory of your own communication skills—consider your verbal, written, and

nonverbal skills. Now ask a person you trust (e.g., partner, parent, best friend) to do the same for you. If there is disagreement in the assessment of your communication skills, talk it out. Then make a plan for how you can improve your communication skills.

6. Think through the five principles of communication. Do you agree with these principles? Why or why not?

7. Describe the various ways that miscommunication can occur. Which barriers to communication do you find yourself exhibiting? What can you do to minimize these barriers?

8. Think about your verbal communication skills. On a scale of 1 to 5 where 5 is excellent and 1 is poor, how would you rate yourself? In what areas of verbal communication do you need to improve? What types of street words or language do you commonly use? Do you have a tendency to use verbal fillers (e.g., um, uh) when you speak? Do you have an accent that might be distracting to listeners? How quickly do you speak? Do you articulate well so that you are easily understood?

9. Describe the various forms of listening. Which do you tend to engage in most? Which is most difficult for you? Why is that? What bad listening habits do you have? When do you listen best (describe the circumstances)? What do you look like (e.g., think of your posture, your facial expressions, your gestures) when you are attending? following? reflecting?

10. How are culture and communication intertwined? How can you maximize intercultural communication? When is this important to do? Explain. When is racism found in verbal communication? How can you minimize this from happening? Why is this particularly important for leaders in parks, recreation, and leisure services? Share your thoughts about gender variations in language. Do you agree with Tannen? Why or why not? How can sexism be minimized in language? Why is this important for leaders?

11. Explain the special nature of facilitation and processing. When are they used? What makes them different from "regular" communication? What are the essential skills for facilitators? How are your skills in these areas? Describe each of the types of facilitation. Which do you think are more effective in what types of circumstances? What are the different levels of processing and learning? Draw a diagram of how this works.

References

Appelbaum, S., Audet, L., and Miller, J. (2003). Gender and leadership? Leadership and gender? A journey through the landscape of theories. *Leadership & Organization Development Journal, 24*(1/2), 43–51.

Beavin, J. and Chovil, N. (2000). Visible acts of meaning: An integrated message model of language in face-to-face dialogue. *Journal of Language and Social Psychology, 19*(2), 163–194.

Brandwein, M. (1999). *Communicating with youth.* Presentation at the Southwest YMCA Camping Conference, January 11, 1999. Davis, OK.

Brocato, R. (2003). Coaching for improvement: An essential role for team leaders and managers. *The Journal for Quality and Participation, 26*(1), 17–23.

Cameron, E. (1998). *Facilitation made easy.* London, UK: Kogan Page.

DeVito, J. (1999). *Essentials of human communication* (3rd ed.). New York, NY: Longman.

Gass, M. (1995). *Book of metaphors: Volume II.* Dubuque, IA: Kendall Hunt.

Groves, K. (2005). Gender differences in social and emotional skills and charismatic leadership. *Leadership & Organization Development Journal, 11*(3), 30–46.

Gudykunst, W. (2004). Bridging differences: *Effective intergroup communication* (4th ed.). Thousand Oaks, CA: Sage Publications.

Johnson, D. and Johnson, F. (1991). *Joining together: Group theory and group skills* (4th ed.). Englewood Cliffs, NJ: Prentice Hall.

Joseph, E. and Winston, B. (2005). A correlation of servant leadership, leader trust, and organizational trust. *Leadership & Organization Development Journal, 26*(1/2), 6–22.

Koch, S. (2004). Constructing gender: A lens-model inspired gender communication approach. *Sex Roles, 51*(3/4), 171–186.

Kratzer, J., Leenders, R., and van Engelen, J. (2005). How team communication affects innovation. *MIT Sloan Management Review, 40*(4), 7.

Limon, M. and La France, B. (2005). Communication traits and leadership emergence. *Southern Communication Journal, 70*(2), 123–133.

Luckner, J. and Nadler, R. (1997). *Processing the experience: Strategies to enhance and generalize learning* (2nd ed.). Dubuque, IA: Kendall Hunt.

Martin, B., Cashel, C., Wagstaff, M., and Breunig, M. (2006). *Outdoor leadership: Theory and practice.* Champaign, IL: Human Kinetics.

Nelson, D. and Quick, J. (2005). *Understanding organizational behavior* (2nd ed.). Mason, OH: South-Western.

Neuliep, J. (2006). *Intercultural communication* (3rd ed.). Thousand Oaks, CA: Sage Publications.

Payne, H. (2005). Reconceptualizing social skills in organizations: Exploring the relationship between communication competence, job performance, and supervisory roles. *Journal of Leadership & Organizational Studies, 11*(2), 63–77.

Pell, A. (1999). *The complete idiot's guide to team building.* Indianapolis, IN: Alpha Books.

Preston, P. (2005a). Persuasion: What to say, how to be. *Journal of Healthcare Management, 50*(5), 294–296.

Preston, P. (2005b). The power image: Strategies for acting and being powerful. *Journal of Healthcare Management, 50*(4), 222–225.

Priest, S. and Gass, M. (1997). *Effective leadership in adventure programming.* Champaign, IL: Human Kinetics.

Tannen, D. (1990). *You just don't understand: Women and men in conversation.* New York, NY: William Morrow & Co.

Ting-Toomey, S. (1999). *Communicating across cultures.* New York, NY: The Guilford Press.

Verderber, R. and Verderber, K. (1992). *Inter-Act: Using interpersonal communication skills* (6th ed.). Belmont, CA: Wadsworth Publishing Company.

Vinnicombe, S. and Singh, V. (2002). Sex role stereotyping and requisites of successful top managers. *Women in Management Review, 17*(3/4), 120–129.

Worchel, S. and Simpson, J. (Eds.). (1993). *Conflict between people and groups.* Chicago, IL: Nelson-Hall Publishers.

York, S., Jordan, D., and Safford, S. (1995). *Leadership series facilitator's guide.* Unpublished manuscript.

Leader Profile

Arthur K.C. Wong
Recreation Specialist, Department of Parks and Recreation • Oahu, HI

Arthur has had 25 years in this position, and 33 years in the parks, recreation, and leisure services profession

Volunteer leadership positions he has held include:

- President, Hawaii Recreation and Park Association (HRPA)
- State Conference Chair, HRPA
- Pacific Southwest Regional Council member
- Board of Trustees, National Recreation and Park Association (NRPA)
- Chair, Diversity Committee, NRPA
- Chair, Board of Managers, Windward YMCA in Kailua, HI

What is the meaning of leadership?
Leadership is the ability to guide or influence people. A leader may not always be in the forefront of every situation, but he or she is usually someone with whom people have trust. His or her word is as good as gold.

What are the most important leader qualities?
A leader must be honest, trustworthy, and dependable. He or she also must have a vision and be able to translate this vision to his or her staff in a way that is meaningful to all.

What advice do you have for students who aspire to leadership in parks, recreation, and leisure services?
First, in whatever position you are in, aspire to do your best. Second, have a vision of how to improve yourself as well as your section, division, or department. Third, help others do their job well—They will respect you for that.

Favorite book(s): I read magazines—short articles, usually for leisure—travel, recreation, tennis.

Favorite activities: Tennis, travel, and karaoke.

Chapter Six
Nonverbal Communication

Learning Opportunities

Through studying this chapter readers will have the opportunity to

- Articulate the types and functions of nonverbal language
- Explain and demonstrate nonverbal skills in body language
- Describe the role of leadership in elements of nonverbal language, such as chronemics and physical appearance
- Identify the cultural, gender, and power issues inherent in nonverbal communication
- Understand the use and importance of quality writing skills in effective leadership

As mentioned in the previous chapter, communication consists of interwoven verbal and nonverbal messages sent back and forth between at least two people. The two avenues of communication are inseparable. Our nonverbal language is continuous—we can never "shut it off." Researchers have noted that verbal messages convey content and tend to impact us on a cognitive level, while nonverbal messages convey information about relationships and tend to impact us on an emotional level (Mottet, Beebe, Raffeld & Paulsel, 2004). Furthermore, we know that *nonverbal display rules* (unspoken social rules that dictate when, where, and how we nonverbally express which emotions to whom) are learned within a culture as one grows up. It has been estimated that we transmit between 60% and 75% of what is said nonverbally (Nelson & Quick, 2005). This is an amazing figure when one thinks about how much we talk!

While nonverbal language and ascribed meanings vary by culture and subculture (e.g., tapping one's temple with the forefinger means "You're crazy!" in Europe, while in the Netherlands it means, "How clever!"), it tends to be the more trusted aspect of communication. People are more apt to believe the nonverbal message than the verbal message if there are any perceived contradictions. In addition, interpreting (i.e., decoding) nonverbal language provides insight into others' states of mind, intent, and personal meanings inherent in the communication. It also helps us to understand their sense of self-identity. While commonly the more trusted form of communication, nonverbal language is also perceived as an ambiguous element of language. This may arise from the fact that interpretations of nonverbal communication differ based on gender, age, ethnicity, power relationships, and other aspects of culture.

Higher levels of self-confidence have been associated with better nonverbal encoding and decoding skills (Aguinis & Henle, 2001), while depression and a lack of self-esteem have been related to poor decoding skills (Boone & Buck, 2003). Thus, to effectively use one's knowledge of nonverbal communication, leisure services

Photo courtesy of Deb Jordan

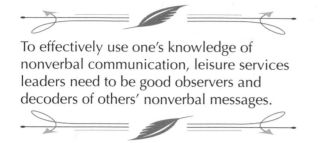

To effectively use one's knowledge of nonverbal communication, leisure services leaders need to be good observers and decoders of others' nonverbal messages.

leaders need to be good observers and decoders of others' nonverbal messages. In addition, leaders need to be effective senders of such messages (e.g., be aware of their own nonverbal messages). Remember, nonverbal language is continuous—we shout messages without even speaking a word! Being able to correctly observe and interpret another's nonverbal language will help in understanding the entire message being sent. In addition, a leader can strengthen or emphasize what is being said by being cognizant of her or his own use of nonverbal language.

In this chapter, nonverbal language will be discussed, including the use of one's body in communication, symbolic communication, and written language, an underemphasized and much needed skill of all leisure services leaders. Nonverbal communication serves several functions within communication interactions.

Functions of Nonverbal Communication

Nonverbal communication enhances the spoken word. It may assist in impression management, indicate membership, regulate communication, provide feedback, repeat or emphasize a verbal message, act as a substitute

for words, and express a variety of social relationships (Neuliep, 2006; Schyns & Mohr, 2004).

Impression Management

Impression management includes those behaviors in which a person engages to control or influence the way others perceive her or him. This includes efforts to increase one's credibility (e.g., status and prestige) as well as efforts to maintain a level of deception (e.g., telling a lie). To some extent people continually engage in efforts related to managing how others perceive them. Generally, we want people to think we are confident, competent, and likeable. For instance, every time a leisure services leader steps in front of a group of participants to lead an activity, the preparation she or he undergoes, the choice of clothing she or he wears, and the techniques and leadership styles utilized all contribute to managing her or his self-impression in front of others.

Sign of Membership

An individual may indicate membership within a certain group or club (either a formal, well-established group or an informal group) by engaging in certain nonverbal behaviors and displaying certain symbols. Young people in gangs do this (e.g., crossing one's arms in a particular manner, wearing gang-associated colors indicates membership in a particular gang) as do professionals in particular organizations (e.g., secret handshakes, wearing agency-associated clothing such as uniforms or suits). Nonverbal communication can send messages of belonging, inclusion, group pride, and cohesion.

Nonverbal language can indicate levels of readiness for participation.

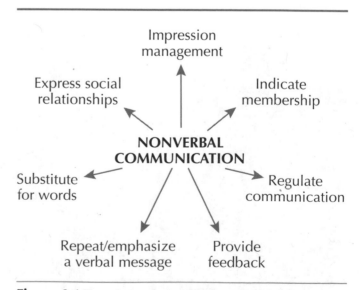

Figure 6.1 Functions of nonverbal communication

Regulate Communication

One of the more subtle yet powerful functions of nonverbal communication is to regulate the flow of conversation. Through this mechanism, people understand when to remain silent while others finish their thoughts and when to take their turn in the conversation. Without this function people would interrupt others frequently and would not know when to stop or start speaking. Regulating communicationn is most evident when engaging in casual conversation with others. One might hold up a finger to prevent another from speaking, use one's eyes to hold one's turn in the conversation, or to lightly touch the other to interrupt.

Provide Feedback

For leaders, nonverbal messages from participants are crucial to effective leadership. The feedback one receives through participant facial expressions, level of fidgeting, and other nonverbal cues helps a leader know when to change approaches, speed up, slow down, or continue to follow the path she or he has chosen. Similarly, feedback informs speakers involved in casual conversations about listener comprehension and readiness for additional information.

Repeat or Emphasize Verbal Message

All of us have had experience with repeating or emphasizing spoken words with nonverbal language. For instance, a pounding fist emphasizes the verbal message as does pointing, gesturing with one's arms, smiling, and an "open" stance. Many leaders are skilled with a certain "look" (i.e., facial expression) that communicates, "I mean business" and induces rapid compliance in listeners.

Substitute for Words

Often nonverbal language substitutes for spoken words—these are called *emblems*. Emblems include the thumbs up sign for "I agree" or "good job," the "okay" sign made with the thumb and index finger, and nodding one's head to indicate "yes." Emblem meanings are culturally based. For instance, in Greece the thumbs up sign means "to get stuffed" (with food); in France, the "okay" gesture means zero (in some cultures it is an obscene gesture); and in Bulgaria a head nod means "no" (a side-to-side shake means "yes").

Express Social Relationships

Nonverbal language helps to explain and define relationships in groups. This includes communicating power and dominance, compliance with another's wishes, sharing emotions, and social intimacy. Just by looking at how people interact we can often tell if they are casual acquaintances, close friends, or significant others. People demonstrate these relationships through proximity, touch, and eye contact and other nonverbal actions.

Power and Dominance

People use nonverbal language to influence other people using power differences. Examples of this include standing (especially with crossed arms or hands on hips) over someone who is sitting; pointing at someone in close proximity; and patting a person on the head—all of these are expressions of power. Power and dominance issues are evident in nonverbal interactions between females and males, people of varying ethnic backgrounds, and in parent-child relationships (Aguinis & Henle, 2001). At times, leaders demonstrate their power through nonverbal

Leaders use nonverbal language to help get their message across.

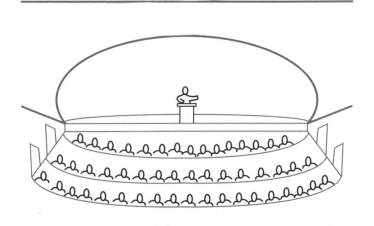

Figure 6.2 Power and dominance are made evident in a leader's use of personal space and spacial arrangements.

language to induce compliance from participants, to gain respect, or to demonstrate their credibility to their superiors.

Compliance

Compliance is generally thought of as yielding to another's request or demand. Like verbal language, nonverbal interactions are reciprocal; therefore, for efficient smooth communication, if one acts in a dominant manner the other party usually will be compliant. Nonverbal compliance may be indicated by smiling, bowing one's head, lowering one's eyes, or making a sweeping gesture with one hand as if indicating, "As you wish."

Affect Management

Affect management refers to the management or regulation of the emotional component of communication. Leaders often manage affect when tempers rise and conflict occurs. Nonverbal language can help to mediate intense surges of emotion. Smiling, sitting with an open posture (with arms and legs uncrossed), and lightly touching another on the forearm are all nonverbal behaviors that may help to diffuse strong emotions. Nonverbal communication may also be used to "hype up" participants and encourage excitement. Wide-open eyes, a big smile or grin, and large gestures such as waving the arms about can incite a group to "get rowdy."

Social Intimacy

Another subfunction of expressing social relationships is maintaining or regulating the amount and tenor of intimacy or familiarity experienced by two parties. Shaking hands sends a different message than does giving a hug; warm, friendly eye contact results in perceptibly different responses than an aggressive stare. When cultural differences are considered, nonverbal language says much about the relationship between those communicating.

❖   ❖   ❖

The need for leisure services leaders to receive and accurately decode as well as appropriately encode and send nonverbal messages was mentioned earlier. As one begins efforts to increase skills in this area, developing keen observation skills becomes important. It is interesting to note that research has shown that females tend to be better at decoding than males (Groves, 2005; Rosip & Hall, 2004). This has been generally attributed to the notion that in the predominant U.S. culture (like many others), women have less social power than men, and therefore pay closer attention to all communication cues.

People from different cultures may have difficulty with interpretation of commonly used nonverbal language in others' cultures. Research has shown, for instance, that international college students are significantly less accu-

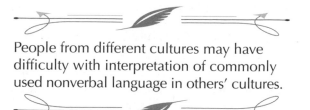

People from different cultures may have difficulty with interpretation of commonly used nonverbal language in others' cultures.

rate in reading the nonverbal body language of Euro-American and African-American students and identifying other's nonverbal cues (Bailey, Nowicki & Cole, 1998). Thus, when working with groups that include international participants, or people who have recently emigrated to the United States, leaders will want to be well-aware of their understanding of the nuances of verbal and nonverbal language.

Body Language

Research indicates that age (Schyns & Mohr, 2004), gender (Groves, 2005; Rosip & Hall, 2004), and well-being (Carton, Kessler & Page, 1999) relate to the ability to accurately interpret nonverbal body language. Because nonverbal display rules (when one should and should not engage in nonverbal behaviors) are learned, younger people may be less skilled in correctly interpreting and using

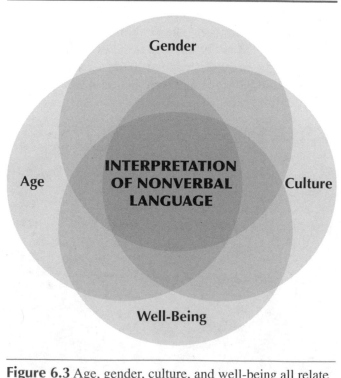

Figure 6.3 Age, gender, culture, and well-being all relate to the ability to correctly interpret nonverbal language.

body language. In addition, individuals who are depressed have poorer decoding abilities than the mentally and physically well (Rashotte, 2002).

According to Aguinis and Henle (2001), women who are in leadership positions face a paradox as it relates to nonverbal behaviors. For instance, in the predominant U.S. culture, leaders are expected to show visual dominance (e.g., make strong eye contact), be verbally assertive, have strong yet relaxed facial features, and take up a good deal of physical space. At the same time, women are supposed to (based on gender role stereotypes that still hold true) avoid making too much eye contact, use a lilting voice tone, and take up as little space as possible. In many cases a woman who uses strong leadership behaviors is perceived as being overly aggressive. Yet, if she demonstrates expected gender role behaviors, she may not be viewed as a leader. Being aware of this paradox can help both women and men better understand the importance of being open to all styles of leadership.

Many who study nonverbal communication report that it consists of several elements of body language as well as paraverbal communication. The most common elements of nonverbal communication investigated include use of space (i.e., proximity), touch, eye contact, facial expressions, gestures, posture, physical appearance, use of time (i.e., chronemics), and paraverbal language (i.e., sounds made by people that are not distinguishable as words, yet have definite meaning—uh, um, uh huh, tsk, pshaw).

Proximity

Proximity refers to the use of space, both used and filled with one's body, as well as with furniture or possessions. In other words, it is the study of how much space a person takes up with her or his body when sitting, walking, or standing. In addition, proximity addresses how an individual uses and fills up space with possessions such as books, papers, coats, and briefcases.

In the communication process, dominant people control more space than less dominant people. This means that dominant individuals take up more space by, for example, sitting with their arms spread out. Furthermore, they might lay their belongings on the backs of empty chairs to claim additional space, and they tend to use large amounts of office space by spreading out the placement of furnishings. In addition, high dominant people tend to establish themselves physically above others—their chair might be raised higher than others, they might stand while others are sitting, or in some other fashion literally raise themselves above others. Leaders who wish to send a message of power and dominance, then, will want to position them-

selves higher than participants, and take up space with their bodies.

Higher dominant individuals are accorded greater personal space than submissive people. Others allow dominant people to move into their space relatively freely, while the opposite is not necessarily true. This might be seen in agencies where the executive director might simply walk into an employee's office without knocking, yet the employee would never think of entering the director's office without first knocking and being invited in.

The elements of gender, ethnicity, and power interact with all aspects of communication. Relative to use of space, women use less personal space than do men; they take smaller steps, sit "smaller" in chairs (e.g., they keep their arms and legs close together), and either take up less space in offices or create multiple intimate spaces in large offices by erecting walls with plants or furniture (Hall, 1999). Power differences can also be seen when examining the use of space by members of various ethnic groups. For example, Asians tend to consume less space when standing, walking or sitting than do Europeans; and Euro-Americans tend to take up more space when doing these things than do other U.S. ethnic groups.

Consider the use of personal space in talking to others. In the dominant U.S. culture, personal distance (i.e., how far away we prefer people to be when we talk with them) is 18 to 36 inches. Therefore, when talking with others in a social setting we expect them to remain at least 18 inches away from us. If nonfamily or individuals with whom we are less intimate get closer than this we feel uncomfortable and tend to back away in efforts to maintain the 18 to 36 inch social distance. In other cultures, however, such as in some Middle Eastern cultures, social speaking distance is much closer and individuals may be offended if the one to whom they are speaking is at "arm's length." As with all elements of communication, in examining spatial differences, understanding cultural norms becomes important in interpreting whether an individual is "in your face" or simply acting within her or his cultural norms.

Some interesting research has recently been conducted looking at *seating dynamics*. This examines the relationships and interactions of people based on where

Understanding cultural norms becomes important in interpreting whether an individual is "in your face" or simply acting within her or his cultural norms.

they sit relative to one another—the "second in command" usually sits to the leader's right. Nelson and Quick (2005) report that to encourage cooperation, people should be seated side-by-side, facing the same direction (as if they are looking at the same point in space from the same perspective). To facilitate open communication, people should be seated at right angles to one another. Thus, if seated a table, one person would sit at the head of the table and another person along the side. Lastly, if a leader desires to foster competition, individuals should be placed across from one another where they look directly each individuals. This information has great impact on issues related to conflict resolution, among other leader functions.

To be effective, leisure services leaders need to consider and be aware of the conscious use of space in leading activities and participants. One should match the use of space to the needs of the situation. For instance, when leading large groups a leader will want to be visible; this may mean standing on top of something to be higher than participants, moving to one side of the room, or a combination of manipulating lateral and vertical space. When desiring to calm individuals down or in dealing with people who are shorter than the leader (e.g., a person in a wheelchair, a short adult, a child) a leader should remember the impact of "towering" over the participant and consider sitting or bending down to the level of the individual. This is particularly important in conflict management and problem-solving situations.

Touch

When researching touch in nonverbal communication, investigators measure the intensity (e.g., light, resting touch or heavy, pressing touch), direction (i.e., who touches whom), duration (i.e., how long the touch lasts), frequency (i.e., how often touches occur), and the instrument of touch (e.g., hand or object). Touch commonly occurs in the course of regular conversations to signal an upcoming change in speaking turn. For instance, if another individual is speaking and I have something I would like to say, I might lightly place my hand on the forearm of the speaker indicating that I have something I would like to interject. Touch is also used when comforting others, managing behaviors, or demonstrating activity rules.

Cultural, gender, and power differences exist related to touch. Higher dominant individuals tend to touch others' possessions more often than do low-power people. This is also true for touching people. Females are touched more than males and males are more apt to touch females than other males (Kalbfleisch & Cody, 1995). In some cultures, touch—such as hand-holding between people of the same sex—is acceptable and indicates a bond of friendship. In other cultures, this type of touch is considered taboo.

Touch can be a very powerful tool and can be used to soothe hurt feelings, to exert power, or to gain attention. Of all the nonverbal tools at a leader's disposal, touch requires the most judicious use. A touch on the arm, pat on the back, or congratulatory hug can easily be misinterpreted and/or misused. For survivors of sexual abuse, even an "innocent" touch on the shoulder may be interpreted or experienced as a sexual advance or personal invasion.

It is best, therefore, prior to touching anyone to ask the individual for her or his permission to be touched. For instance, if a youngster has been hurt by another child's remarks, and comes to the leader with tears in her or his eyes, before reaching out to hug that child, the leader should ask if the child wants a hug. Or, if in explaining an activity the leader needs to reposition someone she or he should ask, "Is it okay if I touch your arm?" prior to doing so. Furthermore, it is best to touch participants only in the view or presence of others. This way, if a question about the appropriateness of a touch arose at a later time, witnesses would be available to speak to what occurred.

The leader must understand the assumed power that goes with her or his position. Any touch from a leader has the potential of being received in a way different than intended. Leaders who are aware of when and how they use touch tend to be safe and appropriate in their contacts.

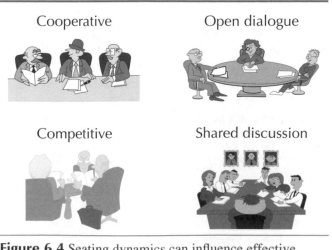

| Cooperative | Open dialogue |
| Competitive | Shared discussion |

Figure 6.4 Seating dynamics can influence effective communication.

Touch can be a very powerful tool and can be used to soothe hurt feelings, to exert power, or to gain attention.

Eye Contact

In the dominant U.S. culture people believe eye contact is important in open and honest communication. Schyns and Mohr (2004) found that appropriate eye contact is related to perceptions of charismatic leadership. It has been said that the "eyes are the window into the soul" and many believe that the eyes allow another to see earnestness and sincerity. In typical conversations people engage in more eye contact when listening than when speaking. Eye contact while listening indicates active listening and listening for understanding. It shows that the listener is fully engaged; it is difficult to daydream while looking an individual straight in the eyes. Leaders engage in eye contact when speaking as well as when listening. Effective leaders will scan the room as they talk to invite feedback and keep participants engaged in the event or activity. Eye contact from the leader helps participants feel welcomed and valued. As an example, Radford (1998) found that eye contact was one of the crucial determinants in whether college students would approach a reference librarian. If the librarian looked at the student (even if she or he was busy at the moment), the student felt as though the librarian was approachable and available. Leaders in parks and recreation will likely get a similar reaction from participants when they make eye contact with them.

An effective leader will have some level of understanding of the cultural, gender, and power differences in how much and when eye contact is used. For instance, in some Asian cultures individuals do not make eye contact when talking to elders and authority figures. In the United States, this is also true for American Indians and African Americans (Neuliep, 2006). In this instance direct eye contact is considered aggressive and disrespectful. In the dominant U.S. culture women and low-power individuals spend more time gazing at others (engaging in eye contact) than do men and high-power people. This has been attributed to the need of low-power individuals to attend to the moods and desires of high-power people in attempts to ensure others' needs are met (Plant, Kling & Smith, 2004). Understanding these types of differences will help in minimizing misinterpretation and miscommunication when interacting with others.

Facial Expressions

When decoding nonverbal communication patterns people look at the whole picture—they make quick observations of how an individual stands, her or his posture, any gestures used, and the degree and intensity of eye contact. People tend to key in on facial expressions in an attempt to discern levels of empathy and to correctly understand the message being sent. Facial expressions include smiles,

Effective leaders will scan the room as they talk to invite feedback and keep participants engaged in the event or activity.

forehead and face "scrunches" (often associated with not understanding something or disgust), frowns, and other facial expressions one can make with eyes, mouth, nose, eyebrows, and forehead.

Much understanding of messages (particularly as they are reflected back to us in terms of feedback) comes through correctly interpreting another's facial expressions. Interestingly, unlike body language, which is highly cultural in interpretation, there are six facial expressions that are universally understood: happiness, sadness, fear, anger, disgust and surprise (Ekman, 1999). As leaders teach or instruct in activity leadership they look at participants to assess the messages being sent through facial expressions—boredom, fatigue, engagement, impatience, and so forth. Once these nonverbal messages are received and interpreted, the leader can make adjustments in her or his style of leadership, the pacing, or whatever best fits the situation.

There is quite a bit of "smile research" reported in the literature. Individuals who smile are perceived as being more charismatic than those who do not smile. Rashotte (2002) reported that a "friendly smile" shows a general cheerful disposition and leads to a belief that the smiling person is friendly and approachable (i.e., important leader traits). Hall (1999) and Cashdan (1998) reported that women smiled more than men, and Cashdan attributed

Photo courtesy of Deb Jordan

Facial expressions are powerful mediums through which we receive messages.

those smiles to women's desire for affiliation and relationships. Both women and men who smiled more than others were perceived to be more caring and popular than those who did not smile as much. We know that leaders who smile are viewed as caring, friendly, approachable, and likeable by others.

Appropriately used smiles (as with all nonverbal language) can aid in de-escalation of conflict, set the stage for a friendly and comfortable atmosphere, and make people feel welcomed. At the same time, leaders should be aware that smiles can be used inappropriately. For instance, if a leader smiles when being firm in an attempt to stop certain behaviors, conflicting messages might be sent. Conflicting messages can be confused, misinterpreted, or ignored by the recipient.

Gestures

The spreading motions of one's hands made when describing the "fish that got away" is an example of an illustrative gesture. Illustrative gestures can augment or replace verbal language. Large sweeping gestures with the arms often serve these functions. Generally, the more power one has, the larger and more sweeping the gestures one uses. This is related to proximity discussed earlier. People who take up a small amount of space will tend to keep their hands, arms, and possessions close to their bodies. In using large spaces, leaders use more expansive gestures.

Gestures may be a representation of something else (e.g., a person might put their thumb to their ear with their little finger to their mouth to represent being on the telephone) or used to get a group's attention, emphasize a point, provide clarity, or serve as a coping mechanism (Roth, 2001). For example, if a leader wants the group's

It is important to know the meaning of nonverbal gestures in various cultures to ensure positive leadership.

attention she or he might clap her or his hands; to emphasize a particular point a leader might pound her or his fist; if a leader asked participants to go into the next room and someone asked "Where?" the leader could point in the appropriate direction; and if one were really nervous or bored, she or he might drum fingers on the table, or exhibit a tic of some sort.

Because gestures are culturally based there is much room for misinterpretation in crosscultural interactions. As an example, gangs have very elaborate nonverbal communication patterns. Gestures are particularly important as symbols of gang membership and status. These gestures have meaning relative to membership, brother- or sisterhood, safety, and upcoming activities. There have been many instances of nongang members inadvertently using a gang-only gesture and being severely beaten for their transgression.

Experts suggest that leaders use strong, dynamic gestures in a relaxed atmosphere (Preston, 2005). Combined with open and excited facial expressions, this helps a leader to exude confidence and competence to the audience. Of course, it is important that one's gestures be in agreement with the message being sent so as not to confuse the goal of the communication.

Posture

The manner in which one walks, sits, and stands constitutes posture. Most people believe that they can tell (from looking at and decoding body posture) if a person is happy, depressed, anxious, confident, or experiencing a host of other moods. The tallness with which one stands, the bounce in one's step, and overall tenseness of one's body serve as various nonverbal cues.

Research shows that leaders tend to stand erect, yet sit casually without slouching (Aguinis & Henle, 2001). Dubrin (2004) suggests that a leader's feet should be flat on the floor and free from foot tapping. A leader's posture matches other nonverbal behaviors and demonstrates an interest in participants. Leaders will want to become aware of the messages they send with their bodies. A slight forward lean toward a group or individual indicates warmth, trust, and intimacy (Floyd & Erbert, 2003). Most partici-

Leaders need to be aware of the messages they send with their bodies. Most participants receive their motivation for behaviors from watching leaders and other participants.

pants receive their motivation for behaviors from watching leaders and other participants. A leader who exudes confidence, energy, and an upbeat attitude usually will engender similar attitudes and feelings in others.

Olfactics (or Personal Odors)

Recent research suggests our sense of smell is another tool used in decoding nonverbal messages (Gudykunst, 2004; Neuliep, 2006). For Middle Eastern and Latin cultures, personal body odors are more important than to people in other cultures. Individual scents help individuals to identify one another and indicate a level of intimacy. In other settings, particular smells are related to illness, fear, and social availability (e.g., both women and men are said to give off pheromones that are attractive to potential partners). Further, it is not uncommon to hear individuals remark that someone they do not like "smells funny."

Another aspect of olfactics of which leaders will want to be aware is the use of perfumes and colognes as an element of one's personal hygiene. While many people use these products to enhance their personal scent, to others the smells can be offensive or overpowering. There are many who have allergies to perfumes and colognes, and particularly when in confined spaces, this can be problematic. Effective leaders are aware of the cultural group and participants with whom they will be working and attend to their personal scents as appropriate.

Physical Appearance

While not a direct result of communicating through body movements, one's physical appearance certainly sends messages. The type of clothing one wears, choice of hair style and color, and use of makeup all communicate something about the individual. While certain hair styles might be in fashion (e.g., purple spikes) and send messages of individuality or rebellion against "the establishment," those same hair styles may not communicate confidence and competence in a leader. Dubrin (2004) and Preston (2005) have indicated that effective leaders who maintain a professional, clean, and neat appearance are perceived as being meticulous and careful.

As with other elements of nonverbal communication, one must recognize cultural differences in personal appearance. Clothing or hair styles that might be considered antiestablishment when worn by one person could be an expression of cultural pride in another. Clothing, hair style, tattoos, and body jewelry all may signify confidence, individuality, or group membership. Members of athletic swim teams, for instance, have been known to shave their heads prior to an important swim meet in a show of team spirit, cohesion, and to get "psyched up." Observers know at a glance that those with shaved heads are on the team and share a common goal.

As leaders develop their own understanding of what it means to be a professional and to engender an atmosphere of respect, credibility, and competence, it becomes clear where the lines should be drawn. For example, leaders who wear neatly pressed uniforms (e.g., shorts and collared shirts), wear their hair in "mainstream" fashion, and use makeup sparingly are typically perceived as more competent, credible, and worthy of respect than leaders who look unkempt or excessively fashionable.

Chronemics

Another related element to nonverbal communication that affects all leisure services leaders is *chronemics*, or the use of time. In the predominant U.S. culture, time is perceived as being linear (i.e., it has a beginning and an end; once it is past it is gone forever) and is valued (i.e., people perceive their time as important to them). As such, being on time for meetings, events, and other gatherings is considered both polite and important. A consistently punctual leader is usually perceived as being respectful of others and as having credibility and competence.

As with other elements of nonverbal communication, the way one uses time can express power relationships. Making an individual wait until 2:20 p.m. when she or he had an appointment at 2:00 p.m. may be an indication of a power ploy—the individual who controls the resources (in this case, time) is more powerful than the other. If being late for an appointment is inevitable, alerting the one being inconvenienced by having to wait is the courteous and respectful thing to do.

In addition to time being used as a power issue, time must also be considered within the context of culture. In Native American, Latin, Middle Eastern, and some African cultures, for example, time is perceived as cyclical (i.e.,

Figure 6.5 Time is viewed from two cultural perspectives.

it follows natural rhythms) and "being on time" may mean "within an hour or two" (or even within a day or two!). The primary focus on time is to enjoy the present—Things will get done "in their own time." Understanding differences allows a leader to prepare for and make a more accurate interpretation of what has occurred and react accordingly.

Because there are both cultural and individual differences in perception of time, one cannot assume that all staff or participants share values related to punctuality. Therefore, planning and conducting activities that allow for adding participants as they arrive will be important when leading activities with mixed groups. In this manner, people who arrive early and late can be accommodated and not left to feel disrespected.

Paraverbal Language

Nonverbal language consists of many elements—those that do not involve sounds such as body movements and physical appearance, and those that include sounds, but are not distinguishable as spoken words. Pitch, rate, volume, inflection, accents, silences and pauses, and miscellaneous sounds are all considered aspects of paraverbal language.

Pitch

Pitch may be described as a musical note that a voice most closely resembles. Women generally have higher pitched voices than men; boys' voice pitch lowers when they reach puberty. For most people, lower-pitched voices are easier to distinguish from other sounds and to understand, and are more comfortable on the ear than are higher-pitched voices. As we age, however, our ability to distinguish lower pitches diminishes and we can have difficulty in discerning meaningful words. Leaders should know the population with whom they will be working and make adjustments accordingly.

In the U.S. culture we have come to associate authority with lower-pitched voices. This is evidenced in television commercial voice-overs, radio disc jockeys, and even in the voices people use when trying to stop misbehaviors (e.g., lifeguards tend to lower their voices when they shout, "Walk, don't run!" at the pool). On the other hand, higher pitched and softer voices are desirable when trying to soothe participants. Elevator voice recordings, recorded voices welcoming travelers to rest stops, and computer-generated voices at places like Disney World tend to be female voices. One key to successful communication is the ability to change pitch as the situation war-

rants. Leaders will want to be aware of the pitch of their own voice and adjust it to meet the needs of the situation.

Rate

Speech rate varies across individuals, by geographic region, and by culture. Some people speak quite rapidly (often a stereotype of those reared in the northeastern United States) while others speak much more slowly (considered typical of those who live in the southern United States). We have come to liken speech rate to speaker competence and intelligence, often assuming (to a point) that the quicker one speaks, the more competent and intelligent that individual is (DeVito, 1999). In reality, speech rate has little to do with competence or intelligence. In general, people can listen faster than most people can talk. Thus, there is ample time for distractions to sneak in and minds to wander during slower rates of speech. Understanding the perception of speech rate may help a leader in selecting an appropriate rate of speech when speaking to different groups.

Volume

The loudness of one's voice and the way a person projects her or his voice are related to volume. A solid volume is often interpreted as strength and sincerity (Gudykunst, 2004). Some people talk loudly while others speak so softly that it is difficult to hear them. To be effective in accomplishing tasks, leaders need to practice using a well-modulated voice that becomes louder or softer as the situation calls for it. Projecting one's voice requires maintaining a conversational tone and inflection, yet increasing in volume. This increase in volume is not the same as shouting or yelling. Shouting or yelling often has a negative, punishing tone to it, while increased volume simply allows people who are at a distance from the leader to hear what she or he is saying. Effective leaders position

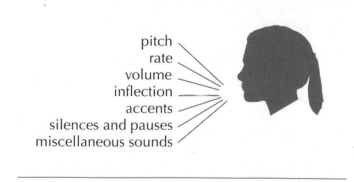

Figure 6.6 Paraverbal language consists of several elements.

One key to successful communication is the ability to change pitch as the situation warrants. Leaders will want to be aware of the pitch of their own voice and adjust it to meet the needs of the situation.

themselves in such a way that their voice carries (e.g., if outside, the wind should be behind the leader) and check in with participants to be sure that everyone can hear well.

Inflection

No matter the language one speaks, it is usually evident to others who speak the same language whether the person speaking is asking a question or making an assertion. The manner in which one's voice goes up or down in pitch at the end of a sentence usually indicates the type of statement being made. In the dominant U.S. culture a question "goes up" at the end while a statement or assertion tends to drop at the end. People who speak with an "up" inflection at the end of statements are often perceived as less capable and less sure of themselves than those whose speech drops at the end of a sentence. Inflection is somewhat regionalized; for example, people living in the south tend to use sentences that end going "up." This has been referred to as "uptalk" and leaders will want to be aware of their use of this technique—overused, it could negatively impact participant perceptions of leader competence.

Accents

Some people believe that everyone has an accent or characteristic way of pronouncing certain words. Others believe that only those other than themselves have accents. It is likely that every person pronounces certain words in particular ways which tend to be distinct to a particular region of the country. As with speech rate, many have come to associate particular accents with competence and intelligence of the speaker. Stereotypes abound and leaders would be wise to be aware of them. For example, a flat, Midwestern-type accent is often perceived with a good deal of authority and believability, while those with southern "drawls" often find their intelligence questioned.

Silences and Pauses

Silences and pauses are used in communication so frequently that many of us do not even notice them. Those who use silences and pauses effectively can hold the attention of a group and draw them into the communication process. One effective use of silence is after asking a question. Educational research has shown that most teachers ask a question, pause momentarily, then move on if an individual does not have an immediate answer. Typically, however, it takes several seconds for people to gather their thoughts and respond in an appropriate fashion. Waiting for five to ten seconds to elapse before rephrasing a question or going on to someone else would be useful for leaders who wish to engage others in meaningful dialogue. It can take practice to let the silence be (five to ten seconds can seem interminable!), but it is an important communication tool for a leader to master. Give people time to think before they respond—Thinking is a good thing!

Miscellaneous Sounds

In everyday speech people commonly use sounds such as "umm," "ahh," and "hmm" to serve as space-fillers and turn-holders. In conversation, when an individual pauses in midsentence to complete a thought she or he will often use a sound to prevent another individual from entering the conversation. Should another individual wish to enter the conversation, but realize the time is not yet right, she or he may insert one of these sounds to indicate that she or he desires a turn speaking next. In this way, paraverbal language helps to regulate communication.

In addition to the typical sounds used to hold one's speaking turn, we also make other paraverbal sounds, "tsk," "pshaw," and "huh?" that serve an important function in communication. Depending upon their use (e.g., timing when in conversation) these sounds may serve to indicate a particular thought or emotion (e.g., disbelief, discounting, confusion). There are many other sounds that are used to emphasize a point, serve in the place of words, convey an emotion, or save one's turn. Overuse of these sounds can make a person sound unsure, so a leader who understands the use of these sounds will be a more effective communicator than one who does not understand the use of paraverbal language.

❖ ❖ ❖

In addition to body language, physical appearance, and paraverbal language, communication occurs through use of symbols. In leisure services settings symbols are used

Give people time to think before they respond—Thinking is a good thing!

in everyday situations: on letterhead, staff uniforms, promotional materials, and agency vehicles. As with all types of communication, a message is sent via these symbols; how they are received and interpreted depends upon several factors.

Symbolic Language

Symbolic language uses symbols to convey a message. This may be seen in the use and proliferation of logos (on T-shirts, posters, promotional materials, agency vehicles) and signs which have a clear meaning. For instance, if a group were to see a set of golden arches up the road, most would realize that a McDonald's restaurant was ahead. Similarly, the symbol of a red circle with a diagonal slash mark through it has an international meaning of "No whatever-is-in-the-circle."

Symbols as language can be very powerful and are often used as indications of membership in an organization. Athletic teams wear logos and symbols on their clothing which helps team members (and others) to identify one another. This is also true of corporations, gangs, neighborhood associations, and parks and recreation departments. Symbolic language has great significance for a sense of belonging and inclusion.

Recently there has been much attention focused on the use of symbols that perpetuate derogatory or stereotypical portrayals of ethnic groups. This is most commonly

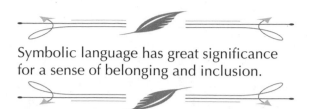

Symbolic language has great significance for a sense of belonging and inclusion.

seen related to schools, colleges, and professional sports teams with team logos and mascots. An example of this is the controversy over the name, logo, and fan chants of the Atlanta Braves baseball team. The "tomahawk chop" is a nonverbal gesture made by fans that to some Native Americans is denigrating and perpetuates stereotypes. To some fans, it is nothing more than a unique rallying cry.

The messages sent by the visual depictions of an organization are strong and memorable. Leaders of leisure services agencies will want to consider implications of using certain symbolic language to represent the agency prior to selecting a representative symbol. Will it project the desired image? Does the meaning change across cultural groups? Is it easily and uniquely recognizable?

Written Language

Communication skills for leaders include the ability to speak well, listen attentively, use paraverbal language effectively, understand symbolic communication, and write in a professional manner. Often at the direct leadership level verbal and nonverbal language skills are emphasized and little or no mention is made of writing skills. One reason for this might be because the writing required of leaders can be infrequent and less valued than physical leadership skills. With the advent of computer technology, however, business and professional writing skills have become even more essential for all leisure services professionals.

Many leisure services leaders hold the erroneous assumption that writing skills do not matter and that the departmental secretary will serve as the editor and proofreader of all paperwork. This is far from the truth. Many agencies do not have access to this type of editorial assistance, and clerical personnel are not always skilled in these areas. Furthermore, the general public will be exposed to a leader through her or his writing promotional copy, business letters, forms, signs in the facility, client reports, and even websites and will form opinions about her or his knowledge, credibility, and personality based on this contact. Learning how to write professionally is essential to effective and competent leadership. Leisure services leaders at all levels write their own reports, memos, and

Figure 6.7 Examples of symbolic language

business letters; they must have good writing skills to do this efficiently and effectively.

Specifically, writing will occur in reports (e.g., accident/incident reports, inventories, client progress reports, contracts, manuals), letters (e.g., to potential employers, registrants, sponsors, parents, and equipment manufacturers), and in promotional materials (e.g., signage, schedule books, flyers, special event information, and public service announcements). While each of these requires slightly different types of writing, each demands basic skills in grammar, composition, spelling, and layout.

Writing may occur on hard copy (e.g., paper, letterhead) or on computer (e.g., electronic mail, web pages). In either case, good writing requires practice and feedback. It is very easy to send incomplete or sloppy work out on electronic mail, for example. Leaders who commit to a sense of professionalism, however, follow basic rules of writing in composition, grammar, and spelling in all communications. Effective written material should be:

- readable and accessible by the intended audience
- precise and to the point
- accurate and detailed
- expressed in complete thoughts
- worded in the active voice
- well-focused relative to the purpose of the communication
- gender-neutral and inclusive

In written communication using appropriate grammar, proper spelling, complete sentences, and nonsexist

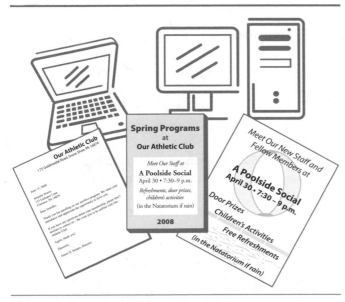

Figure 6.8 Writing skills required of leaders come in many forms.

and inclusive language are important to communicating the intended message. Once written materials are complete they are usually available for a variety of constituents to review, and they become permanent records. Leaders would be wise to remember that many individuals (e.g., participants, the general public, employers) will develop their first impression of the leader through samples of the leader's writing. Competence, intelligence, and sensitivity are a few of the positive characteristics people ascribe to authors of materials. Taking the time to write and design written materials professionally and continually seeking improvement in that area are signs of mature leaders.

Electronic Communication (e-mail, Listservs and text messages)

In this computer age, electronic mail and text messaging have become an important means of communicating both within and outside of organizations. In many respects, e-mail and text messaging have taken the place of telephone calls and face-to-face meetings. Advantages to using these media include the ability to communicate across time zones at one's convenience, having a written record of a transaction, the ability to include many people in one communication (i.e., broadcast messages), and the ability to include detailed instructions or a response to a question. Disadvantages to using e-mail and text messaging include the fact that these are two-dimensional—recipients may have a difficult time accurately decoding the message because it lacks the nonverbal and paraverbal elements. Further, many people do not have access to e-mail and text messaging, business e-mail has legal risks associated with it, and these are not secure methods of communication (i.e., they may be easily hacked). In addition, if one is upset it is too easy to send a "flame"— an emotionally laden, intimidating, or threatening message.

Regardless of the drawbacks, e-mail and text messaging are heavily used; thus, leisure service leaders will want to be aware of the etiquette required for using these media. Just as with other forms of the written word, effective e-mail and text communicators think, plan, and take care when they articulate their thoughts. To be most effective, senders should keep e-mail messages succinct; use proper grammar, spelling, and punctuation; include an appropriate subject heading; respond as quickly as possible; indicate if a response is required of the message; and use both upper and lower case letters just as would be used on hard copy (using all uppercase letters in electronic mail is very difficult to read and is viewed AS SHOUTING!).

It is very important that *before* sending an e-mail message to check the spelling and grammar; to reread the message for tone, style, and content (read it from the recipient's point of view—how will she or he interpret it?); and to review the message for completeness. Be aware of sending along too many attachments as some organizational servers can only handle small files. In addition, make certain any attachment is pertinent to the message and free from viruses. Avoid sending personal messages and electronic chain letters to business associates, no matter how uplifting or funny.

Remember, *no privacy protection* exists on office cellphones and computers; an employer has the right to examine any agency computer and phone use—including e-mail messages sent and received—of all her or his employees. If a leader works for a governmental agency, e-mails likely fall under the Open Records Law. Further, if inappropriate or libelous messages are sent, both the sender and the agency could be held liable (*E-mail manners*, 2004). Many local and state governments have developed comprehensive e-mail policies that outline how and when e-mail should be used, and the messages retained. Many of these policies are also used in the business and nonprofit sectors. Thus, the use of computers at work should be for business use only. In fact, a good way to remain alert to appropriate use is to take the position that anything you write in e-mail would be welcome on the agency bulletin board.

A *Listserv* is an electronic database managed by an individual or organization. A Listserv serves a particular function for a certain group of people. For instance, there is a Listserv geared for leisure services practitioners; another for those in therapeutic recreation, and yet another for parks and recreation educators. One subscribes (there may or may not be a fee for the service) to the list, and then receives messages pertinent to people with that shared interest. Each member of the list can write and send messages to multiple persons at once.

Listservs can be wonderful tools to access people all over the world. People use Listservs to aid in problem solving, conduct research, share important news stories, create new ideas for programs, post job openings, and share information of interest to list members. Having said that, one should use all Listservs wisely. A Listserv is not a place to advertise or make promotional notices for products, and one should avoid sending a reply to an entire list if the message is meant for only one person.

Listserv (and e-mail) users will want to be sure to post all personal contact information about themselves (i.e., name, address, phone, fax, e-mail address) at the bottom of their messages. This way, others can respond through whichever mechanism is most appropriate (e.g., phone, personal e-mail, the group Listserv). In addition, Listserv members should follow the list rules for avoiding bouncing messages. For instance, if one were to post an

Face-to-face contact, a telephone call, or a formal letter are often more appropriate than electronic media.

"out-of-office" message that was to be automatically sent out any time an incoming message was received, then for every Listserv posting the entire list would receive your out-of-office message. Messages end up being bounced back and forth, and this can effectively block or shut down the entire list. Most Listserv managers suggest unsubscribing to a list, or "postponing," if you intend to be out of the office for an extended period of time and then resubscribing upon your return.

Lastly, we are all cautioned to use electronic communication for those purposes for which it is best suited. Face-to-face contact, a telephone call, or a formal letter are often more appropriate than electronic media. Leader convenience is not the best reason for choosing one communication medium over another. Think through the reasons for the communication, the audience, the ease of sending an accurate message, and make wise choices about the medium.

Summary

Nonverbal communication is a complex aspect of the communication process. It serves to aid in impression management, as a sign of membership in a group, and to help regulate the communication interaction. Communication provides feedback, emphasizes a verbal message, holds a turn while in conversation, and serves as a substitution for words. In addition, nonverbal communication expresses a variety of social relationships such as power and dominance, compliance, affect management, and social intimacy. It tends to be the most trusted form of communication.

Elements of body language such as proximity, the use of touch, eye contact, facial expressions, and gestures constitute nonverbal language. Other elements include olfactics, physical appearance, the use of time, and paraverbal communication. Effective leaders are aware of their own and other's uses of these aspects of the communication process. In addition, they recognize and acknowledge cultural differences in nonverbal language so as to avoid embarrassing situations.

Symbolic language utilizes signs and symbols to portray messages. Examples of this are found in leisure services agency logos and on traffic control signs. Electronic media are alternative communication channels. Leaders need to learn to wisely use e-mail, text messaging, and Listservs as parts of their communication repertoire. In addition to wise use of symbolic language and electronic media, good professional writing skills are required of direct leaders. Effective leaders constantly look for ways to improve their communication skills.

Beginning the Journey

Chapter 5 opened the door to the discussion of communication, but offered only half of the communication equation. In this chapter you've had an opportunity to explore the influence of nonverbal communication—both from an individual and a cultural perspective. It's all part of the journey to leadership. Continue your journey as you work through the following questions:

1. What are nonverbal display rules? Identify at least five display rules for your cultural group. What happens if you break these rules? Why do you think that nonverbal language is generally the most trusted form of communication? Talk about the dilemmas this can present given that nonverbal language is also the most ambiguous form of communication.

2. How can you use nonverbal communication to enhance your skills as a leader? Relate your response to the various functions of nonverbal communication. Examine your own nonverbal language right now—what are you saying and to whom?

3. Why are females generally better at decoding nonverbal messages than males? How can this be an advantage for female leaders? Talk about the difficulties people might face in decoding nonverbal language if they either speak a different language or are from a country different than yours. Now chat with a classmate about how age interacts with nonverbal decoding skills. What does this information mean for you as a leader in parks, recreation, and leisure services?

4. Describe the notion of proximity. How can you use this to make your leadership most effective? What should you bear in mind as you make decisions related to proximity? How do gender, ethnicity, and power interact with proximity? What are seating dynamics and how can you use your knowledge of this to positively impact your leadership? Think of specific situations as you talk about this.

5. In what types of leadership situations is touch used? Describe the cultural influences on touching. What are the warnings we should all be aware of related to the use of touch? Practice becoming aware of how much and when you touch others (and they touch you). How does it make you feel? When should touch be avoided? How can you differentiate appropriate touch from inappropriate touch?

6. How do leaders use eye contact when leading? What are the cultural, gender, and power differences in eye contact? When would a leader want to avoid eye contact? How should a leader interpret other's use of eye contact?

7. Practice people-watching and observe the facial expressions of others. What kind of emotions are they expressing? Identify the six facial expressions that are common across cultures. Ask someone else to model these expressions in random order and quiz yourself on what emotion they are expressing. What role does smiling play for a leader? How is your smile? Do you have different kinds of smiles that are useful for different situations? When is it best *not* to smile in leadership settings?

8. What are the different reasons that we use gestures? What kinds of gestures do you think a leader should have in her or his repertoire? Do you use gestures effectively? How can you improve your use of gestures? Lead a game for a group of friends and have them key in on the gestures you use. Were they effective? Distracting? Do you have special gestures that have meaning only for a certain group (e.g., friends, family, teammates)?

9. What does the posture of a leader look like? Is there more than one leader posture? Draw this posture or find a picture from a magazine or a photo of it. Do you exhibit this on a day-to-day basis? How can you show an interest in others by your posture?

10. Draw or take a picture of the ideal parks, recreation, and leisure services leader. Do you look like that? What do you need to do to be perceived by others (based on your appearance) as a leader in our field? Have you ever been treated differently because of the way you dressed, wore your hair, or exhibited body art (e.g., tattoos, piercings)? What are the lessons you learned from this (in

terms of leadership) and how we should treat participants who have unique appearances?

11. What is chronemics and what does it have to do with leadership? What are your strengths and weaknesses related to time—are you punctual? a procrastinator? consistently a few minutes late? always early? Do you prefer to "go with the flow?" How does your use and perception of time impact the way others view you as a leader? What adjustments do you need to make to be perceived more as a leader?

12. What elements of communication constitute paraverbal language? How do these relate to leadership? Make specific recommendations to a leader that will help her or him make wise use of paralanguage. Do you follow these suggestions in your role as a leader?

13. Make a recording of your voice (at least five to ten minutes long). Do you consider your voice to be high-pitched, medium-pitched, or low-pitched? What do others think? Can you modulate the pitch to increase the perceived authority in your voice?

14. Listen to the recording of your voice—how would you describe your rate and volume? Do you have a tendency to speak too quickly or too slowly? Can people hear you from across the room? Practice projecting your voice in a noisy gymnasium, outdoors, at a pool, and other common recreation settings.

15. What is uptalk and how does it affect perceptions of leadership? Make a recording of your voice making a firm statement, asking a question, saying something with an exclamation point, commanding someone to do something, and speaking in a soothing manner. How does your inflection change for each of these verbal patterns? Can you manipulate your voice so that people can hear what you are saying in the inflection you use?

16. Listen to the recordings that you've made of your voice—what type of accent do you have? How can you make this work to your advantage as a leader? Do you use silences and pauses in an appropriate way? Try this: ask a friend a question that requires thinking and then wait a full five to ten seconds before you say anything else (time yourself). Was the silence that followed the question comfortable or uncomfortable for you?

17. What common paralanguage space savers do you have a tendency to use when you are talking? Do you overuse these sounds? When someone says "um" very frequently in communication, what is your perception of them? How does an effective leader use miscellaneous sounds in communication?

18. What is symbolic language and how do you use it every day? How can leaders use symbolic language to strengthen their leadership? How does this type of language impact public perceptions of the agency or organization for which you work?

19. How are your written communication skills? What opportunities do you take to improve your written language? Which form of written language do you use most (e.g., letters, memos, texting, e-mail)? What are the "rules of etiquette" for that form of written language? What specific elements of written language do you need to improve? How will you go about this before you graduate?

References

Aguinis, H. and Henle, C. (2001). Effects of nonverbal behavior on perceptions of a female employee's power bases. *The Journal of Social Psychology, 141*(4), 537–549.

Bailey, W., Nowicki, S., and Cole, S. (1998). The ability to decode nonverbal information in African American, African and Afro-Caribbean, and European American adults. *Journal of Black Psychology, 24*(4), 418–431.

Boone, R. and Buck, R. (2003). Emotional expressivity and trustworthiness: The role of nonverbal behavior in the evolution of cooperation. *Journal of Nonverbal Behavior, 27*(3), 163–172.

Carton, J., Kessler, E., and Pape, C. (1999). Nonverbal decoding skills and relationship well-being in adults. *Journal of Nonverbal Behavior, 23*(1), 91–100.

Cashdan, E. (1998). Smiles, speech, and body posture: How women and men display sociometric status and power. *Journal of Nonverbal Behavior, 22*(4), 209–228.

DeVito, J. (1999). *Essentials of human communication* (3rd ed.). New York, NY: Longman.

Dubrin, A. (2004). *Leadership: Research findings, practice, and skills* (4th ed.). New York, NY: Houghton Mifflin.

Ekman, P. (1999). Facial expressions. In T. Dalgleish and T. Power (Eds.), *The handbook of cognition and emotion* (pp. 301–320). Sussex, UK: John Wiley & Sons.

E-mail manners. (2004). Retrieved 7 July, 2006, from http://www.netmanners.com

Feldman, R., Tomasian, J., and Coats, E. (1999). Nonverbal deception abilities and adolescents' social competence:

Adolescents with higher social skills are better liars. *Journal of Nonverbal Behavior, 23*(3), 237–249.

Floyd, K. and Erbert, L. (2003). Relational message interpretations of nonverbal matching behavior: An application of the social meaning model. *The Journal of Social Psychology, 143*(5), 581–586.

Greer, C. and Plunkett, W. (2000). *Supervision: Diversity and teams in the workplace* (9th ed.). Upper Saddle River, NJ: Prentice Hall.

Groves, K. (2005). Gender differences in social and emotional skills and charismatic leadership. *Leadership & Organization Development Journal, 11*(3), 30–46.

Gudykunst, W. (2004). *Bridging differences: Effective intergroup communication* (4th ed.). Thousand Oaks, CA: Sage Publications.

Hall, J. (1999). Status, gender, and nonverbal behavior: A study of structured interactions between employees of a company. *Personality and Social Psychology Bulletin, 25*(9), 1082–1091.

Kalbfleisch, P. and Cody, M. (Eds.). (1995). *Gender, power, and communication in human relationships*. Hillsdale, NJ: Lawrence Erlbaum.

Mottet, T., Beebe, S., Raffeld, P., and Paulsel, M. (2004). The effects of student verbal and nonverbal responsiveness on teachers' liking of students and willingness to comply with student requests. *Communication Quarterly, 52*(1), 27–38.

Nelson, D. and Quick, J. (2005). *Understanding organizational behavior* (2nd ed.). Mason, OH: South-Western.

Neuliep, J. (2006). *Intercultural communication* (3rd ed.). Thousand Oaks, CA: Sage Publications.

Plant, E., Kling, K., and Smith, G. (2004). The influence of gender and social role on the interpretation of facial expressions. *Sex Roles, 51*(3/4), 187–195.

Preston, P. (2005). Nonverbal communication: Do you really say what you mean? *Journal of Healthcare Management, 50*(2), 83–86.

Rashotte, L. (2002). What does that smile mean? The meaning of nonverbal behaviors in social interaction. *Social Psychology Quarterly, 65*(1), 92–102.

North Carolina Department of Cultural Resources. (2002). *E-mail as a public record in North Carolina: Guidelines for its retention and disposition*. Raleigh. NC: Government Records Branch of the Archives and Records Section.

Rosip, J. and Hall, J. (2004). Knowledge of nonverbal cues, gender, and nonverbal decoding accuracy. *Journal of Nonverbal Behavior, 28*(4), 267–286.

Roth, W. (2001). Gestures: Their role in teaching and learning. *Review of Educational Research, 71*(3), 365–392.

Schyns, B. and Mohr, G. (2004). Nonverbal elements of leadership behaviour. *Zeitschrift fur Personalforschung, 18*(3), 289–304.

Radford, M. (1998). Approach or avoidance? The role of nonverbal communication in the academic library user's decision to initiate a reference encounter. *Library Trends, 46*(4), 699–717.

Ting-Toomey, S. (1999). *Communicating across cultures*. New York, NY: The Guilford Press.

Leader Profile

Barbara Manzo
Deputy Director, Lee County Parks and Recreation • Florida

Barbara has had 17 years in this position, and 36 years in the parks, recreation, and leisure services profession.

Volunteer leadership positions she has held include:

- President, New York State Recreation and Parks Society
- President of Florida Recreation and Parks Association (FRPA)
- President of the FRPA Foundation, Inc.
- Board of Directors, US Tennis Association, Florida

What is the meaning of leadership?
The ability to win people over, to excite them about an idea and make them want to follow you knowing that you will be fair and treat them with respect. Good leaders surround themselves with talented people who are "smarter" than them and understand that they cannot know everything.

What are the most important leader qualities?
Honesty, integrity, loyalty, passion and a genuine concern for humankind…. It is also the ability to listen, make decisions, change, make mistakes, learn from them and move on.

What advice do you have for students who aspire to leadership in parks, recreation, and leisure services?
Some people are born leaders and others have to work at it. But if you want to be a leader start in the trenches, gain the respect of your peers and make your intentions known. Take on every challenge handed to you and ask for some new ones. Being a leader means taking responsibility for your actions— both good and bad. It means standing up for what you believe in. If you can handle this and more, then you have the potential to be a leader.

Favorite book(s): I love to read and I belong to a book club; choosing just one book is tough. However, the book that has affected me the most in the last four years is *My Sister's Keeper* by Jodi Piccoult, a fiction loosely based upon facts that is very timely with some of the controversial issues facing us today.

Favorite activities: Travel, bowling, golf, cooking and many others.

Chapter Seven
Managing Difficulties

Learning Opportunities

Through studying this chapter readers will have the opportunity to:

- Become exposed to the advantages of conflicts and problems.
- Understand how difficulties escalate across a spectrum of struggle intensity.
- Discover various approaches to handling difficulties.
- Integrate knowledge of the sources of conflict with conflict management strategies.
- Explore the methods of leader involvement in mediating difficulties.

Photo courtesy of Paul Jordan/WEBSPORTSPHOTO

Leaders of parks, recreation, and leisure services face a variety of problems, conflicts, and difficulties in their positions. Examples of common difficulties include equipment that breaks down, a participant with a question about payment of an invoice, clients who refuse to participate, and disagreements between participants in structured programs (e.g., arguments, fistfights in sport leagues). Such difficulties range from simple problems related to equipment to complex conflict resolution issues involving multiple parties. Difficulties and struggles are a normal and natural aspect of working with people in various environments and are found in every leisure services setting. Therefore, developing an understanding of difficulties and how to manage them is a vital skill for leisure services leaders.

Conflicts and other difficulties are natural processes that are inherent in all important relationships. A conflict may be viewed as a struggle between two or more interdependent people who perceive differences in goals. Conflicts may be task-oriented (i.e., related to the job to be done) or relationship-oriented (i.e., related to the people involved). Task conflicts often result in positive changes, while relationship conflicts often result in increased anxiety and stress among group members. Regardless of the type of conflict, communication is integral to its development and resolution. Communication creates conflict, reflects conflict, and acts as a vehicle for the productive management of conflict. Conflict, like communication, is a mutual activity; it takes two (or more) people for conflict to exist.

Conflict is beneficial in many ways. According to several authors, conflict

- causes people to examine their self-concepts
- forces individuals to seek evidence to support their positions
- provides a sense of identity
- stimulates creativity
- strengthens commitment to shared goals
- helps in establishing a vision for the future. (Choudrie, 2005; McGrane, Wilson & Cammock, 2005)

Difficulties and struggles are a normal and natural aspect of working with people in various environments and are found in every leisure services setting.

Others have indicated that conflict aids in problem awareness, leads to improved solutions, and serves as a catalyst for change. Conflict is necessary for healthy group development as it is vital to growing and maturing relationships. Without conflict, relationships stagnate and wither away (Blackard, 2001). As discussed in Chapter 4, each stage of group development requires some degree of conflict for the group to move into the next phase of maturity.

While conflicts are beneficial in many ways, relationships continually embroiled in conflict are not healthy. Likewise, instances where conflicts are lacking or consistently avoided are not desirable. As stated by Worchel and Simpson, "…it is not the conflict that is the problem, but rather the management and response to conflict that determines the health of the unit" (1993, p. 79). Leisure services leaders can exert a positive influence on the outcome of conflicts faced in leisure settings.

Leaders have the authority and responsibility to "make things happen" and manage the difficulty to the satisfaction of all. The appropriate management of dif-

ficulties by leisure services leaders can lead to improved quality of services, better communication, and a more committed and productive staff.

What Are Conflict Resolution and Difficulty Management?

Conflict resolution refers to the process of resolving disagreements with the use of specific conflict resolution skills. Some researchers refer to this as *conflict transformation*. Transformation refers to moments in the conflict process when parties reach new understandings—of self, others, the goal, etc. (Bodtker & Jameson, 2001; Putnam, 2004). Conflict resolution or transformation skills include expressing emotions clearly, defining the problem specifically, reflective listening, and creative brainstorming. The skills are often presented in a step-by-step framework for addressing the problem (Arnold, Heyne & Busser, 2005; Johnson & Johnson, 2003). Depending upon the situation, the skills of the disputants, and the seriousness of the problem, the involved individuals may work to solve their own problem (negotiation), or they may ask someone else to serve as a conflict manager (mediation). Whatever the technique, conflict resolution or transformation aims to create a win-win solution.

Whatever model one utilizes to better understand how issues develop into conflicts, it should be noted that most researchers agree that the process is generally linear, yet also loops back on itself. If managed at any one stage, one "spins off" of the conflict development and management loop; if things are not resolved one continues on to the next stages.

The Struggle Spectrum

Keltner (1994) presented a "Struggle Spectrum" which illustrates the development of various types of difficulties faced by people in conflict. The difficulties range from mild differences to a violent interaction (e.g., physical fighting). As one can imagine, maintaining and diffusing conflicts at an early stage of struggle is important. Once a struggle moves to later stages, goals are no longer intertwined and escalation is likely. Leisure services leaders should be prepared for all degrees of conflict.

Consider the following example of the development of a conflict. Two young children are playing a board game. Mikaela moves her piece down the board and Raj thinks Mikaela went out of turn. Raj tells Mikaela to go back, because she went out of turn (i.e., mild difference). Mikaela does not believe she was out of order and says

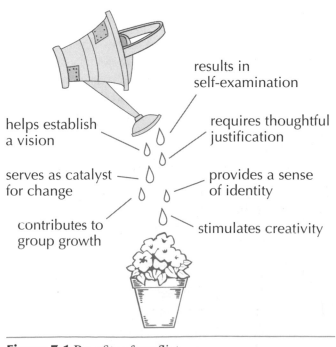

results in self-examination

requires thoughtful justification

helps establish a vision

serves as catalyst for change

provides a sense of identity

contributes to group growth

stimulates creativity

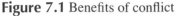

Figure 7.1 Benefits of conflict

The appropriate management of difficulties by leisure services leaders can lead to improved quality of services, better communication, and a more committed and productive staff.

she will keep her piece where it is. Raj is not successful in getting Mikaela to remove her piece and begins to get angry (i.e, disagreement)—the conflict escalates.

At this point Raj yells for the activity leader to come over and restate the rules: "If you go out of turn you have to move your piece back." Mikaela still disagrees that she is out of order (i.e., argument) and refuses to move her piece. Both children are now visibly upset and yelling at one another. Raj resorts to whining and making nonverbal threats (e.g., closed fist, angry facial expression) to try to persuade Mikaela to move her piece off the board (i.e., campaign). Raj is unsuccessful and shouts for the activity leader again. Raj tells the leader to tell Mikaela to stop cheating, take her piece off the board, and rule that Mikaela lost. Raj wants the staff member to make the decision related to who is correct (i.e., litigation). This effort also fails. Raj resorts to dumping the game board upside down and striking Mikaela (i.e., violence).

This movement from mild difference to violent interaction can occur very rapidly—in a matter of minutes. If the youngsters (or the leader) had basic conflict management skills, they could have resolved the issue of turn taking early and continued to play in harmony. Without these skills, the situation escalated out of control.

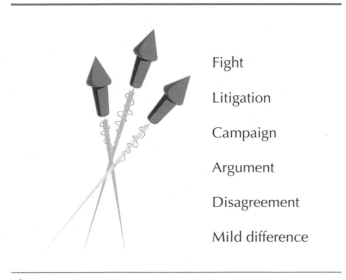

Fight

Litigation

Campaign

Argument

Disagreement

Mild difference

Figure 7.2 Development of conflict

Escalation

Throughout the previous scenario, the situation escalated— It got worse. The conflict was not successfully managed during any of the many levels of conflict and it moved quickly through the process until it reached a point of violence. In any conflict, regardless of cause, there are certain behaviors that almost guarantee escalation of the problem and other behaviors that will generally have the opposite effect. Whether or not the steps of a conflict resolution or transformation process are being followed, individuals can choose to make matters worse or move toward diffusing the conflict by exhibiting certain behaviors. Conflicts are likely to get worse when

- People raise their voices.
- People make themselves physically larger (e.g., by standing up).
- Personal space is invaded (e.g., "getting in someone's face," pointing a finger).
- Other people get involved in the problem and take sides.
- Past conflicts are brought up (especially if the phrases "you always" and/or "you never" are used).
- One or both disputants feel threatened in some fashion.
- Disputants act out anger, fear, or frustration.

De-escalation

Escalation serves to increase the complexity and heighten emotions involved in a conflict; de-escalation helps to mitigate emotions and reduce complexity. De-escalation strategies, even if used by only one of the disputants, make a conflict far more manageable. In the same way that escalating behaviors are consciously chosen, individuals can also consciously de-escalate conflicts by choosing to

- Speak in a calm and evenly modulated voice.
- Define the conflict as a mutual problem.
- Sit down and maintain an open posture.
- Allow for a comfortable distance between disputants.
- Talk directly to the person with whom the conflict exists.
- Exhibit genuine caring/empathy.
- Focus on the problem at hand and stay away from personality issues.
- Identify and express emotions appropriately. (Gudykunst, 2004; Johnson & Johnson, 2003)

De-escalation strategies, even if used by only one of the disputants, make a conflict far more manageable.

Reasons and Sources of Conflict

Conflicts and problems arise for a variety of reasons. Understanding these reasons will help leisure services leaders to manage difficulties in which they are involved, and to facilitate others to manage their own differences. Some researchers studying the issue see conflicts arising out of three basic sources: *distribution of resources, individual psychological needs,* and *value differences* (Arnold, Heyne & Busser, 2005; McGrane, Wilson & Cammock, 2005). Other authors suggest two reasons for conflict—*structural issues* (which include processes and procedures for how we go about resolving the conflict, as well as the substance of the conflict) and *interpersonal concerns* (those conflicts that arise between two or more people due to personalities or other interpersonal issues; Choudrie, 2005). No matter how we envision conflicts, these sources and reasons exist for people of all ages and lifestyles. We will look at the three basic sources of conflict in the following sections.

Distribution of Resources

Conflicts over resources generally manifest in power struggles where one person perceives an inequity in the distribution of resources. Young children might engage in

conflicts over control of toys or equipment, teens might experience difficulties over control of certain parts of town (e.g., "turf" issues), and adults might engage in struggles over money and time. Resources include both tangible resources such as equipment and court time and intangible resources such as self-esteem, authority, and prestige or status. Leaders can minimize resource conflicts by ensuring that tangible (e.g., equipment) and intangible resources (e.g., leader attention) are plentiful and equitably distributed.

Individual Psychological Needs

In addition to competing for resources, people engage in conflicts due to individual social and psychological needs. Competing or incompatible goals, power discrepancies, personality clashes, conflicting motivators, threats to one's self-esteem, a potential "loss of face," and unmet needs (e.g., the need for security and the need for belonging) all fit within this category. If the disputing individuals experience different needs and do not recognize their own needs, conflict is likely. For instance, if one participant in a group has a need to express her or his creativity while another group member operates out of a need for physical rehabilitation, conflict might arise over how to achieve both goals. Leisure services leaders would be well-served to consider individual needs when leading various programs.

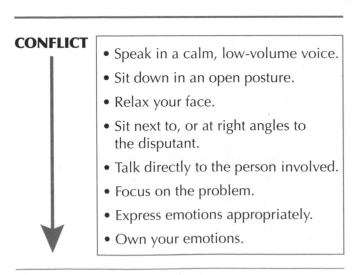

CONFLICT

- Speak in a calm, low-volume voice.
- Sit down in an open posture.
- Relax your face.
- Sit next to, or at right angles to the disputant.
- Talk directly to the person involved.
- Focus on the problem.
- Express emotions appropriately.
- Own your emotions.

Figure 7.3 Process of de-escalation

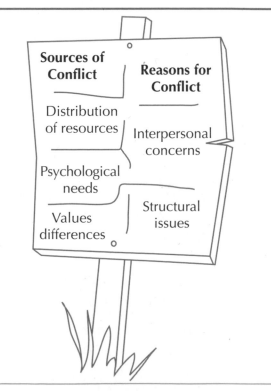

Figure 7.4 Sources and reasons for conflict

Value Differences

The third source of conflict is differences in values. Value differences typically arise out of cultural viewpoints, religious beliefs, or personal belief systems. Common values that vary from one individual to another include those related to the rights of others, work, leisure, honesty, faith, loyalty, the law, and the environment. Since values are vital to one's identity and developed over years of exposure and reinforcement, conflicts over values can be very difficult to resolve. In addition, many of us do not have a complete understanding of others' values (especially if we do not share a common culture), and this lack of understanding can lead to problems.

Factors That Influence Conflict Intensity

Many factors contribute to the likelihood of difficulties occurring. For instance, the more opportunities one has for interactions with others, the more likely that conflict of some type will arise. The visibility of differences between those interacting, such as age, gender, and race/ethnicity, also impacts the likelihood of conflict—the more visible and obvious the differences, the more likely a conflict is to occur. In addition to the tangible factors leading to conflict, perceived incompatibility also influences the nature and strength of difficulties (Chuang, Church & Zikic, 2004; Davidson, 2001).

Approaches to Conflict

Whether addressing issues related to conflict management or problem solving, similar approaches to managing difficulties may be taken. Not all approaches are equally beneficial in all situations, and there are times when some approaches are actually detrimental to relationships and the successful management of the conflict. Nonetheless, the approaches are valid for leisure services leaders in different situations. Using Blake and Mouton's (1964) managerial grid model, a "conflict resolution grid" was developed along two axes: assertiveness (i.e., concern for self) and cooperativeness (i.e., concern for others). From this model, five common approaches to managing conflicts were identified: *avoidance, accommodation, competition, compromise,* and *collaboration* (Blake & Mouton, 1964; Brahnam, Margavio, Hignite, Barrier & Chin, 2005).

Avoidance

Avoidance results when a person employs low-assertive and low-cooperative behaviors. These conflict managers do not feel very good about themselves, nor about the others

Since values are vital to one's identity and developed over years of exposure and reinforcement, conflicts over values can be very difficult to resolve.

involved in the conflict. Many of us are well-skilled at conflict avoidance. When a difficulty arises, individuals skilled in avoidance techniques might engage in denial ("What problem? There is no problem!"), shift topics ("Problem? Say, did you hear about the new facility being built down the road?"), make noncommittal comments ("Problem? It certainly does need to be addressed."), make irreverent remarks ("Problem? Ah, they'll get over it!"), or ignore the issue completely.

An avoidance approach is an unassertive method for dealing with very real issues. It often indicates a lack of respect for oneself and fear of dealing with the issue or person involved. Often, the leader uses this approach to preserve harmony, when fearful that others will cease liking her or him, and when she or he does not want to take the time needed to address the concern. Avoidance usually results in a lose-lose situation—no one comes out ahead and the difficulty remains.

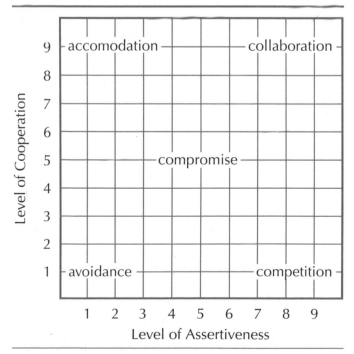

Figure 7.5 The five common approaches to managing conflicts may be placed on an assertiveness-cooperation grid.

Accommodation

As seen in Figure 7.5, accommodation is an approach that is low in assertiveness, yet high in cooperation. In this instance, rather than avoiding the issue, the facilitator attempts to cooperate with (i.e., do a favor for or yield to) others. Accommodation involves doing as the other needs or requests; it obliges the other party with little regard for one's own needs or wants; it is a self-sacrificing behavior. It can be characterized as "whatever you want" or "whatever you say." For instance, a leader might handle a conflict over a shared facility by giving in to the most vocal and persistent participant rather than actually addressing the issue at hand. Accommodation often results in a win-lose relationship and may reflect a lack of self-confidence.

Competition

An individual utilizing a competitive approach to conflict operates from a high assertive, low cooperative perspective. Essentially, an individual looks out for her or his best interests without regard for others. Competitive reactions to difficulties may be seen in verbal aggression and confrontation between two or more individuals; this is often characterized as a one-up relationship. In a competitive approach to conflict, each party seeks to overpower and dominate the other. Personal criticism and attacks are utilized, as well as hostile jokes or questions, and each party often denies responsibility for the situation. Competitive reactions to conflict may be observed in arguments by young children over who gets to play with which toy — a great deal of grabbing, shoving, and screaming occurs. Adolescents often engage in competitive approaches to conflicts during the break for independence. Adults also often engage in a competitive approach to problem solving if they believe their needs are more important than others. Competitive conflict resolution is perceived as a win-lose relationship. While it serves the needs of one, it is unhealthy for all disputants.

Compromise

As noted in Figure 7.5, compromise is a middle position where an individual acts somewhat assertively and somewhat cooperatively (but not overly so). In compromise each side gives in or concedes some aspects of its position to the other. It reflects a give-and-take philosophy with a goal of obtaining an equal exchange in the resolution or management of the conflict — even if it is less than desirable. Often, when they compromise participants feel as though neither party has achieved a satisfactory conclusion to the issue. An example might be a disagreement over which activity to play for the last twenty minutes of a session. The parties might agree to play two games for ten minutes each — not enough time for either participant to truly enjoy her or his favorite activity. This approach may be viewed as a lose-lose or weak win-win conflict management approach.

Collaboration

Collaboration is the most preferred difficulty management technique. A person behaving collaboratively acts both assertively and cooperatively. She or he is concerned for herself or himself as well as the other parties involved. Collaboration involves each individual working toward meeting the goals of the other. Unlike compromise in which each party gives up something to move ahead, in collaboration each party works together to combine resources to move ahead. In collaboration both parties work jointly and accept responsibility for the final decision. It is a win-win position for all involved. An example of collaborative problem solving might be in meeting two different needs — one group member has a need for status, another a need to complete the task. They might work together to accomplish the task and then address the status issue through publicly identifying those directly responsible for the task completion.

Intercultural Conflicts

As a leader who wants to make the best use of her of his resources and skills, understanding the advantages and disadvantages of each approach to conflict resolution is important. In addition, a leader needs to be aware of her or his own biases, the environment in which the conflict arises, and any intercultural influences that may be operating.

Earlier we explored the notion that cultures differ along a very important dimension — collectivism and individualism. In addition to these foundational values, cultures also differ along other dimensions: *uncertainty avoidance* (i.e., the degree to which people prefer unstructured or structured situations); *power distance* (i.e., the degree to which power differences exist); *masculinity* (i.e., the degree to which values associated with the roles of men prevail over values associated with the roles of women); and *long-term orientation* (i.e., the degree to which values are oriented to the future rather than the present or the past; Chuang, Church & Zikic, 2004; Gudykunst, 2004).

A lack of appreciation for these basic cultural values can lead to conflict and confusion in the resolution process. Research has shown that people in individualist cultures prefer to use active, assertive, and confrontational tactics (i.e., a competitive approach) for resolving conflicts. These individuals seek fairness and justice in conflict resolution. People in collectivist cultures, on the other hand, prefer passive, collaborative, and avoidance tactics

A leader needs to be aware of her or his own biases, the environment in which the conflict arises, and any intercultural influences that may be operating.

to "save face" and maintain interpersonal harmony (Chuang, Church & Zikic, 2004; Davidson, 2001).

As an example, in individualist cultures, adolescent—adult conflict is viewed as a natural and important rite of passage. As teenagers begin the drive for independence, a certain level of conflict is anticipated and accepted—we believe that is the only way for adolescents to break away and develop themselves as individuals. However, in collectivist cultures, people dislike social disorganization and disagreements. Social structures, institutions, and customs have been established to avoid or reduce these types of conflicts. Adolescence is not a time of breaking away, but rather a time of learning interdependence—about one's role and responsibilities within the community (Friederike & Krahe, 1999).

Chuang, Church, and Zikic (2004) found that age, gender, race/ethnicity, and tenure (i.e., length of time working in an organization) influence the way a group functions. While sometimes differences can lead to a constructive combination of diverse perspectives, they can also lead to mistrust and disagreements. This is because people from various demographic groups have a definable culture (e.g., age, gender, race/ethnicity) and differ in several respects. Differences exist in the members' willingness to take risks, attention to and concern for detail, respect for people, team orientation, outcome orientation, and aggressiveness.

In highlighting one of the ways in which racial/ethnic groups differ, Davidson (2001) reported that a person's racial background influences how an individual perceives and reacts to others—particularly in a conflict situation. For example, Davidson found that African Americans are louder, and use more forceful speech and animated nonverbal behaviors than Whites when in conflict situations. This is a result of a cultural position that values the capacity to express one's feelings with authenticity. For African Americans (in general) loud and animated self-expression demonstrates trust, respect, and caring in the interaction. On the other hand, the predominant White culture in the United States has been influenced by the Northern European culture where control and moderation of expressive behavior is valued as a means of maintaining order.

Thus, the strong expression of emotions and conflict is discouraged.

Gender is one of the most studied cultural groups in terms of conflict development and resolution, and the research findings have been mixed (Brahnam, Margavio, Hignite, Barrier & Chin, 2005; Klenke, 2003). Some have found that women and men differ in their preferred approaches to dealing with conflict while others have found no differences. In the research that shows differences women have exhibited more collaborative, accommodating, and avoiding strategies while men prefer competitive and confrontational behaviors. This is attributed to the differences in gender role expectations where men are expected to be masculine (i.e., dominant, powerful, aggressive) and women are expected to be feminine (i.e., yielding, considerate, nurturing). Klenke (2003) reported that as long as people use conflict management styles that were congruent with their gender roles, they were evaluated favorably.

Leaders must develop effective cross-cultural conflict resolution skills. Ting-Toomey (1999) suggests these skills include analyzing conflict goals (in terms of one's cultural perspective), mindful and active listening skills, refraining from quick judgments (especially based on one's own cultural mores), analyzing conflict and conflict resolution assumptions among the parties involved, trust-building skills, and being able to adapt one's communication style. In addition, it becomes incumbent upon the leader to develop an understanding of the various cultural groups with which she or he works. Learning about other cultures helps reduce conflicts and helps to make conflict resolution a win-win situation for all involved.

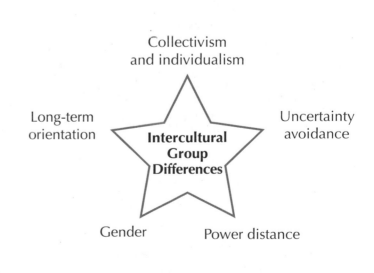

Figure 7.6 Dimensions of intercultural group differences

Effective Conflict Management

To effectively manage various difficulties, leaders must understand that people in conflict will perceive problems very differently. Perceptions are based on personal filters (i.e., how one sees the world), first impressions of those involved, and past experiences. Leaders who are aware of their own feelings relative to the situation (e.g., stress, personal fatigue, timing), who focus on the entire situation, who seek to change positions and understand varying viewpoints, and are aware of their own biases and prejudices related to the persons involved tend to be more effective than others in managing difficulties (Song, Xile & Dyer, 2000; Ting-Toomey, 1999).

A leader who is a constructive conflict manager has many traits: an ability to understand and deal with difficult emotions; empathy and the ability to earn trust; openness and sensitivity to others; emotional balance (i.e., understands own feelings and their impact on the situation); self-awareness and integrity; the ability to take a non-judgmental stance; the capacity to learn from experiences; a willingness to be assertive; the ability to think creatively and deal with complex factual material; and an ethic of thoroughness and professionalism.

Constructive Management of Difficulties

Learning to manage conflicts and solve problems requires ongoing skill development. Dealing with conflict management and problem solving can be a very emotional and complex situation—for both the conflict manager and others directly involved. Managing difficulties well requires self-awareness, creative thinking, knowledge of management techniques, and strong communication skills.

☑ Analyze conflict goals in terms of one's own culture

☑ Use mindful and active listening skills

☑ Refrain from quick judgments

☑ Analyze conflict and conflict resolution assumptions

☑ Build trust

☑ Use adaptable communication

☑ Possess/Develop cultural competence

Figure 7.7 Cross-cultural conflict resolution skills

The following guidelines may help leaders in successful conflict management:

- Address the emotional issues first by acknowledging and validating each person's feelings (e.g., "You seem very angry right now, is that true?").

- Clarify what you see, how you judge, and how you react to people and situations (e.g., I have a tendency to judge quickly so I should take a moment to gather my thoughts before making up my mind.).

- Practice "no-fault" thinking (i.e., This situation is not the fault of any one person; it exists and must be addressed.).

- Understand and take charge of your own feelings and behaviors (e.g., I am fatigued and might not see things as clearly as I should.).

- Step back and take a balanced view of the situation (i.e., identify all the viewpoints).

- Observe and analyze the conflict from three perspectives: mine, yours/theirs, and the "fly on the wall" (i.e., a person who is not invested).

- Respond positively to what is done and what is said (e.g., "I appreciate your willingness to work through this.").

- Remember that managing conflict is a process and takes time—What occurs during the management process is just as important as the end result.

Figure 7.8 A constructive conflict manager has many traits.

- Keep process activities and statements in the first person; use "I" statements (i.e., an "I message" is a four-part statement: "I feel (name the emotion) when (this occurs) because (identify the effect on self), and I would like (this to happen).").
- Beware of and avoid power plays and power issues between disputants.

❖ ❖ ❖

Constructive management of problems and conflicts involves being self-aware as well as being willing to consider all sides of an issue. Remember that a bit of the truth is found within each person's perception of the situation, and perceptions are very real to each individual. Discounting individual comments and insights as "wrong" or "stupid" may lead to a future unwillingness to address conflict in a proactive and straightforward fashion.

Seven-Phase Model of Managing Difficulties

Having discussed the inevitability and nature of conflict, the five basic approaches one can take to managing conflict, and general guidelines for addressing conflict, we will now turn our attention to the actual management of those conflicts and problems. A standard approach to addressing various difficulties moves from identifying the issue, through several interim stages, to implementing and evaluating the proposed management solutions.

A seven-phase model to successful management of various types of difficulties has been developed by combining the models offered by many authors (Marcotte, Alain & Gosselin, 1999; Sharma, Petosa & Heaney, 1999). It provides an effective step-by-step approach to address almost every type of conflict.

Prelude—Consider the Cultural Influences

As a prelude to the conflict resolution process, it is important to take a few moments and consider the people involved in the dispute. Who are they and what do they bring to the table? What history, previous experiences, and biases do they have as a part of who they are? What cul-

Seeking information from as many individuals as possible (while at the same time keeping an open mind) helps to present a clear and relatively complete picture of the actual situation.

tural values do they hold and how might these manifest in the resolution process? Is it necessary to help the disputants understand one another's foundational values? How might differing communication styles impact the conflict management process? After developing a sense of the individuals involved, the step-by-step process may now begin.

Phase 1—Define the Objectives for the Solution

First, the objectives for the solution should be congruent with agency objectives. This means that a leader must have a solid understanding of the agency mission and philosophy to ensure that solutions fall within the scope of agency values and practice. Both short-term and long-term issues should be identified and articulated: How does managing this issue in this manner relate to the existing values structure of the agency? How does addressing this issue in this manner relate to the long-term goals of the agency?

Once goals, objectives, and values are clearly stated it will be important to agree to the process of conflict management. Agreeing to and openly articulating where, when, how long (it might take multiple sessions), and how the process will occur is necessary to serve as a basis for the work ahead. All involved parties must agree to and operate within the same ground rules to progress smoothly.

Phase 2—Identify the Problem

Next, collect facts surrounding the conflict. The goal of this phase is to diagnose the various elements of the problem—to identify and determine the underlying causes of the problem. Is this a relationship or task issue? Is it based on values, resources, or internal identity issues? Many problems are not as straightforward as they might appear. For instance, if two individuals are arguing over a minor rule infraction, the real issue might be that one participant feels ignored and disrespected by the other. In this example, as in many situations, psychological needs may manifest themselves in seemingly unrelated ways.

Seeking information from as many individuals as possible (while at the same time keeping an open mind) helps to present a clear and relatively complete picture of the actual situation. It also will be helpful to list the driving forces that seem to perpetuate the problem. When does the difficulty arise? What seems to escalate the problem? When does the problem dissipate? This information will be helpful in the next step: data analysis and interpretation.

Phase 3—Analyze and Interpret Data

After identifying and stating the problem, those involved in facilitating and managing conflicts will be interested in analyzing and interpreting the data. To do this it is helpful to determine the factors that seem to influence and change the conflict. A conflict manager will want to make observations of both positive and negative factors involved in the changes surrounding the conflict. Using past experiences and good judgment in examining the entire situation will be needed at this stage. Once all the information has been gathered, what does it all mean? Understanding the context in which an issue arose and the people involved are important elements of this stage. How do the involved parties experience the conflict? What is the real issue? What does each disputant have at stake?

Phase 4—Facilitate Creative Solutions

Facilitating creative solutions often is the most enjoyable aspect of managing conflicts and problems. New and creative ideas are sought and welcomed. In fact, at this stage, the negative emotions often associated with the issues at hand are set aside to allow for freedom of expression and a sense of play in the brainstorming process.

Brainstorming is the most commonly used technique to facilitate the development of creative solutions. A common error in brainstorming, however, is to undervalue the process by justifying and qualifying suggestions as they are made. To be effective, the following brainstorming principles should be strictly followed:

- Arrange the group so that each member can see one another. A circle arrangement is often the best option. Being able to make eye contact with others in the group lends itself to supporting an open atmosphere. An open and safe atmosphere is vital to effective brainstorming.

- Be aware of the impact of the physical environment on the brainstorming process. Room temperature, lighting, and comfortable seating impact the flow of creative thought.

- Generate a large quantity (rather than quality) of ideas at this point. Aiming for quantity tends to encourage new thoughts and keeps the pace moving quickly (which is desirable).

- Welcome freewheeling and zany ideas; in fact, the crazier and more creative the ideas, the better. It is often out of one of the most "impractical" ideas that elegant solutions are found.

- Avoid critical judgments and qualifiers attached to ideas. Encourage individuals to present their ideas and then move on to the next brainstorming idea. Lengthy justifications and explanations tend to inhibit the creative process. Likewise, if group members feel that as soon as they say something another person is going to judge it "stupid" or "weird," people will stop participating.

- Strive to combine and piggyback on ideas. Once ideas are out on the floor they belong to the group and adding to them, looking at them backwards, combining two or more, or modifying them in some other fashion all lead to creating additional creative ideas. Everything goes!

- Encourage and help everyone to fully participate. There are many occasions when the best ideas for a solution come from the most unexpected (and often quietest) source. The facilitator might consider a system of some sort whereby a large group is divided into smaller groups and then brought back together; or a situation where everyone shares one idea before any one person may share additional ideas. Encouraging and facilitating participant involvement and managing idea flow are both important in effective brainstorming.

- Use analogies, metaphors, or "animal viewpoints" to encourage different ways of looking at the situation. An analogy is where the situation is likened to something else as in, "A problem is like meatloaf because it is constituted of many different ingredients which can be examined to see the individual components." A metaphor is a figure of speech in which a word or phrase that ordinarily designates one thing is used to designate another, thus making an implicit comparison, as in "a sea of troubles." Finally, animal viewpoints ask individuals to examine the situation from the perspective of a worm, fish, bird, turtle, or other animal. All of these techniques allow for unique and creative perspectives to be brought to bear.

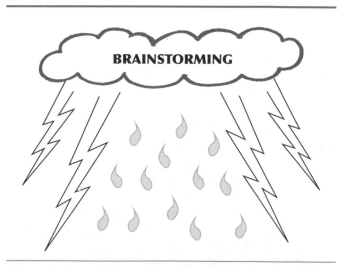

Figure 7.9 Brainstorming is like a thunderstorm where ideas flow like raindrops and creativity flashes like lightning.

- Write ideas on an overhead or flip chart for viewing as they are generated. This enables group members to piggyback on ideas and helps people to retain information.

Phase 5—Select from Among Alternatives

Once brainstorming is complete the next step is to select one or more choices from the brainstormed list. This can be a difficult process. One should engage the critical thinking abilities of the participants to delineate and evaluate the advantages and disadvantages of each possible solution. Examine the pros and cons of each possible solution, no matter how zany the idea. Stopping short often results in premature selection of a solution which may not be the best option. When evaluating the possibilities, the facilitator will want to assist participants in considering the consequences and viability of each option. In addition, it may be important to rearticulate the decision-making method and degree of group involvement in the decision-making process. Listing the pros and cons on overheads or flip charts in view of everyone often helps with critical-thinking processes.

Phase 6—Generate Strategies and Implement Decisions

Once a solution has been selected, participants will need to brainstorm strategies, actions, and timing to implement the decision. The conflict management process will be wasted if a selected solution is not tried and given a chance to work. Again, brainstorming is effective at this stage. Strategies to initiate implementation of a conflict management decision are very important to resolving the issue in a satisfactory manner. Effective leadership involves giving the strategy time to work. It can take several trials or some time for people to get used to the implementation of the new strategy. Leaders would be wise to give the solution time to work before judging its effectiveness.

Phase 7—Evaluate the Process and Outcome

After the solution has been implemented, leaders and participants will want to evaluate both the problem management process and the outcome. Were the objectives met? Was the issue managed to the satisfaction of all participants? Is the momentum back on the right track? At this stage, checking in with task issues, human relations, and conceptual issues will allow those involved to determine the level of success.

❖ ❖ ❖

Following techniques to manage difficulties may appear to be a relatively mechanical process, but it involves many different leadership skills. Effective communication and group dynamics skills are integral to successful problem management. In addition, personal leadership style and competencies such as assertiveness are also beneficial to the difficulty management process.

Assertiveness in Managing Difficulties

Assertiveness involves a range of behaviors that arise out of particular attitudes related to perception of self and the handling of various situations. Being assertive means standing up for one's own rights while being sensitive to the rights of others and accepting responsibility for the consequences of one's actions. Crawley (1994) suggested a four-stage continuum of behaviors: aggressive, passive, manipulative, and assertive.

Aggressive Behaviors

Aggressiveness is based on a lack of respect for others. It involves standing up for personal rights in a way that violates the rights of others. Aggression aims to dominate and win, usually through humiliating, degrading, or overpowering others so that they become unable to stand up for themselves. Aggressive people often get what they want and perceive themselves as powerful. Others will frequently resent an aggressive person and respond in equally negative fashions. While all of us act aggressively

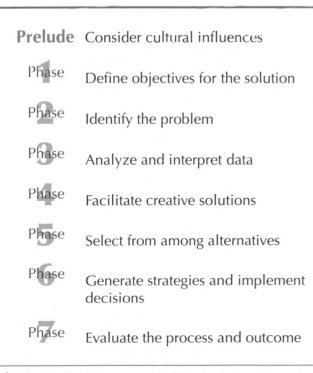

Prelude	Consider cultural influences
Phase 1	Define objectives for the solution
Phase 2	Identify the problem
Phase 3	Analyze and interpret data
Phase 4	Facilitate creative solutions
Phase 5	Select from among alternatives
Phase 6	Generate strategies and implement decisions
Phase 7	Evaluate the process and outcome

Figure 7.10 The seven-phase model for managing problems.

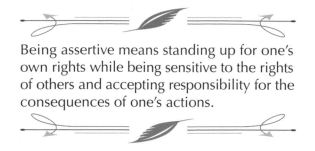

Being assertive means standing up for one's own rights while being sensitive to the rights of others and accepting responsibility for the consequences of one's actions.

at some time, aggressive leaders will rarely retain personal credibility or respect from the group.

Passive Behaviors

Passive behavior involves violating one's own rights by failing to express (or disregarding) one's own feelings and thoughts. Being passive shows a lack of respect for oneself. The goal is to appease others and avoid conflicts. Some passive people feel that their behavior leads to a quiet life free of unpleasant conflicts and problems. On the other hand, many individuals do not respect people who do not stand up for themselves, and may take advantage of passive people. Passive leaders are usually ineffective, particularly when attempting to facilitate problem management.

Manipulative Behaviors

Being manipulative is based on a lack of respect for self *and* others. It involves expressing one's needs in an underhanded fashion to coerce particular responses from others,

usually to one's personal benefit. Manipulative people may succeed in persuading others to behave in certain ways and may even be successful at dodging unpleasant situations. However, being manipulative often results in resentment by others and a loss of respect. Manipulative leisure services leaders quickly lose the respect of participants and are often stymied by group members in their leadership efforts.

Assertive Behavior

Assertiveness indicates a respect for self and others. It involves standing up for one's own rights in direct, honest, and appropriate ways which honor cultural differences and do not violate other's rights. When a leader is assertive, others understand her or his needs and respect her or him as an individual. Because assertiveness may lead to confrontation and denied requests, effective assertiveness makes use of the four-part "I" statements discussed on page 147.

Selecting appropriate assertive behaviors can result in positive approaches to various types of difficulties. Leisure services leaders can help participants develop assertive behaviors and make use of them in the conflict management process. The use of assertive behaviors often aids in the handling of the emotional aspects, which are an integral aspect of all conflicts and problems. An assertive leader is more effective in all aspects of working with groups than leaders who utilize other types of behaviors.

Emotions and Managing Difficulties

The emotional element of conflict and other difficulties is often neglected in the conflict management process. In the predominant U.S. culture, people are taught to conceal their emotions—people view an emotional person as weak. Nonetheless, emotions persist in conflict situations, and if not acknowledged and addressed they can be detrimental to successful problem management.

Bodtker and Jameson (2001) suggest that emotion has three elements: a behavioral element, which is the way the emotion gets expressed; a physiological component, which is the way the emotion makes us physically feel; and a cognitive/moral element, which relates to how we assess a particular situation (e.g., good/bad, right/wrong). The meanings of the emotions we experience are socially and culturally based. Different cultural groups express emotions differently and society tells us what emotions are acceptable in what circumstances (e.g., We should be happy at weddings and sad at funerals). To further assist

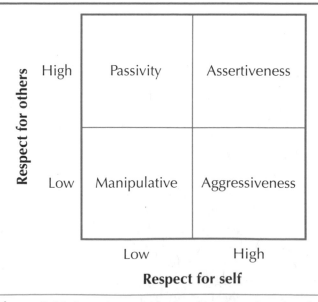

Figure 7.11 Assertiveness is a combination of respect for self and others.

in the understanding of emotions in conflict, Bodtker offers five principles of conflict-based emotion.

Principle 1: Conflict is marked by a triggering event that elicits emotion.

Principle 2: Intensity levels of emotion vary throughout the conflict process.

Principle 3: The experience of emotion is fundamentally a values-based process.

Principle 4: Conflict is identity based; we become emotional when something is personally at stake for us.

Principle 5: Conflict is relational; power and social status are often the source of conflict.

One of the more prevalent emotions in conflict management is anger. Anger has been given a "bad rep" in that many believe that anger is never appropriately expressed—being angry may even be perceived as irrational. As many therapists will attest, however, well-handled anger can be beneficial in many settings. Appropriately used, anger promotes an acknowledgment of problems and elaborates on positions held by those involved (Tjosvold, 1993). It also fuels ongoing improvement as parties work toward managing the issues that triggered the initial bouts of anger.

Anger may be viewed as similar to physical pain in that it sends a signal that helps individuals determine the source of irritation—the underlying causes of the problem. Furthermore, anger focuses and motivates people, and moves people to action (Tjosvold, 1993). It is difficult to do nothing when an individual expresses anger about a situation.

In cooperative relationships anger can serve to reaffirm interdependence, strengthen the need for collaboration, energize the parties involved, and increase both self-awareness and awareness of others. Expressing anger allows for a ventilation of emotions, which can be relaxing and serve as a physical release. As with all emotions, there are appropriate and inappropriate ways to express anger. Leisure services leaders who understand how to use anger as well as how to help others manage it will be increasingly effective in helping to manage conflicts. To express anger constructively leaders should

- Establish a cooperative context (i.e., show a commitment to the relationship and avoid provoking anger simply because of the ability or position to do so).
- State and explain their position (i.e., describe feelings, be specific, take responsibility for one's own anger, be consistent in verbal and nonverbal messages, use assertion).

Appropriately used, anger promotes an acknowledgment of problems and elaborates on positions held by those involved. It also fuels ongoing improvement as parties work toward managing the issues that triggered the initial bouts of anger.

- Avoid "out of control" expressions of anger (e.g., shouting, throwing items, projecting blame).
- Question and understand differing views (e.g., check assumptions, be sensitive to other viewpoints, check the reactions of those listening).
- Integrate and create options (e.g., use constructive conflict management, ask for help in developing solutions).
- Agree and "shake hands" (i.e., once the issue has been successfully managed, put the anger away, avoid hanging on to it, make the expression of anger cathartic).
- Reflect and learn (e.g., celebrate joint success, reflect on the experience, determine the lessons learned that can be used in the future).

Using anger within the context of assertive behaviors can enhance successful conflict management. People have a right to know how each disputant feels (as well as what she or he thinks) about a particular situation. In helping others to manage their anger and other feelings in a constructive fashion, leaders may engage in behaviors known as mediation.

Photo courtesy of Gwynn Powell

Emotions, when well used, can be a good thing.

Mediation and Leadership Responsibilities

Conflict management typically begins when at least one disputant recognizes the need to find a solution to the problem and initiates the process. Although it is almost always best for individuals to resolve their own conflicts, many occasions arise in which the use of a mediator is the best choice for finding the elegant solution. Leaders in parks, recreation, and leisure services are often called upon to mediate conflicts at a variety of levels. The goal is to achieve an elegant solution—one that satisfies all parties, maintains a positive atmosphere, and strengthens relationships.

A mediator facilitates the resolution process of the parties involved in the dispute to enable them to reach an agreement by themselves. In this manner, mediation involves a third party helping individuals move through the conflict management process. It might be wise to consider mediation when:

- Relationships are important and people care about one another.
- Those involved want to retain control of the outcome (i.e., they want to avoid having an outsider dictate the way to manage the problem).
- Both sides have a good case and it is difficult to discern which is "better."
- Speed and timing are important (i.e., the issue must be addressed now).
- Confidentiality is important.
- Both sides see a need to let off steam (i.e., a third party can help to keep things from getting overly personal).
- Neither side wants things to go further up the [grievance] line (Johnson & Johnson, 2003; McFadzean, 2002; Putnam, 2004).

Furthermore, a mediator can be helpful when one disputant feels that the other person involved in the dispute is in a more powerful position than she or he. Although this power discrepancy (which may be related to size, age, sex, personality, seniority, or other reasons) may be more perceived than real, it is a limiting factor in face-to-face negotiation when those involved in the conflict manage the situation themselves.

Mediation is also useful when the parties do not communicate openly with one another; the parties do not have the skills, desire or trust to manage the difficulties effectively; or the parties cannot find an acceptable solution themselves. The presence of a mediator may also be

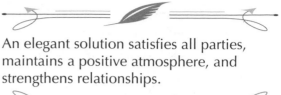

An elegant solution satisfies all parties, maintains a positive atmosphere, and strengthens relationships.

helpful when the conflict is a long-standing one, when past efforts to negotiate have failed, or when one of the involved parties seems reluctant to engage in negotiation.

The Mediation Process

Because they are similar in aim, the mediation process provides guidance to the conflict management process. The conflict manager begins the process by explaining how it works and expressing appreciation to all parties for being willing to work out the problem. Establishing ground rules (a matter of good manners) for the mediation meeting is also important. Participants need to agree not to interrupt each other, to be honest, and to try to find a solution together. Throughout the process the conflict manager asks clarifying questions to ensure that points are clearly understood and makes certain that each disputant gets relatively equal time.

The mere presence of an independent third party may help with the resolution of a dispute (Bercovitch & Houston, 2000). Mediator presence often helps in reducing emotions and objectifying the situation. A leader serving as a mediator should strive to maintain an emphasis on establishing meaningful communication between the disputants, who eventually will identify their own mutually acceptable (i.e., elegant) solution. The mediator helps the participants through the following process:

Step 1—Set the Tone

State your positive intentions; front-load for success. For example: "I think we have a problem and I'd really like to work together with you to solve it for everyone involved," or "Thank you for taking the time to meet with me today. I look forward to solving this problem together."

Step 2—Define and Discuss the Conflict

Using "I" messages and active listening, define and discuss the conflict. Each disputant should have an opportunity to state her or his views and to restate what the other person has said. Each person should be given equal and uninterrupted time to state her or his view of the conflict.

The mediation process provides guidance to the conflict management process.

Step 3—Summarize Progress

Once it appears that the conflict has been described from both points of view, each person should spend a few minutes summarizing the situation from her or his viewpoint. The mediator serves to prevent interruptions and assist in clarification, if needed.

Step 4—Explore Alternative Solutions

Ask and answer the question, "What can I do to solve this problem?" Avoid criticizing ideas and list as many alternatives as possible. Using and following the principles of brainstorming might be helpful during this stage. Explore possible solutions for each part of the conflict and discuss possible future consequences for each idea. Keep in mind that effective solutions must be agreeable to both parties (specifically regarding what will happen, who will do it, and when) and balanced (each person should contribute to the solution).

Step 5—Set a Time for Follow-up

Before ending the mediation session, agree on a time to check back with those involved to make sure the solution is working. This encourages all parties to be accountable and helps to address any unexpected problems which may arise.

❖ ❖ ❖

Following and practicing mediation steps and the conflict management process can be helpful to mitigate all types of difficulties a leader might face in leisure services settings. The steps to mediation provide a logical framework from which to address a variety of issues. It would be wise to remember that while the model steps to mediation and conflict management are straightforward, in real situations the process might not be as clear cut. People react to various situations in unique and unpredictable ways and these behaviors can cause glitches in the conflict management or mediation process. Levine (1998) suggests adopting an attitude of resolution when addressing conflicts. "When you choose an attitude of resolution, you implicitly become a leader. In your leadership roles, when dealing with differences at work and at home, it becomes up to you to keep moving toward resolution" (p. 106).

"When you choose an attitude of resolution, you implicitly become a leader. In your leadership roles, when dealing with differences at work and at home, it becomes up to you to keep moving toward resolution."

The Mediation Process

A very simple process for leader-facilitated mediation has been presented by Koch and Jordan (1993). It is a quick and positive process for resolving conflicts. The first step is to have two (or more) disputants who are interested in resolving an issue. Next, the disputants must agree to certain conditions:

1. to work to solve the problem;
2. to speak honestly; and
3. not to interrupt, use name calling, or become physically violent.

The role of the mediator is to facilitate the process, not to resolve the issue for the disputants. In this respect, the mediator provides the structure and the opportunity for the disputants to work through the issues. The following steps, facilitated by the mediator, can help to reach an agreeable solution:

1. Have the disputants move with the mediator to a private place and sit down side-by-side facing the same direction.
2. Remind the disputants of the conditions stated above.
3. Ask Person 1 to tell what happened and how she or he feels.
4. Repeat with Person 2.
5. Ask Person 1 what she or he can do to help solve this problem.
6. Repeat with Person 2.
7. Get agreement from each disputant regarding what each is willing to do.
8. Ask if the disagreement is resolved.
9. Ask each person what she or he could do differently if a similar disagreement should arise again.
10. Congratulate the disputants for managing the problem!

Figure 7.12 An in-depth look at a mediation process

Summary

While not often perceived as such, conflicts and problems can be very positive—they may serve to jump-start a group, encourage creative thinking, and help individuals clarify their positions. Difficulties range on a spectrum from mild differences to violence; movement from one extreme position on the continuum to the other extreme can occur quite rapidly. This is known as escalation. Escalation can occur when people raise their voices, make themselves larger, involve outsiders, bring up past issues, and/or feel threatened in some manner. Leisure services leaders can be instrumental in helping to de-escalate conflict by engaging in specific behaviors.

Reasons for conflict arise out of differences in perceptions of the distribution of resources, different psychological needs, and conflicting values. Values conflicts tend to be the most difficult to address because they affect individuals at their core. With knowledge about how conflicts can escalate and why people face conflict, leaders can choose an approach to facilitate the successful management of that conflict. There are five common approaches to conflict: avoidance, accommodation, competition, compromise, and collaboration. These approaches vary in terms of level of assertion and level of cooperation required of the disputants. Collaboration is often the most highly sought after approach as it leads to successful management of conflicts. Various cultures differ in uses of conflict resolution approaches.

A seven-phase model of conflict management was presented where one moves from defining the objectives for the solution to evaluating a decision after it has been implemented. The process involves all disputants and can provide a structure for addressing each party's needs. All perspectives of conflict resolution require assertiveness. Assertiveness falls along a four-point continuum along with aggressiveness, passive behaviors, and manipulative behaviors.

To facilitate the management of difficulties leisure services leaders may be called upon to serve as mediators for participants. Mediators address emotional issues of the situation, practice no-fault thinking, take a balanced view of the situation, use positive "I" statements, and address the situation from three perspectives: yours, mine, and the casual observer. Mediation is a process whereby the leader facilitates the conflict management process with those involved; when followed and practiced a leader can be highly effective.

Beginning the Journey

Any time there are people gathered, there is potential for misunderstandings and conflicts. Effective leaders know how to address conflicts and difficulties and work through them to the satisfaction of all parties. As you continue on your personal leadership journey, consider your knowledge and experience in dealing with conflicts. Perhaps the following thought-provoking questions will help.

1. What is the difference between a conflict and a problem, and which tends to be more complex? Why? How is conflict beneficial? When is conflict not healthy?

2. What is conflict resolution? What is the ultimate goal of conflict resolution? What are the basic skills of conflict resolution? What kind of practice have you had in resolving conflicts? Draw a flow chart of the conflict-resolution process. Is it in a straight line? Does it flow back on itself? Is it curvilinear? What skills do you need to improve most?

3. Describe the struggle spectrum. Think of a recent conflict you had with someone. What level of struggle did you get to before it was resolved? Have you ever been engaged in a conflict where the result was a fight? How was the conflict resolved at that point? Can you recall each step as it developed?

4. How do conflicts escalate? What does this mean? How do conflicts de-escalate? What does this mean? What role does a leader play in conflict escalation and de-escalation? Role play an imaginary conflict with someone else. One of you make it escalate while the other focuses on de-escalation by following the suggested behaviors. Try this (de-escalation) the next time you are involved in a conflict.

5. Think of recreation-specific situations and the common causes of conflicts. Make a list of the different reasons that conflicts arise. What role can you, as the leader, play in minimizing conflicts now that you understand these reasons? Explain the factors that can influence the intensity of difficulties.

6. Draw the conflict resolution grid and identify the axes. Mark on the grid where the five common approaches to resolution fall. Which one of these approaches to conflict resolution do you tend to utilize most? How can you tell? Do you favor one approach over others in certain situations? Describe these differences.

7. Think about your own cultural background and the assumptions that are inherent in your belief systems and values. Now, think about a culture that is different from yours. How might these cultural differences contribute to difficulties in resolving conflicts? What are the primary differences between collectivist and individualist cultures in terms of dealing with conflicts? What are the skills needed for effective intercultural conflict resolution? What do you need to focus on to become a skilled intercultural conflict manager?

8. What kinds of traits does a leader with effective conflict resolution skills have? Which of these traits are strong suits for you, and which do you need to work to improve? What guidelines would you offer to a younger leader for constructive management of difficulties?

9. Draw a flow chart of the seven-phase model to manage difficulties. Explain the process and listen to yourself as you talk it out. Which step do you think is the most difficult to work through and why? Which of the seven steps do you think is most crucial to successful conflict management? Why do you think this? Describe the process of brainstorming to help in this area. What are the critical guidelines for effective brainstorming?

10. On the continuum of assertiveness, where do you usually fall? Are you comfortable with assertiveness? When are you usually most passive? How can you use this range of skills to aid you in developing your conflict management skills? Are you able to distinguish between assertiveness and aggressiveness? Why is understanding this continuum important for a leader?

11. Think of a variety of situations in which you have been involved and your emotions have been stirred up. In what situations were you able to most appropriately express your emotions? When is it appropriate for a leader to show anger? How should you go about doing so? What techniques do you utilize when others are expressing extreme emotions (e.g., anger, irritation, frustration, hurt, glee) to help moderate those emotions?

12. What is mediation and what is the role of a leader in mediation? When would it be a good idea to consider mediation? Describe the steps to mediation. Practice this with at least two other people. Thinking back to what you learned about seating dynamics, how might you position individuals who are in the midst of mediation? What does it mean to "adopt an attitude of resolution?"

References

Arnold, M., Heyne, L., and Busser, J. (2005). *Problem solving: Tools and techniques for the park and recreation administrator* (4th ed.). Champaign, IL: Sagamore.

Bercovitch, J. and Houston, A. (2000). Why do they do it like this? *Journal of Conflict Resolution, 44*(2), 170–202.

Blackard, K. (2001). Assessing workplace conflict resolution options. *Dispute Resolution Journal, 56*(1), 57–62.

Blake, R. and Mouton, J. (1964). *The managerial grid.* Houston, TX: Gulf Publishing.

Bodtker, A. and Jameson, J. (2001). Emotion in conflict formation and its transformation: Application to organizational conflict management. *International Journal of Conflict Management, 12*(3), 259–275.

Brahnam, S., Margavio, T., Hignite, M., Barrier, T., and Chin, J. (2005). A gender-based categorization for conflict resolution. *The Journal of Management Development, 24*(3), 197–208.

Brewer, N., Mitchell, P., and Weber, N. (2002). Gender role, organizational status, and conflict management styles. *International Journal of Conflict Management, 13*(1), 78–94.

Choudrie, J. (2005). Understanding the role of communication and conflict on reengineering team development. *Journal of Enterprise Information Management, 18*(1/2), 64–78.

Chuang, Y., Church, R., and Zikic, J. (2004). Organizational culture, group diversity, and intra-group conflict. *Team Performance Management, 10*(1/2), 26–34.

Cox, T. (1993). *Cultural diversity in organizations.* San Francisco, CA: Berrett-Koehler Publishers Inc.

Crawley, J. (1994). *Constructive conflict management.* San Diego, CA: Pfeiffer & Co.

Davidson, M. (2001). Know thine adversary: The impact of race on styles of dealing with conflict. *Sex Roles, 45*(5/6), 259–276.

Friederike, B. and Krahe, B. (1999). Strategies for resolving interpersonal conflicts in adolescence. *Journal of Cross-Cultural Psychology, 30*(6), 667–683.

Gudykunst, W. (2004). *Bridging differences: Effective intergroup communication* (4th ed.). Thousand Oaks, CA: Sage Publications.

Johnson, D. and Johnson, F. (2003). *Joining together: Group theory and group skills* (8th ed.). Boston, MA: Allyn & Bacon.

Keltner, J. (1994). *The management of struggle.* Cresskill, NJ: Hampton Press.

Klenke, K. (2003). Gender influences in decision-making processes in top management teams. *Management Decision, 41*(10), 1024–1030.

Koch, S. and Jordan, D. (1993, July/August). We can work it out: Resolving staff conflicts. *Camping Magazine*, 21–25

Levine, S. (1998). *Getting to resolution*. San Francisco, CA: Berrett-Koehler Publishers.

Marcotte, D., Alain, M. and Gosselin, M. (1999). Gender differences in adolescent depression: Gender-typed characteristics or problem-solving skills deficits? *Sex Roles, 41*(1/2), 31–48.

McFadzean, E. (2002). Developing and supporting creative problem solving teams: Part 2 – Facilitator competencies. *Management Decision, 40*(5/6), 537–552.

McGrane, F., Wilson, J., and Cammock, T. (2005). Leading employees in one-to-one dispute resolution. *Leadership & Organization Development Journal, 26*(3/4), 263–279.

Putnam, L. (2004). Transformations and critical moments in negotiations. *Negotiation Journal, 20*(2), 275–295.

Sharma, M., Petosa, R. and Heaney, C. (1999). Evaluation of a brief intervention based on social cognitive theory to develop problem-solving skills among sixth-grade children. *Health Education and Behavior, 26*(4), 465–477.

Song, M., Xile, J. and Dyer, B. (2000). Antecedents and consequences of marketing managers' conflict-handling behaviors. *Journal of Marketing, 64*(1), 50–66.

Ting-Toomey, S. (1999). *Communicating across cultures*. New York, NY: The Guilford Press.

Tjosvold, D. (1993). *Learning to manage conflict: Getting people to work together productively*. New York, NY: Lexington Books.

Worchel, S. and Simpson, J. (Eds.). (1993). *Conflict between people and groups*. Chicago, IL: Nelson-Hall.

Leader Profile

Tracey Crawford, CTRS, CPRP
Superintendent of Recreation • North Suburban Special Recreation Association, IL

Tracey has 12 years in this position, and 18 years in the parks, recreation, and leisure services profession

Some of the leadership positions she has held include:

- Illinois Parks and Recreation Association President (and almost every other office position possible)
- Illinois Therapeutic Recreation Society Section Representative
- Steering Committee, National Institute for Recreation Inclusion
- Program Chair, National Institute for Recreation Inclusion
- National Recreation and Park Association (NRPA) program committee member
- President, National Therapeutic Recreation Society, NRPA
- Chair, National Therapeutic Recreation Society Institute
- Great Lakes Regional Council (of NRPA) Board Member

What is the meaning of leadership?
Leadership is the ability to inspire and motivate people to move toward a cause. True leaders are able to navigate and move their team through change and still keep a clear direction in front of them. They are able to clearly articulate choices to the team, solicit input, and move the group toward the chosen direction.

What are the most important leader qualities?
Know that things are constantly changing. Change is the norm—It has become the new constant. Leaders need to be able to make tough decisions when no one else wants to make them. Integrity, honesty loyalty, commitment… the biggest quality is the desire to want to be a leader. You really have to want it. You have to be able to keep that in front of you—surround yourself with clear indicators of why you want to be a leader.

What advice do you have for students who aspire to leadership in parks, recreation, and leisure services?
Get to know yourself and give yourself time to know yourself. This means know what you are passionate about; know what it is you like, dislike, and why you are doing what you are doing. Take time to learn what you really believe in. To do that, get involved in as much as you can—You won't know what you want to do until you try a lot of different things. Open your mind and welcome opportunities—it's the only way to figure out what your passion is, what you are "supposed" to do. We often try to choose our niche too early; most of us find our niche after years of trying new things. Again, open your mind, expose yourself to everything possible—put yourself out there.

Favorite book(s): The Lion, the Witch, and the Wardrobe by C.S. Lewis.

Favorite activities: Reading, and reading several books at once—all genres; listening to books on tape. I find myself listening to books I might not read—I'll listen to anyone read me a story.

Chapter Eight
Managing and Motivating Participant Behaviors

Learning Opportunities

Through studying this chapter readers will have the opportunity to:

- Explore various approaches to behavior management;
- Examine a variety of behavior management techniques for inclusion into one's own repertoire;
- Consider methods of selecting behavior management techniques;
- Explain how motivation is related to behavior management; and
- Put into practice motivation techniques as preventative behavior management.

Photo courtesy of Deb Jordan

People expect to be free from the pressures of work and free to do as they please when engaged in leisure and recreation activities. In fact, *freedom from* and *freedom to* are integral elements of several leisure theories. These expectations are part of what leads to the need for managing and motivating participant behaviors—people often let down their "social guard" when recreating.

Everyone is different in this respect; people have different expectations, preferences, and behavior styles when involved in parks, recreation, and leisure activities. Because of these differences people sometimes behave in ways that are not always considered acceptable. In other words, people do not always do and behave as leaders ask or as they would like—this is true for children, adolescents, adults, and the elderly.

Over the past several years in society tremendous changes have taken place in individual viewpoints, social mores, and social values. In addition, there is general agreement in society that a shared sense of morality has lessened. People are more apt to engage in confrontational, rude, and violent behaviors than in the past. Since leisure settings are reflections of the larger society, these changes in social mores may lead to increased violence and aggression in recreational venues. Examples include road rage and violence at all levels of sports (e.g., player to player, player to official, fans to fans, fans to officials). Having said that, these types of incidents are still relatively isolated and it is more likely that a recreation leader will face more basic behavioral disruptions in the course of leadership.

This chapter will define terms, explore approaches to behavior management, and present various behavior management systems. As a part of behavior management, motivation theories will be addressed, as well as specific techniques for motivating participants.

Definitions

The term *behavior management* has been used interchangeably with other words such as discipline and behavior modification, yet each term has different meanings. They all relate to the desire to maintain individual behaviors in a desirable and socially acceptable fashion.

Behavior Management

Behavior management is the preferred term for altering or maintaining positive relationships and actions in recreation and leisure services leadership. It tends to be most accurate in terms of identifying what the leader wants to accomplish. Leaders do not necessarily want to control other's behaviors, but rather to guide others' actions to conform to an established set of expectations. Behaviors are actions or reactions of people in response to external or internal stimuli. Therefore, it makes sense that to manage or guide those behaviors, the internal and/or external stimuli need to be addressed. By far, prevention is the best behavior management tool available to minimize undesirable conduct.

Discipline

Discipline, one element of behavior management, refers to one person initially controlling behaviors of another through the process of training. To *discipline* usually implies to control by enforcing compliance or order on someone. The ultimate goal is self-discipline, where each individual controls her or his own behaviors to meet internal and external expectations. Interference from a leader

Leaders do not necessarily want to control other's behaviors, but rather to guide others' actions to conform to an established set of expectations.

is rarely needed when individuals are self-disciplined. When used, leader imposed discipline commonly involves the use of punishment to gain submission to rules and authority.

If external discipline measures are needed, leaders are encouraged to use principle-centered discipline (Laursen, 2003). Principle-centered discipline encourages leaders to identify the principles on which they base their views of desirable (and undesirable) behaviors. One suggested principle is to provide a safe and consistent environment with the aim of developing self-control and self-discipline. Holding the philosophy that people are basically good (rather than bad) and "catching" them doing something right are additional core principles.

Behavior Modification

Behavior modification is a term commonly used in the therapeutic element of the leisure services field. It has its foundation in operant conditioning and utilizes a great deal of reinforcement toward the ultimate goal of controlled, constructive, predictive, and orderly behaviors (Carter, Van Andel & Robb, 2003). Leaders use positive and negative reinforcements to increase desirable behaviors and decrease undesirable behaviors. Leisure services providers often use behavior modification when working with clients who have few or low level social skills, or who engage in self-destructive behaviors.

Table 8A Behavioral changes over the years

In the Past	Today
• Youth were considered innocent.	• Youth are streetwise.
• Physical punishment was condoned.	• Corporal punishment is banned.
• Public agencies were immune from most lawsuits.	• Lawsuits are likely no matter the type of agency.
• Leadership was autocratic.	• Leadership is participatory.
• Problem youth were separated from the mainstream.	• Problem and troubled youth are integrated in schools and neighborhoods.
• Acts of violence were relatively uncommon.	• Acts of violence are commonplace; violence has moved from fists to guns.
• Severe behavior problems were limited to inner cities and slums.	• Severe behavior problems are found everywhere.

Adapted from Ramsey, R. (1994). *Administrator's complete school discipline guide*. Englewood Cliffs, NJ: Prentice Hall.

behavior management:
Goal is to maintain positive relationships with all.

discipline:
Uses training to move from external control of behaviors to internal control, or self-discipline.

behavior modification:
Uses reinforcement and operant conditioning to increase desirable behaviors and decrease undesirable behaviors.

Figure 8.1 Definitions of key concepts

Both adults and children receive benefits from structured environments and routines that serve as the basis for positive behaviors. In addition, the environment, facilities, program, and other participants benefit from guiding participant behaviors in positive directions. While adults often engage in the same undesirable behaviors as children (e.g., whining, fighting, shouting, being disrespectful to the leader, refusing to participate, not listening to instructions), when adults engage in these behaviors they are not labeled as misbehaving; children, however, commonly are so labeled. Thus, misbehavior is simply a label adults place on certain types of actions exhibited by young people.

Generally, actions defined as misbehaviors are goal-directed rather than directed at the leader personally. The person misbehaving is usually trying to meet personal needs rather than purposefully disrupt the activity or compete with the leader. The manner or approach used to meet those needs might be perceived as immature or considered antisocial; this is what usually leads to the negative label of misbehavior.

It is not uncommon for recreation leaders to define any disruption to an activity or leadership opportunity as misbehavior, yet all disruptions are not behavior problems. Experienced leaders expect some disruptions, no matter the age of the participants. Disruptions may be no more than evidence of exuberance, excitement, or high-intensity interest. In addition, people with developmental, emotional, behavioral, or learning disabilities may be perceived as misbehaving because they do not act in a manner consistent with their chronological age or as society deems appropriate. As leaders gain experience, it becomes easier to distinguish behavior management issues from simple participant excitement.

Power and Behavior Management

As with all aspects of leadership, effective leaders need to be self-aware with regard to their views of behavior management. Knowing one's "hot buttons," understanding the impact of previous experience on personal views of behavior, and one's basic philosophy of behavior management can help in times of uncertainty. For instance, if a leader is unaware of her or his views of appropriate behavior, it can be tempting to "pull rank" over participants when dealing with undesirable behaviors. The leader may try to argue, bully, or intimidate participants into appropriate behaviors. These types of behaviors are examples of leader power over participants and are often a result of a lack of leader self-knowledge and self-confidence.

Leader power exists—it comes from the position one holds and might include the power to eject someone from a facility, deny access to equipment, force an individual to attend a group session, or to otherwise interfere or intervene with another's leisure experience. It is important to remember that even if leader power is not used in a negative way with participants, the perception of leader power exists. Inappropriate and negative use of one's power may lead to participant resentment or retaliation where a power struggle between participants and leaders occurs. Power struggles rarely lead to successful behavior management and generally do not facilitate an individual learning self-discipline.

To facilitate positive leisure experiences, leaders would be wise to be aware of their position of power and use it in a fashion to help participants achieve their leisure goals and improve their personal social skills. In relation to discipline, power can be viewed as being on a continuum with the leader retaining all the power (i.e., external discipline) on one extreme and the participants having full control over power to discipline themselves (i.e., internal power) on the other end. Self-discipline is the most effective for managing behaviors, involves less leader intervention, and can lead to life-long personal development.

Approaches to Behavior Management

Many approaches to behavior management have been developed over the years. Many of the models were established through the study of sociology, psychology, and education and have roots in behaviorism, humanism, and other aspects of social psychology. This section will provide snapshot information about several of the more commonly used behavior management models in leisure services.

Preventative Management

An effective leader experiences fewer disruptions from participants than does an ineffective leader due to the

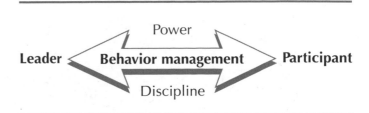

Figure 8.2 Discipline and power relate to behavior management.

skilled use of behavior management techniques. In fact, (Barbetta, Norona & Bicard, 2005) suggest that effective leadership is the best approach to behavior management. Effective leaders tend to intuitively use preventative management techniques to minimize or prevent behavior difficulties from occurring. This technique includes using effective leadership techniques, beginning with preparation, to keep participants engaged in fun and exciting experiences throughout the event.

In addition to exhibiting strong leadership abilities, preventative management utilizes selection of developmentally appropriate activities, sequencing, pacing, and frequent monitoring of participants so that potential problems can be addressed before they occur. Frequent monitoring enables a leader to observe participants acting in desired manners and praise them for it (i.e., catch them doing something right). The use of clear rules and appropriate praise are also elements of a preventative management approach. As an example, a leader using a preventative management approach would ensure that there is enough equipment for full participation and that the activity space is well-defined. This would minimize participants vying for use of equipment or having a long wait time, and would help participants to know activity boundaries.

Moral Education

Many favor the use of moral education as a model to change behaviors. It has drawbacks relative to participant understanding, however. Youngsters may not have the cognitive development to make sense of a leader using this approach. In their attempts to alter behaviors, leaders ascribing to this theory commonly use discussions of

Long wait times can result in bored and disengaged participants.

Effective leadership is the best approach to behavior management.

real-life dilemmas and role-playing as techniques to help participants understand why their behaviors are undesirable and why they should change those behaviors. For instance, a leader using this approach with a child who has just bitten another child might sit the biter down and have a heart-to-heart discussion about the negative aspects of biting or hurting someone. The leader might ask, "How would you feel if someone bit you?" Moral education also may include participant involvement in agency leadership and policy development when rules, policies, and procedures are developed.

Affective and Communication Models

Affective and communication models of behavior management target one's emotions and feelings about various behavioral issues. Within this category leaders work with participants on values clarification and interpersonal skills training. Feelings and emotions are addressed as the leader attempts to determine causes for undesirable behaviors. In addition, the leader stresses active listening in these models because open communication is a prerequisite for trust, expression of emotions, and dealing with problems openly. For example, if a leader were to follow this approach when dealing with an argumentative adult, she or he might ask the individual to come into the office and talk things through. Through active listening, the leader would try to determine what participant feelings (e.g., frustration, anger) were causing or exacerbating the conflict and work with the individual to minimize such issues from recurring.

Behavior Modification

As mentioned earlier, behavior modification has its basis in operant conditioning, popularized through B. F. Skinner's early experiments. Using this approach effective leaders would begin with direct instruction (relative to the desired behaviors) with involved participants. Once initial instruction occurs, behavior modification relies heavily on the effective use of positive and negative reinforcement techniques to alter behaviors. In addition, time-out is commonly used as a negative reinforcement tool. People who use behavior modification are well-rehearsed in techniques such as shaping, chaining, fading, and extinction.

Assertive Discipline

Assertive discipline is a structured, systematic approach whereby a leader responds to behaviors confidently and quickly (MacIntyre, 2005). This model of discipline requires that leaders be assertive in addressing undesirable behaviors. Leaders need "to be firm, stand up for personal rights and express thoughts, feelings, and beliefs in direct, honest, and appropriate ways which do not violate another person's rights" (Silberman & Wheelan, 1980, p. 8). The associated discipline uses behavior modification techniques designed to achieve desired results. Open and honest communication, often framed in a series of "I" statements, is the hallmark of this model. For instance, a leader facing a verbally abusive parent at a youth sports event might approach the parent and say, "When that language is used with the coaches, it sets a bad example for the youth. In addition, it disrupts the game. I need you to stop the verbal abuse so that the game may continue uninterrupted. If you do not stop, you will be removed from the field."

Reality Therapy

The premise of reality therapy is that for people to change their behaviors, they must first be *aware* of what they are doing. This approach utilizes confrontational questioning in one-on-one and group settings. An example of confrontational questioning would be to ask a person whining about wanting her or his turn what she or he is doing. A typical exchange would be, "I want my turn.… [with a whine in the voice]" The leader again would ask, "What are you doing just now?" This would continue until the participant recognized and acknowledged that she or he was whining. The leader then might choose to use logical consequences—any time a person whined, she or he would not get what was desired.

Social Skills Training

One of the most prevalent myths surrounding participants in leisure services settings is that they have received quality and appropriate social skills training at home and school. Leaders expect participants to be nice, ask for things politely, and know how to interact appropriately with others. This, however, is an incorrect assumption. Many participants (of all ages) do not have the appropriate and necessary social skills to function well in diverse social situations (Farmer, Goforth, Hives, Aaron, Kjackson & Sgammato, 2006). Therefore, leaders who adhere to

Table 8B Key differences in approaches to behavior management

Behavioral Management Approach	Goal of Approach	Primary Process
Preventative management	Minimize the likelihood of behavior problems from occurring	Leader preparation, adequate resources, effective leadership techniques
Moral education	Teach about appropriate behaviors through morality	Use real dilemmas and role playing techniques to elicit underlying morality of the undesirable behavior
Affective and communication models	Achieve open communication with participants	Address emotions and underlying issues; use values clarification and interpersonal training
Behavior modification	Increase positive behaviors and decrease negative behaviors	Use of positive and negative reinforcement; shaping, chaining, fading, and extinction
Assertive discipline statements	Let others know how their behaviors are affecting others	Use of "I" to express oneself assertively
Reality therapy	Help others recognize how they are being perceived by others	Use of reflecting questions to try to help the individual better understand what they are *really* doing
Social skills training	Teach more appropriate social (i.e., interpersonal) skills	Use modeling, practicing, and coaching behaviors to teach participants appropriate interpersonal skills
Behavioral and family therapy	Make changes in the emotional and/or cognitive identity of an individual	Therapeutic processes and medications may be used by licensed therapists to initiate deep internal changes

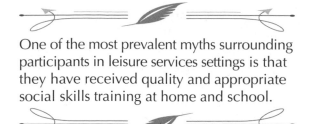

One of the most prevalent myths surrounding participants in leisure services settings is that they have received quality and appropriate social skills training at home and school.

this model of behavior management would utilize direct instruction, modeling and practicing skills, and coaching behaviors. Helping individuals develop affiliations with supportive peers, avoiding placing problem participants together, and providing opportunities for participants to highlight the areas in which they are skilled are other social skills training techniques. As an example, a leader might help a person who gets into numerous fights to learn basic conflict management skills. Opportunities to practice and use the skills would also be made available until the person became proficient at conflict management.

Behavioral and Family Therapy

In cases of extreme participant actions, leaders may refer clients for cognitive, behavioral, and/or operant conditioning therapy. These are considered forms of psychotherapy and because of this only certified, licensed, or trained therapists should use them. Leisure services professionals might be involved in therapy interventions through making referrals for those participants in need.

❖ ❖ ❖

As with learning about various models and theories of leadership, learning about models and approaches to behavior management is useful for recreation and leisure services leaders. The models provide a basic foundation for the approach a leader takes when utilizing various behavior management techniques. Often, leaders use a combination of two or more approaches to behavior management. Many of the specific behavior management techniques provided in this chapter are used with various underlying approaches. We will now move into investigating the purposes and necessity of behavior management.

Purposes of Behavior Management

As a leader considers the use of an approach to behavior management and the implementation of specific techniques, she or he must understand the purpose behind managing behaviors. Is it to maintain control of a situation? for participant safety? to enhance leader/participant power

differences? Agencies frequently establish expectations for behavior management. Individual leaders then implement those policies based on the requirements of the immediate situation.

Typically, behavior management is desirable for safety reasons. Effective use of behavior management techniques ensures safety of self, other participants, the facility, and equipment. Furthermore, the use of behavior management techniques allows for the smooth conduct of recreation and leisure activities. If people's actions are managed well, a leader is free to give instructions and work with participants as needed. A more manageable and enjoyable experience results for all involved.

At the direct leadership level, leaders may desire to manage others' behaviors for many reasons. While controlling others' behaviors can be difficult (since each individual is truly the only one who can make choices relative to her or his own behaviors), a certain level of control may be achieved, particularly with children. This is often accomplished through controlling access to equipment and limiting the open hours of a facility. When "in control" a leader usually is directive and authoritarian in her or his leadership style; it is clear who is in charge.

At other times a direct leader may wish to use behavior management to instruct or educate others. Participants learn what is appropriate and inappropriate through leader explanations of acceptable behavior. Once participant behaviors are managed effectively, it becomes easier to teach tasks needed to accomplish an activity or be successful with people skills. To achieve long-term educational goals a leader would typically engage in ongoing coaching and guiding behaviors.

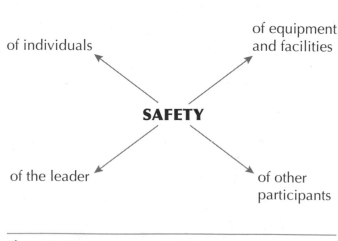

Figure 8.3 Reasons to use behavior management

Factors Affecting Behavior Management

While general rules of thumb can be established for handling most situations, people are much too diverse and every case too unique to make hard-and-fast rules about how to handle undesirable behaviors. This is not to say that rules cannot be made and followed consistently and equitably. Rather, leaders must consider all aspects of a situation before making a judgment relative to the undesirable behavior and subsequent intervention.

Leaders can expect a wide variety of behaviors from people from all walks of life—all age groups, socioeconomic classes, cultural backgrounds, and so on at times engage in disagreeable ways. Many times the behaviors being exhibited mask problems such as abuse, victimization, pain, or low self-esteem. Thus, leaders will want to consider a range of demographic elements (e.g., developmental ability, age, health, gender, and cultural background) when making decisions regarding behavior management. A leader should also consider environmental influences such as temperature, lighting, activity sequencing and pacing, and spatial arrangements. These issues should not be used to excuse undesirable behaviors, but rather to develop a deeper understanding as to the causes of inappropriate actions. Understanding underlying causes helps a leader in advising participants how to handle themselves more appropriately. Understanding helps the leader to make changes in leadership style or programming approach to better set up participants for success.

Developmental Ability

To be most effective when utilizing behavior management techniques, leaders should bear in mind that as people pass through the various developmental stages (see Chapter 3) they grow cognitively, affectively, physically, socially, and morally. At certain times in life some people will not have the sophistication to fully understand the repercussions of certain behaviors. At other times they may not be physically capable to do as asked. Those with emotional, behavioral, or developmental disabilities often cannot make appropriate judgments relative to their own behaviors and may require particular attention from the leader.

Age

Combined with knowledge of developmental stages, understanding the influence of age helps when deciding which behavior management approach would be most effective with a given individual. For example, young children may be unable to articulate their needs and may

While general rules of thumb can be established for handling most situations, people are much too diverse and every case too unique to make hard-and-fast rules about how to handle undesirable behaviors.

act out to gain what they desire. Particularly when in the heat of the moment, leaders should remember that children are not miniature adults; therefore, the expectations of and consequences for undesirable behaviors must be different for youngsters than for adults.

In addition to children, leaders may find that other age groups have difficulty in clearly articulating their needs. For instance, due to changing bodies and relationships with others, adolescents may be unaware of their own needs. Thus, they have a difficult time in asking for what they need and want from adults. In addition, the need to break away from adult authority may result in impulsive and undesirable behaviors by teens. Leaders will need to consider all the impacts one faces at different life stages before deciding on appropriate behavior management techniques.

Health/Disability Status

One's physical and mental health as well as disability status can be the underlying cause of behaviors that manifest as inappropriate. For instance, a person who has had a recent stroke or brain injury may exhibit argumentative and aggressive behaviors; so too will individuals on some medications and illegal drugs. Depression can result in an individual engaging in undesirable behaviors, especially among adolescents and the elderly. People who are in pain (e.g., physical, emotional) due to such ailments as a toothache, malnutrition, or Alzheimer's disease may also act out. Individuals with attention deficit disorder (ADD) and attention deficit hyperactivity disorder (ADHD) sometimes have difficulty with impulse control. This is also true of

Leaders should remember that children are not miniature adults; therefore, the expectations of and consequences for undesirable behaviors must be different for youngsters than for adults.

those with emotional or behavioral disorders. Addressing the underlying cognitive, mental, and physical issues often resolves the behavioral concerns.

Gender

Gender subtly influences approaches to behavior management. Leaders may not recognize its influence in their perceptions and use of various behavior management techniques, but it exists nonetheless. In many instances it is considered acceptable for males to engage in certain behaviors (e.g., a "boys will be boys" attitude) but unacceptable for females to engage in similar behaviors (e.g., it is "not ladylike"). Because of this, leaders often apply or enforce rules differently for females and males. Boys are often allowed more freedom in their conduct than girls. For instance, it may be more acceptable for males to be more aggressive than girls. Leaders will want to be aware of different standards based on the participant's gender and make adjustments to avoid falling into stereotypical behaviors and expectations of participants.

Cultural Background

Society has become increasingly diverse, and it is more important than ever for recreation leaders to have a basic understanding of cultures other than their own. Based on culture, one behavior might be considered offensive, while in another culture the behavior is perfectly acceptable. For instance, machismo may be a significant factor in the behavior of Mexican-American males (Ryska, 2001). To an Anglo, the manifestation of machismo might be perceived as a behavior problem, while it is viewed as an essential aspect of identity for the individual Mexican-American participant. As another example, refusal to participate might be perceived by a leader as misbehavior, yet the religious beliefs of the individual involved may not permit engagement.

Further, one should recognize that people from various cultures do not handle all situations alike. For instance, in the predominant U.S. culture people are expected to make eye contact with others, particularly when being addressed by a leader due to a behavior problem. However, for some people of Native American heritage, making eye contact is considered rude and aggressive, particularly when being addressed by a leader (as an authority figure). In addition to differences in eye contact, cultural differences may be found in the use of vocalizations (e.g., loudness, pace, intonation) and in the use of physical contact between peers and others (e.g., shoulder punches, chest bumps). These differences do not necessarily equate to inappropriate or undesirable behaviors in and of themselves.

❖ ❖ ❖

In addition to misinterpretations based on culture, gender, age, health, or developmental stage, other factors influence individuals engaging in undesirable behaviors. Often the factors that affect behavior management contribute to underlying reasons why people act out. Understanding these reasons can help a leader in difficult situations.

Why Behavior Management Is Needed

As microcosms of society, leisure services settings are not immune from the larger problems that occur in home, school, and work settings. In any experience involving people, the potential for display of inappropriate behaviors exists. Behavior management helps to maintain safe and enjoyable leisure environments. Problem behaviors range in severity from minor disruptions (e.g., a participant talking out of turn) to very serious situations (e.g., a fight with weapons). Some of the more common problem behaviors that face direct leaders in leisure service settings include:

- stealing
- fighting
- talking back, refusing to participate
- destroying equipment, disrupting activities
- disrespecting leaders
- racial intolerance, demeaning others

- using profanity and rude language, lying
- inflexibility/poor adaptability
- whining, arguing/verbal abuse
- demanding a leader's attention
- sexual harassment

Why do people act in these inappropriate ways? Why do both adults and young people engage in undesirable and antisocial behaviors? People act out for a variety of reasons: they might be tired, in a bad mood, or simply uninterested

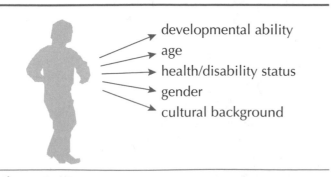

developmental ability
age
health/disability status
gender
cultural background

Figure 8.4 Factors to consider when choosing behavior management techniques.

in the activity. As one might imagine, there are as many individual reasons for undesirable behaviors as there are people. Table 8C lists several underlying reasons that help explain why people act out. Some reasons relate to effective leadership and can be addressed through improving leadership skills. Other reasons relate to individual participant issues and have to be addressed on a different level.

More than half of the reasons identified relate to effective leadership and can be mitigated through an improvement in leadership skills. Another 20% relate to actions of both the leader and the participant, which also can be influenced through effective use of leadership skills. Effective leadership, therefore, can have a tremendous impact on participant success and enjoyment.

Principles of Behavior Management

To be prepared for a variety of situations, each leisure services leader will want to develop a repertoire of behavior management techniques to be used with adults and young people. To be most effective this repertoire should match the leader's style as well as the policies and aims of the agency. The agency in which one works sets the tone for how staff members approach behavior management. Through agency norms, expectations are established related to personal behaviors exhibited by both staff and participants (e.g., verbal abuse, fighting, disrespect, stealing). Policies provide guidelines for staff, indicating how and when staff should step in to resolve escalating conflicts, call for assistance, and handle other behavioral concerns.

Many behavior management techniques exist and all have different success rates depending upon the situation. A leader will want to develop a range of behavior management techniques which suit her or his preferred style of leadership. If a particular technique is not effective with a participant, the leader can try another approach. It is not uncommon for a leader to utilize several techniques before finding one that is effective for a particular individual and situation.

Behavior management techniques vary from unobtrusive (i.e., it is difficult to observe the leader taking action) to very obtrusive (i.e., it is obvious that the leader is trying to gain control), and there are many variations of each. If a leader considers the factors involved, attempts to determine the underlying cause(s), and adheres to the following principles, effective management of behaviors is likely.

Make It an Agency Process

Behavior management should be systematic; every agency should have a philosophy of behavior management and train its staff accordingly. This philosophy usually involves a proactive component as well as an intervention plan. Typically the agency develops guidelines related to intervention and enforcement to share with staff via training or a staff manual. Resources to help resolve causes of misbehaviors and ways to help people meet their needs are commonly included in the behavior management system.

Assess Self-Awareness

Leaders should make an assessment of their own personal history with behavior management, motivations, "hot

Table 8C Reasons people act out

• Unmet needs	• To test personal power
• Did not understand, so did not pay attention	• Personality conflicts among participants
• Physical discomfort	• Low self-esteem
• Boredom	• Immaturity
• Overstimulation, too many distractions	• Underskilled for activity; to avoid failure
• Because the leader seemed to pick on someone	• Problems at home and/or workabout youth
• Fear (e.g., of abandonment, intimacy)	• Leader was not perceived as genuine
• Curiosity/testing the leader	• Leader did not explain well enough
• Conflicts with agency personnel	• Not enough equipment for all
• Lack of appropriate social skills	• No participant input into programs
• Depression, poor mental health	• Leader would put people down; leader did not care
• Medical problems (e.g., vision, hearing, ADD)	• Leader was not interactive enough
• To get the leader's attention	• Inappropriate labeling of participants
• Feelings of not belonging	

Ambrose & Kulik, 1999; Macciomei & Ruben, 1999

A leader should develop a range of behavior management techniques which suit her or his preferred style of leadership. If a particular technique is not effective with a participant, the leader can try another approach.

buttons," experiences, and beliefs. Further, leaders will want to examine their individual role in each behavior management situation asking questions such as: What is my impact on this situation? Have I used my skills to their fullest? Have I allowed personal biases or emotions to cloud my judgment? Have I obeyed the rules I expect others to follow? What have I done to contribute to this situation? What can I do to extract myself and others from this situation? What can I learn from this situation?

Be Proactive

Leaders who consistently model and send positive messages tend to have participants with few behavior problems. Ramsey (1994) suggested that the following messages permeate an agency to establish an atmosphere of mutual respect:

- All people have value as human beings and deserve respect as worthwhile persons.
- There is more than one way to be human, to learn, and to contribute.
- People are more alike than different.
- There is strength in diversity.

Establishing an atmosphere of respect and identifying expectations related to responsibility for one's actions are proactive behavior management techniques. One of the simplest and most effective proactive steps leaders can take is to learn participant names, pronounce them correctly, and use them often. In addition, Boardman (2004) suggests that leaders engage in "behavior management by walking around." This allows for frequent and genuine interactions between the leader and participants, and enhances the likelihood that the leader will be able to reinforce desirable behaviors.

Be Prepared

Disruptions of some magnitude occur in every leadership opportunity. To be ready for such events, effective leaders prepare for the activity, transitions, and conclusions. In addition, leaders maintain a repertoire of behavior management techniques with which they feel comfortable. Arranging space and equipment in such a way as to avoid tempting misuse or misbehaviors, and playing "What if?" (see Chapter 12) so that all contingencies have been considered are aspects of being prepared. Establishing routines, consistent responses, and clear expectations also are integral to preparation. A well-known adage highlights the importance of planning: "Proper prior planning precludes poor performance."

Leaders who consistently model and send positive messages tend to have participants with few behavior problems.

Offer Corrective Feedback

In the course of engaging in behavior management techniques some type of corrective feedback must be given to the participants involved. Corrective feedback is the communication passed from leader to participant related to a particular incident. It ensures a cycle where all participants are actively involved in the communication process. Most suggest that to be effective in helping to change behaviors, corrective feedback should be given immediately after the behavior occurs. There are times, however, when it would be best to wait before giving feedback (Omer, 2001). If a leader is busy with the group, recognizes that she or he is having an emotional response to the situation, or is unsure what to do, it might be best to indicate to the participant that feedback will come at a later (designated) time. This gives the leader time to consider an appropriate response. It also often results in the participant

PRINCIPLES OF BEHAVIOR MANAGEMENT

1. Make it an agency process
2. Assess self-awareness
3. Be proactive
4. Be prepared
5. Offer corrective feedback
6. Handle situations immediately
7. Avoid neglecting the entire group
8. Focus on the behavior, not the person
9. Protect and maintain the dignity of the participant
10. Help and nurture the target of misbehaviors
11. Be consistent and fair
12. Target underlying causes of undesired behaviors
13. Avoid a power struggle

Figure 8.5 Principles of behavior management guide effective leaders.

reflecting on the behaviors in question while waiting and wondering how the leader will respond. This personal reflection by the participant can be an influential learning experience.

Other guiding principles in giving corrective feedback include:

- giving the feedback in private
- being very specific about the behavioral concerns
- focusing the comments on the behaviors rather than the person
- stating the feedback in "I" messages
- ensuring feedback is understandable to the recipient

Avoid Neglecting the Entire Group

If the leader leaves the group unattended to deal with one individual, the message will be that to get the leader's personal attention one should engage in undesirable behaviors. In addition, ignoring the group while handling one person might lead to safety concerns, and it is unfair to group members. Further, the disruption caused by the leader when addressing misbehavior should not be larger than the disruption caused by the misbehaving person (Macciomei & Ruben, 1999).

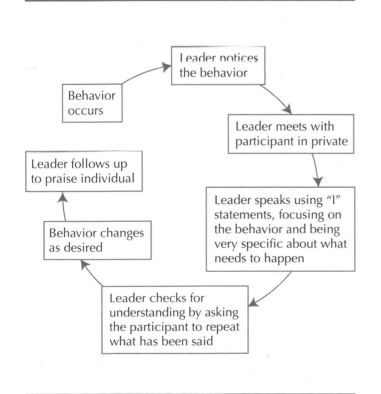

Figure 8.6 Corrective feedback has several steps.

Focus on the Behavior, Not the Person

Leaders should make it apparent that their concerns are with participant behaviors, and not the participant as a person. Messages perceived as personal attacks on participants will result in defensiveness, hostility, and a lack of cooperation. For example, "Pat, pushing people is unacceptable behavior" targets the behavior while, "Pat, you are bad!" is aimed at the person. Leaders should be very clear that they are concerned with the behaviors and not a character flaw in the individual.

Protect and Maintain the Dignity of the Participant

When utilizing behavior management techniques with a specific individual, a leader should strive to avoid addressing her or him in the presence of others (although this is not always possible). Humiliation will not only cause the individual in question to react negatively, but also may cause the entire group to rebel. Whenever possible, those engaging in undesirable behaviors should be taken aside and the issue dealt with away from the eyes and ears of others. Maintaining one's dignity and saving face should be an important element in addressing concerns in a positive fashion/manner.

Help and Nurture the Target of Misbehaviors

If the target of inappropriate behaviors is another participant (e.g., through harassment, name calling, fighting), attend to and nurture the victim. Particularly in instances of personal attacks, leaders have a tendency to admonish or punish the one misbehaving and ignore the target of those actions. Attend to the needs of the emotionally or psychologically injured person, just as one would a physically injured person; empathize and nurture the person who is hurt. This accomplishes several things—it lets the target of the negative behaviors know that the leader does not condone the actions of the attacker, it gives the victim positive leader attention, it helps to soothe hurts, and it models preferred behaviors.

Attend to the needs of the emotionally or psychologically injured person, just as one would a physically injured person; empathize and nurture the person who is hurt.

Be Consistent and Fair

While children may be the most vocal about their displeasure if they perceive that something is unfair or not being consistently applied, adults will also resent inconsistencies and unfairness. Being consistent and fair while keeping in mind the uniqueness of all situations and people can be a challenge for a leisure services leader. Consistency provides a sense of security as participants can count on a leader to act or react certain ways in particular situations.

Target Underlying Causes of Undesired Behaviors

Acting-out behaviors have been likened to medical signs that a person exhibits while ill. The signs need to be treated, *and* the cause of the illness must be determined. This is true of behavior problems as well. If we only address the behaviors without examining the underlying causes, undesirable behaviors will continue and may escalate. As mentioned earlier, leaders will want to consider physical, emotional, social, and psychological issues that might be manifesting in the disagreeable conduct.

Avoid a Power Struggle

Engaging in argumentative behaviors with participants—no matter their age—is counterproductive. Leaders would be wise to hold their emotions in check so as to avoid a power struggle. One way to deal with a participant who seems to insist on a power struggle is to provide options so that it is the participant's choice as to what occurs. For instance, asking a participant to hold a ball still or put it away provides her or him with a choice. Simply telling the person to put the ball away will likely be perceived as a command and could result in a power struggle.

❖ ❖ ❖

These basic principles work within the various approaches to behavior management discussed earlier and help lay the groundwork for a successful leadership experience. Leaders will want to implement these principles using a style comfortable to them—not all leaders are equally skilled in the use of all techniques, nor do all techniques suit each person. Specific management techniques build on the principles of behavior management and are described in the next section.

Behavior Management Techniques

Having prepared well for the leadership opportunity and taken a proactive position with regard to behavior management with a group, we now consider individual behavior management techniques. As mentioned earlier, techniques for managing behaviors range from simple and unobtrusive to complex and obtrusive. It is usually wise to try unobtrusive measures first to manage behaviors; only if those attempts prove unsuccessful should a leader then move into the more complex and obtrusive techniques. In this section behavior management techniques are presented in order from unobtrusive to obtrusive.

Unobtrusive or Preventative Techniques

Some preventative and unobtrusive techniques have already been addressed in this chapter. Depending upon the approach to behavior management one utilizes, the style of behavior management will differ. Preventive techniques minimize the likelihood of behavior problems occurring. These techniques include:

- defining limits
- planning for contingencies in advance (i.e., playing "What if?")
- providing ongoing clarification as needed
- establishing routines
- being sure that participants are challenged at an appropriate level
- being inclusive of all participants
- being clear and explicit in communication
- front-loading for success

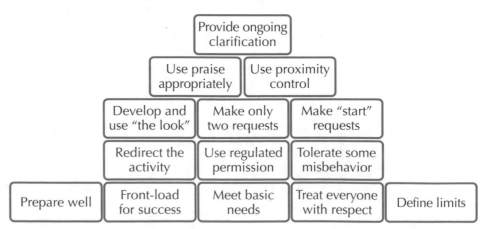

Figure 8.7 Unobtrusive techniques minimize undesirable behaviors from occurring.

- giving and expecting respect
- treating people with dignity
- avoiding some activities
- meeting basic needs (e.g., physical, safety, belonging, achievement, self-actualization).

Behavior management aims to induce compliance or to influence participants to behave in a particular fashion. Eventually, the goal is to influence participants to want to behave as expected on their own. While the sophistication level might differ, these techniques produce similar positive reactions in people of all ages, backgrounds, and abilities.

Use a Question Format

While leaders do not wish to appear to beg for compliance or behavior norming, phrasing a directive in the form of a question softens it and may make it more palatable than if it were a straightforward directive. A question format is less authoritarian than a directive, and is usually more easily accepted by participants.

Use Eye Contact

Using eye contact and perfecting "the look" lets participants know that the leader is aware of their actions, and a firm look sends a message to stop. Remember, however, the cultural differences in the use and meaning of eye contact—effective leaders are culturally aware in their behavior management techniques.

Use Distance and Proximity Control

Quite often, simply moving closer to an acting out participant may cause her or him to cease the undesirable behaviors. Doing so in an unobtrusive fashion to avoid drawing undue attention to the target individual.

Make Two Requests—No More

As long as the leader knows that a participant understands the request, two requests to stop a behavior are sufficient. Ask twice and then intervene with the preferred leader follow-up behaviors (e.g., logical consequences, punishment). Making more than two requests can lead to a leader-participant power struggle—this is something to avoid!

Allow Time for Compliance

After a request has been made, allow a minimum of five to ten seconds (with no other leader-participant conversation) for the person to change her or his behavior. There are times when five to ten minutes should be allowed—it depends on the individual and the situation.

Make More Start Than Stop Requests

Avoid a negative tone by asking participants to begin a specific action rather than stop one. For instance, if a person was running around a pool, rather than asking that individual to stop running (which leaves all sorts of wonderful options open such as cartwheeling, skipping, or hopping), the leader might ask the person to start walking heel-to-toe around the pool.

Make Specific and Descriptive Requests

Comprehension is very important in influencing desired behaviors. A request from a leader should be specific, literal, and descriptive to minimize the need for clarification. Check for understanding by asking the individual to repeat what you have said. Simply asking, "Did you hear me?" or "Do you understand?" is not enough to know if comprehension occurred. Consider language barriers and cultural meanings of words and phrases. In addition to verbally making the request, it may be important to demonstrate the desired actions.

Use Genuine Reinforcement of Positive Behaviors

When participants comply, praise those actions using "I" statements. Participants can tell when a leader makes positive comments solely to influence them to behave a certain way. Leader authenticity is desired and effective leaders are genuine with their voice and actions.

Redirect the Activity

Often participants act out due to difficulties with the activity—they are bored, do not understand how to play, or the activity is not meeting their present needs (e.g., if a person needs to expend energy, a quiet board game will not keep her or him engaged). Changing the activity in midstream to accommodate needs is an effective way to redirect behaviors. Leaders should take cues from the participants as to what type of activity to begin next. This requires constant monitoring of the group and making adjustments by the leader.

Use Regulated Permission

Regulated permission accommodates a participant's immediate needs. For example, if the participants are not on task because they have a physical or emotional need to run around and make noise, a leader using regulated permission would encourage three to five minutes of running around and making noise. After the designated time period has passed, participants would be guided into the next task.

Tolerate Some Misbehavior

People will not always act in ways acceptable to the leader. If the undesirable behaviors do not cause difficulties for others or present a safety concern, it may be appropriate to ignore the behaviors. When people are in groups they expect others will fidget, whisper, and move about. Leaders would be wise to remember the cliché: "Choose your battles."

Use Praise

Praise as a form of feedback should be specific and related to behaviors rather than a person. Because praise is a feeling, value, or thought of the leader, it is best to couch it in "I" statements rather than "you" statements (Macciomei & Ruben, 1999). In this way the issue remains with the person who owns it. For instance, state "I appreciate you helping to put away equipment; it makes my job easier" rather than "You did a good job with the equipment today." The "you" message may imply that something is amiss on days the person did not help and can lead to guilt, hurt feelings, and a feeling of being criticized. It also may communicate a lack of respect for others. An "I" message alerts participants that the leader is human and has needs, too. Guidelines for effective praise may be found in Table 8D.

Discernible Techniques

Discernible techniques are those that fall between being unobtrusive and outright obvious interventions. They are often integrated into basic leadership skills and techniques for teaching an activity or task, and therefore, tend to be more pointed than unobtrusive techniques. Discernible behavior management techniques are more noticeable than unobtrusive techniques, but not as obvious as obtrusive methods. Leaders typically use these techniques when the unobtrusive techniques have failed to result in desirable behaviors.

Positive Discipline

Discipline refers to a set of techniques used in behavior management to maintain orderly social behaviors so that meaningful learning can occur (KidsSource, 2003). It often includes direct instruction, the use of punishment, and an overall tone of leader control to induce compliance in others. Positive discipline helps to move the sense of control from the leader (i.e., external to the individual) to the individual (i.e., internal). See Table 8E for characteristics of positive discipline.

Modeling

By demonstrating desired behaviors and then allowing individuals to practice these behaviors, participants learn

---

Table 8D Giving appropriate praise

Giving praise is very similar to giving general feedback. There are several principles to bear in mind to ensure that praise is both appropriate and effective in reaching desired goals. Usually praise contains both affect (i.e., feelings) and content (i.e., the message) and is targeted at a specific individual or group.

- Be specific and target the behaviors, rather than the person; avoid global statements. Rather than commenting, "Wow! You did great today!" tell the individual what exactly she or he did great.

- Use "I" statements when identifying affect (e.g., "I appreciate the way you picked up the equipment today!").

- When you indicate that something is "good," be sure to indicate what was good about it. For instance, in the example above, did the leader appreciate the way the group picked up equipment because the group did it without being asked? or because it was done quickly, quietly, or neatly? or because the leader wasn't feeling well and the group helped her or him out? or because it showed responsibility or commitment? or….

- Know when to use praise in public and when it is best done privately. For example, to praise one person loudly in front of others who have been acting out may cause an increase in undesirable behaviors by the others. If an individual might be embarrassed by public recognition, it may be best to give praise privately.

- Be sure that verbal praise is "in sync" with nonverbal language. People are more apt to believe the nonverbal message over the verbal one if there are inconsistencies.

- Follow verbal praise with consistent treatment of the individual.

- Be genuine and truthful in your praise of another; avoid exaggerations. Most people are perceptive and can recognize exaggerated praise; it is often interpreted as "buttering up" the target of the praise and can backfire.

- Understand cultural nuances surrounding praise. In many cultures, giving praise to one person is undesirable and is thought to draw undue attention to that individual. In this instance, praising the group may be best.

- Try to catch people doing something right and use praise often. This helps to articulate expectations and desirable behaviors.

- Avoid using words like "perfect!" Perfection is rare, and this type of praise may give a false sense of ability. After all, one cannot improve on perfection. Instead, use phrases that accurately describe the situation.

- Give praise when it is due and try to use it often—Remember the above principles, however.

to understand leader expectations. When using modeling, for example, a leader might have participants learn and practice how to quiet down when the leader needs their attention. Modeling occurs as participants observe leaders and staff. If leaders say one thing and do another, or break established rules, they will have little credibility or authority in terms of behavior management.

Rules

Rules set the stage for the the managed presentation of recreation and leisure services activities. Rules do not have to be overly constraining and ruin people's fun. Rather, rules are designed, implemented, and enforced to manage what otherwise could be chaos and to give participants a sense of personal security. In most leisure services settings participants express many different interests and desires simultaneously. Without rules, very few people would have their needs met. The following principles apply to the successful use of rules.

Rules should have reasons. Arbitrary rules serve no purpose other than to enhance leader power. When participants realize this, the leader loses much respect and authority. Have reasons for rules and share those reasons with participants. Most rules are designed to keep participants, leaders, equipment, and facilities safe from harm.

Design rules in conjunction with participants. As much as possible, develop rules with participants. When developed cojointly by participants and leaders, participants are much more likely to understand and follow rules.

State rules in positive terms. Avoid a long list of "No" statements as rules: No gum. No candy. No drinks. No running. No shouting. This leaves one wondering just what she or he *is* allowed to do. In addition, it establishes a negative tone and often results in the leader looking for people to break rules. As much as possible, state all rules in a positive fashion: Please protect the grass by walking only on the sidewalk. Please keep voices at a conversational level.

Keep rules clear and succinct. The more descriptive, short, and sweet a rule is, the easier it is to understand. Keep individual rules unambiguous and concise, and state rules the same way.

Design rules to be equitable. Rules should be designed to affect all participants in a similar fashion and be enforced equitably. For instance, the rule of "no hats inside" could be discriminatory to Jewish men who wear yarmulkes for religious reasons. When developing rules leaders and participants need to consider all the elements of a situation and make a judgment related to how a particular behavior will be handled based on those factors.

Use rules to define responsible behaviors. If participants do not know what behaviors are expected, they will be unable to fully comply with the rules.

Clarify, practice, and monitor rules. Leaders can help participants meet rule expectations by continuously clarifying them. In addition, participants will need time to practice following and meeting the rules. Both participants and leaders can monitor progress related to rules. Further, as rules become outdated or irrelevant, they should be modified or omitted.

Ensure appropriate rules for participants. Be sure that rules appropriately match participant developmental stage. Expecting too much from participants can set them up for failure.

Rules must be enforceable. Unenforceable rules often arise out of leader emotions and are simply threats. To be effective, design rules that can be enforced and follow the organization philosophy.

Follow through with enforcement. Rules not enforced or enforced only sporadically tend to be ineffective. Be prepared to enforce the

---

Table 8E Positive discipline

- Successful experiences are provided, highlighted and modeled.
- Honest answers are given by the leader.
- Responsibility for things that really matter is put in the hands of the participants.
- Self-discipline is the ultimate goal and efforts lead participants toward achieving this.
- Leaders hold realistic expectations of participants based on their knowledge of human development.
- Personalization and individual attention are given to each participant.
- Second chances are given; people are allowed to make mistakes.
- The process is systematic.
- Active listening is utilized.

- The leader gives recognition for effort as well as achievement.
- Encouragement is used regularly.
- Equal access is ensured for all participants.
- Flexibility is utilized to accommodate each situation.
- Structured choices are provided to participants.
- Self-evaluation related to one's behaviors is conducted on a continuous basis.
- Authentic feedback is provided as opportunities arise.
- Acceptance of failed efforts as a part of learning is emphasized.
- The leader emphasizes genuine respect for differences.

rules with everyone—even your best friend or favorite participant.

Give a warning. People of all ages tend to respond better to directions if given a heads-up that something is about to (or should) change. For instance, when it is necessary to put equipment away or swim time is about over, alerting participants ahead of time is a courteous way to help them make the psychological switch from involvement to ceasing activity. Expecting anyone to put a ball away *now* or get out of the pool *now* without advance notice is almost guaranteeing a lack of compliance.

Have only a few rules. If participants feel overwhelmed by the sheer number of rules they may feel overly constrained and not trusted. Have as few rules as possible and follow through on them.

❖ ❖ ❖

Bearing in mind these principles when developing rules will help make the policies that exist useful and doable (see Figure 8.8). Rules provide structure and help teach about expectations of leaders. Use rules, but use them consciously and judiciously.

Positive Reinforcement

Positive reinforcements increase the frequency of desired behaviors when used appropriately (Macciomei & Ruben, 1999; Sherrill, 1998). Primary reinforcers include edible and sensory reinforcers (e.g., candy, a pat on the back). Secondary reinforcers include tangible materials (e.g., trophies, certificates, stickers), privilege reinforcers (e.g., being first, being allowed to play longer), activity rein-

forcers (e.g., playing special activities, choosing the activity), generalized reinforcers (e.g., tokens, points), and social reinforcers (e.g., a verbal "nice job" or a smile).

Rewards are an integral aspect of positive reinforcement, yet there are many disadvantages in using rewards to increase (or decrease) particular behaviors. Many believe that when used too frequently, rewards tend to lose their value to participants. Also, if used inappropriately rewards may be perceived as bribes. Participants can often acquire rewards on their own—rewards are not contingent upon the leader. Furthermore, it is not uncommon for misbehaviors inadvertently to be rewarded and desired behaviors to go unrewarded. Eventually the absence of a reward may feel like punishment. A leader will want to consider all the options before deciding to use rewards as an integral part of behavior management.

Punishment

Punishment is anything that decreases a particular behavior. Typically, punishment has a negative connotation and involves taking away privileges or reinforcements; to be punished is not a desirable thing. Jones and Jones (1995) oppose the use of punishment because it does not teach about the more desirable behaviors, it simply penalizes the individual for particular conduct. In addition, punishment has been shown to inhibit learning and allow the one being punished to project blame on the punishers.

Macciomei and Ruben (1999) reported that use of punishment can lead to the four Rs: *resentment, revenge, rebellion,* and *retreat.* Further supporting the position against punishment in behavior management, Gordon (1989) reported that youth often cope with punishment by

Rules should have reasons.
Design rules in conjunction with participants.
State rules in positive terms.
Keep rules clear and succinct.
Design rules to be equitable.
Use rules to define responsible behaviors.
Clarify, practice, and monitor rules.
Ensure appropriate rules for participants.
Rules must be enforceable.
Follow through with enforcement.
Give a warning.
Have only a few rules.

Figure 8.8 Rules for rules

Photo courtesy of Deb Jordan

Different people are reinforced by different things. Reinforcement can come from accomplishment.

- resisting
- defying
- being negative
- rebelling
- sassing
- retaliating
- striking back
- hitting
- being combative
- breaking rules or laws
- lying
- deceiving
- getting angry

- blaming others
- bullying others
- withdrawing
- trying to be in a position of "one-up" on everyone
- giving up
- feeling defeated
- becoming fearful and shy
- becoming ill
- becoming overly submissive
- using drugs

Obviously, none of these coping mechanisms are considered positive responses. If the goal of behavior management is to change behaviors and influence participants to behave in positive ways, punishment may not be a useful tool.

Consequences

Consequences differ from punishment and range in how obvious they appear to observers in leader interventions. In behavior management terms, consequences are external reactions to activity or behavior choices. There are three basic types of consequences:

1. *arbitrary consequences,* which have nothing to do with the undesirable behavior. As an example, if a participant does not put the equipment away when asked, she or he must do ten push-ups;

2. *logical consequences,* which are connected to the action through reason or logic. For example, if an individual does not put equipment away when asked, she or he must put away not only the equipment she or he was using, but must also pick up all the other equipment as well; and

3. *natural consequences,* which occur as a natural outcome of the action. As an example, if participants did not put away equipment when asked, putting away equipment would take longer, and participants would be late for and perhaps unable to engage in the next activity. The leader does not impose natural consequences—they occur as a natural outcome of the action.

There are proponents both for and against the use of the three types of consequences in behavior management. Most agree that arbitrary consequences have the least value

in terms of long-term effectiveness of managing participant behaviors. Logical and natural consequences have some impact on successful behavior management.

As with rules, there are principles for applying effective consequences. Generally, the use of consequences should reflect the behavior management philosophy of the agency. If education is the primary objective of behavior management, certain types of consequences would be more effective than if the primary goal were simple crowd control. Consider the following principles when implementing consequences:

Catch participants doing something right. If the underlying premise of behavior monitoring is to catch participants doing something right, there will be fewer behavior problems than if the leader was looking for participants to do something wrong. Reinforce the appropriate and desirable behaviors so that these will occur with increased frequency.

To be most effective, consequences should be appropriate to the rule infraction. "Make the punishment fit the crime" is an adage that has application here. Demanding that participants wash a car, sit in time-out for 30 minutes, or run laps for using profanity is usually not very effective in reducing the use of profanity. Consider how and when the profanity was used, how it affected other participants and the success of the program, and how it impacted the effectiveness of leadership before identifying and applying potential consequences.

Consequences should be clear and understood. Well-informed participants can make better choices relative to their behaviors than those not informed. When enforcing rules be sure to explain the consequences of breaking those rules and be sure that participants understand them by asking clarifying questions.

Accepted consequences are balanced and doable. Building on the notion of ensuring that the consequence matches the infraction, consequences tend to be accepted when they are balanced and doable. Doable consequences are those that are enforceable. For instance, an untrained, emotionally-responding leader might say to a child, "If you don't stop talking I'm going to tape your mouth shut!" Suffice it to say that taping the mouth shut of another is very unwise; that type of response tells more about the emotional reaction of the leader than any actual consequence. Participants know that a leader is not going to tape their mouths shut; this type of threat is ineffectual and may result in overall reduced leader effectiveness.

Leave emotions out of it. Emotional leaders tend not to think clearly and often act in unprofessional and potentially damaging ways. People very rarely direct behavior at the leader. Acting out usually occurs because a need is not being met, problems at home or school are interfering with an individual, or the participant is uncomfortable. Therefore, effective use of consequences should be free of leader emotions. If the leader remains calm, the participant remains calm, and the consequences are more palatable.

Do not withhold physical necessities. Some leaders (e.g., uninformed sport coaches) punish or instill arbitrary consequences of withholding physical needs such as water, food, and shelter if a player acts in an undesirable fashion. This is a very dangerous practice. If when standing in line for water, for instance, participants begin to push one another, a logical (although inappropriate) consequence might be to remove the pusher from the line and not let her or him have water. Withholding water from an individual has the potential to cause life-threatening illnesses and should be avoided. This is particularly true in a warm, humid environment where participants have been active.

Ask for participant involvement. Oftentimes, asking the participant what consequences should follow a rule infraction is effective because it puts the responsibility on the participant rather than the leader. The leader can then modify the suggestion to be sure it meets the other principles of using consequences.

Behavior Contract

Participants of all ages have successfully used contracts for behavior management. A contract should be a shared effort, outlining expectations of both the participant and the leader. The leader assumes responsibility for helping the participant achieve her or his behavioral goals by being there, giving nonverbal signals, or engaging in some other tangible action to aid in behavior control.

Effective use of consequences should be free of leader emotions. If the leader remains calm, the participant remains calm, and the consequences are more palatable.

A behavior contract is a formal (preferably written) agreement between the leader and a participant in which the participant agrees to behave in a certain fashion. Desired behaviors are identified, as are the consequences for failing to meet contract stipulations. It is most effective when negotiation of all behavior contracts is systematic. The process of developing a behavior contract would include several steps.

First, the leader would explain what a contract is and show examples of types of contracts. To ensure understanding the leader then would ask the individual to describe another example of a behavior contract. Next, the leader would explain the need for a contract and identify the specific behaviors to be addressed in the contract. Both leader and participant negotiate the elements of the contract: timeline, criteria for achievement, leader's role, evaluation procedures, and date for renegotiation. The contract is then written out; if the participant is old enough the leader might consider having her or him write it out. Once written, both the leader and the participant sign the contract, and each of them keep a copy.

✔ Catch participants doing something right.

✔ To be most effective, consequences should be appropriate to the rule infraction.

✔ Consequences should be clear and understood.

✔ Balanced and doable consequences are usually accepted.

✔ Leave emotions out of it.

✔ Do not withhold physical necessities.

✔ Ask for participant involvement.

Figure 8.9 Principles of using consequences

---

① Explain what a social contract is

② Ask the participant to explain it in her or his own words

③ Explain the need for the contract

④ Identify the specific behavioral changes desired

⑤ Establish a timeline

⑥ Identify criteria for accomplishment

⑦ Spell out consequences for nonperformance

⑧ Note the leader's role in the process

⑨ Develop an evaluation process

⑩ Choose a date for follow-up

⑪ Make two copies

⑫ Leader and participant each sign and keep a copy

Figure 8.10 Steps to develop a social contract

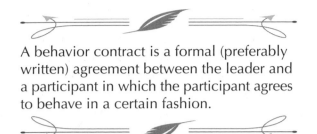

A behavior contract is a formal (preferably written) agreement between the leader and a participant in which the participant agrees to behave in a certain fashion.

To be most effective, contracts should be drawn up privately and in a positive fashion. Reasons for needing the contract as well as each of the contract elements should be articulated. Often, it is helpful to have a bonus clause to reinforce persistent efforts or outstanding behaviors by the participant. Contracts are not always successful—they fail for a variety of reasons, including punitive penalties, lack of understanding, and leader inconsistency. In addition, if the leader is not available to dispense reinforcers when needed or to enforce the contract, it will lose its effectiveness. Social contracts can be effective for a wide range of ages and for people with various cognitive and developmental disabilities.

Obtrusive Techniques

Most obvious to participants and onlookers, obtrusive behavior management techniques often get the attention of the entire group. With these techniques there is little question that the leader has noticed and is acting on inappropriate or undesirable behaviors. Typically, obtrusive techniques are utilized only after exhausting the unobtrusive and discernible behavior management techniques without success.

Time-Out

Time-out is a technique used with both adults and youth. Barbetta, Norona, and Bicard (2005) remind us that time-out should not be a place; rather, it is a process and moment in time where all potential reinforcers are withheld. Thus, sending a young person to time-out in a room where she or he could play video games, listen to music, or watch others engage in activities is not recommended. With adults, time-out is usually referred to as penalty time (as in soccer or hockey) and provides an opportunity for settling down.

As a behavior management technique with youth, time-out tends to be overused. Many parents, teachers, and leisure services leaders use time-outs for every minor infraction, thus decreasing its effectiveness. Often, time-out is used because it is convenient for the leader—the participant is out of the way and not causing problems (at the moment). Because of its minimal effectiveness in changing

Time-out should not be a place; rather, it is a process and moment in time where all potential reinforcers are withheld.

behaviors, however, time-out should be a last effort technique. Leaders should first try the many other management techniques mentioned in this text.

To maximize the effectiveness of time-out, the leader should explain the entire process first: why the person is being put in time-out, where the time-out area is located, and how long the participant will remain in time-out. The time-out setting should be well-lit, ventilated, clean, and void of all potential reinforcers. (Note: a storage closet is usually not an acceptable location.) To avoid having participants vying for time-out, select a place where people do not want to go and is visually isolated from the activity. For safety reasons, the leader should be able to see the area at all times.

One reason that time-outs are not effective is because many leaders expect participants to "sit and think about what they did" for an excessive amount of time (15 minutes or more). Even the best intentioned child (or adult) cannot or will not think about her or his inappropriate behaviors for 15 minutes. A more appropriate reason to use time-out is to remove an individual from an environment where she or he is overstimulated. Time-out becomes a tool to help people "gather themselves" and calm down.

Time-out is a serious behavior management technique and to maintain this tone, the amount of time spent in time-out should be dictated by the leader and not the participant. A good rule of thumb is to require a participant to remain in time-out for no longer than her or his age. Therefore, a five-year-old usually should spend no more than five minutes in time-out (and often, less time is more effective). Certainly, leader judgment should be used and this time adjusted as the situation warrants; seven to eight minutes is usually a maximum length of time for any individual in time-out. Requiring the individual to be quiet for the last 30 seconds before rejoining an activity when released from time-out helps to maintain a controlled activity level (Wolfgang & Wolfgang, 1995).

Physical Intervention

When discussing physical intervention, thoughts often turn to corporal punishment such as spanking or slapping. The use of corporal punishment in any form is an unwise behavior management technique. Concerns over child abuse and lawsuits have effectively resulted in a ban of such contact no matter the situation. Physical intervention in other forms, however, is sometimes necessary. If a participant is likely to hurt herself or himself, others, or property, action to stop the individual must be taken.

Physical intervention ranges from a hand lightly resting on the shoulder to actual "bear" hugs to completely physically restrain the individual. To minimize the likelihood of misinterpretation and misuse, and to protect the leader(s), these types of intervention should be used only in the presence of another adult. In addition, if the situation will allow for it, the participant should be verbally alerted that the leader(s) is about to touch, bear hug, or reach out for the participant.

Any physical interventions used should be in the best interest of the participant, not for the convenience of the leader. Therefore, the care and well-being of the participant should be foremost in the leader's mind. As with the use of all behavior management techniques, physical intervention should be emotion-free. If a leader is caught up in the moment, the possibility of a struggle and inappropriate (e.g., violent) use of intervention arises. It is best to avoid using physical intervention when possible. Typically, these types of techniques are used infrequently and as last resorts. Most physical intervention techniques require special training and must be within the guidelines of the organization. If a leader engages in physical interventions outside the agency or organizational guidelines, she or he could be held personally liable should something go wrong.

Selecting Appropriate Techniques

People are unique; this makes the field of leisure services exciting, challenging, and rewarding. Knowing that all people differ, and that at times people act in undesirable manners, how does a leader know which technique to use when? Several factors help to determine the most effective technique. Leader style, skills, experience, and preferences are determining factors, as are the personality, age, and developmental stage of the participant, and the environment. Leaders will want to use different techniques over time, as techniques tend to lose their effectiveness if used over and over again with the same participants.

Leader knowledge, experience, and comfort level with the various techniques greatly influence the selection of behavior management techniques.

Leader knowledge, experience, and comfort level with the various techniques greatly influence the selection of behavior management techniques. In addition to these factors the needs of the individual participant should be primary in determining which technique to use when. Until one gains experience in behavior management and working with groups, it would be best to have a repertoire of techniques and work through them from unobtrusive to obtrusive until the behavior is changed in the desired fashion.

To help in minimizing the need for extensive use of behavior management techniques, the leader should frontload for success and encourage participants to ask for what they need rather than act out. In addition, participants tend to engage in fewer misbehaviors when the leader meets them as they enter the facility, uses their names, and listens well (Anonymous, 2000). Leaders who recognize their own biases and prejudices and do not take things personally also tend to be more successful than those who do otherwise.

When implementing behavior management, leaders sometimes make mistakes. Mistakes in behavior management techniques are called *miscalls* (Seaman, DePauw, Morton & Omoto, 2003). Miscalls include such errors as overreacting to a withdrawn person and feeling compelled to include them immediately (often accompanied by a leader command for the participant to have fun); the need to have all the attention on oneself (any fidgeting or whispering is taken personally); and displaced anger (aimed at participants). Furthermore, sometimes leaders become tired of being understanding (being understanding requires a commitment and energy), or they may see participants mirror a piece of themselves which they do not like. Other leader miscalls include the need to maintain absolute control; mistaking excitement and enthusiasm for disruptions; blaming participants not at fault; and being incongruent and inconsistent. Being aware of these potential miscues can help a leisure services leader avoid common behavior management errors.

Ineffective Behavior Management Techniques

When leaders get tired or things do not go well, they tend to fall back into old behaviors and techniques—mostly ineffective, and often unprofessional. Among the techniques that do not work and should be avoided are: yelling or blaming an individual; sarcasm, threats or name-calling; physical punishment (lawsuits are likely any time a leader gets physical with a participant); corporal punishment (outlawed in most states); and calling parents (many parents are uninvolved or are unable to be involved to the extent needed). If one keeps in mind the principles and techniques of behavior management and utilizes a range of techniques, it is likely that individuals will modify their behaviors as desired.

Motivation

Behavior management and motivation go hand in hand. If a leader has the skills to motivate participant involvement, there will be fewer behavior problems than if participants are not motivated to participate or behave appropriately. Thus, understanding motivation theories and models provides leaders with background information to better prepare for direct leadership. Motivation is a very complex concept and due to space limitations, only an overview of motivation will be presented.

First, it is necessary to understand that all people are motivated. They may not be motivated to do as the leaders desire, nor to behave as deemed appropriate; yet people are, nonetheless, motivated. Further, people may experience multiple motivations at one time and their motivations, particularly in relation to recreation behavior, change over time (Russell, 2005). Motivation means "to move," from the Latin *movēre*. It refers to an internal process that pushes or pulls us in relation to some external event; it drives us to want something (Ferguson, 2000). All leaders are encouraged to learn more about motivation and motivation theories to be fully effective when working with groups.

Theories of motivation commonly focus on unmet needs. The needs might be physical, social, emotional, or psychological. Generally, the motivation process involves

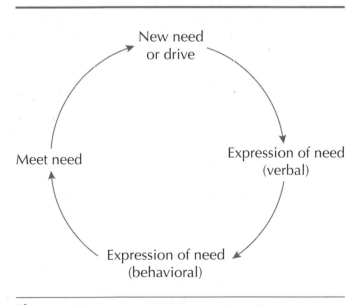

Figure 8.11 The motivation process is cyclical.

New need or drive → Expression of need (verbal) → Expression of need (behavioral) → Meet need →

If a leader has the skills to motivate participant involvement, there will be fewer behavior problems than if participants are not motivated to participate or behave appropriately.

four steps. The following explanation includes an example of a physical need serving as a motivator.

1. An internal drive arises based on a perceived or real need (e.g., hunger), of which the participant may or may not be aware,

2. which serves as an impetus to consider behavioral choices (e.g., go to the refrigerator, go to the store, ask for food)

3. from which a choice of action is made (e.g., ask for food)

4. which is directed toward meeting the need. (Moorhead & Griffin, 2004)

If the choice of actions includes undesirable behaviors either due to a lack of knowledge about appropriate choices, poor social skills, or lack of awareness about the underlying need, then inappropriate behaviors may occur. For instance, if a person was hungry and knew that she or he was not feeling well but did not recognize why, her or his behavioral choices might not be related to the real need of eating something. Thus, frustration might build and misaligned behaviors might occur. A leader, then, might be called upon to help an individual recognize the real need and identify appropriate ways to meet that need.

There are many theories of motivation addressed in the literature that help leaders understand human behavior. A few of the more popular ones in the recreation and leisure profession include Maslow's Hierarchy, McClleland's Trichotomy of Needs, Five Sources of Motivation, and Flow.

Maslow's Hierarchy of Needs

One of the more well-known theories of motivation is Maslow's hierarchy of needs (Ferguson, 2000; Plunkett & Greer, 2000). According to this model, people will act to meet lower order needs before striving for higher order needs. Maslow believed that people are initially motivated by subsistence or physiological needs such as the need for food, water, sleep, sex, and the elimination of physical pain. Therefore, if a participant is hungry or thirsty she or he will be motivated to eat and drink before doing much else. If food and water are not available or if the need goes unrecognized, misbehaviors might result. For instance, people who are hungry may be tired and cranky until they have had something to eat.

Once physiological needs have been met, Maslow suggested that participants are motivated by a need for security. Security includes not only physical safety, but also psychological and emotional safety. Structure, routines, and agency policies can contribute to a sense of safety in recreational settings. Therefore, if an individual feels threatened she or he will act in ways to regain a sense of security. This might include staying close to the leader, fighting back, or withdrawing from the situation.

As social beings, humans have a need for love, belonging, companionship, and social contacts; this is the next level of needs according to Maslow. Wanting to be a part of the group, to fit in, and to be accepted are strong drives once security and physiological needs have been met. Adolescents and teens often act in ways to gain acceptance by a peer group such as dressing alike and having similar hairstyles; joining a sports team; using tobacco, alcohol, or drugs; and engaging in hazing. Young couples often join other couples in recreation activities, and seniors might be active in senior centers or volunteer capacities.

The last two levels of needs in Maslow's hierarchy are the needs for esteem and self-actualization. Esteem needs include the needs for competence, sense of accomplishment or achievement, and recognition by others. Participants strive to master skills and to gain recognition (e.g., attention from the leader, a pat on the back, a trophy) for those skills. If leaders and others do not give such

recognition, participants may act out to gain the leader's attention. People with low self-esteem may be moody, aggressive or withdrawn.

Self-actualization needs may be defined as the needs described by the now-popular phrase, "Be all that you can be." Self-actualized people are independent, motivated and satisfied from within themselves, dare to take risks, and are not afraid of failure. They are creative and enjoy self-expression (often through their leisure). According to Maslow all humans strive to reach this potential.

McClelland's Trichotomy of Motivation

McClelland believes that three factors motivate all people: *achievement, power* and *affiliation.* Others believe the three drivers are autonomy (i.e., independence), competence (i.e., skills), and affiliation (i.e., sense of belonging; Gagne & Deci, 2005). According to McClleland, we continuously work to achieve personal accomplishments and to contribute to society. Opportunities to demonstrate a mastery of skills and continue our learning are ways to meet the need to achieve. In addition, we behave in ways to increase our personal power, prestige, and social status. Lastly, we have a strong need to associate and connect with others—we want others to like us and we need to feel accepted.

Examples in recreation might include a person driven to improve her or his skills at a particular leisure activity (e.g., music, sports, fine arts); an individual who seeks out activities to experience power (e.g., in-line skating, winning a race or award); and a person who engages in recreation activities for the social experience (e.g., quilting bees, fine-arts classes).

As leaders consider the various factors of motivation and the reasons behind people acting the way they do, it is wise to bear in mind that people move up and down Maslow's hierarchy and among McClelland's motivation factors, and may strive to meet several needs at the same time. Therefore, if a participant is acting out it may be helpful to discern which needs are driving the behaviors. By addressing the underlying needs, the undesirable behaviors can be curtailed. For instance, a participant may not have slept well the previous night, feel as though others are picking on her or him, and may feel ostracized from the group. According to McClelland's motivation theory, this individual will strive to "fix" these imbalances through various actions. Some of these actions may be appropriate, while others may be undesirable behaviors.

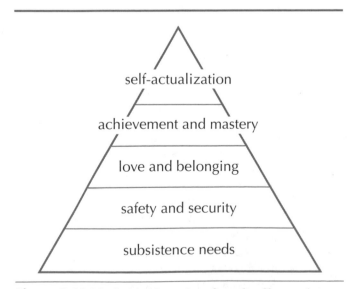

Figure 8.12 Maslow's hierarchy of needs offers a clear look at the primary motivators of participants.

Five Sources of Motivation

Some researchers who examine motivation suggest that there are five sources (Barbuto, 2005; Clark, 2002) that move people to action. They include:

1. *Intrinsic process motivation*—people are motivated to engage in an activity for the sheer fun or joy of it. The activity is the motivation. This may be seen in the play behaviors of people of all ages. There is no ulterior motive for participation; it is simply fun.

2. *Instrumental motivation*—people are motivated by external, tangible rewards such as trophies or prize money. Some theorists combine this type of motivation with the following type and refer to this as external motivation. The activity may be enjoyable, but the drive for participation is an external reward.

3. *Self-concept external motivation*—people are motivated by the social status they will achieve through their behaviors. This is similar to the power motivation suggested by McClelland.

4. *Self-concept internal motivation*—people are motivated to maintain personal standards that help them achieve and maintain a personal identity. We all have a sense of self—who we are, what defines us, who we strive to be. It is the desire and attempt to act in ways that support this sense of self that is described in this type of drive.

5. *Goal internalization motivation*—people are motivated to adopt behaviors that are congruent with their personal values system; they act in ways to achieve a "cause." People at this level are some-what selfless—they act out of a concern to positively impact the world around them.

Flow

Another way to look at participant needs is to examine the concept of flow (Csikszentmihalyi, 1990). Flow shares many elements with the concept of leisure and is frequently discussed in the parks, recreation, and leisure services field. Flow (in its most basic sense) refers to a zone of enjoyment and pleasure that exists between boredom and anxiety. When engaging in leisure activities, people strive for enjoyment and to reach a psychological level where they feel competent. With difficult or challenging activities, a novice participant will probably feel anxious. This anxiety may lead to acting out behaviors as the participant tries to avoid failure. A highly skilled participant engaging in an activity that lacks challenge, however, may experience boredom. As with anxiety, a participant feeling bored might act out in an effort to be more challenged. Therefore, leaders should strive to determine if the activity is overly challenging or too simple for participant skill levels. By adapting activities and the way one leads, flow can be facilitated for many. A leader strives to match participant skill and challenge levels in an effort to help them experience flow.

Facilitating Motivation

If the supposition that all people are motivated is true, then one might wonder about the role of a leader in motivating participants. Leaders can establish an environment that will

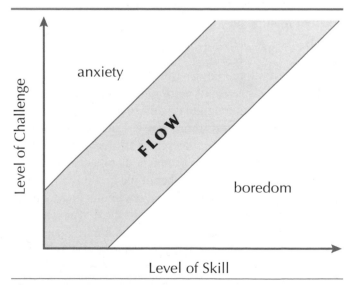

Figure 8.13 McClelland believes all people are motivated by three factors.

Achievement

Affiliation

Power

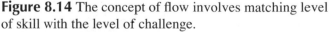

Figure 8.14 The concept of flow involves matching level of skill with the level of challenge.

anxiety

FLOW

boredom

Level of Challenge

Level of Skill

provide an atmosphere to help direct a person's motivation. An environment can be established that will enhance and guide participant motivation to match the behavioral expectations of the leader, group, and society. Leaders can enhance participant motivation by manipulating physical, psychological, and socioemotional environments.

Physical Environment

The physical environment can be manipulated through use of room colors, posters, lighting, noise, temperature, and external stimuli. For instance, the color red increases heart rate and respiration—it serves to excite people. Most blue tones, on the other hand, act as a calming influence. Green influences hunger. Bright lights affect participants differently than does subdued lighting. Room temperature can affect the level of alertness (e.g., warm temperatures often cause people to become sleepy, cooler temperatures make people more alert). Music affects people differently, establishing various moods. Smells also induce different reactions from people as does a "homey" vs. sterile environment.

Psychological Environment

Leaders can manipulate the psychological environment by creating conditions that encourage achievement, mastery of skills, esteem, and knowledge. Motivating participants may occur through ensuring an appropriate level of challenge and difficulty in activities to achieve success. By maintaining and communicating expectations of success, a leader also can manipulate the psychological environment. Allowing opportunities for participants to make choices and providing immediate feedback also influence the psychological environment. By ensuring participant readiness and utilizing appropriate behavior management techniques a leader manipulates the psychological environment.

Socioemotional Environment

The socioemotional environment includes the elements that affect one's sense of belonging and affect (i.e., feelings). Leaders can manipulate this environment by managing group size for different activities and by helping participants see links between their efforts and outcomes. Providing a supportive environment that meets one's need to belong and feel like a member of the group is an important element of the socioemotional environment. Modeling interest, enthusiasm, and intensity in the activity, and outlining meaningful objectives in which participants are interested are two other techniques that might increase the effectiveness of this environment.

People become involved in activities if they think they can be successful. Therefore, if activities are designed for participant success based on developmental stage,

Leaders can enhance participant motivation by manipulating physical, psychological, and socioemotional environments.

motivating need, and other factors, it is likely that they will be motivated to participate rather than act out. In addition, participants will be motivated to the degree that they value the rewards of participation. The more an individual values a particular activity, the more she or he will behave in appropriate ways. Furthermore, the quality of relationships involved in an activity is also a motivating factor. Leaders

---

Table 8F Principles of motivation

Remembering the following principles of motivation may help when desiring to facilitate intrinsic motivation and positive behavior management in participants (i.e., self-instilled):

- All people are motivated.
- People are motivated for their reasons, not yours.
- There is no single best or all-purpose motivational pattern (i.e., Everyone is different).
- Motivational strength overused, or used when inappropriate, can become a weakness (e.g., a person who is motivated by perfection might end up never completing her or his tasks because the jobs are never perfect enough).
- People use different behaviors to meet their needs.
- People are naturally motivated to meet their needs.
- People choose whether to live by needs alone (e.g., some people think that if their needs are met—physiological, safety, belonging, achievement, and self-actualization— that is all that counts).
- People cannot live by needs alone (e.g., values help to temper the need motivations to fit within social dictates).
- Productive motivation begins with awareness (i.e., once an individual is aware of her or his primary motivators, she or he can be very productive in how that motivation is used).
- People have natural ways of behaving which can be predicted.
- When you understand someone, you can better predict her or his behavior.
- Motivation is where our behavior begins and returns; that is, motivation is an ongoing cycle that influences every aspect of our lives (Merwin & O'Connor, 1988).

who strive for high-quality relationships with participants will be more successful than those who do not (Boardman, 2004).

Summary

In this chapter you have had an opportunity to discuss and explore several approaches to behavior management: preventative management, moral education, affective and communication models, behavior modification, assertive discipline, reality therapy, and behavior and family therapy. Each of these approaches provides a philosophical orientation to how a leader handles the management of other's behaviors. A leader may follow one approach or a combination of several in behavior management efforts.

Just as there are many ways in which people differ from one another, there are also many contributing factors to how and why people act out. Age, health, developmental ability, cultural understanding, and gender all play a role in how people act in leisure settings. Through understanding the underlying principles of behavior management, leaders can accommodate and acknowledge differences in people while attending to the undesirable behaviors. A variety of specific behavior management techniques were presented, from unobtrusive to discernible to obtrusive in nature.

Because motivation and behavior management are closely related, Maslow's hierarchy of needs and McClelland's theory of motivation were presented, as was a brief introduction to flow. Comprehending what motivates people and how to facilitate that motivation are great aids in managing participant behaviors. As with all leadership skills, each leader will integrate various motivation techniques and methodologies into her or his particular leadership style as appropriate. Managing behaviors is necessary to facilitate high-quality recreation experiences for participants. In that sense, rules and guidelines serve not to constrain individual leisure and ruin people's fun, but rather to manage diverse situations in the best interest of all.

Beginning the Journey

Perhaps you have noticed by now that almost all of the chapters in this text address some aspect of working with people. It makes sense, because people are our business. All of these skills are necessary for a successful journey to leadership, as is a basic understanding of the underlying theories and concepts that help explain it all. Try answering the following questions as a tool to your own development.

1. Define the following terms in a way that makes sense to you: behavior management, discipline, behavior modification. How do these apply to all age groups? Give examples of how the elderly, adults, teens, and children act in undesirable ways. Discuss what is meant by goal-directed behaviors. How does power relate to behavior management issues?

2. Develop a chart of the eight approaches to behavior management. When drawing this chart, include columns where you explain or describe the approach, highlight the key elements of that approach, identify the advantages and disadvantages of using each approach, and describe/identify the leadership skills one would need to be effective in using this approach.

3. Why is behavior management needed? What is the ultimate goal of behavior management? Discuss the three primary purposes of behavior management. Reflect on and describe examples of behavior management situations that either you've seen or been involved with and put them on a continuum from minor to major infraction. How were those situations resolved?

4. As a leader, you'll have to decide which behavior management approaches and techniques to utilize. What factors will you need to consider in your decision making? Explain thoroughly and give examples of how these factors relate to behavior management.

Engaging and empowering youth can be strong motivating factors.

5. Have a look at Table 8C. How would you categorize these reasons for acting out? Which of them can the leader manage and minimize most easily? How would the leader control or manage these issues? Brainstorm at least three things you can do as a leader to alleviate each of these issues.

6. Reflect on a job (paid or volunteer) you have had in the field of parks, recreation, and leisure services. What was the organizational approach to behavior management? If it was not articulated, you may have to think this through and extrapolate from situational cues. When you were involved personally in behavior management situations, did you use the self-awareness questions found on page 168? In what ways are you proactive in your behavior management? Describe typical preparations you undertake when you are leading to minimize behavior problems.

7. Review the elements of effective corrective feedback. Give yourself corrective feedback for something you recently did. Practice giving and receiving corrective feedback to a classmate. Be sure to incorporate what you know about listening, nonverbal behavior, and other aspects of leadership as you practice this. Take notes about what you did as you engaged in corrective feedback.

8. Which behavior management principles do you think are most critical and why? Which of these principles do you adhere to regularly? Which do you need to further develop to enhance your skills as a leader?

9. Explain the differences between unobtrusive, discernible, and obtrusive behavior management techniques. Which behavior management techniques are already a part of your repertoire? Do you have a tendency to overuse or underutilize any of these techniques? Why do you think this happens? Create a pocket-sized card with the full range of behavior management techniques listed, from unobtrusive to obtrusive, and laminate it for future use and reference.

10. What will help you decide which behavior management technique to use and when? How can you minimize your need to use obtrusive behavior management techniques? What should you do if you make a miscue or miscall in behavior management? What are miscalls?

11. Why is information about motivation included in this chapter? What is motivation? What are your strongest motivators? What are you most motivated to do? Why? What are you least motivated to do? Why? Describe the scenario in which you are most motivated. How can you facilitate your own motivation? Is it important for leaders to be motivated? Explain.

12. Describe Maslow's hierarchy of needs. Explain McClelland's theory of motivation. How do the two theories compare? Which do you think better explains the motivation process? Why? What is flow? In detail, describe a time when you experienced flow (describe the situation and the feelings you experienced). Is flow easily achievable? How can you, as a leader, facilitate the flow experience for others?

13. How can a leader facilitate other people being motivated? What does it mean to "set someone up for success?" How does that relate to motivation? How do leader-follower relationships motivate (positively or negatively) people?

References

Ambrose, M. and Kulik, C. (1999). Old friends, new faces: Motivation research in the 1990s. *Journal of Management, 25*(3), 231–292.

Anonymous. (2000). Behavior management 101: Ideas and tips for managing challenging behavior. *Camping Magazine, 73*(3), 26–27.

Barbetta, P., Norona, K., and Bicard, D. (2005). Classroom behavior management: A dozen common mistakes and what to do instead. *Preventing School Failure, 49*(3), 11–19.

Barbuto, J. (2005). Motivation and transactional, charismatic, and transformational leadership: A test of antecedents. *Journal of Leadership & Organizational Studies, 11*(4), 26–34.

Barbuto, J., Fritz, S., and Marx, D. (2002). A field examination of two measures of work motivation as predictors of leaders' influence tactics. *Journal of Social Psychology, 142*(5), 601–615.

Boardman, R. (2004). Behavior management by walking around. *Reclaiming Children and Youth, 13*(1), 48–50.

Carter, M., Van Andel, G., and Robb, G. (2003). *Therapeutic recreation: A practical approach* (3rd ed.). Prospect Heights, IL: Waveland Press.

Clark, J. (2002). *Leadership and motivation*. Retrieved July 12, 2006, from http://www.isma.org.uk/stressnw/leadmot1.htm

Csikszentmihalyi, M. (1990). *Flow: The psychology of optimal experience*. New York, NY: Harper & Row.

Farmer, T., Goforth, J., Hives, J., Aaron, A., Kjackson, F., and Sgammato, A. (2006). Competence enhancement behavior management. *Preventing School Failure, 50*(3), 39–44.

Ferguson, E. (2000). *Motivation: A biosocial and cognitive integration of motivation and emotion.* New York, NY: Oxford University Press.

Gagne, M. and Deci, E. (2005). Self-determination theory and work motivation. *Journal of Organizational Behavior, 26,* 331–362.

Gordon, T. (1989). *Teaching children self-discipline.* New York, NY: Times Books.

Jones, V. and Jones, L. (1995). *Comprehensive classroom management.* Boston, MA: Allyn and Bacon.

KidsSource. (2003). *Positive discipline.* Retrieved July 13, 2006, from http://www.kidsource.com/kidsource/content/positive.discipline.html

Laursen, E. (2003). Principle-centered discipline. *Reclaiming Children and Youth, 12*(2), 78–82.

Macciomei, N. and Ruben, D. (Eds.). (1999). *Behavioral management in the public schools.* Westport, CT: Praeger.

MacIntyre, T. (2005). *Assertive discipline.* Retrieved July 13, 2006, from http://maxweber.hunter.cuny.edu/pub/eres/EDSPC715_MCINTYRE/AssertiveDiscipline.html

Moorhead, G. and Griffin, R. (2004). *Organizational behavior: Managing people and organizations* (7th ed.). Boston, MA: Houghton Mifflin.

Omer, H. (2001). Helping parents deal with children's acute disciplinary problems without escalation: The principle of nonviolent resistance. *Family Process, 40*(1), 53–66.

Ramsey, R. (1994). *Administrator's complete school discipline guide.* Englewood Cliffs, NJ: Prentice Hall.

Russell, R. (2005). *Leadership in recreation* (3rd ed.). New York, NY: McGraw Hill.

Ryska, T. (2001). The impact of acculturation on sport motivation among Mexican-American adolescent male athletes. *The Psychological Record, 51*(4), 533–544.

Seaman, J., DePauw, K., Morton, K., and Omoto, K. (2003). *Making connections: From theory to practice in adapted physical education* (2nd ed.). Scottsdale, AZ: Hathaway Publishing.

Sherrill, C. (1998). *Adapted physical activity, recreation, and sport: Crossdisciplinary and lifespan* (5th ed.). Boston, MA: WCB/McGraw Hill.

Silberman, M. and Wheelan, S. (1980). *How to discipline without feeling guilty.* Champaign, IL: Research Press Company.

Wolfgang, C. and Wolfgang, M. (1995). *The three faces of discipline for early childhood.* Boston, MA: Allyn and Bacon.

Section III
Synergy in Leadership: Pulling It All Together

Synergy describes the notion that the sum of the parts is larger, bigger, and more powerful than the whole. It implies an important linking together of the various pieces. Issues of diversity, values, ethics, risk management, direct leadership techniques, and social and professional concerns are vital to all discussions surrounding leadership. Successful, effective leaders have a solid understanding of how these elements impact leadership situations.

Everyone learns in her or his own way. Some quickly grasp abstract concepts and build practical knowledge on that base, while others learn through experience and backtrack to related conceptual issues. In this text, an attempt has been made to provide a mix of information—conceptual, theoretical, and practical—that might meet the needs of a diverse readership. Readers are encouraged to review sections that may have been a bit muddied in earlier study and to place the information in context with current learning and goals. Leadership development and learning both occur through book knowledge as well as through experiential efforts—Material must be continually reviewed to fully make sense.

As one reads the chapters in this section and begins to pull together the material from throughout the text, the synergy that develops from these efforts will aid in the development of holistic leadership skills. An effective leader exhibits competence in conceptual skills, interpersonal skills and technical skills, and understands how the three skill areas are linked. In addition, successful leaders know and understand their own abilities and limitations in each of these areas.

Leader Profile

Jane H. Adams
Executive Director, California Park & Recreation Society

Jane has over 19 years in this position and more than 34 years in the parks, recreation, and leisure services profession.

Volunteer leadership positions she has held include:

- President, National Recreation and Park Association
- Board Member, American Park and Recreation Society, NRPA
- President, American Academy for Park and Recreation Administration
- Chair, Council of State Affiliate Executive Directors
- President, Missouri Park and Recreation Association
- Dean's Leadership Council, Penn State University Department of Health and Human Development

What is the meaning of leadership?
Leadership is being aware of who you are and what you can bring to the organization. It is about being available to others. It is a journey towards "wholeness" as a person. It is also a process to inspire others to work towards a common vision or mission. It is about having focus, the ability to communicate, and listen.

What are the most important leadership qualities?
Leaders must be authentic and credible. They must have a vision and the ability to communicate it to others. They have to be able to make it "real" to the people involved, and they have to be able to articulate how everyone working together can make a difference. Additionally, a leader has to be flexible and be willing to demand at times.

What advice do you have for students who aspire to leadership in parks, recreation, and leisure services?
Actively participate in your state and national park and recreation associations! It is through these organizations that we get to practice leading and following. It is also an excellent way to meet that future employer. Volunteer for extra assignments at work. Be willing to make mistakes and learn from them. Finally, be willing to move to another part of the country or state in order to get the job you want. Write down your professional goals—Where do you want to be in 5 or 10 years? Track your progress and get involved in those activities that help you achieve your goals.

Favorite book: Synchronicity: The Inner Path of Leadership by Joe Jaworski

Favorite activities: I am an avid reader; I love to cook, hike, and golf. I also have two new favorites—biking and swimming.

Chapter Nine
Diversity and Leisure Services Leadership

Learning Opportunities

Through studying this chapter readers will have the opportunity to

- Understand the importance of diversity for effective leadership.
- Examine the construct of culture and how it impacts leisure services leadership.
- Increase knowledge of the dimensions of diversity.
- Recognize the impacts of unearned privilege on access to resources.
- Examine several techniques for leaders to effectively meet the needs of a variety of constituents.

Photo courtesy of Deb Jordan

People go to leisure services settings to engage in enjoyable activities, to be with others with whom they feel safe and whose company is stimulating, and to perhaps learn new skills or knowledge. Leisure services leaders strive to facilitate the various types of leisure experiences participants seek. Leaders have a responsibility to ensure (as much as possible) that every leisure participant has the opportunity to reach her or his desired potential in leisure. For this to occur, the environment must be conducive to a feeling of belonging, personal growth, and must offer a variety of experiences. In many cases, such an atmosphere is lacking. Consider the following scenarios:

- Women from a local college basketball team are at the recreation facility over winter break shooting hoops during an open gymnasium period. A group of young men come in and run them off saying, "Let us men show you girls how the game is really played—Basketball is a man's game."

- An African-American family enters the library and a friendly librarian steps up and offers to show them where the books are shelved that would be of interest to them—She takes the family to the section that deals with African-American history.

- A group of boys ages 11 to 13 are engaged in a rough-and-tumble game on the football field. When the recreation supervisor asks them what they are playing they shout, "Smear the queer!"

- A 68-year-old man signs up for a beginners' racquetball class. The person at the front desk mutters, "Man, you're a little too old to start something new like this, aren't you?"

- A person who uses a wheelchair wants to play racquetball and is told she cannot because "black rubber soles are not allowed on the court" and the tires on her chair are black rubber.

In each of the above situations, potential participants were faced with prejudice and discrimination which interfered with their leisure experiences. Whether based on age, gender, ethnicity, disability or perceived sexual orientation, prejudice and discrimination have the potential to inhibit and constrain the leisure of those being labeled. As facilitators of leisure experiences, recreation and leisure services leaders should protect, facilitate, and enhance the leisure experiences of members of all groups.

Because leisure services leaders work with people of all backgrounds, they need an understanding of diversity to be effective. Having some knowledge of the different ways in which people learn, communicate with one another, and participate in leisure can help a leader be responsive to the needs of all participants. An attempt has been made throughout each chapter of this text to address issues of diversity as they apply to the material being discussed. To supplement that material, this chapter provides additional information about various elements of diversity and multiculturalism to assist leaders to better understand the issues involved.

Understanding the Basics

As with all constructs it is important to gain an understanding of how terms are used. This chapter utilizes terms that are used in everyday language, but for which people often hold different meanings. In this text, *diversity* refers to celebrating differences among people in a way that allows people to better understand and appreciate those differences (and similarities) in the pursuit of social justice. Respect for others' cultural viewpoints and a desire for equality and fairness among all, are primary goals of diversity. *Dimensions of diversity* refer to the various demographic dimensions, traits, or characteristics on which we differ. We all have core (primary) and secondary characteristics upon which others make assumptions and pass judgments about us. Dimensions of diversity include such things as sex, age, class, religion, and level of education (Loden & Rosener, 1991; Schwartz & Conley, 2000).

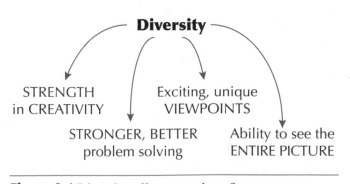

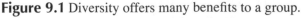

Figure 9.1 Diversity offers many benefits to a group.

As facilitators of leisure experiences, recreation and leisure services leaders should protect, facilitate, and enhance the leisure experiences of members of all groups.

The assumptions and judgments others make about us based on our dimensions of diversity are known as *stereotypes*. Stereotypes are part of a process whereby we make observations about and perceive others in particular ways and then attribute specific traits to those people—all based on their apparent membership in a particular group. Stereotypes are usually simple and exaggerated, are automatically and unconsciously activated, and may be either negative/hostile or positive/benevolent (Fujimoto & Hartel, 2004). For instance, we would hold a negative stereotype if we believe that all members of a cultural group are substance abusers. A positive/benevolent stereotype might be judging an individual as highly intelligent simply because we think that she or he belongs to a particular cultural group. According to King, Chipman, and Cruz-Janzen (1994), stereotypes are perpetuated by

- denying they exist (e.g., "This is the 21st century. People don't believe in stereotypes any more.")
- ignoring them or accepting them when they occur (e.g., in response to a sexist remark—"Uh huh, that's true.")
- denying that they affect our lives (e.g., "Stereotypes don't affect me—I'm accepted for who I am.")
- denying that they affect other's lives (e.g., "They need to stop playing victims. People don't get fired from jobs because of stereotypes.")
- supporting them through our own behaviors, for example: exclusion and tokenism, stereotyping, biased language, imbalance and inequality, giving value to only one side of the story, spreading misinformation, isolation, and segregation.

Prejudice—a preconceived belief or preference for one person, place, or thing over another—closely relates to stereotyping. It includes an emotional element; often an irrational judgment (usually consisting of hatred or fear) of a group of people and individual members of that group (Kurtz-Costes & Pungello, 2000). *Discrimination* describes the acts taken on the basis of prejudice—differential treatment of one group that often creates a situation of disadvantage for another group.

General descriptions of various cultural groups will be presented in this chapter. *Culture* is defined as the sum total of the way people act and live their lives. It explains a person's response to the ultimate query, "Who am I?," and consists of shared assumptions, beliefs and values (usually unspoken); learned responses; and ways of being, knowing and doing. Because culture is both personally and socially constructed, such things as language, material objects, rituals, institutions, and art transmit culture from one generation to the next (Friedman & Antal, 2005; Hofstede, 2001).

Culture is a dynamic, complex, multidimensional, and continuous process—an orientation to life that includes an intertwined system of values, attitudes, and beliefs that give meaning to individual and collective identity (Sagie & Aycan, 2003; Yan & Wong, 2005). Althen (1994) thinks of culture as an iceberg. The tip of the iceberg represents the aspects of culture which are visible to others—words, behaviors, customs, and traditions. Yan and Wong (2005) and others refer to this as *surface culture*. Just under the surface of the water are the beliefs held by the cultural group: they surface in varying situations, but for the most part, remain hidden. Far under the water are the worldviews, values, assumptions, and thought processes of the culture; these are very difficult to access and understand by people who do not belong to that cultural group (and sometimes by cultural group members themselves). This is sometimes referred to as *deep culture*.

By understanding that people differ in beliefs, values, assumptions, customs, and ways of knowing we begin to comprehend the complexities of working with people in leisure services settings. While humans are similar to one another in many respects, there are also significant ways in which people differ from one another. Leaders who are able to work with both the similarities and differences in people are likely to experience success in their leadership efforts. This is termed *cultural competence,* and it is possible for an individual to become competent in multiple cultures (Goldberg, 2000).

Cultural Competence

Leadership is about working with people, and to effectively work with people we need to appreciate who they are, their values (i.e., what is important to them), and belief structures. When we truly appreciate others it is easier to understand and accept their preferred styles of communication, social interactions, their motivations, and recreation and leisure preferences and behaviors. Yan and Wong (2005) present three major dimensions involved in becoming culturally competent: (a) awareness of and sensitivity to one's own values, biases, and perceptions of power differences; (b) knowledge of individual cultures; and (c) skills in verbal and nonverbal communication.

To begin, leaders who wish to become culturally competent first need to conduct an internal self-analysis. To do this we must work on becoming aware of the messages we learned as children, the assumptions we hold about various cultural groups, our reactions (on both emotional and cognitive levels) to people who are different from us, our expectations of others, what we value most, and our worldviews (e.g., collectivism/individualism, power distance, masculinity/femininity, uncertainty avoidance). For instance, this self-analysis might help us understand that an insistence that everyone should be able to help themselves and "pull themselves up by their bootstraps" is likely derived from an individualist perspective, and that a person with a collectivist perspective would not likely share this belief because community is what is most important in helping someone.

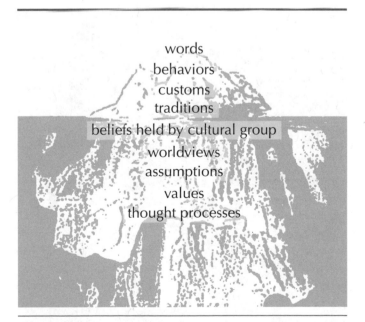

words
behaviors
customs
traditions
beliefs held by cultural group
worldviews
assumptions
values
thought processes

Figure 9.2 Culture may be perceived as an iceberg with various elements above and below the water line.

Leaders who are able to work with both the similarities and differences in people are likely to experience success in their leadership efforts. This is termed *cultural competence,* and it is possible for an individual to become competent in multiple cultures.

The second phase in becoming culturally competent is to gain knowledge and learn about various cultures. It is difficult to claim that we understand people from cultures other than our own if we know nothing about them. Learning about the history, language, politics, traditions, customs, values, worldviews and other elements of a culture sets the stage for us to develop an understanding and appreciation of distinct cultural groups. For example, did you know that during the days of slavery African Americans could be hanged for looking a White person directly in the eyes when they were being spoken to? Knowing this could help in understanding why some African American children do not look adults (particularly Whites) directly in the eyes when being addressed.

Developing a wide repertoire of communication skills will serve all leaders well. With regard to cultural competence, skills in many forms and styles of communication are important to ensure effective and suitable interactions. Further, communication is the basis for the development of relationships; thus, it is necessary to feel confident that what is being received is the message we meant to send. For instance, something as simple as tossing something (e.g., a pen) to a person from Latin America could be perceived as rude; handing such things to an individual is much more polite (*Spanish culture*, 2006). Speaking loudly or softly, directly or indirectly, and using nonverbal gestures and symbols in culturally appropriate ways will enhance our communication and leadership.

Several authors suggest a six-stage model that describes a continuum of cultural competence. Individuals, agencies, and society experience this continuum of integrating diversity in daily living. The stages include

1. Denial of the existence of other cultural groups (This can result in avoidance of people who belong to other cultural groups.)

2. Defensiveness or superiority (i.e., "People in the other group are different from me, but my group is better.")

3. Minimization (i.e., "Okay, there may be some differences, but they really don't matter as we are all human beings.")

4. Acceptance (Recognition of differences; differences are important to people and valued.)

5. Adaptation (Empathy is experienced; able to understand a person through her or his culture's life experiences.)

6. Integration (Differences are fully accepted and reconciled; a multicultural society exists.)

Dean (2001) presents the intriguing idea that it is not necessarily desirable or possible to become culturally competent. Cultures are dynamic, evolving constructs and thus difficult to ever fully "capture." Rather than giving up on understanding issues related to diversity, however, he suggests we should maintain an awareness of our own lack of competence with regard to culture. In this way, we keep our focus on striving for knowledge, understanding, and skills related to our own (as well as others') culture. It is extremely difficult (if at all possible) to separate ourselves from our own cultural baggage by focusing on our own attitudes, knowledge and skills, but we can minimize the impact our "baggage" will have on our interactions with others.

Changes in Diversity Issues

In the past, when people used the word "culture" they were referring only to traits deemed characteristic of people who belonged to various racial groupings (e.g., African, Caucasian, Asian). In recent years we have seen an expansion of the definition of culture to include many additional dimensions of diversity (e.g., gender, ethnicity, sexual orientation, physical/cognitive abilities and qualities, age, religion). This means that it is now believed that people with disabilities have an identifiable culture, as do the elderly, as do people who are gay, and so on.

One position suggests that the impacts of discrimination result from power differences between cultural

Photo courtesy of Deb Jordan

Understanding the basics about accessibility is necessary for inclusive leaders.

groups. These differences arise out of historical and political factors associated with the particular culture (Ting-Toomey, 1999). For example, between African-American people and Euro-American people, prejudice and discrimination arise out of a power relationship more so than a racial relationship (i.e., Whites were slave owners, African Americans were the slaves). In the United States, Euro-American people continue to have more power (e.g., better and easier access to resources such as money, good jobs, and housing; more political clout) than do African Americans. Discrimination that goes beyond personal attitudes and is perpetuated by the norms of the dominant culture is referred to as *institutional discrimination.*

Recognizing that power differences exist hand-in-hand with discrimination often helps in understanding the need to disassemble such system-wide prejudicial attitudes. As a leader in the broad field of human services it is important to support social justice issues such as equal access to basic needs (e.g., housing, food, transportation) and leisure experiences for all people. To do this, effective leaders must understand diversity. Knowing how to best serve people of different backgrounds and cultures is the first step to celebrating diversity in leisure services leadership. Consider the following information from the U.S. Census Bureau:

> between the years 2000 and 2050 it is estimated that in the United States the Asian-American population will increase from 3.8% to 8.0%; the Hispanic-American (including Latino) population will see an increase from 12.6% to 24.4%; the African-American population will grow from 12.7% to 14.6%; non-Hispanic Whites will decrease from 81% to 72%; and all other races (including people reporting more than one race)

> will grow from 2.5% to 5.3%. (*U.S. interim projections,* 2004)

These changes will be due to birth rates as well as immigration. In fact, one report suggested that immigration to the United States is at its highest ever (*Rate of immigration,* 2002). Over one million immigrants have entered the United States every year since 1992; most have been from Latin America (e.g., Mexico) and Asia (e.g., India, Philippines; Meyers & Yau, 2004). Some of these immigrants are voluntary (e.g., they emigrated to the United States in search of a better life), while others are involuntary (e.g., a result of war, starvation, or persecution). These two types of immigrant populations will arrive with and face different issues in their new home country. In addition, many will face language issues. According to Barnes and Bennett (2002), 61% of Vietnamese, 51% of Chinese, and 24% of Filipinos immigrants are not fluent in English. Leisure services leaders will be faced with addressing and meeting the needs of very diverse constituent groups.

Leaders in certain regions of the United States and particular states will face more challenges than others in terms of developing cultural competence. For instance, compared to other regions, the southern United States has the highest poverty rate, the largest percentage of African Americans, the highest disability rate, and ranks second largest in terms of overall population growth. It also has the highest rate of grandparents who are now parenting their grandchildren. Since 1990 the western region experienced the largest growth in the overall population as well as in the older population (e.g., Nevada experienced a 72% total increase); the largest number of Asians and fewest number of Blacks live in the west (*U.S. interim projections,* 2004).

California is one of the most diverse states. It houses the largest Asian, Hispanic, and American Indian populations, the second largest Black population (behind New York), the most legal immigrants, and the highest percentage of individuals who do not speak English. New York ranks second to California in most of these statistics; West Virginia leads the nation in percentage of population with a disability (24.2%)—that is almost one in every four people (*U.S. interim projections,* 2004).

Dimensions of Diversity

Several years ago Loden and Rosener (1991) presented a model of diversity that has become quite popular in helping to understand the impact of diversity on all aspects of life. They categorized dimensions of diversity as being either primary or secondary and provided evidence of how we

Melting pot:
No one culture is distinguished from another.

Salad bowl:
Cultures are distinct, yet added together to make one coherent group.

Figure 9.3 Two views of cultural relationships

tend to ascribe more worth to one element or dimension of diversity than another. Further, people are a composite of many elements of diversity and each dimension can serve to mitigate or enhance positive and negative social responses. For instance, not only is a person Hispanic or Native American but also she is a particular age, has a certain level of education, has an identified family structure, and so on. How others react to this person will be based on all of her dimensions of diversity.

Many people perceive the dimensions of diversity as bipolar; that is people tend to classify individuals as belonging to one or another category (either/or). This polarization of the dimensions of diversity is seen in the obvious and subtle valuing of one element of diversity over another. For instance, being Euro-American is more highly valued (i.e., group members have access to better and more resources) than being African American; male is more highly valued than female; and being able-bodied is more highly valued than having a disability.

Core (Primary) Dimensions

Most of us expect other people to be just like us in ways such as likes, dislikes, values, assumptions, and behaviors. This is referred to as the *assumption of similarity;* it is often the cause of misunderstandings because we base our expectations and judgments of their behaviors on these perceptions (Friedman & Antal, 2005). For instance, if we hear someone using a speech pattern that we perceive as street language and full of slang or unfamiliar words, we may perceive that person as "less than" (e.g., less educated, less potential, less income) people who speak (and look) more like us. Because people are distinct from one another and live with different elements of diversity, we have sets of experiences that lead to developing unique ways of looking at and living in the world. We filter information differently based on our cultural perspective. Leaders who bear this in mind as they interact with others tend to be effective in their interactions.

The primary dimensions of diversity—the traits we observe upon meeting people—are extremely difficult (if not impossible) to change. To maintain order and process information efficiently, we often put people into perceptual categories based on these core dimensions. The meanings and values that we ascribe to these various elements of personhood can result in prejudice and discrimination. Some authors suggest that we try to build our own self-esteem by developing positive opinions of our own cultural group and negative opinions of others (Kurtz-Costes & Pungello, 2000). This is similar to the ideas discussed in the chapter on group dynamics—we think positively of the

group of which we are members and less positively of other groups.

Sex/Gender

Sex refers to biological differences between females and males present at birth that exist throughout life (i.e., our chromosomal makeup). Gender—the way we perceive femaleness (i.e., what it means to be a girl or woman—femininity) and maleness (i.e., what it means to be a boy or man—masculinity)—is socialized throughout life. One can be female in sex yet masculine in gender, or male and feminine.

Sex and gender remain important variables in terms of perceptions of competence and potential. Koch (2004) and Oakhill, Granham, and Reynolds (2005) have found that we immediately and unconsciously activate gender-based stereotypes upon learning whether an individual is female or male and upon hearing a role (i.e., occupation). People expect women to be nurturing and strong in relationships while men are expected to be focused on getting the job done. Further, when a person hears a role or occupation such as "nurse," she or he assumes the individual is female; hearing the role "auto mechanic" brings to mind a male (Koch, 2004).

The prevailing attitude in the United States favors the male sex and masculine gender. As examples, most administrative and managerial positions are held by men; in 2004 Caiazza, Shaw, and Werschkul reported that

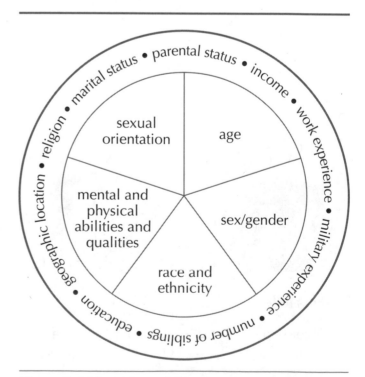

Figure 9.4 Dimensions of diversity wheel

women make only 76 cents for every one dollar that men earned. Further, males who behave in a characteristically masculine fashion have greater power than females and people who are feminine. This attitude is visible in many settings, including leisure services settings; an example is the basketball scenario presented at the beginning of this chapter. The men believed they had the right to take the court away from the women and did so without hesitation.

Age

People often overlook age when addressing issues of prejudice and discrimination, yet there are clear instances of age being used to label people and constrain them from reaching their full potential. Many people hold negative/hostile stereotypes of teenagers (e.g., they are self-serving and lazy) while others hold negative/hostile beliefs about older people (e.g., they have diminished mental and physical capabilities). Jumping to conclusions about an individual's abilities or interests based on age, or treating people in a certain manner because of their age, may limit full involvement in the leisure experience.

Age is a dimension of diversity that has an impact on leadership styles, communication, expectations, as well as challenges and opportunities (remember the discussion of human development provided in Chapter 3). All leaders are aided by knowing the nature of their constituents, and there is information available that provides some context in this area. We know that approximately 26% of the U.S. population is under the age 18; 62% are between the ages of 18 and 64, while 12% are ages 65 and older (Meyer, 2001). The 50- to 54-year-old age group experienced a 55% increase during the 1990s. In the 21st century, of course, we can expect this age bubble to continue to move up the population scale. There are more older women

than men because women tend to live longer than men. A common stereotype about the older population is that most elderly live in long-term care facilities. Hetzel and Smith (2001) reported that, in fact, the percent of people ages 65 years and older who lived in care facilities dropped from 5.1% to 4.5%. In 1990, 24.5% of the 85 and older population lived in long-term care facilities; in 2000, that had dropped to 18.2%. The older generation is living longer, healthier, and more independent lives. Thus, parks and recreation leaders will be working more frequently with older individuals in a variety of recreational settings.

Ethnicity/Race

Historically, people have used the term *race* when referring to a group of people who share a genetic makeup which results in biological characteristics used to distinguish one group from another (e.g., people of Asian heritage have eyefolds and small noses; people of Spanish or Latin descent have dark skin, hair, and eyes). The accuracy of the term *race* has been questioned, however, as new research indicates that all humans are biologically related to one another and that the majority of people are biologically mixed. For instance, more than 40% of Japanese people are of mixed races (Lassiter, 1998) and over 60% of Native American people are racially mixed (Ogunwole, 2002).

Ethnicity refers to the commonalties shared and passed down through history and tradition from one generation of people to the next. Ethnicity more accurately describes the culture with which one identifies than does race. Several components constitute ethnicity: a historical link, shared geographic beginnings, linguistic commonalties, shared religious beliefs, common social class, mutual political interests, and a joint moral (i.e., values) base. Individuals who have most or all of these seven aspects of ethnicity in common would be considered to share an ethnic heritage and culture (Carlson, Uppal & Prosser, 2000).

Understanding that within racial groups there may be different ethnic traditions assists leaders in understanding those with whom they work. For instance, there are over 500 federally recognized and over 100 state recognized American Indian tribes (Ogunwole, 2002). Each tribe has distinct cultural traditions that influence the way they live in and respond to the world. The same distinctions can be seen among Hispanics, who may come from Mexican, Puerto Rican, Cuban, or Central or South American traditions—each is unique.

The assumption made by the friendly librarian in the scenario at the beginning of this chapter that an African-American family would only be interested in books about African Americans is a subtle form of prejudice based on race/ethnicity. Before asking the family about their interests,

Age is one of the primary dimensions of diversity.

the librarian made an unfounded judgment and limited the family's exploration of the library. This faulty assessment was likely based on both skin color and assumptions about the ethnicity of the family.

Sexual Orientation

Sexual orientation refers to one's identity as gay, lesbian, bisexual, transgendered (GLBT), or heterosexual. This dimension of diversity is the most easily hidden of all core elements of diversity (i.e., one cannot tell if someone is straight or gay simply by looking at her or him), yet it engenders strong social reactions. Being heterosexual is more valued and acceptable than being gay, lesbian, bisexual, or transgendered. Estimates of the U.S. population who are gay or lesbian range from 3% to 10% and transgendered people at 1%.

Research about the lives of GLBT people reveals unique concerns of this group. Over 90% of youth in high school report hearing homophobic remarks in school, and over one-third report hearing those types of remarks from teachers or staff (Peters, 2003; Roberts, 2001). In addition, verbal and physical abuse are prevalent toward people who are not heterosexual. *Homophobia*—the unrealistic fear of homosexuality or homosexual people—often results in those who are not heterosexual experiencing isolation, loneliness, homelessness, and making detrimental personal behavior choices (e.g., drug and alcohol abuse, unsafe sex, increased suicide rates).

People of all sexual orientations engage in a variety of leisure activities and are involved in every type of leisure services organization. Leisure services leaders have

Photo courtesy of Deb Jordan

People who share ethnic identities have a common history, shared geography, language, and religion. They also share a social class, often have mutual political interests, and a joint values base.

long catered to the needs of heterosexuals—family programming, husband-and-wife activities, dances—while essentially ignoring the needs of GLBT participants. At the same time, the GLBT community may be underserved in recreation settings because it is a virtually invisible population (Caldwell, Kivel, Smith & Hayes, 1998; Jaffe, 1998).

To be most effective, leaders would be wise to recognize the specific needs of all constituents. Addressing the sense of isolation, loneliness, and social rejection, particularly experienced by young people, would combat some of the concerns and challenges faced by people who are GLBT. These group members often experience tremendous stresses as they discover their sexuality in an atmosphere of hate and misunderstanding. The early chapter scenario of young boys playing a game called "smear the queer" is an example of homophobic attitudes found throughout society—even in children's games.

Physical/Cognitive Abilities and Qualities

In this dimension of diversity cognitive and physical disabilities are addressed, as are other physical qualities that might foster negative reactions—obesity, wearing thick glasses, having severe acne, or being "ugly" in cultural terms. Too often people with disabilities and other less than perfect physical qualities are ignored as far as equal access to services and leisure services opportunities. Assumptions and prejudgments about desires and capabilities are often made upon seeing a person who is obese, a person with Down syndrome, a person who has autism, or a person who is blind.

We will all interact with individuals who have disabilities. Almost 29% of people in the United States have a disabling condition of some sort—that is two of every seven people. Of those, 16.6% have a physical disability, 10.2% have a mental disability, and 8.0% have a sensory impairment (Wang, 2005). Over 13% of people with disabilities cannot leave their home without assistance, and 5.7% have difficulty with self-care. In terms of residence, Wang indicated that West Virginia had the highest prevalence of people with disabilities, followed by Kentucky, Arkansas, Mississippi, and Alabama. The states of Alaska, Utah, and Minnesota have the lowest population percentage of people with disabilities.

People with disabilities are often excluded from consideration in parks, recreation, and leisure service organizations; they experience social isolation and negative health conditions at a greater rate than those who do not have a disability. Not all people with disabilities require accommodations for full involvement in recreation activities, but some will have this need. As depicted at the beginning of this chapter, prohibiting a person who uses a wheelchair from full participation in leisure due to the fact that her or his wheelchair has rubber tires is an example of discrimination.

Secondary Dimensions

Secondary dimensions of diversity include elements of self which are not necessarily visible and which may change over the course of one's life. Elements that fit into this classification of diversity include marital status, parental status, socioeconomic status (class), educational level, type of occupation, military experience, types of leisure engagement, geographic location, and religion. As with the core dimensions, throughout various cultures, facets of each of these secondary diversity dimensions are more highly valued than others and receive unspoken privileges.

As we get to know more about a person than cannot be seen with our eyes (i.e., secondary dimensions of diversity), we usually modify our first impressions. For instance, if we recently met an individual who is Asian-American (stereotype: highly intelligent), female (stereotype: feminine), 16 years old (stereotype: college-oriented), heterosexual (stereotype: normal), and able-bodied (stereotype: healthy), our first impression would likely be positive toward this individual; she fits the American model of a contributing member of society. As we get to know this teen better, however, if we learn that she had a baby last year (sterotype: teen parent status) and has used illegal drugs, many of us would modify our first impression to include stereotypes of irresponsibility, sexual promiscuity, and "slacker." Whether or not any of these assumptions were accurate could not be determined until we learned much more about this individual.

Diversity and Privilege

It has been mentioned that each element of diversity has a preferred state of being which is valued more highly than another. For example, in the dimension of physical/cognitive abilities and qualities the preferred state is able-bodied and attractive (according to cultural standards). Being able-bodied and attractive is more highly valued and desired than being disabled and unattractive. Attractive, able-bodied people are well-treated by society and receive many unearned privileges because of their physical appearance. *Unearned privileges* are special advantages, permissions, rights, or benefits granted to an individual based on physical appearance (or other dimensions of diversity; McIntosh, 1989). Such an advantage, permission, right, or benefit often excludes others, resulting in discrimination.

People in each of the privileged classes on the valued end of the diversity continuum are socialized to not see the privileges bestowed upon them; most are very unaware of their own privileges based on the dimensions of diversity they represent (Davidson, 2001). Again, we have a tendency to see this as simply the way things are. The awareness and knowledge of personal privilege, however, is believed to be necessary to reduce prejudice and discrimination.

In an attempt to establish an important way to remind us of our privileges, some years ago McIntosh (1989) presented a number of examples of unearned privileges based on skin color (e.g., White privilege). Examples of other types of unearned privileges based on other elements of diversity follow.

White privilege includes:

- being able to go shopping at the mall without being harassed or followed by security personnel
- being certain people did not get out of the swimming pool when I got in because of my skin color
- being able to swear, dress grubby, and not answer letters without others attributing these behaviors to the bad morals, poverty, or illiteracy of my race
- getting a job without coworkers thinking I got it because of my race

Male privilege includes:

- being assured of not waiting in long lines to use a public restroom
- being rude and short with people without being referred to as a bitch
- being physically athletic without someone questioning my sexuality
- having the ability to get a hair cut and clothes pressed at a lower cost than a woman

Unearned privileges are special advantages, permissions, rights, or benefits granted to an individual based on physical appearance (or other dimensions of diversity). Such an advantage, permission, right, or benefit often excludes others, resulting in discrimination.

Privileges of being heterosexual include:

- the protection of marriage, should it be desired
- acceptance to engage in some public displays of affection with my significant other
- receiving less costly family rates at parks, recreation and leisure services settings
- being fired from my job (or not being hired in the first place) because of my sexuality is unlikely

Privileges of being thirty-something include:

- the assumption of being capable, college-educated and having some level of knowledge and intellect
- good insurance rates on my automobile
- full access to all rides at an amusement/theme park
- being assured that people will listen to my opinion

Privileges of being attractive and able-bodied include:

- being assured of getting prompt, efficient service at a restaurant
- local recreation and leisure services facilities are fully accessible

Demographic privileges are unearned and are a result of social valuing.

- when I have a flat tire alongside the road, someone is likely to stop and help
- leisure services leaders will be pleasant with me and comfortable in my presence

Privileges of being in the upper class include:

- chances of getting a bank loan for a vacation are fairly assured
- can find housing in an area where safety is not a concern
- my family will never go without heat or food for lack of paying a bill
- can afford to use whichever local leisure services facilities as I wish

Each of the dimensions of diversity includes unearned privilege and power based solely on exhibiting that element of diversity with which one was born. This results in unearned advantage for some and disadvantage for others. If people are to be treated fairly and without bias, an acknowledgment of these privileges must occur. Effective leaders understand that those privileged by chance of birth are afforded privileges, while others are essentially being penalized for their birth situation. This is an example of institutionalized discrimination and it exists throughout society.

What Leaders Can Do

An awareness of differences is the first step to working effectively with culturally diverse people. Consider the following story as presented by Edwards (1991) and cited in Sims and Dennehy (1993, p. 2):

> The second grade teacher posed a simple problem to the class: "There are four blackbirds sitting in a tree. You take a slingshot and shoot one of them. How many are left?"
>
> "Three," answered the seven-year-old European with certainty, "One subtracted from four leaves three."
>
> "Zero," answered the seven-year-old African with equal certainty, "If you shoot one bird, the others will fly away."

This story illustrates how two different people can view the world differently from one another—and how both can be correct. Neither one is more correct than the other, and everyone is enriched by understanding both viewpoints. Most situations have more than one right answer; recognizing this benefits leaders in their efforts to

An awareness of differences is the first step to working effectively with culturally diverse people.

resolve conflicts, engage in problem solving, and make decisions. Diversity in people and viewpoints offers strength in creativity, problem solving, and seeing the big picture (Chuang, Church & Zikic, 2004; Dunphy, 2004).

Another reason to acknowledge differences is because people who are in the minority face frustration, confusion, and loneliness when they perceive themselves to be different from the dominant group (Knouse & Dansby, 1999). These stresses arise from differences in values, norms, roles, attitudes, negative stereotypes, constantly interpreting what is occurring, and from being on constant alert or guard (Friedman & Antal, 2005). Leaders who recognize these types of stresses will likely feel empathy, acknowledging the possible frustrations participants might face. A connection with participants facing these pressures would help with achieving social integration and meeting each individual's leisure goals.

Leaders concerned with becoming culturally competent can take several steps on a personal and organizational level to increase their competence, including engaging in discovery/enlightenment, conducting a cultural audit, exploration, and audit check. *Discovery/enlightenment* refers to an individual who becomes personally aware of diversity as an important issue. This personal and organizational awareness becomes a basis for future growth.

Next, an individual and organization should engage in *conducting a cultural audit*. An individual takes a personal inventory of her or his own cultural beliefs, values, and understandings. In addition, she or he examines her or his own biases, prejudices, and discriminatory behaviors. An organization or agency can engage in this same type of audit. The organization takes a corporate inventory of beliefs, practices, policies, and underlying currents to ascertain the organizational attitude toward diversity.

The next step is *exploration*. As an individual, one will explore the myriad opportunities available to grow and develop in one's cultural competence. Through exploration, one takes advantage of opportunities to be exposed to diversity, learn more about other cultures, and examine one's own culture. In addition, one should pay particular attention to how dimensions of diversity interrelate in any one individual. Likewise, an organization can engage in similar avenues of exploration. What resources are available to the organization to help it grow in its awareness

and understanding of diversity? Perhaps training staff, expanding programs, and/or changing policies are required for organizational growth.

Lastly, an individual and organization cannot grow in their cultural competence without conducting an *audit check* or evaluation. To do so, the individual must ask, "What have I done to grow? In what ways have I grown? What more do I need to do to become culturally competent?" An organization might ask, "How have we grown? Is it enough to serve our constituents? How can we continue to improve our cultural competence?"

You have already begun the personal journey and growth process through your readings and your efforts to learn more about others. To provide more along these lines, the next section of this text addresses specific leadership issues for each core element of diversity. Remember as you read that each one of us is a composite of many dimensions of diversity and they will all influence our notions of who we are.

Considering Sex/Gender

At different stages of development females and males are both similar and different. When young, physical differences between the sexes are minimal. Then girls move ahead of boys for a couple of years, after which boys move ahead of girls, at least in terms of physical size and strength. In late adulthood physical prowess is again somewhat equalized. Across the lifespan, there are no cognitive differences based on sex or gender. Social and emotional differences exist in as much as people have been socialized into gender roles. If one is feminine she or he might seem yielding, emotional, unassertive, "soft," and interested in social activities rather than physical games. If one is more masculine in demeanor one might be physical, assertive, boisterous, and "tough." These views are culturally bound, and not every member of a cultural group buys into these notions. Females and males and those who are feminine or masculine may be interested and motivated in similar or dissimilar leisure pursuits.

Leading People of Both Sexes

Having grown up in a common society, people usually share a common culture and thus share the socialization messages of childhood. Some messages stick with us more strongly than others, but we have all been influenced by our upbringing in society. In their personal development leisure services leaders will want to examine their own biases and assumptions relative to sex-appropriate and sex-inappropriate thoughts, attitudes, and behaviors.

Many leaders treat females and males differently. For example, some tend to take a "boys will be boys" approach and tolerate certain behaviors and attitudes in males but not in females. Being conscious of language usage (see Chapter 5) may be the first step to equitable leadership for the sexes. Recognizing that all people, regardless of sex, have the right to equal leisure opportunities should help guide a leader in her or his choice of behaviors and words. Examples of sex bias are evident at every age. For example, when treating a young child who scraped her or his knee on the sidewalk, does the leader comfort the child, put a bandage on the injury and send the child off with a hug (a common leader treatment of a little girl), or does the leader tell the child to stop crying, grow up, and get back out there and play (a common response to a little boy)?

Considering Age

At various ages across the life span people have different abilities, skills, and needs. As we age we gain maturity in physical size, physical abilities, emotional and social skills, and cognitive abilities. Our ability to reason, use language, and manipulate objects also increases with age—to a point. When reaching old age, physical abilities decline, as do some cognitive functions. (Review Chapter 3 for additional information about differences in abilities across the life span.) In recreation and leisure services, interests and motivations change across the life span. The changes may be associated with life stage (e.g., primary school, first job, establishing a family, retirement) or age groups.

Leading People of Varying Ages

When talking with and leading the very young, remember that they are literal in their understanding. The use of adages or clichés can be very confusing to youngsters during this period. Teens often wrestle with issues of self-identity, esteem, and gaining a sense of belonging while also struggling with expressing individuality. Middle-aged adults face concerns about family and stability and often seek leisure as a diversion or stress reliever. Older seniors should be treated with dignity and respect; activities should be adapted for changing physical and cognitive needs. Leaders who choose age-appropriate and developmentally appropriate activities, communication styles, behavior management options, and problem-solving approaches will likely be successful with a cross-section of participants.

Considering Race/Ethnicity

Ethnic identity is incredibly complex, with as much *within* group diversity as *between* group diversity. For instance, many people have a tendency to talk about Asian people

Leaders who choose age-appropriate and developmentally appropriate activities, communication styles, behavior management options, and problem-solving approaches will likely be successful with a cross-section of participants.

as though they represent one culture. Within the Asian population, however, there are Chinese, Filipino, Thai, Korean, Japanese, Vietnamese, Hmong, Laotian, and other distinct cultural groups. As another example, within the Caucasian population, some are acculturated in rural areas while others only know inner city life. Thus, leaders should gain information about the racial/ethnic groups with which they work, because each culture is very complex in its attitudes, beliefs, value structures, and leisure preferences. Within each culture individuals are unique—not all Hispanic women believe in the same issues or have the same concerns, for instance. Gender, age, first language, religion, cognitive and physical abilities and qualities, and sexual orientation all interact with one's ethnicity to result in differences within groups. Learning through observations, interactions, and personal research can help to gain a solid understanding of various ethnic groups.

Leading People of Various Racial/Ethnic Backgrounds

As more and more people immigrate to the United States, many leisure services leaders will be faced with developing

Photo courtesy of Deb Jordan

Learning about various ethnic groups will help a leader become culturally competent.

and providing services for people who speak English as a second language (ESL). As recent arrivals to the United States, these individuals may experience feelings of alienation, distrust, and of not fitting in. Their orientation to family and what are considered sex-appropriate behaviors may be different than the dominant structure in the area in which they live. Stresses and pressures associated with these feelings may inhibit full participation and enjoyment of leisure. Leaders who are aware can choose activities and leadership techniques to address these concerns.

Recognize that various ethnic groups differ in perception and use of time, view of the collective versus the individual, ability to handle ambiguity, sense of family, status differences, understanding of masculinity and femininity, use of language and patterns of communication, leisure preferences, and values. Ethnic groups do not differ in terms of intellectual, physical, or emotional abilities and needs. Learning about specific ethnic groups will reveal appropriate leader approaches. Certainly leisure services leaders need to go beyond celebrating ethnic festivals, hanging posters of famous people of color, and eating ethnic foods in their efforts to demonstrate diversity. Understanding a culture necessitates delving well beneath the tip of the iceberg. It requires that a leader strive to become culturally competent.

When working with people who speak ESL, leaders should bear in mind that speaking more loudly does not increase comprehension, although it can increase listener anxiety. Being patient, speaking slowly, using gestures, and leading through physical demonstration will help in leading people who have limited comprehension of English. Involve groups in the planning and implementation of recreation and leisure opportunities; help them to experience ownership. Leaders will want to check for understanding by asking individuals to demonstrate desired behaviors and avoid questions that can be answered with "yes" or "no." These are effective leadership techniques no matter the participants.

Considering Sexual Orientation

Gay, lesbian, bisexual, and transgendered people differ from heterosexuals in terms of emotional and sociosexual attraction, but not in terms of leisure preferences. No differences based on sexual orientation exist in physical, cognitive, or emotional abilities. Specific needs of GLBT participants generally fall in the area of emotional support and social opportunities. Many leisure services providers specifically cater to the needs of gays, lesbians and bisexuals, particularly in tourism. An increasing number of public agencies also respond to the needs of gay and transgendered youth.

Parks, recreation, and leisure services leaders should be aware that GLBT youth face physical and verbal abuse on a regular basis (GLBT adults may also face abuse, but it tends to be more subtle). Peters (2003) reported that 42% of gay, lesbian, and bisexual youth are physically harassed on a regular basis, while over 83% are verbally harassed on a regular basis (often in schools, and from teachers as well as peers). This often continues into college where estimates range from 55% to 72% of gay students reporting verbal or physical abuse on campus (Ryan & Futterman, 2001). Over 20% are kicked out of their homes once their sexuality is known. In addition, gay, lesbian, and bisexual youth often engage in risky behaviors such as drug and alcohol abuse, unsafe sex, and suicide attempts (Caldwell, Kivel, Smith & Hayes, 1998; Jaffe, 1998). Gay, lesbian, bisexual, and transgendered youth are 2 to 3 times more likely to attempt suicide, and over 50% have contemplated it (Bagley & Tremblay, 2000). Furthermore, it is reported that while GLBT youth may comprise only 10% of the population, they constitute 30% of completed suicides (Owens, 1998).

Leading People Who Are Gay, Lesbian, Bisexual or Transgendered (GLBT)

As with the other dimensions of diversity, an effective leader will take stock of her or his own biases related to people who are GLBT. Because homosexuality tends to be hidden, there exists a common misperception that "there are no gay people in our community." By all figures used to estimate the number of people in the United States who are GLBT it stands to reason that every parks, recreation and leisure services facility provides services to people who identify as such.

While being GLBT is generally not acceptable in any racial or ethnic group, such individuals may face additional social sanctions depending upon their race/ethnicity. Ryan and Futterman (2001) describe such individuals as a minority within a minority. In many ethnic groups, identifying as lesbian or gay may represent a rejection of one's ethnic heritage (to that ethnic group). Thus, ethnic minority gay youth may face additional vulnerabilities.

To be effective in addressing the needs of all constituents, leaders should be sensitive to the issues and assumptions that exist in the local community and strive to develop and maintain a safe environment for all community members. Support, tolerance, and acceptance are critical leader skills when working with the GLBT population. These skills include:

- avoiding the assumption that all people are heterosexual
- modeling acceptance of people who are GLBT

Leaders should be sensitive to the issues and assumptions that exist in the local community and strive to develop and maintain a safe environment for all community members.

- being both proactive and reactive to disparaging remarks made by uninformed individuals

- using inclusive language (e.g., partner or significant other rather than spouse);

- protecting and supporting an individual should she or he become the target of abuse

- knowing where and when to provide information about support systems in the community

Considering Physical/Cognitive Abilities and Qualities

At various times in U.S. history people with disabilities have been viewed as subhuman (e.g., vegetables), menaces to society (e.g., scary), objects of pity, holy innocents (e.g., special or exceptional), diseased organisms, objects of ridicule, and eternal children (Havens, 1992). While changing throughout most of the United States, vestiges of these attitudes remain. Estimates of people with disabilities in the United States range from 21 million to 50 million people (Waldrop & Stern, 2003; Wang, 2005). Numbers are varied due to differences in the way questions are asked. It is generally agreed that approximately

- 30% of all people in the U.S. exhibit various health impairments

- 17% are physically disabled

- 10% have cognitive or mental disabilities

- 8% have sensory impairments

- 6% have other disabilities

- 46% of those in the United States report having more than one disability

Boys tend to have more disabilities than girls, but in older adulthood women have more disabilities than men. Larger numbers of people with disabilities live in rural, rather than urban areas, and families in which there is a person with a disability tend to have lower incomes than other families (Wang, 2005). Members of American Indian and Alaska Native ethnic groups had the highest rates of disability among racial/ethnic groups.

Americans with Disabilities Act (ADA)

The Americans with Disabilities Act of 1990 (P.L. 101-336) is considered to be the civil rights bill for people with disabilities. It was designed to end discrimination against a person on the basis of her or his disability. Leisure services leaders in direct contact with people who have disabilities should be well-aware of the spirit of the ADA so as to facilitate a full range of leisure experiences for all people. People have a disability if they have: (a) a physical or mental impairment that substantially limits one or more major life activities; (b) a record of having such an impairment; or (c) been regarded as having such an impairment.

According to the ADA, service providers (including those who provide parks, recreation, and leisure services) shall **NOT**:

- deny a qualified person with a disability the opportunity to participate in or benefit from services available to people without disabilities,

- offer less effective opportunities for people with disabilities;

- provide separate aids, benefits, or services for people with disabilities unless those aids are necessary to make services available;

- perpetuate discrimination in any form; nor

- use facilities or sites that result in the exclusion of people with disabilities.

Furthermore, the ADA suggests that people with disabilities who participate in parks, recreation, and leisure services have various rights (McGovern, 2005):

- The right to participate in the most integrated setting. In effect, every opportunity offered to people without disabilities must also be offered to people with disabilities.

- The right to participate in any desired activity as long as they meet the essential eligibility requirements (e.g., age, size, competitive league skill level).

- The right to reasonable accommodations provided by the activity organizer or sponsor. Accommodations might include changes in rules, a sign language interpreter, or the use of adapted equipment.

- The right to adaptive equipment or assistive technology.

- The right to an assessment or evaluation to determine reasonable accommodations.

- The right to avoid being disparately impacted—this means that a rule may not have a more negative impact on people with disabilities than it does on those who are not disabled.

- The right to pay the same fees for the same programs as others. Recreation providers may not charge an individual with a disability additional fees to cover the cost of an accommodation. Fees and charges have to be equitable based on program policy.

- The right to require that affiliated programs and services provide accessible facilities. For example, if a private youth sports league uses public facilities for a nominal fee or no charge, they must abide by the ADA and provide accessible programs, services, and facilities to all.

- The right to request a change in rules and policies as long as it does not fundamentally alter the nature of the activity.

- The right to receive accommodations for behavioral issues. For instance, if an individual engages in negative behaviors as an outgrowth of her or his disability, the provider must determine what accommodations are necessary to facilitate inclusion (perhaps an aide or one-on-one assistance from staff would control the undesirable behaviors).

A similar list of ADA-based rights apply to employees. To be exempt from these rights providers may demonstrate an "undue burden." This is not easy to demonstrate, but may be due to economics (i.e., the cost of the accommodation is untenable), administrative issues (i.e., the needed expertise cannot be found), or if the change would

Photo courtesy of Deb Jordan

It is important for leaders to know how to work with all people—including those with visual impairments.

fundamentally alter the nature of the activity. Furthermore, only two types of entities are exempt from these provisions—private clubs where membership requires a personal nomination and substantial fee, and religious organizations.

In terms of general leadership, leisure services leaders are required by law to lead programs and services in such a way as to fully include people with disabilities in activities. Specific leader actions will vary based on different types of disabilities and individuals. Some people with disabilities engage in behaviors of learned helplessness—they use their disability as an excuse to receive special attention and assistance. In this case, leaders should be aware of these behaviors and avoid enabling this condition.

Inclusion

Inclusion is a philosophy or value that emphasizes a proactive approach to including all people in all programs and services. Most often, it is a term used to describe the physical and social inclusion of people with disabilities into parks and recreation programs and services. Anderson and Kress (2003) suggest this involves including people with disabilities across five dimensions:

- having the same choices and opportunities as every other person

- being accepted and appreciated for who a person is

- being with people who share the same interests (rather than the same disability)

- having accessible recreation facilities, areas, and equipment

- providing necessary individual adaptations, accommodations, and supports so that every person can benefit equally from recreational involvement with friends

Parks and recreation organizations and agencies are fairly well aware of the need for changes to structures and buildings to enhance *physical inclusion*, and many have long-term plans to accomplish those tasks. This might include widening doorways; installing entrance ramps; changing a playground surface; hardening a nature trail; or adding Braille signage, voice recognition software, or installing TTY lines. Physical inclusion is, perhaps, the easiest to attain because the needs are visible and tangible. In addition to physical inclusion, parks and recreation providers need to address *functional inclusion*, where staff have the knowledge and skills to accommodate all individuals in programs and services. This encompasses leaders who develop their own awareness, knowledge, and skills about working with people with disabilities. Leaders are encouraged to seek exposure, training, and practice in working with people with disabilities. A third type of inclusion, *social inclusion*, is the most difficult to achieve. This describes an individual's ability to gain acceptance and be able to participate in positive interactions with peers during recreation activities (Nolan, 2005), and is often out of the direct control of the recreation leader. Leaders can, however, influence groups through role modeling, policies, staffing, and the exercising of their group dynamic skills.

Generally, the inclusion process will begin with an individual making a request for an accommodation. Organizational staff follow up with a contact and make an assessment to determine what types of adaptations or modifications are necessary. The leader, participant, and parent/guardian/aide (if needed) jointly develop the inclusion plan. The plan will stipulate the needed support(s) such as assistive technology, one-on-one aide, alteration of rules or policies, sign language interpreter, or other mechanism to facilitate full inclusion and involvement. The plan is implemented, observations made and documented, and then evaluated on a periodic basis (Anderson & Kress, 2003; Carter & LeConey, 2004). Parks and recreation leaders will be integrally involved throughout this process.

One visible sign of being inclusive is using "person-first" language and avoiding identifying a person as their disability. Examples of this include using phrasing such as "the person who is blind" rather than "the blind person," and "Mario who has CP (i.e., cerebral palsy)" rather than "the CP guy." The one exception to this person-first language is for those who face a significant hearing loss. Deaf people have expressed a preference for being referred to as "deaf people" and identify with a distinct deaf culture.

In addition to using person-first language, rather than using terminology that highlights the limitations a person might have, it is best to use a more accurate description. For instance, Keiko might use a wheelchair, but she is not "confined" to it. Carlos does not "suffer" from mental retardation; rather, he is a person with mental retardation. Being aware of how language is used demonstrates a commitment to treating all people with dignity and respect.

Leading People with Physical Challenges

Physical challenges include disabilities such as cerebral palsy, muscular dystrophy, spinal cord injuries, amputations, arthritis, epilepsy, and multiple sclerosis. The impacts of these physical disabilities are as varied as those who are disabled. Leaders should learn about the person, her or his disability, and how the two interact before deciding what assistance or modifications are needed. For instance, some individuals with paraplegia seem very limited by their disability, while for others their physical limitation interferes very little with their activities. Difficulties associated with these disabilities may be attributed to physical issues as well as the emotional and social struggles each person faces. Leaders should (in private) ask the person with the disability what adaptations (if any) work best for her or him—generally people with disabilities know their own needs. As much as possible, enable the person with the disability to do what her or his peers do in the most integrated setting; preferences for leisure activities are influenced more by age and gender than by disability.

To be fully accepting and inclusive of people with physical disabilities, leaders should treat individuals with disabilities the same as individuals without disabilities. Communicate with them in the same way, hold them to the same expectations, observe and enforce the rules with the same level of alertness. One should avoid overprotecting individuals who have disabilities and offering too much help (usually well-intentioned, but often condescending). Finally, leaders serve as models in helping other

Photo courtesy of Deb Jordan

Adaptive equipment, such as this sports chair, enables people with spinal cord injuries to engage in active recreation.

As much as possible, enable the person with the disability to do what her or his peers do in the most integrated setting; preferences for leisure activities are influenced more by age and gender than by disability.

participants feel comfortable with those who have disabilities. This might include helping to raise individual awareness about preconceptions of people with disabilities or informally teaching about disabilities.

Leading People with Chronic Health and Sensory Challenges

Many health conditions are not visible. If it is important for leaders to be aware of them for safety reasons; however, the conditions should be identified through noninvasive and nonthreatening means. Leaders should be aware that, at times, people with chronic diseases such as cardiac disease, cancer, asthma, HIV, AIDS, multiple scelorsis, or diabetes may be limited in their ability to participate in certain activities. Generally, participants will inform leaders of limitations they may have, but leaders should be alert to observable difficulties as well. Simple adaptations such as slowing the pace of activity, taking additional breaks, or allowing additional team members may address the physical concerns. As is true for all participants, leaders should know the location of completed medical and permission forms at all times. This way, if an emergency should arise, specific health information is available to medical professionals when needed.

Sensory impairments include visual impairments, which range from total blindness to tunnel vision and varying degrees of light perception; and hearing impairments, which include difficulty with hearing certain tones, being unable to distinguish sounds from background noises, and deafness. Most people will face some level of disability related to vision or hearing as they age.

For participants with chronic health impairments, leaders need to be aware of medical limitations and at

Many people who use wheelchairs lead active lives.

the same time be careful of being overprotective. If there are questions related to participant safety, the advice of a physician or other experts should be sought. If an injury occurs, treating all participants by following universal precautions (i.e., protection against the transmission of bodily fluids) is an absolute necessity. If everyone is treated in this fashion, there is no discrimination, and more importantly, the leader and the participant are both protected from potentially serious health concerns.

For those who have sensory impairments, leaders should be articulate and speak clearly. Bear in mind that due to challenges in learning from the environment, some young people with sensory impairments may be developmentally delayed compared to their peers. People who are visually impaired (as well as those who do not have a clear view of the leader) will appreciate the limited use of directional terms. This means being careful in telling a participant to move "over there" (Where is "there?") or "go to the corner" (Which corner? Where is it in relation to me?). Furthermore, leaders who wear brightly colored or decorative clothing may inadvertently cause visual difficulties for people who have partial sight and are distracted by such patterns.

If participants are hearing impaired or deaf and lip read, it is important for the leader to stay in front of them and avoid mumbling or exaggerating lip movements. Be careful of turning away from a person who is lip reading and avoid using gestures that block a clear view of one's face and lips. Written instructions may be helpful for people with hearing impairments, and physical demonstrations involving the participants may be helpful for those with visual impairments. In addition, some deaf people may have sign language interpreters. Leaders should avoid speaking to the interpreter; instead, look at and talk to the deaf person—that individual will look at the interpreter as needed.

Leading People with Temporary Physical Disabilities

Temporary disabilities affect many of us over the course of our lives. These include those of us who have broken or sprained limbs, are recovering from health problems such as a heart attack or a severe illness, and those temporarily limited in sight (e.g., their glasses are broken, their vision is impaired by injury). Because the disabilities are temporary, it is not uncommon for leaders to overlook the needs of those who are impacted. While people with temporary disabilities are not covered under the ADA, they may be in need of appropriately adapted or modified leisure experiences. Simply telling an individual with a temporary disability to sit on the sidelines and watch is not being inclusive.

Leading People with Mental Retardation

Mental retardation is a disability that is characterized by significant limitations in intellectual functioning and adaptive behaviors, and originates before a person reaches the age of 18 (*Definition of mental retardation*, 2005). Adaptive behaviors include such skills as being able to express oneself, understanding directions, and being capable of engaging in activities of daily living (e.g., eating, preparing meals, dressing, toileting, using transportation).

According to Ford-Martin (2002) mental retardation is commonly classified into four categories. Those classified as having *mild* mental retardation function on a second through sixth grade level. These individuals adjust to fairly high levels of independence within a community. Approximately 85% of people with mental retardation fall in this category. Those classified as having *moderate* mental retardation are those who typically work and live in a supervised group home. For people with this level of mental retardation the primary focus is on developing self-help skills. The third and fourth classifications of mental retardation are *severe* and *profound* mental retardation. These include those who may not be able to take care of their own basic needs. A significant level of supervision is required throughout the lifetime of these individuals (Carter, Van Andel & Robb, 2003).

Recently, the American Association of Mental Retardation developed an alternative classification system for people with mental retardation. This system focuses on the capabilities rather than limitations of people with mental retardation. The categories focus on the level of support required, and may be more helpful to those in parks and recreation. Those who require *intermittent support* may need assistance only occasionally—perhaps during times of stress or when facing an unfamiliar situation. Others require *limited support*—perhaps for particular tasks or times of the day. Those with severe and profound mental retardation may have a need for *extensive* or *pervasive support*. These individuals require assistance in their daily lives for most adaptive behaviors (Ford-Martin, 2002).

For people with mental retardation (and other developmental disabilities) leaders should strive to keep instructions concrete and straightforward, avoid abstractions, and avoid figurative speech. Using contact with actual equipment rather than illustrations or representations helps some people with cognitive and developmental disabilities understand activity instructions. Because cognitive processing takes time for these individuals, allowing plenty of time for changeovers, transitions, and changes in routine is helpful.

In addition, using the participant's name prior to giving instructions helps to secure and maintain attention. Repetition develops routines and helps people with cognitive disabilities to remember activity rules and directions. Leaders who include the ongoing practice of social skills and a broad range of fine-motor and gross-motor skill involvement in activities for individuals with mental retardation tend to be effective in their leadership efforts.

Leaders will want to be cognizant of the impact of external stimulation on this population of individuals. People with cognitive and developmental disabilities may react strongly and aggressively if exposed to an overabundance of stimulation (e.g., flashing lights, loud and conflicting noises, bright colors, lots of activities) at one time. Helping people with cognitive and developmental disabilities to focus will often facilitate their success. In addition, leaders may find that individuals with mental retardation work well with a personal aide who is there to ensure success and understanding.

Table 9A Three classifications of mental retardation

Classification	General Abilities
Mild (Intermittent support)	Function at second through sixth grade level; can reach some level of independence
Moderate (Limited support)	Can develop self-help skills; require assistance with daily living skills
Severe/Profound (Extensive/ Pervasive Support)	Unable to care for self; require significant level of assistance for all activities.

Photo courtesy of Deb Jordan

Many people with mental retardation participate in recreation events such as Special Olympics.

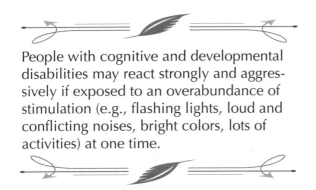

People with cognitive and developmental disabilities may react strongly and aggressively if exposed to an overabundance of stimulation (e.g., flashing lights, loud and conflicting noises, bright colors, lots of activities) at one time.

Leading People with Behavior Disorders

The most common behavior disorder in children is attention-deficit/hyperactivity disorder (ADHD; *Mental health disorders*, 2006). Other behavioral disorders include conduct disorder and oppositional defiant disorder. Behavior disorders seem to affect boys more than girls and may manifest in many ways. An individual with *ADHD* may have difficulty sitting still, paying attention, or controlling her or his impulses. Young people with *conduct disorder* might engage in antisocial behaviors such as running away, stealing, or hitting others. Those with *oppositional defiant disorder* might exhibit uncooperative, defiant, and negative behaviors—particularly to those in authority positions.

Leaders may encounter individuals with some type of behavioral disorder in any type of recreational setting. As with leading people with physical disabilities, it is important for the leader to become acquainted with the particular behavioral disorder to best meet the needs of each individual. Most people with behavioral disorders require some level of structure in leisure activities; well-established rules are welcome. For example, open gym time may not provide enough structure to allow those who have behavioral disorders to succeed. In addition, leisure services leaders should clearly inform participants of expectations and available leader assistance.

Along with behavior management techniques, modeling and reinforcing appropriate behaviors are important for people who have behavioral disorders. As activities and rules change, leaders should plan for a gradual transition to allow people time to adjust to the shifts in actions and mind-sets. Leader fairness and consistency are vital to this population, as is understanding that participant-expressed anger and aggression are not necessarily directed at anyone in particular. For people with behavioral and emotional disorders, leaders should use touch and physical intervention with discretion; it may be that the disorder is a result of inappropriate touching and abuse. Consistency and caring are important leader traits for success in working with people who have behavioral or emotional disorders. A common support provided for individuals with behavior disorders is a personal aide. Thus, leaders may need to plan for the presence and inclusion of this individual in activities and events.

General Leadership Hints When Working with People with Disabilities

At some time, all leisure services leaders will work with people who have some type of disability. A minimum level of personal awareness, knowledge and skills are required to work effectively with persons with disabilities. It will be helpful to become familiar with one's own biases, discomfort and fears of working with those who have disabilities. Often those who are able-bodied fear causing physical harm to an individual who has a disability; this can cause some level of unease. If there are concerns about hurting an individual, ask that person if such actions would be harmful. Most people with disabilities are well aware of their own limitations and are not afraid to share that information.

Becoming a Pluralistic Leader

Pluralistic leaders believe in and commit to leadership that reaches all constituents. They support a vision that includes diversity across all dimensions. Pluralistic leaders attempt to be pluralistic in their lives, not just on the job. They support an ethical commitment to the fair treatment of all and the elimination of discrimination. To make this happen, pluralistic leaders must have a broad knowledge of the dimensions of diversity, be open to change based on new knowledge about personal limitations, and be culturally competent.

Pluralistic leaders understand the interdependence of all people—peers, employers, participants, and various stakeholders. Leaders who are committed to diversity are well-aware of promotional materials and agency presentation of people (e.g., representation of people with disabilities, people of color, females, and people of various ages on paper and electronic materials). In addition to checking organizational materials, pluralistic leaders are willing to "call" people on their prejudice and attitudes in a way that educates rather than berates.

If leisure services leaders believe that all people deserve equal access to full leisure experiences, they will strive to make leadership and programming equitable in all settings. Underlying principles that may help with promoting equal access to leisure include the beliefs that

• Diversity is important for social, political, economic, and moral reasons.

- Historically, the greater leisure services system has not served all equally well.
- All people are unique and different from other people.
- All people are whole people with many different qualities.
- All people have unknown potential for growth and development.
- Multicultural presentations of leisure are appropriate for all.
- Pluralistic leadership is effective leadership.
- Leadership is a crosscultural encounter. (adapted from Loden, 1995; Protheroe & Barsdate, 1991)

To be a pluralistic leader, one must be accepting of all people and respect the ideals of effective leadership. If leisure services leaders strive to meet the need for dignity and respect of all humankind, effective and successful leadership will occur. All people, no matter their differences, inhabit the same small world (made smaller by the incredible potential of the Internet). Therefore, learning to live and lead one another with sensitivity can serve to improve the human condition.

Summary

This chapter has presented information to supplement the material found throughout the text relative to leading diverse populations. Culture as the shared beliefs, attitudes, values, and traditions of an identifiable group of people was discussed in terms of culturally sensitive leadership. There are generally two approaches to dealing with diversity: to focus on diversity and celebrate it, and to simply work toward shared goals and ideals without

To be a pluralistic leader, one must be accepting of all people and respect the ideals of effective leadership.

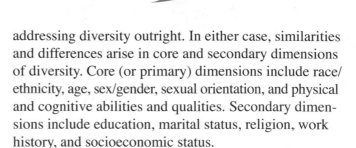

addressing diversity outright. In either case, similarities and differences arise in core and secondary dimensions of diversity. Core (or primary) dimensions include race/ethnicity, age, sex/gender, sexual orientation, and physical and cognitive abilities and qualities. Secondary dimensions include education, marital status, religion, work history, and socioeconomic status.

Within each dimension of diversity, society attributes a value; those who have characteristics of the more highly valued traits tend to receive very subtle privileges. Through the system of privilege, people are treated differently based on core and secondary dimensions of diversity. Understanding this helps leisure services leaders to address diversity and be inclusive of everyone. Knowing about differences (and similarities) assists leaders in selecting activities, communicating with participants, managing behaviors, programming, and working with groups. Becoming a pluralistic leader is a goal of those who wish to strive for the ideals of transformational leadership.

Beginning the Journey

Diversity is an area of growth and development through which all of us work on our own time and in our own ways. There is no doubt, however, that an understanding of diversity and some level of cultural competence are crucial for all leaders. Thus, as you proceed on your personal journey to leadership, you are encouraged to work through the critical questions below.

1. Develop a glossary of terms and define the following terms so that a typical 12-year-old could understand them: diversity, stereotypes, dimensions of diversity, prejudice, discrimination, culture, surface culture, deep culture, cultural competence.

2. How is power related to discrimination? What is meant by "discrimination is systemic?" Why should leisure services leaders be concerned with diversity issues? Study the demographics of your local community and develop a demographic table. Identify the breakdowns for ethnicity, age, sex, physical and cognitive disabilities, and sexual orientation (you may have to guesstimate sexual

---

Pluralistic Leaders:

- believe in and are committed to inclusive leadership
- live values that support diversity
- are pluralistic in all aspects of their lives
- have a broad knowledge of diversity
- are open to change
- are self-aware and willing to learn
- are culturally competent

Figure 9.5 Pluralistic leaders make conscious decisions about integrating diversity into their lives.

orientation figures using the national average of 10%). Provide raw data and percentages for these categories. How will or should this information influence recreation leaders in your area?

3. Identify and explain the primary dimensions of diversity. Why are these considered core dimensions? Describe yourself along these dimensions. Based on societal norms and stereotypes, on which dimensions do you match the more highly valued characteristic? the lesser valued? How does this contribute to your sense of identity? How does this impact or influence you as a leader?

4. Identify and explain the secondary dimensions of diversity. Why are these considered secondary dimensions? Describe yourself along these dimensions. Based on societal norms and stereotypes, on which dimensions do you match the more highly valued characteristic? the lesser valued? How does this contribute to your sense of identity? How does this impact or influence you as a leader?

5. How does privilege interact with the dimensions of diversity? Examine your core and secondary dimensions of diversity. What privileges do you have because of who you are? What privileges do you find yourself having to earn? Ask a friend to help you identify the privileges you have based on your dimensions of diversity. Add to the privilege lists identified in the text (pp. 197–198).

6. How and why is diversity a good thing? How can you, as a leader, become more culturally competent? Explain the six-step process to develop cultural competence on page 192. Go through the steps for yourself. Write up and share your cultural audit with a classmate. Help each other identify ways to explore opportunities to become more culturally competent.

7. Summarize the primary/core dimensions of diversity. Now develop a chart that lists them, explains them, and identifies specific leader implications.

8. What is inclusion? Describe and give examples for three types of inclusion. What does inclusion have to do with leadership in parks, recreation, and leisure services? What skills and knowledge do you need to gain as a leader to become effective with inclusion? Given your current situation, how can you gain these skills and knowledge?

9. What is a pluralistic leader? How can you become one? Why is this desirable? What responsibilities exist for a pluralistic leader? Is pluralism important to a leader of recreation and leisure services? Why or why not?

References

Althen, G. (Ed.). (1994). *Learning across cultures*. Washington, DC: NAFSA Association of International Educators.

Anderson, L. and Kress, C. (2003). *Inclusion: Including people with disabilities in parks and recreation opportunities*. State College, PA: Venture Publishing, Inc.

Bagley, C. and Tremblay, P. (2000). Elevated rates of suicidal behavior in gay, lesbian, and bisexual youth. *Crisis, 21*(3), 111–117.

Barnes, J. and Bennett, C. (2002). *The Asian population: 2000*. Washington, DC: U.S. Census Bureau.

Caiazza, A., Shaw, A., and Werschkul, M. (2004). *Women's economic status in the States: Wide disparities by race, ethnicity, and region*. Washington, DC: Institute for Women's Policy Research.

Caldwell, L., Kivel, N., Smith, E., and Hayes, D. (1998). The leisure context of adolescents who are lesbian, gay male, bisexual, and questioning their sexual identities: An exploratory study. *Journal of Leisure Research, 30*(3), 341–355.

Carlson, C., Uppal, S., and Prosser, E. (2000). Ethnic differences in processes contributing to the self-esteem of early adolescent girls. *The Journal of Early Adolescence, 20*(10), 44–67.

Carter, M. and LeConey, S. (2004). *Therapeutic recreation in the community: An inclusive approach*. Champaign, IL: Sagamore.

Carter, M., Van Andel, G., and Robb, G. (2003). *Therapeutic recreation: A practical approach* (2nd ed.). Prospect Heights, IL: Waveland Press.

Chuang, Y., Church, R., and Zikic, J. (2004). Organizational culture, group diversity, and intra-group conflict. *Team Performance Management, 10*(1/2), 26–34.

Davidson, M. (2001). Know thine adversary: The impact of race on styles of dealing with conflict. *Sex Roles, 45*(5/6), 259–276.

Dean, R. (2001). The myth of crosscultural competence. *Families in Society, 82*(6), 623–630.

Definition of mental retardation. (2005). Retrieved July 19, 2006, from http://www.aamr.org/Policies/faq_mental_retardation.shtml

Dunphy, S. (2004). Demonstrating the value of diversity for improved decision making: The "Wuzzle-Puzzle" exercise. *Journal of Business Ethics, 53*, 325–331.

Ford-Martin, P. (2002). *Mental retardation*. Retrieved July 19, 2006, from http://www.healthatoz.com/healthatoz/Atoz/ency/mental_retardation.jsp

Friedman, V. and Antal, A. (2005). Negotiating reality: A theory of action approach to intercultural competence. *Management Learning, 36*(1), 69–86.

Fujimoto, Y. and Hartel, C. (2004). Culturally specific prejudices: Interpersonal prejudices of individualists and intergroup prejudices of collectivists. *Cross Cultural Management, 11*(3), 54–69.

Goldberg, M. (2000). Conflicting principles in multicultural social work. *Families in Society, 81*(1), 12–21.

Havens, M. (1992). *Bridges to accessibility*. Dubuque, IA: Kendall/Hunt.

Hetzel, L. and Smith, A. (2001). *The 65 years and over population: 2000*. Washington, DC: U.S. Census Bureau.

Hofstede, G. (2001). *Culture's consequences: Comparing values, behaviors, institutions, and organizations across nations*. Thousand Oaks, CA: Sage Publications.

Jaffe, M. (1998). *Adolescence*. New York, NY: John Wiley & Sons.

King, E., Chipman, M., and Cruz-Janzen, M. (1994). *Educating young children in a diverse society*. Needham Heights, MA: Allyn and Bacon.

Knouse, S. and Dansby, M. (1999). Percentage of work-group diversity and work-group effectiveness. *The Journal of Psychology, 133*(5), 486–494.

Koch, S. (2004). Constructing gender: A lens-model inspired gender communication approach. *Sex Roles, 51*(3/4), 171–186.

Kurtz-Costes, B. and Pungello, E. (2000). Acculturation and immigrant children: Implications for educators. *Social Education, 64*(2), 121–125.

Lassiter, S. (1998). *Cultures of color in America*. Westport, CT: Greenwood Press.

Loden, M. (1995). *Implementing diversity*. Chicago, IL: Irwin.

Loden, M. and Rosener, J. (1991). *Workforce America: Managing employee diversity as a vital resource*. Homewood, IL: Business One Irwin.

McGovern, J. (2005). *Recreation rights under the ADA* [electronic version]. *National Center on Physical Activity and Disability, 12*. Retrieved July 19, 2006, from http://www.ncpad.org/fun/fact_sheet.php?sheet=53&section=389

McIntosh, P. (1989, July/August). White privilege: Unpacking the invisible knapsack. *Peace and Freedom*, 10–12.

Mental health disorders: Behavior disorders. (2006). Retrieved July 21, 2006, from http://healthsystem.virginia.edu/uvahealth/adult_mentalhealth/bdhub.cfm

Meyer, J. (2001). *Age: 2000*. Washington, DC: U.S. Census Bureau.

Meyers, D. and Yau, J. (2004). *U.S. Immigration Statistics in 2003*. Retrieved July 18, 2006, from http://www.migrationinformation.sytion.org/USfocus/display.cfm?id=263

Nolan, V. (2005). *Best practices of inclusive services: The value of inclusion* [electronic version]. *NCA Online, 12*. Retrieved July 19, 2006, from www.ncaonline.org/monographs/19inclusion.shtml.

Oakhill, J., Granham, A., and Reynolds, D. (2005). Immediate activation of stereotypical gender information. *Memory & Cognition, 33*(6), 972–983.

Ogunwole, S. (2002). *The American Indian and Alaska Native population: 2000*. Washington, DC: U.S. Census Bureau.

Owens, R. (1998). *Queer kids*. Binghamton, NY: The Haworth Press.

Peters, A. (2003). Isolation or inclusion: Creating safe spaces for lesbian and gay youth. *Families in Society, 84*(3), 331–337.

Protheroe, N. and Barsdate, K. (1991). *Culturally sensitive instruction and student learning*. Arlington, VA: Educational Research Services.

Rate of immigration to the United States highest in 150 years. (2002). Retrieved July 18, 2006, from http://www.ncpa.org/iss/imm/2002/pd060502d.html

Roberts, E. (2001). Lesbian, gay, bisexual, and transgendered youth issues. *SEICUS Report, 29*(4), 37–41.

Ryan, C. and Futterman, D. (2001). Social and developmental challenges for lesbian, gay, and bisexual youth. *SEICUS Report, 29*(4), 5–18.

Sagie, A. and Aycan, Z. (2003). A cross-cultural analysis of participative decision-making in organizations. *Human Relations, 56*(4), 453–460.

Schwartz, S. and Conley, C. (2000). *Human diversity: A guide for understanding* (4th ed.). New York, NY: McGraw-Hill.

Sims, R. and Dennehy, R. (Eds.). (1993). *Diversity and differences in organizations*. Westport, CT: Quorum Books.

Spanish culture and nonverbal communication: Latin America vs. United States. (2006). Retrieved July 8, 2006, from http://www.spanishprograms.com/spanish-culture.htm

Ting-Toomey, S. (1999). *Communicating across cultures*. New York, NY: The Guilford Press.

U.S. interim projections by age, sex, race, and Hispanic origin. (2004). Retrieved July 20, 2006, from http://www.census.gov/ipc/www/usinterimproj/

Waldrop, J. and Stern, S. (2003). *Disability status: 2000*. Washington, DC: U.S. Census Bureau.

Wang, Q. (2005). *Disability and American families: 2000*. Washington, DC: U.S. Census Bureau.

Yan, M. and Wong, Y. (2005). Rethinking self-awareness in cultural competence: Toward a dialogic self in cross-cultural social work. *Families in Society, 86*(2), 181–188.

Leader Profile

Lonny Zimmerman, M.A., CPRP
Manager, Adaptive Recreation Division, City of Las Vegas, Department of Leisure Services

Lonny has been in this position for two years and has more than 16 years in the parks, recreation, and leisure services profession.

Volunteer leadership positions he has held include:

- President, Nevada Parks and Recreation Society
- Board of Directors, American Park and Recreation Society, NRPA
- Chair, National Institute on Recreation Inclusion
- President Lakeside, Nevada Chapter of Disabled Sports USA
- World Inclusion Panel Member

What is the meaning of leadership?
Leadership is defined by the character of the individual. From a management perspective it is realizing that I am here to serve my employees; they are not here to serve me or my needs. Leaders often have to stand alone and make unpopular decisions; oftentimes it's that standing alone that allows the progression of the entire department. Leadership is being committed to the ideals of the organization and carrying out those ideals. It's the ability to understand that you may have to accept the responsibilities for others' actions and maintain the course and direction of the organization through good and, more importantly, troubled times. True leaders are those who continue to work even when the lights and cameras have been put away and attention to a specific event or activity has waned.

What are the most important leadership qualities?
Confidence, integrity and a humanistic quality that allow individuals to be themselves. A true leader develops the organization's goals and objectives with the assistance of his or her staff, and does not surround himself or herself with people who are followers. Leaders understand that it is their job to train and prepare leaders of the future. The quintessential quality of leadership is the ability to admit fault and accept responsibility.

What advice do you have for students who aspire to leadership in parks, recreation, and leisure services?
Understand the mission, goals, and objectives of your agency; commit yourself to fulfilling those goals; stay true to yourself and your organization. Many of the battles fought internally and externally will be fought alone—the more of a leader you become, the more detractors you will have. If you're true to the mission, goals, and objectives of your agency, you will always be able to weather the storm of controversy. True leadership is often not the most popular position on a given subject, but it is typically the correct position.

Favorite books: Hot Zone and Daemon in the Freezer both by Richard Preston (nonfiction); The Fragile Alliance by Charles Meeks (academic); and Angels and Demons by Dan Brown (fiction).

Favorite activities: Golf; and when the sun sets, I love to read.

Chapter Ten
Values and Ethics in Leisure Services Leadership

Learning Opportunities

Through studying this chapter readers will have the opportunity to

- Understand the role of ethics and values in leisure leadership.
- Explain the ethic of care in leisure leadership.
- Explain the rights and justice position of ethics.
- Discuss ethical issues as related to participants.
- Consider the place of values and ethics in one's own life.

Photo courtesy of Gwynn Powell

Leadership is based on relationships; it always occurs in the context of other people. It is a complex moral relationship between people based on trust, obligation, commitment, and emotion in a shared vision of what is good (Johnson, 2001). Because of these connections, ethics lie at the very heart of all leadership. Relationships between leaders and followers, leaders and participants, and leaders with groups of participants are integral to all leisure services settings. The values and beliefs that individual leaders hold are made evident in their choice of words and actions. Leisure services leaders tend to be very visible people. Through leading and being in front of groups, leaders expose themselves—and their beliefs, values, and ethics—to the scrutiny and judgment of others. In general, people look for high ethical standards in leaders. Leaders need strong values and ethics to guide them in dealing with constituents.

One learns (and models) ethics through a variety of avenues: upbringing, formal education, modeling, professional training, social interaction, and life and work experiences (Hardy & Carlo, 2005). While these methods of transmission may be culturally based, it is important to note that right and wrong, and good and bad, go beyond culture. What is right and what is wrong is right and wrong for humanity, not just for select individuals who happen to fall into the "right" category. Many authors recognize universal ethics such as compassion, honesty, fairness, responsibility, and respect (Kidder & Born, 1999; Oliver, 1999). Other universal truths include such values as doing no harm, respecting living things, and respecting others' property.

Oftentimes the terms ethics and morals are used synonymously. Ethics, however, are not the same as morals; they are a product of morality. Morals represent a personal philosophy of right and wrong, and ethics represent actions based on those morals. Ethics are characterized by high standards based on morals. The stronger the ethical behaviors, the higher the integrity, the more positive the character and the more effective the leader (Storr, 2004).

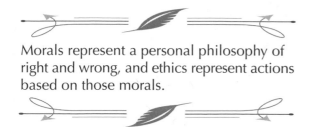

Morals represent a personal philosophy of right and wrong, and ethics represent actions based on those morals.

This chapter presents material about ethics, morals, values, and beliefs as it pertains to leisure services leadership. You will quickly discover that there are no easy answers—ethical dilemmas are very difficult to address and work through to the satisfaction of all involved. Often no one right answer exists, and the multiple response choices have different impacts on different groups of people. After discussing background information in the early part of the chapter, several case studies are presented for you to read and work through. This will enable you to practice basic steps to ethical decision making, and become better acquainted with your own position related to particular ethical dilemmas.

The Role of Values and Ethics in Leisure Leadership

Leaders demonstrate their commitment to consistent expectations by clarifying meanings, unifying constituents, and intensifying actions. They do this through living their values and morals. Repeated over time, these lead to trust and credibility—the foundations for successful leadership (Storr, 2004).

Leaders lead by example; people continuously watch and take note of leader actions. Leader behaviors must be

Photo courtesy of Gwynn Powell

Fun is often a foundational value in parks, recreation, and leisure services settings.

consistent with the words she or he uses or else respect and trust will be lost. Leaders' words and actions exemplify the values important to them and the agency they represent. In their positions, the expressed morality of leaders has an impact on the morality of followers. Leaders are, after all, role models. All participants, especially children, observe, discuss, and imitate leader behaviors. Everything a leader does while in contact with participants—responses to participant questions, giving instructions and directions, discussions, problem management, every comment and every action—carries moral weight and illustrates the character of the leader.

Earlier in this text various models of leadership were discussed, including transformational leadership. Transformational leaders ask group members to

transcend their own self-interests for the good of the group, organization, or society; consider their longer-term needs to develop themselves, rather than the needs of the moment; and become more aware of what is really important. (Bass, 1990, p. 53)

Similarly, service to others is a core value of servant leadership (Russell, 2002). In asking group members to take this type of position, leaders espouse their own beliefs about what is important. This is one way that leaders influence the values and ethics of others.

Without followers, of course, there are no leaders. Followers legitimize leadership by attributing leaders with credibility, trust, and loyalty, and by accepting the leader's ability to influence them. Leaders act in ways to make these things occur. In this way leadership and followership are interdependent, reciprocal, and active systems. Followers ascribe leader legitimacy to the leader who demonstrates expertise, innovation, initiative, and stewardship (Coughlan, 2005). Thus, legitimacy comes from the beliefs of followers that leaders are competent (i.e., experts), personally compelling and dynamic (i.e., entrepreneurial or charismatic), and trustworthy (i.e., stewards).

Everything a leader does while in contact with participants—responding to participant questions, giving instructions and directions, discussions, problem management, every comment and every action—carries moral weight and illustrates the character of the leader.

Legitimacy comes from the beliefs of followers that leaders are competent (i.e., experts), personally compelling and dynamic (i.e., entrepreneurial or charismatic), and trustworthy (i.e., stewards).

Ethics as Guides

Leaders use ethics to guide themselves when existing rules do not fit the situation and when the situation is too ambiguous to know what rule to apply. In addition, leaders can consciously use ethics to set examples for others. Strong ethical values raise the level of conduct for both leaders and participants because, as Calabrese and Roberts (2001) found, followers model the behaviors of the leader.

Leaders generally perform three functions relative to values and ethics:

1. Define and communicate ethical behavior constantly through their words and actions.
2. Translate that definition so that everyone understands the ethical position taken—this builds trust.
3. Facilitate resolution of ethical conflicts that arise—This strengthens relationships and the agency or organization.

Leaders have a responsibility to speak out for ethical behaviors and justice. Leaders must live exemplary ethics. Leaders show what they value by their actions, how they spend their time, the clothes they wear, the priorities on their agendas, the questions they ask, people they see, places they go, and behaviors and results they recognize and reward (Grundstein-Amado, 1999; Minkes, Small & Chatterjee, 1999). For instance, a leader who spends the majority of her or his time visiting with participants, smiling, and making everyone feel welcome likely values relationships. On the other hand, a leader who prefers to complete paperwork and tends to avoid close relationships with participants may more highly value tasks or solitude over relationships.

Leaders exemplify what is important, and it is through living their values that leaders influence followers. Leaders have a powerful impact on those they serve. The values leaders hold permeate everything they do and say. This can be beneficial in that values help guide the leader's

- perception of situations and problems to be faced
- approach to possible solutions to those dilemmas

- view of others
- perception of individual and group success as well as how to achieve success
- determination of what is and is not ethical behavior
- acceptance or refusal of organizational pressures and goals. (Mattison, 2000)

Leaders build trust and loyalty by behaving ethically and consistently from a solid values base. Trust is the keystone of shared values and ethics between leaders and followers (Klenke, 2005; Storr, 2004). Thus, effective leaders at all levels must be trustworthy and loyal. To determine sources of ethical influence, researchers asked people to rank the importance of various individuals in influencing their ethical conduct. The respondents' rankings (from most to least important):

1. behaviors of their superiors
2. behaviors of peers in the agency in which they worked
3. ethical practices of the profession to which they belonged
4. society's moral climate
5. existence of formal agency policies related to ethical standards. (Hitt, 1990)

Furthermore, it was reported that people have a tendency to live up to or down to the leader's standards. (You may have heard this called a *self-fulfilling prophecy*.) Others have researched similar questions and found that values and ethics are stable over time (Oliver, 1999).

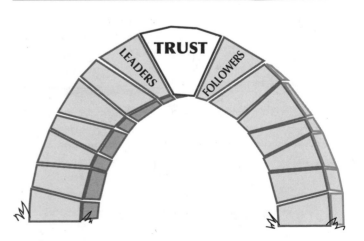

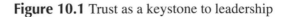

Figure 10.1 Trust as a keystone to leadership

Foundational Values

Values are traits, characteristics, and beliefs people esteem highly in themselves and others. When people value something, they judge it to have worth—it is important to the individual. Values include intangible things such as religious beliefs, honesty, and trustworthiness. These intangibles provide guidance to people's lives in terms of: (1) modes of conduct or behaviors (i.e., beliefs about how we should behave), and (2) desired end-states or goals (i.e., what we strive for). Individuals, groups, and agencies or organizations all have underlying values. Some are clearly articulated and others are unspoken expectations.

It is important for leaders to be in a state of *value congruence* with their agency. This means that the values a leader holds as an individual should be in sync with the values of the agency or organization for which she or he is working. Being in a state of incongruence can lead to frustration, confusion, and anxiety. Those who are unclear in the values they hold to be important may experience values confusion. These people often demonstrate inconsistencies in behaviors, lack persistence, and may appear apathetic. Individuals who clearly understand their own values tend to be positive, enthusiastic, and follow through on tasks (Kidder & Born, 1999).

It is desirable that leaders be aware of and clear about their own values so that they can be most effective in their dealings with participants. In fact, Klenke (2005) talks about a leader being well-aware of her or his own "moral compass." Self-awareness and personal reflection are used as ways to better understand personal values, and

Individuals who clearly understand their own values tend to be positive, enthusiastic, and follow through on tasks.

are two of the most commonly cited tools of a successful leader (Swenson-Lepper, 2005; Tubbs, 2006).

Research has been conducted that asked leaders and followers about the importance of values for leaders. Several authors reported that important values for leaders include

- the need for achievement
- orientation toward both task and people
- a willingness to take risks
- a willingness to trust others. (Bryant, 1998; Sosik, 1997)

In addition to having a good understanding of their own values, beliefs, and morals, effective leaders exhibit high levels of self-efficacy. *Self-efficacy* refers to the belief that one is responsible for (and in charge of) her or his own fate. These leaders accept the consequences (both good and bad) of their actions and aim to learn from both their successes and their mistakes. Leaders with these traits tend to cope well with stress, are perceived as highly effective, and are well-liked.

Perceptions of Ethics

Leaders rely on their values and sense of ethics to help them in all leadership actions and decisions. While we learn values from our families, friends, and social institutions (i.e., religion, politics), values and morals evolve as one matures both as a person and as a leader. As discussed in Chapter 3, a common evolution through moral development is to move from seeking pleasure and/or avoiding pain, to abiding by rules and authority, to conforming to social norms and mores, to living through one's own conscience (i.e., being authentic and inner-directed; Wark & Krebs, 2000). Mature and effective leaders tend to be inncr-directed and self-monitored relative to moral positions—they rely on their own values to define right and wrong. Consider the following scenario:

> A leader is responsible for closing and securing the recreation center each evening. One evening this leader has general admission tickets to a concert, which were extremely difficult to get.

Figure 10.2 Self-awareness and personal reflection are important tools of a leader.

To remain open until closing time would make the leader late for the concert and pose difficulties in getting good seats (or even getting in). Unable to get anyone to cover the shift and close up for the evening in her or his place, the leader had to work and now considers closing up early.

A leader who acts out of a moral base of seeking pleasure and/or avoiding pain would attempt to decide which pleasure or pain would be greater—closing early, getting to the concert, and likely losing her or his job; or staying until closing, retaining the job, but likely missing the concert. A leader who abides by rules and authority might wrestle with closing early based on the rules and policies of the agency. Agency policy indicates that the center should be closed early only in case of dire emergency; therefore, a leader at this stage might follow the rules and remain open. At the next level of moral development a leader would determine the ethics of closing early based on the moral tone of society. Generally, society dictates a sense of industriousness and a strong work ethic. Closing early for personal gain is not a socially accepted practice; the leader would keep the center open. A leader who is ethically directed from within would likely choose to remain open out of a sense of professionalism and a recognition that to close early would negatively impact others, and which demands that the center remain open until official closing time. This leader has a level of self-sacrifice in her or his position of leadership.

In addition to these stages of moral development, different people base their perception of ethics on different sources: religious beliefs, reason and logic, what is best for the greatest number of people, the end results, and hedonism. *Hedonism* is when one acts out of a desire for the highest level of self-pleasure and/or self-gain. People often place their perceptions of right and wrong on a psychological continuum with absolute "right" on one end, and complete hedonism (thus, "wrong") on the other. Ethicists spend their time studying and examining these various viewpoints in attempts to better understand the human condition. One of the difficulties with studying ethics is that it is not an exact science. Ethics are based on beliefs about what is good and right, not facts or scientific proof.

Ethics cover broad issues such as the environment, the conduct of business, and how one manages and engages in one's personal affairs. A prerequisite for success in working within one's personal ethical framework is *ethical sensitivity*. This refers to the ability to perceive that a situation has ethical components to it (Swenson-Lepper, 2005). Before one can apply values, morals, or ethics to a given situation, she or he must recognize that something being done (or about to happen) may affect the

Mature and effective leaders tend to be inner-directed and self-monitored relative to moral positions—They rely on their own values to define right and wrong.

welfare of someone else, either directly or indirectly, by violating a commonly held social standard. Without some level of ethical sensitivity a leader may be perceived as being uncaring, selfish, or indifferent to the needs of others.

Swenson-Lepper (2005) suggests a leader who has ethical sensitivity has five related abilities: the ability to

1. Understand the special circumstances of a situation including the people involved, the actions taken, and the setting or context.

2. See possible ethical issues or problems in the situation and understand that involved individuals have rights and responsibilities.

3. See possible consequences (positive and negative) of the ethical choices.

4. See how others would be affected by those choices and indicate how those individuals would be affected given their respective rights and responsibilities.

5. Understand and interpret how the four factors (i.e., situation, ethical issue, consequences, and stakeholders) interact to compose a larger system.

Our abilities to perceive ethical issues are influenced by a variety of forces such as culture, professional environment, agency or organizational environment, and personal

Religious institutions

Philosophy

2 + 2 = 4

Reason and logic

Figure 10.3 Sources of ethics are varied.

characteristics. We can develop our sensitivity to ethical issues through working with others, being alert to the underlying causes of conflict, and through an awareness of divergent thinking related to social issues. To encourage reflection on ethics in general, you will find an illustration of organizationally based environmental ethics in the following section.

Organizational Environmental Ethics

Environmental ethics are those actions we take that relate to the state and conservation of natural resources. While not directly related to leisure services leadership, there is quite a bit that leisure services leaders can do to help maintain healthy parks, open spaces, and living spaces (e.g., rural, suburban, urban). If all leisure services leaders engaged in some of the following behaviors and encouraged participants to do so when appropriate, as a profession, we could make a difference:

- Reuse paper in the office (e.g., write notes and lists on the back side of used paper). Keep a scrap paper box next to the copy machine, and use that paper on which to write notes.

- Use a washable rag rather than paper towels to clean up messes.

- Use the air conditioner in your car infrequently (and the agency's vehicles)—Roll down the windows instead.

- Drive only when absolutely necessary (e.g., walk or ride a bike for the shorter distances).

- Replace incandescent light bulbs with fluorescent bulbs. Dispose of fluorescent bulbs properly; they contain mercury.

- Turn off lights when leaving a room for more than three minutes.

- Turn off computers overnight (or when not in use).

- Recycle as much as possible. The following items are recyclable in most towns: aluminum (e.g., beverage cans), plastic (e.g., soda bottles, cleaning supply bottles), paper (use both sides first), newspaper, cardboard (e.g., supply boxes), magazines, junk mail, and glass.

- Plant trees on agency property—Make it an annual event.

- Plan, conduct, and promote environmentally friendly activities for all participants.

- Encourage participants (through small incentives) to use nonmotorized transportation to your center (e.g., walking, biking, inline skating, cross-country skiing).

- Compost organic waste from employee lunches and participant treats.

Promoting Positive Social Values

Many consider engaging in leisure to be a freeing experience; some expect to be free from all obligations and constraints. To be totally free of constraints, however, would mean that individuals would be acting outside of the social contract. This social contract comprises the laws, norms, and mores of society to which members of that social group tacitly agree. By agreeing to live within these boundaries, society avoids chaos and maintains an acceptable sense of community and civility. Thus, we know that leisure without any constraints is highly undesirable. During times of total disregard for social and ethical boundaries, illegal and immoral activities commonly take place.

As purveyors of leisure and the good life, leisure services leaders have a responsibility to promote positive social values. Zhu, May, and Avolio (2004) suggest leaders are obligated to set a moral example for others. Living and leading ethically helps to maintain a humane society, and a safe and enjoyable leisure setting. Underlying values, morals, and ethics serve not only to guide leaders in their actions but also to guide others and minimize social chaos. Chaos occurs when there is a lack of social order and values to bind people together. If there were no value for other people, their property, or even activity rules, leadership would be extremely difficult; participants would be unhappy, unfulfilled, and perhaps injured; and property might be damaged. An ethical leader has a responsibility to establish a standard of behaviors that will lead others to live their lives within an ethical framework.

In the United States the values of justice, human rights, equity, freedom, diversity of opinion, and quality of life are primary values, and all of them impact leisure (Oliver, 1999). Each of these values provides guidelines for decision making and action related to moral issues. For example, in playing competitive games leaders will often strive to organize teams equitably in terms of the skill levels of players. Furthermore, most leisure services professionals believe in individual freedom to choose from

As purveyors of leisure and the good life, leisure services leaders have a responsibility to promote positive social values.

alternative leisure pursuits. We also believe that each individual is responsible for her or his actions, and that leisure is an avenue to achieve quality of life. These positive social values are within reach of all leisure services leaders.

Ethical Decision Making

In addition to utilizing values and ethics as a way of maintaining the social contract, leisure services leaders use values when facing the many ethical dilemmas in their careers. When addressing ethical conflicts, leaders need to consider the factual, conceptual, and moral issues involved. *Moral issues* include a prescription for conduct (i.e., an "ought" or "should" statement), leader impartiality (i.e., remaining objective), a sense of overriding importance, and independence from arbitrary authority or rules (Stainer, 2004). When attempting to determine how to approach ethical issues, the leader asks: What is good? What is right?

Kidder and Born (1999) conceptualized ethical dilemmas as arising out of one of four basic tensions: (a) *individual vs. collective*, where the needs of the individual or a small group are considered against the claims of the larger society; (b) *truth vs. loyalty*, where personal honesty or integrity is at odds with responsibility and promise-keeping; (c) *short-term vs. long-term*, where the real and important requirements of the present are considered against foresight, stewardship, and deferred gratification; and (d) *justice vs. mercy*, where fairness, expectations, and an equal application of the rules are opposed to empathy, compassion, and a desire to make exceptions.

As part of the decision-making process, we first need to identify the tension that exists. Once we have identified the tension within the dilemma, we have several ways of thinking about that issue: (1) We can consider the end, and decide that whatever we do, the end justifies the means. This usually means that we are looking for the greatest good for the greatest number in our decision. (2) We can consider the rules of the situation, and take the approach that every action can be morally right or wrong. We might ask ourselves, "What if everyone else were to make this same decision and/or do this same thing—Is this the kind of world I want to live in?" (3) Lastly, we can take a care-based approach where we either "Do unto others as they would do unto us" or more aptly, "Do unto others as they would want to be done unto" (Kidder & Born, 1999).

Ethical Decision-Making Process

There are many different ways to think about ethical issues, but to help solve a real dilemma, we need some sort of framework to follow. Johnson (2001) and Stainer (2004) propose a multi-step approach to ethical decision making. They advocate sound moral reasoning; moral motivation, which is a desire to follow moral principles and a belief that moral principles take precedence over other issues; and moral action, the implementation of the decision. Following is a brief discussion of the recommended steps.

Three Considerations to Guide Decisions

(1) We can consider the end, and decide that whatever we do, the end justifies the means. This usually means that we are looking for the greatest good for the greatest number in our decision.

(2) We can consider the rules of the situation, and take the approach that every action can be morally right or wrong. We might ask ourselves, "What if everyone else were to make this same decision and/or do this same thing—Is this the kind of world I want to live in?"

(3) Lastly, we can take a care-based approach where we either "Do unto others as they would do unto us" or more aptly, "Do unto others as they would want to be done unto."

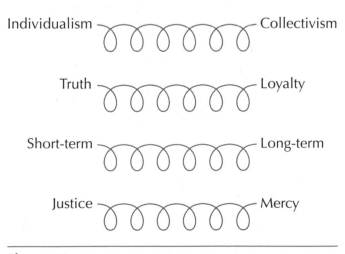

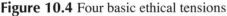

Figure 10.4 Four basic ethical tensions

Step One

Realize that there is a problem and that it has an ethical component. While this step might appear to be obvious, as was mentioned earlier, people have different levels of ethical sensitivity. Checking in with trusted colleagues and determining the values embedded in the situation will help at this initial stage.

Step Two

Determine the individuals involved in the situation. This includes not only identifying the names of the individuals but also coming to an understanding of their positions and roles. Recognizing cultural influences and individual histories will aid the leader in fully realizing this step.

Step Three

Gather relevant information from the involved parties. As with the previous step, this information might include facts, cultural worldviews, personal perceptions, and other aspects of the incident. Accurately identifying the real ethical dilemma is important to eventually finding a workable resolution.

Step Four

Test for right-versus-wrong elements of the situation. One way to do this is to take the "gut test"—if something does not feel right in your gut (i.e., using your intuition), the action is probably not a good one. In addition, if you would not want the action to become public, it is probably a wrong action.

Step Five

Test for right-versus-right values embedded in the situation. Part of the reason that ethical issues can be so difficult to resolve is because multiple actions can be right. This is the point at which the leader needs to highlight the core values. If multiple core values are at odds with one another, the leader and parties involved will need to consider the ideal or most important value as well as who is more negatively and positively impacted than the others. Once this information surfaces, decisions about actions can be considered.

Step Six

Apply the most relevant and useful ethical standards to the situation—remembering to consider the involved parties, the context, the ethical issue, and the potential consequences. Oftentimes the leader will need to reflect on her or his personal values and morals, as well as those of the agency and the community.

Step Seven

Look for a third way… it is not uncommon for people to consider an ethical issue from "my view" and "your view"—this can set up an either/or (i.e., "I'm right and you are not") mindset that can be counterproductive. By looking for "a third way" the leader can view the situation from a totally unique perspective. This requires an open frame of mind and creative thinking.

Step Eight

Make the decision, take action, and reflect on its impact. If the situation is well-considered, the outcomes will likely be positive and the decision, successful. If unanticipated consequences occur, a wise leader will learn from the process and retain the information and experience for use in addressing future ethical dilemmas.

Questions for Pause

Several authors recommend that a leader ask herself or himself some very practical questions as they wrestle with ethical dilemmas:

1. Is the action legal?
2. Would doing it make me feel bad?
3. Is it consistent with agency/organization values and policies?
4. Would I want my parents or children to read about it in the newspaper?
5. Would failing to act make the situation worse or allow a "wrong" to continue?
6. Does it follow the "Platinum Rule" (i.e., "Do unto others as they would want to be done unto")?
7. Will the decision be viewed as valid and correct after several years have passed?
8. Under what conditions would I make exceptions to this decision? (Johnson, 2001; Murphy, 1998)

As can be seen, ethical decision making is not an easy or a clear-cut process. Ethical dilemmas will present some of the most wrenching problems faced by leisure services leaders. Leaders who are clear in their own values and moral position, and who take either a transformational or servant leadership approach to leadership, will usually be respected and appreciated for their consistent manner in handling difficult situations.

Leaders who are clear in their own values and moral position and who take either a transformational or servant approach to leadership will usually be respected and appreciated for their consistent manner in handling difficult situations.

Ethic of Rights and Justice, or Ethic of Care?

As mentioned earlier, ethics arise out of morals, and morality is viewed as one's sense of what is right and good, and what is wrong or bad. In the predominant U.S. culture, ethics involve what is fair and right for the individuals involved. This approach has been termed the *ethic of rights and justice* (Kujala & Pietiliainen, 2004). Thus, to determine the ethics of a situation a leader would attempt to determine what is fair, right, and just for those involved in the dilemma. Leaders apply rules across the board because, "It wouldn't be fair to the others if you weren't held to the same standard." Rules exist to be applied in difficult situations, and to apply them uniformly in every situation is considered right and just. Leaders have policies, procedures, and rules to follow which they impart to others. An ethic of rights and justice is typified by a values base of rules and authority.

Another view of ethics based more on individual relationships is an *ethic of care* (Gilligan, 1982; Kujala & Pietiliainen, 2004). Whereas the ethic of rights and justice defines what is right by equal application of rules in an attempt to remain impartial and fair, an ethic of care defines what is right by the needs of the individuals involved. Seeing and responding to the needs of others, having the utmost regard for the dignity and intrinsic value of each person, and acting out of a need to maintain connections describes an ethic of care (Furman, 2004). Therefore, if one were to subscribe to an ethic of care, one would respond to moral and ethical issues out of caring and concern for others and not necessarily by following exactly what is right and fair through the application of rules and policies.

An ethic of care has two elements:

1. the disposition, personality, or desire to care about and fulfill the needs of others, which assumes a commitment to an ideal of caring where everyone in the world cares for other beings; and

2. an obligation to care for, which is caring expressed in action (Kracher & Wells, 1998). From this perspective day-to-day interactions with others create a web of reciprocal caring. The caring might be manifested in caring for others physically, psychologically, emotionally, or spiritually.

"Caring for" involves a measure of self-sacrifice on the part of the caregiver, and many would suggest that leaders need an element of self-sacrifice to be successful. By their very nature, human relationships require a level of caring—being receptive, accepting, and on-call for others—which requires commitment and practice. Therefore, leaders require commitment and practice in caring and being open in order to achieve the ideals of an ethic of care.

Leader Traits and Ethics

Followers indicate that they admire leaders who exhibit the following characteristics: authenticity and integrity (i.e., truthful, trustworthy, has convictions), competence (i.e., capable, effective, qualified), and leadership (i.e., inspiring, decisive, provides direction; Zhu, May & Avolio, 2004). Participants measure leader integrity through the leader's actions and behaviors; they look to see if leader actions match leader words, if leaders are consistent, and if leaders can articulate their own values.

Authenticity and Integrity

Authenticity is being true to oneself—being genuine and living life honestly. To be authentic, leaders need to ensure

Figure 10.5 Ethics of rights vs. ethics of care—differing views of ethical positions

Participants measure leader integrity through the leader's actions and behaviors; they look to see if leader actions match leader words, if leaders are consistent, and if leaders can articulate their own values.

that their thoughts, words, actions, and intentions are consistent (Zhu, May & Avolio, 2004). Authentic ethical conduct represents behaviors consistent with stated and lived values and moral intentions. Related to this is integrity—the value placed on self. Integrity requires a level of self-awareness and self-value. Respected people know their own values, take a stand for what they believe in, and profess their own standards. These individuals are said to have personal integrity. To be ethical leaders, leaders must first know their own values and what is important to them. Once a leader knows and understands these values, the leader with integrity lives by these values—and does so consistently. Leaders who have integrity make and keep commitments to themselves and others; they are trustworthy.

Winning trust is a long-term process which needs continual nurturing and development. Attributes that lead to trust include integrity, reliability, openness, and consistency. In the trust-building process participants will consider their history with the individual leader as well as the leader's reputation. Because of this, leaders need to avoid perceptions of impropriety in all settings. A solid values system, honesty, a straightforward demeanor, and living up to one's promises are all needed to achieve personal integrity. When weighing and judging the integrity of an individual, we often ask about the strength of her or his convictions—Does the person stand up for what she or he believes in? Does it feel safe to be with that person?

Hitt (1990) presented the relationship of trust and leadership in this syllogism:

- Trust is required for effective leadership.
- Without personal integrity, there can be no mutual trust.
- Therefore, without personal integrity, there can be no effective leadership. (p. 206)

In addition to trust, other elements of integrity include competence, authenticity, openness, responsibility, and a solid sense of self or identity (Kanungo & Mendonca, 1996; London, 1999). *Identity* is knowing who one is and

who one is not; it provides a sense of wholeness and integration; it is grounded in a hierarchy of values; and it allows one to sustain sameness and continuity of essential patterns in the face of changes. All leaders need a sense of authenticity—the capacity to be oneself and not the roles one fills. In addition, authenticity allows one to communicate expectations, give and receive honest feedback, and admit mistakes. Integrity involves multiple components:

- responsibility
- realizing that each person lays the groundwork for what she or he will be
- awareness that one has the freedom to choose
- faithfulness to one's convictions
- putting all of oneself into little as well as big things
- being accountable for decisions and their consequences
- realizing that one can be accountable for inaction as well as action
- admitting mistakes and correcting them (Mattison, 2000; Zhu, May & Avolio, 2004).

When a leader with integrity is presented with a problem, participants and followers can be assured that the same standards utilized to make simple decisions will be utilized in considering difficult situations. The leader is honorable in her or his actions and words and this is evident to all.

Principled Leadership

Several authors have discussed principled leadership in examining the relationship of ethics and personal integrity to the role requirements of leaders (Covey, 1991; London, 1999). Generally, principles are natural laws of the universe that pertain to all human relationships. Principles apply at all times and in all places; they are manifested in values, ideas, norms, and teachings that empower people. Principles are objective and external to an individual.

In discussing principled leadership in businesses and organizations, Covey (1991) suggested four levels of principled leadership: (a) personal (i.e., trustworthiness), (b) interpersonal (i.e., trust), (c) managerial (i.e., empowerment), and (d) organizational (i.e., alignment). First, leaders develop a personal trustworthiness—Others can depend on them to do what is right and be consistent in behaviors and words. As leaders become comfortable with their own values and moral base, trust begins to develop between themselves and others. Once personal and interpersonal values are established, principled leaders then use their values base to empower others—in their own ethical positions as well as in day-to-day tasks. Becoming aligned with organizational values follows as leaders influence and are influenced by the agency with which they work.

London (1999) suggested that principled leaders promote ethics in all aspects of their lives. To do this, they follow the Japanese notion of *kyosei*—the belief that all people can live and work together for the common good. Individuals show this by taking responsibility for themselves and others, and treating others with respect and kindness. Principled leadership includes core values of integrity, honesty, concern for people, and openness to new ideas.

Principle-centered leaders are characterized by the specific traits:

- self-aware
- purposeful
- life-long learner
- service oriented
- positive
- strong believer in others
- balanced
- adventurous
- synergistic
- sensitive
- flexible

Principled leadership sets up a leader for success. Principled leaders earn the respect and trust of participants, engage in positive decision making, establish solid interpersonal relationships, and accomplish tasks. A principle-centered leader is often characterized as being highly professional in her or his handling of people and tasks.

Codes of Ethics

Professionalism describes how members of a profession integrate obligations with knowledge and skill in ethical relationships with clients and customers. It allows participants to measure leaders against established professional standards. These standards are often presented as codes of ethics. Wood and Rimmer (2003) suggest that having a code of ethics is a tangible sign that a profession, agency, or organization is thinking about ethics and their value.

A code of ethics is a written statement concerning what is good and right behavior; it is designed to capture the key values of the organization or agency and make them public (Coughlan, 2005; Wood & Rimmer, 2003). Generally, the statements found on a code of ethics provide guidance when there is no clear response to a particular type of situation. The language is usually stated as "oughts" and "shoulds" and is a public reminder of core values. A code of ethics is considered useful if it is clear, comprehensive, and enforceable; this latter characteristic is often the most difficult to achieve.

The National Recreation and Park Association (NRPA), the primary professional organization to which leisure and recreation practitioners and academicians belong, developed a code of ethics to guide the profession. Initially the code of ethics was developed in response to concern about the professionalization of leisure services practitioners. It was revised in recognition of the various ethical issues that members of the profession face almost daily.

The following is the NRPA *Professional Code of Ethics*:

> The National Recreation and Park Association has provided leadership to the nation in fostering the expansion of recreation and parks. NRPA has stressed the value of recreation, both active and passive, for individual growth and development. Its members are

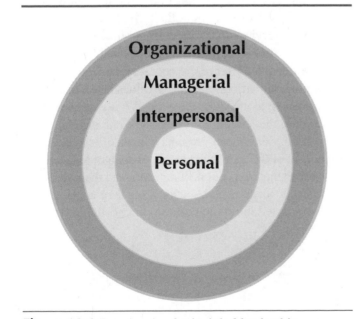

Figure 10.6 Four levels of principled leadership

Principled leadership sets up a leader for success. Principled leaders earn the respect and trust of participants, engage in positive decision making, establish solid interpersonal relationships, and accomplish tasks.

dedicated to the common cause of assuring that people of all ages and abilities have the opportunity to find the most satisfying use of their leisure time and enjoy an improved quality of life.

The Association has consistently affirmed the importance of well-informed and professionally trained personnel to continually improve the administration of recreation and park programs. Members of the NRPA are encouraged to support the efforts of the Association and profession by supporting state affiliate and national activities and participating in continuing education opportunities, certification, and accreditation.

Membership in NRPA carries with it special responsibilities to the public at large, and to the specific communities and agencies in which recreation and park services are offered. As a member of the National Recreation and Park Association, I accept and agree to abide by this Code of Ethics and pledge myself to:

- Adhere to the highest standards of integrity and honesty in all public and personal activities to inspire public confidence and trust.

- Strive for personal and professional excellence and encourage the professional development of associates and students.

- Strive for the highest standards of professional competence, fairness, impartiality, efficiency, effectiveness, and fiscal responsibility.

- Avoid any interest or activity which is in conflict with the performance of job responsibilities.

- Promote the public interest and avoid personal gain or profit from the performance of job duties and responsibilities.

- Support equal employment opportunities. (2006)

In addition to striving to meet the code of ethics of the profession, leisure services leaders may wish to be guided by the code of ethics developed for citizen board members. The following code of ethics may be useful in working with town boards, staff, subcommittees, or other special groups that provide leadership to some aspect of leisure services. The Code of Ethics for Parks and Recreation Board Members is as follows:

As a Park and Recreation Board member representing all residents of my community, I recognize that:

1. I have been entrusted to provide/recommend park, recreation, and leisure services to all residents of my community. These services are available to everyone regardless of age, sex, race, religion, national origin, physical or mental ablility.

2. I will respect ideas and opinions expressed by fellow board members, professional staff, and citizens to ensure the best interests of the community.

3. I will respect and support decisions made by the board.

4. I pledge to devote the time and effort necessary to ensure thoughtful and informed decisions by the board.

5. I will adhere to the highest standards of integrity and honesty in all my endeavors to safeguard the public trust.

6. I will work to accomplish the mission of the organization and strive to maintain the trust of those who elected or appointed me and those whom the organization serves.

7. I will serve the interest of all people, avoid acts of favoritism toward special interests and avoid use of the board for personal advantage.

8. I understand that my authority is restricted to official meetings and authorized actions of the board.

9. I acknowledge that board members establish/ recommend policy while administrators and staff carry out approved policy.

10. I will support policy that ensures that all board meetings are open to the public except in cases where closed meetings are explicitly authorized. (*Citizen Branch Code of Ethics*, 2006)

These two codes of ethics may serve as guideposts for leisure services leaders in their efforts to work with and provide services to a variety of publics. It remains up to the individual leader, however, to act in ways that are above reproach and serve the needs of their participants. Developing and articulating one's values and moral base is the first step to utilizing ethics in such a way as to benefit not only the leader, but those she or he serves. The remainder of this chapter presents a series of ethical dilemmas typical of the type faced in the practice of leisure services leadership. You are encouraged to read them through, determine the ideals and obligations, and then work through the issues based upon the highest ethical standards.

Case Studies

No Form, No Trip

You are the leader responsible for gathering children attending a summer recreation program and preparing them for an off-site field trip. You sent home parental permission forms last week and again yesterday, informing the youngsters in no uncertain terms that they would not be able to go on the trip without a signed form. Agency policy is "no form, no trip." A child walks up to you, who you know is from a struggling single-parent family, and tells you the form was lost, but "Dad said I could go." By now 26 of the 29 children in the program are on the bus having handed in their signed forms. The youngster without the form begins to cry asking, "Why won't you let me go? My dad said I could go." It is time for the bus to leave. What is your decision relative to this youngster going on the trip?

Wiped Out?

You are responsible for the supervision of a weight room where adults are free to drop in and work out on the various weightlifting machines. Agency policy is that everyone must have a towel in the facility, and lifters are asked to wipe down the machines after each use to clean off their sweat. If it is determined that lifters have not been wiping down the machines, they can be denied access for a period of time. This is the second day in a row that a participant (Caucasian) has sought you out to complain that another weightlifter (African American) is not wiping down the machines after use. The complainant asks you to deny weight room access to the other lifter per the rules. You spot-check the use of the room and every time you have been in the weight room you have observed the African-American participant clearly wiping down each machine. You suspect the accusations are racially motivated. How do you handle this situation?

Just Toughening 'Em Up

You are responsible for the youth soccer league and part of your job duties include recruiting and training volunteer coaches. You also visit various fields as games get underway to ensure that things are running smoothly. One team has been overwhelming other teams throughout the season, and you go to one of their games. While at the game you observe the coach yelling and shouting at the players, grabbing the youths by their shirts and shaking them when they do not perform well. At halftime the coach spends the first ten minutes berating the youngsters for their sloppy work. You ask to see the coach off to the side and you indicate that yelling at the children in this manner is not appropriate—this is an educational/recreational league. The coach responds by saying, "I've been doing this all year. It toughens 'em up—This is why we are the best team in the league." The game and the coach's behaviors resume. How do you handle this situation?

The Old Folks

You are a counselor at a senior camp where people over the age of 55 attend a residential camp for a week in May. Activities include horseback riding, arts and crafts, aquatics, archery, and fine arts. It has been made clear in all of the literature, as well as on the first day of camp, that because the camp was outdoors and people would be sleeping in wood cabins, smoking materials would be allowed in only one designated area. The designated smoking area is away from the other buildings to minimize fire hazard, and somewhat out of the way of camp activities. By registering, people agreed to abide by the restricted smoking policy. You return to a cabin after lunch on the third day and discover two of the participants smoking in a no smoking area. You remind them of the policy and

they tell you, "We've been smoking all of our lives and aren't going to stop now. The smoking building is too far away, and we will not be shunned to some far corner of camp. We've been smoking here every day since we got here and nothing has burned down." How do you handle this?

What Are Friends For?

You work at a very popular theme park. As an employee you receive one free guest pass after every eight months of employment. You have been with the company just over nine months. You, of course, can get into the park with your employee badge at any time. Three of your best friends are in the area to visit you and want to get into the park, but they don't have enough money. One of these friends has lent you her car on numerous occasions and reminds you of this as the three ask you to use your guest pass to get them in free. They want you to say that they are potential employees who are here checking out the opportunities. The friends have driven 500 miles to visit you and are in the area for only four days. How do you handle this situation?

Summary

Values and ethics define a person; the role she or he fills serves as the medium through which those values and ethics are lived. Followers expect and look for high standards, clear ethics, and appropriate values in leaders. There are four primary avenues through which people learn ethics: modeling, discipline and training, socialization, and social interaction. Parks, recreation, and leisure services leaders can be involved in all of these functions.

Ethics serve as guides for behaviors—they explain and describe how things ought to be. Everything a leader does, says, and wears influences the perception of others about that leader. Ethics are the guideposts that help people make decisions, promote positive social values, and explain how to interact with others. In these interactions there are two basic approaches: an ethic of care and an ethic of rights and justice. Different leaders take different approaches based on their own knowledge, style, and values system. An individual who has a clear values system and who has great personal integrity in working with others is identified as a highly principled leader. To aid in subscribing to strong ethics in the course of one's career, oftentimes professional associations develop a code of ethics. In this chapter, the code of ethics for parks, recreation, and leisure services professionals (and board members) was presented as a model of what professional ethics look like.

Beginning the Journey

All successful leaders have an identifiable sense of personal values and ethics for which they stand. Effective leaders have a consistent values base, and others can see those values exhibited through a variety of ways. As you persevere in your journey to leadership, consider the following questions and relate them to your own values and ethical positions.

1. What are ethical beliefs? How and where do you learn them? What are universal ethics and why are they considered universal? How do leaders demonstrate their ethics and values? What leadership-related values do you exhibit?

2. How do ethics serve as guides for leaders? Explain/describe the three leader functions relative to values and ethics in your own words.

3. Why must leaders have strong ethics? What does it mean to have strong ethics? Why is trust a keystone of shared values and ethics?

4. What is a value? How do values relate to ethics? Why is it desirable for leaders to be aware of and clear about their own values and ethics? Why are self-awareness and reflection important tools for leaders (relative to ethics)?

5. How do values help to guide a leader? Revisit Kolhberg's stages of moral development (pp. 49–51) and identify the stage from which you most commonly operate. Are you satisfied with where you are? If not, what can you do to change your moral stage?

6. What is a social contract? How does it come into play when discussing values and ethics? What are positive social values? How do recreation leaders promote positive social values? Why are these values important in our field?

7. Describe the four common tensions faced in ethical dilemmas. Give an example from your own experience of ethical dilemmas that represents each tension. Which did you find easiest to resolve? Which were most difficult? Why?

8. Explain the three approaches to addressing ethical dilemmas. Develop a slogan or bumper sticker that captures the essence of each approach. Which approach do you prefer? On what values is this approach based?

9. Draw a picture or diagram of the ethic of rights and justice and the ethic of care. On what key issues do these ethical positions differ? Explain in your own words the two elements of the ethic of care. How is leader self-sacrifice related to these two ethical stances?

10. What is integrity? Do you have it? How do you know? How do others know whether or not you are a person of integrity? How do authenticity and a sense of identity fit within the notion of integrity?

11. Describe/explain what is meant by principle-centered leadership. Of the definitions of leadership presented in Chapter 2, which do you believe present leaders as principled? Explain.

12. Explain the NRPA Code of Ethics to someone who is not familiar with NRPA or the profession. Then ask them what impression they get of the parks and recreation field from this code. How will you use this code to enhance your sense of leadership in or for the profession? Go online and find a code of ethics for your area of interest (e.g., therapeutic recreation, outdoor recreation). Do you agree with all the components? Why or why not?

References

Bass, B. (1990). *Bass & Stogdill's handbook of leadership* (3rd ed.). New York, NY: The Free Press.

Bryant, M. (1998). Cross-cultural understandings of leadership. *Educational Management & Administration, 26*(1), 7–20.

Calabrese, R. and Roberts, B. (2001). The promise forsaken: Neglecting the ethical implications of leadership. *The International Journal of Educational Management, 15*(6/7), 267–275.

Citizen Branch Code of Ethics. (n.d.). Retrieved July 21, 2006, from https://www.nrpa.org/content/default.aspx?documentId=704

Coughlan, R. (2005). Codes, values and justifications in the ethical decision-making process. *Journal of Business Ethics, 59*, 45–53.

Covey, S. (1991). *Principle-centered leadership.* New York, NY: Summit.

Furman, G. (2004). The ethic of community. *Journal of Educational Administration, 42*(2), 215–235.

Gilligan, C. (1982). *In a different voice: Psychological theory and women's development.* Cambridge, MA: Harvard University Press.

Grundstein-Amado, R. (1999). Bilateral transformational leadership: An approach for fostering ethical conduct in public service organizations. *Administration & Society, 31*(2), 247–260.

Hardy, S. and Carlo, G. (2005). Identity as a source of moral motivation. *Human Development, 48*, 232–256.

Hitt, W. (1990). *Ethics and leadership.* Columbus, OH: Batelle Press.

Johnson, C. (2001). *Meeting the ethical challenges of leadership.* Thousand Oaks, CA: Sage.

Kanungo, R. and Mendonca, M. (1996). *Ethical dimensions of leadership.* Thousand Oaks, CA: Sage.

Kidder, R. and Born, P. (1999). Resolving ethical dilemmas in the classroom. *Educational Leadership, 56*(4), 38–41.

Klenke, K. (2005). Corporate values as multi-level, multi-domain antecedents of leader behaviors. *International Journal of Manpower, 26*(1), 50–65.

Kracher, B. and Wells, D. (1998). Employee selection and the ethic of care. In M. Schminke (Ed.), *Managerial ethics* (pp. 81–98). Mahwah, NJ: Lawrence Erlbaum.

Kujala, J. and Pietiliainen, T. (2004). Female managers' ethical decision-making: A multidimensional approach. *Journal of Business Ethics, 53*, 153–163.

London, M. (1999). *Principled leadership and business diplomacy.* Westport, CT: Quorum Books.

Mattison, M. (2000). Ethical decision making: The person in the process. *Social Work, 45*(3), 201–212.

Minkes, A., Small, M., and Chatterjee, S. (1999). Leadership and business ethics: Does it matter? Implications for management. *Journal of Business Ethics, 20*(4), 327–335.

Murphy, P. (1998). *Eighty exemplary ethics statements*. Notre Dame, IN: University of Notre Dame Press.

National Recreation and Parks Association. (2006). *Professional code of ethics*. Retrieved July 21, 2006, from http://www.nrpa.org.

Oliver, B. (1999). Comparing corporate managers' personal values over three decades, 1967–1995. *Journal of Business Ethics, 20*(2), 147–161.

Russell, R. (2002). A review of servant leadership attributes: Developing a practical model. *Leadership & Organization Development Journal, 23*(3/4), 145–157.

Sosik, J. (1997). Effect of transformational leadership and anonymity on idea generation in computer-mediated groups. *Group & Organization Management, 22*(4), 460–887.

Stainer, L. (2004). Ethical dimensions of management decision-making. *Strategic Change, 13*(6), 333–342.

Storr, L. (2004). Leading with integrity: A qualitative research study. *Journal of Health Organization and Management, 18*(6), 415–434.

Swenson-Lepper, T. (2005). Ethical sensitivity for organizational communication issues: Examining individual and organizational differences. *Journal of Business Ethics, 59*, 205–231.

Tubbs, S. (2006). Exploring a taxonomy of global leadership competencies and meta-competencies. *Journal of American Academy of Business, 8*(2), 29–34.

Wark, G. and Krebs, D. (2000). The construction of moral dilemmas in everyday life. *Journal of Moral Education, 29*(1), 5–10.

Wood, G. and Rimmer, M. (2003). Codes of ethics: What are they really and what should they be? *International Journal of Value-Based Management, 16*(2), 181–195.

Zhu, W., May, D., and Avolio, B. (2004). The impact of ethical leadership behaviors on employee outcomes: The roles of psychological empowerment and authority. *Journal of Leadership & Organizational Studies, 11*(1), 16–25.

Leader Profile

Joseph Wynns, CPRP
Director, Indianapolis Department of Parks and Recreation

Joe has seven years in this position and 34 years in the parks, recreation, and leisure services profession.

Volunteer leadership positions he has held include:

- Board of Trustees, National Recreation and Park Association
- Board of Directors, American Academy for Park and Recreation Administration
- Chair, Urban Park and Recreation Alliance
- Member, The Roundtable Associates, Inc.
- Board of Trustees, Indiana University Executive Development Program
- Black Coaches Advisory Board
- Indiana Sports Corporation Youth Committee member

Prior to becoming the director of the department, Joe worked as the Deputy Director, Administrator, Recreation District Manager, and Recreation Center Director. He also served as the director of the Youth and Family Services Department, and was a teacher and football coach in the public school system.

What is the meaning of leadership?
Leadership is bringing different people with different interests to a common goal.

What are the most important leadership qualities?
A leader must be ethical and possess visionary and decision-making skills, in addition to strategic thinking and an understanding of the organization's performance.

What advice do you have for students who aspire to leadership in parks, recreation, and leisure services?
Before one can lead, one must have a good understanding on how to follow. Through "follow-ship," one learns the important skill sets that are needed to become a good leader.

Favorite book: Who Moved My Cheese? by Spencer Johnson

Favorite activities: Cycling and bird watching

Chapter Eleven
Risk Management in Direct Leadership

Learning Opportunities

Through studying this chapter readers will have the opportunity to

- Understand the four elements of negligence.
- Evaluate levels of required supervision for various situations.
- Describe and identify the components of a supervision plan.
- Relate the conduct of an activity to personal leadership skills.
- Select the appropriate forms for managing leisure services risks.

A typical configuration of a recreation or leisure activity consists of one or more participants, the environment (e.g., indoors, outdoors), equipment, and the leisure services leader or leaders who conduct or facilitate the activity. Any time people are involved in an activity, whether self-led or supervised, illnesses, injuries, and mishaps can be expected to occur. The potential injuries from these unexpected incidents may range from very minor to extremely serious. Examples of common situations where injuries or illnesses arise include when an individual looks away at the moment a ball is being thrown to her or him, a player falls as she or he runs, a participant has a seizure and hits her or his head on a hard surface, and an individual suffers heatstroke at an outdoor art festival.

U.S. society has become very litigious; when people are injured or personal property is damaged, the injured person has a tendency to want to sue an individual or organization for medical and other costs. Parks, recreation, and leisure service entities are not immune from this litigious state of mind. Lawsuits in the field have increased due to several reasons: increased participation in leisure, greater awareness of better and safer ways to play, an increase in year-round activities, new technology and more sophisticated equipment, social attitudes, and increased accessibility to legal services (Hronek & Spengler, 2002).

Minimizing the likelihood of injuries, and thus lawsuits, is important for several reasons. First, being named in a lawsuit can be devastating (both personally and professionally) for the individuals named as well as financially draining for the agency or organization involved. In addition, lawsuits beget lawsuits—if an individual or organization is successfully sued once, other lawsuits may follow. Most importantly, recreation and leisure services professionals have an ethical and professional responsibility to maintain safe environments and activities for participants involved in programs and using facilities.

This chapter will assist the reader in understanding basic concepts related to legal liability and managing the risks typically involved in direct leadership settings. Because laws and the interpretation of laws differ from

Photo courtesy of Steven Nanton

Recreation and leisure services professionals have an ethical and professional responsibility to maintain safe environments and activities for participants involved in programs and using facilities.

state to state and between governmental, nonprofit, and commercial entities, this chapter provides a general understanding of negligence and related concepts only. Recreation and leisure services professionals would be wise to check with a local attorney for information related to their particular situation in their home state.

Criminal Law and Tort Law

There are two basic types of law: tort law and criminal law. For the most part, *criminal law* deals with intentional acts against the public at large addressed in the state and federal penal code. Incidents that fall under criminal law are followed up in the criminal court system—someone is arrested and punishment is meted out by the state or federal government through the court system. Examples of violations of criminal law include theft, sexual assault, and driving violations (e.g., speeding tickets).

Tort law deals with civil issues—those issues that arise out of living in a community. It involves both intentional and unintentional acts based on a breach of some type of contract. Because tort law involves the civil system, issues that arise out of tort law lead to lawsuits through which people seek to be compensated for losses they have incurred. An example of a violation of tort law is failing to keep sidewalks free of ice, snow, and debris resulting in an injury to a member of the public.

Often parks, recreation, and leisure services leaders are surprised to learn that in tort law a person may be sued by anybody for any thing at any time (Cotten & Wolohan, 2007). This means that the possibility of being sued exists for all of us, whether we are leisure service professionals, business people, or homeowners. For instance, a person could be sued for having a hair color and style (e.g., magenta, bowl cut) that distracted someone who, as a result, collided with a fence and was injured. This type of lawsuit may not hold up in court, but the damage of initiating the lawsuit may have already been done. By being named in a lawsuit, one's name might be in the newspaper; an attorney would need to be engaged (and paid); and the

time necessary to address the lawsuit could interfere with one's work, family, and other obligations.

Leisure service professionals must attend to all aspects of programs and services to maximize safety and minimize the risk of being sued. To accomplish this, one needs an understanding of legal concepts and their impact on leisure services leadership. An agency director would want to address many administrative concerns, such as civil rights, property laws, employment laws, and Occupational Safety and Health Administration (OSHA) regulations. Due to the focus of this text, however, this chapter will briefly discuss negligence, supervision, conduct of an activity, and the use of forms in minimizing risks—those legal concerns of direct interest to face-to-face leaders.

A person may be sued by anybody for any thing at any time.

Negligence

Negligence describes an act that results in personal injury to another or her or his property (Cotten & Wolohan, 2007; van der Smissen, 2007). It typically refers to a situation where an individual was careless in the course of her or his duties resulting in injury to another party. For negligence to exist, four elements must be present: *duty, an act/standard of care, proximate cause,* and *injury/damage.* Without all four elements, negligence (and therefore standing for a lawsuit) does not exist.

Duty

The term *duty* refers to an obligation to another individual based on a legal relationship (van der Smissen, 2007). This legal relationship might be mandated by law, inherent in the relationship, or voluntarily undertaken. For negligence to exist there must be a violation or breach of that duty or obligation. Typically in leisure services settings a leader and participants are involved in the conduct of a leisure or recreational pursuit. In this case there is a legal relationship (i.e., duty) between the leisure services professional and the participant. The leisure services leader has a duty, or obligation, to provide reasonably hazard-free activities and facilities to all participants and other staff.

In any legal relationship, whereby one person owes a responsibility or has a legal obligation to another person, a duty exists. Examples of legal duty may be found in the following relationships: teachers and students have a relationship whereby the teacher is responsible for the students; parents are responsible for children; lifeguards owe a responsibility to swimmers; coaches have obligations to players; and leisure services leaders owe a level of duty to participants. If there is no special relationship, and thus no duty, there is no negligence.

In direct leadership positions the duty owed an individual includes a responsibility to act in a safe and prudent manner, to warn of hidden and visible hazards, and maintain a safe environment. This duty is owed when participants are using leisure facilities, in the conduct of activities, and in the general provision of leisure services.

Act/Standard of Care

The *act* refers to the actions of a person (leisure services leader) in light of the duty owed to participants. A certain *standard of care* is required to maintain a hazard-free environment for all participants. In legal terms, in an assertion of negligence, a leisure services leader will be held to the same standard that a reasonable and prudent (i.e., careful) professional maintains. This standard of care may be established by statute, ordinance, or regulation; by an organization or agency; or by the profession. For instance, the American College of Sports Medicine (ACSM) has established standards for fitness leaders, the National Council on Therapeutic Recreation Certification (NCTRC) publishes standards for therapeutic recreation specialists, and the American Red Cross has well-established standards for lifeguards. If professional standards exist, leaders will be held to those standards.

Thus, a leisure services leader must act in the same way that another person competent for the position would act. If a leader does not meet these expectations, duty has been breached and negligence could be found. In most cases, interns and volunteers are held to the same standard of care as a professional (Cotten & Wolohan, 2007).

Three elements determine what is reasonable: the *activity, environment,* and *participants* (van der Smissen, 2007). These are discussed in further detail later in this chapter. In addition to examining these elements, reason-able care is measured in part by foreseeability. *Foreseeability* refers to the responsibility of the leader to foresee, or anticipate, that a dangerous situation might arise if "X" were to occur (Peterson & Hronek, 2003). Generally, it is accepted that identifiable, foreseeable risks are associated with all activities. Thus, leaders will want to be competent in anticipating what risks are associated with which activities. If an event is not foreseeable (by a reasonable, prudent professional) then the conduct of that activity is likely not unreasonable. For example, it is usually foreseeable that where water exists (e.g., pond, lake, swimming pool, river) drowning may occur, no matter the swimming abilities of participants. In the game of dodge ball where a small playground ball is hurled at opponents, it is similarly foreseeable that someone will be hit in the face and possibly injured. On the other hand, it is not generally foreseeable that in the excitement of bowling a strike, a person would jump up and down thereby fracturing her foot.

To fully understand the level of care we owe participants, it is important to be aware of what is known as the "Rule of Seven" (Peterson & Hronek, 2003). This states that

- Children under the age of seven are not responsible for their own welfare. They are considered too young and immature to recognize dangerous situations. Thus, leaders have a tremendous legal responsibility to these youngsters.

- Children between seven and fourteen years of age are considered partially responsible for their own well-being. They can understand some warning signs and can extrapolate potential dangers in many situations.

- Youth ages fourteen through the age of majority (18 or 21, depending upon the state) are mostly responsible for their own welfare. Generally, the courts have found that this age group has enough experience and intellectual capacity to understand risks and hazards.

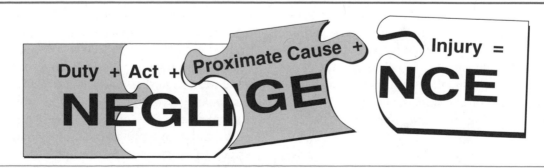

Figure 11.1 For negligence to be found, all four elements must exist.

These general principles might be mitigated if an individual has a social, mental, or cognitive disability. Leaders must know their participants and provide appropriate levels of supervision and care.

Negligent acts may occur due to acts of *omission*, where a leader does not do something she or he should do, or acts of *commission*, where a leader either does something she or he should not do, or does something she or he is supposed to do, but incorrectly. Three ways that a leader might behave or act inappropriately in her or his position include *nonfeasance, misfeasance,* and *malfeasance.*

Nonfeasance. *Nonfeasance* implies neglect of duty or not doing something one should. Nonfeasance is perceived as passive negligence because it results out of uninvolvement; a leader does not do something she or he should do, or she or he neglects her or his duties altogether (Peterson & Hronek, 2003). Examples of nonfeasance include failing to maintain a facility by passively allowing it to age without regular maintenance or upkeep, resulting in injury; or abandoning a group for which one has a responsibility (even for a short while) during which time a participant is injured while the leader is gone.

Misfeasance. Those acts whereby a leader did not exercise due care for the rights of the participants are termed *misfeasance.* This type of breach of duty includes both a failure to act when one should have (i.e., act of omission) as well as the improper conduct of an act (i.e., act of commission; Peterson & Hronek, 2003). An example of misfeasance by omission would be a situation at a resident camp where several youth engage in a fist fight (resulting in physical injury) while two adult leaders rest nearby—aware of, yet choosing to ignore the events. In this case, the leaders failed to exercise due care for the rights of the victim, resulting in misfeasance. The leaders justified their inaction in stopping the fight based on the fact that the youth receiving the beating had been teasing and picking on the other youngsters earlier, and in their words, "He deserved it [the beating]." This was evidence of very poor judgment by the leaders.

As an example of misfeasance by improper conduct (i.e., an act of commission), a recreation therapist was helping to transfer a person who uses a wheelchair to her bed. In the course of the transfer, the therapist used an incorrect technique and the individual with the disability fell to the floor, suffering a broken leg. The transfer act was appropriate, but done incorrectly. This was misfeasance during an act of commission.

Malfeasance. Doing something that one ought not to have done and which may also be illegal is considered *malfeasance* (Peterson & Hronek, 2003). For instance, malfeasance would have occurred if a leisure services leader slapped a participant who was using foul language. Striking

Negligent acts may occur due to **acts of omission**, where a leader does not do something she or he should do, or **acts of commission**, where a leader either does something she or he should not do, or does something she or he is supposed to do but does it incorrectly.

any individual is an unacceptable practice, unlawful (i.e., battery), and should not have been done. It is an act of commission for which the leader could be held liable.

Proximate Cause

In addition to duty and a breach of that duty (i.e., standard of care), proximate cause must also exist for negligence to be proven. Proximate cause refers to the actual cause of the injury or damage (van der Smissen, 2007). For negligence to be attributed to an action, it must be shown that the injury was the direct result of the action (remember, actions may be acts of omission or commission). Often a defense attorney will attempt to prove that there was an intervening act that came between a negligent act and the injury. If an intervening act is found, the negligent act would not have been the proximate cause, and there would be no negligence.

In the bed transfer example of misfeasance, the incorrect technique used during the transfer was what caused the fall, and thus the injury. The improper technique was the proximate cause of the broken leg. Imagine the same staff member doing the same incorrect technique, but rather than dropping the patient, the brakes on the bed failed and that was the reason the person fell to the floor breaking her leg. The failed bed brakes would have been the proximate cause of the injury and not misfeasance (i.e., using the incorrect technique) on the part of the recreation therapist.

Injury/Damage

The fourth element that must exist for negligence to be found is actual injury (to a person) or damage (to physical property; van der Smissen, 2007). The injuries might be physical (e.g., fracture, sprain, head injury), emotional/mental (e.g., anguish, humiliation, embarrassment, emotional trauma, psychogenic shock), or economic (e.g., replacement cost for equipment, loss of one's job, future medical bills). Interpretation of injury or damage differs by state with some more loosely defined than others; it is wise to become familiar with the guidelines in one's home state. Recreation and sport activities that have required medical attention (and thus, met one critical element of negligence) were (in order from highest to lowest frequency of incidence): basketball, football (touch and tackle combined), softball and baseball, roller and in-line skating, soccer, and exercising with weights or equipment (Dougherty, Goldberger & Carpenter, 2002).

❖　❖　❖

Understanding the four necessary elements of negligence is critical to beginning the process of reducing and minimizing risks and hazards. Duty, an act/standard of care, proximate cause, and injury/damage must all exist for a claim of negligence to be upheld. Duty is established based on relationships, the act is what the leader did or did not do, and proximate cause and injury/damage are "after the fact" constructs. To best minimize risks, the area in which parks, recreation, and leisure services leaders might choose to focus is on the act/standard of care. There are many components that fit within this element of negligence and they are addressed in the remainder of this chapter.

Types of Supervision

Leader supervision of leisure services events is a very important element in managing risks related to standard of care. Dougherty, Goldberger, and Carpenter (2002) reported that 23% of lawsuits against recreation and sport managers were due to supervision-related issues. The duty to supervise depends on the relationships or duty owed between the person supervising (i.e., the leader) and the participants. Recreation and leisure services agencies and organizations require supervision of activities they sponsor and conduct, usually by an activity or program leader.

Various elements of a recreation or leisure activity help to determine the nature of the required supervision. It is important to recognize generalities that impact the type of supervision required (see Table 11A, p. 240) so as to make wise decisions relative to appropriate level of supervision. In parks, recreation, and leisure services settings there are times when the leader (employee) is considered *in loco parentis*. In other words, the leisure services leader acts in the place of the parent or guardian in the care and safety of a minor (i.e., youth under the age of 18 or 21, depending upon the state in which one resides). Acting *in loco parentis* actually demands of the leader a level of care and supervision of the child *greater* than that owed to the child by her or his parents.

As an example, a family with two youth, ages 13 and 14 years, might go camping at a state park campground. They set up the family tents well away from the shower house/bathroom to better enjoy the natural surroundings. Many parents would consider the ages of their young teen-

agers and allow the adolescents to walk to the shower house without being accompanied by parents. The parents' judgment seems reasonable; to allow young teens to walk to the shower house in this type of setting without being escorted is not uncommon.

Now imagine the same situation, but rather than with parents, a group of young teenagers are on a camping trip sponsored by the local YMCA. The counselors would be acting *in loco parentis,* yet in this instance, it would be best if the adolescents were accompanied to the shower house. The many possible ways for young people to get into mischief remain the same in both situations: the teenagers might decide to tour the campground and see what "fun" they might induce, a stranger might interfere with the safety of the teens, or the youth might get lost. In the first scenario the parents would be distraught over the incident, yet no legal or civil action would likely be undertaken for their failure to properly supervise their children. In the second scenario, however, if an injury should occur to one of the teens, the counselors and the YMCA could be held legally responsible for that incident.

In direct leadership situations, whether *in loco parentis* or as a professional, an inherent duty to supervise exists. Further, when activities are sponsored and led by agency personnel, participants have an expectation of safe conditions (Dougherty, Goldberger & Carpenter, 2002). To ensure these safe conditions three types of supervision are utilized in situations dependent upon various elements: *general, transitional,* and *specific* (Gaskin & Batista, 2007). Parks and recreation leaders must fully understand the

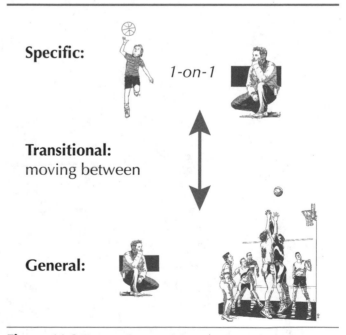

Figure 11.2 Types of supervision

In direct leadership situations, whether *in loco parentis* or as a professional, an inherent duty to supervise exists. Further, when activities are sponsored and led by agency personnel, participants have an expectation of safe conditions.

three types of supervision and the activity being supervised to know which type of supervision is required when. Failure to afford participants the appropriate type of supervision may result in increased risk of injury to participants and lead to claims of negligence.

General Supervision

General supervision describes situations where a leader oversees a broad area. The focus of general supervision is on the conduct and demeanor of participants or on the physical environment itself. For example, a leisure services leader might provide general supervision to adults who are playing beach volleyball. When focused on player conduct and demeanor a supervisor would notice if a

player was playing overly aggressively, or who appeared to mentally "check out" of the activity. In either case, the supervisor might wish to visit with the individual and ask her or him to settle down or to pay closer attention to avoid injury. A supervisor focused on the physical environment would watch the court and nearby areas for potential hazards. If another ball, Frisbee, or other object were to enter the playing area the supervisor would halt play and remove the hazard.

In general supervision, visual and voice contact are easily maintained with participants in the area being supervised, and the ratios of leaders to participants can be quite high. Examples of general supervision include teachers overseeing a playground, coaches supervising an athletic practice, leisure services leaders supervising an open gymnasium period, a recreational therapist supervising clients on a community outing, and a docent supervising a museum visit. In all of these instances the ratio of leader to participants might be 1:20 or more.

Transitional Supervision

Transitional supervision is used when shifting from general to specific supervision and vice versa (Gaskin & Batista, 2007). In conducting an activity, many situations may arise which demand a change in the level of supervision: the teaching of new skills, the introduction of new or unknown participants, or a change in environmental conditions. For example, moving from warming up in an athletic practice to learning and practicing new drills could require a change from general to specific supervision. A change in weather conditions might warrant more specific supervision as might participant fatigue, participant atten-

Leaders have a responsibility to use appropriate supervision to ensure participant safety.

Foreseeable hazards exist in many areas, and leaders are expected to warn participants of such conditions.

tion levels, activity difficulty, and familiarity with the play space or activities.

Specific Supervision

Leisure services leaders are required to engage in specific supervision when there is instruction involved, when participants are low skilled, and when participant behaviors so indicate. Specific supervision involves direct contact with participants by the leader (Gaskin & Batista, 2007). Direct contact does not necessarily imply physical contact; close visual and voice contact are elements of specific supervision as well. There are times, however, when physical contact by a leader is necessary (e.g., spotting in gymnastics; spotting individuals on a ropes or teams course, or in rock climbing). Any time the risk of injury increases, the level of supervision owed to participants increases. See Table 11A (page 240) for examples of the impacts of change in participants, activity, and environment on the needed type of supervision.

Leaders as Supervisors

Whenever a leisure services professional leads a sponsored activity, she or he owes a legal duty to the participants to conduct activities in a safe and conscientious manner. As described in the previous explanations of the various types of supervision, leisure services leaders are viewed as supervisors of participants, activities, and areas. As supervisors, if a question of negligence arises, the leader will be measured against a standard of a reasonable and prudent professional. Reasonable and prudent professionals are competent and are positioned in appropriate locations relative to participants and potential hazards.

Competency

Competency refers to the condition of being qualified to perform an act. Leisure services leaders are expected to be competent in a variety of areas such as direct leadership techniques, behavior management, human development, and emergency care. The competence of a supervisor is measured by several components which include, but are not limited to: knowledge, age, experience, credentials, and attentiveness to duty (Gaskin & Batista, 2007).

Knowledge

To minimize liability, it is important for supervisors to be knowledgeable about the participants, the activity, and the environment. This knowledge must extend to include the proper ways of conducting activities as well as ways to ascertain potential hazards. More will be said about the three areas of knowledge in a later section of this chapter which discusses the conduct of an activity.

Age

The age of the leader must be appropriate to the activity requirements. Age is considered to be correlated to maturity level and is very important in many situations. Leader age may be mandated by certification or accreditation standards. For instance, to be an American Red Cross Canoe Instructor an individual must be a minimum of 21 years of age. Another age consideration is based on the difference between the ages of the leader and participants. This issue arises when participants are adolescents and leaders are in their late teens/early twenties — the age difference is minimal and difficult supervisory issues can result.

Experience

Level of experience is another important factor when selecting the appropriate supervisor for a particular task. The more complex a task or the higher the risk of injury, the more experience a leader should have before being put in a position of responsibility. If leader experience level is weak and the situation requires a good deal of attention, it might be best to pair that leader with a more experienced person until the less-seasoned leader develops the necessary skills and judgment.

Credentials

If national or industry standards require certifications or licensure for particular positions, persons filling such slots should hold those credentials. Industry standards are not mandated by any national entity, but are commonly accepted as minimum standards for a person filling a particular position. As an example, since the 1990s it has

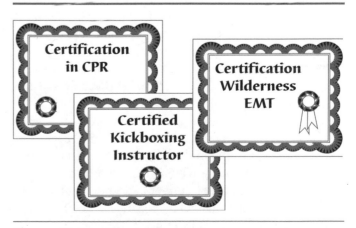

Figure 11.3 Leaders who are acting in a supervisory capacity must be competent.

Industry standards are not mandated by any national entity, but are commonly accepted as minimum standards for a person filling a particular position.

become common practice for individuals who work with youth in leisure services agencies to hold certificates of completion for training in universal precautions (e.g., blood-borne pathogens) and mandatory child abuse reporting. Competent leaders in supervisory roles would have and maintain these and other certifications.

Attentiveness to Duty

Any time an injury occurs, questions will be raised about the leader's attentiveness to the situation. For instance, a lifeguard on duty should have her or his attention on the swimmers and others at the waterfront at all times. An inattentive lifeguard, perhaps visiting and talking to people, may miss potential hazards resulting in unsafe conditions for participants. Being attentive to one's responsibilities is important for all parks, recreation, and leisure services leaders. Attentiveness is always important, whether supervising people in a gymnasium, childcare center, library, nature center, or on an amusement ride.

Supervisor Location

Supervisor location is as important as supervisor competence in minimizing risks. Supervisors must be accessible to participants and the area they are supervising to meet expectations of their jobs. A well-located supervisor can manage problems and foresee potential hazards more easily than one who is in the wrong place, too far away, or out of view. When considering placement, one should think about proximity—the relative closeness of the leader to potential trouble spots and to initiating emergency systems. Being in the right place at the right time should not be by chance. Rather, supervisor location should be purposeful and deliberate relative to participant, activity, and facility needs.

In addition to physical proximity, being able to make visual and voice contact with participants in all corners of the environment is important to being able to act promptly and appropriately. Being within visual contact allows the supervisor not only to see current happenings but also to foresee or anticipate what might occur next. Voice distance without visual contact is limiting as the supervisor is unable to glean all the necessary information to make decisions regarding a particular situation.

Depending upon the activity, the environment, and the participants, the location of the supervisor may vary. Supervising with a focus on participants requires a level of visual contact with participants so as to be able to make judgments relative to their actions. Focusing on the area or physical environment necessitates a leader be within easy viewing of the area to be supervised.

There are occasions when the visual contact should be continuous (e.g., at a waterfront) and other times when it need not be continuous and uninterrupted. For instance, if a leisure services leader were supervising participants in an open gymnasium period or painting in an arts-and-crafts room, being able to see the space and checking in on the participants periodically could be sufficient.

Supervisor Functions

In addition to being competent, being in the appropriate location, and determining and applying appropriate types of supervision to participants, there are additional functions of an activity supervisor (i.e., direct leadership). Supervisors have five primary functions:

- Manage participant behaviors.
- Render emergency care.
- Enforce rules equitably.
- Be alert to dangerous conditions.
- Maintain responsibilities for participants off premises. (Hronek & Spengler, 2002)

Manage Participant Behaviors

The leader acting as the supervisor must maintain control of a group through appropriate behavior management techniques. Through appropriate behavior management a leader helps to maintain safe activity conditions, to minimize hazards, and to maximize participant enjoyment.

Render Emergency Care

Should something go awry and a participant require emergency care, it is the responsibility of the supervisor or direct leader to provide that aid. This is not to say that the supervisor must physically provide first aid, but rather

Through appropriate behavior management a leader helps to maintain safe activity conditions, to minimize hazards, and to maximize participant enjoyment.

take responsibility for enacting the emergency medical system (e.g., calling 911) and protecting the individual from further harm. Many leisure services agencies require first-aid and CPR certifications as prerequisites for employment. These two certifications are quickly becoming industry standard in all aspects of parks, recreation, and leisure services.

Enforce Rules Equitably

A third responsibility of a supervisor is to establish, communicate, and enforce all rules equitably. This allows for differences in participant skill levels, developmental stages, and environmental conditions while maintaining a safe environment. If a rule is not enforced in one instance because the situation involves a friend or because the leader is simply trying to be "nice," difficulties could arise that might result in a claim of negligence.

Be Alert to Dangerous Conditions

A supervisor must always be alert to dangerous conditions. Dangerous conditions might arise out of participant behaviors (e.g., inattentiveness, acting out), staffing situations (e.g., not enough staff, improperly located staff), the activity (e.g., inherently dangerous, improperly conducted, overly difficult), and the environment (e.g., wet floors, extreme temperatures). Leisure services leaders are expected to be constantly on the watch for changing conditions and to foresee and avoid potential hazards.

Maintain Responsibility for Participants Off Premises

Leader responsibility for participants exists whether one is on agency premises or off-site. Whenever participants are off-premises and involved in a sponsored activity, a supervisor has a responsibility to minimize hazards and present activities in a safe fashion. Trips to the pool, to the ball field, or to the concert hall all demand ongoing supervision while in transit and at the new location.

Develop and Utilize a Supervision Plan

An additional function of a supervisor, which is often handled by administrators, is to develop and follow a supervision plan. A written plan may serve to educate and train new leaders and supervisors as well as remind existing supervisors of proper procedures. A written plan can minimize the confusion over type of supervision, supervisor location, and necessary supervisor credentials. According to several authors, a plan for supervision should answer the following questions:

- How many supervisors are required for what types of events? What are the qualifications of a super-

Leisure services leaders are expected to be constantly on the watch for changing conditions and to foresee and avoid potential hazards.

visor for this situation (e.g., age, certifications, experience)? How will appropriate supervisors be identified?

- What types of supervision are required under what circumstances? Should general, transitional, or specific supervision be practiced?

- Where should supervisors be located? Being specific about approximate or relative locations helps to minimize confusion for supervisors. Location might be defined in relation to participants, the activity, or the area. For example, when leading young children in a pool area, activity leaders (not lifeguards, who remain at their posts) might be directed to be located in the midst of the children. When supervising participants on a softball field, leaders might be directed to walk around the facility in an identified pattern so that their location is fluid.

- When should a supervisor step in? Knowing when to directly interfere and when not to is something that is learned through experience and often part of agency policy. When in the learning stages, a leader may find that while stepping into a situation might irritate participants, it is generally wiser to interfere than not.

- What are the expectations of a supervisor? All supervision plans should articulate and describe the expectations of a supervisor. For example: Are supervisors expected to physically break up an altercation, perform first aid, deal with the media, expel participants, call their supervisor when…, clean bathrooms, and lock or unlock doors? (Gaskin & Batista, 2007; Simmons, 1998)

Having a written supervision plan will help not only as a training aid for supervisors but also as a guide for understanding leader expectations should a participant be injured, or equipment or facility damaged. As long as the supervision plan is followed appropriately, the risk of liability is minimized. Having a written supervision plan and not following it, however, may lead to additional concerns related to claims of negligence.

Conduct of the Activity

The conduct of an activity is the very essence of recreation and leisure services leadership. Leisure services leaders conduct a large variety of activities for all types of people. The manner in which activities are conducted (and supervised) has a tremendous impact on the safety, well-being, and enjoyment of the participants (and the leader!). Conducting an activity improperly can lead to injury and lawsuits; in fact, Dougherty, Goldberger, and Carpenter (2002) report that 24% of lawsuits in recreation and sport are related to the conduct of the activity.

> The manner in which activities are conducted (and supervised) has a tremendous impact on the safety, well-being, and enjoyment of the participants (and the leader!).

Thus, it is absolutely critical for recreation and leisure services providers to remember that there is no compromise for safety. There are times when leisure services leaders find themselves in situations where they have to play the "bad guy" by enforcing unpopular safety rules; this can be an uncomfortable feeling, particularly when leading a group of one's peers. It must be understood, however, that the leader has ultimate responsibility for the safety of each participant in the group. If safety rules or guidelines are not followed consistently and a participant is injured, the leader and the organization could be at risk for negligence.

If, for instance, people were allowed to stand on an earth ball (a large four-foot to six-foot diameter ball) "just this once," and an individual was injured during that play, the leisure services leader could be held liable—negligence could be found for failure to follow safety rules. Leisure services activities have safety rules and guidelines to minimize risks, not to constrain participants from having fun. If activity rules seem overly stringent, perhaps they warrant a review in a staff meet-

ing, but activity leaders should not feel free to disregard rules because some participants complain. Remember, there is no compromise for safety.

In the process of leading activities, leisure services leaders have a responsibility to follow professional standards and practices to keep participants safe and free from harm. As mentioned earlier the safe conduct of an activity requires a knowledge of the *participants*, the *activity*, and the *environment* in which the activity is held (Simmons, 1998; van der Smissen, 2007).

Knowledge of Participants

To conduct an activity safely, leisure services leaders must have a solid understanding of the participants and their level of readiness for the upcoming activity. Leaders must understand individual differences based on developmental abilities, previous experience, physical condition, and physical and emotional capabilities. Leaders should be cautioned, however, not to make generalizations about people, as many individuals fall well above and well below the norm of a particular group. Information should be gathered to support all evaluations made of participants and stereotypical judgments should be avoided.

A competent leisure services leader will use this information in her or his decision making related to types

Table 11A Leader supervision constantly changes

	Specificity of Supervision		
Participants	**Highest** ←	→	**Lowest**
Age	very young	teen	adult
Developmental abilities	low	moderate	high
Skill level	low	moderate	high
Previous exposure	none	some	lots
Activity			
Complexity	high	moderate	low
Difficulty	high	moderate	low
Inherent risk	high	moderate	low
Environment			
Maintenance and condition	poor	good	excellent
Participant familiarity with space	none	some	lots
Leader			
Skills	low	moderate	high
Maturity	low	moderate	high
Experience	low	moderate	high
Competence	low	moderate	high

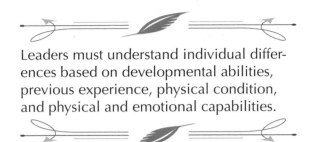

Leaders must understand individual differences based on developmental abilities, previous experience, physical condition, and physical and emotional capabilities.

of equipment (e.g., Koosh ball or Whiffle ball, safety scissors or regular scissors), the selection of teammates and opponents (e.g., to help balance skill, physical size, and maturity levels), and the nature and enforcement of activity-related rules (e.g., younger children generally require more explicit and clearly stated rules than do older individuals).

Developmental Abilities

Generally, developmental abilities are defined by considering participant age, maturity, coordination, and physical size. Age alone can provide some information about the probable maturity level of the participants, but combined with observations of actual maturity, kinesthetic awareness and physical size, developmental abilities provide a much more accurate assessment of what can be expected of participants. For example, when working with adults who have mental retardation, knowledge of their developmental abilities (i.e., what level of cognitive, emotional and physical capabilities they have) tends to be a more accurate assessment of ability than age or physical size.

Previous Experience

Leisure services leaders are expected to have knowledge of participants' general intelligence, experience, and knowledge base related to the planned activities. Knowing these things can be helpful in deciding how to conduct an activity—which rules to state, when and how to state them, and the type of supervision required. It is not always wise to accept participants' statements about their skill levels, however. When faced with potential embarrassment, many participants will exaggerate their skills and previous experience with a particular activity.

For example, when asking a group of individuals (no matter their age) at a pool if they can swim, almost every one will either answer in the affirmative or remain silent. However, when those individuals are swim-tested, it is not at all uncommon for a leader to discover that at least one of them does not know how to swim. Therefore, while it is appropriate to solicit a verbal self-report as to previous experience and skill level from participants, in activities with high inherent risks, a physical test of abilities should be conducted.

Physical Condition

It is the leisure services leader's responsibility to know about obvious and hidden physical limitations of participants which might interfere with full or safe participation in the activities. This includes a general knowledge of physical conditions such as obesity, recent illnesses, and pertinent previous injuries. Obviously, one should use her or his judgment; it is not necessary to know if someone has a bad knee if the activity is a card game, but the leader might need to know about joint injuries if the activity is a walk or hike. For day-to-day drop-in types of activities, a standard medical information form completed at registration and kept on file is usually sufficient. This way, if an injury should occur, a general medical history is available for those who will be treating the participant.

Physical and Emotional Capabilities

For safety reasons and maximum enjoyment it is helpful to know about the physical and emotional capabilities of group members. If an activity results in emotional stress which might negatively affect one's mental or physical health, the leader may wish to avoid that activity. Inclusion and therapeutic recreation specialists will want to be particularly alert to this type of situation.

Leisure services leaders are expected to have a general knowledge of the emotional states of participants. For instance, participants involved voluntarily often have a more positive and alert emotional state than do those who are "forced" to participate (e.g., children who are made to participate by parents who need childcare). Furthermore, leaders should be alert to any participants who might have a propensity for violence or are especially agitated during the session.

Developmental abilities
Previous experience
Physical condition
Physical and emotional capabilities

Figure 11.4 For safety reasons, leaders must know general information about their participants.

Knowledge of the Activity

In addition to having a solid knowledge of the participants, a leisure services leader is expected to have knowledge of the activity to be conducted. Knowledge of the appropriate equipment, activity objectives, rules, and safety concerns will aid a leader in making decisions as to the appropriate timing of the activity. This knowledge will help her or him foresee hazards and take protective action.

Rules and Level of Skills Needed

Knowledge of the activity rules and level of skills needed to safely participate allows the leader to select activities which match the needs and skill levels of those who wish to engage in such activity. Furthermore, a leader who knows the activity rules can ensure safe practice by communicating and enforcing those rules to all participants.

Actual Instruction and Safety Needs

A leader has a responsibility to teach safely, to teach safety, and to warn of hazards in the conduct of an activity. To safely conduct an activity, a leader needs to know how to provide directions based on the developmental level of participants and what the potential safety concerns may be. For instance, people who are members of the community theater may be exposed to many hazardous situations. They need to be informed about all potential safety concerns such as moving about a darkened stage, physical requirements of moving sets, and the use of materials that may be toxic (e.g., paints, solvents). Neglecting to inform participants about potential hazards could lead to liability problems.

Leaders must know the activity and its requirements.

Knowledge of the appropriate equipment, activity objectives, rules, and safety concerns will aid a leader in making decisions as to the appropriate timing of the activity. This knowledge will help her or him foresee hazards and take protective action.

Sequencing and Progression

Leaders also take responsibility for sequencing activities appropriately and developing a sound progression of activities. A competent leader will know when to introduce new skills within an activity. If a group struggles to grasp basic skills, she or he will not move on to the next skill level. For example, one would not introduce dive rolls to people who cannot yet do forward rolls. Activities should be led in a progression, with activities that are complex and rigorous following those that are simpler and easier to grasp. An example of this would be teaching Newcomb (i.e., volleyball that involves catching rather than hitting the ball over the net) prior to teaching volleyball.

Knowledge of the Environment

In addition to understanding participants and having a solid knowledge of the activity, knowing about the environment and equipment (e.g., advantages and disadvantages of the space, hazards, layout) is necessary. The environment must be appropriate for the activity being conducted. For example, playing rugby on an asphalt surface would not be appropriate because it could lead to severe injury. While most activity instructions do not include information about preferred playing surfaces, leaders should consider the nature of the activity and make an appropriate judgment about environmental requirements.

Playing Area

If indoors, a leisure services leader should be knowledgeable about the playing area; if outdoors, the leader should be knowledgeable about the grounds and surrounding area. This knowledge should include the leader having a sense of the layout, the number of participants that can be accommodated, structures in the area, and location of emergency exits. Ascertaining this information usually requires a walking tour of the area to look for existing and potential hazards. Omitting this physical inspection of the environment could lead to unsafe leadership situations. It is expected that leaders will ensure playing areas are safe from

If indoors, a leisure services leader should be knowledgeable about the playing area; if outdoors, the leader should be knowledgeable about the grounds and surrounding area.

hazards and potential dangers. This includes avoiding wet surfaces, litter and broken glass, low-hanging branches from trees, extraneous equipment lying about, and poor lighting.

Equipment

Typically, the conduct of leisure activities involves some type of equipment (e.g., balls, hoops, paint brushes) and structures (e.g., goal posts, fences, playground structures). As with the grounds, it is necessary to conduct an inspection of these items prior to the conduct of an activity. Using defective equipment may be cause for claims of negligence; leaders are expected to be aware of (and take action to remove) any defect in equipment used in leisure services activities. In addition to being free from defect, the leader should be sure that the items are being used as they were intended.

Facilities and Environment

Legal concerns about leisure services facilities and environment fall into two general categories—*agency or organizational liability* for maintenance of facilities and *leader liability* for conducting an activity on unsafe premises. Parks, recreation, and leisure services agencies and organizations owe a duty to their constituents to maintain safe properties, and yet, this tends to be a problematic area for us. Dougherty, Goldberger, and Carpenter (2002) report that 53% of lawsuits in recreation and sports are due to claims about unsafe areas and facilities. An example of the duty parks and recreation leaders owe to participants includes the expectation that picnic pavilions will be free from dangerous structural problems (e.g., wooden picnic tables free from splinters, concrete flooring free of large cracks and uneven surfaces), and environmental hazards (e.g., beehives, wasp nests). If these expectations are not met, issues of legal liability (i.e., negligence) could be the result.

An activity leader is liable for the conditions of premises being used in the conduct of an activity, whether public (e.g., a city park) or privately owned (e.g., fitness trails on commercial property). A leader must avoid placing or leading activity participants in unsafe situations. If a hazard is found, either in the facility or environment, a leisure services leader is responsible to first report and document the hazard. Once discovered, a leader must avoid conducting an activity in the vicinity of the hazard. In an unsafe area a leader's choices would be

- Stop the activity.
- Modify the activity so the hazard is not an issue.
- Make a temporary repair, warn the participants, and continue. (Hronek & Spengler, 2002)

This last option is viable only if the leader knows how to (and is capable of) making a safe and appropriate repair.

To minimize risks to participants and to minimize risks of negligence to the leaders, it is important to hold periodic and scheduled inspections of facilities and outdoor environments. Furthermore, it is critical to inspect a site immediately prior to its being used for an activity, especially if a leader has any reason to suspect that the nature or care of the facility has changed since the most recent inspection.

For example, a day camp utilizes a public park area for its programming and activity efforts. Camp runs daily, Monday through Friday, and grounds inspections are performed every Monday morning before the campers arrive. The Fourth of July holiday occurs on a Wednesday and the park is a favorite spot for public celebration. On Thursday morning the camp director and all the counselors should conduct a thorough grounds inspection because glass and aluminum beverage containers and trash would likely be found throughout the park. This type of litter can pose hazards to participants in the pursuit of leisure.

❖ ❖ ❖

Safe and responsible conduct of an activity demands that leisure services leaders be aware of three activity elements: knowledge of participants, knowledge of the activity, and knowledge of the environment. With this information leaders can make appropriate judgments related to activity selection and appropriate direct leadership techniques.

In addition to having a basic understanding of legal issues related to negligence, leisure services leaders may

To minimize risks to participants and to minimize risks of negligence to the leaders, it is important to hold periodic and scheduled inspections of facilities and outdoor environments.

wish to use forms and records to minimize risks. A sample risk management checklist is provided in Figure 11.5. While the use of various forms, particularly releases and waivers, has been questioned, there is value in their appropriate use (Cotten & Wolohan, 2007; Peterson & Hronek, 2003). This next section will provide an introduction to the more common forms used in recreation and leisure service settings as elements of a risk management plan.

The Use of Forms in Risk Management

The purpose of using most forms in risk management is to limit the liability of individual employees and the agency or organization. While questions have arisen over the effectiveness of waivers and release forms, the courts have found them to be useful in determining participant understanding of the risks involved in the activity. In other words, at times risk management forms are used for informational and public relations purposes. All forms being developed by an agency should be examined by an attorney or risk management specialist prior to use. This will help to ensure appropriate language and consistency with state or local laws.

All risk management forms should be legible (e.g., 10 point font or larger) and written in clear, unambiguous language. To be valid, forms should be dated and signed by the participant; it also must be shown that the forms were understood by the person signing them. In this effort, it may be best to not only have the participants read the forms before signing, but also have the leader read the content of the forms aloud to participants and provide an opportunity for participants to ask questions.

Waivers are considered legal contracts into which minors cannot legally enter. It is important to note, while parents or guardians are often asked to sign waivers on behalf of their minor children, parents or guardians may not sign away their children's rights (Cotten & Wolohan, 2007; Peterson & Hronek, 2003). This means that although a parent may sign a form waiving the right to collect monetary damages in the case of injury to her or his child,

once the minor child reaches the age of majority, that child may sue on her or his own behalf. Therefore, leisure services agencies and organizations should save forms and records for a minimum of five years, and it would be wise to save those that involve minors for five years past the year the child reaches the age of majority.

Types of Forms

A variety of forms commonly used by parks, recreation, and leisure services agencies attempt to inform participants of potential hazards and to minimize risks of negligence to the agency. Some forms are primarily used to inform about upcoming activities, while others ask those who sign them to voluntarily relinquish their right to sue in the event of an injury due to the negligence of the leader.

Accident/Incident Report

Accident/incident reports are used for several reasons: to document treatment of an injury for insurance needs, to provide agency statistics, and to assist in legal situations. This report form is one of the most important forms utilized by recreation and leisure service personnel. This report documents an accident or incident where an individual injury or property damage results. To be useful, accident/incident reports must be completed within a short time of the event, thorough, and free from speculation. A "just the facts" approach should be taken with all legal forms, and in particular, this form.

When describing an accident or incident, the leader completing the form should use dry, objective language. In response to "What led up to this incident?" Rather than stating on an accident/incident report, "People were goofing around when they should not have been…," one would write, "Horseplay occurred between several participants and they were told on three occasions to stop." State facts without being subjective and limit speculation.

Well-designed accident/incident reports will have a space for the person completing the form to illustrate or draw the scenario, body part injured, or physical layout of the environment in which the incident occurred. In addi-

While parents or guardians are often asked to sign waivers on behalf of their minor children, parents or guardians may not sign away their children's rights.

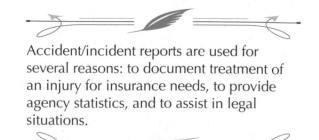

Accident/incident reports are used for several reasons: to document treatment of an injury for insurance needs, to provide agency statistics, and to assist in legal situations.

tion, information about the environment, the participants and witnesses, a factual description of what occurred, and the disposition of the incident should be provided (e.g., the participant was sent home, EMS was activated, damaged equipment was removed from the area).

Risk Management Checklist

Staff

Is the staff mature, responsible, respectful, and professional?	
Does the staff know and understand emergency procedures?	
Is the staff certified and/or properly trained to conduct the activity?	
Does the staff have good judgment (i.e., "Know what they know and what they don't know.")?	
Do staff members always put the safety of participants first?	
Do staff err on the side of safety?	
Do the staff provide proper supervision to all activities/ participants?	
Are the staff attentive to the program and participants?	
Has the staff played "What if?"	
Do staff members have access to medical forms?	

Activity

Is the activity developmentally appropriate?	
Does the activity require general or specific supervision?	
Do you have the appropriate number of staff needed for this activity?	
Has the activity been presented or taught in sequential order?	
Do you have enough materials to offer the program safely?	
Is there potential for participant-induced hazards (e.g., horseplay, fights)?	
Is the activity being conducted on or in a suitable area?	
Is safety emphasized when giving activity instructions?	
Have potential activity-associated risks been identified?	

Participants

Do the participants have a sense of self-care?	
Why are the participants in attendance?	
Do the participants understand the importance of safety?	
Do participants follow instructions?	
What is the group atmosphere like (e.g., respectful, careless, wild, calm)?	
What are the group norms with regard to treatment of group members?	
Do you have participants who:	
— abdicate self-responsibility?	
— consider themselves immortal?	
— are disengaged?	
Do participants have previous injuries or medical conditions that warrant consideration (e.g., epilepsy, allergic reaction to bee stings, bad knees, asthma)?	
Does each participant have a medical history form, release of treatment form, and release of participation form on file?	
Are participants properly attired for the activity and weather conditions?	

Equipment

Is the equipment in good working condition?	
Is the equipment being used as it was intended?	
Is the equipment appropriate for this age and group?	
Does this equipment have inherent hazards (e.g., earth ball, scuba gear)?	
Is it possible that this equipment will break or stop functioning in the middle of an activity?	
What are possible misuses of this equipment?	
Is it appropriate for participants to play on or with this equipment unsupervised?	
Is a first-aid kit available?	

Facility, Structure, and Grounds

	Facility/ Structure	Grounds
Are the lights in working order, and play areas well-lit?		
Is the play area clear of debris (e.g., paper, trash, broken glass, dirt)?		
Is the floor/are the grounds clear of water?		
Is the floor/are the grounds slippery?		
Is the ground surface smooth and free from holes and divots?		
Are obstacles clear from the playing area (e.g., unused equipment, tables, chairs, benches)?		
Are the grounds an appropriate place for this activity?		
Are the facilities appropriate for all weather conditions?		
Is there indoor access in case of inclement weather (e.g., humidity, lightning)?		
Does the leader have a clear view of all play areas?		
Is the area secure from unauthorized visitors?		
Are the structures in good working order?		
Do structures have any inherent hazards (e.g., exposed bolts, splinters, rough surfaces)?		
Where is the area in relation to potential danger zones (e.g., roads, bodies of water, electrical wires)?		
Is the facility clean?		
Where is the nearest emergency telephone?		
Is there access to drinking water?		

NOTES:

Figure 11.5 Risk management checklist

Assumption of Risk/ Agreement to Participate

An assumption of risk or agreement to participate form documents that participants know and understand the inherent hazards and possible injuries of participating in an activity. All activities have risks, although many are so common as to not warrant such a form. For instance, playground activities, swimming pool use, and attendance at athletic events are so common in society, there is little chance that an individual would not know and understand the risks involved in participation. Other activities, however, are less common and the average person would not be expected to know and understand the inherent risks. In these instances, an agreement to participate or assumption of risk (AOR) form would be desirable.

To be useful an AOR should describe in detail the nature of the activity, the expectations of the participants, and information about potential hazards. If on a canoe trip death by drowning is possible, include that information on the form. Some parks, recreation, and leisure services professionals have expressed concerns that identifying the extreme physical hazards of an activity might drive participants away, but this has not been the case (Herbert, 1997). A failure to describe and articulate all risks could limit the usefulness of this form.

In addition to describing the nature of the activity and all of its potential dangers, information about the expectations of the participants should be included. In this statement, participants are informed that they will be expected to follow rules and respond to the activity leader when called upon to do so. If participants need to provide written documentation of previous experience or skill level, include this requirement in the AOR. An agreement to participate form should also include a statement about the condition of the participants. If participant skill levels vary, this should be stated. If participants are expected to be in good physical health, this should also be stated.

Parental (Guardian) Permission

Parental or guardian permission forms solicit permission from parents and guardians for their children to engage in particular activities. Commonly, these forms are used as public relation tools to inform parents or guardians about upcoming events. Often, a generic permission form is used, but at times it is necessary to utilize activity specific forms. For instance, when a child is to be transported away from the primary location for a field trip, to engage in aquatic activities, or to participate in an activity which might be physically or emotionally trying for a youngster, specific forms identifying the particulars should be used. If a parent/guardian does not give permission or if a youngster does not return a signed form, she or he should not be allowed to participate.

Media Release

A media (e.g., photograph, video, recording) release form protects privacy and property interests. Particularly in the field of therapeutic recreation, issues of privacy are paramount. Permissions must be gained prior to publishing client photographs or video where individuals might be identifiable. Failure to do so could result in a lawsuit based on invasion of privacy.

Property rights relate to photographs and other recordings in that it is plausible that this type of media could be sold to a publisher resulting in a financial gain for the seller. Generally, the subject of the photo has rights to the use of her or his likeness in money-making ventures. It is always wise to gain permission from the subjects for use, whether it be issues of privacy or property.

Medical History

A medical history form is an important form to have on hand for extended sponsored activities (e.g., day camp, adult softball leagues, drop-in recreation), activities that require agency-provided travel (e.g., field trips), and activities where the participants have special needs (e.g., health concerns, physical/developmental/behavioral disabilities). In addition to the expected medical history, these forms commonly include a physician's signature (indicating good overall health), medical insurance information, and a permission-to-treat statement. A permission-to-treat statement authorizes medical treatment should the partici-

Figure 11.6 Recreation leaders will use a variety of forms designed to minimize risks.

pant be unable to speak for herself or himself. In the case of minors, parents or guardians indicate their permission to have their child treated should they be unavailable for immediate consultation.

For these forms to be effective, they must be readily available and be within the vicinity of the participant. For example, medical history forms should go with the group on a field trip and be located in a nearby office when activities are on-site.

Release/Waiver

In common usage the terms *release* and *waiver* are used interchangeably, and while the law makes a technical distinction between the two, for purposes of this text the terms will be used as one. A release or waiver is based in contract law. By signing a release or waiver, the participant indicates that she or he knows and understands the risks involved in an activity, chooses to engage in the experience in spite of those risks, and then through this contract, agrees not to hold the leader and agency liable for negligence. In most cases, as long as the contract was entered into legally and the language was clear and unambiguous, the waiver or release will be considered valid.

Summary

Understanding the basics of legal liability is critical to being a successful leader. Sound knowledge helps to minimize problems and increases enjoyment of leaders and participants. One of the primary tenets of legal liability is that anyone can sue any body for any thing at any time. In this light, leisure services leaders should strive to minimize leader negligence. For negligence based in tort law to exist, four elements must be present: duty, act/standard of care, proximate cause, and injury/damage.

A lack of supervision is the primary complaint identified in lawsuits. To be effective, leisure services leaders need to know when to use general, transitional, and specific supervision. The nature of the participants, activity, environment and leader combine to determine which level of supervision is required in what instance. Supervisors have five basic functions and are expected to be competent and in an appropriate location relative to the participants and area being supervised. A comprehensive supervision plan will go a long way in minimizing risks.

In conducting an activity, a leader is expected to have solid knowledge of the participants, activity, and the environment. With this knowledge, activity selection is easier, site inspections are focused, and the leader can make sound (and safe) decisions. Leaders use many forms in their efforts to minimize risk to an individual leader and

A release or waiver is based in contract law. By signing a release or waiver, the participant indicates that she or he knows and understands the risks involved in an activity, chooses to engage in the experience in spite of those risks, and then through this contract, agrees not to hold the leader and agency liable for negligence.

agency. These include parental permission forms, medical history forms, accident/incident reports, assumption of risk forms, releases/waivers, and media release forms.

This chapter introduced the concepts surrounding leadership and liability. Recreation and leisure services students and practitioners are encouraged to seek additional information pertinent to their own state and country, and continue to study this area.

Beginning the Journey

Risk management can seem like a rather technical area of study. Nonetheless, it is still an important content area for an effective leader to master. As you consider your own knowledge and understanding of risk management and fit that in with your journey to leadership, contemplate the following reflective questions.

1. What are the differences between criminal and civil (i.e., tort) law? With which one do parks and recreation professionals have the most concern? Were you surprised to learn that "any one can be sued by any body for any thing at any time?" Why or why not?

2. What is negligence and how does it relate to parks and recreation leadership? What are the four components of negligence? Describe each one to someone who does not understand legal issues.

3. Does a recreation leader *always* have a duty to participants? Explain your thoughts. How is the "reasonable and prudent professional" measured? Can you match up to this standard? What do you need to do to reach this standard?

4. Give an example of nonfeasance, misfeasance, and malfeasance. What can you do to minimize the likelihood of being charged with one of these acts? What is an act of omission? an act of commission?

5. How do proximate cause and injury/damages relate to leadership situations?

6. Draw a picture of the three different types of supervision. Which should you use in what situations? What is *in loco parentis* and what does it have to do with recreation leadership?

7. How does a supervisor demonstrate her or his competence? How competent are you to serve in a supervisory role? Explain. Go to a local agency or organization that provides leisure services and conduct a "supervisor audit." Go through the points raised in your text and evaluate the site based on these. What recommendations would you make for changes in the supervision system apparently in place at this site?

8. Study the functions of a supervisor so well that you can "rattle off" and describe them to someone who is being trained as a new supervisor. What would you suggest be included in a supervision plan? Develop an outline for a supervision plan and strive to complete it so that you can use it with an agency.

9. What are the three knowledge areas in which a leader is expected to be proficient in the conduct of an activity? On an index card develop a list of questions that you can use when in leadership situations to help you gain the information you need about the conduct of the activity. Be sure to include questions for all three areas.

10. Visit a variety of parks, recreation, and leisure services settings and collect the various risk management forms they use. Read and study them thoroughly and determine which meet the criteria for effective forms. Keep them for later use as you move into the profession. Besides the forms mentioned in the text, what other forms do you think are critical to maintain good risk management? How and when would they be used?

References

Cotten, D. and Wolohan, J. (2007). *Law for recreation and sport managers* (4th ed.). Dubuque, IA: Kendall/Hunt.

Dougherty, N., Goldberger, A., and Carpenter, L. (2002). *Sport, physical activity, and the law* (2nd ed.). Champaign, IL: Sagamore.

Gaskin, L. and Batista, P. (2007). Supervision. In D. Cotten and J. Wolohan (Eds.), *Law for recreation and sport managers* (4th ed., pp. 119–132). Dubuque, IA: Kendall/Hunt.

Herbert, D. (1997). Struggling with legal issues in a non-legal environment. *The Sports, Parks & Recreation Law Reporter, 10*(4), 59–60.

Hronek, B. and Spengler, J. (2002). *Legal liability in recreation and sports* (2nd ed.). Champaign, IL: Sagamore.

Peterson, J. and Hronek, B. (2003). *Risk management for park, recreation and leisure services* (4th ed.). Champaign, IL: Sagamore.

Simmons, R. (1998). The duty to provide proper instruction: An important component of risk management. *The Sports, Parks & Recreation Law Reporter, 12*(3), 38–40.

van der Smissen, B. (2007). Elements of negligence. In D. Cotten and J. Wolohan (Eds.), *Law for recreation and sport managers* (4th ed., pp. 36–45). Dubuque, IA: Kendall/Hunt.

Leader Profile

Andy Fernandez, CTRS
Manager, Adaptive Recreation, City of Eugene, Oregon Adaptive Recreation Services

Andy has 2 years in this position and more than 15 years in the parks, recreation, and leisure services profession.

Volunteer leadership positions he has held include:

- Accessibility Chair, Local Host Committee, National Recreation and Park Association Congress
- Program Co-Chair, National Institute on Recreation Inclusion
- Board of Directors, Pacific Southwest Regional Director, National Therapeutic Recreation Society (NTRS)
- NTRS representative to 1996 Paralympians World Congress
- President, Colorado Therapeutic Recreation Society
- U.S. Senator John Ensign's Disability Task Force Member
- FreeWheelin' Foundation Advisory Board member

What is the meaning of leadership?
Leaders are those who, when things are at their worst, are at their best.

What are the most important leadership qualities?
Ability to think outside the box, have an open mind, seize opportunity, be willing to risk failure, learn from mistakes, and share with others. Most importantly, a leader must stay positive, even in the face of adversity and criticism. It sounds simple, but most of us look for someone to motivate us and ensure us that we can do it—especially when we think we cannot.

What advice do you have for students who aspire to leadership in parks, recreation, and leisure services?
One of the biggest differences between you and the professionals you are studying is experience. Leaders have had to make tough on-the-job decisions and have been involved in scenarios and situations that have tested their skills and abilities. Every good leader learns from those experiences—the good, bad, and ugly—and then uses them as a tool for the next difficult decision or judgment call. Get involved early, take on responsibility, and get the experience you will need to use to your advantage later in your career.

Favorite books: **Baby and Childcare** by Dr. Benjamin Spock and *The Fool's Progress* by Edward Abbey

Favorite activities: Cycling and spending time with my family

Chapter Twelve
Direct Leadership Techniques

Learning Opportunities

Through studying this chapter readers will have the opportunity to

- Describe the many steps of preparing for leadership.
- Understand the importance of knowing demographic information about the group one is about to lead.
- Learn about four different levels of recreation goals.
- Practice writing goals and objectives.
- Outline a method of game and song leadership.
- Explore the idea of leading meetings.
- Consider key points to successful oral presentations.

One of the most exciting and enjoyable aspects of leisure services leadership is putting into practice all of the leader competencies one has learned. Being in front of a group, sharing one's talents and enthusiasm, teaching new skills, and helping people to achieve a higher quality of life is the highlight of the profession for many leisure services leaders. Part of this is because direct leaders have a tremendous impact on the groups and individuals they lead. A leader's personality and leadership style can incite people to stretch themselves and truly enjoy all of their leisure experiences—this is accomplished through direct leadership.

Direct leadership techniques are those methods and approaches used when leading individuals and groups in parks, recreation, and leisure settings. Direct leadership involves the act of working with a person or persons directly in a face-to-face situation. In the delivery of leisure services, examples of direct leadership include game and song leading, facilitating a leisure education session, giving a guided tour, coaching a youth sport, and leading exercise classes.

To be successful in leisure services, direct leadership skills are necessary. Understanding what goes on "in the trenches" and being successful at working directly with people are two of the most important aspects of success for leaders in the leisure services field. These techniques and skills are used in all leisure settings and with all ages of people.

Photo courtesy of Nina Roberts

To be successful in leisure services, direct leadership skills are necessary. Understanding what goes on "in the trenches" and being successful at working directly with people are two of the most important aspects of success for leaders in the leisure services field.

Being responsible for direct leadership involves establishing the environment, leading people in a variety of recreation and leisure activities, exploring different leadership styles, and applying theoretical concepts to situations that exist in the provision of leisure services. Successful leadership consists of three phases: *preparation, priming the group,* and *delivery.* Each of these phases will be discussed in this chapter.

Leadership Preparation—Phase I

Leadership and being an effective leader do not simply happen; a leader must make them happen. Every leader has her or his own style, methods, and competencies which make leadership work for her or him. Yet, within those personal styles, methods, and competencies common elements of leadership can be identified that help prepare a leader for successful face-to-face leadership.

Everyone has been in situations where ineffective leadership was recognized (e.g., the activity flopped, was disorganized, the environment was chaotic, people were bored), yet few have gone the next step to determine exactly what it was that led to that evaluation. If the leadership presentation and interactions were closely examined, one would likely notice that a hallmark of a good leadership was lacking—being prepared.

It becomes evident very quickly when a leader is ill-prepared for an activity or session. Whether it is facilitating a staff meeting, leading a group of senior citizens in low-impact exercises, or leading songs while waiting for an overdue bus, effective and ineffective leaders can be spotted easily. The ineffective leader comes in, sits down, and says, "So, what are we here to talk about?" An effective leader has an agenda prepared and a copy at each place. An ineffective leader fumbles about trying to decide how she or he wants the room to be set up, an effective leader has the chairs and room arranged prior to participant arrival. An ineffective leader does not know any songs and is trying in vain to maintain order; an effective leader is one around whom the children flock as they take turns leading songs.

This section of the chapter will help set the stage for effective leisure services leadership. Setting the stage is about being prepared. Among other things, good leaders are prepared for the people, the activities, and the unexpected. Leaders interact with people; most recreation leaders work primarily with groups, although there are situations where a leader works with only one or two leisure participants at one time. As a part of leader preparation, understanding something about the participants and the group will help ensure effective and upbeat leadership.

Group Composition

Knowing something about the group one is about to lead makes direct leadership much easier than if one goes in without any information whatsoever. The more a leader knows about a group, the better decisions she or he can make relative to appropriate leadership styles, type of communication, potential difficulties, and the probable needs and desires of the participants. As previously discussed, people of different ages, physical and/or mental abilities, sex, gender, sexual orientation, and ethnic background respond differently to different styles and techniques of leadership. To be best prepared, leisure services leaders might want to ask and answer several questions about the group composition prior to beginning. Questions might include the following:

- How large is the group?
- What is the approximate percentage of females and males in the group?
- What is the mix of ages of participants?
- Do any group members require special considerations due to physical or mental ability differences?
- How experienced are the participants with the planned activities?
- What are the group members' reasons for participation?
- Do group members know one another?
- Are medical histories available to the leader?

How large is the group?

Group size will impact preparation, implementation, and leadership style. Typically, large groups require more

Preparation can include ensuring that all participants are focused on the same task.

structure than small groups for a leader to maintain control. They also require additional equipment, time for breaking into smaller groups (if needed for the activity) and receiving instructions. Additional leaders may also be needed to help with supervision of activity leadership. On the other hand, smaller groups tend to complete activities more quickly than do larger groups and demand a higher level of social intimacy and attention from the leader.

What is the approximate percentage of females and males in the group?

This information is sometimes helpful in determining attitudes and comfort levels of participants. As previously discussed, females and males are socialized differently from one another, communicate somewhat distinctly, and have differing expectations of leaders. The effects of socialization last a lifetime, and this knowledge, combined with other information about a group, may give the leader a fairly good picture of what to expect. For instance, if there is a large percentage of boys in a group of thirteen- to fifteen-year-olds, a leader might expect an overall desire for sports and active leadership. On the other hand, if the group consists of women over fifty years old, there might be a stronger desire for socially oriented activities and a more subdued leadership style.

What is the mix of ages of participants?

Knowing the approximate ages (or age cohort) of group members helps a leader select appropriate leadership techniques based on knowledge about developmental maturity, level of sophistication, types of preferred activities, and appropriate complexity of rules. It has already been noted that leading children is different than leading teens and adults. A wide range of ages in one group presents special challenges for a leader to fully engage all participants as much as possible. For example, how a leader presents activity instructions, approaches behavior management, makes decisions, and addresses participant motivation all vary depending upon the ages of the participants.

Do any group members require special considerations due to physical or mental ability differences?

Full involvement of all group members should be a goal of parks, recreation, and leisure services leaders. A leader should always be prepared to adapt activities for someone with special needs; it is helpful to know of specific needs in advance. This information is not always available, however, and simply because one hears that none of the participants have special challenges does not negate the need to be prepared to adapt or change activities and leadership

techniques. For instance, if a leader knows in advance that one group member has poor hearing, she or he can prepare to present activity instructions through physical demonstration as well as verbally. In addition, it may be important to minimize potential noise distractions (e.g., poor acoustics, music playing in the background). Again, no matter what a leader knows ahead of time, she or he should be prepared to make changes based on the actual needs of the participants.

How experienced are the participants with the planned activities?

A leisure services leader can be much more effective if she or he knows whether participants are beginners, experts, or if the group is of mixed abilities. With this knowledge leadership techniques and activities can be modified appropriately to match skill levels and participant goals. As an example, novices may require closer leader supervision, more repetition, and more structure than those who have expertise in a particular activity. In addition, sequencing, pacing, and progression are impacted by previous participant experience, as are risk management concerns.

What are the group members' reasons for participation?

People participate in leisure activities for a variety of reasons: because they were invited to participate, their parents desired it, peer pressure, or they wanted to participate (also for a variety of reasons). Each reason has different implications for the level of readiness and motivations of participants as well as approaches leaders may take in their leadership efforts. If, for instance, a child has been forced to attend because her or his parents needed the supervised childcare, the child may not be positively motivated to participate. She or he may require much leader intervention to participate in an appropriate manner and gain maximum benefits of involvement.

Do group members know one another?

Group members who know one another have likely established some elements of group dynamics. Levels of trust, group roles, decision-making processes, and norms have probably been developed to some extent. This may be an advantage or disadvantage for the leader, depending upon the goals of the group, leader, and agency or organization. In previously formed groups the leader may be perceived as an outsider and may have to work to gain influence and be fully effective. In groups not yet formed, the leader often is influential in deciding the norms and internal processes from the beginning.

Are medical histories available to the leader?

The importance of this information may depend upon the nature of the organization and activity. In a therapeutic recreation setting knowing medical histories could be critical to successful leadership. In all settings, medical history forms for participants and staff members should be a prerequisite to field trips and other off-site trips or activities. A leader who has access to medical background information (as necessary) would be able to make decisions about both activities and leadership approaches that would be most effective and safe for all participants.

❖   ❖   ❖

Learning about a group prior to leading leisure service activities is one step to effective and successful leadership. A concerned leader will gather information about group composition and weigh it in relation to her or his own experiences, abilities, and limitations to determine appropriate styles and techniques to utilize. The more a leisure services leader knows about the people she or he is about to lead, the easier, more enjoyable, and successful she or he will likely be in guiding any activity.

Figure 12.1 Knowing the composition of one's group is a prerequisite to effective leadership.

A concerned leader will gather information about group composition and weigh it in relation to her or his own experiences, abilities, and limitations to determine appropriate styles and techniques to utilize. The more a leisure services leader knows about the people she or he is about to lead, the easier, more enjoyable, and successful she or he will likely be in guiding any activity.

Risk Management Considerations

In addition to understanding as much as possible about the participants one is about to lead, it is very important to consider and address issues of risk management. Knowing about the group can help a leader understand concerns of risk management related to the participants, the environment, and her or his own leadership skills and approaches. Effective risk management will protect not only the leader but also the participants, equipment, and facility.

As a competency of direct leadership, effective risk management begins with the development of policies and procedures designed for the health and safety of everyone and everything. Addressing the considerations identified in the following questions prior to engaging a group in leadership will help a leisure services leader ensure safe leisure activities.

Have you gone through the risk management checklist?

An example of a risk management checklist is presented in Chapter 11. To be fully prepared as a leader, all areas should be checked for and cleared of potential hazards. Both a visual and hands-on check should be conducted on a periodic basis as established by agency/organizational policies, and a visual check should be conducted in an activity area prior to each and every activity session.

Are the staff assigned to this direct leadership opportunity right for the job?

As a direct leader, knowing about the skills, temperament and limitations of oneself, as well as peer leaders, is vital to the safe conduct of activities. Utilizing individual strengths and managing limitations helps to spur staff growth and maintains a level of quality and safety for which all parks, recreation, and leisure services leaders should strive.

Knowing about the group can help a leader understand concerns of risk management related to the participants, the environment, and her or his own leadership skills and approaches.

Do you know enough about the participants to be safe?

Learning about group composition not only makes a leader's job easier but it is also an important risk management tool because it helps in activity selection and sequencing, decision making, behavior management, communication, and so on. A review of the chapter on human development and the planning questions in the previous section may help to ensure a thorough understanding.

Are the activities appropriate for the group?

Once having learned about the group composition and having checked safety issues, a leader may now turn her or his attention to the activities. Effective leaders will want to be sure that activities are age and developmentally appropriate, culturally sensitive to differences among group members, and meet the goals of the session.

What if...?

If done thoroughly, the preparation phase of direct leadership can be a lengthy process. In fact, preparation time often exceeds the time spent in direct leadership. With experience and practice solid preparation can become second nature. In addition to addressing preparation issues already mentioned, another aspect of direct leadership that is critical to being well-prepared is playing "What if?" *"What if?"* is an activity and a process that helps a leader to prepare for the unexpected.

Brainstorming questions, scenarios, and potential issues before they happen is a key to facilitating enjoyment, maintaining safety, and managing participant behaviors. Until one is practiced at it, it is best to engage as many people as possible in the generation of "What if?" questions and related issues. In addition to generating questions and issues, it is important to identify appropriate responses. Simply raising the questions without appropriate answers does little for leader readiness. Many "What if?" questions can be asked in preparation for the delivery of leisure services. For instance:

- *What if* someone has to go to the bathroom in the middle of presenting an activity? It is fairly com-

mon for many children to have to go to the bathroom when one child expresses the need. Will the entire activity be stopped for the whole group to go? Does the child have to be escorted to the restroom? (If in a public setting, this would be wise.) Is it possible for participants to come and go as they need? Where is the bathroom in relation to the activity space (e.g., distance, street-crossing hazards)?

- *What if* a participant forgets her or his lunch at an all-day event? If an activity is a full-day activity and a lunch is forgotten, leaders will want to be prepared to assist the hungry participant. Do the leaders bring extra fruit and bread to share? Does the agency provide emergency money for such contingencies? Will all participants be asked to share? Or is the participant left to go hungry?

- *What if* a minor does not bring a completed parental permission slip for a field trip? Parks, recreation, and leisure services organizations usually have strict policies on this issue. Permission slips are required for liability reasons, and allowing a child to participate without one can put the leader and agency at risk. What is your agency or organizational policy? Is the child sent home? What if parents are not at home? Is there someone available to stay with the child?

- *What if* a participant arrives early or late? Participants arrive at structured leisure activities at various times; some arrive 15 to 20 minutes early, while others arrive 15 to 20 minutes late. What do the

Figure 12.2 *What if?* prepares the leader for the unexpected.

early or late arrivals do? Are staff assigned to assist them? How long will an activity be postponed while waiting for latecomers?

- *What if* the facility is not accessible and a person who uses a wheelchair arrives to participate? Do you turn them away? Find an alternative location? Find some way to make a quick modification? Let them figure it out themselves?

- *What if* someone is not wearing appropriate footwear? What are the safety and participation implications?

- *What if* someone refuses to participate? Should she or he be "forced" to participate?

- *What if* someone gets injured or becomes ill? Is the emergency medical system in place? Do all leaders know what to do?

- *What if* a fight starts? Do the leaders break it up, call police, or report it? to whom?

- *What if* it begins to rain on an outdoor activity? Is the activity over? Is the activity moved? If so, to where? How will this be accomplished?

- *What if* the equipment breaks? Are there replacements available? Can it be repaired? Are repair materials and tools handy?

- *What if* the power goes out? What are the safety and participation implications?

- *What if...?*

❖ ❖ ❖

Asking and answering "What if?" questions will help to minimize hazards, maximize participant satisfaction, and make leadership easier and more enjoyable. After learning everything possible about the group, going through the risk management checklist, and playing "What if?" the next element of preparation is to consider and develop goals and objectives for the leadership session. Understanding participant goals and articulating leader goals and objectives will provide the focus and direction for the leisure experience.

Understanding participant goals and articulating leader goals and objectives will provide the focus and direction for the leisure experience.

Goals and Objectives

While therapeutic recreation specialists commonly articulate goals and objectives for clients, in many other areas of our field, direct leaders do not engage in this practice. For many years now, school teachers have been articulating and writing goals and objectives for their students, but in the leisure services field the connection between effective teaching and effective leadership is often missed. However, just as effective teaching is effective leadership, effective leadership involves effective teaching. During activities parks, recreation, and leisure services leaders may teach participants songs, games, or new leisure skills; thus, teaching is integral to leadership.

Goals and objectives are the bedrock of effective and sound leadership. They provide the structure around which leisure activities are built and help leisure services leaders define their tasks. An effective and well-prepared leader knows what she or he hopes to accomplish prior to engaging in the leadership experience. Among other impacts, this knowledge influences participant involvement, how instructions are given, and what group leadership techniques are used.

Goals

A goal may be short-term or long-term; it is a course of action that one intends to follow—an aim. Objectives are the steps to reaching the goal. A well-prepared leader is one who has a solid sense of the goals and objectives she or he hopes to accomplish. A lack of goals and objectives may result in aimless activities, unsatisfied participants, and ineffective leadership. Russell (2005) suggested four types of goals.

Societal goals. Societal goals are aims or ideals of a community; they often relate to issues of social justice and environmental stewardship. These goals tend to be culturally relevant (meaning they change with the times), and may or may not be in the best interest of all community members. Examples of societal goals include the goals of stopping child violence, preventing teenage parenthood, and maintaining a litter-free neighborhood. These goals may directly or indirectly impact the provision of leisure services. In fact, it is quite common for leisure programs to follow in the wake of articulated social goals. An example of this is the rise in 24-hour programming in response to shift work.

Professional goals. These goals relate to several subcomponents that expressly impact face-to-face leaders: professionalism, performance standards (including certification), and ethical behaviors. A high level of dedication and commitment to the organization and the profession will facilitate personal development in these areas. Leaders who have professional goals strive to meet professional standards as evidenced by ongoing personal evaluations and gaining appropriate certifications. In addition, exhibiting personal values and ethics that are in line with those adopted by the profession are other types of professional goals.

Agency or organizational goals. Agency or organizational goals are those espoused by the parks and recreation agency or organization. Often, these goals are identified in the mission statement or a statement of purpose. Agency/organization goals might include things such as: to make a profit; to provide the highest quality services at the lowest price; and to see that all people, no matter their socioeconomic status, receive the benefits of leisure services. As an example, one goal of Special Olympics International (SOI) is to provide sports training to help develop physical fitness for people over eight years of age who have mental retardation. This goal drives the specific program goals and objectives of SOI. If an agency is tax supported, its goals typically will be in line with the prevailing societal goals and norms of the local community.

Participant goals. Participant goals are quite diverse. People may desire to participate in leisure to exercise, to learn a new skill, to be with others, to do something different, to experience excitement, to respond to peer or parental pressure, and for many other reasons. As the leader, it usually is best to focus on one or two participant goals in the planning and leading of programs. As an example, an SOI participant may have a personal goal to improve skills specific to a particular sport—in order to address this participant goal, a leader will first have to be aware of the participant's desire for improvement.

To provide structure and focus to leisure experiences, an effective leader identifies the goals and objectives of each activity. Oftentimes goals and objectives are established for an entire day, week, or session. For maximum effectiveness it is important that a direct leader's goals and objectives be compatible with the goals and objectives of the agency/organization for which she or he is working. Goals are broad statements that describe the anticipated or desired behaviors of participants. Common participant leisure goals include the following:

- *Skill/Knowledge development.* Skill development can include physical skills such as dancing, fly fishing, jumping, or painting; it can also include cognitive skills such as critical thinking, recognition, or memory. Knowledge development includes such elements as local history, rules of a game, or obtaining factual information about natural phenomena such as stargazing or plant succession. A session or activity that has skill or knowledge development as a goal will encourage teaching and practice sessions. A skill and/or knowledge development goal will tend to dictate that information and activities be presented in such a progression as to allow participants time to develop an understanding of basic material and competencies prior to moving on to more complex skills and knowledge.

- *Interpersonal skills* (e.g., decision making, problem solving, communication) and social goals (e.g., being with others, sharing, helping) are common reasons people participate in a wide variety of leisure experiences. Enhancing the likelihood that these types of goals will be met is often a secondary aim of leisure services leadership. This may be accomplished through manipulating the physical environment and purposefully planning activities that will enhance these types of goals.

- *Democratic living skills* (e.g., cooperation, ideals of fair play, equality) may be the focus of leisure activities for a variety of people. Through leisure, where fun and enjoyment are the primary foci, lessons about being a good sport, how to win

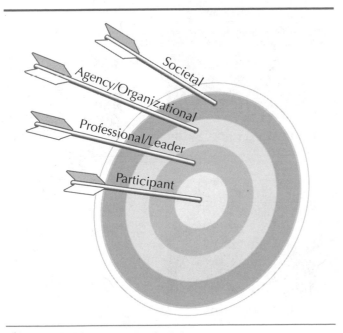

Figure 12.3 Four types of goals

Goals are broad statements that describe the anticipated or desired behaviors of participants.

graciously, lose with dignity, and work together are learned and practiced.

- *To have fun and serve as diversionary (i.e., non-utilitarian) activity* is a perfectly legitimate goal of recreation and leisure activities. In fact, many participate in leisure experiences with having fun as the primary goal. This enhances health and quality of life in a number of ways.

- *Health benefits.* Many people engage in leisure for the physical exercise and mental health benefits derived from participation. Physical exercise makes participants feel better physically, emotionally and mentally. The health and wellness benefits of many leisure activities are tremendous. Physical exercise is often seen as a secondary goal or positive "bonus benefit" of leisure participation by many participants.

People engage in leisure for a variety of reasons and have a variety of goals for which they aim. As a leader, it is pefectly acceptable (although it can be confusing, initially) to work toward more than one goal at a time. To meet each goal leisure services leaders develop objectives, which are the stepping stones to achieving goals.

Objectives

Objectives serve as the practical and identifiable steps to reaching goals. If one were to picture a staircase, objectives would be the individual steps and the goal would be at the top of the stairs. Each step can have three different types of objectives: *cognitive, behavioral,* and *affective* (Bloom, 1956). *Cognitive* objectives are those that deal with thinking, *behavioral* objectives deal with physical actions and skills, and *affective* objectives deal with feelings and emotions.

In leisure services all three objectives are addressed through direct leadership although one may be more emphasized than another. For instance, in working with the frail elderly one might focus on cognitive objectives dealing with mental stimulation and memory retention; participants in rehabilitation may focus on objectives such as coordination and strength; and when working with children with developmental disabilities a leisure services leader might focus on affective objectives such as sharing and cooperation.

As steps to goals, objectives are statements that indicate very specific actions to be taken to help meet the goal. They are necessary elements of program or treatment plans. In leadership, articulating the goal or general purpose of what one does first is important for structure; clearly stating the related objectives helps make goals achievable.

While writing objectives can be a challenge to learn, practicing and learning how to write them are well worth the effort. To those just learning how to write objectives, practice and feedback become very important to successful writing and use of objectives. In essence, objectives may be defined as specific, measurable statements needed to

Skill Development

Interpersonal Skills

Democratic Living Skills

To Have Fun

Health Benefits

Figure 12.4 Common types of participant goals

reach a goal. In that light, objectives must be related to goals. Thinking *SMART* helps a leader to remember that objectives are:

S = Specific
M = Measurable
A = Achievable
R = Realistic
T = Trackable

If any one of these individual components is missing or weak, the objectives will not be as effective as they need to be. Writing down objectives as they are developed aids in focusing the leader, and provides a framework and reasoning for leadership actions taken. The aim of writing objectives, whether they be cognitive, behavioral, or affective, is to design them in such a way that if they were turned into a question, an individual could answer without hesitation, "Yes" or "No." If the best answer is "sort of" or "maybe," the objective is not written as specifically as needed.

ABCDs of Writing Behavioral Objectives

To aid in the development and writing of objectives, some people find it helpful to follow the ABCD method. Remember, objectives go hand-in-hand with goals. Thus, prior to writing objectives, one must know the goal for which one is striving. Since objectives are the steps to achieving goals they must be specific, measurable and meaningful. Objectives are used to serve as guideposts to measure whether or not an individual has done the action named in the objective.

Writing an objective is much like writing a sentence—there is a *subject, verb, object,* and *modifier*—and every objective must have all these components. In this case, the subject is *who* will do the behavior, the *what* is the verb (or behavior the subject will be doing), the *how* is the object that explains the behavior to be done, and *how well* corresponds to the modifier. These elements are the *ABCD*s of writing objectives and are further defined here:

As steps to goals, objectives are statements that indicate very specific actions to be taken to help meet the goal.

A = Audience

The audience identifies *who* is doing the action or behavior described in the objective. The audience should be identified as specifically as possible. Audiences commonly found in leisure and recreation objectives include campers, children, participants, swimmers, clients, runners, players, adults, guests, customers, teens, and other terms that describe an individual or group of people. For example,

The participant....

B = Behavior

The behavior is the *action* the audience must do — It is the verb and is required in a behavioral objective. There should be only one verb or behavior in each objective; otherwise, the objective is extremely difficult to measure. Common behaviors in leisure and recreation objectives include throw, hop, jump, count, answer, demonstrate, build, run, lift, read, speak, introduce, play, sing, take initiative, control her or his emotions, collaborate, and other actions or behaviors common to the accomplishment of a particular leisure task. For example,

The participant *will introduce three group members to the rest of the group....*

C = Condition or Criterion

A condition helps to *describe* the behavior in specific terms. Anything that serves to further identify the behavior in the objective is considered a condition. Often, a condition can be recognized by the way it describes how or when an action is to be accomplished. For instance, if an

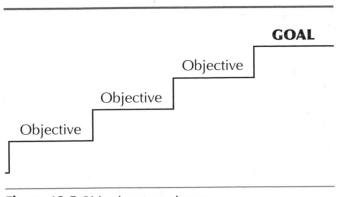

Figure 12.5 Objectives as stairsteps

Cognitive   Behavioral   Affective

Figure 12.6 Three types of objectives

objective specified that the audience was to throw a ball, how would participants throw it (e.g., overhand, underhand, with two hands)? In addition, what kind of ball must they throw (e.g., a football, basketball, playground ball, tennis ball, Koosh ball)? When will the throwing occur (e.g., by the last session, before the session is over, by the end of the season, at the beginning)?

Several authors further characterize this element of an objective by identifying possible types of conditions or criteria (Shank & Coyle, 2002; Stumbo & Peterson, 2004). The types of conditions are listed along with an example (in the parentheses):

- Amount of time (…within five minutes)
- Degree of accuracy (…within two feet of the end line)
- Degree of assistance (…without any assistance from the leader)
- Form (…using the correct formation as described in the playbook)
- Number of trials (…4 out of 5 times)
- Percentages or fractions (…70% of the time)
- Specific subskills (as evidenced by being able to make eye contact, remember the other person's name, respond appropriately to another person's statements, and so forth)

Continuing with the objective we are developing, an example would be

The participant will introduce three group members to the rest of the group *by saying each person's name and identifying her or his favorite leisure activities….*

D = Degree

The degree in an objective describes *how well* the behavior will be accomplished. To what degree of competence will the audience be held? Various ways of stating degrees include such things as 90% of the time, with fewer than four errors, without any leader prompts, without losing her balance, and so on. The degree must match the behavior—it should answer the question, "How well must the audience do the behavior?" Therefore, if the action is throwing, how well must the person throw (e.g., hitting the target 8 out of 10 times)? If singing is the behavior, how well must the individual sing (e.g., without any mistakes)? If playing jacks and the goal is improved social skills, the degree might be "without arguing over lost points." As an example,

The participant will introduce three group members to the rest of the group by saying each person's name and identifying those members' favorite leisure activities *without making a mistake.*

❖ ❖ ❖

Leaders who get in the practice of writing goals and objectives will be well prepared to address the needs and wishes

---

Table 12A Sample verbs for use in writing objectives

Cognitive (thinking and knowledge)		Behavioral (actions and skills)		Affective (feelings and attitudes)	
analyze	exemplify	catch	recognize	accept	express loyalty
apply	explain	draw	roll	acknowledge	follow
assess	identify	grasp	run	advocate	group
combine	illustrate	hit	sing	assist	obey
compare	interpret	hop	sit	assume responsibility	organize
conclude	justify	jump	skip	be aware	prefer
construct	label	leap	smell	care for	rank
contrast	list	listen	stand	choose	respond
define	name	observe	step	comply	show concern
describe	plan	pick up	strum	contribute	support
design	recall	pivot	swim	control	value
differentiate	select	plant	swing	cooperate	volunteer
evaluate		play	talk	express emotions	
		read	touch		

The degree must match the behavior— It should answer the question, "How well must the audience do the behavior?"

of their participants. The preparation that is done as goals and objectives are written help a leader to consider many of the "What if?" questions. Competence in writing goals and objectives demonstrates a professional commitment to the groups with which a leader works. In particular, those in therapeutic recreation or who are working in the inclusion field will need to develop some proficiency in this skill area to meet the needs of the participants (and meet the requirements of the treatment or inclusion plan). Figure 12.7 presents a flow chart to aid in writing objectives.

Setting the Tone

Setting the tone is a very important skill, and the responsibility for it rests with the leader. This stage of leadership begins in leader preparation and continues through the second phase of Priming the Group. It is integral to the planning and preparation component of leadership. One way leaders begin to set the tone is by manipulating the environment. Leaders manipulate (in a positive sense) situations, people, and activities all the time. In fact, those who are highly skilled at positive manipulation are often very successful leaders; participants seem to lead themselves. Positive manipulation, then, is the artful handling of an environment or situation to positively influence a leisure experience.

An effective leader manipulates the environment to set the mood, to encourage participation, and to make general leadership easier. Leaders purposefully arrange the physical environment to enhance the socioemotional and psychological elements of leisure settings. The *socioemotional* element is concerned with individuals' feelings of belonging, affection, comfort, and acceptance. All of these elements are very important to successful leisure service experiences. Positive affect is developed through manipulating the physical and activity environment. The *psycho-*

Positive manipulation, then, is the artful handling of an environment or situation to positively influence a leisure experience.

logical environment involves feelings of identity, achievement, and mastery. By changing the physical environment, leaders can contribute to meeting the diverse needs of participants.

An effective leader might consider altering the physical environment in the following ways:

- The use of color in leisure settings is a subtle, but highly effective way to manipulate the physical environment for social and psychological purposes. "Hot" colors (e.g., red, orange, yellow) tend to increase both cognitive and behavioral activity levels, while "cool" colors (e.g., green, blue, violet)

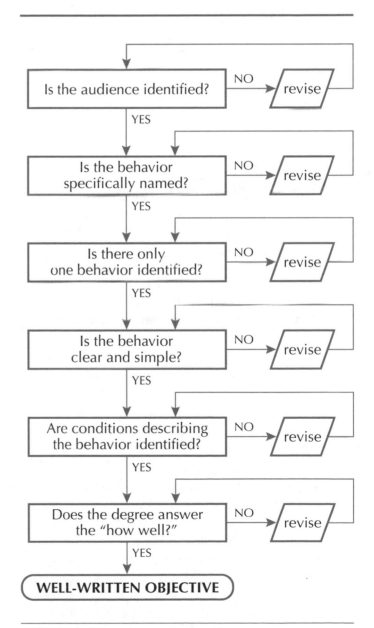

Figure 12.7 To determine if an objective is well-written and meets needed criteria, ask these questions (adapted from Mager, 1984)

tend to induce a calmer, more quiet response. In addition, bright colors tend to excite participants while pastels and muted colors help to maintain a more relaxed atmosphere. Leaders would be wise to decide what is appropriate to meet the desired goals and objectives, and manipulate the environment to meet them.

- Lighting is another physical element that can be manipulated; it is often used to enhance socioemotional responses in participants. Bright, white lights set a mood of excitement and alertness while softer lighting can set a mood for intimacy and group closeness. For example, we rarely see bright fluorescent lights at dance clubs—It makes more sense to have bright lights for a crafts project.

- Noise, sounds, and music also affect the mood and atmosphere of a leisure setting. Amusement parks, malls, and eating establishments have been using various types of sounds, noises, music, and colors to enhance our buying and eating habits for years. Loudness, style of tunes, and tonal quality all impact how people feel about others, the activity, and the situation.

- Artwork, murals, posters, pictures, and the use of various media contribute to the atmosphere as well. Involving participants in the creation of wall hangings can enhance a variety of emotions and, at the same time, create a feeling of ownership. Often, leaders cannot change the color of the activity space, but the effect can be accomplished through the use of colorful pictures, posters, and wall hangings.

- Arrange space and equipment for maximum safety. This involves following a risk management checklist and putting away or guarding hazards (e.g., benches or chairs in a gymnasium). Separating incompatible structures and activities is an important consideration in arranging space for safety.

- Arrange space and equipment for maximum efficiency by having equipment and structures to be used in a convenient location. Has the needed gear and equipment been arranged nearby, yet is it out of the way of other activities?

- Arrange activity space and equipment for maximum effectiveness. It is not particularly effective to have an activity that utilizes loud music next to an area to be used for individual skill instruction (this seems to happen all too frequently). A tip for leisure services leaders is when giving instructions (or simply trying to talk to an individual) for an activity in an area where there are many potential distractions, arrange and focus the group on the leader. As the leader, stand in a corner or constrained space and arrange the group so they face you and are less likely to be distracted by other stimuli.

- Consider the type, size and shape of the open space. How will it be utilized to its maximum benefit and usefulness for the anticipated participants?

❖ ❖ ❖

Helpful Hints

- Do unto others as they would want to be done unto.
- Involving participants (especially children) in decision-making processes takes extra time; do it anyway.
- Ask questions that will require more than a yes/no response.
- Never ask a question if you are not prepared for the answer.
- If out-of-doors, let the group face the leader; the leader faces the sun.
- Avoid wearing dark glasses (unless for safety), it hides your eyes from participants.
- Flexibility and being able to respond in ambiguous situations are hallmarks of good leaders.
- Always end an activity while the participants are having fun.
- Safety should never be compromised, nor negotiated.
- End an activity on a positive note, even if the participants were not always positive.
- Love the person; it is okay to dislike the behavior.
- Provide structured choices.
- Power is like love—the more one gives away, the more one has.
- Be aware of your surroundings, arrange participants to minimize outside distractions.
- All children need to run, jump, and scream—Let them.
- Always be honest with children, teens, and adults.
- Adult logic and reasoning does not always make sense to a child.
- Participants will be excited about things leaders are excited about.
- Remind yourself (and other adults) to *play* every once in a while.

Figure 12.8 Helpful hints for successful leadership

As one can see, from manipulating the physical environment to articulating goals and objectives, playing "What if?" when attending to risk management concerns, and learning about the group one is about to lead, there is quite a bit to do prior to ever meeting the group. This preparation phase is essentially the first "contact" a leader has with a group and is very important to the overall success of the leader. Once well-prepared, a leader is then ready to meet the participants and engage in the second phase of direct leadership—priming the group.

Priming the Group—Phase II

Phase II of leadership in parks, recreation, and leisure services is priming the group for an activity, song, or other type of leisure session. Completing preparation steps first will provide the information a leader needs for selecting the types of leadership techniques that will be most effective in the anticipated situations. Priming the group includes getting a group's attention, dividing a group into subgroups, and learning participant names.

In general, it is best to think of ways to accomplish the priming tasks that are fun, experiential (i.e., active and interactive), and integrated into the actual activity. This will help to keep things from feeling choppy, thereby increasing leader effectiveness and participant satisfaction. The examples for the various priming elements provided below are appropriate for adults, children, and people of different physical and mental abilities. Understanding the group culture helps make for an understanding leader. It is during these initial priming minutes that the tone is set for the remainder of the leadership interaction. In addition, it is during this phase that leaders will make an impression (first, and often lasting) on participants; thus, this is a critical phase for successful leadership.

Getting a Group's Attention

Prior to beginning an activity with a group, part of the leader's role is to get the group's attention. Initially, getting a group's attention may be a bit chaotic. Particularly in large groups, there is a lot of noise, fidgeting, and movement as people expectantly await the start of an activity.

Priming the group includes getting a group's attention, dividing a group into subgroups, and learning participant names.

An effective leader strives to use this excitement as the group moves into the conduct of the activity itself.

Recreation and leisure activities should be fun and enjoyable for all; fun is one of the defining elements of a recreation experience. Therefore, techniques where a leader stares a group into quiet submission, incessantly blows a whistle, or berates individuals with voice tone and, "Quiet please," are antithetical to meeting the goal of having fun and promoting the leisure ideal.

Basic principles for activities used in priming a group include being:

- fun
- unexpected
- respectful
- experiential

Making some type of loud noise is a common method of getting a group's attention. If this is the leader's preferred technique, it should be as fun and unique as possible. One noisemaker to avoid is a traditional whistle; a traditional whistle is loud, piercing, and reminds many people of authority figures (e.g., referees, police officers) for whom they do not necessarily hold positive leisure connotations. Using a nontraditional noisemaker such as a party horn, a drum, or a dinner (or cow) bell maintains a level of fun, is unique, and is usually unexpected. It is best to use a noisemaker that utilizes low tones and pitches; high-pitched whistles and horns are difficult to hear for some people. In addition, the louder high-pitched whistles

Recreation and leisure activities should be fun and enjoyable for all; fun is one of the defining elements of a recreation experience.

Photo courtesy of Gwynn Powell

When a group is in a circle formation, everyone is on equal footing.

Basic principles for activities used in priming
a group include being:

- fun
- unexpected
- respectful
- experiential

are, the more shrill and displeasing they sound. Leisure
services leaders will want to experiment with a variety
of noisemakers, and use them sparingly—Frequent use of
a noisemaker may lessen its effectiveness at getting a
group's attention.

Dividing Groups

For some activities or because of the nature of the participants it may be necessary to divide the group into smaller
subgroups. Again, leaders are challenged to remember that
leisure settings should have an element of joy and fun—
even when dividing a group into subgroups. Following the
same guidelines as mentioned for getting a group's attention, dividing a group should be fun, enjoyable, experiential, and leave people with their dignity; this requires
conscious thought and planning on the part of the leader.
It is particularly helpful if the methods used for dividing
a group relate to the goals and objectives of the session.
If a primary goal is to enhance social skills, the leader will
want the group to divide in such a way as to facilitate
social interactions. If skill development is a goal, dividing
a large group into groups where skills can be developed
(e.g., people of like skills and abilities together in one
group) will be important. Likewise, if maximum participation is a goal, then subgroups should reflect that need.
There are many ways to divide a large group into smaller
groups that are creative, equitable, and do not negatively
impact participant self-esteem. It is the leader's responsibility to learn, practice and select methods that enhance,
rather than detract from, the larger leisure experience.

Several techniques for dividing groups should be
avoided in most leisure settings: using team captains,
counting off, and dividing by sex. At one time in many of
our lives we have experienced someone dividing a group
by using team captains. As a child (or adult), being the last
one chosen can be a hurtful and humiliating experience.
There are few, if any, circumstances in leisure services
that warrant using this method to divide a large group
into smaller ones.

Another undesirable technique used to divide a large
group is by counting off. This is commonly used in school
systems, and when used with children often will evoke a

There are many ways to divide a large
group into smaller groups that are creative,
equitable, and do not negatively impact
participant self-esteem. It is the leader's
responsibility to learn, practice and select
methods that enhance, rather than detract
from, the larger leisure experience.

flurry of activity as youngsters quickly try to realign so
as to be in the same group as their best friend. Used with
adults, counting off may be viewed as childish and paternalistic. An advantage to counting off when dividing a
group, however, is that it is a time-efficient way to break
a large group into smaller ones. If time is running short,
counting off may be an acceptable technique to dividing
a group; it should be used sparingly.

Yet another less than desirable technique of dividing
a large group into several small groups is to divide by
sex—females in one group and males in the other. Unless
for an activity-based purpose or to meet a particular goal,
this method of pitting females and males against one
another often perpetuates stereotypes of "us versus them"
and may establish a negative tone within the group.

Learning Names

Success in leadership is a combination of many things, one
of which is earning the respect of participants. People like
and respect those whom they believe like and respect
them. One way to show this is by using people's names,
and by using and pronouncing names the way people wish
to be called. For example, an individual who introduces
herself as Tomika should be called Tomika, not Tommi
or some other derivative that the leader feels is cute, nice,
or easier to pronounce.

Learning names is a task often overlooked (it is assumed it will simply happen) or completed very quickly
and without a lot of innovation. This may be due to time
constraints, inappropriate assumptions, or inexperience on
the part of the leader, but learning names of individuals
is vital to the enjoyment and productivity of the group.
Calling, "Hey, you in the green-striped shirt" is both
disrespectful and oftentimes ineffective in actually getting
that person's attention. Leaders have the opportunity to
facilitate the learning of participant names for themselves
as well as other participants. Leaving the learning of names
up to individual participants may result in group members
who are uncomfortable, lack trust among themselves, and

Success in leadership is a combination of many things, one of which is earning the respect of participants. People like and respect those whom they believe like and respect them. One way to show this is by using people's names, and by using and pronouncing names the way people wish to be called.

are slow to come together; this may result in the leisure environment feeling somewhat stilted and uncomfortable. A leader can remedy this situation through planning and using creative activities to facilitate the learning of everyone's names.

At this stage the leisure services leader has completed preparation for the leadership session and has primed the group. It is now time to provide activity instructions or directions to participants. Leaders are reminded that throughout this process, considerations and modifications should be made to accommodate the needs of the group based on the characteristics of the participants.

Delivery—Phase III

Once the preliminary tasks of being prepared, getting a group's attention, dividing a group, and learning names has occurred, it is time to move into the delivery phase of the activity. Delivery refers to the aspects of activity and song leadership that involve introducing an activity and giving directions or instructions to participants so they can play.

Leading games and activities is part art and part science. The art of leadership includes the intangible qualities of leadership that are critical to success such as using sound judgment; integrating one's personality into activity leadership; and having a positive, upbeat attitude. These leadership elements are difficult to teach and are acquired and internalized over time.

The science aspect of activity leadership can be readily taught. It involves following a series of steps and much proper planning. Children and adults can be taught these steps as they begin to lead others in a variety of games, sports, arts-and-crafts, and drama events.

Introducing an Activity

Introducing an activity, song, or leisure experience continues to refine the tone that was established when the

Learning names of individuals is vital to the enjoyment and productivity of the group.

group was learning names and dividing into smaller subgroups. Typically, a leader does four things when introducing an activity: (a) identifies herself or himself, (b) identifies the activity, (c) explains the object or goal of the activity (e.g., to score goals, to cooperate, to run from here to there), and (d) tells a short story (i.e., fact or fiction) to help set the mood of the activity.

Leader Introduction

An oversight of many leisure services leaders is to neglect to introduce or reintroduce themselves when they work with participants. Staff members who have worked at a particular organization or agency for a long time often have the mistaken belief that everyone knows their names. Since group members continuously change in leisure settings, the leader will want to ensure that everyone knows her or his name; thus, it may be best to introduce oneself at the beginning of each session.

Name the Activity

After introducing oneself to participants most leaders will then tell participants the name of the activity or song. This is to help participants understand and put into context what is coming next. Bear in mind that although some people might say that they have played "this game" all of their lives, they may know a version different from the one you are about to introduce. Leaders should not assume people know how to play even "standard" activities or sing common songs. There are many local variations in activities, and various tunes and melodies for common songs.

Identify the Goal of the Activity

Prior to beginning an activity, it is best to remind or tell participants about the aim of the activity. This serves to

The art of leadership includes the intangible qualities of leadership that are critical to success such as using sound judgment, integrating one's personality into activity leadership, and having a positive and upbeat attitude.

ensure that everyone is aiming for the same goal. While the leader may have "to enhance social interaction among participants" as a goal, the goal that is shared with participants at this point is the goal of the activity. For example, although a leader may select checkers as an appropriate activity to increase fine-motor control in the hands, at this time participants would be told that the goal of checkers is for one player to take all of her or his opponent's pieces before the opponent takes her or his pieces.

Tell a Story

After clearly stating the goal of the activity, it becomes important to further establish the mood (i.e., the leader has already altered the physical environment to maximize the desired activities and affect). This is often accomplished through telling a short story (i.e., 60 seconds or less). The story might be fact or fiction, and its purpose is to engage participants, to draw them in, to get them "psyched." Using all of her or his enthusiasm, a leader might personalize the story (e.g., "I used to play this when I was younger," "My great-great grandmother taught me this."), make it pure fantasy (e.g., "Picture the days of long ago, when dragons ruled the skies;" "A UFO landed in a field and creatures I had never seen before got out of the spaceship"), or teach with the story (e.g., "This game originated in Africa and was played by people during the harvest season."). The story helps to set the mood and accomplish the leader's goals for the day.

Giving Directions

Once the activity has been introduced it is time to give participants the directions for how to play. As stated earlier, a leader should be careful not to assume, and not to allow others to assume, that they know how to play a particular activity. Games, activities, and songs have many variations, and it is usually important for participants to be playing by the same rules. In stating directions or guidelines for an activity, a leader might remember the following acronyms: *KISS, KIP* and *PLAY*.

KISS

Keep It Short and Simple is the most important guideline for giving directions for activities and songs. An effective leader will speak in clear, unambiguous language, say what she or he means, then stop. This of course, requires that a leader be very familiar with the activity. A leader who is unfamiliar with the activity instructions often will hesitate, give contradictory instructions, and otherwise confuse the participants. Well-prepared leaders will have played the activity and practiced their leadership of it prior to leading it.

KIP

Keep It Positive is another guideline for effective leadership. This refers to stating the rules of an activity in a *do* rather than *do not* fashion. For example, teen centers often post rules—no smoking, no drugs, no cursing, no fighting, no horseplay. This long list of what one cannot do can set a negative tone before the leader even introduces herself or himself.

Without explicit directions about the desired behaviors, people will often generate their own ideas. In addition, constantly being told to not do things may leave a person feeling small and powerless. If leaders state rules in a positive fashion, they will likely be better respected and, therefore, effective. Leisure services leaders should get into the habit of telling people what they can do when leading activities.

PLAY

PLAY means just what is says. Once the leader gives enough instruction to participate safely and within necessary guidelines, leaders should stop talking and allow participants to play, sing, experience, or otherwise participate. Whether it be a crafts class for senior citizens, sports in a youth league, or aquatic movement in a rehabilitation setting, leisure services leaders need to get out of the way and let people play. Play is when participants are engaged in the leisure experience, and it is when objectives and goals are being met; it is influenced by leadership.

Photo courtesy of Deb Jordan

At times, the best way to give instructions for an activity is to model it with the participant.

Leading Songs

Leading songs is much like leading activities in that the techniques described above work equally well with either. The important thing to recognize about song leading is that one does not have to know how to sing (e.g., be able to carry a tune) to be an effective song leader. Many great recreational song leaders are not at all musically inclined.

Music, particularly singing, is an element that in and of itself is joyful and uplifting; it is difficult to sing and be somber. Singing can be a magical element in any setting and with all ages. Singing can be used during down time, as a start up activity, and as part of closing an event or day. It can help get participants energized, calm them down, or get them in a particular mood.

As with activity leadership, when leading songs leaders should begin with a leader introduction, name the song, tell a story, and then give directions. If a round is to be sung, it will be necessary to divide into a number of groups. Leaders may choose to divide the group into subgroups after learning names or after singing the entire song through once.

Sing the Song Through Once in Its Entirety

So that participants have a context, it is usually best for the leader to sing the entire song through once, using hand and body motions as appropriate. This might be done alone, or with the assistance of participants from the group; more than three assistants may make it difficult for listeners to make out the words of the song.

Steps to Leading Songs

When analyzed step-by-step, leading songs commonly follows these steps:

1. Once the participants have heard and seen the song (and motions) the leader sings a verse and has the group repeat line-by-line.

2. Depending upon the length of the song and the abilities of the group, the leader may wish to sing two lines at a time and have the group repeat.

3. Sing the entire song through with the participants.

4. If there are hand or body motions in the song, the leader goes through the song again, using the

One does not have to know how to sing (i.e., be able to carry a tune) to be an effective song leader. Many great recreational song leaders are not at all musically inclined.

motions. Making one motion at a time and having the group imitate it allows for learning by demonstration. Depending upon the length of the song and the abilities of the group, the leader may wish to sing two lines at a time with the motions and have the group repeat and imitate.

5. Sing and act out the entire song. The song should be sung a minimum of twice through to help all participants to best learn the song.

Teaching a Song in a Round

There are a few extra steps to teaching and leading a song to be sung in a round:

1. A round is usually sung as many times as there are groups. This evens things out so that every group has an opportunity to sing the song through the same number of times.

2. Follow the steps listed for song leading

3. Once the entire group has "a handle on" the song, divide the group into appropriate numbers. Three groups are most common, but depending upon the age group and the song, this may be adjusted up or down.

4. It is the leader's job to engage all participants in singing their part of the round at the appropriate times. An engaging leader will use her or his entire body to engage the group. By physically moving from group to group, using grand arm and hand

Photo courtesy of Deb Jordan

Music can be joyous and uplifting, and all leaders can become good song leaders.

gestures, and mouthing the words in front of each group so the members are sure when it is their turn to sing, a leader can enthusiastically engage the subgroups.

Transitions

Transitions are psychological links between two or more different experiences which help smooth out leadership and interactions with the group. Transitions provide the connection between activities, programs, or sessions in a leisure setting. They serve to maintain momentum in activities, help to reassert leader positioning, and provide a psychological bridge so participants feel comfortable with where they are and where they are going. Commonly, transitions are verbal links made by the leader; they occur between the phases of activity leadership and between activities themselves.

Transitions often link activities together by what is similar between them. For instance, if the group was moving from playing wallyball to playing crab soccer, a leader might make a transition by commenting on the use of the ball: "We just finished playing a game that used a small ball; now we are going to play an activity that uses a large ball." Leaders may also use transitions to comment on what is different between activities: "We just finished playing a game where we used our hands; now we are going to play an activity where we use our feet." Some transitions include a combination of commenting on similar and dissimilar elements: "We just finished playing a game that used a small ball where we got to use our hands; now we are going to play an activity that uses a large ball, and instead of our hands, we'll use our feet."

Whatever the preferred technique, transitions are important to the effective leadership of any activity or session. Transitions are used within activities, between activities, and even between activity sessions. Effective use of transitions tends to lead to increased participant satisfaction.

Concluding a Leadership Session

Some activities come to their own natural conclusion with very little effort on behalf of the leader. Others require the leader to provide direction to the wrap-up of the activity or session. Usually, it is best to stop playing while people are still having fun. This way participants will want to re-engage in that leisure experience at another time. A solid and well-planned method to conclude activities or leisure sessions is just as important as a strong beginning to the activity. Poor conclusions occur when there is a lack of planning and a lack of focus by the leader. Weak conclusions are endings that leave participants hanging, wondering if the session is really over, or if there is more yet to come.

The conclusion is a leader's last opportunity (at this session) to influence the leisure experience. It is a time that can be used to bring people together, to summarize, to leave people with positive feelings, and to leave participants wanting more. If the event or day has been competitive, for example, and individuals are feeling less than friendly and supportive toward one another, at the conclusion the leader might emphasize the strengths of each group member. In addition, the leader can guide the group into summarizing the events of the day and do a quick review of how things went.

Furthermore, a conclusion serves as an opportunity for participants to leave the experience on an upbeat note. It is fine to acknowledge difficulties, whether they are leader or participant generated, yet speaking in positive terms will leave participants feeling good about the experience. "I know we had a difficult time getting started, but once we got going, the group came together and...."

One of the more critical elements of a successful conclusion is that it be definitive. People need to know something is over when it is over. Whether the leader leads the group in a rousing cheer or comments about things accomplished, a concluding statement should be made which leaves no room for doubt about the session being over.

❖ ❖ ❖

The direct leadership techniques of preparation, priming the group, and delivery are used in activity leadership, the

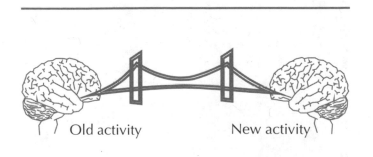

Figure 12.9 Transitions serve as psychological bridges between steps of an activity and between different activities.

Whatever the preferred technique, transitions are important to the effective leadership of any activity or session. Transitions are used within activities, between activities, and even between activity sessions.

It is best to stop playing while people are still having fun. This way participants will want to re-engage in that leisure experience at another time. A solid and well-planned method to conclude activities or leisure sessions is just as important as a strong beginning to the activity.

implementation of treatments, instructional sessions, and other leader-to-participant interactions. Consciously engaging in these three phases of leadership will facilitate successful leadership experiences. Other settings exist where leaders will be involved in direct leadership with others—holding meetings and making oral presentations. This next section of this chapter presents information to help leaders be successful in these two venues.

Conducting Successful Meetings

In addition to leading activities and songs, leisure services leaders will often be asked to lead or facilitate meetings. Meetings might be held with sport league coaches, fellow staff, boards of directors, treatment teams, and the public, among others. Having appropriate leadership skills to facilitate a meeting in a firm task- and people-focused fashion is necessary for effective and efficient meeting leadership. Time, resources, and people are much too valuable to waste in disorganized or unnecessary meetings.

Leisure services leaders and participants are often involved in multiple tasks simultaneously; therefore, it is desirable to hold meetings that are purposeful, succinct, and held only when necessary. Meetings are called for a variety of reasons, which include: when various components of a team project need to be coordinated (e.g., special event); when information needs to be shared among a group of people with similar responsibilities (e.g., youth sport coaches) and leaders need to share information with everyone; when messages sent out via email are getting too complicated, lengthy, or generating confusion; when it is necessary to engage in a rich or in-depth multi-directional conversation; and when problems or difficulties arise (Schlegel, 2005). Certainly, leaders will want to avoid calling meetings when there is no agenda (i.e., nothing to talk about)—even if a meeting is regularly scheduled for that date and time. Announcements often can be made quite efficiently via written memoranda or through electronic postings.

It is desirable to hold meetings that are purposeful, succinct, and held only when necessary.

Generally, meetings are either formal or informal in structure. The nature of the meeting usually dictates the level of formality. For instance, advisory board meetings for public parks and recreation departments are often required by law or ordinance to follow a formal, predefined structure. These meetings typically fall under open meetings laws, which stipulate when and how business can be conducted.

Formal meetings commonly follow *Robert's Rules of Order* to maintain flow and an organized structure. These meeting rules control who speaks when, how to make and decide a motion, what material may be considered at what time during the meeting, and they serve to manage other meeting functions in an organized and predictable manner. There are several good resources available in local libraries and bookstores that explain *Robert's Rules of Order* in an easy-to-follow format. Informal meetings are a bit more free-flowing and allow people to freely interact as needs arise. Many leaders prefer to conduct meetings by loosely following *Robert's Rules of Order* to maintain an organized and friendly tone.

Prior to the Meeting

Meeting leaders are expected to accomplish several tasks—some are addressed prior to a meeting being held, other tasks occur during the meeting, and there are follow-up tasks to attend to as well. An effective and efficient

Figure 12.10 All leaders are involved in meetings.

leader plans ahead for all meetings—even emergency meetings. During the planning phase the leader decides the purpose of the meeting, who is to be in attendance, where the meeting will take place, how the room is to be arranged, when the meeting is to be held (and for how long), and how the meeting is to be conducted. In addition, the leader will provide meeting participants with needed information such as resources and an agenda prior to the meeting—this requires careful forethought.

Bearing in mind that people are very busy, an effective and efficient leader will notify participants of a meeting at least one week ahead of the meeting date. This notification should include the meeting date, time, location, general purpose, and any background information. It is also common at this phase to include a tentative agenda and request additional agenda items from attendees. An agenda serves to provide enough information so that meeting participants arrive at the meeting prepared to address the issues. Handouts and background information supplement the agenda and help attendees to all start "on the same page." By sending these materials out well ahead of the meeting time and date, participants can prepare and be conscientious in their treatment of each item.

The Meeting Agenda

If any changes are made to the original, a final agenda should be received by all invited participants a minimum of two days ahead of time unless an emergency meeting is being called. When developing the agenda it will be necessary to make an educated guess regarding the length of time needed for each item during the meeting; the leader will strive to select material to fit within the allotted time period without rushing through agenda items. An agenda typically includes the following information:

- The heading centered at the top of the page: AGENDA

- The name of the group that is meeting: centered at the top of the page

- Date of the meeting: centered at the top of the page

- Time of the start and end of the meeting: centered at the top of the page

- Location of the meeting: centered at the top of the page

- Purpose statement: the general purpose of the meeting. This provides a focus to the meeting and helps to keep participants on track.

- Introduction of any guests (e.g., reporters, members of the general public, invited speakers)

- Acceptance of minutes: At the beginning of each meeting it is common to review and accept the

Bearing in mind that people are very busy, an effective and efficient leader will notify participants of a meeting at least one week ahead of the meeting date.

minutes from the previous meeting. Oftentimes, corrections are made, noted in the current minutes, and then the old minutes are accepted. If this is the first meeting of the group, there will be no previous minutes to approve.

- Old business: Any business not finished from a previous meeting is placed on the agenda. This includes items that were tabled, those that required additional discussion or fact-finding, or items that were carried over from the last meeting. If this is the first meeting of a group, there will be no old business.

- New business: This includes any material to be addressed in the current meeting, not previously discussed.

- Other items: This could include general reports from subcommittees or miscellaneous items that do not fit well in another above category.

- Announcements: information to be shared for which discussion and group decisions are not needed. Typically, dates and times of upcoming events, due dates, and factual information (e.g., the location of the policy manual) are listed as announcements.

During a meeting the agenda is used as a guide to help participants (and the leader) focus on the tasks to be addressed in the meeting. While agendas can be extremely helpful when used in this fashion, leaders would be wise to remember that flexibility remains important. A change in the agenda or flow of the meeting does not necessarily mean the meeting is being run poorly—it may simply indicate a responsiveness to the needs of those in attendance. See Figure 12.11 for a sample agenda.

During the Meeting

The leader sets the tone for each and every meeting. As with activity and song leadership, some of the tone may be partially accomplished through the physical environment. The arrangement of the meeting room serves to direct communication and reinforce the nature of the meeting. Many meetings are held sitting at a long rectangular conference table, with the leader seated at one end (i.e., the head of the table). This arrangement directs communication and attention to the leader and minimizes, but allows, conversations between participants. A meeting held at a round table, on the other hand, encourages equal participation among those in attendance. Other meetings that have a strong one-way information sharing purpose (i.e., the leader has information to pass on to participants) may be held in a room arranged like a traditional classroom (i.e., theater style) with the leader at the front of the room and participants in desks or chairs, all facing the leader. The purpose of the meeting, leader style, and desired participant involvement combine to influence meeting room arrangement. Regardless of the seating arrangement, a leader may wish to provide extra sets of agendas and background information for those who forget to bring their copies with them.

In addition to determining room arrangement, a meeting leader also sets the tone with regard to punctuality, staying on task, and developing and maintaining an atmosphere of friendliness and respect. To help establish an atmosphere of trust and participation, it is useful to begin with introductions—even if it is believed that everyone knows one another. Next, go over the agenda and ask for changes or additions to it. Establish or reiterate the meeting ground rules—the need to stay on task and the mechanism in place to assist that occurrence, the use of *Robert's Rules of Order*, a reminder that the leader's job is to facilitate movement in thoughts and ideas, and so on.

Some leaders find it helpful to set aside a couple of minutes at the beginning of a meeting to socialize. By allowing the first few minutes of a meeting for socializing, the need to visit and catch up with one another is addressed. It is important to be clear about the intent of this time so that the actual business component of the meeting can begin on time. For many, beginning a meeting late is an indication of a lack of respect for the participants and the value of their time. For these individuals nothing is worse than to have to wait for latecomers. Leaders might begin with a reminder about announcements (found on the agenda), and make it clear that everyone is responsible (for themselves) to know what occurs at meetings once a meeting is scheduled to begin.

Prior to beginning the actual conduct of the meeting it is necessary to identify an individual to record minutes. This individual may be a secretary, clerical staff member or any member of the group—it is common for individuals in meetings to rotate turns in taking minutes. *Minutes* are the official record of

---

National Hispanic Cultural Center
Advisory Board Meeting
AGENDA
28 August 2008
NHCC, 1701 4th Street, SW
6:30–8:00pm

Purpose of the meeting: Regular monthly meeting of the NHCC Advisory Board.

I. Call the meeting to order
II. Roll call
III. Introduction of guests
IV. Acceptance of previous minutes
V. Old Business
   A. Update on planning for upcoming events
      1. Locations (offsite locations or within the Center)
      2. Programs
      3. Financing
      4. Marketing and promotion
      5. Additional help or resources needed
   B. Building renovations
      1. Progress and timelines
      2. ADA compliance
VI. New Business
   A. Financial issues
      1. Budget update
      2. Grants in progress
      3. Fundraising efforts (donations and sponsorships)
      4. Program fees
   B. Volunteers
      1. Recruitment
      2. Training and staff development
      3. Recognition for service
   C. Upcoming and future exhibits
VII. Additional agenda items and items for future agendas
VIII. Announcements
     Staff changes, new hours, visiting scholars, next meeting

This agenda is available in alternative formats.
Esta agenda está disponible en español.

Figure 12.11 Sample agenda

The purpose of the meeting, leader style, and desired participant involvement combine to influence meeting room arrangement.

what occurred during the meeting and will serve to inform others of those events.

During a meeting the leader's job is to facilitate communication and complete the agenda. To accomplish this it is necessary to direct and manage the flow of conversation and the tone of the meeting. The agenda will help to focus participants on the meeting tasks, and as much as is reasonable, it should be followed. Having an agenda and not following it at all can leave meeting participants feeling unsettled and confused.

In addition to allowing the agenda to serve as a meeting guide, part of the leader's role is to manage the flow of communication during the meeting. This does not mean that a leader must use an autocratic leadership style; rather, it means that the leader controls the flow of the meeting. To accomplish this there are times when the leader will be required to interrupt others while they are speaking. The leader owes a responsibility to each member of the meeting team to encourage equal involvement. Thus, at times the leader will invite comments from specific individuals while at other times the leader may need to intervene if any one individual seems to be monopolizing the meeting.

If it is necessary to interrupt someone who is transgressing into an unrelated tangent, someone who is repeating thoughts already heard (unless doing so for clarification) or someone who is rudely addressing other meeting participants, a leader should do so with respect. For example, "Excuse me, I appreciate your participation in this meeting, but we need to return to the agenda" may serve to get things back on track. If necessary, the leader may call a short recess and speak to the offending individual away from others and ask her or him to allow for other voices to be heard.

Part of the responsibility owed to each person in the meeting is to include everyone in the meeting activities. A meeting leader may need to draw certain individuals into the meeting by asking for their opinions directly or by taking turns around the room voicing opinions or sharing information. By playing the role of gatekeeper, the leader can be sure that each person is heard on each agenda item. Once agenda items are discussed, information shared, and motions and decisions made, the leader should move the group on to the next agenda item. By moving through

The leader owes a responsibility to each member of the meeting team to encourage equal involvement. Thus, at times the leader will invite comments from specific individuals while at other times the leader may need to intervene if any one individual seems to be monopolizing the meeting.

each agenda item this way, the meeting can end at its scheduled time.

Many meetings have a set, or standing, meeting time (e.g., the second Tuesday of every month) and are slated to last 60 minutes. Whenever the meeting is scheduled to end, the meeting leader should make all attempts to end the meeting at that time. Participants will have planned other tasks and meetings around this one and this should be respected. If people do not trust that the leader is going to end the meeting on time, they may act out in a variety of ways. To conclude a meeting on time, it is not uncommon to have to eliminate some items from of the agenda; a good deal of leader flexibility is needed throughout the meeting. If there is ample reason to run overtime, the leader should alert meeting participants as soon as this becomes apparent so that arrangements may be made to either move items earlier on the agenda, or for people to make arrangements to change their schedules. In any event, the leader should strive to end the meeting on an upbeat note.

A Note about Diversity

A diverse work group tends to balance one another and be effective in accomplishing tasks. At the same time, cultural differences in the ways people view the world can impact the way meetings are conducted, or the perceptions of those in attendance. Gardenswartz and Rowe (1998) offer general guidance with regard to some of these differences:

- If some in attendance hold the view that one does not challenge the group leader, the boss, or an elder, they may not be comfortable in sharing alternative viewpoints; they may also remain quiet even though they might have a solution to a particular problem. A leader will want to be clear about expectations for participation. It may be important to explain the need for full involvement in terms of the benefits to the agency or organization.

- If only a few individuals hold a collectivist perspective while the majority holds an individualist perspective, misunderstandings could occur due to people being unwilling to stand out or seek individual recognition. By focusing on the efforts of one as contributing to the whole, a leader may capitalize on this viewpoint.

- People for whom "losing face" is a concern may not be willing to take risks due to a concern of failing. By recognizing mistakes as part of development and clearly articulating this to group members (and demonstrating this philosophy with words and actions), group members will begin to develop trust and be more willing to take risks.

- If there are differences within the group with regard to a view of time (i.e., linear and punctual vs. more cyclical and "loose"), a leader will want to be very explicit about expectations and follow through with any rules related to starting on time. By positioning a need for punctuality (if this is the case) within a framework of respect for others in the group, this issue can often be alleviated.

After the Meeting

Schlegel (2005) cautions leaders to be aware of the "meeting-after-the meeting." This is the informal "hanging out" that occurs after a meeting has officially ended. In some cases where open meeting laws apply, these non-public meetings can be problematic in terms of legality. During these small gatherings, questions, issues, or concerns are expressed that were not communicated in the meeting itself; these types of conversations can undermine what was accomplished in the larger group. It is best to curtail these unofficial meetings, if at all possible. Ask the individuals to bring the issues up to the entire group or offer another mechanism for their voices to be heard. At the least, a leader will want to be aware of the issues that people raise and try to integrate those concerns in future meetings.

Periodically leaders will want to evaluate the meetings, particularly regularly scheduled meetings. This may be done verbally, in writing, or both. By asking staff members how they think meetings are going, the leader receives valuable participant input and can make adjustments in future meetings. Ask participants to respond to such questions as: What are we spending too much time on? not enough time on? What types of things should be covered that we are not covering? Are people satisfied with the meetings? Why or why not? Do individuals feel that their voices are heard? that they are treated with respect? By involving meeting participants in developing evaluation questions and conducting an evaluation every fourth or fifth meeting, a leader can improve her or his own meeting leadership.

By recognizing mistakes as part of development and clearly articulating this to group members (and demonstrating this philosophy with words and actions), group members will begin to develop trust and be more willing to take risks.

Minutes

Minutes are the official record of what occurred during the meeting. To be as useful as possible, minutes should be distributed to meeting participants, as well as those who were unable to attend the meeting, within one week after the meeting was held. It was stated earlier that minutes are recorded during the meeting by either a secretary or a participating group member. This individual takes notes throughout the meeting and, after the meeting, summarizes them in a concise fashion. Common practice is for the leader or committee chair to review draft minutes for accuracy and completeness before sending the minutes on to others. The intent is to provide minutes that are detailed enough so that those who were not in attendance can understand the gist of what occurred and what actions were taken, yet succinct enough so as not to be overwhelming to the reader.

Typically minutes mirror the agenda and include the following items:

- Centered on the page the heading: MINUTES
- The name of the group that met: centered at the top of the page
- Date the meeting was held: centered at the top of the page
- Time of the actual start and end times of the meeting: centered at the top of the page
- Location of the meeting: centered at the top of the page
- Roll call: List the names of those present, those absent, and those excused
- List names of guests in attendance: A guest is any invited or drop-in individual who is usually non-voting, yet has a particular interest in the meeting information.
- Acceptance of minutes: At the beginning of each minutes it is common to indicate that the previous minutes were reviewed and accepted. Minutes are either "accepted as is" (with no corrections), or "with corrections (as noted)."

- Action items: Action items are identified throughout the minutes and stand out from other material. They serve as reminders to participants to complete a task. Action items are tasks that need specific action by participants by a specific date (often prior to the next meeting). For instance, "ACTION ITEM: Each group member will develop a team roster and bring enough copies of it to share with other coaches at the next meeting."

- Old business: A summary of information identified as old business on the agenda. If a lengthy discussion occurred over a particular item, it is common to record it as, "A lengthy discussion ensued surrounding risk management around the pool area. It was decided that…." If, for example, two or three major issues or viewpoints were discussed in the meeting, those might be summarized in this section.

- New business: As with old business, this section of the minutes includes discussion and decisions that were raised in the meeting under this heading.

- Other items: A summary of the miscellaneous items that did not fit well in another category.

- Announcements: A reminder list of announcements from the agenda, plus any new announcements that were raised at the meeting.

- Next scheduled meeting: Commonly listed at the bottom (and in the same place on every set of minutes) is the date, time, and location of the next meeting.

- Submitted by: Whether minutes were recorded by agency staff or a meeting group member, it is important to identify the name of the recorder. In this way, should a question or need for clarification arise, the appropriate individual might be found easily. See Figure 12.12.

To share in ownership of meetings, some meeting leaders like to rotate responsibility for facilitating meetings. To accomplish this, the leader works in conjunction with the meeting facilitator in developing the agenda and in establishing meeting protocols and ground rules but allows that individual to facilitate the business of the meeting. This helps others to understand the importance of the meetings and to appreciate the work that goes into preparing for them. Another technique is to delegate certain components of the meeting to individual participants so that several people are actively involved in the meeting process. The leader should bear in mind that, ultimately, it is her or his responsibility to facilitate the meetings as efficiently and effectively as possible.

Virtual Meetings

Virtual meetings are those conducted with meeting participants at a physical distance from one another. They follow the same general guidelines as face-to-face meetings. Virtual meetings might be in the form of teleconferences, which are conference calls (e.g., everyone is on a phone); videoconferences where members who are geographically spread out can see and interact with one another in real time through video technology; or online meetings that utilize Internet software to have written real-time conversations or chats (i.e., instant messaging).

Any time a teleconference call is utilized, a moderator should be identified. This individual is usually the person who sets up the date and time of the call, establishes the common number to dial into, and ensures that all parties have the necessary information to join in the call. If more than three people are going to be involved, it is common practice to use a teleconference service. An operator accepts the individual calls and establishes the multi-line connections. Since the parties cannot see one another and because voices can sound alike on the phone, prior to speaking teleconference members will want to identify themselves by name; for example, "This is Franco, I think that we…"

For a videoconference to be effective and efficient, individual desktop computers might have cameras mounted on them which allow for this modality to be used, or a specially "wired" room may be utilized which allows people to see and be seen through phone, video, and other high-speed connections. In these situations cameras and phone or voice-over-internet-protocol (VOIP) are available in each room, and all parties can see and hear one another.

Instant messaging can be effective for short term "conversations," but it can be time-consuming to type messages for a complex or lengthy meeting. In addition, the receiver may not be able to determine the intended "tone" of the sender in the written message. Further, a number of people may try to communicate at once resulting in confusion or stilted communication. Thus, Internet-based instant messaging is best used only for short meetings where there is a well-defined goal and a limited number of participants.

Virtual meetings can be advantageous in that meetings can be called quickly, people can meet while at

Virtual meetings are those conducted with meeting participants at a physical distance from one another.

MINUTES
YWCA Board Meeting
Marriott–Airport, Kansas City, MO
3 October 2009
5:30 p.m. – 8:30 p.m.

1.0 Meeting was called to order at 5:35 p.m.

Present: Chris Brown, Wan-Chung Wong, Georgia Neilson, Daleesha Pullman, Noe Garcia, Mikael O'Brien, Roberta Kimberowski (ex-officio)

Guest: Jorge Watson (The *Local Times* Newspaper)

Absent: None

1.4 Roberta Kimberowski moved, Chris Brown seconded, to accept minutes of 3 and 4 January 2008 as is. Motion carried.

1.5 Changes in the agenda

Noe Garcia asked to begin meeting with information about Expansion Project.

Discussion about mission statement was moved up on the agenda to item 2.8.

Discuss dates/location of next meeting—added to the agenda.

Discussion—Expansion Project: YWCA began first week of project, re: gathering of YWCA constituencies. Strategic Planning group examining YWCA as it is now, examining mission of YWCA, barriers to success. First year of grant is to investigate constituencies (community agencies, resources) to determine YWCA needs and opportunities. Look at the development and implementation of new models rather than simply expanding the existing model. Suggestions to allow for models that get at youth worker development education vs. nonprofit management/administration education (existing YWCA certification). Agencies express desire for entry level professionals who are grant writers, managers, fund raisers; not direct care youth workers.

Mailing List: Noe Garcia distributed mailing list (names and quantity) information. Agency personnel make up ½ to ¾ of the list. A list of about 800 names are on a library list; Daleesha Pullman has another 100 or so. Possibility of readership survey, agency survey for interest in the newsletter. All 12 YWCA affiliated agencies are on the list. Do not know if all youth/human service agencies are on the list. Discussion ensued about methods for maintaining current lists.

ACTION ITEM: Georgia Neilson will follow up on this and report back by e-mail by the end of the month.

Newsletter is being developed for YWCA by Daleesha Pullman and Wan-Chung Wong with help from the editor of the *Local Times* newspaper; the first one is being sent out this month. It will include information updates, new Board members, article on the conference, update on YWCA happenings, article on planned giving opportunities. Readership consists of: 5-year donor list, alums, members. Intent is to distribute the newsletter quarterly (perhaps only 3 this year). Suggestion to focus each issue on different concerns.

Newsletter should:

(1) include information to explain the mission of the YWCA,

(2) promulgate knowledge that influences profession practice (how-to material),

(3) promote the advancement of knowledge through research—practitioner friendly, i.e., implications for professional practice.

Use regular columns to meet needs of quick information needed now. Layout will help with catching, drawing in leaders, telling them "this piece is readable."

The purpose statement of the Newsletter is being revised to reflect the following thoughts: the Advisory Board will seek to encourage a free exchange of ideas from a variety of perspectives. The submission and equitable treatment of all material submitted. Within the editorial content of the newsletter freedom of press, intellectual discourse, dialogue, breadth of ideas, inquiry must be allowed. The newsletter will seek to address a variety of issues, perspectives, and view points without bias. The newsletter will serve as a forum to discuss issues, concerns, concepts that reflect a diversity of ideas, perspectives and viewpoints. Once accepted by the YWCA Board, this statement will be included on the first page.

There is a need to conduct a reader survey—who reads, why, what they get out of it, etc., could use focus groups. A thorough and useful survey would take a year of development.

ACTION ITEM: Mikael O'Brien will gather background information so we can reconsider in the future.

ACTION ITEM: Potential dates for next YWCA meeting: February 3, 4, 5 or 10, 11, 12. Arrive Friday evening, meet all day Saturday, leave Sunday morning, Wan-Chung Wong will check on dates/location and get back to us within two weeks.

Meeting adjourned 8:25 p.m.

Minutes submitted by Roberta Kimberowski

Figure 12.12 Sample minutes

their desks (or at least away from a single location), they tend to take less time than in-person meetings, and people who might not ordinarily speak out at a face-to-face meeting might be more prone to share and stand their ground on various issues (Adler & Elmhorst, 1999). Drawbacks to virtual meetings include less access to immediate feedback and increased chance of miscommunication. In addition, if individuals do not have access to the required technology, don't know how to use it, or experience technical problems during the meeting, they will be severely limited in their ability to participate. Nonetheless, virtual meetings are on the increase as travel becomes increasingly expensive and technology continues to advance.

❖ ❖ ❖

Leaders in all settings within parks, recreation, and leisure services will lead both formal and informal games, songs, activities, therapy sessions, and meetings. Another type of leadership activity commonly engaged in by leaders is the formal oral presentation. Generally, formal presentations require the same preparation and skills as other types of leadership.

Effective Oral Presentations

Leaders make oral presentations all the time—whenever they teach a song or give activity instructions they are engaged in presenting information to others. Leaders also may be called upon to give a more formal presentation at a staff meeting, an in-service training, or to the city council. The good news is that many of the same principles that apply to leading an activity also apply to making an oral presentation. An effective oral presentation requires thorough preparation, practice, and a solid delivery.

Preparation

As with activity leadership, preparation for an oral presentation requires knowing one's self, the audience, the purpose and goals, and the environment (or setting). Knowing one's self involves acknowledging personal abilities and limitations including one's technical skills, interpersonal skills, and conceptual skills. Effective presentation skills include

- *Technical skills* such as knowledge of the topic, technical equipment used as part of the presentation, speaking ability, and making appropriate use of the space and room arrangement
- *Interpersonal skills* such as active listening, having a positive attitude, understanding the audience, empathy and the ability to connect with others

Many of the same principles that apply to leading an activity also apply to making an oral presentation— thorough preparation, practice, and a solid delivery.

- *Conceptual skills* such as the ability to apply one's knowledge of diversity, creativity, goal setting, and group dynamics to the presentation

Know the Topic

Every oral presentation requires that the presenter have a solid knowledge base of the topic to be shared. Whatever the topic, knowing the pertinent facts and figures, understanding how the material is applicable to the audience, and being able to relate to similar topics is necessary. This can require hours of background work ahead of the actual presentation. Because they are confident in the content of the presentation, well-prepared speakers tend to be smooth in their articulation of ideas and readily handle questions from the audience.

Know the Reason for the Presentation

When you make your presentation are you trying to: persuade the audience? inform the audience? motivate the audience? teach the audience? The purpose of the presentation impacts the delivery, content, and timing. It will change the way the speaker shares ideas, the order in which the material is presented, the methods used to deliver the talk, and even the level of formality used in the presentation.

Know the Audience

As with preparing to lead an activity, knowing something about the audience aids leaders in presenting suitable information in the most appropriate style. This includes knowing what will get and keep the audience's attention, when and how to best involve the audience in the presentation, and how to anticipate potential questions. Anticipating questions is very much like playing "What if?" in activity preparation. For example, "What if someone asks me for a concrete example?" "What if someone doesn't understand something on the handouts?" "What if someone challenges the facts and figures I have?" By preparing in advance a leader can be confident that she or he will be able to respond correctly and with composure.

Know the Technology

While presentations may be made without the use of supporting technology, it is not uncommon for a presenter to use a computer program, overhead projector, the Internet, a DVD, or simple handouts to provide additional information related to the presentation. Whatever one chooses to use, a well-prepared leader will want to be familiar enough with the equipment (e.g., LCD projector, computer, overhead projector, document camera) so that she or he can successfully troubleshoot it should something go awry. This includes knowing how to hook up one's computer with a projector, knowing how to mirror the monitors, knowing how to change a light bulb in the projector, and knowing how to use the software. Regardless of the level of familiarity with technology, having a backup of the presentation in an alternative medium, or at least on an alternative storage device (e.g., CD, flash drive, hard drive) is important.

Organize the Presentation

Depending upon method of delivery, the audience, the purpose of the presentation, time constraints, and so on, a leader might present information in a slightly different flow. In general, however, organizing a presentation involves preparing an introduction, the body of the presentation, and the conclusion. It is important to develop these components with time periods in mind. For instance, if making a 30-minute presentation, one might want to limit the introduction to no more than five minutes, plan for 15 minutes devoted to the body of the presentation, five minutes for questions, and five minutes for a wrap-up.

An effective introduction gets the attention of the audience and sets the stage for the material to come. Many have been told that it is best to begin with a joke, but this should only be done if it fits the audience, purpose, and personal skills of the leader. Usually it is best to simply provide a quick overview of what is to be shared and give some context to the content of the talk. The introduction is essentially the "first impression" one makes with the audience and should be treated with due diligence.

Preparation

Delivery

Transitions

+ Conclusions

EFFECTIVE PRESENTATION

Figure 12.13 Effective presentations involve the same elements as activity leadership.

Practice. Practice. Practice.

Few people can effectively improvise a presentation. The rest of us have to thoroughly prepare and practice ahead of time to ensure that our presentation will fit within the given time limits, feel comfortable with the flow and organization of our talk, and know the material well enough that we will not be tempted to read from our notes.

If possible, practice in the room in which you will be presenting and with the equipment you will be using. At the very least, arrive at the presentation site 15 to 30 minutes ahead of time to check the room arrangement, the lighting (and your ability to adjust the lighting), the room temperature, and that the support equipment and materials are ready and working.

❖ ❖ ❖

Preparation is a key element in making a successful presentation. As with all types of leadership, paying attention to the details on the front end makes the actual presentation run smoothly and professionally. Thinking through the why, what, where, when, with whom, and how of making a presentation will assist a leader in being perceived as credible, trustworthy, and competent—all desired qualities for any successful leader. After the background work has been done, a leader is ready to deliver the presentation; just as with the preparation phase, there are many factors to consider in the delivery stage.

Delivery

The delivery phase of an oral presentation consists of several components, some of which include: one's personal appearance and presence, the style of communication one uses, the grammar and language one chooses, the effective use of questions and pauses, and the other elements of communication embedded in an oral presentation.

Personal Appearance and Presence

While it may not be necessary to be dressed in formal business attire, no matter the setting a presenter will want to be dressed neatly and appropriately for the session. A good rule of thumb is to dress "one notch above" how the audience will be dressed. This aids in speaker credibility and the comfort level of the audience. Thus, if one is presenting at a staff meeting in the middle of the summer and

An effective introduction gets the attention of the audience and sets the stage for the material to come.

everyone will be dressed in shorts and t-shirts, the presenter might consider wearing in a collared short-sleeve shirt and dress shorts. If the presentation is to be to the board of directors, treatment team, or city council, business attire might be more appropriate.

In addition to dress, the way a person carries her or himself makes an impact during a presentation. Standing tall, smiling, keeping one's hands out of one's pockets, not fidgeting, using appropriate gestures, and making eye contact send a message of confidence and credibility to the audience. If using a podium, stand up straight behind it and avoid leaning either on the top or on the side. If the speaker is short and the podium tall, she or he may wish to stand on a small step. On the other hand, if the speaker is quite tall, she or he may wish to have the podium raised. If moving about the room is appropriate to one's personal style and the type of presentation, do so smoothly and beware of turning your back to the audience.

Personal Style and Language

One's personal comfort level, communication skills, the session purpose, and the audience will influence the speaking style and language one uses during an oral presentation. Generally, effective presentations come across as personal conversations with each member of the audience. In that regard, relaxing, projecting one's voice, and making eye contact are all valuable presentation skills.

The presenter will want to be aware of how she or he uses nonverbal and paraverbal language; these types of communication should coincide with the content of the talk, rather than serve as a distraction. Further, the language and grammar one uses during a presentation should be considered. Proper grammar is always a must, regardless of the audience. Further, the language and terminology should be applicable to those in the audience. Avoiding jargon and big words will support the conversational links to members of the audience and tends to increase speaker comfort.

Be Aware of the Anchor

The anchor is anything that tends to draw a presenter toward it throughout the presentation. It might be a podium, overhead projector, chalkboard, flip chart, spot on the floor, or even a person. Anchors serve as essentially a "home base" for the presenter; making use of an anchor can be both a positive and negative technique. Used positively, it gives the presenter a sense of security and a place to get re-centered. It might be the location where the presenter lays her or his notes. Further, it provides a place to which the audience knows the speaker will eventually return; it helps with audience focus. Overusing the anchor by rarely or never moving away from it, however,

Generally, effective presentations come across as personal conversations with each member of the audience. In that regard, relaxing, projecting one's voice, and making eye contact are all valuable presentation skills.

can result in a presentation that appears stiff, stilted, and unbalanced. A lack of an anchor can make the leader seem "lost."

Kinesthetic Awareness

Being aware of one's location with regard to the audience, room, and any technology is important. This involves recognizing the impact of the presentation on the audience and can be answered by exploring several questions: Are you too far away to connect with people? Are you so close that people are intimidated? Do you turn your back to the audience? How does this impact the ability of the people to hear you? Will the microphone cord reach the places you intend to roam? Have you moved in such a way that people are facing a distraction (e.g., the sun, bright lights, people passing by)?

Be alert to the layout of the room as well as the equipment and supplies in the room. Prior to beginning a presentation, a leader will want to identify the location of any tripping hazards such as electrical cords, sports equipment, or ground or floor hazards; in addition, knowing the location of light switches and thermostats may be important. Finally, kinesthetic awareness involves paying attention to one's location in relation to any visual aids being used. For instance, presenters will want to avoid blocking any type of projection with their body—from a computer projector, overhead projector, document camera, or the like. By keying in on the nonverbal feedback given by the audience, a presenter can help to keep clear of creating these types of obstructions.

The Use of Notes

Because a goal of an effective presentation is to come across as a conversation, the unpracticed use of notes can be awkward. This is not to say that a presenter should not use notes, rather that the type of notes used should fit the nature and style of the presentation. Some people prefer 3-by-5–inch or 5-by-7–inch note cards, others prefer loose full-size sheets of paper, while others use full-size paper arranged in a three-ring binder. The key, of course, is to practice with one's notes to ensure smooth transitions from one page to the next.

It is wise to number the cards or pages just in case they are dropped or blown around by the wind or a fan. Stapling multiple pages together may work, but each time the presenter flips to the next page there is much paper rustling and opportunity for audience distraction. Some people put tabs on page edges to assist with turning; others color-code pages to help them know when they move from one section of the presentation to the next.

When developing notes, leaders typically try to write enough to help with them remember content, but not so much as to lose key points in the text. Using a variety of pen colors or highlighters can help to draw one's attention to the desired information. Some people even put reminders in their notes to smile, pause, and ask the audience a question.

❖ ❖ ❖

The delivery of an oral presentation is very similar to the leadership skills and techniques one would use to lead an activity or teach a song. All communication skills as well as the knowledge about human development and diversity, motivation, and behavior management come together to provide an individual with the ability to successfully make a presentation to informal and formal groups of all sizes. In addition to the personal skills one brings to a presentation, leaders commonly use a wide variety of visual aids to assist in the delivery of the message.

Visual Aids

Using visual aids in an oral presentation can augment the message and help the audience to remember key points. Visual aids include handouts, flip charts, posters, the use of a chalkboard or dry erase board, overhead transparencies, or computer-generated slide shows. Choosing the appropriate tool takes careful thought and consideration. Examining some of the following questions may help with making the determination regarding which, if any, type of visual aid will be utilized. What type of presentation is it? What type of technology is available? What are the characteristics of the presentation space (e.g., outdoors, indoors, conference room, lecture hall)? How will the audience be arranged in relation to the presenter and the visual aid? Who is the audience; what are their characteristics? Will the visual aids be static (i.e., prepared ahead of time) or dynamic (i.e., developed with the audience during the presentation)? How long is the presentation? What are the leader's strengths and limitations with regard to technology?

One rule of thumb for all visual aids is that they should be so well done that the presenter will never have to apologize for such matters as poor quality, illegibility, spelling or grammatical errors, or complexity such that

All communication skills as well as the knowledge about human development and diversity, motivation, and behavior management come together to provide an individual with the ability to successfully make a presentation to informal and formal groups of all sizes.

the material cannot be understood. For instance, if a photograph does not reproduce well on a paper handout, omit it. If a particular color is so light as to not show up well when projected, change the color or do not use that slide. If the information is too small to be seen (e.g., on a screen) either increase the size, put it on a handout, or find a way to present the material without it. Ask a colleague to proofread all materials to ensure proper spelling and grammar. (Computer spell-checkers don't catch all mistakes!) In addition, by starting early and letting materials "rest" for several days, the presenter can look at the information with fresh eyes to catch errors in thought or mechanics.

Handouts

Low-tech visual aid tools in the form of handouts can serve multiple purposes. They can be detail laden, a simple outline, or miniature copies of a computer-generated slide show with space for taking notes. Regardless of the level of detail, basic principles apply to all handouts. First, they should be professional in appearance—clear, clean, readable copy (including any photographs or graphics). Second, no more than two different types of fonts should be used on handouts, and they should be no smaller than 10 points. To anticipate audience members who might have a vision impairment, having a couple of handouts that present the material in at least 18-point font would be wise.

A question often arises as to the timing of distributing handouts. Providing handouts at the beginning of a presentation will result in people looking through the material before the leader covers it. This might be a desirable situation as it provides context and facilitates note taking during the talk. Distributing handouts in the middle of a presentation as the related topic arises can be disruptive to the flow of the presentation, and it does take time. If this is the chosen timing, the presenter will want an assistant or two to help pass out the materials. Some speakers only make handouts available at the end of the talk. In this way, the handouts serve as a "take-away" item that reinforces what was shared and discussed in the session. Consideration of the purpose of the handouts and the presentation will help the leader make the best decision regarding distribution.

Flip Charts

Easily portable and useful for keeping ideas in view, flip charts can be appropriate tools to augment a presentation. When hung around the room, printed flip chart pages enable a group to refer to previously voiced ideas in a concrete way. If the intention is to use the flip charts to develop notes and graphics during the presentation, leaders will want to check ahead of time to ensure availability of an appropriate quantity and quality of working markers or pens. In addition, some method of hanging the pages (e.g., tape, pins) will be needed if the presenter intends to hang the pages around the room. One should bear in mind that some walls do not hold sticky substances and some locations will not allow the use of tape or other such substances on the walls.

Because of their size, flip charts are best suited for a relatively small audience. The presenter can have some pages prepared ahead of time and simply flip the pages to subsequent ideas, or she or he can write on the flip charts as the audience provides ideas or responses to questions. If multiple flip charts (or at least pages from a flip chart pad) are shared with small groups in the audience, interaction and participation may be enhanced. Either way, the leader will want to ensure that the person serving as the scribe has legible and large handwriting.

Overhead Transparencies

To some people transparencies are considered outdated or "old school;" however, they still have their place in oral presentations. They can be used either as a static tool or as a dynamic, interactive tool. When used as a static aid, the presenter prepares and prints transparencies prior to the presentation. Each premade transparency essentially serves as one slide (as found in a computer-generated slide show). The print size needs to be at least 28-point font (if the room is large, 36 or 44 point font might be best) to be visible from a distance, and the slides are most easily visible with black print on clear acetate. Color graphics or transparencies can also be used; the leader will want to ensure clear, sharp focus of all printed material.

Like flip charts, transparencies can be used dynamically and involve audience interaction and participation; with a water-soluable marker the leader can transcribe ideas and suggestions from the audience while in the midst of a presentation. This can help to keep people connected with the leader and the material. Unlike a flip chart, however, once there is no more room on the slide it is removed from the audience's view. The only way to refer to earlier

material is for the leader to re-present the previously created slides.

Because of the white background (created by the light shining through the acetate), overhead transparencies tend to be easily viewed in a bright or well-lighted room. When using overhead transparencies an effective presenter will want to either turn off the machine if there is a time between slides, or place a piece of paper over the projector—this eliminates the group looking at a big white square in the front of the room and helps to keep the focus on the presenter. Overhead projectors have fans that can be noisy, and this should be taken into account when making a decision about the most appropriate visual aid tools.

Computer-Generated Slideshow

In the technological age, the use of computer-generated slideshows such as those made with PowerPoint and Keynote are considered the standard for most presentations. Of course, such a presentation requires a computer (some handheld devices also have this capability) and a projector of some sort. Computer-generated slides offer sharp, clear images in full color; they can also be connected to the Internet and the presenter can utilize real-time web surfing.

If a leader chooses to use this type of presentation aid, she or he should have a solid knowledge of both the technology and the software to be used. It is important to avoid relying on information technology (IT) staff to set up and prepare one's presentation. Too often IT staff are unavailable, cannot be found, or are not familiar with the software or computer being used. Thus, a thorough

---

Choosing Appropriate Visual Aids

- What type of presentation is it?
- What type of technology is available?
- What are the characteristics of the presentation space (e.g., outdoors, indoors, conference room, lecture hall)?
- How will the audience be arranged in relation to the presenter and the visual aid?
- Who is the audience; what are their characteristics?
- Will the visual aids be static (i.e., prepared ahead of time) or dynamic (i.e., developed with the audience during the presentation)?
- How long is the presentation?
- What are the leader's strengths and limitations with regard to technology?

Figure 12.14 Choosing appropriate visual aids requires careful thought and consideration.

understanding of the tools used for the presentation is critical. Should something go awry (which is not uncommon), being able to make adjustments "on the fly" can make the difference between an effective presentation and no presentation at all.

General ideas to bear in mind when developing a tech-based presentation include keeping it simple, maintaining consistency, minimizing special effects, and using an appropriate number of slides. Keeping it simple entails choosing an appropriate slide background—a light background with dark print is most easily visible in a bright room while a dark background with light print is most easily visible in a dark room. Further, a simple background is more comfortable to view than is a slide background that is "busy" or complex. Most types of software provide templates that aid with background, print color, and text alignment; it is often wise to choose a standard template.

In addition to a simple background, a good rule of thumb regarding amount of text is to use no more than six words on a line and no more than six lines to a slide. Try to avoid so much text that punctuation is required. Designing content in such a way as to highlight key points rather than tell the entire story is an efficient use of this technology. Avoid reading the slide to the audience. The slide offers a visual focal point; the information is presented by the speaker. To be visible from a distance, text should be no smaller than 32-point font, depending upon the font style (serif or sans serif; bold or plain). It is best to avoid special effects, such as italics or shadowing, on slide text. Any photos should be focused and visible from the farthest point in the room—the graphics should

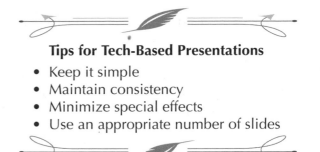

Tips for Tech-Based Presentations
- Keep it simple
- Maintain consistency
- Minimize special effects
- Use an appropriate number of slides

speak for themselves; if the leader has to verbally describe a graphic, it would be best to avoid using it.

Another element of simplicity is consistency. Once a slide background and text (or template) is selected, use it throughout the slide show. Use the same color scheme on every slide—and be sure to use contrasting colors. Standardize the position of the information on the slides. For example, if you put text on the left and graphics on the right side, try to maintain that same relationship throughout. If you do choose to change, avoid changing every other slide. The graphics, photos, or clip art should balance the slide and supplement the message. If the audience has to guess why a particular graphic was included or figure out what it is, choose an alternative or omit it.

One of the added features of tech-based slide shows is the opportunity to include a variety of transitions within and between slides, as well as movies, animation, and sounds along with text. Leaders are cautioned to be extremely judicious in utilizing these features; they can be very distracting. Within-slide transitions are those that allow content to appear and disappear at different times. If used, choose one style and be consistent. Between-slide transitions should be simple and unnoticeable—the transitions should flow as the ideas flow—smoothly and simply. Incorporating short movie clips into a presentation can be effective to enhance a message or serve as an example (as long as the software is available and functional), but in general, sounds and animations detract from the overall message.

Deciding on an appropriate number of slides for a particular presentation is an important consideration. If one has too many slides, she or he might rush the presentation, or the flow might be choppy as the presenter tries to keep up with the slides. On the other hand, not having enough slides can leave an audience confused and wondering why the technology was used at all. In general, three to four slides per minute works well. This allows enough time for the audience to see the slide, acknowledge the content, and return their attention to the presenter for additional information. Clearly, there are times when a slide might be shown for longer (or less time) than this; it will depend on the purpose of the slide, the content, and your point.

Figure 12.15 Effective presentations make use of a variety of visual aids.

Effective oral presentations using computer presentation tools require solid preparation and practice. Whenever possible, one should practice with the equipment to be used ahead of time. Get to the presentation site early, check the lighting, set up the computer and projector, and run through the entire slide show. Make several backups of the presentation and have them with you. Put a copy of the presentation on a flash drive, a CD, and the computer hard drive; another idea is to e-mail yourself your presentation. If Internet access is available, you will be able to download your presentation no matter your location. Be sure to have the original files or any photos or graphics (e.g., jpg, mpg) on the same backup storage devices in stand-alone files. It is not uncommon for a technical glitch to render imported graphics unviewable; a simple delete and reinsert often fixes the problem.

❖　❖　❖

Wise use of visual aids to augment a presentation can enhance the intended message and convey credibility to the audience. This, of course, assumes that one makes the appropriate choice of aid and that the leader has done a thorough job of attending to the details. One key to remember is that a presenter wants the audience to remember the material, and not the show (either for positive or negative reasons).

Summary

This chapter has established the groundwork for direct leadership techniques. There are three phases to direct leadership skills: preparation, priming the group, and delivery. An effective leader is one who is prepared, knows the group with which she or he will be working, and has followed risk management procedures. In addition, preparation entails establishing goals and objectives, setting the mood by manipulating the environment, and playing "What if?"

Once having taken care of preparations, a leader primes the group. Priming the group involves using fun, experiential and unique techniques or activities to get the group's attention and divide the group into smaller groups. It is best to avoid using team captains or counting off as ways of dividing a group because of negative effects. Learning names is very important to group satisfaction and is part of the priming stage.

The delivery phase of direct leadership includes the leader introducing both herself or himself and the activity, identifying the goal of the activity, telling a story and giving directions. When giving directions it is best to follow the KISS, KIP and PLAY methods. Within and between activities, transitions are used; transitions are

psychological bridges used both within and between activities. Conclusions are as important as beginnings in leisure experiences and may be used to maintain positive affect and to bring individuals back for more.

As an additional role and responsibility of many direct leaders, formal leadership opportunities were discussed, including the conduct of meetings. Suggestions about meeting preparation, conduct, and what to do upon the completion of a meeting were presented. The importance of developing and distributing agendas and minutes and the notion of virtual meetings were shared. Lastly, information and techniques related to formal oral presentations were provided. Preparation and attention to detail are extremely important for effective oral presentations. Leaders will make decisions about content, tone, style, audience interaction, and the use of visual aids.

Beginning the Journey

As you put together all that you have learned and implement that knowledge in actual leadership, you enter another phase of the leadership journey—that which is gained through practice. Practice and exposure to other leaders are vital avenues of learning for all potential leaders. Think about the following questions as you prepare to lead others in recreation activities.

1. What are direct leadership techniques? Give examples of direct leadership experiences in your life. Why is it important for all parks, recreation, and leisure services leaders to be skilled in direct leadership techniques? What are the three phases of successful direct leadership?

2. Describe the nature of the Leadership Preparation phase. What does it entail? What information do you need about a group to make yourself most effective as the leader? Are there other questions you should ask besides those provided in this chapter? What are they? What is the ultimate goal of asking all these questions about groups?

3. Explain the need for reviewing risk management concerns in direct leadership. Imagine a parks and recreation setting in which you are working. With a classmate, generate a list of 10 to 20 "What if?" questions that could be asked to help you prepare for leadership. Do this for several distinct age groups and settings.

4. What are goals and objectives, and how are they used in recreation leadership? Describe the four types of goals; which do you think are most impor-

tant to a typical recreation leader? Why do you believe that?

5. Go to a local parks, recreation, or leisure services agency or organization and ask the director to share the organizational goals. Next, ask a staff member about her or his goals for an activity she or he will be leading. Follow up with some participants and ask them about their goals. What are the goal relationships (e.g., cooperative, competitive, independent)? Comment on your findings in terms of challenges to effective leadership.

6. What is the relationship of objectives to goals? What does the acronym SMART mean? What is the ABCD method of writing behavioral objectives? For practice, write one goal and at least three objectives that would meet that goal using each of the objective writing techniques. Which of these methods do you find easiest to follow when writing objectives? Continue practicing with goals and objectives; have a classmate follow the objective flow chart and check your work. Get into the habit of writing at least one goal and three objectives per week related to recreation and leisure, and turn them in for feedback.

7. What is Setting the Tone? Rate your own skill level at doing this. Are you conscious of how you set the tone every time you work with a group? How can you improve at this skill? Identify specific things you can do and say to set the tone in a certain way. It might be helpful to make a chart—identify the tone you want to set, what you might say, and the manipulation of the environment.

8. What is involved in Priming a Group? Identify at least five methods you can use to get a group's attention. Identify at least five ways you can divide a group, and when you might use each method. Do the same thing for learning names. Why is learning names an important skill for leaders? How can you improve your ability to learn names?

9. Describe what goes into the delivery phase of direct leadership. Develop and laminate an index card that has the steps to leading activities on one side and leading songs on the other. Keep this for future reference. At which of these skills are you best? Which need more work? How and where can you practice these skills? Practice these at home in front of a mirror. Remember to incorporate what you have learned about verbal and nonverbal communication for effective leadership as you practice.

10. How and why are transitions used? What happens if you don't use transitions? Why is the conclusion of an activity so important? Reflect on your previous leadership experiences—How skilled are you at concluding a session? What do you need to do to improve? What is the most important aspect of a conclusion? Explain your thoughts.

11. Make a list of leader Dos and Don'ts for meeting leadership. What do effective and efficient meetings look like? How do you, as the leader, facilitate this? Write a sample agenda for an upcoming meeting. Take minutes at that meeting, and then write up the minutes. Share those with a classmate for feedback.

12. What are virtual meetings and what are the pros and cons of holding virtual meetings? What challenges do virtual meetings hold for leaders?

13. Attend a formal oral presentation and critique it. Describe the level of preparation that was evident. Did the leader fidget? Did she or he make appropriate use of the visual aid tools? Did she or he know how to use those tools well? Did the visual aid material enhance or detract from the message? What take-away lessons did you learn to enhance your own skills?

References

Adler, R. and Elmhorst, J. (1999). *Communicating at work* (6th ed.). New York, NY: McGraw Hill.

Bloom, B. (1956). *Taxonomy of educational objectives*. New York, NY: Longman.

Gardenswartz, L. and Rowe, A. (1998). *Managing diversity: A complete desk reference and planning guide* (2nd ed.). Dubuque, IA: McGraw-Hill Professional.

Mager, R. (1984). *Measuring instructional results* (2nd ed.). Belmont, CA: Pitman Learning, Inc.

Russell, R. (2005). *Leadership in recreation* (3rd ed.). New York, NY: McGraw Hill.

Schlegel, J. (2005). *Running effective meetings*. Retrieved July 27, 2006, from www.salary.com/advice/layouthtmls/advl_display_nocat_Ser265_Par384.html

Shank, J. and Coyle, C. (2002). *Therapeutic recreation in health promotion and rehabilitation*. State College, PA: Venture Publishing, Inc.

Stumbo, N. and Peterson, C. (2004). *Therapeutic recreation program design* (4th ed.). San Francisco, CA: Benjamin Cummings.

Leader Profile

Lori Daniel, CPRP
Recreation Services Manager, City of Aurora, Colorado Recreation Services

Lori has over 33 years in this position, and over 34 years in the parks, recreation, and leisure services profession.

Volunteer leadership positions she has held include:

- President, National Recreation and Park Association
- Board of Trustees, National Recreation and Park Association
- Board of Directors, American Camp Association
- Accreditation Visitor, American Camp Association
- Board of Directors, American Academy for Park and Recreation Administration
- Board member, Colorado Association of Community Educators

What is the meaning of leadership?
Leadership is beyond managing and supervision. It is a mindset that one acquires—from others by example; from leadership experiences throughout life and one's career; from continuous learning that leads to leading; from the passion and joy of helping make a difference and contributions in your job, career and profession. Leadership is leading others and/or an organization from here to there to achieve a mission, goals and objectives. To quote Blaine Lee: "Great leaders are like conductors, they reach beyond the notes to reach the magic in players."

What are the most important leadership qualities?
Integrity, honesty, fairness, and commitment; inspires trust; continually develops; and is their own person; focuses on people, keeps their eyes on the horizon; is innovative and friendly, but not a buddy; sets and practices standards and expectations.

What advice do you have for students who aspire to leadership in parks, recreation, and leisure services?
Get involved in professional organizations from the get-go, starting with your university recreation club, state park and recreation, and the national association. Accept leadership roles and/or appointments to learn side-by-side from other professionals. Attend local, state, regional and national events/ training as often as you can (e.g., volunteer to go) for networking and for continuing professional development. Seek a mentor whom you can call on and learn from…. Achieve and retain certification (e.g., Certified Park and Recreation Professional); it makes an important statement about you and your standards. Accept that leadership and career development are *LIFELONG*.

Favorite books: Any book, tape, or DVD of Garrison Keillor's *A Prairie Home Companion*

Favorite activities: Camping, driving vacations, and now attending the grandchildren's sports and recreation events.

Chapter Thirteen
Selected Social and Professional Issues Affecting Leisure Services Leaders

Learning Opportunities

Through studying this chapter readers will have the opportunity to

- Understand the impact of social and professional issues on leisure services leaders.
- Describe the signs of child abuse and explain the role of the leisure services leader in reporting suspected abuse.
- Examine the importance of taking universal precautions when dealing with blood-borne pathogens.
- Discuss the nature of professional certifications.
- Identify various certifications and professional memberships a leisure services leader may obtain.

To reach their professional potential, leisure services leaders need a solid awareness and understanding of the social and professional issues facing the field. *Social issues* have an impact, both good and bad, on the quality of life and social mores of the community. Social issues include poverty, homelessness, crime and violence, and the decline in national fitness levels. *Professional issues* affect the professions within parks, recreation, and leisure services. Professional issues include developing a set of professional ethics, credential and accreditation requirements, and understanding the role leisure plays in quality of life. All of these concerns affect leadership in parks, recreation, and leisure services.

Leisure services settings are microcosms of society. This means that what occurs in larger society, both positive and negative, also occurs in or has an impact on leisure services settings. Social issues such as unemployment, HIV/AIDS, child abuse, and violence all impact leisure in some respect. Higher rates of unemployment affect individuals' ability to pay for and travel to leisure services, thereby limiting the unemployed individual's quality of life. HIV/AIDS impacts the way leisure services leaders treat small wounds and injuries and constrains the participation of some people. Leisure services leaders may be involved in reporting issues of child and elder abuse. Other forms of violence also impact leisure services in the need for conflict resolution and in addressing participant safety. Even the impact of natural disasters such as Hurricane Katrina in 2005 is felt throughout the leisure services delivery system.

Professional issues such as certification, licensure, and accreditation also impact the ongoing growth and development of leisure services leaders. Working with a variety of people in different types of situations may require leisure services leaders to fulfill many roles: instructor, information provider, mediator, facilitator, mentor, director, entertainer, counselor, problem solver, presenter, and authoritarian, among others. Filling these many roles requires a breadth of knowledge and a variety of skills. Engaging in continuing education and earning

Photo courtesy of Paul Jordan/WEBSPORTSPHOTO

applicable credentials help to ensure up-to-date knowledge and skill levels in these areas.

Effective leaders are aware of how social and professional issues affect their personal leadership styles and the profession in general. In increasing their awareness, leaders can direct their own continuing education to meet personal needs, the needs of constituents, and the profession as a whole. This chapter addresses only a small selection of social and professional issues that influence leader effectiveness. All leaders are encouraged to learn as much as possible about the impacts of social and professional issues on the delivery of leisure services.

Social Issues

Many diverse social issues influence the delivery of leisure services. These issues are often reflected in local, state, and national news and political affairs. They include such concerns as the effects of human-made and natural disasters, war, and immigration. Other social issues that affect leisure services leadership include obesity and overall health, gang problems, infant mortality, poverty, and other social indicators. Effective parks and recreation leaders are aware of these social dilemmas and make attempts to address them through programming, leadership, and administrative structures. In an attempt to raise the level of awareness about social issues in general, the following section will provide information about a few issues that directly impact leadership in leisure services: child abuse, elder abuse, and universal precautions and blood-borne diseases.

Child Abuse

Child abuse is an issue facing all parks, recreation, and leisure services providers who work with or provide services for children. Child abuse affects leisure services professionals in two ways. First, leaders must be aware of the impact they have on children when providing services, managing behaviors, and leading activities to avoid being perpetrators of abuse (or perceived as such). Second, the children involved in leisure services activities may be victims of abuse and require leader intervention as a mandated or volunteer reporter.

The Child Abuse Prevention, Adoption, and Family Services Act of 1988 (P.L. 100-294 as amended by P.L. 104-235) defines child abuse and neglect as:

> At a minimum, any recent act or failure to act on the part of a parent or caretaker, which results in death, serious physical or emotional harm, sexual abuse or exploitation; or

Effective leaders are aware of how social and professional issues affect their personal leadership styles and the profession in general.

> An act or failure to act which presents an imminent risk or serious harm. (Child Welfare Information Gateway, 2006)

The regulations indicate that child maltreatment includes physical, emotional and sexual abuse, while neglect is the failure to care for a child's basic needs (i.e., physical and emotional needs). In leisure services settings, child abuse may be passive (e.g., someone observes a child being abused) or active (e.g., some form of abuse is directed at a particular child).

Types of Child Abuse in Leisure Services Settings

Child abuse can take several forms: passive abuse or neglect, which is the most commonly occurring type of maltreatment (63%); then verbal, physical, emotional, and sexual abuse. *Verbal abuse* is the most commonly occurring type of active abuse and the least often reported. It includes such things as name calling (e.g., "You jerk!" "What a baby!"), hurtful comments regarding performance (e.g., "You couldn't hit that ball if you tried." "You stink at this."), swearing (using profanity) at participants, and comments designed to demean a child's integrity (e.g., "You are a liar—I've never heard you tell the truth;" or "The only way you ever win is when you cheat.").

Physical abuse arises out of any physical touch that is hurtful, or activities purposefully designed to cause pain to the participant. Grabbing, shoving, slapping, spanking, and excessive exercise as a method of discipline could all be considered physical abuse. Approximately 30% of all youth endure physical abuse of some type (*Child abuse*, 2006).

Emotional abuse of children often involves having unrealistic goals and expectations for them. Examples of this type of abuse include pushing a child to achieve excellence in every activity, aggressively urging a youngster to score the most points, and not allowing children to make mistakes. Statistics report that approximately 5% of youth are emotionally abused.

Sexual abuse may be any form of sexual contact or implied sexual contact between an adult and child. Examples include all forms of sexual harassment, implicit or explicit sexual comments and innuendoes, and sexual touch. Approximately one in five girls and one in seven boys are sexually abused during their lifetime (Tabachnick, 2005)

Contributing Factors

A variety of larger social problems contribute to abuse of young people. If these contributing factors were satisfactorily addressed, a good deal of child abuse could be mitigated. Leisure services plays a role in addressing many of these issues through the provision of services. Research has shown that social problems such as poverty, substance abuse, mental health problems, unemployment, financial difficulties, isolation, and a lack of social support all contribute to increased incidences of child maltreatment (*Child abuse*, 2006). Once child abuse begins, it often becomes cyclical; reports indicate that a victim of abuse is four times more likely to become an abuser than a person who has not experienced abuse (*Child abuse*, 2006).

Consequences

Child maltreatment affects the individual child, her or his siblings, and society in general. The detrimental effects of child abuse result in an individual with a whole host of long-lasting personal problems which negatively influence long-term success and life quality. Very often, victims of child maltreatment suffer from low self-esteem, depression, sleep and eating disorders, substance abuse, and suicidal tendencies at various times throughout their lives. The effects of the mistreatment may be observed in behavioral extremes, impulsiveness, social withdrawal, or excessive anxiety (*Child Maltreatment*, 2006; Levesque, 2000). Because of our unique position in working with people,

Research has shown that social problems such as poverty, substance abuse, mental health problems, unemployment, financial difficulties, isolation, and a lack of social support all contribute to increased incidences of child maltreatment

leisure services leaders may be in positions to recognize and help alleviate many of these effects.

Other results of child abuse for the victim include delayed development (e.g., physical, emotional, social), an inability to concentrate, substance abuse, and sexual promiscuity (often at a very young age). Individuals abused as children develop a distrust of adults and peers, which negatively impacts interpersonal skills. This often translates into a lack of successful peer relationships (*Child abuse*, 2006; *Child maltreatment*, 2006). The consequences of child abuse are powerful, long-lasting, and extremely harmful.

Signs of Child Maltreatment

A prominent role for leisure services leaders in addressing child abuse is in the prevention, recognition, and reporting of suspected cases of abuse. As mentioned, maltreatment may be physical, emotional, sexual, or a combination of the three. Neglect may be emotional, physical or both. While emotional abuse may not manifest itself in observable injuries, all types of abuse and neglect have some discernable characteristics.

Indicators of Physical Abuse

Some physical injuries may simply be signs of an active, exploring child; it is not uncommon for a child to break an arm or require stitches from a fall. A pattern of injuries, including bruises, fractures, wounds, and burns (particularly those caused by cigarettes), however, can be signs of physical maltreatment. Head and internal injuries are common results of physical abuse, rather than typical childhood exploratory injuries. Behavioral characteristics of abused children may include overly passive or aggressive behaviors, a fear of physical contact such as a touch on the shoulder or pat on the back, regressive behaviors (i.e., the child reverts to acting much younger than her or his years), or a child acting frightened of her or his parent(s) or guardian(s). If a physical injury is apparent, a concerned leader needs to consider first if the injury could have occurred as described by the child(ren) or witnesses.

Table 13A The four categories of maltreatment identified by law

Type of Abuse	Examples	
Verbal abuse	• Yelling • Name calling • Verbal put-downs	
Physical abuse	• Slapping • Grabbing • Excessive exercise	• Pinching • Pushing
Emotional abuse	• Unrealistic goals • Attacking character • Developing and breaking trust	
Sexual abuse	• Sexual harassment • Sexual innuendos • Sexual touch	

A prominent role for leisure services leaders in addressing child abuse is in the prevention, recognition, and reporting of suspected cases of abuse.

Second, the leader must decide if the child is developmentally mature enough to have caused the injury as indicated.

Signs of Emotional Abuse

Emotional abuse may be the most difficult to ascertain because there is no obvious physical injury or pain. However, emotional abuse can be just as harmful to a child as physical maltreatment. Children who are emotionally maltreated or neglected may mistrust adults and peers, have low self-esteem, and have poor interpersonal skills. An inability to cope with everyday stresses and frustrations, unexplained aggressiveness, and hyperactivity may also indicate emotional abuse. Some children may withdraw, be apathetic or unresponsive about everything, and lack decision-making skills. Many victims of emotional abuse or neglect turn to substance abuse as a means of escape or to draw attention to themselves.

Signs of Sexual Abuse

In some recreational settings leisure services leaders may observe what appear to be signs of sexual abuse. This is most often the case in situations where children change their clothes in front of activity leaders (e.g., when preparing to go swimming) or in situations of extended contact (e.g., at a resident camp). Injuries to the genital or anal areas; torn, stained, or bloody undergarments; sexually transmitted diseases (STDs); and pregnancy at a young age are all signs of sexual abuse. Children who are so abused often feel extreme rage, anger, and frustration at what is happening to them. Signs of sexual abuse may be manifested in feelings of humiliation, a sense of a lack of control over self, and irrational thinking. Many children who are sexually abused become inappropriately sexually aggressive. They may project sexual desires onto a leisure services leader, their own peers, or younger children. Sexual promiscuity and substance abuse are also signs of being victimized in this fashion.

Signs of Neglect

Leisure services leaders are often aware of various issues of child abuse but may be less aware of the impact of child neglect on the healthy development of young people. Being alone for long periods of time without adult super-

vision is commonly perceived as neglect. Neglect may also occur when adults present in the household ignore the children. Common signs of neglect include poor personal hygiene, inappropriate or inadequate clothing, frequent hunger, and lethargy or exhaustion. In addition, poor academic performance, a high rate of school absenteeism, and delinquent behaviors also may be indications of child neglect. In a leisure services setting, children who are neglected might not want to leave at closing hours or may ask the leader if they can go home with her or him.

Characteristics of Maltreating Adults

Often, one can make a determination of child maltreatment by combining knowledge of injuries to a child and information about the adults involved. Because child maltreatment tends to be cyclical, a history of abuse or neglect as a child is a common characteristic of an abusing or neglectful adult. The use of excessively harsh discipline (e.g., screaming, hitting with an object, overreacting to minor mishaps) is quite common, as is a history of mental illness, alcohol and/or drug abuse, and a chaotic home life. Social isolation also characterizes maltreating adults—they may have little or no contact with others, either purposefully or because they live far away from others and lack transportation. Adults who experience undue stress related to finances and other factors are more likely to engage in child maltreatment than adults who do not experience such stresses (*Child abuse*, 2006; *Child maltreatment*, 2006).

Reporting Suspected Abuse

Certainly, being aware of the potential for child abuse and recognizing the signs and indications are important for leisure services leaders. Once maltreatment has been observed or suspected, leisure services leaders must then take the next step—reporting the suspected abuse. Reporting suspected child abuse can be one of the most heart-wrenching situations in which leisure services leaders find themselves. Concern for the safety and well-being of the child is often tempered with the question, "What if I am wrong?" To aid in the decision-making process, all states have passed laws dictating who must report suspected child abuse, to whom, and when. These laws protect the child and afford some liability protection to the individual making the report should an error be made.

Mandatory Reporters

Mandated reporting laws and definitions of mandatory reporters are defined by each state. They may include teachers, physicians, police, and other social service professionals (including those in leisure services). Each state has reporting laws and legislation which identify the defi-

To aid in the decision-making process, all states have passed laws dictating who must report suspected child abuse, to whom, and when. These laws protect the child and afford some liability protection to the individual making the report should an error be made.

nition of child abuse and procedures for reporting it. Therefore, leisure services leaders should be cognizant of the specifics relative to their own state. Each state has laws regarding the following:

- *what* must be reported
- *who* must report: usually teachers, physicians, and police; many states list any childcare provider and twenty states name "any person."
- *when* it must be reported (e.g., immediately by phone; when a reporter has "reason to believe" or "reasonable cause to suspect" maltreatment)
- reporting *procedures* and to whom the report is made. The most common child protection agencies that receive child abuse reports include social service agencies, police departments, health departments, and juvenile court systems.
- the existence and operation of a *central registry*: names of accused individuals are entered into a central registry for ease of intervention and follow-up.
- *protective custody* for children and *immunity* for good faith reporters (i.e., immunity from civil and criminal prosecution)
- *sanctions for failure to report:* In many states, a failure to report child abuse is a misdemeanor that may result in a fine and/or jail time. (*Child abuse*, 2006)

In trying to determine the reasons behind mood swings, extremes in behavior, or participant difficulties, a leisure services leader may engage in conversation with a youngster which results in the knowledge that the youth is being or has been maltreated. The child might begin to share this information by asking the leader to promise not to tell anyone. Leaders must recognize and tell the child that this type of promise is not possible. For the safety of the child and by law, once abuse is suspected or known, a report must be made. Leaders should be very careful of promises (which cannot be kept) made to young people when faced with this issue. A lack of trust and feelings of humiliation and shame often accompany such revelations, and leaders need to be very cognizant of the long-term impacts on, and the feelings of, the young person involved.

The Process of Reporting

Once an individual suspects child abuse, a report must be made. While the procedure in each state varies somewhat, the typical reporting process is as follows:

a. A report is made by a volunteer or mandated reporter who has "reasonable suspicion" of abuse occurring.
b. The report is screened through an intake process by child protective services (CPS) personnel.
c. A decision is made to send out an investigator (usually within 24 hours of the initial report).
d. A case record is made.
e. Findings are recorded.
f. Case and intervention plans are developed and implemented.

To initiate legal action, should it be deemed necessary, CPS personnel must first substantiate the claim of maltreatment. The ultimate goal of many state CPS agencies

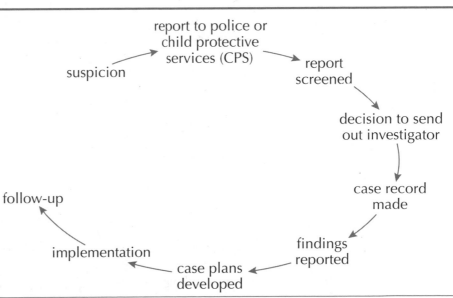

Figure 13.1 Once a mandatory reporter of child abuse reports a suspected case, the process moves forward.

is to maintain the integrity of the family unit and its cultural practices; therefore, disposition of child maltreatment cases may include parental support classes, family counseling, and temporary removal from the home. Ultimately, if no other intervention works, a child may be permanently removed from the home and put into the foster care/adoption system.

After Making the Report

Once a report has been made, a leisure services leader should strive to treat the child as before—with respect and understanding. Once the child knows that an adult is aware of the "secret," she or he may increase in acting out or engaging in inappropriate behaviors; this is often a result of the fear and anxiety of what will occur as CPS becomes involved. A leader will want to be as sensitive as possible to the needs of the youngster, whether it is a need to be alone, to talk, or simply to be in the company of supportive and caring adults. Talking about and sharing accounts of abuse should be initiated by the young person, not by leisure services leaders. Very few leisure services leaders are trained as social workers or therapists, and thus are limited in how they can help an abused youngster. Leaders can, however, be good listeners, make referrals, and establish opportunities for the abuse victim to feel in control and experience success in recreational activities.

Leisure services leaders can positively impact children who have been maltreated by designing and leading activities to help rebuild a sense of trust in others. To initiate this, leaders will need to be consistent, dependable, and reliable for these youths. Active listening and responding to stated needs—a genuine caring about the child—is vital for aiding wholesome child development. Designing activity and leadership opportunities so that youths have a high likelihood of success and are not judged by how well they perform is also important. Effective leadership techniques for victims of child abuse usually require heightened awareness and sensitivity toward the participant.

Because children who are maltreated often lack appropriate interpersonal skills, leisure services leaders should model and design opportunities for the development and practice of social skills (e.g., sharing, coping

Leisure services leaders can positively impact children who have been maltreated by designing and leading activities to help rebuild a sense of trust in others.

with disappointments and frustrations, communication). Basic life skills such as self-esteem, communication, conflict resolution, decision making, stress management, and leisure education are needed by children from abusive backgrounds (and many others as well). By providing a wide variety of opportunities for those youths to construct and try out their own ideas, leisure services leaders can begin the process of empowering abuse victims to regain self-respect.

Leader Caveats

Caveats are warnings to be careful. When addressing and considering the concerns surrounding the issue of child abuse, several caveats for leaders arise. By their positions (e.g., camp counselor, locker-room attendant, playground supervisor, trip leader), leisure services leaders are often in situations where their actions could be perceived as suspicious by those observing. In addition, by their actions (e.g., some behavior management techniques, motivational methods, specific supervision), leisure services leaders may come under scrutiny for allegations of child maltreatment.

To avoid any claim of misconduct while maintaining safe and effective leadership, leaders should continually examine their own behaviors with children. It may be helpful to imagine what a behavior or situation might look like to someone out of earshot and at a distance. No matter how innocent a particular behavior (e.g., hugging a crying child), from across the room it may look very different. Therefore, leaders should be very aware of their actions, words, and intentions at all times (and crying children may still need to be hugged).

Reaching out and touching children (and adults) tends to draw attention from observers. Parents and schools teach children about "good" touching (e.g., nonsexual hugs, pats on the back, high fives) and "bad" touching (e.g., sexual, hurtful). Leaders also need to know what constitutes good and bad touches.

Touching should be appropriate for the situation. For example, it is generally acceptable for a hug to follow bandaging a scraped knee and a pat on the back to be given as congratulations for a job well done. One should ask an individual for permission to touch her or him before doing so—"Would you like a hug?" "Is it okay if I give you a pat on the back?" This way, if such touching is not comfortable for the child, she or he can tell you so—allowing children to define the boundaries of touching will help to minimize misinterpreted intentions.

When in public settings outside the usual recreational setting (e.g., on a field trip, at a local waterpark), it is often necessary for safety and liability reasons to accompany small children to the restroom or locker room. To protect oneself from perceptions of impropriety, accompany multiple children simultaneously or ensure that other adults are nearby. In this way, if a child must be assisted with dressing or attending to personal needs, witnesses are available to observe and confirm leader actions.

Other situations raise concerns and awareness of child abuse such as behavior management (e.g., when using touch or physical intervention) and any time one is alone with a child (e.g., in the office, equipment room, vehicle). To minimize concerns about child maltreatment in these situations, it would be wise to be aware of who is doing what where, the setting itself, and who is around. These concerns are valid because some research shows that, while uncommon, at times children will lie about maltreatment (Wilson, 2002). To be effective and still meet the human needs of young people, then, leaders will want to do what they can to protect themselves and their young charges from any perception of wrongdoing.

Elder Abuse

While we generally think of youth and children when discussing abuse, many adults, particularly the elderly, are also victims of abuse and neglect. It is estimated that up to 10% of persons ages 60 and older experience some

form of maltreatment (National Center on Elder Abuse, 2006), and the numbers are increasing. Because of this, every state now has laws that address issues of elder abuse. Maltreatment of elders includes financial exploitation, physical abuse (this can include confinement as well as more familiar forms of physical abuse), emotional and verbal abuse, sexual abuse, and neglect. Neglect can be both passive (e.g., ignoring or abandoning the person) and active (i.e., the willful deprivation of a physical or emotional need).

The abuser is most often a member of the family—most commonly a spouse, adult child, or grandchild who lives with the victim; both women and men are abusers (National Center on Elder Abuse, 2006). Elder abuse is also perpetrated by nonfamily member caregivers such as home health aides or hospital aides. According to *Elder abuse* (2006), victims tend to be white women in their mid to late 70s. Commonly, the abuse victim suffers from some form of dementia or physical disability that makes her dependent on others for personal care. She is often isolated and fearful of reporting the abuse.

As with child abuse, several states identify mandatory reporters of adult abuse, and you will want to be aware of the laws in your state. Most commonly, mandatory reporters include "persons delivering professional services to older persons" (*Elder abuse*, 2006) such as those working in social services, adult care, education, medicine, and state services to seniors. Thus, it may well be that therapeutic recreation specialists would fall under the mandatory reporter laws. Of course, anyone can report suspected abuse.

Those in parks, recreation, and leisure services who work with the elderly in senior centers, care facilities, hospitals, and home settings will want to be alert to signs and symptoms of maltreatment with adults. The observable signs and symptoms of maltreatment (e.g., unexplained bruises, burns, untreated sores, soiled clothing, changes in behaviors) are similar to those found in child maltreatment cases. Reporting procedures have not yet been codified in most states, but it would be safe to follow the same procedures outlined for the reporting of child abuse.

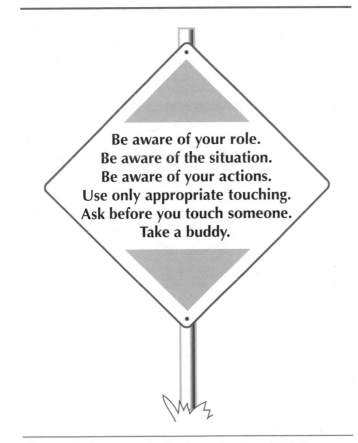

Be aware of your role.
Be aware of the situation.
Be aware of your actions.
Use only appropriate touching.
Ask before you touch someone.
Take a buddy.

Figure 13.2 Caveats for leaders related to child abuse

While we generally think of youth and children when discussing abuse, many adults, particularly the elderly, are also victims of abuse and neglect.

Universal Precautions and Blood-Borne Pathogens

Leisure services leaders need a basic awareness of the prevention of transmission of blood-borne pathogens to help keep themselves and participants safe. A knowledge of universal precautions facilitates this. Blood-borne pathogens include diseases such as Hepatitis B, tuberculosis, and HIV/AIDS. These diseases are transmitted through contact with an individual's blood or other bodily fluids (e.g., mucous from sneezing, spittle from coughing, vomit, urine, feces). In leisure services settings there are many instances when contact with another person's bodily fluids may occur such as when a child wets the bed at camp, a participant gets a bloody nose from being hit with a ball, or an individual vomits due to illness or overexertion.

Leisure services leaders commonly provide minor first aid to slightly injured participants, thereby being exposed to blood. Those in therapeutic recreation settings may deal with many bodily fluids in the normal course of their work. Many blood-borne pathogens are impossible to detect simply by looking at someone and the diseases have varying degrees of danger to those exposed to them (e.g., hepatitis B, hepatitis C, HIV/AIDS can all be debilitating over the life course; all of these diseases are incurable). The possible transmission of HIV frightens many; however, other communicable diseases such as hepatitis B, hepatitis C, and tuberculosis are much easier to transmit from one individual to another than is HIV. Therefore, while we may attribute an increase in awareness of blood-borne pathogens to the rise of HIV/AIDS, the resulting precautions make tending to ill or injured persons safer for everyone.

To protect oneself, the individual who is ill, and others from blood-borne communicable diseases, a leader will want to take universal precautions when providing assistance. Universal precautions are those actions taken by a person who is handling bodily fluids in any situation (e.g., cleaning up after a bladder accident, rendering medical aid to another) to protect herself or himself against unknown (and often invisible) diseases. HIV, hepatitis, and tuberculosis infections do not discriminate. In the United States, youth and heterosexual women constitute the fastest growing group of individuals infected with HIV.

It is best to presume that everyone is contagious and capable of infecting others. Following universal precautions ensures the same treatment of everyone—use rubber gloves, a medical mask, and take care in disposing of soiled bandages and other materials. The Occupational and Safety Health Act (OSHA), provides guidelines for managing blood-borne pathogens in various situations. The guidelines include

- Educate staff and participants about the identity and proper disposal of contaminated materials.
- Remove from any activity any individual who has evidence of bleeding or blood on herself or himself (or clothes) until it can be cleaned up.
- Ensure that any area used for first aid is not used for eating, smoking, applying cosmetics, inserting contact lenses, or any other activity that could increase the risk of infection.
- Ensure an adequate supply of disposable personal protective gear (e.g., gloves, masks) for use during first aid.
- Encourage hepatitis-B vaccinations of all staff likely to come into contact with bodily fluids.
- Establish a thorough record-keeping process to document all levels of exposure.

The key in protecting all involved is to assume that all body fluids have potential to infect someone. Further,

Thorough washing of hands

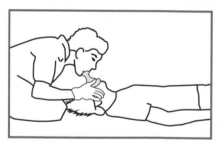
Disposable gloves and resuscitation mask

Protective eyewear, mask, and gloves

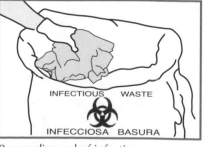
Proper disposal of infectious waste

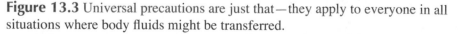

Figure 13.3 Universal precautions are just that—they apply to everyone in all situations where body fluids might be transferred.

leaders should be just as concerned with protecting an injured participant from their (the leader's) germs and bacteria as with being protected from the participant. Universal precautions are called universal because they apply to everyone—even the leader.

Professional Issues

Professionalism includes a knowledge of the impact of social issues on leisure services participants, the leader, and the profession. In addition, a leisure services provider who strives to be the best leader possible seeks out professional contacts and pursues continuing education. Competence requires remaining involved in the evolution of the profession and a commitment to lifelong learning. One can demonstrate a commitment to the profession and ongoing learning through professional certifications, licensure, and membership in professional associations.

Professional Certifications

Certifications related to the field of parks and recreation can be sought in two general areas—professional expertise and health and safety. Many entry-level and mid-level positions in leisure services require a minimum of certifications in various health and safety areas (e.g., CPR, first aid). Other certifications enhance a leader's competence and verify a commitment to the profession, and employers often look for individuals with certifications to fill positions. All certifications require testing. Some require written tests which examine knowledge and understanding of material; others require both written and physical skill tests on which individuals must demonstrate proficiency.

Certification describes the process whereby an individual voluntarily submits her or his credentials for review based upon clearly identified competencies, criteria, or standards. This type of credentialing ensures that staff employed in leisure services meet high standards of performance. In addition, certifications often help when liability and negligence concerns arise. In many instances, certifications have become industry standard; the expectation or norm in the profession is for staff to be certified as a condition of employment. Generally, certifications in basic first aid and CPR are required of direct leadership staff and are considered minimum industry standards for direct leisure services leaders in many subfields (e.g., therapeutic recreation, outdoor leadership).

Becoming certified assures employers that certified applicants meet prescribed education, experience, and continuing education requirements and have shown dedication to professionalism through voluntary credentialing.

Leaders should be just as concerned with protecting an injured participant from their (the leader's) germs and bacteria as with being protected from the participant. Universal precautions are called universal because they apply to everyone—even the leader.

Certification does not guarantee a particular level of performance, however. Great variation in ability and performance exists among certified individuals. Credentials such as certifications and licenses are awarded by a wide variety of local, state, national, and international agencies and organizations.

Certified Park and Recreation Professional (CPRP)

The National Recreation and Park Association (NRPA) certifies leisure services professionals indicating that those individuals have been exposed to a basic body of knowledge through formal education and experience. In 1981 parks and recreation professionals and educators developed a National Certification Board consisting of individuals who provide guidance to the organization certification program. The certification process: (a) formally recognizes individuals who fulfill requirements of certification; (b) encourages professional growth and individual study; and (c) provides a standard of knowledge desirable for leisure services professionals.

Many professional positions in parks, recreation, and leisure services now prefer or require certification prior to employment. Through NRPA, a leisure services professional may be certified as a Certified Park and Recreation Professional (CPRP), Provisional Park and Recreation Professional (PPRP), or Associate Park and Recreation Professional (APRP). The latter two certifications are considered temporary and may be obtained while working toward CPRP status.

Certification describes the process whereby an individual voluntarily submits her or his credentials for review based upon clearly identified competencies, criteria, or standards.

An individual certified as a CPRP has graduated from an accredited university and passed a written test in several core knowledge areas of job-related tasks common to entry-level professionals. The core areas tested include *conceptual foundations; the leisure services profession; leisure services delivery system; programming strategies; assessment, planning, and evaluation; administration/ management; legislative and legal aspects; and field experiences*. The certification is valid for two years, and a certified individual needs to earn 2.0 continuing education units (CEUs) over that time to maintain certification. Exams are given in various cities around the country and are typically offered twice a year. When ready, one should contact her or his state parks and recreation association (or NRPA) for application materials and testing dates and locations.

Two temporary certifications include the Provisional Park and Recreation Professional (PPRP) and the Associate Park and Recreation Professional (APRP) certification. The PPRP provides certification to an individual who meets all education and experience qualifications, but has not yet had a chance to sit for the CPRP national exam. The APRP is designed for an individual who has less than a four-year degree. Specifically, one must have a two-year degree (usually an associate's degree) and experience in the field to receive this level of certification. One does not sit for the exam at this level. It is expected that both PPRP and APRP certificate recipients will complete their educational and exam requirements to attain the full CPRP certification.

Certified Therapeutic Recreation Specialist (CTRS)

The National Council for Therapeutic Recreation Certification (NCTRC) is a nonprofit organization that was formed in 1981. It follows the credentialing process utilized by the Council for Advancement of Hospital Recreation and the National Therapeutic Recreation Society in the design of its certification. It is designated as a certification program for individuals desiring to work in the field of therapeutic recreation. NCTRC establishes and tests the acceptable standards for therapeutic recreation personnel. Healthcare accrediting bodies and state and federal regulatory groups recognize the NCTRC as the credentialing authority for therapeutic recreation personnel in the United States.

According to its mission statement, the NCTRC exists to protect the public and promote the provision of quality therapeutic recreation services by: (a) establishing standards for certification and recertification; (b) granting recognition to individuals who voluntarily apply and meet established standards for certification and recertification; and (c) monitoring adherence to the standards. NCTRC

evaluates the educational and experiential qualifications of therapeutic recreation professionals as part of the certification process (National Council for Therapeutic Recreation Certification, 2005).

To be eligible to sit for the CTRS exam, an individual must hold a baccalaureate degree from an accredited college or university and have successfully completed a minimum of a 360-hour, ten consecutive week internship under the supervision of a CTRS. The CTRS exam covers the following material: *background information, diagnostic groupings and populations served, assessment, planning programs and treatments, implementing programs and treatments, documentation and managing services, organizing and managing services,* and *professional issues.* Initial CTRS certification is valid for five years; to renew, one needs a combination of professional experience, continuing education credits, and/or reexamination.

Certified Recreational Sports Specialist (CRSS)

Another setting-specific certification is offered through the National Intramural-Recreational Sports Association (NIRSA). NIRSA offers a certificate to qualified professionals working in the field of intramural and recreational sports (i.e., campus recreation). The certification was developed in 1979 to help maintain a high quality of professional competence of recreational sports specialists; to provide a means of identifying individuals who possess the necessary knowledge and expertise required in the field; to promote the educational standards set forth for recreational sports professionals; and to encourage professional growth and development of recreational sports personnel.

In addition to current certification in CPR and first aid, a written examination is required which covers the following knowledge areas: *programming, management and operations, risk management and legal concepts, program evaluation, participant rights, history and philosophical foundations,* and *professional ethics.* There are several categories of eligibility to sit for the exam, and interested individuals are encouraged to contact NIRSA for additional information (see p. 301).

Specialty Certifications

Several different types of certifications exist that enhance the leadership skills and professional commitment of entry-level leisure services personnel. Individuals may be certified as youth coaches, sports officials, Special Olympics coaches and officials, aerobics instructors, outdoor leaders, ropes course facilitators, and many other leadership positions. In addition, leaders may earn a certificate of attendance for receiving instruction related to child

Several different types of certifications exist that enhance the leadership skills and professional commitment of entry-level leisure services personnel.

abuse, elder abuse, and universal precautions. A sampling of specialty certifications related to parks, recreation, and leisure services are further explained in the following sections.

Nonprofit Management

American Humanics (AH) is a national program offered through many universities to aid in preparing and certifying students for entry-level positions in nonprofit human service agencies and organizations. In cooperation with nonprofit partners, AH has developed a series of competencies (typically translated into curriculum requirements) suited for those desiring to go into the field of nonprofits. Upon completion of the competency requirements, participation in co-curricular experiences, and a 300-hour internship in the nonprofit sector, a student may receive an American Humanics Certificate in Youth and Human Service Nonprofit Management and Leadership. More information about AH may be found on their website at http://www.humanics.org/.

Youth Sports

Individuals interested in working in youth sports as coaches, directors of coaches, or officials may wish to be certified as a youth sports coach (at various levels) or official. The YMCA offers these types of certification nationally. National, state, and local organized youth sports programs and the National Youth Sports Coaches Association (NYSCA) also offer certification. As part of the National Alliance for Youth Sports, the NYSCA promotes national standards for youth sports, including

- selecting the proper environment for each child (i.e., considering age, developmental stage, type of sport, rules in the sport, and level of physical and emotional stress)
- selecting youth sports programs designed to enhance the emotional, physical, social, and educational well-being of children
- encouraging a drug, tobacco, and alcohol-free environment for children
- recognizing that youth sports are only a small part of a child's life

- insisting that coaches are trained and certified
- exhibiting the ideals of fair play by being positive role models
- insisting on safe playing facilities, healthful playing situations, and proper first aid
- providing equal sports play opportunities for all youth regardless of race, creed, sex, economic status, or ability
- involving only substance-free adults at all youth sports activities. (National Alliance for Youth Sports, 2006)

Youth sports coaches training programs vary in length from clinics of six hours to full-training programs up to 20 hours. Information usually covered in such training includes psychology of coaching youth sports, rules of the game, developmental characteristics of youth, working with officials, injury prevention and treatment, child abuse prevention, substance abuse, and ideas for planning practices. By contacting the national office, leisure services leaders can find information about state contacts and local certification. More information may be found on the National Alliance for Youth Sports website at www.nays.org

Officials and coaches training is commonly offered through the regulating body of a particular sport, such as Amateur Softball Association of America (www.softball.org), and the American Association of adaptedSports (www.aaasp.org). Interested leisure services leaders are encouraged to seek additional information from those organizations related to the sport in which they have an interest. Websites of regulating bodies and associations can be a good place to start.

Special Olympics International

Special Olympics International (SOI) offers training to individuals who desire to coach and/or officiate Special Olympic athletes in a wide variety of sports programs. In the SOI system each sport is categorized by level of international involvement. For instance, Official Sports are those that are played in at least twelve countries. They include: aquatics, track and field, basketball, bowling, cycling, equestrian, soccer, gymnastics (both artistic and rhythmic), roller skating, softball, tennis, volleyball, power lifting, golf, alpine skiing, cross-country skiing, figure skating, floor hockey, and speed skating. Those sports with a smaller following are also supported by SOI, and are called *national sports*. They include: badminton, bocce, sailing, snow shoeing, table tennis, and team handball. Every two years (at the closing of the World Games), sports are evaluated for inclusion in these categories.

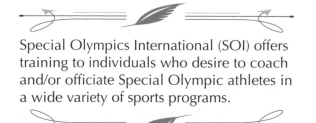

Special Olympics International (SOI) offers training to individuals who desire to coach and/or officiate Special Olympic athletes in a wide variety of sports programs.

Special Olympics International offers several levels of coaching training—a General Orientation (in which all prospective coaches enroll), a Skills Course, Principles of Coaching Course, Tactics Course, and a Comprehensive Mentoring Course. The General Orientation Course is an introductory-level course designed for volunteers and professionals who wish to coach Special Olympics athletes. The training commonly includes background information about Special Olympics International and its sports program, support services available for the coach, hints for recruiting athletes and assistant coaches, ability grouping, challenges, and benefits. The other courses cover additional areas as indicated by their titles.

SOI offers a variety of coaching and training courses, and the revised training system (implemented in 1999) enables prospective coaches to acquire the skills needed through meeting and verifying competencies. Thus, once an individual has attended the General Orientation course, other competencies may be met in a wide variety of ways.

In addition to coaching certifications, Special Olympics offers a Special Olympics officials certification. This certification may be obtained through clinics and practicum experiences at local, area, and chapter competitions. Material covered in training sessions includes the philosophy of Special Olympics International, information related to ability grouping for competition, general medical information, and rules interpretation specific to each sport. For information about coaching or officials training for SOI, interested individuals should contact their state Special Olympics office. Contact information may be found through links on the SOI website at www.specialolympics.org.

Aerobics Leader Certification

As it becomes more evident that a qualified aerobics instructor should know more than simply how to move to music, training for aerobics leaders has essentially become a prerequisite for employment in this area. A variety of national and local agencies and hospitals conduct certification programs which commonly cover a wide spectrum of material. Information contained in typical aerobics instructor training include components of an exercise class, basic exercise selection, practical applications of exercise science, nutritional information, biomechanics

of movement, exercise physiology, choreography, music selection, and safety and liability. Course lengths vary from 25 to 100 hours depending upon the organization providing the certification. Several national agencies provide certification in aerobics leadership (including aerobics instructor, personal trainer, step instructor, weight training instructor, and kickboxing instructor). Two professional associations with related training include the Aerobics and Fitness Association of America (AFAA; www.afaa.com) and the American College of Sports Medicine (ACSM; information online at www.acsm.org).

Ropes Course Facilitator

While there is no one nationally accepted certification program for ropes course leaders, formal training and certification are highly desirable prior to leading groups on ropes or teams courses. In fact, there are many nationally accepted practices regarding safety and technical skills associated with a ropes course. Typically, ropes course facilitators require training in basic adventure programming, facilitation skills, group dynamics, safety and rescue, ropes and knots, program planning, working with people with disabilities on ropes courses, and structure maintenance. Ropes course facilitator training typically requires a practicum of some type. Length of course varies from one day to two weeks depending upon the breadth and complexity of the material to be covered. For certification and course information, leaders are encouraged to contact the Association for Challenge Course Technology (ACCT; www.acctinfo.org) and Project Adventure (www.pa.org).

YMCA of the USA Training Program

The YMCA of the USA offers various types of training at program schools across the country which lead to various certifications. All sessions are open to YMCA volunteers and staff members, and some training (at local YMCAs) is open to the general public. The YMCA of the USA trains people in many diverse areas including CPR and first aid, "Working With" programs for specific populations (e.g., different age groups, people with disabilities, program volunteers, military families), aquatics, camping, childcare, community development (e.g., substance

While there is no one nationally accepted certification program for ropes course leaders, formal training and certification are highly desirable prior to leading groups on ropes or teams courses.

abuse prevention, prejudice awareness, conflict and violence prevention and management), health and fitness (e.g., Fitness Leader, Fitness Instructor, Personal Trainer, Healthy Back, Prenatal/Postpartum Exercise), youth sports, and teen leadership. In addition, the YMCA of the USA provides leadership and management training for directors in their Executive Development Program. Course hours and prerequisites vary with course sessions, but typically run from four hours (e.g., the "working with" programs) to 28 hours (e.g., aquatics). Additional information may be found at www.ymca.net.

Mandatory Reporter Training

Colleges, universities, and many nonprofit organizations now offer training related to information needed by mandatory reporters of child and/or elder abuse. Typical training sessions are two to four hours in length and are good for three to five years. These are noncertification courses that provide information about recognizing signs of child abuse, what to do if a child reports abuse, and identifying resources for intervention.

Universal Precautions

Similar to mandatory reporter training, several different agencies offer training and awareness sessions about universal precautions. As noted earlier in this chapter, universal precautions are those steps taken when handling an individual's bodily fluids to minimize the transmission of disease. Typical noncertification courses are two to four hours in length and are good for three to five years. The American Red Cross offers a Preventing Disease Transmission course designed for this purpose (http://www. redcross.org).

CPR, First-Aid, and Safety Education

The American Red Cross and the American Heart Association are internationally known for developing health and safety standards and training. Both programs continually update and improve their standards and educational programs based on current science. The most commonly sought certifications are related to emergency care; these types of certifications are often required as conditions of employment for those working in parks, recreation, and leisure services. Table 13B (p. 298) summarizes the types of CPR and first aid training available through these two agencies.

Aquatics Certifications

Anyone desiring to work in or near water, whether it be a swimming pool, waterpark, or natural waterfront, will be required to hold one or more aquatic certifications. As with first-aid and safety education, the American Red Cross

Anyone desiring to work in or near water, whether it be a swimming pool, waterpark, or natural waterfront, will be required to hold one or more aquatic certifications.

is the most widely recognized and accepted certification program for aquatic certification needs. Aquatic safety programs range from basic "drown proofing," to teaching swimming, to advanced water rescue techniques. Some certifications appropriate for parks and recreation leaders are mentioned here.

Lifeguarding

Lifeguard training is a 33-hour course designed for individuals wishing to lifeguard at all types of bodies of water. Prerequisites for this course include the requirement that candidates be a minimum of fifteen years of age and pass a water-skills test. Course content includes professional rescue techniques, interacting with the public, preventing aquatic injuries, patron surveillance, being prepared for emergencies, first aid for injuries and illnesses, handling spinal injuries, and what to do after an emergency. Three certifications are provided upon completion of this course: Lifeguard, First Aid, and CPR for the Professional Rescuer. Separate courses for Waterpark Lifeguarding and Waterfront Lifeguarding specifically address the setting-based challenges of those venues.

Water Safety Instructor (WSI)

In the 30-hour water safety instructor (WSI) program, individuals learn to teach learn-to-swim and community water safety courses. Prerequisites include a minimum age of 17 years, completion of a three-hour precourse session, and completion of instructor candidate training. Focused on teaching swimming skills, the content of this course includes teaching progressions, the development of lesson plans, recognition of skill errors and the ability to give corrective feedback, motor learning and hydrodynamic principles, cultural diversity, fitness and training, and disabilities and other conditions. The course begins with a preliminary written swimming and water safety skills test as a prerequisite for continuation.

Lifeguarding Instructor

In this 15-hour program, individuals learn to teach American Red Cross lifeguarding and water safety courses (i.e., basic water safety and emergency water safety). Course content includes course administration and planning, teaching progressions for lifeguarding and water safety skills, and recognizing common skill errors and providing corrective feedback. Lifeguard training is a prerequisite to enroll in this course.

Safety Training for Swim Coaches

This course provides practical information for swim coaches to help them prepare for emergencies.

❖ ❖ ❖

In addition to these aquatic certifications, the American Red Cross also offers certifications related to equipment and

---

Table 13B Selected American Red Cross and American Heart Association CPR, first-aid, and safety trainings

American Red Cross	American Heart Association
CPR for the Professional Rescuer (9 hours): Covers principles of CPR for adults, children and infants, two-person CPR, ventilation with airbag and mask, and how to minimize disease transmission. Valid for one year.	**Basic Life Support (BLS) for Healthcare Providers** (4.5 hours): Covers adult and child CPR (including two-person scenarios and use of a bag mask), foreign-body airway obstruction, and automated external defibrillation (AED). Valid for two years.
AED—Adult and Child (4.5 hours): CPR and safe use of an automatic external defibrillator (AED) on adults and children. Valid for one year.	**Heartsaver CPR** (3 hours): CPR and relief of choking in adults and children. Optional units include infant CPR and choking, adult/child with bag mask, and infant with bag mask. Valid for two years.
Adult CPR (4 hours): Involves practicing an emergency action plan—caring for breathing emergencies, airway obstruction, cardiac emergencies—and information about how to prevent heart attacks. Valid for one year.	**Heartsaver AED** (3.5 hours): Covers CPR, AED use, and relief of choking in adults and children. Optional units include infant CPR with mask, and infant CPR. Valid for two years.
Child and Infant CPR (5 hours): Course addresses basic life support for persons under the age of nine years as well as how to prevent injuries to infants and children in and around the home and play areas. Valid for one year.	**Heartsaver First Aid** (7.5 hours): General principles of illness and injury management, medical emergencies, injury emergencies. Optional units include environmental emergencies, CPR, and AED use. Valid for two years.
First Aid/CPR/AED for Schools and the Community (9 hours): Covers bleeding, shock, broken bones, seizures, illnesses, poisoning, and other emergency situations. Adult CPR, and Infant and Child CPR are included in this certification. The first-aid certification is valid for three years, and the CPR certifications are valid for one year.	**Heartsaver Pediatric First Aid** (7.5 hours): Illness and injury management in the pediatric patient, first-aid basics, medical emergencies, injury emergencies, and environmental emergencies. Optional units include asthma care training for childcare providers, child and infant CPR, and child and infant AED. Valid for two years.
Emergency Response (23.5 – 35 hours depending on the modules included): Covers CPR for Adults, CPR for Infants and Children, First Aid, and material related to prevention of injury and illness. Optional units include emergency childbirth and first aid for when help is delayed for more than 30 minutes. The first-aid certification is valid for three years, and the CPR certifications are valid for one year.	**Advanced Cardiovascular Life Support** (13.5 hours): Enhanced skills in treatment of adult victim of cardiac emergencies. Integration of basic life support with advanced life support interventions, and the importance of team interaction and communication during resuscitation. Valid for two years.
Sports Safety Training (6.5 hours): Focuses on first aid needed for common sports injuries. Includes injury prevention information, basic first aid, and Adult CPR. Optional units include Infant and Child CPR. The safety certification is valid for three years, and the CPR certification is valid for one year.	**Pediatric Advanced Cardiovascular Life Support** (14 hours): Enhanced skills in the efficient and effective management of critically ill infants and children. This course is generally for those in healthcare professions and in healthcare settings. Valid for two years.
CPR/First-Aid Instructor (16 hours): Course prepares individuals to teach the CPR/First Aid courses. The CPR certification is good for one year, and the first-aid certification is valid for three years.	**Core Instructor Course:** Designed to provide a foundation for teaching and facilitating learning. Upon completion of this course the candidate completes a specific course (as identified above), is monitored as an instructor, and, if appropriate, awarded the instructor certification. Valid for two years.

Sources: http://www.americanheart.org and http://www.redcross.org

facilities: Small Craft Safety, Basic Sailing, and Aquatic Examiner. Future parks and recreation leaders are encouraged to determine which certifications would best prepare them for internships or jobs they are considering.

Outdoor-Related Certifications

Anyone desiring to work as an outdoor leader will want to hold one or more outdoor-related certifications. These can be taken from a wide variety of national programs (e.g., the National Outdoor Leadership School, American Canoe Association) and will enhance one's professional qualifications tremendously. Only a few of the many available certifications are mentioned here.

Leave No Trace

The National Outdoor Leadership School (NOLS), in conjunction with other organizations, developed the Leave No Trace (LNT) program several years ago. It promotes and inspires responsible outdoor recreation through education, research, and partnerships. Course content focuses on low-impact camping skills, wildland ethics, and teaching techniques. A student may wish to become a *LNT Master* through a five-day course designed for people actively teaching others outdoor recreation skills or providing recreation information to the public. Individuals certified at this level can offer *LNT Trainer* courses. More information may be found on the web at www.lnt.org.

Canoe and Kayak Certifications

The American Canoe Association offers a wide variety of solo and tandem canoeing and kayaking courses. These courses cover instruction and certification for flat water, moving water, whitewater, coastal kayaking, and river safety and rescue. In addition to receiving basic instruction, outdoor leaders can seek certification in becoming an instructor and instructor-trainer for these courses. More information may be found online at www.americancanoe.org.

Wilderness Emergency Care

Currently three major organizations certify individuals in backcountry emergency care—the Wilderness Medical Institute (through the National Outdoor Leadership School), Wilderness Medicine Associates, and Stonehearth Open Learning Opportunities (SOLO). The programs they offer are fairly similar and include five levels of certification: Wilderness First Aid, Advanced Wilderness First Aid, Wilderness First Responder, Wilderness Emergency Medical Technician, and Wilderness Transition. Specific information may be found online at www.nols.edu/wmi or www.wildmed.com or www.soloschools.com.

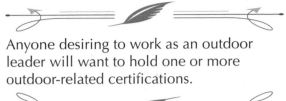

Anyone desiring to work as an outdoor leader will want to hold one or more outdoor-related certifications.

At 16 to 24 hours in length, the basic *Wilderness First Aid* course covers a wide range of wilderness medicine topics at an introductory level; it is most appropriate for dayhikers and those taking short trips. The *Advanced Wilderness First Aid* course (40 hours) is designed for outdoor leaders who will be leading short trips that are easy to access from a roadhead. This course focuses on stabilization, treatment and evacuation guidelines for patients in backcountry environments. These two levels of certification are common requirements for those working in camps.

The *Wilderness First Responder* course (80 hours) is designed for a variety of outdoor leaders and professionals. It consists of classroom skills, scenarios, mock rescues, and many decision-making situations. It covers material needed by those who will be traveling away from easy-and-quick access to city emergency care. For most wilderness-based outdoor leadership job positions, Wilderness First Responder is the minimum required certification.

Wilderness EMT is a 180-hour course covering classroom education, practical skills, scenarios, and full-scale mock rescues. Individuals who complete the course can sit for both the Wilderness EMT and national EMT exams. A successful student will be certified as a Basic EMT, Wilderness EMT, and will be recorded on the National Registry of EMTs. The *Wilderness Transition* course is designed for an individual who already holds a valid EMT certification. It helps an EMT transition from urban emergency care to backcountry emergency care.

❖ ❖ ❖

As can be seen from the certifications mentioned here, there are many avenues for professional education for leisure services leaders. This list of certifications is by no means exhaustive; several associations and organizations offer other leadership level certifications which would enhance various types of leisure services positions. Entry-level leisure services personnel are strongly encouraged to seek out appropriate certifications and training to enhance their competence and professional growth.

Professional Associations

Like gaining appropriate certifications, membership in one or more professional associations is indicative of a commitment to the profession and an interest in ongoing growth and development. Membership in professional associations provides an opportunity to network with practitioners and educators, gain new information, and promote one's own organization or agency. National associations for all interest areas in the leisure services profession exist. This diversity in professional associations allows one to join and network with other professionals who share interests and concerns specific to particular leisure services specialty area(s). This networking provides opportunities for individuals to share problems, solutions, issues, and learning experiences with one another.

In addition to networking with other professionals, many professional associations develop and promote standards of practice. This is evidenced in the various certification and accreditation programs offered by professional associations such as the CPRP, CTRS, and CRSS certifications. Many professional associations hold periodic conferences where educational sessions are offered to delegates. Individuals can gain continuing education units (CEUs) during these conferences to maintain certification and show evidence of ongoing development.

Other benefits of joining professional associations include access to research findings about practical issues; access to liability, health, and retirement benefits; subscriptions to professional journals or magazines, and the opportunity to become involved in developing the profession through association leadership. Furthermore, many professional associations offer educational scholarships to college students. Some of the more common professional organizations that serve individuals in the parks, recreation, and leisure services field follow.

American Alliance for Health, Physical Education, Recreation and Dance (AAHPERD)

1900 Association Drive
Reston, VA 22091
(800) 213-7193
http://www.aahperd.org

AAHPERD promotes interests in health and safety education, intramurals, aging, fitness research, physical education, adapted physical education, sport, dance, leisure and recreation, and outdoor education and recreation. The major publication of AAHPERD is the *Journal of Physical Education, Recreation and Dance*, although it also publishes several other periodicals. The American Association for Physical Activity and Recreation (AAPAR) is the substructure of AAHPERD dedicated to promoting the field of leisure and recreation within the membership of AAHPERD.

Membership in one or more professional associations is indicative of a commitment to the profession and an interest in ongoing growth and development.

American Camp Association (ACA)

Bradford Woods, 5000 State Route 67N
Martinsville, IN 46151
(765) 342-8456
http://www.acacamps.org

The American Camp Association assures the quality of organized camps and conference centers. Membership in ACA is open to individuals and organized camps that promote camp activities, including those involved in providing camp programs at private, youth serving, church, and agency/nonprofit organizations. ACA holds an annual convention, manages and publishes camp and leadership-related books and resources, and produces its primary publication, *Camp Magazine*, on a bimonthly basis. In addition, ACA conducts an internationally recognized accreditation process for camps and conference centers.

American Therapeutic Recreation Association (ATRA)

1414 Prince Street, Suite 204
Alexandria, VA 22314
(703) 683-9420
http://www.atra-tr.org

Started in 1984, the American Therapeutic Recreation Association is one of the newest professional organiza-

Professionalism is the hallmark of a leader who is committed to best practices.

tions available to those interested in therapeutic recreation. As a nonprofit organization, it promotes the needs of therapeutic recreation professionals in healthcare and human service settings. To this end, ATRA offers a Code of Ethics for professionals, workshops, and educational information. Its major publication is the *Therapeutic Recreation Annual.* According to ATRA the primary purposes of treatment services (i.e., recreation therapy) are: to restore, remedy, or rehabilitate; to improve functioning and independence; and to reduce or eliminate the effects of illness or disability.

Association for Experiential Education (AEE)
3775 Iris Ave, Suite 4
Boulder, CO 80301
(866) 522-8337
http://www.aee.org

The AEE has its roots in adventure education and commits to furthering experience-based teaching and learning in all settings. AEE has several professional and special interest groups within it, including experience-based training and development; schools and colleges; women in experiential education; therapeutic adventure; and Natives, Africans, Asians, Latinos(as) and Allies of AEE (NAALA). Members include people involved in school-based settings, recreation programs, challenge course providers, human service providers, correctional and mental health institutions, youth service agencies, programs for people with disabilities, environmental centers, outdoor adventure organizations, and universities.

AEE provides program accreditation and peer review for adventure programming and experiential education programs internationally. AEE publishes and sells several books and other publications for those interested in out-

door and experiential education. Membership benefits include receiving the *Journal of Experiential Education* (three times a year), newsletters, and discounts on AEE publications and conferences. A Listserv is available for those interested in learning more about the issues affecting experiential education. In addition, international and regional conferences are offered throughout the United States on an annual basis.

National Intramural-Recreational Sports Association (NIRSA)
4185 SW Research Parkway
Corvallis, OR 97333-1067
(541) 766-8211
http://www.nirsa.org

NIRSA strives to foster the growth of quality recreational sports programs (e.g., campus recreation) by providing for the continuing growth and development of recreational sports professionals. Membership includes professionals involved in recreational sports programming at the collegiate level (e.g., intramurals, sports clubs, campus recreation), in the military, correctional facilities, and public schools. Individuals working in these settings are typically involved in informal sports, programming, fitness, recreation facility operations, fiscal and personnel management, intramurals, wellness programs, and the administration of outdoor recreation programs. Membership benefits include publications such as the *NIRSA Journal* (three times a year), a newsletter, and conference proceedings. In addition NIRSA offers research grants, job listings, annual national and regional conferences, officiating instruction, and certification for recreational sports officials.

National Recreation and Park Association (NRPA)
22377 Belmont Ridge Road
Ashburn, VA 20148
(703) 858-0784
http://www.nrpa.org

The National Recreation and Park Association (NRPA) is the primary professional association of parks, recreation, and leisure services professionals. It serves professionals, volunteers, students, universities and agencies/organizations. NRPA holds an annual congress and provides a variety of services and publications for its diverse membership body. Its major publication is *Parks and Recreation Magazine*, although it also publishes the *Therapeutic Recreation Journal* and other periodicals. NRPA implements and conducts an accreditation and certification program of colleges and universities to ensure standards commensurate with a high-quality profession.

Within NRPA many branches facilitate meeting the needs of its diverse constituencies. These include the

✓ networking	✓ ongoing education
✓ promote own agency	✓ employment searches
✓ collaborative efforts	✓ liability insurance
✓ opportunity to develop personal leadership skills	✓ subscription to professional journals
✓ discounts on goods and services related to the profession	✓ a set of professional ethics
✓ access to research findings	✓ exposure to new products

Figure 13.4 The benefits of joining and participating in professional organizations are quite varied.

Student Branch (SB), National Therapeutic Recreation Society (NTRS), Society of Park and Recreation Educators (SPRE), American Park and Recreation Society (APRS), National Society for Park Resources (NSPR), Armed Forces Recreation Society (AFRS), Citizen Branch (CB), National Aquatics Branch (NAB), Leisure and Aging Section (LAS), Commercial Recreation and Tourism Section (CRTS), and an affiliate—the Ethnic Minority Society (EMS).

❖ ❖ ❖

In addition to the organizations and associations identified in this section, nearly every state has its own professional association. These associations are typically affiliated with a corresponding national association. For example, the Oklahoma Parks and Recreation Society (ORPS) is a state association linked to NRPA. It views itself as a service organization supported by membership dues and voluntary contributions. A typical state association publishes a state-wide journal or a periodic newsletter. They also host an annual conference and workshops, scholarship program, and other services and opportunities to network within the state.

Similarly, a state association linked with AAHPERD, the Oklahoma Association of Health, Physical Education, Recreation and Dance (OAHPERD) exists to meet the needs of physical education, dance, health, and recreation professionals within the state of Oklahoma. It holds an annual conference, publishes *OAHPERD Journal* biannually, and provides funding for special projects. Likewise, the Texoma Section of the American Camping Association is the state association that provides ACA services to individuals and organizations within two states—Texas and Oklahoma. Fall and winter workshops, educational sessions, and a bimonthly newsletter are products of this association.

Summary

This chapter addressed selected social and professional issues impacting leisure services leaders and the profession. These issues impact both the profession and the individual leadership style of leisure services professionals. Child abuse as a social issue impacts leisure services leaders in two ways: (a) leisure services leaders may serve as those who intervene on behalf of an abuse victim, and (b) leisure services leaders must take care to avoid situations in which they might be perceived as perpetrators of child maltreatment.

Leisure services leaders exhibit a commitment to the field of leisure services through their own competence and continued education. Evidence of this commitment

The National Recreation and Park Association (NRPA) is the primary professional association of parks, recreation, and leisure services professionals.

may be seen through the various certifications one may obtain in efforts to improve leadership skills. In addition to health and/or safety certifications and those associated with particular skill areas, another way in which leisure services leaders illustrate an interest in furthering the profession is through membership in one or more professional associations. Through ongoing practice of skills and involvement in the profession, leisure services leaders improve their professional standing and become more effective leaders.

Beginning the Journey

The beginning of your personal journey to leadership is coming to an end. Next, you move on to furthering your studies of leadership and continuing your self-reflection and personal awareness through the conduct of leadership in the field. As you begin the next phase of your leadership development, you will be integrating personal concerns with professional concerns. The following questions may help as you begin that transition.

1. What is the difference between social and professional issues? Why should parks and recreation leaders be concerned with these types of issues? What would you name as some of the more pressing social issues in your community? What is the role of leisure services leaders related to these issues in your community? Are leisure services leaders doing enough with respect to these issues? What more could/should be done?

2. Do you think that child maltreatment is something that parks and recreation leaders should be concerned with? Where can you find the regulations addressing child abuse in your state? In your state, what is required of you by law if you suspect child maltreatment?

3. What are the differences in types of maltreatment faced by children? Do you believe that child abuse is prevalent in your community? Find the statistics for your local area as well as your state. Compare them to the national statistics about child maltreat-

ment. Discuss the impact of these statistics on the field of parks, recreation, and leisure services.

4. What are the factors that contribute to child maltreatment cases? Identify the consequences of child maltreatment on an individual, the community, and the leisure services profession. What does this have to do with leadership development?

5. How can you tell if a child is being abused or neglected? What types of and how many signs and symptoms would you need to see and hear before you suspect child maltreatment? What are the characteristics of maltreating adults? What is the likelihood that if someone was abused as a youngster, they would abuse as an adult?

6. What is the process of reporting and follow-up by Child Protective Services? Have a discussion with a classmate about what you would do if a child made you promise not to tell and then told you that she or he was being abused. Have you ever had this happen? What did you do?

7. As a recreation leader how can you protect yourself against unfounded suspicions of child abuse? What caveats would you give to other leaders? Why?

8. What is elder maltreatment, and what should you do about it? Are you a mandatory reporter of adult abuse? Where can you find out? What is the reporting process for suspected adult abuse?

9. What are universal precautions? What are bloodborne pathogens? Why do recreation leaders need to be aware of these? In what types of settings are you likely to come into contact with someone else's bodily fluids? What should you do to protect them and you?

10. Why are professional certifications important for parks and recreation leaders? Which certifications do you already hold? Which certifications do you think will be most advantageous for you to have as you go into the field? How do you intend to go about getting those certifications? Go online and find specific information related to the certifications you think you will need in an entry-level position in your area of interest.

11. What are CPRP and CTRS? Who should seek out these certifications? What do you have to do to be eligible for these certifications? What organizations are responsible for awarding these certifications? What do you need to do to maintain these certifications once you've received them?

12. Explain the role of professional associations in terms of facilitating leadership development. Read about the professional associations named in this text, and find others that represent your interest in the field. Identify the three most important professional associations for you to join. Explain why these professional associations are best for you. Make a plan for how and when you will join at least one of these prior to graduation.

References

Child abuse. (2006). Retrieved August 12, 2006, from http://www.acf.hhs.gov/programs/cb/pubs/cm04/index.htm

Child Abuse Prevention, Adoption, and Family Services Act of 1988, Pub. L. No. 100-294. (1988).

Child maltreatment. (2006). Retrieved August 12, 2006, from http://www.cdc.gov/ncipc/factsheets/cmfacts.htm

Child Welfare Information Gateway. (2006). *What is child abuse and neglect?* Retrieved May 13, 2007, from http://www.childwelfare.gov/pubs/factsheets/whatiscan.cfm

Elder abuse. (2006). Retrieved August 12, 2006, from http://www.state.il.us/aging/1abuselegal/abuselegal-main.htm

Levesque, R. (2000). Cultural evidence, child maltreatment, and the law. *Child Maltreatment, 5*(2), 146–160.

National Alliance for Youth Sports. (2006). *National standards for youth sports.* Retrieved November 18, 2006, from http://www.nays.org/TimeOut/National%20Standards.pdf

National Center on Elder Abuse homepage. (2006). Retrieved August 12, 2006, from http://www.elderabusecenter.org/default.cfm

National Council for Therapeutic Recreation Certification (2005). About NCTRC. Retrieved May 13, 2007, from http://www.nctrc.org

Tabachnick, J. (2005). *Prevent child sexual abuse.* Northampton, MA: Stop It Now!

Wilson, T. (2002). *False allegations of abuse.* Retrieved August 12, 2006, from http://members.aol.com/asherah/falsealleg.html

Index

21st Century Leisure: Current Issues, 2nd ed.
by Valeria J. Freysinger and John R. Kelly

The A•B•Cs of Behavior Change: Skills for Working With Behavior Problems in Nursing Homes
by Margaret D. Cohn, Michael A. Smyer, and Ann L. Horgas

Activity Experiences and Programming within Long-Term Care
by Ted Tedrick and Elaine R. Green

The Activity Gourmet
by Peggy Powers

Adventure Programming
edited by John C. Miles and Simon Priest

Assessment: The Cornerstone of Activity Programs
by Ruth Perschbacher

Behavior Modification in Therapeutic Recreation: An Introductory Manual
by John Datillo and William D. Murphy

Benefits of Leisure
edited by B.L. Driver, Perry J. Brown, and George L. Peterson

Benefits of Recreation Research Update
by Judy M. Sefton and W. Kerry Mummery

Beyond Baskets and Beads: Activities for Older Adults with Functional Impairments
by Mary Hart, Karen Primm, and Kathy Cranisky

Beyond Bingo: Innovative Programs for the New Senior
by Sal Arrigo, Jr., Ann Lewis, and Hank Mattimore

Beyond Bingo 2: More Innovative Programs for the New Senior
by Sal Arrigo, Jr.

Boredom Busters: Themed Special Events to Dazzle and Delight Your Group
by Annette C. Moore

Both Gains and Gaps: Feminist Perspectives on Women's Leisure
by Karla Henderson, M. Deborah Bialeschki, Susan M. Shaw, and Valeria J. Freysinger

Client Assessment in Therapeutic Recreation Services
by Norma J. Stumbo

Client Outcomes in Therapeutic Recreation Services
by Norma J. Stumbo

Conceptual Foundations for Therapeutic Recreation
edited by David R. Austin, John Dattilo, and Bryan P. McCormick

Constraints to Leisure
edited by Edgar L. Jackson

Dementia Care Programming: An Identity-Focused Approach
by Rosemary Dunne

Dimensions of Choice: Qualitative Approaches to Parks, Recreation, Tourism, Sport, and Leisure Research, 2nd ed.
by Karla A. Henderson

Diversity and the Recreation Profession: Organizational Perspectives
edited by Maria T. Allison and Ingrid E. Schneider

Effective Management in Therapeutic Recreation Service, 2nd ed.
by Marcia Jean Carter and Gerald S. O'Morrow

Evaluating Leisure Services: Making Enlightened Decisions, 2nd ed.
by Karla A. Henderson and M. Deborah Bialeschki

Everything from A to Y: The Zest Is up to You! Older Adult Activities for Every Day of the Year
by Nancy R. Cheshire and Martha L. Kenney

The Evolution of Leisure: Historical and Philosophical Perspectives
by Thomas Goodale and Geoffrey Godbey

Experience Marketing: Strategies for the New Millennium
by Ellen L. O'Sullivan and Kathy J. Spangler

Facilitation Techniques in Therapeutic Recreation
by John Dattilo

File o' Fun: A Recreation Planner for Games & Activities, 3rd ed.
by Jane Harris Ericson and Diane Ruth Albright

Functional Interdisciplinary-Transdisciplinary Therapy (FITT) Manual
by Deborah M. Schott, Judy D. Burdett, Beverly J. Cook, Karren S. Ford, and Kathleen M. Orban

The Game and Play Leader's Handbook: Facilitating Fun and Positive Interaction, Revised Edition
by Bill Michaelis and John M. O'Connell

The Game Finder—A Leader's Guide to Great Activities
by Annette C. Moore

Getting People Involved in Life and Activities: Effective Motivating Techniques
by Jeanne Adams

Glossary of Recreation Therapy and Occupational Therapy
by David R. Austin

Great Special Events and Activities
by Annie Morton, Angie Prosser, and Sue Spangler

Group Games & Activity Leadership
by Kenneth J. Bulik

Growing With Care: Using Greenery, Gardens, and Nature With Aging and Special Populations
by Betsy Kreidler

Hands On! Children's Activities for Fairs, Festivals, and Special Events
by Karen L. Ramey

Health Promotion for Mind, Body and Spirit
by Suzanne Fitzsimmons and Linda L. Buettner

In Search of the Starfish: Creating a Caring Environment
by Mary Hart, Karen Primm, and Kathy Cranisky

Inclusion: Including People With Disabilities in Parks and Recreation Opportunities
by Lynn Anderson and Carla Brown Kress

Inclusive Leisure Services: Responding to the Rights of People with Disabilities, 2nd ed.
by John Dattilo

Innovations: A Recreation Therapy Approach to Restorative Programs
by Dawn R. De Vries and Julie M. Lake

Internships in Recreation and Leisure Services: A Practical Guide for Students, 3rd ed.
by Edward E. Seagle, Jr. and Ralph W. Smith

Interpretation of Cultural and Natural Resources, 2nd ed.
by Douglas M. Knudson, Ted T. Cable, and Larry Beck

Intervention Activities for At-Risk Youth
by Norma J. Stumbo

Introduction to Outdoor Recreation: Providing and Managing Resource Based Opportunities
by Roger L. Moore and B.L. Driver

Introduction to Recreation and Leisure Services, 8th ed.
by Karla A. Henderson, M. Deborah Bialeschki, John L. Hemingway, Jan S. Hodges, Beth D. Kivel, and H. Douglas Sessoms

Introduction to Therapeutic Recreation: U.S. and Canadian Perspectives
by Kenneth Mobily and Lisa Ostiguy

Introduction to Writing Goals and Objectives: A Manual for Recreation Therapy Students and Entry-Level Professionals
by Suzanne Melcher

Leadership and Administration of Outdoor Pursuits, 2nd ed.
by Phyllis Ford and James Blanchard

Leisure Services in Canada: An Introduction, 2nd ed.
by Mark S. Searle and Russell E. Brayley

Leisure and Leisure Services in the 21st Century: Toward Mid Century
by Geoffrey Godbey

Other Books by Venture Publishing, Inc.

The Leisure Diagnostic Battery: Users Manual and Sample Forms
by Peter A. Witt and Gary Ellis

Leisure Education I: A Manual of Activities and Resources, 2nd ed.
by Norma J. Stumbo

Leisure Education II: More Activities and Resources, 2nd ed.
by Norma J. Stumbo

Leisure Education III: More Goal-Oriented Activities
by Norma J. Stumbo

Leisure Education IV: Activities for Individuals with Substance Addictions
by Norma J. Stumbo

Leisure Education Program Planning: A Systematic Approach, 2nd ed.
by John Dattilo

Leisure Education Specific Programs
by John Dattilo

Leisure in Your Life: An Exploration, 6th ed.
by Geoffrey Godbey

Leisure Services in Canada: An Introduction, 2nd ed.
by Mark S. Searle and Russell E. Brayley

Leisure Studies: Prospects for the Twenty-First Century
edited by Edgar L. Jackson and Thomas L. Burton

The Lifestory Re-Play Circle: A Manual of Activities and Techniques
by Rosilyn Wilder

Marketing in Leisure and Tourism: Reaching New Heights
by Patricia Click Janes

The Melody Lingers On: A Complete Music Activities Program for Older Adults
by Bill Messenger

Models of Change in Municipal Parks and Recreation: A Book of Innovative Case Studies
edited by Mark E. Havitz

More Than a Game: A New Focus on Senior Activity Services
by Brenda Corbett

The Multiple Values of Wilderness
by H. Ken Cordell, John C. Bergstrom, and J.M. Bowker

Nature and the Human Spirit: Toward an Expanded Land Management Ethic
edited by B.L. Driver, Daniel Dustin, Tony Baltic, Gary Elsner, and George Peterson

The Organizational Basis of Leisure Participation: A Motivational Exploration
by Robert A. Stebbins

Outdoor Recreation for 21st Century America
by H. Ken Cordell

Outdoor Recreation Management: Theory and Application, 3rd ed.
by Alan Jubenville and Ben Twight

Parks for Life: Moving the Goal Posts, Changing the Rules, and Expanding the Field
by Will LaPage

Planning and Organizing Group Activities in Social Recreation
by John V. Valentine

Planning Parks for People, 2nd ed.
by John Hultsman, Richard L. Cottrell, and Wendy Z. Hultsman

The Process of Recreation Programming Theory and Technique, 3rd ed.
by Patricia Farrell and Herberta M. Lundegren

Programming for Parks, Recreation, and Leisure Services: A Servant Leadership Approach, 2nd ed.
by Debra J. Jordan, Donald G. DeGraaf, and Kathy H. DeGraaf

Protocols for Recreation Therapy Programs
edited by Jill Kelland, along with the Recreation Therapy Staff at Alberta Hospital Edmonton

Puttin' on the Skits: Plays for Adults in Managed Care
by Jean Vetter

Quality Management: Applications for Therapeutic Recreation
edited by Bob Riley

A Recovery Workbook: The Road Back from Substance Abuse
by April K. Neal and Michael J. Taleff

Recreation and Leisure: Issues in an Era of Change, 3rd ed.
edited by Thomas Goodale and Peter A. Witt

Recreation and Youth Development
by Peter A. Witt and Linda L. Caldwell

Recreation Economic Decisions: Comparing Benefits and Costs, 2nd ed.
by John B. Loomis and Richard G. Walsh

Recreation for Older Adults: Individual and Group Activities
by Judith A. Elliott and Jerold E. Elliott

Recreation Program Planning Manual for Older Adults
by Karen Kindrachuk

Recreation Programming and Activities for Older Adults
by Jerold E. Elliott and Judith A. Sorg-Elliott

Reference Manual for Writing Rehabilitation Therapy Treatment Plans
by Penny Hogberg and Mary Johnson

Research in Therapeutic Recreation: Concepts and Methods
edited by Marjorie J. Malkin and Christine Z. Howe

Simple Expressions: Creative and Therapeutic Arts for the Elderly in Long-Term Care Facilities
by Vicki Parsons

A Social History of Leisure Since 1600
by Gary Cross

A Social Psychology of Leisure
by Roger C. Mannell and Douglas A. Kleiber

Special Events and Festivals: How to Organize, Plan, and Implement
by Angie Prosser and Ashli Rutledge

Stretch Your Mind and Body: Tai Chi as an Adaptive Activity
by Duane A. Crider and William R. Klinger

Therapeutic Activity Intervention with the Elderly: Foundations and Practices
by Barbara A. Hawkins, Marti E. May, and Nancy Brattain Rogers

Therapeutic Recreation and the Nature of Disabilities
by Kenneth E. Mobily and Richard D. MacNeil

Therapeutic Recreation: Cases and Exercises, 2nd ed.
by Barbara C. Wilhite and M. Jean Keller

Therapeutic Recreation in Health Promotion and Rehabilitation
by John Shank and Catherine Coyle

Therapeutic Recreation in the Nursing Home
by Linda Buettner and Shelley L. Martin

Therapeutic Recreation Programming: Theory and Practice
by Charles Sylvester, Judith E. Voelkl, and Gary D. Ellis

Therapeutic Recreation Protocol for Treatment of Substance Addictions
by Rozanne W. Faulkner

The Therapeutic Recreation Stress Management Primer
by Cynthia Mascott

The Therapeutic Value of Creative Writing
by Paul M. Spicer

Tourism and Society: A Guide to Problems and Issues
by Robert W. Wyllie

Traditions: Improving Quality of Life in Caregiving
by Janelle Sellick

Trivia by the Dozen: Encouraging Interaction and Reminiscence in Managed Care
by Jean Vetter

Venture Publishing, Inc.
1999 Cato Avenue
State College, PA 16801

Phone: 814-234-4561
Fax: 814-234-1651